John Dewey

The Later Works, 1925–1953

Volume 7: 1932

EDITED BY JO ANN BOYDSTON

TEXTUAL EDITOR, BARBARA LEVINE

With an Introduction by
Abraham Edel and Elizabeth Flower

Southern Illinois University Press
Carbondale and Edwardsville

The text of this reprinting is a photo-offset reproduction of the original cloth
edition that contains the full apparatus for the volume awarded the seal of
the Committee on Scholarly Editions of the Modern Language Association.
Editorial expenses were met in part by a grant from the Editions Program of
the National Endowment for the Humanities, an independent Federal agency.

The paperbound edition has been made possible by a special subvention from
the John Dewey Foundation.

The Library of Congress catalogued the first printing of this work (in cloth)
as follows:

Dewey, John, 1859–1952.
    The later works, 1925–1953.

    Vol. 7 has introd. by Abraham Edel and Elizabeth Flower.
    Continues The middle works, 1899–1924.
    Includes bibliographies and indexes.
    CONTENTS: v. 1. 1925—v. 2. 1925–1927—[etc.]—v. 7. 1932.
    1. Philosophy—Collected works.   I. Boydston, Jo Ann,
1924–.   II. Title.
B945.D41   1981   191   80-27285
ISBN 0-8093-1200-x (v. 7)

ISBN 0-8093-1575-0 (paperback)

Contents

Introduction

By Abraham Edel and Elizabeth Flower

Little is known about how John Dewey and James Hayden Tufts came to publish an ethics book together in 1908, nor even about the steps by which twenty-four years later (1932) they issued a revised and almost wholly rewritten edition. In 1891 Dewey, as head of the philosophy department at the University of Michigan, appointed Tufts, whose interests were in ethics and social philosophy, to that department.[1] Two years later, Tufts resigned to study in Freiburg. He had previously studied theology with William Rainey Harper at Yale, and when Harper became president of the new University of Chicago, he brought Tufts there.[2] Tufts then urged the appointment of Dewey to head the philosophy department. The ten years Dewey spent at Chicago were obviously the period in which their mutual interests had free play. This intellectual and personal friendship was strong enough to support what subsequently must have been largely collaboration at a distance, for Dewey moved to Columbia, while Tufts remained at Chicago. Charles Morris, drawing on his own recollections of Chicago, says:

> Tufts's ethical interests antedated his contacts with Dewey, but he found in Dewey the complement to his own ethical interests. He once said to me that after every half-hour conversation with Dewey he felt like writing a book. It was Tufts who suggested to Dewey the plan of the famous *Ethics*, with Dewey to write the more analytic second part, and he to write the historical and much of the applied parts.[3]

1. George Dykhuizen, *The Life and Mind of John Dewey* (Carbondale and Edwardsville: Southern Illinois University Press, 1973), pp. 64–65.
2. Charles Morris, *The Pragmatic Movement in American Philosophy* (New York: George Braziller, 1970), p. 183.
3. Ibid., pp. 183–84. More specifically, they did the introduction together, and Dewey, in addition to the second part, did the first two chapters in the third part, dealing largely with the theory of society and politics. This held for both editions.

The 1932 edition of Dewey and Tufts's *Ethics* is our major concern here, particularly the contribution Dewey makes to ethical theory. While this is largely in Part II, it cannot, in the nature of their enterprise, be divorced from the history of morality in Part I, nor from the application to social problems in Part III. Indeed, the attempt to integrate the three distinct inquiries in one work was what attracted reviewers of the 1908 volume in the first place. The 1932 edition was not as widely reviewed as the first, nor were the basic theoretical changes adequately noted.[4]

Behind the changes made in the 1932 edition lies an exciting drama that covers a quarter of a century and reaches back even before 1908. The characters of the drama include not only philosophers and scientists grappling with theoretical problems, but history itself in an eventful era. The first edition came in a period when industrialism was moving into high gear and challenging social institutions that had not accommodated to its demands, when people still looked on the future as an era of unfolding progress and democratic growth, when a revolution in mathematics and physics had not yet penetrated philosophic thought, when ethics and social philosophy were still reflecting the effort to reconcile Darwinism and traditional religion, when imperialist struggles to divide the world among the major powers had begun to change the temper of political relations and to introduce a new order of violence. There was not yet awareness of how radically the world was changing. By 1932, all is different. Industrialism has moved into overdrive and an urban society is clearly in the making. But it also is a period of world depression. The expectation of peaceful progress has been shattered by World War I, and the vista of slow democratic growth interrupted by the advent of Russian communism, Italian fascism, and the imminent threat of German nazism. A new physics has replaced the

4. Milton Halsey Thomas, in his *John Dewey: A Centennial Bibliography* (Chicago: University of Chicago Press, 1962), pp. 30–31, 99, lists twenty reviews of the first edition but only four of the second. For a complete listing of reviews, see Textual Commentary, footnote 20. A suggestion that the differences were worth exploring was made by Herbert W. Schneider in *Dialogue on John Dewey*, ed. Corliss Lamont (New York: Horizon Press, 1959), p. 131. Schneider said ". . . somebody should get a Ph.D. for comparing the second edition with the first. I don't think anybody's done that; and Dewey made some radical changes." Our inquiries along this line suggest that it is at least complex enough for post-doctoral research.

Newtonian outlook and a new logic is shaking philosophy; philosophy is gaining independence from religion and itself becoming a profession. The social sciences have been staking claims for the study of human life and thrusting different perspectives of method and research into the arena. Ethics is in a particularly precarious position: formerly it had coasted on the comfortable assumption that people agreed about morality but only argued about how it was to be justified. Now it is startled into the perception that there are fundamental conflicts on moral questions.

While this Introduction shows some of the general features of Dewey's ethical theory as well as the distinctive features that set it off from other types of ethics, it emphasizes the changes that mark the journey from the first to the second edition. These are responses to the growth of the social sciences and the lessons of historical experience in the intervening quarter of a century. Section I of this Introduction presents Dewey's continuing psychological commitments and identifies the basic theses in the 1908 *Ethics* that were destined for change in the 1932 version. Section II explores the changes in the sociocultural dimension of the ethical theory. Section III deals with changes in ethical concepts that grow out of or are made possible by the transformation in the other dimensions. Throughout, influences and "critical points" are noted. Finally, Section IV draws lessons from Dewey's experiences with ethical theory, the way in which a theory crystallizes out of a multitude of historical, social, and intellectual influences.

I.   The analysis of conduct and its psychological background, which is central to the 1932 *Ethics*, has not changed from the 1908 *Ethics*.[5] It had been well developed even before that, in the seminal article on "The Reflex Arc Concept in Psychology" (1896; EW 5:96–109) in which Dewey by means of a feedback model integrates stimulus, central processes of awareness, and motor response. This gave shape to permanent features

5. *The Middle Works of John Dewey, 1899–1924*, ed. Jo Ann Boydston (Carbondale: Southern Illinois University Press, 1978), vol. 5. Subsequent references to other *Middle Works* volumes, as well as to *The Early Works of John Dewey, 1882–1898*, and *The Later Works of John Dewey, 1925–1953*, all edited by Jo Ann Boydston and published in Carbondale by the Southern Illinois University Press, will be indicated by EW, MW, and LW.

in his thought, both epistemological and ethical: First is the basic presence of a problematic structure underlying consciousness and inquiry. A second is the active character of inquiry. A third is the reconstructive nature of the process, including some novelty in the solution or evaluation and the experimental status of its stabilization. A fourth is the attentiveness to time as internal to the process, and so to its context and conditions and in turn to its consequences, not as an external interfering factor. And a fifth is the integrated organic character of the whole process: conduct unifies different aspects of the situation—intention, motive, volition, satisfaction, experience, character, self—as dimensions and not as elements functioning separately.

Dewey had early begun to use this psychological model for ethics, in his *The Study of Ethics: A Syllabus* (1894; EW 4:219–362). This had dealt chiefly with what Dewey called *psychological ethics*; the 1908 *Ethics* added a full measure of *social ethics* by tracing the social component in ethical theory, by dealing with the history of ethics from primitive to modern times, and by adding specific discussion of social problems. It is important to note that Dewey's distinction between psychological and social ethics is never equivalent to familiar distinctions between individual and social ethics as separate branches of ethics. For Dewey psychological and social ethics are two ways of studying *ethics as a whole*. Conduct is a transaction between the organism and an environment both natural and social. Psychological ethics studies the processes of the individual in that transaction; in that sense it gives the form that ethics takes. Social ethics studies the transaction in its environmental scope and historical depth; it furnishes the content.

As contrasted with these continuities in Dewey's ethical thought, the 1932 *Ethics* makes two very serious revisions from the 1908 *Ethics*. One deals with the sociocultural dimension in ethical theory, the other with the relations of ethical concepts. The views that undergo change may be summarized as follows.

In the first decade of the twentieth century the historical development of morality was generally seen in "linear" terms: morality had evolved from customary group morality to a reflective individual morality. The efficacy of reflection (intelligence) in facing moral problems was of course a central concern in both editions of the book, but the 1908 *Ethics* construed the contrast of the reflective and the customary in a very special way. Since reflective thought is in some sense an *individual* matter, custom tended to be cast as a *group* or social matter. (Of course, habit characterizes an individual as well as a group, but custom, construed as valued habits, tended to be considered as group anchored.) Custom was seen as *conservative*, while reflection appeared dominantly to be *reconstructive* and concerned with the change that the resolution of problems required. It followed that a society which was steered by custom tended to be *stationary* rather than *progressive*. Further, a progressive society embodied greater *intelligence* in its operations than a stationary one. Finally, as society became more progressive, its morality was more differentiated from other institutional aspects (law, etiquette, religious edict, etc.) and stood out as *independent*.[6]

In the 1908 *Ethics* the conceptual equipment of ethical theory presents *good* as central: goodness lies not just in satisfaction of impulse but in the impulse itself being transformed by the funded experience of consequences and so refers to the value that an impulse has in the whole system of conduct. *Right* (obligation, as well as duty and law) is oriented rather to control, centering on relations to others and what they require. But it is filtered through the good: "Duty is what is owed by a partial isolated self embodied in established, facile, and urgent tendencies, to that ideal self which is presented in aspirations which, since they are not yet formed into habits, have no organized hold upon the self and which can get organized into habitual tendencies and interests only by a more or less painful and difficult reconstruction of the habitual self" (1908; MW 5:326). Duty is thus a phenomenon of the expansion of ends and the reconstruction of character. *Vir-*

6. This evolutionary picture, with its "cake of custom" conception of early man, was part of the general attempt in the late nineteenth and early twentieth century to trace lines of evolution in various institutions. On Spencerian assumptions of evolution as progress and moving from unorganized homogeneity to organized differentiation, current forms tended to be viewed as culminations: e.g., an evolution of kinship from a postulated initial group promiscuity through stages of polygyny and polyandry to the monogamous family; law from customary status to individualized contract; religion from indiscriminate belief in animism through polytheism to monotheism; morality from custom and collective group responsibility to individual (growingly rational) reflection in an independent morality.

tue by contrast is directly related to the common good, not routed through the individual self: virtues are traits of character that support the common good (MW 5 : 359). (Approbation and disapprobation are secondary phenomena of affective recognition and response to that common good.) In the case of good and right, reference to the social or common good enters more indirectly. The good is cast formally in terms of satisfaction of the self in conduct, with a demand for the permanently satisfying as against presently satisfying ends; but an explicitly accompanying hypothesis states that permanently satisfying ends will prove to be social ends. In the case of duty, the social has to be sought in content; the form is still the relation of ideal and present self. In general, then, the 1908 *Ethics* formulates its ethical concepts in terms of psychological ethics, connected to the good as central.

Such are the two major themes that are destined for change by 1932. The "linear" theory of the evolution of morality had to be unpacked for almost a quarter of a century before its aftereffects disappeared. Only then could the revision in the relation of ethical concepts be rapid and decisive.

II.   Defects early emerged in the linear theory of moral evolution that underlay the 1908 *Ethics*. One was in the assumption that the same pattern of development was to be found in the evolution of a society's morality and the maturation of individual life from childhood to adulthood (a kind of "ontogeny recapitulates phylogeny" thesis). A second was the assumption that the mentality of primitive man was different from that of modern man. Even in the 1908 *Ethics* and in the near period before and after it, Dewey voiced some reservations about the comparison of individual development and historical evolution. While he did not take up cudgels against the comparison, he did insist throughout on the separate study of each, particularly in the impact such doctrines had on education. And as for the historical evolution, while Dewey did not in 1908 question the past existence of an epoch of customary as distinct from reflective morals, he did point to the large degree of the customary in current morality. Even further, he regarded an individual-oriented morality as itself a social pattern rather than the individualistic replacing the social (MW 5 : 389). The other defect in the theory of moral evolution—the assumption that primitive mentality was different from modern—gave way as scientific anthropology fought it out in the second and third decades of the century.

Looking back, we may wonder why it took Dewey almost a quarter of a century for the sociocultural presuppositions of the 1908 ethical theory to be thoroughly replaced and an amended ethical theory crystallize. The answer lies in the complexity of the relations between the customary and the individual-reflective. It was no easy task to alter the conception of custom and its constituent idea of habit in such a way that reflection could penetrate and be at home within the customary. It involved altering the meaning of what it is to be an individual, and so coming to grips with the individualism that had come to dominate Western thought since the seventeenth century. This further involved assessing the opposition of individual and social as categories in social and moral thought. In addition, a view of reflection had to be worked out which would reckon with diverse philosophical speculations about reason and rationality and the methods of advancing knowledge. Only at the end could Dewey utilize the results of these inquiries to reconstruct the ethical theory that formulates and guides moral inquiry.

These tasks are accomplished by the time of the 1932 *Ethics.* The notion of reflection has matured in a carefully etched conception of intelligence. Independence as a mark of an advanced morality has given way to the dangers of isolating morality: moral reflection reaches into any and every area of life to find what is relevant to specific problems; morality is not an isolated sphere applying its own principles. Individualism is recognized as a specific trend in thought, feeling, and practice, under specific historical conditions of Western man. Whether the movement of morals is from social to individual—that is, from a kind of moral status to a kind of moral contract—or the reverse, depends on the demands of particular historical conditions and contexts. Focus is no longer on a world development of mankind but on Western man and the sources relevant to the shape that his development happened to take. There is no longer a prescribed global pattern, nor a set pattern for any people that is historically bestirred. Social and individual are now aspects of any moral thought or action; no issue can seriously be posed as individual versus social; the alleged conflict of individual and society is always the tension between specific individuals and specific institutional demands under specific conditions or between different groups within society. The social good is no longer a distinctive content in moral judgment, but almost a defining breadth in the idea of morality itself—a broader as against a narrower outreach in a human being. Intelligence has taken over the mantle of reason, and custom is no longer limited to an unreflective drag upon it. Habit enters more actively into the consolidation of reflection, though old habits are ever on trial, taxed by new conditions that unhalting change brings and will bring about; custom may thus at times be confirmed by reflection, even though reflection will never find its rest.

To see the impact of these changes within the ethical theory, we have to understand how the changes themselves took place. They issued from the expansion of knowledge in different disciplines over the quarter of a century, from the vigorous impact of historical events during that period, and from Dewey's own reflective philosophical analysis of theoretical traditions in moral philosophy. Our first attention goes to changes in the disciplines that operated within the ethical theory. Just as the changes in Dewey's psychology prepared the way for his psychological understanding of ethics prior to the 1908 edition and the social science of that early period joined the psychology in his ethical theory of the 1908 edition, so the advances of social science in the subsequent period together with Dewey's response to historical events prepared the ground for the ethical theory of 1932.

The transformations that emerged out of the abandonment of the thesis of moral evolution from the customary to the reflective can be presented by selective comment on the constituent issues we have discovered: moral evolution and historical perspective; social and individual; custom and habit; intelligence.

Moral Evolution and Historical Perspective. The new anthropology that set the path of critical thought for several decades and upset the premises of the uncritical evolutionism was largely associated with the school of Franz Boas. His *The Mind of Primitive Man* (1911) riddled the notion that there was a uniform primitive mentality different from the modern; it recognized a broad similarity of individual capacities in primitive and modern people, differentiated largely by traditional patterns, opportunities, and areas of attention. Dewey was clearly exposed to this thought.[7] Eventually, in an article on "Anthropology and Ethics" (LW 3 : 11–24),[8] Dewey examined in detail different interpreters of moral evolution and concluded against the isolation of moral conceptions and practices from institutional and intellectual changes; he found no determinate evolutionary pattern, whether away from or toward greater individuality, unambiguously borne out by the facts; he stressed the plurality of influences and the need for specific investigations. This paper marked the end of the historical substructure of the 1908 *Ethics*. It should be taken together with Dewey's *The Public and Its Problems* (LW 2 : 235–372), also published in 1927, which provided fresh categories for replacing the individual-social dichotomy.

Once the linear view of moral evolution was rejected, the 1932 *Ethics* turned to specific historical inquiry and evaluation free of a specific commitment about social and individual in general. Thus individualism could be examined in different historical contexts for the conditions under which it developed. The use of "social" in a general way yielded to the study of specific groups. Static societies could be examined without assuming that they had to be in an earlier developmental stage—for example, strong reliance on custom in China need not be an index of moral backwardness. What replaced the linear view was simply a more genuinely sociohistorical analysis of the social phenomena in their specific sociohistorical contexts.

Although the 1932 *Ethics* does not discuss this changed approach to history, it can be seen clearly in particular historical chapters as compared with those of 1908. Where the chapters

7. Dewey gave a seminar with Boas at Columbia in 1914–15 on "An examination of the evolutionary and historical methods in the study of the intellect"; surviving notes (Center for Dewey Studies, Southern Illinois University at Carbondale) taken by Homer Dubs in Dewey's own course "Moral and Political Philosophy" (1915–16) show detailed consideration of different patterns of evolutionary thought. Dewey refers to Boas's book (New York: Macmillan Co., 1911) in a 1923 syllabus for a course at Columbia on "Social Institutions and the Study of Morals" (MW 15 : 235) and lists the book in the 1932 *Ethics*. From various reflections and reminiscences in papers by Dewey and by Tufts and from students' lecture notes at different times, we can trace in firm detail not only where the 1908 view of moral evolution was accepted but also the successive steps by which from 1908 to 1932 it was dissolved.
8. This article appeared as a chapter in William Ogburn and Alexander Goldenweiser's *The Social Sciences and Their Interrelations* (Boston: Houghton Mifflin Co., 1927).

are rewritten or fresh (that on Hebrew morality, the added chapter on the Roman contribution, and the treatment of modern trends), a shift takes place from simply presenting the emergence of a higher consciousness and personal morality to an explanatory inquiry into the impact of social conditions. Why, for example, did the Hebrews, beginning as nomads like their neighbors, develop morality as they did? The point is not merely economic and social background expanded and put into the foreground; it is that emerging moral forms are now seen not as general stages of moral evolution but as specific responses to challenges in the specific historical problems and conflicts. Rome in light of its distinctive problems of empire developed the jural aspect of morality; and the early modern development had its varied roots that merged in the tide of individualism.

Historical events between 1908 and 1932 also contributed to the change of perspective. The traumatic impact of World War I in particular undermined the general assumption of progress, with rational democratic advance as the mark of civilization. Instead of rationality, now came violence and the growth of dictatorship. A popular work like Oswald Spengler's *Decline of the West*, with its theory of the inevitable decline of every civilization and its use of war and violence and authoritarianism as the indicators of imminent collapse, expressed a general pessimism. Prophecies of the doom of democracy, in the shadow of fascism and nazism, came largely after the 1932 *Ethics*, in the period between Hitler's ascent to power and World War II; but World War I, with subsequent turmoil and revolution, together with economic crisis and depression, were enough. While Dewey did not in any way abandon his commitment to democracy, democracy could no longer be assured of triumphant historical emergence. This made more significant his view of an open world and man's responsibility to take the reins.

Dewey had long argued for the importance of ideas and decisions and actions in shaping social direction. Spread large on the canvas of history was the same structure that had emerged from his earlier exploration of psychology and the place of thought: the trio in social psychology—impulse, habit, and intelligence—now appear in history as needs, custom, reconstruction. In both cases, the reflection that exhibits intelligence at work or prompts reconstruction is the conflict of habits in the matrix of old or new needs, and when it does not issue in smooth change it can become a critical or even a revolutionary situation.

It is interesting to compare Dewey's historical model with the Marxian. Dewey does hold that the problem-producing factors in history, setting the stage for necessary change, are economic, in the sense of production and technology. And he is ready to say that the economic does determine the character of life—but only where the reflective or ideational is held back or rendered impotent. Where for the Marxians the relations of production of a preceding period impede necessary changes, Dewey thinks in more general terms of institutional habits of the past as conservative and needing reconstruction. Both hold to the importance of ideational factors. Lenin, for example, feels it necessary in 1908 to appeal to philosophy (in his *Materialism and Empirio-Criticism*) to rally his followers. But whereas Lenin locates the ideational in the firm conceptions of the vanguard group or party that leads the proletariat, Dewey focuses on the awakening of a whole people in the revolutionary situation that economic changes generate. Whether he is viewing the Far East, Soviet Russia, Mexico, or Turkey (in travels from 1919 to 1929), he describes the basic fact of a revolution not in terms of those who set it into motion or their opinions and hopes, but as "psychic and moral rather than merely political and economic, a revolution in the attitude of people toward the needs and possibilities of life" ("Leningrad Gives the Clue," LW 3:204). In Leningrad, the atmosphere of change in the people is more striking than any theoretical formulations about it. In rural Mexico he is impressed by the phenomenon of night schools, to which Indians walk miles, each bringing a candle to light the night's studies. His papers on China analyze the play of ideas in shaping action within the ongoing massive movements that battleships, railways, machines, chemicals, precipitated, upsetting thereby Chinese habits and institutions of long standing. The 1932 *Ethics* does not expound Dewey's interpretation of history, but depends on it clearly enough throughout.

Social and Individual. The 1932 *Ethics* gives a definitive verdict on "social" and "individual": "We shall accordingly substitute the consideration of definite conflicts, at particular times and places, for a general opposition between social and individual. Neither 'social' nor 'individual,' in general, has any fixed meaning" (327). This verdict was a foregone conclusion at least since *Reconstruction in Philosophy* (1920, based on earlier lectures in Japan; MW 12:77–201). There Dewey dismissed discussion in terms of such conceptual generalities as a waste of energy; it should give way to "specific inquiries into a multitude of specific structures and interactions" (MW 12:193).

> Just as "individual" is not one thing, but is a blanket term for the immense variety of specific reactions, habits, dispositions and powers of human nature that are evoked, and confirmed under the influences of associated life, so with the term "social." Society is one word, but infinitely many things. It covers all the ways in which by associating together men share their experiences, and build up common interests and aims; street gangs, schools for burglary, clans, social cliques, trades unions, joint-stock corporations, villages and international alliances. The new method takes effect in substituting inquiry into these specific, changing and relative facts (relative to problems and purposes, not metaphysically relative) for solemn manipulation of general notions. (MW 12:194)

And again, "What upon one side looks like a movement toward individualism, turns out to be really a movement toward multiplying all kinds and varieties of associations" (MW 12:196).

There had, however, been an asymmetry in Dewey's previous treatment of *individual* and *social*. He had never believed in the atomic individual entrenched in the philosophies of Hobbes and Locke, the individual as a self-enclosed unit in terms of which all institutions have to be justified. As early as 1888 he had pointed out that the essence of social contract theory was not the contracting but the fact that men are taken to be isolated unsocial individuals until a contract is formed (*The Ethics of Democracy*, EW 1:232); he argued that such an approach equated democracy with anarchy and compelled the manufacture of a common will. On the other hand, the general idea of the social is put to frequent work. Individuals are social beings, selves are social products, and we have seen how even in the 1908 *Ethics* while accepting the linear moral evolution he rebelled against the idea that the culminating individualism is itself other than a social pattern.

It is important to repeat that in 1908 *social* was not just a general category but a hard working concept; by contrast, *individual*, rejected as a category, was kept simply for its work in relation to reflection, initiative, variability, and the like. In the discussion of the good it is hypothesized that only the social good fulfills the conditions ethics requires (MW 5:261); and that "The genuinely moral person is one, then, in whom the habit of regarding all capacities and habits of self from the social standpoint is formed and active" (MW 5:271). In an earlier work by Tufts and Helen Thompson,[9] the idea of individualism had been traced through the seventeenth and eighteenth century particularly to see how the way was opened for the social good as the criterion and end of action. This point emerges in the 1908 *Ethics*: if moral evolution moves from the social to the individual, the content of the moral consciously adopted by the moral individual becomes increasingly social.

After the clear adoption of the new line in *Reconstruction in Philosophy*, it remained a task of the '20s to reconstruct the concepts of individual and social. The former was the easier task. Individuality as a kind of self, nurtured by the institutions and associations and educational processes of a society, maturing capacities of reflective thought, critique, initiative, and providing variability as against fixed ways, becomes the heir of the tradition of individualism. It is suggested by the discussion of intelligence in *Human Nature and Conduct* (1922; MW 14), which is an introduction to *social* psychology, and is fully expounded in the contrast of *Individualism, Old and New* (1930; LW 5:41–123). The reconstruction of *social* requires more: its use as a general category is not to be abandoned, but its use in specific analysis has to be undertaken by some fresh ideas. *The Public and Its Problems* (1927; LW 2:235–372) carries out the reconstruction. The distinction between individual and social is replaced by that between *private* and *public*, at least for working purposes in political and social theory. When the consequences of action extend

9. *The Individual and His Relation to Society as Reflected in British Ethics* (New York: Augustus M. Kelley, 1970). Originally published in two parts in 1898 and 1904.

beyond agent or agents and are recognized as serious by a wider group, a public is formed:

> The line between private and public is to be drawn on the basis of the extent and scope of the consequences of acts which are so important as to need control, whether by inhibition or by promotion. We distinguish private and public buildings, private and public schools, private paths and public highways, private assets and public funds, private persons and public officials. It is our thesis that in this distinction we find the key to the nature and office of the state. (LW 2:245)

And again, "The public consists of all those who are affected by the indirect consequences of transactions to such an extent that it is deemed necessary to have those consequences systematically cared for" (LW 2:245–46). On this view, publics can rise, change, and disappear; there can be larger more comprehensive publics and narrower ones. The determining consequences take shape in terms of the conditions and instrumentalities of the time. The conceptual shift reformulates questions and opens the way to experimental answers in the light of conditions and consequences as they actually are found to take place.

In April of the following year, 1928, Dewey published an article on "Social as a Category." [10] He distinguishes between operative social phenomena and the general category. On the whole it contains few new points, but it confirms the social character of human phenomena, and reckons with the place of thought, even of subjectivity, and morality itself. In a sense, it is bidding goodbye to the category by elevating it.

Dewey's round-up of these issues is, of course, *Individualism, Old and New*. It contains all the lessons whose emergence we have considered: the rejection of a static atomic individualism, the rejection of the opposition of the collective and corporate to the individual, the cultural character of relations of individuals, the insistence that altruism cannot constitute a solution, the basic role of historical and social conditions. Significantly, as he approaches the conclusion he calls on us to "forget 'society'

---

10. Republished as "The Inclusive Philosophic Idea" in *Philosophy and Civilization* (New York: Minton, Balch and Co., 1931), pp. 77–92 (LW 3:41–54).

and think of law, industry, religion, medicine, politics, art, education, philosophy—and think of them in the plural" (LW 5 : 120). He does not offer a blueprint for social change but a rounded conception of individuality to guide it.

The 1932 *Ethics* therefore has little need to argue the reconstructed ideas of the social and the individual. It can exhibit a greater concreteness in explicating the idea of the common good and in invoking sociohistorical contexts to illuminate controversies in moral theory. The idea of the common good is now enriched by specific ideas of sharing and participating (345). And it becomes intelligible why morality is neither wholly social nor wholly individual. It becomes clear after the new analysis of *social* and *individual* that in periods of stability problems of morality concern more how individuals should adjust to institutions of society, while in periods of flux they center more on the value of social arrangements and yield critiques of traditions and inherited ways (314). And throughout ideas are analyzed in terms of the needs and problems of specific periods and the quality of life that one or another solution will engender.

Custom and Habit. The theory of moral evolution had assigned custom a cluster of attributes such that they were the exact opposite of the features that characterized reflective thinking, for the movement of evolution was from customary morality to reflective morality. Since the latter called the tune, custom had to involve group cohesion instead of individual independence, automatic acceptance instead of thoughtful consideration, static conditions instead of dynamic progress. When the underlying theory was abandoned, the idea of custom was bound sooner or later to be thoroughly shaken. Custom was defined as valued social habit, and habit itself within the individual had these conservative and automatic properties.

This view of custom and habit as inherently conservative remained in Dewey's thought as late as *Reconstruction in Philosophy* (1920; MW 12:77–201). For example, technologies are said to promote the experimental attitude once arts are removed from "the rule of sheer custom" (MW 12:89). He regards classical Greek philosophy as a metaphysical substitute for custom, guaranteeing the moral and social values that were being threatened (MW 12:89). Custom makes claims of finality and immutability and breeds a pervasive authoritarian tradition (MW 12: 91). When the bonds of customary institutions are relaxed, the contract theory of the state rapidly gains a place (MW 12:104).

Yet within a couple of years the whole theory of habit is profoundly altered—in *Human Nature and Conduct* (1922; MW 14). This book is obviously the end product of at least three decades of concern with the character of psychology, with the successive strata of psychological theories and outlooks. It carries further the biological and social aspects of psychology. In its cast of characters, Impulse represents biology, Habit is the surrogate for the social, and Intelligence expresses the individual reflecting. The startling feature is that Habit is the star in this array. It gives social shape to impulse; impulse is therefore secondary and dependent, although biologically first. Intelligence operates in the matrix of conflicting habits and serves to disrupt unsatisfying habits. But the expansion of habit goes far beyond serving as the matrix. Habits constitute the self, character is the interpenetration of habits; even in the operation of intelligence "Concrete habits do all the perceiving, recognizing, imagining, recalling, judging, conceiving and reasoning that is done" (MW 14:124). Intelligence itself is on the way to being construed in terms of a special set of habits. The notion of custom is released from the charge of being the drag of the past. Reason can be seen as "a custom of expectation and outlook, an active demand for reasonableness in other customs" (MW 14:55–56). The rise of this new custom in human affairs has a revolutionary influence on other customs.

Somewhere between 1919, when the lectures that became *Reconstruction in Philosophy* were delivered in Japan, and the lectures that issued in 1922 in *Human Nature and Conduct*, Dewey's view of habit and custom was itself reconstructed. The change appears to have been stimulated by contact with a large-scale instance of what happens to custom in a situation of revolutionary change, for from Japan Dewey went to China where he spent two years. His papers about China show a clear concern with the understanding of custom and its operations. His arrival coincided with the student movement which at that point was directed against the central government's attempt to compromise with the Japanese invaders. Dewey is particularly interested in what will happen to Chinese modes of thought among the new

forces that were arising. He recognizes the unparalleled contribution of customary ways in Chinese endurance over four thousand years, especially in maintaining the soil from exhaustion.
He begins to see the conservatism of the Chinese as more intellectual and deliberate rather than as merely clinging to custom.
To think of reflection confirming the customary and custom embodying reflection clearly goes counter to Dewey's previous and
habitual view of custom.[11]

Whatever may have been the actual role of these experiences
in Dewey's thought, clearly the ground was broken for a new
view of custom and habit, and the mature analysis of *Human
Nature and Conduct* marks the difference between the older
view that permeates the 1908 *Ethics* and the treatment of custom
in morality in the 1932 *Ethics*. Meanwhile, however, the concept
of reflection has grown into the enhanced idea of *intelligence*.

Intelligence. Reason and rationality, the favorites of
most ethical theories, play only a limited role in Dewey's ethics,
largely because Dewey and Tufts have reservations about the
part reason has played in the history of ethics. Stoic, medieval
and Kantian theory made it into an independent source of moral
authority expressing cosmic or natural law or the conflict of
moral law and natural desire. In the 1908 *Ethics* reason is low
keyed—not a peremptorily prescriptive superego, nor an isolated and commanding power, simply the way of coping with
needs that stem from conflict and complexity for patterns of control in a changing world, to be worked out with appropriate ten-
tativeness for subsequent experience.

The more commonsensical idea of reflection, which does play
a central role in 1908, is developed in the years that followed,
through Dewey's explorations of method in the growth of knowledge, of logic, and of science. It moves to a larger scale in *How
We Think* (1910; MW 6:177–356). The decision to use *intelligence* rather than traditional ideas of reason or rationality was a
deliberate one both for Tufts and for Dewey. It came to a head
between 1917 and 1919. In his "The Moral Life and the Con-

11. See Dewey's papers on: "Chinese National Sentiment," MW 11:215–27;
"What Holds China Back," MW 12:51–59; "As the Chinese Think," MW
13:217–27; also, *Letters from China and Japan*, by John Dewey and Alice
Chipman Dewey, ed. Evelyn Dewey (New York: E. P. Dutton and Co., 1920).

struction of Values and Standards" (1917),[12] Tufts has as one of
several topics "intelligence and reason, through which experience is interrelated, viewed as a whole, enlarged in imagination." [13] He examines different aspects of thought that, he decides
explicitly, had better be termed "intelligence" than "reason." In
morals, both imply considering a proposed or performed act as
a whole, in its relations, and with a view especially to consequences; intelligence involves not only empirical observation on
past experience, already formulated concepts, and deduction,
but "that rarer quality which in the presence of a situation dis-
cerns a meaning not obvious, suggests an idea, 'injustice,' to interpret the situation." [14] Thus in intelligence there is a synthetic
or creative element as well as an analytic one, that goes beyond
the narrower sense of reasoning and includes imagination and
feeling. It reckons also with other possible acts and their consequences, going beyond habit and prejudice, and reaches into social intercourse by envisaging effects on others. "Intelligence"
thus points to constructive and creative efforts, to new sources of
interest and open fields for development.

Dewey's development of the distinctive character of intelligence is evident in *Reconstruction in Philosophy* (1920), in the
analysis of intelligence in *Human Nature and Conduct* (1922),
and in *The Quest for Certainty* (1929; LW 4). The last is devoted
wholly to intelligence and the life of intelligence, set in contrast
to the chief philosophic aberration, the search for immutable and
authoritative truth. Nowhere, however, is the point made more
succinctly stated than in his outline for the lectures in Japan [15]
that became *Reconstruction in Philosophy*. Lecture 5 is entitled
"The Changed Conception of Experience and Reason." It re-
traces old ground: how experience, which in ancient times meant
an accumulation and gradual organization, yielded a practical
insight like that of the builder and physician; how it became under British sensationalist psychology a tool for skeptical criticism rather than construction. Reason was for the ancients a fac-

12. In *Creative Intelligence: Essays in the Pragmatic Attitude*, by John Dewey et
    al. (New York: Henry Holt and Co., 1917), pp. 354–408.
13. Ibid., p. 358.
14. Ibid., p. 364.
15. "Dewey's Lectures in Japan" in Notes and News, in the *Journal of Philosophy*
    16 (19 June 1919): 357–64 (MW 11:341–49).

ulty of insight into universals, laws, and principles; for Kant it was a faculty of organizing chaotic details of experience. But modern psychology, under biological influence, brought out the active and motor factors in experience. Experimental method then emphasized projection and invention rather than accumulation from the past. "Reason thus becomes Intelligence—the power of using past experience to shape and transform future experience. It is constructive and creative" (MW 11:346). Hence the shift from Reason to Intelligence is not simply a verbal shift, nor the discovery of a fresh faculty; it is a philosophic turn to pragmatism, resting on a new psychology.

This critical shift lights up many points in the 1932 *Ethics* and solidifies the conception of ethics as dealing with reconstruction and resolution of conflicts and problems in particular situations. This is not the application of rules that simply sum up past experience, nor the resistance to temptation to transgress established rules. (Dewey's strong preference for "principles" over "rules," because the former are guides to analysis, itself parallels the use of intelligence as against following prescriptive reason.) It provides the key to his analysis of freedom and responsibility, for freedom is essentially the capacity to learn and to make creative and innovative use of learning in guiding conduct. The pragmatic emphasis is on responsibility as prospective rather than retrospective, on using praise and blame to cultivate attitudes of attention and response rather than as recrimination for the past, on sensitivity, learning and self-development rather than external manipulation.

III.   Whereas the changes in the sociocultural dimension from 1908 to 1932 were slow, uneven, and not for the most part self-consciously announced, those in the analysis of ethical concepts were declared as it were fully-born, and with dramatic effect. The three major ethical concepts of good, right and obligation, and virtue, originally analyzed in terms of the good, were now declared independent, each resting on a different force in human life. Since Dewey had never dealt with ethical concepts in isolation from the character of human life and conduct, this shift from a fundamental focus on the good to a set of independent factors represents a fresh way of looking at what goes on in the moral aspects of life.

Dewey had always called attention to the interaction of organism and environment (natural and social) in understanding the activity of the individual. He analyzed the relation in depth, showing how the relevant environmental factors were selected in terms of the processes and awareness of individuals; for example, breathing is a cooperative activity of lungs and air, mining involves awareness of the minerals and their use. His earlier writing and lecturing even suggests transferring an organic model to the whole picture with selected environmental features operating almost as organs with respect to the individual; later, concepts of interaction and then transaction take over. Nevertheless, as long as he was doing chiefly psychological ethics, supported by the individualism of the theory of moral evolution, the ethical concepts were interpreted wholly in terms of inner-individual processes. Now, however, the view is no longer simply of an individual affecting and being affected by the natural and social environment; it is rather a direct focus on the full complexity of natural and social relations that occur in the field itself.

The new view was set forth in "Three Independent Factors in Morals" (LW 5:279–88), a lecture Dewey gave in France in 1930. The morality of ends, with the central idea of the good, is based on multiple impulses, appetites and desires; without foresight the stronger wins out, but, with foresight of consequences, judgments of comparison become possible, which can be examined and corrected in the light of envisaged consequences, objectives, or ends. Such ends, hierarchically ordered as goods, may be molded into the idea of a single good to which all reasonable acts lead. The second theoretical form that morality took is that of laws or the jural. This comes from the basic phenomenon of group life, each trying to secure the acceptance of his purposes and plans by others; this generates an established system of order or right, that is, requirements clothed with authority. Dewey says:

The whole point for which I am contending is simply this: There is an intrinsic difference, in both origin and mode of operation, between objects which present themselves as satisfactory to desire and hence good, and objects which come to one as making demands upon his conduct which should be recognized. Neither can be reduced to the other. (LW 5:285)

A third independent variable in morals reflects praise and blame, spontaneous approval and disapproval. These are natural responses to the acts of others, and out of them come our ideas of virtue and vice.

Dewey traces finally the conflict of the three factors. What is desired may be prohibited, and what is prohibited may happen to be approved. To recognize the reality of conflict is a gain in theory and morality. The generic facts of conflict and problems and reconstruction had of course been fully recognized in the 1908 *Ethics*. Indeed generic conflict and generic reconstruction are the essential features of consciousness which shape the operation of intelligence. What is new is the discovery of *systematic* conflict between the basic idea-systems and so between the forces in human life that underly the idea-systems. This reveals the inner tension and indeterminateness that characterize moral situations and call for moral, not analytic or conceptual, resolution.

Dewey sees different historical schools emphasizing one of the variables and to some extent subordinating the others. Thus we have development of the good in Greek philosophy and Utilitarianism, development of the right in Roman Stoicism and Kant, eighteenth-century British sentiment theory developing sympathy and approval into virtue and vice. And just as Dewey looks to universal psychological and social phenomena as a base for the concepts and theories, so he looks to specific sociohistorical conditions that incline thinkers to prefer one to another of the independent factors. For example, the Greeks developed the good in teleological terms in a unified way because in their political institutions in the small city it was possible to consider their decisions as expressing the reasoned thought of the group in pursuit of purposeful goals. In the Roman empire, however, the need was for central control and order; law was seen as manifesting an ordered cosmic reason; focus accordingly was on functions, duties, relations.

The 1932 *Ethics* develops all these ideas. In the concluding summary of Part II (308–9), Dewey recapitulates the pervasiveness of human desires, wants and needs demanding satisfaction; the unavoidability of associated living with its companionship and competition, its relations of cooperation and subordination; and the mass of phenomena of approval and disapproval, sympathy and resentment. He concludes that this furnishes a permanent structure that is neither arbitrary nor artificial. He has, however, suggested a mode of relating the three factors: the categories are independent, but this does not prevent the content from being interdependent. Thus while Right or Law as a category is independent of Good, what is to be accepted as right has to undergo evaluation in terms of the good. This is, of course, the endless process of evaluation in facing particular situations. In the case of virtue, the independence of the category means a reversal of the position taken in 1908. There contribution to the social good determined the set of virtues; the affections or sentiments had to fall in line. In 1932, the affective is regarded as basic expression yielding praise and blame, appreciation and depreciation. Its relation to the content of the good at any time is, like that in the case of right, itself a moral process of evaluating our responses and reactions, and thereby developing a standard for dealing with them in the light of ends.

The changes in conceptual structure that are carried through in the 1932 *Ethics* consolidate the central Deweyan outlook on ethics: that it is the concrete task of bringing the broadest lessons of experience and the resources of inventiveness to the solution of particular problems, not the application of a fixed and pre-set code of moral universals.

Let us now look at the important specific changes within each of the factors and where possible see what influenced the revision. The most dramatic change is in the interpretation of right, duty, law, obligation. The sharpest reversal of the position of 1908 is in the theory of virtue. The notion of the good, when these other concepts have drifted out from its control, becomes more attentive to its inner tensions—as if, having lost its empire it has now to put its own house in order.

The revised basis for the theory of right is the independent naturalness of exercising claims: "the exercise of claims is as natural as anything else in a world in which persons are not isolated from one another but live in constant association and interaction" (218). These claims arise in the relations of people, the "inherent relationships persons sustain to one another," such as parent and child in the parental relation, or in the case of friends what they owe to one another "because of the very nature of the friendly relation" (218). Generalizing, Dewey concludes that "Right, law, duty, arise from the relations which human beings intimately sustain to one another, and that their authoritative force springs from the very nature of the relation that binds people together" (219). Such a picture of every individual living in a network of relations is a far cry from the individual's inner tension of long-range ideal and established value of 1908, or from the widely prevalent contractualism of wills in individualist ethics.

A conceptual shift very like this was proposed early on by Tufts in "The Moral Life and the Construction of Values and Standards" (1917). Tufts asserts that the significance of the social factor for morals has not yet in certain respects been adequately understood. He goes on "So far as the moral aspect is concerned I know nothing more significant than the attitude of the Common Law as set forth by Professor Pound. This has sought to base its system of duties on relations." [16] Roscoe Pound, in "A Feudal Principle in Modern Law" (1914),[17] contrasts the feudal principle operative in the Common Law with the individualism accentuated by the entry of Roman Law. The feudal principle affixes duties and liabilities independently of the will of those bound, in virtue of relations that hold between people. The individualism that threatened to dominate the nineteenth and early twentieth century, with its high evaluation of individual liberty and property, determined duties on the basis of transactions. In the nineteenth century, says Pound, the Roman idea of contract became popular in jurisprudence, and (quoting Maitland) contract became "the greediest of legal categories." Pound calls attention to the differences in linguistic formulation of the two approaches: the contractualist speaks of a letting of services, the other of the relation of master and servant; the one, of domestic relations, the other of family law. Pound suggests that the concept of contract suffices for a pioneer agricultural society but that in industrial urban society "classes and groups and relations must be taken account of no less than individuals." [18]

Tufts is ready to draw a far-reaching conclusion for ethics

16. Tufts, "The Moral Life and the Construction of Values and Standards," *Creative Intelligence*, p. 361.
17. *International Journal of Ethics* 25 (October 1914): 1–24. (Tufts was then managing editor of the journal.) Republished as the first chapter of Pound's *The Spirit of the Common Law* (Boston: Marshall Jones Co., 1921). Dewey showed a marked interest in philosophy of law during the early part of the second decade of the century. He chaired a Conference on Legal and Social Philosophy in 1913 at which Pound talked on "The Philosophy of Law in America." The Conference continued for several years.
18. Ibid., p. 24.

from this material: "if right and duty have their origin in this social factor there is at least a presumption against their being subordinate ethically to the conception of good. . . . If they have independent origin and are the outgrowth of a special aspect of life it is at least probable that they are not to be subordinated to the good unless the very notion of good is itself reciprocally modified by right in a way that is not usually recognized in teleological systems."[19] He concludes that right has an independent place in the moral consciousness.

Dewey's attitude to contractualism had long been apparent. He had criticized it for its assumed atomic individualism, but Maine's thesis that the movement of progressive societies had been from status to contract was one of the mainstays of the linear theory of moral evolution. Now, with the linear theory gone and individualism wholly refashioned, nothing stood in the way of the sociological study of actual relations and needs as furnishing materials for ethical evaluation of rights, duties, laws, obligations.

The change in the theory of virtue from 1908 to 1932 reversed the position of the cognitive and the affective. In the 1908 *Ethics* the good determines which character traits are conducive of the social good, and this determination legislates for our affective reactions of appreciation, praise, blame, etc. In 1932 these affective reactions are conceived as prior and independent. They are psychological reactions under social influences, and so in a changing world have to be constantly scrutinized since they may reflect older habits that require alteration. Active moral judgment is accordingly needed to bring them in relation with the right and the good. Dewey, in a letter to Professor Horace S. Fries[20] after the publication of the revised edition of 1932, attributed this shift to his restudy of eighteenth-century British moral philosophy; he realized that their theories of the role of sympathy and the moral feelings had tapped a stratum quite coordinate with the teleological theories and the deontological theories, and that it reflected an independent root.

Finally, perhaps the most complicated changes concerned the

---

19. Tufts, *Creative Intelligence*, p. 363.
20. Dewey to Fries, 26 December 1933, Horace S. Fries Papers, State Historical Society of Wisconsin, Madison, Wis.

idea of the good itself. In contrast to 1908, concentration upon the moral good, the reference to character and through a standard for character upon the realizing of a whole self, has been removed in 1932 from the account of the good. Character is more instrumental, the good is more pluralistic and equated with the cultivation of interests. The concept of the good is functional: it remains moored to desires and wants and the like, from which ends emerge, and the task of the concept is to usher in reflection and its process of end-formation. The primary role of good is thus to evaluate among alternatives in conflict and to shape ends in decision.

Such a focus on the valuational nature of judgments of the good leads already in the second decade of the century to a protracted concern with the concept of *value*. It finds expression in a set of papers and controversies that extends well over two decades before culminating (after 1932) in his *Theory of Valuation* (1939) and continues intermittently even after that. Where in his books, particularly of the 1920s, Dewey discusses the good as an ethical concept, the valuational function dominates.

The career of the concept of value in the first third of the twentieth century and Dewey's part in it is another story. What concerns us here is that, throughout his writing about value, Dewey wages a persistent and unrelenting struggle for two related theses: the thorough penetration of the valuational component (the critical preferential judgment, the weighing decisional element) in all judgments of value—they are not to be equated with simply pleasures, desires, satisfactions, even prizings; and the insistence that judgments of value are active and play a part in modifying antecedent values. The first of these is seen in his opposition to the notion of intrinsic value. At times he seems ready to allow immediate prizing to be distinguished from valuation (as comparing by the consideration of consequences); but even then he tries to minimize the significance of prizing by seeing it as a judgment *about* value rather than as a value judgment (a judgment of valuation). More eagerly, he tries to reduce it to a bare statement of satisfaction, especially when he comes on the suggestion that the very meaning of *good* is to be reduced to a primary *better*. The second thesis points directly to the underlying psychological assumption that we enter upon valuation when we have a problem-situation in which our value judgment is decisional and so active, and (the first thesis) that it is ultimately preferential in character. The expanded theory of what goes on in valuation and the critique of foreshortened views of it is finally worked out in *Theory of Valuation*. But the valuational role of *good* in the moral situation as one of decision, in which what is indeterminate is made determinate as an end, is firmly central in the 1932 *Ethics*.

IV.   Three themes in Dewey's experiences with ethical theory are among those deserving special attention for the lessons they may bring to contemporary issues: (1) Genetic method; (2) The relation of theory and practice; (3) Scientific presuppositions within ethical theory.

(1) Dewey attributes to Darwin's influence the awakening to genetic and experimental ideas as the best way of asking questions and looking for explanations. He regularly couples the genetic and the experimental, for he regards an historical approach as the nearest way in which the study of man can get to discovering the consequences of institutions and ideas; the physical sciences can experiment more directly and repetitively and can be given universal form.

The charge against genetic method that it substitutes historical-causal explanation for normative judgments of adequacy or truth cannot be sustained. Genetic inquiry is not simply giving historical fact but by the discovery of historical relationships it is clarifying and extending the meaning of the original "it" whose history was sought. He sometimes compares the original subject inquired into—for example an idea as it is presented in consciousness—to a fossil we discover whose full meaning will come only as we gain knowledge in depth of what it represents historically. The growth in genetic method is therefore a growth of meaning that may help to reformulate the initial inquiry.

Of course the notion of historical context is extremely complicated, and its components have to be distinguished in use. In examining an idea, for example, one element is historical *origins* or causal genesis. Another, and perhaps central, is its *functions*, which obviously sweeps in *consequences* in the temporal milieu. This in turn is enriched by bringing out the element of *selective interest* which gives purposive guidance among the consequences. The extension that the reference to context gives may be *spatial* as well as *temporal*, bringing in the circumambient phenomena that illuminate: for example, a picture of a person running will not tell us whether he is in a marathon, trying to catch a bus, or escaping from a bull. Temporally, an event is illuminated by being set as part of a narrative in which it has interrelations to other events. Finally, identifying the context as including a background of culture and theory opens the door to full sociocultural interpretation under the rubric of "context"—that is, by relation to people around the agent in both space and time and their ways and characters and institutions.

Dewey's lecture on "Context and Thought" (LW 6 : 3 – 21), the George Holmes Howison Lecture for 1930 at the University of California, is a belated attempt to analyze the idea of context itself; but its fuller meaning has to be extracted from his numerous case studies.

(2) The relevance of moral theory to concrete issues is a crucial question. This is presently called "applied ethics" which might suggest that a moral theory—say Utilitarianism, Kantianism, etc.—is adequate to provide ready-made answers to current problems. That this is not Dewey's attitude is readily gathered from Part III of the 1932 *Ethics*, in which Dewey and Tufts discuss the treatment of social problems. No ethical theory, no moral system, no set of moral rules, can deliver an answer to the problems which a particular situation poses; there is no such moral machinery. The preliminary step is the diagnosis, the analysis of what kind of problem is involved, its locus in the situation, what resources are available to handle conflicting claims, goods, values, and what is required in a constructive effort to resolve the problem-situation. Principles are leads and theories propose methods, but the work of analysis has to be done in each case. The element of the novel in situations and of the innovative in method make ready-made solutions inappropriate.[21]

What assurance does Dewey have that genetic inquiry will not itself produce a set of moral rules, of continued stability, to pro-

---

21. We are indebted to Jo Ann Boydston for calling our attention to the following remark of Dewey's about the 1908 *Ethics*, from a 6 May 1915 letter to Scudder Klyce: "My only claim is that the objection brought usually against it is true. I have not given or tried to give any 'solutions'. But it doesnt seem to have occured to the objectors that to say that the moral life is a sries of problems and that morality *is* their solution as they arise would naturally preclude me from profferring solutions" (Scudder Klyce Papers, Library of Congress, Washington, D.C.).

vide a stable content for morality? It is one thing to call attention to the pervasiveness of change, and to the corrigibility of beliefs, but it cannot be antecedently settled whether or not there are constancies reached by scientific inquiry itself. Constancies that held for the past—for example, moral rules found in all past cultures—turn out to be highly general and thin in content. And Dewey's interpretation of ethical concepts—particularly value— turns them toward guidance of the future, toward decision, rather than summing the past. Hence we have here an assurance of change, complexity, and an ample measure of indeterminateness that will constantly require sensitive attention and revision. Dewey has clearly decided, as is evident in his *Experience and Nature* (1925; LW 1), that the world contains a measure of both the stable and the precarious. Once we are rid of dualisms that give us a separate domain of certainties about essences, and once we have rejected teleologies that bid us interpret every event in fixed terms, then the degree of the stable and the precarious becomes a lesson of experience. And the lesson is one of change, novelty, the complexity of the particular, the plurality and partial character of systems, the accidental character of interlockings. There is no separate realm of the accidental (as in the ancient Aristotelian division) but the precarious and the indeterminate are found throughout. Hence to invest moral theory—the technique of guidance in the effort to control—in a specific set of fixed rules is untrue to what the world requires. Constant awareness is the price not just of liberty but of knowledge and morality.

(3) That the 1932 *Ethics* assumes the input of scientific knowledge in an ethical theory and its relevance to every step of the way from the original perception of what a problem is, the clarification of ideas used by the theory, to the assessment of what resources can be invoked and where applied, as well as understanding where the possibilities of growth lie, needs no elaboration here. One of the strengths of Dewey's method, even in criticizing other naturalistic ethics, is to press on into their scientific presuppositions. For example, they build their ethics on basic notions of pleasure, or of interest or desire, or of purpose, or the occurrence of emotion or feeling. Dewey calls for a psychological examination of the context in which pleasure arises and the functions it serves, or what the occurrence of a desire is a response to, or what the theory of emotion tells us about the presence and

direction of a feeling. His assumption of an underlying problem-situation to which such occurrences are addressed opens the way to inquiry for explicit criteria of resolution and so gets beyond the simple reckoning of pleasures or desires satisfied or feelings expressed.

To gear an ethical theory to the growth of knowledge and to be ready to modify and improve it as knowledge grows is thus a fundamental point in Dewey's ethics. But such a commitment involves the task of seeing precisely where the different items of knowledge impinge within the theory, and that is a task of developing, refining, and reconstructing ethical theory itself. The 1932 *Ethics* has to be read in this light. The study of the development of Dewey's ethical theory from 1908 to 1932 shows how this theory of the interplay of science and ethics holds for his ethical theory.

Dewey and Tufts were unready to prepare a third edition in the 1940s, although Dewey defended his approach in controversy with the then prevailing analytic schools.[22] In the 1980s, when the normative problems of practice engage us anew, Dewey's ethical theory is freshly relevant with its attentiveness to the particular, to change, to the incorporation of the best available knowledge, to the role of ethical theory as enlightenment, to the summoning of innovative thought and intelligence.

22. See Textual Commentary, p. 477.

Ethics

Preface to the 1932 Edition

It is a fair question whether to call this edition of 1932 a revision or a new book. The basic plan remains the same; perspective and setting have changed. About two-thirds of the present edition has been newly written, and frequent changes in detail will be found in the remainder.

The twenty-four years since 1908 have seen a great increase of interest in the field of ethics. At the time of publication of the original edition few in America were writing on moral problems. Since then a number of texts for college and university use attests the importance of the subject in educational curricula; economists, sociologists, political scientists, and historians discuss the moral as well as the technical aspects of their subject-matter; several volumes approaching moral questions from the point of view of the general reader have appeared. In a world where wars may wreck any national or individual life, where wealth and insecurity go hand in hand, where class still divides, and religion no longer speaks with unquestioned authority, the need of study and reflection becomes increasingly evident.

It is equally evident that if the authors were to arrogate the decision of difficult questions they would thereby defeat the purpose of ethical study. The aim in this, as in the earlier edition, is to induce a habit of thoughtful consideration, of envisaging the full meaning and consequences of individual conduct and social policies, and to aid the student with tools and method. As tools, the processes in which morals took form, and certain of the notable conceptions by which the moral consciousness has been interpreted. As method, the open mind toward new values as well as toward those tested by experience, and persistent effort to pursue analysis and inquiry until underlying principles or assumptions are reached and examined.

As regards details, changes in Part I will be found in Chapters

1, 3, and 6. A new chapter on the Roman contribution has been added, and the chapter on the Modern Period has been almost entirely rewritten. Part II has been recast; the method of presentation has been changed and the material practically all rewritten. Part III with the exception of pages 438–443 is new.

It is a pleasure to acknowledge suggestions from many colleagues who used the earlier edition. Among these, the late Professors G. H. Mead and Addison W. Moore, Professors Aikens, Ames, Burtt, Fite, Piatt, Sharp, Smith, and W. K. Wright. For experience in both sides of questions in industry the author of the economic chapters is grateful to the firms engaged in the men's clothing industry in Chicago, particularly to the firm of Hart, Schaffner, and Marx as represented by Dr. E. D. Howard, and to the Amalgamated Clothing Workers as represented by their president, Mr. Sidney Hillman, and the Chicago manager, Mr. Levin. And finally for suggestions as to both style and substance and for generous help in proof reading to Dr. M. C. Tufts.

J. D.

J. H. T.

March, 1932

Preface to the First Edition

The significance of this text in Ethics lies in its effort to awaken a vital conviction of the genuine reality of moral problems and the value of reflective thought in dealing with them. To this purpose are subordinated the presentation in Part I of historic material; the discussion in Part II of the different types of theoretical interpretation, and the consideration, in Part III, of some typical social and economic problems which characterize the present.

Experience shows that the student of morals has difficulty in getting the field objectively and definitely before him so that its problems strike him as real problems. Conduct is so intimate that it is not easy to analyze. It is so important that to a large extent the perspective for regarding it has been unconsciously fixed by early training. The historical method of approach has proved in the classroom experience of the authors an effective method of meeting these difficulties. To follow the moral life through typical epochs of its development enables students to realize what is involved in their own habitual standpoints; it also presents a concrete body of subject-matter which serves as material of analysis and discussion.

The classic conceptions of moral theory are of remarkable importance in illuminating the obscure places of the moral life and in giving the student clues which will enable him to explore it for himself. But there is always danger of either dogmatism or a sense of unreality when students are introduced abruptly to the theoretical ideas. Instead of serving as tools for understanding the moral facts, the ideas are likely to become substitutes for the facts. When they are proffered ready-made, their theoretical acuteness and cleverness may be admired, but their practical soundness and applicability are suspected. The historical introduction permits the student to be present, as it were, at the social situations in which the intellectual instruments were forged. He appreciates their relevancy to the conditions which provoked them, and he is encouraged to try them on simple problems before attempting the complex problems of the present. By assisting in their gradual development he gains confidence in the ideas and in his power to use them.

In the second part, devoted more specifically to the analysis and criticism of the leading conceptions of moral theory, the aim accordingly has not been to instill the notions of a school nor to inculcate a ready-made system, but to show the development of theories out of the problems and experience of every-day conduct, and to suggest how these theories may be fruitfully applied in practical exigencies. Aspects of the moral life have been so thoroughly examined that it is possible to present certain principles in the confidence that they will meet general acceptance. Rationalism and hedonism, for example, have contributed toward a scientific statement of the elements of conduct, even though they have failed as self-inclosed and final systems. After the discussions of Kant and Mill, Sidgwick and Green, Martineau and Spencer, it is possible to affirm that there is a place in the moral life for reason and a place for happiness,—a place for duty and a place for valuation. Theories are treated not as incompatible rival systems which must be accepted or rejected *en bloc*, but as more or less adequate methods of surveying the problems of conduct. This mode of approach facilitates the scientific estimation and determination of the part played by various factors in the complexity of moral life. The student is put in a position to judge the problems of conduct for himself. This emancipation and enlightenment of individual judgment is the chief aim of the theoretical portion.

In a considerable part of the field, particularly in the political and economic portions of Part III, no definitive treatment is as yet possible. Nevertheless, it is highly desirable to introduce the student to the examination of these unsettled questions. When the whole civilized world is giving its energies to the meaning and value of justice and democracy, it is intolerably academic that those interested in ethics should have to be content with conceptions already worked out, which therefore relate to what is least doubtful in conduct rather than to questions now urgent. Moreover, the advantages of considering theory and practice in direct relation to each other are mutual. On the one hand, as against the *a priori* claims of both individualism and socialism, the need of the hour seems to us to be the application of methods of more deliberate analysis and experiment. The extreme conservative may deprecate any scrutiny of the present order; the ardent radical may be impatient of the critical and seemingly tardy processes of the investigator; but those who have considered well the conquest which man is making of the world of nature cannot forbear the conviction that the cruder method of trial and error and the time-honored method of prejudice and partisan controversy need not longer completely dominate the regulation of the life of society. They hope for a larger application of the scientific method to the problems of human welfare and progress. Conversely, a science which takes part in the actual work of promoting moral order and moral progress must receive a valuable reflex influence of stimulus and of test. To consider morality in the making as well as to dwell upon values already established should make the science more vital. And whatever the effect upon the subject-matter, the student can hardly appreciate the full force of his materials and methods as long as they are kept aloof from the questions which are occupying the minds of his contemporaries.

Teachers who are limited in time will doubtless prefer to make their own selections of material, but the following suggestions present one possible line of choice. In Part I, of the three chapters dealing with the Hebrew, Greek, and modern developments, any one may be taken as furnishing an illustration of the method; and certain portions of Chapter 9 may be found more detailed in analysis than is necessary for the beginner. In Part II, Chapters 11–12 may be omitted without losing the thread of the argument. In Part III, any one of the specific topics—*viz.*, the political state, the economic order, the family—may be considered apart from the others. Some teachers may prefer to take Parts in their entirety. In this case, any two may be chosen.

As to the respective shares of the work for which the authors are severally responsible, while each has contributed suggestions and criticisms to the work of the other in sufficient degree to make the book throughout a joint work, Part I has been written by Mr. Tufts, Part II by Mr. Dewey and in Part III, Chapters 20 and 21 are by Mr. Dewey, Chapters 22–26 by Mr. Tufts.

It need scarcely be said that no attempt has been made in the bibliographies to be exhaustive. When the dates of publication of the work cited are given, the plan has been in general to give, in the case of current literature, the date of the latest edition, and in the case of some classical treatises the date of original publication.

In conclusion, the authors desire to express their indebtedness to their colleagues and friends Dr. Wright, Mr. Talbert, and Mr. Eastman, who have aided in the reading of the proof and with other suggestions.

J. D.
J. H. T.

Introduction

§ 1. Definition and Methods

The place for an accurate definition of a subject is at the end of an inquiry rather than at the beginning, but a brief definition will serve to mark out the field. Ethics is the science that deals with conduct, in so far as this is considered as right or wrong, good or bad. A single term for conduct so considered is "moral conduct," or the "moral life." Another way of stating the same thing is to say that ethics aims to give a systematic account of our judgments about conduct, in so far as these estimate it from the standpoint of right or wrong, good or bad.

The terms "ethics" and "ethical" are derived from a Greek word *ethos* which originally meant customs, usages, especially those belonging to some group as distinguished from another, and later came to mean disposition, character. They are thus like the Latin word "moral," from *mores*, or the German *sittlich*, from *Sitten*. As we shall see, it was in customs, "ethos," "mores," that the moral or ethical began to appear. For customs were not merely habitual ways of acting; they were ways approved by the group or society. To act contrary to the customs of the group brought severe disapproval. This might not be formulated in precisely our terms—right and wrong, good and bad,—but the attitude was the same in essence. The terms ethical and moral as applied to the conduct of today imply of course a far more complex and advanced type of life than the old words "ethos" and "mores," just as economics deals with a more complex problem than "the management of a household," but the terms have a distinct value if they suggest the way in which the moral life had its beginning.

To give a scientific account of judgments about conduct, means to find the principles which are the basis of these judgments.

Conduct or the moral life has two obvious aspects. On the one hand it is a life of purpose. It implies thought and feeling, ideals and motives, valuation and choice. These are processes to be studied by psychological methods. On the other hand, conduct has its outward side. It has relations to nature, and especially to human society. Moral life is called out or stimulated by certain necessities of individual and social existence. As Protagoras put it, in mythical form, the gods gave men a sense of justice and of reverence, in order to enable them to unite for mutual preservation.[1] And in turn the moral life aims to modify or transform both natural and social environments, to build a "kingdom of man" which shall be also an ideal social order—a "kingdom of God." These relations to nature and society are studied by the biological and social sciences. Sociology, economics, politics, law, and jurisprudence deal particularly with this aspect of conduct. Ethics must employ their methods and results for this aspect of its problem, as it employs psychology for the examination of conduct on its inner side.

But ethics is not merely the sum of these various sciences. It has a problem of its own which is created by just this twofold aspect of life and conduct. It has to relate these two sides. It has to study the inner process *as determined by the outer conditions or as changing these outer conditions*, and the outward behavior or institution *as determined by the inner purpose, or as affecting the inner life*. To study choice and purpose is psychology; to study choice as affected by the rights of others and to judge it as right or wrong by this standard is ethics. Or again, to study a corporation may be economics, or sociology, or law; to study its activities as resulting from the purposes of persons or as affecting the welfare of persons, and to judge its acts as good or bad from such a point of view, is ethics.

In approaching the study of ethics we shall employ the comparative and genetic methods. We cannot assume that our own morality is the only type that needs to be considered. Customs of primitive folk are doubtless not an adequate guide for present-day conduct, nor are our problems identical with those of ancient Hebrews, Greeks, and Romans. Yet despite civilization we are still fundamentally human. Like primitive folk and the an-

1. Plato, *Protagoras*, sec. 320 ff.

cients we are born with a certain bodily structure, depend on parental care, are divided into men and women, use language, learn to think. We have to get a living, and have to get on with our fellows. But as compared with earlier times, we find ourselves confronted with such complex and difficult situations that there is much doubt and perplexity as to our standards.

When we deal with any process of life it is found to be a great aid for understanding present conditions if we trace the history of the process and see how present conditions have come about. And in the case of morality, in particular, there are four reasons for examining earlier stages. The first is that we may begin our study with a simpler material. Moral life at present is extremely complex. Professional, civic, domestic, philanthropic, ecclesiastical, and social obligations claim adjustment. Interests in wealth, in knowledge, in power, in friendship, in social welfare, make demand for recognition in fixing upon what is good. It is desirable to consider first a simpler problem. In the second place, this complex moral life is like the human body in that it contains "rudiments" and "survivals." Some of our present standards and ideals were formed at one period in the past, and some at another. Some of these apply to present conditions and some do not. Some are at variance with others. Many apparent conflicts in moral judgments are explained when we discover how the judgments came to be formed in the first instance. We cannot easily understand the moral life of today except in the light of earlier morality. The third reason is that we may get a more objective material for study. Our moral life is so intimate a part of ourselves that it is hard to observe impartially. Its characteristics escape notice because they are so familiar. When we travel we find the customs, laws, and moral standards of other peoples standing out as "peculiar." Until we have been led by some such means to compare our own conduct with that of others it probably does not occur to us that our own standards are also peculiar, and hence in need of explanation. It is as difficult scientifically as it is personally to see ourselves as others see us. It is doubtless true that to see ourselves merely as others see us would not be enough. Complete moral analysis requires us to take into our reckoning motives and purposes which may perhaps be undiscoverable by the "others." But it is a great aid to this completer analysis if we can sharpen our vision and awaken our attention by a comparative study. A fourth reason for a genetic study is that it emphasizes the dynamic, progressive character of morality. To examine the present merely may easily give the impression that the moral life is not a *life*, a moving process, something still in the making—but a changeless structure. There is moral progress as well as a moral order. This may be discovered by an analysis of the very nature of moral conduct, but it stands out more clearly and impressively if we trace the actual development in history. Before attempting our analysis of the present moral consciousness and its judgments, we shall therefore give an outline of earlier stages and simpler phases.

§ 2. The Moral as a Growth

At present biologists, psychologists, and sociologists are far from agreement as to the relative part played in the individual's make-up and character by heredity, environment, and the individual's own choices and habits. Similarly in the history of races and cultures, the importance of race, of economic and other social forces, and of great men, is variously estimated by anthropologists, historians, and other students of this complex problem. For our purpose we shall assume that all these factors enter into moral growth, although it may sometimes be convenient to distinguish what nature does, what society does, and what the individual does for himself, as he chooses, thinks, selects, and forms habits and character.

We may also find it convenient to distinguish *three levels* of behavior and conduct: (1) behavior which is motived by various biological, economic, or other non-moral impulses or needs (e.g., family, life, work), and which yet has important results for morals; (2) behavior or conduct in which the individual accepts with relatively little critical reflection the standards and ways of his group as these are embodied in customs or *mores*; (3) conduct in which the individual thinks and judges for himself, considers whether a purpose is good or right, decides and chooses, and does not accept the standards of his group without reflection.

Although this separate consideration of these levels has convenience in gaining clear conceptions of stages and factors in moral growth, it is important to remember that no individual of maturity is wholly at any single level. We are all born into families; we all pursue activities which develop thinking; we all are members of some social group and are subtly molded by its standards; we all on some occasions think and choose.

If, instead of considering separately the factors and forces in moral growth, we look at the process of growth as it now goes on in a child, and as to some extent it has gone on in the history of those peoples which have had most to do with the present moral life of Europe and America, we may describe this as a process in which man becomes more *rational*, more *social*, and finally more *moral*. We examine briefly each of these aspects.

The first need of the organism is to live and grow. The first impulses and activities are therefore for food, self-defense, and other immediate necessities. Primitive men eat, sleep, fight, build shelters, and give food and protection to their offspring. The rationalizing process will mean at first greater use of intelligence to satisfy these same wants. It will show itself in skilled occupations, in industry and trade, in the utilizing of all resources to further man's power and happiness. But to rationalize conduct is also to introduce new ends. It not only enables man to get what he wants; it changes the kind of objects that he wants. This shows itself externally in what man makes and in how he occupies himself. He must of course have food and shelter. But he makes temples and statues and poems. He makes myths and theories of the world. He carries on great enterprises in commerce or government, not so much to gratify desires for bodily wants as to experience the growth of power. He creates a family life which is raised to a higher level by art and religion. He does not live by bread only, but builds up gradually a life of reason. Psychologically this means that whereas at the beginning we want what our body calls for, we soon come to want things which the mind takes an interest in. As we form by memory, imagination, and reason a more continuous, permanent, highly-organized self, we require a far more permanent and ideal kind of good to satisfy us. This gives rise to the contrast between the material and ideal selves, or in another form, between the world and the spirit.

The socializing side of the process of development stands for an increased capacity to enter into relations with other human beings. Like the growth of reason it is both a means and an end. It has its roots in certain biological facts—sex, parenthood, kinship—and in the necessities of mutual support and protection. But the associations thus formed imply a great variety of activities which call out new powers and set up new ends. Language is one of the first of these activities and a first step toward more complete socialization. Cooperation, in all kinds of enterprises, interchange of services and goods, participation in social arts, associations for various purposes, institutions of blood, family, government, and religion, all add enormously to the individual's power. On the other hand, as he enters into these relations and becomes a member of all these bodies, he inevitably undergoes a transformation in his interests. Psychologically the process is one of building up a social self. Imitation and suggestion, sympathy and affection, common purpose and common interest, are the aids in building such a self. As the various impulses, emotions, and purposes are more definitely organized into such a unit, it becomes possible to set off the interests of others against those interests that centre in my more individual good. Conscious egoism and altruism become possible. The interests of self and others can be raised to the plane of rights and justice.

All this is not yet moral progress in the fullest sense. The progress to more rational and more social conduct is the indispensable condition of the moral, but not the whole story. What is needed is that the more rational and social conduct should itself be valued as good, and so be chosen and sought; or in terms of control, that the law which society or reason prescribes should be consciously thought of as right, used as a standard, and respected as binding. This gives the contrast between the higher and lower, as a conscious aim, not merely as a matter of taste. It raises the collision between self and others to the plane of personal rights and justice, of deliberate, selfishness or benevolence. Finally it gives the basis for such organization of the social and rational choices that the progress already gained may be permanently secured in terms of acquired habit and character, while the attention, the struggle between duty and inclination, the conscious choice, move forward to a new issue.

§ 3. Divisions of the Treatment

Part I, after a preliminary presentation of certain important aspects of group life, will first trace the process of moral development in its general outlines, and then give specific illustrations of the process taken from the life of Israel, of Greece, of Rome, and of modern civilization.

Part II will analyze conduct or the moral life on its inner, personal side. After distinguishing more carefully what is meant by moral action, it will take up the three chief concepts or categories about which moral theory has centered:—namely, Good, Right (or Duty and Law), and Approbation and Virtue, concluding with discussion of Moral Knowledge and the place of the Self in moral conduct.

Part III will study conduct as action in society. But instead of a general survey, attention will be upon three phases of conduct which are of especial interest and importance. Political rights and duties, the production, distribution, and ownership of wealth, and finally the relations of domestic and family life, all present unsettled problems. These challenge the student to make a careful examination, for he must take some attitude as citizen toward the issues involved.

If we can discover or discern ethical principles these ought to give some guidance for the unsolved problems of life which continually present themselves for decision. Whatever may be true for other sciences it would seem that ethics at least ought to have some practical value. "In this theater of man's life it is reserved for God and the angels to be lookers on." Man must act; and he must act well or ill, rightly or wrongly, If he has reflected, has considered his conduct in the light of the general principles of human order and progress, he ought to be able to act more intelligently and freely, to achieve the satisfaction that always attends on scientific as compared with uncritical or rule-of-thumb practice. Socrates gave the classic statement for the study of conduct when he said, "A life unexamined, uncriticized, is not worthy of man."

Literature

The literature on specific topics will be found at the beginning of each Part, and at the close of the several chapters. We indicate here some of the more useful manuals and recent representative works, and add some specific references on the scope and methods of ethics. Baldwin's *Dic-*

tionary of Philosophy and Psychology has selected lists (see especially articles, "Ethical Theories," "Ethics," "Worth") and general lists (Vol. III.). Runze, *Praktische Ethik*, 1891, has good bibliographies.

ELEMENTARY TEXTS: Drake, *The New Morality*, 1928; Everett, *Moral Values*, 1918; Fite, *Introductory Study of Ethics*, 1903; Mackenzie, *Manual of Ethics*, 1900; Sharp, *Ethics*, 1928; Urban, *Fundamentals of Ethics*, 1930; Wright, *General Introduction to Ethics*, 1929.

REPRESENTATIVE BOOKS AND TREATISES IN ENGLISH: Green, *Prolegomena to Ethics*, 1883 (Idealism); Martineau, *Types of Ethical Theory*, 1885, 3rd ed., 1891 (Intuitionism); Sidgwick's *Methods of Ethics*, 1874, 6th ed., 1901 (Union of Intuitionist and Utilitarian Positions with careful analysis of common sense); Spencer, *The Principles of Ethics*, 1892–93 (Evolution); Stephen's *Science of Ethics*, 1882. The comprehensive work of Paulsen (*System der Ethik*, 1889, 5th ed., 1900) has been translated in part by Thilly, 1899; that of Wundt (*Ethik*, 1886, 3rd ed., 1903), by Titchener, Gulliver, and Washburn, 1897–1901. Among the more recent contributions, either to the whole field or to specific parts, may be noted: Alexander, *Moral Order and Progress*, 1889, 2nd ed., 1891; Dewey, *Outlines of Ethics*, 1891, and *The Study of Ethics: A Syllabus*, 1894; Fite, *Moral Philosophy*, 1925; Höffding, *Ethik*, German tr., 1887; Janet, *The Theory of Morals*, Eng. tr., 1884; Ladd, *Philosophy of Conduct*, 1902; Mezes, *Ethics: Descriptive and Explanatory*, 1900; Moore, *Principia Ethica*, 1903; Palmer, *The Field of Ethics*, 1902, *The Nature of Goodness*, 1903; Taylor, *The Problem of Conduct*, 1901; Rashdall, *The Theory of Good and Evil*, 1907; Bowne, *The Principles of Ethics*, 1892; Rickaby, *Moral Philosophy*, 1888; Nicolai Hartmann, *Ethics*, tr. by Coit, Vol. I., 1932.

HISTORIES OF ETHICS: Rogers, A. K., *Morals in Review*, 1927; Sidgwick, *History of Ethics*, 3rd ed., 1892; Albee, *A History of English Utilitarianism*, 1902; Stephen, *The English Utilitarians*, 1900; Martineau, *Types of Ethical Theory*; Whewell, *Lectures on the History of Moral Philosophy in England*, 1852, 1862; Köstlin, *Geschichte der Ethik*, 2 vols., 1881–92 (ancient theories); Jodl, *Geschichte der Ethik*, 2 vols., 1882–89 (modern); Wundt, *Ethik*, Vol. II.; the histories of philosophy by Windelband, Höffding, Erdmann, Ueberweg, Falckenberg.

SCOPE AND METHOD OF ETHICS: See the opening chapters in nearly all the works cited above, especially Palmer (*Field of Ethics*), Moore, Stephen, Spencer, Paulsen, and Wundt (*Facts of the Moral Life*); see also Ritchie, *Philosophical Studies*, 1905, pp. 264–291; Wallace, *Lectures and Essays on Natural Theology and Ethics*, 1898, pp. 194 ff.; Dewey, *Logical Conditions of a Scientific Treatment of Morality* (University of Chicago Decennial Publications, 1903); Stuart, *The Logic of Self-Realization*, in University of California Publications in Philosophy, I.,

1904; Small, *The Significance of Sociology for Ethics*, 1902; Hadley, Articles on Economic Theory in Baldwin's *Dict.*
RELATION OF THEORY TO LIFE: Green, *Prolegomena*, Book IV.; Dewey, *International Journal of Ethics*, Vol. I., 1891, pp. 186–203; James, same journal, Vol. I., pp. 330–354; Mackenzie, same journal, Vol. IV., 1894, pp. 160–173.

Part I

The Beginnings and Growth of Morality

General Literature for Part I

Hobhouse, *Morals in Evolution*, 2 vols., 1906.

Westermarck, *The Origin and Development of Moral Ideas*, Vol. I., 1906.

Sutherland, *The Origin and Growth of the Moral Instinct*, 2 vols., 1898.

Wundt, *Facts of the Moral Life*, 1902; also *Ethik*, 3rd ed., 1903, Vol. I., pp. 280–523.

Paulsen, *A System of Ethics*, 1899, Book I.

Sumner, *Folkways*, 1907.

Sneath (Editor), *The Evolution of Ethics as Revealed in the Great Religions*, 1927.

Bergemann, *Ethik als Kulturphilosophie*, 1904.

Mezes, *Ethics: Descriptive and Explanatory*, Part I.

Dewey, "The Evolutionary Method as Applied to Morality," *Philos. Review*, XI., 1902, pp. 107–124, 353–371.

Adam Smith, *Theory of Moral Sentiments*, 1759.

Baldwin, *Social and Ethical Interpretations*, 1902.

Taylor, *The Problem of Conduct*, 1901, ch. iii.

Spencer, *Data of Ethics*, 1879; *Psychology*, 1872, Part IX., chs. v.–viii.

Ihering, *Der Zweck im Recht*, 3rd ed., 1893.

Steinthal, *Allgemeine Ethik*, 1885.

Goodsell, *A History of the Family as a Social and Educational Institution*, 1923.

Briffault, *The Mothers*, 1927.

2

Early Group Life

To understand the growth of moral life, whether in the history of civilization or in a child, it is helpful as a first step to look into the life of certain more primitive societies. For these show clearly the great influence of groups on their members.

It is not asserted that all peoples have had precisely the same type of groups, or the same degree of group solidarity. It is beyond question that the ancestors of modern civilized races lived under the general types of group life which will be outlined, and that these types or their survivals are found among the great mass of peoples today.

§ 1. Typical Facts of Group Life

Consider the following incident as related by Dr. Gray:

A Chinese aided by his wife flogged his mother. The imperial order not only commanded that the criminals should be put to death; it further directed that the head of the clan should be put to death, that the immediate neighbors each receive eighty blows and be sent into exile; that the head or representatives of the graduates of the first degree (or B.A.) among whom the male offender ranked should be flogged and exiled; that the granduncle, the uncle, and two elder brothers should be put to death; that the prefect and the rulers should for a time be deprived of their rank; that on the face of the mother of the female offender four Chinese characters expressive of neglect of duty towards her daughter should be tattooed, and that she be exiled to a distant province; that the father of the female offender, a bachelor of arts, should not be allowed to take any higher literary degrees, and that he be flogged and exiled; that the son of the offenders should receive another name, and that the lands of the offender for a time remain fallow.[1]

Put beside this the story of Achan:

Achan had taken for his own possession certain articles from the spoil of Jericho which had been set apart or "devoted" to Yahweh. Israel then suffered a defeat in battle. When Achan's act became known, "Joshua and all Israel with him took Achan, the son of Zerah, and the mantle, and the wedge of gold, and his sons and his daughters, and his oxen, and his asses, and his sheep, and his tent, and all that he had. . . . And all Israel stoned him with stones; and they burned them with fire and stoned them with stones."[2]

The converse of these situations is brought out in the regulations of the Kumi, a Japanese local institution comprising five or more households:

As members of a Kumi we will cultivate friendly feelings even more than with our relatives, and will promote each other's happiness as well as share each other's grief. If there is an unprincipled or lawless person in a Kumi, we shall all share the responsibility for him.[3]

For another aspect of the group take Caesar's description of landholding among the Germans:

No one possesses privately a definite extent of land; no one has limited fields of his own; but every year the magistrates and chiefs distribute the land to the clans and the kindred groups (*gentibus cognationibusque hominum*) and to those (*other* groups) who live together.[4]

Of the Greeks, our intellectual ancestors, as well as fellow Aryans, it is stated that in Attica, even to a late period, the land remained to a large degree in possession of ideal persons, gods,

1. J. H. Gray, *China*, Vol. I., pp. 237 f.
2. Joshua 7:24, 25.
3. Simmons and Wigmore, *Transactions, Asiatic Society of Japan*, vol. xix., pp. 177 f.
4. *De Bell. Gall.*, VI., 22.

phylae (tribes) or phratries, kinships, political communities. Even when the superficies of the land might be regarded as private, mines were reserved as public.[5] The basis on which these kinship groups rested is thus stated by Grote:[6]

> "All these phratric and gentile associations, the larger as well as the smaller, were founded upon the same principles and tendencies of the Grecian mind—a coalescence of the idea of worship with that of ancestry, or of communion in certain special religious rites with communion of blood, real or supposed." "The god or hero, to whom the assembled members offered their sacrifices, was conceived as the primitive ancestor to whom they owed their origin."

Coulanges gives a similar statement as to the ancient family group:[7]

> The members of the ancient family were united by something more powerful than birth, affection, or physical strength; this was the religion of the sacred fire, and of dead ancestors. This caused the family to form a single body both in this life and in the next.

Finally, the following passage on clanship among the Kafirs brings out two points: (1) That such a group life implies feelings and ideas of a distinctive sort; and (2) that it has a strength rooted in the very necessities of life.

> A Kafir feels that the "frame that binds him in" extends to the clan. The sense of solidarity of the family in Europe is thin and feeble compared to the full-blooded sense of corporate union of the Kafir clan. The claims of the clan entirely swamp the rights of the individual. The system of tribal solidarity, which has worked so well in its smoothness that it might satisfy the utmost dreams of the socialist, is a standing proof of the sense of corporate union of the clan. In olden days a man did not have any feeling of personal injury when a chief made him work for white men and then told him to give all, or nearly all of his wages to his chief; the money was

---

5. Wilamowitz-Möllendorff, *Aristoteles und Athen*, II., 47, 93.
6. *History of Greece*, III., 55.
7. *The Ancient City*, p. 51.

kept within the clan, and what was the good of the clan was the good of the individual and *vice versa*. The striking thing about this unity of the clan is that it was not a thought-out plan imposed from without by legislation upon an unwilling people, but it was a *felt-out* plan which arose spontaneously along the line of least resistance. If one member of the clan suffered, all the members suffered, not in sentimental phraseology, but in real fact.[8]

The above passages refer to Aryan, Semitic, Mongolian, and Kafir peoples. They could be matched by similar statements concerning nearly every people. They suggest a way of living, and a view of life very different from that of the American or of most Europeans.[9] The American or European belongs to groups of various kinds, but he "joins" most of them. He of course is born into a family, but he does not stay in it all his life unless he pleases. And he may choose his own occupation, residence, wife, political party, religion, social club, or even national allegiance. He may own or sell his own house, give or bequeath his property, and is responsible generally speaking for no one's acts but his own. This makes him an "individual" in a much fuller sense than he would be if all these relations were settled for him. On the other hand, the member of such groups as are referred to in our examples above, has all, or nearly all, his relations fixed when he is born into a certain clan or family group. This settles his occupation, dwelling, gods, and politics. If it does not decide upon his wife, it at least usually fixes the group from which she must be taken. His conditions, in the words of Maine, are thus of "status," not of "contract." This makes a vast difference in his whole attitude. It will help to bring out more clearly by contrast the character of present morality, as well as to see moral life in the making, if we examine more carefully this group life. We shall find, as brought out in the passages already quoted, that the most important type of group is at once a kindred or family, an economic, a political, a religious, and a moral unit. First, however, we notice briefly the most important types of groups.

8. Dudley Kidd, *Savage Childhood*, pp. 74 f.
9. Russian mirs, South Slavonian "joint" families, Corsican clans with their vendettas, and tribes in the Caucasus have kept the group interest strong, and the feuds of the mountaineers in some of the border States illustrate family solidarity.

§ 2. Kinship and Household Groups

The kinship group is a body of persons who conceive of themselves as sprung from one ancestor, and hence as having in their veins one blood. It does not matter for our study whether each group has actually sprung from a single ancestor. It is highly probable that the contingencies of food-supply or of war may have been an original cause for the constitution of the group, wholly or in part. But this is of no consequence for our purpose. The important point is that the members of the group regard themselves as of one stock. In some cases the ancestor is believed to have been an animal. Then we have the so-called totem group, which is found among North American Indians, Africans, and Australians, and was perhaps the early form of Semitic groups. In other cases, some hero or even some god is named as the ancestor. In any case the essential part of the theory remains the same: namely, that one blood circulates in all the members, and hence that the life of each is a part of the common life of the group. Degrees of kindred are less important. This group, it should be noted, is not the same as the family, for in the family, as a rule, husband and wife are of different kinship groups, and continue their several kinship relations. Among some peoples marriage ceremonies, indeed, symbolize the admission of the wife into the husband's kinship, and in this case the family becomes a kinship group, but this is by no means universally the case.

The feeling that one is first and foremost a member of a group, rather than an individual, is furthered among certain kin groups by a scheme of class relationship. According to this system, instead of having one definite person whom I, and I alone, regard and address as father or mother, grandfather, uncle, brother, sister, I call any one of a given group or class of persons mother, grandfather, brother, sister. And any one else who is in the same class with me calls the same persons, mother, grandfather, brother, or sister.[10] The simplest form of such a class system is that found

10. "In all the tribes with whom we are acquainted all the terms coincide without any exception in the recognition of relationships, all of which are dependent on the existence of a classificatory system, the fundamental idea of which is that the women of certain groups marry the men of others. Each tribe has one term applied indiscriminately to the man or woman whom he actually marries

among the Hawaiians. Here there are five classes based upon the generations corresponding to what we call grandparents, parents, brothers and sisters, children, and grandchildren, but the words used to designate them do not imply any such specific parentage as do these words with us. Bearing this in mind, we may say that every one in the first class is equally grandparent to every one in the third; every one in the third is equally brother or sister to every other in the third, equally father or mother to every one in the fourth, and so on. In Australia the classes are more numerous and the relationships far more intricate and complicated, but this does not, as might be supposed, render the bond relatively unimportant; on the contrary, his relationship to every other class is "one of the most important points with which each individual must be acquainted"; it determines marital relations, food distribution, salutations, and general conduct to an extraordinary degree. A kinship group was known as "tribe" or "family" (English translation) among the Israelites; as genos, phratria, and phyle among the Greeks, gens and curia among the Romans; clan in Scotland; sept in Ireland; Sippe in Germany.

Two kinds of families may be noted as significant for our purpose. In the *maternal family* the woman remains among her own kin, and the children are naturally reckoned as belonging to the mother's kin. The husband and father is more or less a guest or outsider. In a blood feud he would have to side with his own clan and against that of his wife if his clan quarreled with hers. Clan and family are thus seen to be distinct. In the *paternal*, which easily becomes the *patriarchal* family the wife leaves her relatives to live in her husband's house and among his kin. She might then, as at Rome, abjure her own kindred and be formally adopted into her husband's gens or clan. The Greek myth of Orestes is an illustration of the clashing of these two conceptions of father kin and mother kin, and Hamlet's sparing of his mother under similar circumstances, shows a more modern point of view.

It is evident that with the prevalence of the paternal type of family, clan and household ties will mutually strengthen each other. This will make an important difference in the father's relation to the children, and gives a much firmer basis for ancestral

---

and to all whom he might lawfully marry, that is, who belong to the right group: One term to his actual mother and to all the women whom his father might lawfully have married."—Spencer and Gillen, *Native Tribes of Central Australia*, p. 57.

religion. But in many respects the environing atmosphere, the pressure and support, the group sympathy and group tradition, are essentially similar. The important thing is that every person is a member of a kindred, and likewise, of some family group, and that he thinks, feels, and acts accordingly.[11]

§ 3. The Kinship and Family Groups Are Also Economic and Industrial Units

In *land*, as a rule, no individual ownership in the modern sense was recognized. Among hunting and pastoral peoples there was, of course, no "ownership" by any group in the strict sense of modern law. But none the less, the group, large or small, had its fairly well-defined territory within which it hunted and fished; in the pastoral life it had its pasture range and its wells of water. With agriculture a more definite sense of possession arose. But possession was by the tribe or gens or household, not by the individual:

> The land belonged to the clan, and the clan was settled upon the land. A man was thus not a member of the clan, because he lived upon, or even owned, the land; but he lived upon the land, and had interests in it, because he was a member of the clan.[12]

11. The fact that primitive man is at once an individual and a member of a group—that he has as it were two personalities or selves, an individual self and a clan-self, or "tribal-self," as Clifford called it,—is not merely a psychologist's way of stating things. The Kafir people, according to their most recent student, Mr. Dudley Kidd, have two distinct words to express these two selves. They call one the *idhlozi* and the other the *itongo*. "The *idhlozi* is the individual and personal spirit born with each child—something fresh and unique which is never shared with any one else—while the *itongo* is the ancestral and corporate spirit which is not personal but tribal, or a thing of the clan, the possession of which is obtained not by birth but by certain initiatory rites. The *idhlozi* is personal and inalienable, for it is wrapped up with the man's personality, and at death it lives near the grave, or goes into the snake or totem of the clan; but the *itongo* is of the clan, and haunts the living-hut; at death it returns to the tribal *amatongo* (ancestral spirits). A man's share in this clan-spirit (*itongo*) is lost when he becomes a Christian, or when he is in any way unfaithful to the interests of the clan, but a man never loses his *idhlozi* any more than he ever loses his individuality."—*Savage Childhood*, pp. 14 f.
12. Hearn, *The Aryan Household*, p. 212.

Greek and German customs were quoted at the outset. Among the Celts the laws of ancient Ireland show a transitional stage. "The land of the tribe consisted of two distinct allotments, the 'fechtfine' or tribeland, and the 'orba' or inheritance land. This latter belonged as individual property to the men of the chieftain groups." [13] The Hindoo joint family and the house community of the Southern Slavonians are present examples of group ownership. They are joint in food, worship, and estate. They have a common home, a common table. Maxims of the Slavs express their appreciation of community life: "The common household waxes rich"; "The more bees in the hive, the heavier it weighs." One difficulty in the English administration of Ireland was this radical difference between the modern Englishman's individualistic conception of property and the Irishman's more primitive conception of group or clan ownership. Whether rightly or not, the Irish tenant refused to regard himself as merely a tenant. He considered himself as a member of a family or group which formerly owned the land, and he did not admit the justice, even though he could not disprove the legality, of an alienation of the group possession. For such a clan or household as we have described is not merely equivalent to the persons who compose it at a given time. Its property belongs to the ancestors and to the posterity as well as to the present possessors; and hence in some groups which admit an individual possession or use during life, no right of devise or inheritance is permitted. The property reverts at death to the whole gens or clan. In other cases a child may inherit, but in default of such an heir the property passes to the common possession. The right to bequeath property to the church was long a point on which civil law and canon law were at variance. The relations of the primitive clan or household group to land were therefore decidedly adapted to keep the individual's good bound up with the good of the group.

In the case of *movable goods*, such as tools, weapons, cattle, the practice is not uniform. When the goods are the product of the individual's own skill or prowess they are usually his. Tools, weapons, slaves or women captured, products of some special craft or skill, are thus usually private. But when the group acts as a unit the product is usually shared. The buffalo and salmon and

13. McLennan, *Studies in Ancient History*, p. 381.

large game were thus for the whole Indian group which hunted or fished together; and in like manner the maize which was tended by the women belonged to the household in common. Slavic and Indian house communities at the present day have a common interest in the household property. Even women and children among some tribes are regarded as the property of the group.

§ 4. The Kinship and Family Groups Were Political Bodies

In a modern family the parents exercise a certain degree of control over the children, but this is limited in several respects. No parent is allowed to put a child to death, or to permit him to grow up in ignorance. On the other hand, the parent is not allowed to protect the child from arrest if a serious injury has been done by him. The *State*, through its laws and officers, is regarded by us as the highest authority in a certain great sphere of action. It must settle conflicting claims and protect life and property; in the opinion of many it must organize the life of its members where the cooperation of every member is necessary for some common good. In early group life there may or may not be some political body over and above the clan or family, but in any case the *kin or family is itself a sort of political State*. Not a State in the sense that the political powers are deliberately separated from personal, religious, and family ties; men gained a new conception of authority and rose to a higher level of possibilities when they consciously separated and defined government and laws from the undifferentiated whole of a religious and kindred group. But yet this primitive group was after all a State, not a mob, or a voluntary society, or a mere family; for (1) it was a more or less permanently organized body; (2) it exercised control over its members which they regarded as rightful authority, not as mere force; (3) it was not limited by any higher authority, and acted more or less effectively for the interest of the whole. The representatives of this political aspect of the group may be chiefs or sachems, a council of elders, or, as in Rome, the House Father, whose *patria potestas* marks the extreme development of the patriarchal family.

The control exercised by the group over individual members

assumes various forms among the different peoples. The more important aspects are a right over life and bodily freedom, in some cases extending to power of putting to death, maiming, chastising, deciding whether newly born children shall be preserved or not; the right of betrothal, which includes control over the marriage portion received for its women; and the right to administer property of the kin in behalf of the kin as a whole. It is probable that among all these various forms of control, the control over the marriage relations of women has been most persistent. One reason for this control may have been the fact that the group was bound to resent injuries of a member of the group who had been married to another. Hence this responsibility seemed naturally to involve the right of decision as to her marriage.

Legal rights are still largely due to membership in a group. A State may allow a citizen of another country to own land, to sue in its courts, and will usually give him a certain amount of protection, but the first-named rights are often limited, and it is only a few years since Chief Justice Taney's dictum stated the existing legal theory of the United States to be that the Negro "had no rights which the white man was bound to respect." Even where legal theory does not recognize race or other distinctions, it is often hard in practice for an alien, or member of a disesteemed social or economic group, to get justice. In primitive clan or family groups this principle is in full force. Justice is a privilege which falls to a man as belonging to some group—not otherwise. The member of the clan or the household or the village community has a claim, but the stranger has no standing. He may be treated kindly, as a guest, but he cannot demand "justice" at the hands of any group but his own. In this conception of rights within the group we have the prototype of modern civil law. The dealing of clan with clan is a matter of war or negotiation, not of law; and the clanless man is an "outlaw" in fact as well as in name.

Joint responsibility and mutual support, as shown in the blood feud, was a natural consequence of this fusion of political and kindred relations. In modern life States treat each other as wholes in certain respects. If some member of a savage tribe assaults a citizen of one of the civilized nations, the injured party invokes the help of his government. A demand is usually made that the guilty party be delivered up for trial and punishment. If he is not forthcoming a "punitive expedition" is organized against the whole tribe; guilty and innocent suffer alike. Or in lieu of exterminating the offending tribe, in part or completely, the nation of the injured man may accept an indemnity in money or land from the offender's tribe. The same principle carried out through private citizens as public agents, and applied to towns, underlay a peculiar practice in the Middle Ages. "When merchants of one country had been defrauded by those of another, or found it impossible to collect a debt from them, the former country issued letters of marque and reprisal, authorizing the plunder of any citizens of the offending town until satisfaction should be obtained." Transfer the situation to the early clan or tribe, and this solidarity is increased because each member is related to the rest by blood, as well as by national unity. The Arabs do not say "The blood of M. or N. has been spilt," naming the man; they say, "Our blood has been spilt." [14] The whole group, therefore, feels injured and regards every man in the offender's kin as more or less responsible. The next of kin, the "avenger of blood," stands first in duty and privilege, but the rest are all involved in greater or less degree.

Within the group each member will be treated more or less fully as an individual. If he takes his kinsman's wife or his kinsman's game he will be dealt with by the authorities or by the public opinion of his group. He will not indeed be put to death if he kills his kinsman, but he will be hated, and may be driven out. "Since the living kin is not killed for the sake of the dead kin, everybody will hate to see him." [15]

When a smaller group, like a family, is at the same time a part of a larger group like a phratry or a tribe, we have the phase of solidarity which is so puzzling to the modern. We hold to solidarity in war or between nations; but with a few exceptions [16] we have replaced it by individual responsibility of adults for debts and crimes, so far as the civil law has jurisdiction. In earlier times the higher group or authority treated the smaller as a unit. Achan's family all perished with him. The Chinese sense of justice recognized a series of degrees in responsibility dependent on

14. Robertson Smith, *Kinship and Marriage in Early Arabia*, p. 23.
15. Cited from the Gwentian Code. Seebohm, *The Tribal System in Wales*, p. 104.
16. E.g., certain joint responsibilities of husband and wife.

nearness of kin or of residence, or of occupation. The Welsh system held kinsmen as far as second cousins responsible for insult or injury short of homicide, and as far as fifth cousins (seventh degree of descent) for the payment in case of homicide. "The mutual responsibility of kinsmen for *saraad* and *galanas* (the Wergild of the Germans), graduated according to nearness of kin to the murdered man and to the criminal, reveals more clearly than anything else the extent to which the individual was bound by innumerable meshes to his fixed place in the tribal community."[17]

§ 5. The Kinship or Household Group Was a Religious Unit

The kinship or household group determined largely both the ideas and the cultus of primitive religion; conversely religion gave completeness, value, and sacredness to the group life. Kinship with unseen powers or persons was the fundamental religious idea. The kinship group as a religious body *simply extended the kin to include invisible as well as visible members.* The essential feature of religion is not unseen beings who are feared, or cajoled, or controlled by magic. It is rather *kindred* unseen beings, who may be feared, but who are also reverenced and loved. The kinship may be physical or spiritual, but however conceived it makes gods and worshippers members of one group.[18]

In totem groups, the prevailing conception is that one blood circulates in all the members of the group and that the ancestor of the whole group is some object of nature, such as sun or moon, plant or animal. Perhaps the most interesting and intelligible account of the relation between the animal ancestor and the members of the group is that which has been discovered in certain Australian tribes. These folks believe that every child, at

17. Seebohm, *The Tribal System in Wales*, pp. 103 f.
18. "From the earliest times, religion, as distinct from magic or sorcery, addresses itself to kindred and friendly beings, who may indeed be angry with their people for a time, but are always placable except to the enemies of their worshippers or to renegade members of the community. It is not with a vague fear of unknown powers, but with a loving reverence for known gods who are knit to their worshippers by strong bonds of kinship, that religion in the only true sense of the word begins."—Robertson Smith, *Religion of the Semites*, p. 54.

its birth, is the reincarnation of some previous member of the group, and that these ancestors were an actual transformation of animals and plants, or of water, fire, wind, sun, moon, or stars. Such totem groups cherish that animal which they believe to be their ancestor and ordinarily will not kill it or use it for food. The various ceremonies of religious initiation are intended to impress upon the younger members of the group the sacredness of this kindred bond which unites them to each other and to their totem. The beginnings of decorative art frequently express the importance of the symbol, and the totem is felt to be as distinctly a member of the group as is any of the human members.

At a somewhat higher stage of civilization, and usually in connection with the patriarchal households or groups in which kinship is reckoned through the male line, the invisible members of the group are the *departed ancestors*. This ancestor worship is a power today in China and Japan, and in the tribes of the Caucasus. The ancient Semites, Romans, Teutons, Celts, Hindoos, all had their kindred gods of the household. The Roman genius, lares, penates, and manes, perhaps the Hebrew teraphim,— prized by Laban and Rachel, kept by David, valued in the time of Hosea—were loved and honored side by side with other deities. Sometimes the nature deities, such as Zeus or Jupiter, were incorporated with the kinship or family gods. The Greek Hestia and Roman Vesta symbolized the sacredness of the hearth. The kinship tie thus determined for every member of the group his religion.

Conversely, this bond of union with unseen, yet ever present and powerful kindred spirits completed the group and gave to it its highest authority, its fullest value, its deepest sacredness. If the unseen kin are nature beings, they symbolize for man his dependence upon nature and his kinship in some vague fashion with the cosmic forces. If the gods are the departed ancestors, they are then conceived as still potent, like Father Anchises, to protect and guide the fortunes of their offspring. The wisdom, courage, and affection, as well as the power of the great heroes of the group, live on. The fact that the gods are unseen enhances tremendously their supposed power. The visible members of the group may be strong, but their strength can be measured. The living elders may be wise, yet they are not far beyond the rest of the group. But the invisible beings cannot be measured. The long-departed ancestor may have inconceivable age and wisdom. The imagination has free scope to magnify his power and invest him with all the ideal values it can conceive. The religious bond is, therefore, fitted to be the bearer, as the religious object is the embodiment in concrete form, of the higher standards of the group, and to furnish the sanction for their enforcement or adoption.

§ 6. Groups or Classes on the Basis of Age and Sex

While the kindred and family groups are by far the most important for early morality, other groupings are significant. The division by ages is widespread. The simplest scheme gives three classes: (1) children, (2) young men and maidens, (3) married persons. Puberty forms the bound between the first and second; marriage that between the second and third. Distinct modes of dress and ornament, frequently also different residences and standards of conduct, belong to these several classes. Of groups on the basis of sex, the *men's clubs* are especially worthy of note. They flourish now chiefly in the islands of the Pacific, but there are indications, such as the common meals of the Spartans, of a wide spread among European peoples in early times. The fundamental idea[19] seems to be that of a common house for the unmarried young men, where they eat, sleep, and pass their time, whereas the women, children, and married men sleep and eat in the family dwelling. But in most cases all the men resort to the clubhouse by day. Strangers may be entertained there. It thus forms a sort of general centre for the men's activities, and for the men's conversation. As such, it is an important agency for forming and expressing public opinion, and for impressing upon the young men just entering the house the standards of the older members. Further, in some cases these houses become the centre of rites to the dead, and thus add the impressiveness of religious significance to their other activities.

Finally, *secret societies* may be mentioned as a subdivision of sex groups, for among primitive peoples such societies are con-

19. Schurtz, *Altersklassen und Männerbünde.*

fined in almost all cases to the men. They seem in many cases to have grown out of the age classes already described. The transition from childhood to manhood, mysterious in itself, was invested with further mysteries by the old men who conducted the ceremonies of initiation. Masks were worn, or the skulls of deceased ancestors were employed, to give additional mystery and sanctity. The increased power gained by secrecy would often be itself sufficient to form a motive for such organization, especially where they had some end in view not approved by the dominant authorities. Sometimes they exercise strict authority over their members, and assume judicial and punitive functions, as in the Vehm of the Middle Ages. Sometimes they become merely leagues of enemies to society.

§ 7. Moral Significance of the Kindred and Other Groups

The moral in this early stage is not to be looked for as something distinct from the political, religious, kindred, and sympathetic aspects of the clan, family, and other groups. The question rather is, *How far are these very political, religious, and other aspects implicitly moral?* If by moral we mean a conscious testing of conduct by an inner and self-imposed standard, if we mean a freely chosen as contrasted with a habitual or customary standard, then evidently we have the moral only in germ. For the standards are group standards, rather than those of individual conscience; they operate largely through habit rather than through choice. Nevertheless they are not set for the individual by outsiders. They are set by a group *of which he is a member.* They are enforced by a group of which he is a member. Conduct is praised or blamed, punished or rewarded by the group of which he is a member. Property is administered, industry is carried on, wars and feuds prosecuted for the common good. What the group does, each member joins in doing. It is a reciprocal matter: A helps enforce a rule or impose a service on B; he cannot help feeling it fair when the same rule is applied to himself. He has to "play the game," and usually he expects to play it as a matter of course. Each member, therefore, is practicing certain acts, standing in certain relations, maintaining certain attitudes, just because he is one of the group which does these things and maintains these standards. And he does not act in common with the group without sharing in the group emotions. It is a grotesque perversion to conceive the restraints of gods and chiefs as purely external terrors. The primitive group could enter into the spirit implied in the words of the Athenian chorus, which required of an alien upon adoption

To loathe whate'er our state does hateful hold,
To reverence what it loves.[20]

Sympathies and sentiments growing out of common life, common work, common danger, common religion are the emotional bonds of a community. Morality is already implicit, it needs only to become conscious. The standards are embodied in the old men or the gods; the rational good is in the inherited wisdom; the respect for sex, for property rights, and for the common good, is embodied in the system—but it is there. Nor are the union and control a wholly objective affair. "The corporate union was not a pretty religious fancy with which to please the mind, but was so truly felt that it formed an excellent basis from which the altruistic sentiment might start. Gross selfishness was curbed, and the turbulent passions were restrained by an impulse which the man felt welling up within him, instinctive and unbidden. Clannish camaraderie was thus of immense value to the native races."[21]

Literature

The works of Hobhouse, Sumner, Westermarck contain copious references to the original sources. Among the most valuable are:

FOR PRIMITIVE PEOPLES: Waitz, *Anthropologie der Naturvölker,* 1859–72; Tylor, *Primitive Culture,* 1903; Spencer and Gillen, *The Native Tribes of Central Australia,* 1899, and *The Northern Tribes of Central Australia,* 1904; Howitt and Fison, *Kamilaroi and Kurnai,* 1880; Howitt, *The Native Tribes of S. E. Australia,* 1904; N. Thomas, *Kinship Organisations and Group Marriage in Australia,* 1906; Rivers, *The Todas,* 1906, *History of Melanesian Society,* 1914; Morgan, *Houses*

20. *Oedipus at Colonus,* vv. 186 f.
21. Dudley Kidd, *Savage Childhood,* pp. 74 f.

and House-Life of the American Aborigines, 1881, *League of the Iroquois,* 1851, *Systems of Consanguinity, Smithsonian Contributions,* 1871, *Ancient Society,* 1877. Many papers in the *Reports of the Bureau of Ethnology,* especially by Powell in 1st, 1879–80, Dorsey in 3rd, 1881–82, Mindeleff in 15th, 1893–94; Karsten, "Jibaro Indians," *Bulletin* of the Am. Bureau of Ethnol. 79, 1923; Kroeber, "Zuñi Kin and Clan," in *Am. Mus. Nat. Hist.,* Vol. XVIII., 1917; Malinowski, *The Family among the Australian Aborigines,* 1913; Seligman, *The Melanesians of British New Guinea,* 1910, *The Veddas,* 1911.

FOR INDIA, CHINA, AND JAPAN: Lyall, *Asiatic Studies, Religious and Social,* 1882; Jackson, *Cambridge History of India,* Vol. I.; Gray, *China,* 1878; Smith, *Chinese Characteristics,* 1894, *Village Life in China,* 1899; Nitobé, *Bushido,* 1905; L. Hearn, *Japan,* 1904.

FOR SEMITIC AND INDO-GERMANIC PEOPLES: W. R. Smith, *Kinship and Marriage in Early Arabia,* 1885, *The Religion of the Semites,* 1894; W. Hearn, *The Aryan Household,* 1879; Coulanges, *The Ancient City,* 1873; Seebohm, *The Tribal System in Wales,* 1895, and *Tribal Custom in Anglo-Saxon Law,* 1902; Krauss, *Sitte und Brauch der Südslaven,* 1885.

GENERAL: Boas, *The Mind of Primitive Man,* 1911; Lowie, *Primitive Society,* 1920; Goldenweiser, *Early Civilization,* 1922; Frazer, *Totemism and Exogamy,* 1910; Grosse, *Die Formen der Familie und die Formen der Wirthschaft,* 1896; Starcke, *The Primitive Family,* 1889; Maine, *Ancient Law,* 1885; McLennan, *Studies in Ancient History,* 1886; Rivers, "On the Origin of the Classificatory System of Relationships," in *Anthropological Essays,* presented to E. B. Tylor, 1907; Ratzel, *History of Mankind,* 1896–98; Kovalevsky, *Tableau des Origines et de l'Evolution de la Famille et de la Propriété,* 1890; Giddings, *Principles of Sociology,* 1896, pp. 157–168, 256–298; Thomas, "Sex and Primitive Social Control" in *Sex and Society,* 1907; Webster, *Primitive Secret Societies,* 1908; Simmel, "The Sociology of Secrecy and of Secret Societies," *American Journal of Sociology,* Vol. XI., 1906, pp. 441–498; *Enc. of the Social Sciences,* Art. "Anthropology," by Boas, 1930. See also the references at close of Chapters 6, 7.

3. Basic Activities and Agencies

Moral life implies (1) guiding and controlling acts by intelligence, and (2) getting and keeping on good terms with our fellow men—with the community. We may say then that whatever makes for the development of intelligence, and for cooperation and sympathy with our fellows is laying foundations on which morality can build. The foundation is not the structure; there are some very intelligent rascals, and certain gangs show effective cooperation for criminal purposes. Nevertheless intelligence and community life are necessary factors in choosing and doing what is good and right. Nature gives us at birth a certain structure and imposes certain conditions of growth and survival which aid the development of the mind and initiate us into community life. Later conditions of survival include activities of getting food and shelter, and of defense against enemies. If the stock is to survive there must be reproduction and parental care. Moreover, while perhaps they may not be absolutely necessary for survival, many other activities such as games, contests, dances, festal celebrations, songs, and recitals of brave deeds, provide emotional stimulation and satisfaction; they strengthen social feeling and social ties. All these activities and agencies, although not primarily intended to promote morality, are yet important as making for the formation and development of intelligence, character, and right relations between men. They may be called cosmic and social roots of morals. The initial conditions of birth and infancy may be called a biological factor; the other activities may be considered under the topic named in Chapter 1, as rationalizing and socializing agencies.

§ 1. Biological Factors

The most important biological factor is the condition in which the human infant is born and passes his early years. Compare this with the birth and early life of other species. In many of these the young must fend for themselves from the beginning of separate life. The young of birds receive care for a brief period, then leave the nest, find food, and look out for themselves. The more complex system of mammals involves a more intimate and longer continued relation of young to mother. But in the human infant the organism needs, not a few weeks or months, but years of care and protection before it can care for and protect itself. Even after the age when it is barely possible for a child to get food and shelter for himself increasing need of education to meet the demands of civilized life prolongs the period of dependence upon parents.

During this period of infancy and childhood children learn, chiefly from mothers, the ways of behavior, the language, and much of the transmitted wisdom, of their group and people. They feel the mother's affection and develop their own emotional life in response. Before the machine age came in to take most of the arts and crafts away from the home to the factory, girls learned from mothers not only the preparation of food but the textile arts, the making of clothes and candles, knowledge of plants, care of the sick. Boys learned from fathers to hunt or fish, to tend and manage cattle, sheep, and horses, to plow, sow, and harvest, to work wood and metal, to build of wood, brick, and stone.

The effect upon parents, especially upon the mother, of caring for children through infancy and childhood has been scarcely less significant. Such care enlarges affection, it compels thought of the future. It gives a worthwhile object for the work and often for sacrifices when these are necessary, in the daily round. Wish and hope that the boy and girl may have a better start in life than they themselves enjoyed are incentives to the efforts of father and mother. So much follows from the conditions of birth and growth.

But children do not long remain children. Certain activities which men and women undertake in order to get a living, to satisfy curiosity, to make tools, to protect themselves, to feel the thrill of rhythm or of dramatic story, have also an influence in forming character and fitting men and women to live in society. Some of these activities we now consider under rationalizing and socializing agencies.

§ 2. Rationalizing Agencies

1. Earlier forms of occupation, hunting and fishing, call for active intelligence, although the activity is sustained to a great degree by the immediate interest or thrill of excitement, which makes them a recreation to the civilized man. Quickness of perception, alertness of mind and body, and in some cases, physical daring, are the qualities most needed. But in the pastoral life, and still more with the beginning of agriculture and commerce, the man who succeeds must have foresight and continuity of purpose. He must control impulse by reason. He must organize those habits which are the basis of character, instead of yielding to the attractions of various pleasures which might lead him from the main purpose.

The *differentiation of labor* has been a powerful influence for increasing the range of mental life and stimulating its development. If all do the same thing, all are much alike, and inevitably remain on a low level. But when the needs of men induce different kinds of work, slumbering capacities are aroused and new ones are called into being. The most deeply-rooted differentiation of labor is that between the sexes. The woman performs the work within or near the dwelling, the man hunts or tends the flocks or ranges abroad. This probably tends to accentuate further certain organic differences. Among the men, group life in its simplest phases has little differentiation except "for counsel" or "for war." But with metal working and agricultural life the field widens. At first the specializing is largely by families rather than by individual choice. Castes of workmen may take the place of mere kinship ties. Later on the rules of caste in turn become a hindrance to individuality and must be broken down if the individual is to emerge to full self-direction.

2. Aside from their influence as work, *arts and crafts* have a distinctly elevating and refining effect. The textiles, pottery, and skilfully made tools and weapons; the huts or houses when artis-

tically constructed; the so-called free or fine arts of dance and music, of color and design—all have this common element: they give some visible or audible embodiment for order or form. The artist or craftsman must make definite his idea in order to work it out in cloth or clay, in wood or stone, in dance or song. When thus embodied, it is preserved, at least for a time. It is part of the daily environment of the society. Those who see or hear are having constantly suggested to them ideas and values which bring more meaning into life and elevate its interests. Moreover, the order, the rational plan or arrangement which is embodied in all well-wrought objects, as well as in the fine arts in the narrow sense, deserves emphasis. Plato and Schiller have seen in this a valuable preparation for morality. To govern action by law is moral, but it is too much to expect this of the savage and the child as a conscious principle where the law opposes impulse. In art as in play there is direct interest and pleasure in the act, but in art there is also order or law. In conforming to this order the savage, or the child, is in training for the more conscious control where the law, instead of favoring, may thwart or oppose impulse and desire.

3. A child begins very early to explore and test the things and people about him. He is curious. He handles, tastes, looks, listens, and things get meanings. He finds obstacles and is forced to contrive a way to do or get what he wants. When a child in a hunting tribe begins to hunt he must study the ways of wild animals. If he is to get his living from the soil or the sea he will watch the sky, and try to forecast the weather. He will wonder at the movements of sun, moon, and stars. If he becomes a trader he must decide what goods to carry, and will match wits with his customers. All these problems call for *thinking*, that is, for making use of something which he has seen, or known, or known about, before in order to help in meeting this new situation. If we can see that the new object is like some things and different from others that we have known before, that helps to class it. We think that if it moves it is alive, or that if it is sweet it is good to eat, or we think that a man who speaks roughly is angry. Such "general" ideas as "alive," "sweet," "angry" enable us to connect our particular experiences into wholes, to guide our acts intelligently, instead of either blindly following habit, or being dazed by each new event as though we had never seen anything like it

before. Now to guide our lives intelligently toward what is good requires the same kind of thinking. It means looking ahead to forecast all the consequences of a decision. Training in thinking is then forging a tool which is indispensable for the most intelligent morality.

§ 3. Socializing Agencies

1. *Language* might well have been noted under rationalizing agencies, for if not absolutely essential to thinking it is so intimately a part of it by furnishing the symbols and tools with which most thinking does its work that it is virtually indispensable. Its function as a socializing agency is similarly fundamental. It is not the only method of "communicating," i.e., of imparting, or sharing, or making common, some thought or feeling, but it is by far the most usual, and for many purposes the only method. When groups speak different languages it is notoriously difficult for them to unite under a common government. There was good psychology underlying the story of the Tower of Babel, according to which the Lord is said to have scattered the ambitious builders by confounding their language, "and they left off to build the city." Written language enables each generation to profit more fully from the thought and work of previous generations. The sacred Hebrew Scriptures kept the Jews a people after their capital city had been destroyed, Homer unified generations of Greeks, Shakspere and the English Bible have given common imagery to millions of widely scattered dwellers in many lands. Increased means of communication are among the inventions of largest promise for mutual understanding among men.

2. Aside from their effects in promoting intelligence, courage, and ideality of life, industry, art, and war have a common factor by which they all contribute powerfully to the social basis of morality. They all require *cooperation*. They are socializing as well as rationalizing agencies. Mutual aid[1] is the foundation of success. "Woe to him who stands alone, e'en though his platter be

1. P. Kropotkin, *Mutual Aid: A Factor of Evolution*; Bagehot, *Physics and Politics*.

never so full," runs the Slav proverb. "He that belongs to no community is like unto one without a hand." Those clans or groups which can work together, and fight together, are stronger in the struggle against nature and other men. The common activities of art have value in making this community of action more possible. Cooperation implies a common end. It means that each is interested in the success of all. This common end forms then a controlling rule of action, and the mutual interest means sympathy. Cooperation is therefore one of nature's most effective agencies for a social standard and a social feeling.

In *industry*, while there was not in primitive life the extensive exchange of goods which express the interdependence of modern men, there was yet much concerted work, and there was a great degree of community of property. In groups which lived by hunting or fishing, for instance, although certain kinds of game might be pursued by the individual hunter, the great buffalo and deer hunts were organized by the tribe as a whole. "A hunting bonfire was kindled every morning at daybreak at which each brave must appear and report. The man who failed to do this before the party set out on the day's hunt was harassed by ridicule."[2] Salmon fishery was also conducted as a joint undertaking. Large game in Africa is hunted in a similar fashion, and the product of the chase is not for the individual but for the group. In the pastoral life the care of the flocks and herds necessitates at least some sort of cooperation to protect these flocks from the attacks of wild beasts and from the more dreaded forays of human robbers. This requires a considerable body of men, and the journeying about in company, the sharing together of watch and ward, the common interest in the increase of flocks and herds, continually strengthens the bonds between the dwellers in tents.

In the agricultural stage there are still certain forces at work which promote the family or tribal unity, although here we begin to find the forces which make for individuality at work until they result in individual ownership and individual property. Just as at the pastoral stage, so in this, the cattle and the growing grain must be protected from attacks by man and beast. It is only the group which can afford such protection, and accordingly we find the Lowland farmer always at the mercy of the Highland clan.

2. Eastman, *Indian Boyhood*.

War and the blood feud, however divisive between groups, were none the less potent as uniting factors within the several groups. The members must not only unite or be wiped out, when the actual contest was on, but the whole scheme of mutual help in defense or in avenging injuries and insults made constant demand upon fellow feeling, and sacrifice for the good of all. To gain more land for the group, to acquire booty for the group, to revenge a slight done to some member of the group, were constant causes for war. Now although any individual might be the gainer, yet the chances were that he would himself suffer even though the group should win. In the case of blood revenge particularly, most of the group were not individually interested. Their resentment was a "sympathetic resentment," and one author has regarded this as perhaps the most fundamental of the sources of moral emotion. It was because the tribal blood had been shed, or the women of the clan insulted, that the group as a whole reacted, and in the clash of battle with opposing groups, was closer knit together.

> Ally thyself with whom thou wilt in peace, yet know
> In war must every man be foe who is not kin.

"Comrades in arms" by the very act of fighting together have a common cause, and by the mutual help and protection given and received become, for the time at least, one in will and one in heart. Ulysses counsels Agamemnon to marshal his Greeks, clan by clan and "brotherhood (phratry) by brotherhood," that thus brother may support and stimulate brother more effectively; but the effect is reciprocal, and it is indeed very probable that the unity of blood which is believed to be the tie binding together the members of the group, is often an afterthought or pious fiction designed to account for the unity which was really due originally to the stress of common struggle.

Cooperation and sympathy are fostered by the activities of *art*. Some of these activities are spontaneous, but most of them serve some definite social end and are frequently organized for the definite purpose of increasing the unity and sympathy of the group. The hunting dance or the war dance represents, in dramatic form, all the processes of the hunt or fight, but it would be a mistake to suppose that this takes place purely for dramatic purposes. The dance and celebration after the chase or battle may give to the whole tribe the opportunity to repeat in vivid imagination the triumphs of the successful hunter or warrior, and thus to feel the thrill of victory and exult in common over the fallen prey. The dance which takes place before the event is designed to give magical power to the hunter or warrior. Every detail is performed with the most exact care and the whole tribe is thus enabled to share in the work of preparation.

In the act of song the same uniting force is present. To sing with another involves a contagious sympathy, in perhaps a higher degree than is the case with any other art. There is, in the first place, as in the dance, a unity of rhythm. Rhythm is based upon cooperation and, in turn, immensely strengthens the possibility of cooperation. In bas-reliefs upon the Egyptian monuments representing the work of a large number of men who are moving a stone bull, we find the sculptured figure of a man who is beating the time for the combined efforts. Whether all rhythm has come from the necessities of common action or whether it has a physiological basis sufficient to account for the effect which rhythmic action produces, in any case when a company of people begin to work or dance or sing in rhythmic movement, their efficiency and their pleasure are immensely increased. In addition to the effect of rhythm we have also in the case of song the effect of unity of pitch and of melody, and the members of the tribe or clan, like those who today sing the Marseillaise or chant the great anthems of the church, feel in the strongest degree their mutual sympathy and support. For this reason, the Corroborees of the Australian, the sacred festivals of Israel, the Mysteries and public festivals of the Greeks, in short, among all peoples, the common gatherings of the tribe for patriotic or religious purposes, have been attended with dance and song. In many cases these carry the members on to a pitch of enthusiasm where they are ready to die for the common cause.

Melodic and rhythmic sound is a unifying force simply by reason of form, and some of the simpler songs seem to have little else to commend them, but at very early periods there is not merely the song but the recital, in more or less rhythmic or literary form, of the history of the tribe and the deeds of the ancestors. This adds still another to the unifying forces of the dance and song. The kindred group, as they hear the recital, live over together the history of the group, thrill with pride at its glories, suffer at its defeats; every member feels that the clan's history is his history and the clan's blood his blood.

§ 4. Moral Interpretation of This First Level

On this first level we are evidently dealing with forces and conduct, not as moral in purpose, but as valuable in result. They make a more rational, ideal, and social life, and this is the necessary basis for more conscious control and valuation of conduct. The forces are biological or sociological or psychological. They are not that particular kind of psychological activities which we call moral in the proper sense, for this implies not only getting a good result but aiming at it. Some of the activities, such as those of song and dance, or the simpler acts of maternal care, have a large biological element. We cannot call these moral *in so far as* they are purely biological. Others imply a large amount of intelligence, as, for example, the operations of agriculture and the various crafts. These have purpose, such as to satisfy hunger, or to forge a weapon against an enemy. But the end is one set up by our physical or impulsive nature. So long as this is merely *accepted* as an end, and not compared with others, valued, and *chosen*, it is not properly moral.

The same is true of emotions. There are certain emotions on the impulsive level. Such are parental love in its most elemental form, sympathy as mere contagious feeling, anger, or resentment. So far as these are at this lowest level, so far as they signify simply a bodily thrill, they have no claim to proper moral value. They are tremendously important as the source from which strong motive forces of benevolence, intelligent parental care, and an ardent energy against evil may draw warmth and fire.

Finally, even the cooperation, the mutual aid, which men give, so far as it is called out purely by common danger, or common advantage, is not in the moral sphere in so far as it is instinctive, or merely give and take. To be genuinely moral there must be some thought of the danger as touching others and *therefore* requiring our aid; of the advantage as being common and *therefore* enlisting our help.

But even although these processes are not consciously moral they are nevertheless fundamental. The activities necessary for existence, and the emotions so intimately bound up with them, are the cosmic roots of the moral life. And often in the higher stages of culture, when the codes and instruction of morality and society fail to secure right conduct, these elementary agencies of work, cooperation, and family life assert their power. Society and morality take up the direction of the process and carry it further, but they must always rely largely on these primary activities to afford the basis for intelligent, reliable, and sympathetic conduct.

Literature

Bagehot, *Physics and Politics*, 1890; Bücher, *Industrial Evolution*, Eng. tr., 1901, *Arbeit und Rythmus*, 3rd ed., 1901; Schurtz, *Urgeschichte der Kultur*, 1900; Fiske, *Cosmic Philosophy*, Vol. II., "The Cosmic Roots of Love and Self-Sacrifice" in *Through Nature to God*, 1899; Dewey, "Interpretation of Savage Mind," *Psychological Review*, Vol. IX., 1902, pp. 217–230; Durkheim, *De la Division du Travail Social*, 1893; P. Kropotkin, *Mutual Aid: A Factor of Evolution*, 1902; Ross, *Foundations of Sociology*, 1905, ch. vii.; Baldwin, Article "Socionomic Forces" in his *Dictionary of Philosophy and Psychology*; Giddings, *Inductive Sociology*, 1901; Small, *General Sociology*, 1906; Tarde, *Les Lois de l'Imitation*, 1895; W. I. Thomas, *Sex and Society*, 1907, pp. 55–172; Gummere, *The Beginnings of Poetry*, 1901; Hirn, *The Origins of Art*, 1900.

4. Group Morality—Customs or Mores

What does society do more directly to guide and control the behavior of its members, to keep peace, promote welfare, and maintain right relations between its members? To answer this question we must examine what may be called "group morality" which shows how the member is strongly influenced, either consciously or unconsciously, by the group. Inasmuch as the agencies by which the group controls its members are largely those of custom, the morality may also be called "customary morality." Such conduct is what we called in Chapter 1, "the second level." It is "ethical" or "moral" in the sense of conforming to the *ethos* or *mores* of the group.

§ 1. Meaning, Authority, and Origin of Customs

Wherever we find groups of men living as outlined in Chapter 2, we find that there are certain ways of acting which are common to the group—"folkways." Some of these may be due merely to the fact that the members are born of the same stock, just as all ducks swim. But a large part of human conduct, in savage as truly as in civilized life, is not merely instinctive. There are *approved* ways of acting, common to a group, and handed down from generation to generation. Such approved ways of doing and acting are customs, or to use the Latin term, which Professor Sumner thinks brings out more clearly this factor of approval, they are *mores*.[1] They are habits—but they are more. They imply the judgment of the group that they are to be followed. The welfare of the group is regarded as in some sense

1. W. G. Sumner, *Folkways*, p. 30.

imbedded in them. If any one acts contrary to them he is made to feel the group's disapproval. The young are carefully trained to observe them. At times of special importance, they are rehearsed with special solemnity. For an act so sanctioned there is a cumulative pressure: the group all do it and approve it; they always have done it and approved it; it will be well to do it and dangerous not to do it.

The old men, or the priests, or medicine men, or chiefs, or old women, may be the especial guardians of these customs. They may modify details, or add new customs, or invent explanations for old ones. But the authority back of them is the group in the full sense. Not the group composed merely of visible and living members, but the larger group which includes the dead, and the kindred totemic or ancestral gods. Nor is it the group considered as a collection of individual persons. It is rather in a vague way the whole mental and social world. Regard for such a group becomes akin to religious reverence. The fact that most of the customs have no known date or origin makes them seem a part of the nature of things. Indeed there is more than a mere analogy between the primitive regard for custom and that respect for "nature" which from the Stoics to Spencer has sought a moral standard in living "according to nature."

The *basis* of customs is to be sought in several concurrent factors. In the first place every member of a group stands in certain relations of give and take to other members of the group, and usually to the group as a whole.[2] In a family father, mother, children have their respective parts in getting a living. In a maternal clan the uncle has a definite duty to his sister's household. A man makes certain gifts to his chief and gets favors in return. When the group goes fishing or hunting or on a fighting expedition, every man has his place and part. When one man makes a gift to another he expects some gift in return. All such relationships tend to become regular and standardized. They are the machinery of society. Customs are the natural workings of this machinery. Even in modern society the law considers that certain obligations and rights follow from the *status* of the persons concerned, such as parent and child, husband and wife, landlord and tenant. The same principle holds in primitive society.

In the second place some ways of doing things succeed; some

2. B. Malinowski, *Crime and Custom in Savage Society.*

fail. Man hands the successful ways down with his approval; he condemns those that fail.

This attitude is reenforced by the views about good luck and bad luck. Primitive man—and civilized man—is not ruled by a purely rational theory of success and failure. "One might use the best known means with the greatest care, yet fail of the result. On the other hand, one might get a great result with no effort at all. One might also incur a calamity without any fault of his own."[3] "Grimm gives more than a thousand ancient German apothegms, dicta, and proverbs about 'luck.'"[4] Both good and bad fortune are attributed to the unseen powers, hence a case of bad luck is not thought of as a mere chance. If the ship that sailed Friday meets a storm, or one of thirteen falls sick, the inference is that this is sure to happen again. And at this point the conception of the group welfare as bound up with the acts of every member, comes in to make individual conformity a matter for group concern—to make conduct a matter of mores and not merely a private affair. One important, if not the most important, object of early legislation was the enforcement of lucky rites to prevent the individual from doing what might bring ill luck on all the tribe. For the conception always was that the ill luck does not attach itself simply to the doer, but may fall upon any member of the group. "The act of one member is conceived to make all the tribe impious, to offend its particular god, to expose all the tribe to penalties from heaven. When the street statues of Hermes were mutilated, all the Athenians were frightened and furious; they thought they should all be ruined because some one had mutilated a god's image and so offended him."[5] "The children were reproved for cutting and burning embers, on the ground that this might be the cause for the accidental cutting of some member of the family."[6] In the third place, besides these sources of custom, in the usefulness or lucky character of certain acts, there is also the more immediate reaction of individuals or groups to certain ways of acting according "as things jump with the feelings or displease them."[7] An act of daring is applauded,

3. Sumner, *Folkways*, p. 6.
4. *Ibid.*, p. 11.
5. Bagehot, *Physics and Politics*, p. 103.
6. Eastman, *Indian Boyhood*, p. 31.
7. Hobhouse, *Morals in Evolution*, Part I., p. 16. Hume pointed out this twofold basis of approval.

whether useful or not. The individual judgment is caught up, repeated, and plays its part in the formation of group opinion. "Individual impulse and social tradition are thus the two poles between which we move." Or there may even be a more conscious discussion analogous to the action of legislatures or philosophic discussion. The old men among the Australians deliberate carefully as to each step of the initiation ceremonies. They make customs to be handed down.

§ 2. Means of Enforcing Customs

The most general means for enforcing customs are public opinion, taboos, ritual or ceremony, and physical force.

Public approval uses both language and form to express its judgments. Its praise is likely to be emphasized by some form of art. The songs that greet the returning victor, the decorations, costumes, and tattoos for those who are honored, serve to voice the general sentiment. On the other hand ridicule or contempt is a sufficient penalty to enforce compliance with many customs that may be personally irksome. It is very largely the ridicule of the men's house which enforces certain customs among the men of peoples which have that institution. It is the ridicule or scorn of both men and women which forbids the Indian to marry before he has proved his manhood by some notable deed of prowess in war or chase. Among the Trobriand Islanders the power of public disapproval is so great that an offender who incurs it may feel compelled to commit suicide as the only possible course; life becomes intolerable.[8] Even in civilized society no one finds it a light matter to be sent to Coventry or cut dead by all his acquaintance.

Taboos are perhaps not so much a means for enforcing custom, as they are themselves customs invested with peculiar and awful sanction. They prohibit or ban any contact with certain persons or objects under penalty of danger from unseen beings. Any events supposed to indicate the activity of spirits, such as birth and death, are likely to be sanctified by taboos. The danger

8. B. Malinowski, *op. cit.*

is contagious; if a Polynesian chief is taboo, the ordinary man fears even to touch his footprints. But the taboos are not all based on mere dread of the unseen.

They include such acts as have been found by experience to produce unwelcome results.—The primitive taboos correspond to the fact that the life of man is environed by perils: His food quest must be limited by shunning poisonous plants. His appetite must be restrained from excess. His physical strength and health must be guarded from dangers. The taboos carry on the accumulated wisdom of generations which has almost always been purchased by pain, loss, disease, and death. Other taboos contain inhibitions of what will be injurious to the group. The laws about the sexes, about property, about war, and about ghosts, have this character. They always include some social philosophy.[9]

They may be used with conscious purpose. In order to have a supply of cocoanuts for a religious festival the head men may place a taboo upon the young cocoanuts to prevent them from being consumed before they are fully ripe. The conception works in certain respects to supply the purpose which is later subserved by ideas of property. But it serves also as a powerful agency to maintain respect for the authority of the group.

As taboo is the great negative guardian of customs, *ritual* is the great positive agent. It works by forming habits, and operates through associations formed by actually doing certain acts, usually under conditions which appeal to the emotions. The charm of music and of orderly movement, the impressiveness of ordered masses in processions, the awe of mystery, all contribute to stamp in the meaning and value. Praise or blame encourages or inhibits; ritual secures the actual doing and at the same time gives a value to the doing. It is employed by civilized peoples more in the case of military or athletic drill, or in training children to observe forms of etiquette, so that these may become "second nature." Certain religious bodies also use its agency. But in primitive life it is widely and effectively used to insure for educational, political, and domestic customs obedience to the group standards, which among us it secures to the codes of the army, or to those of social

9. Sumner, *Folkways*, pp. 33 f.

etiquette. Examples of its elaborate and impressive use will be given below under educational ceremonies.

When neither group opinion, nor taboo, nor ritual secures conformity, there is always in the background physical force. The chiefs are generally men of strength whose word may not be lightly disregarded. Sometimes, as among the Sioux, the older braves constitute a sort of police. Between different clans the blood feud is the accepted method of enforcing custom, unless a substitute, the wergeld, is provided. For homicide within a clan the remaining members may drive the slayer out, and whoever meets such a Cain may slay him. If a man murdered his chief of kindred among the ancient Welsh he was banished and "it was required of every one of every sex and age within hearing of the horn to follow that exile and to keep up the barking of dogs, to the time of his putting to sea, until he shall have passed three score hours out of sight." [10] It should be borne in mind, however, that physical pains, either actual or dreaded, would go but a little way toward maintaining authority in any such group as we have regarded as typical. Absolutism, with all its cruel methods of enforcing terror, needs a more highly-organized system. In primitive groups the great majority support the authority of the group as a matter of course, and uphold it as a sacred duty when it is challenged. Physical coercion is not the rule but the exception.

§ 3. Conditions Which Bring Out the Importance of Group Standards and Render Group Control Conscious

Although customs or mores have in them an element of social approval which makes them vehicles of moral judgment, they tend in many cases to sink to the level of mere habits. The reason—such as it was—for their original force—is forgotten. They become, like many of our forms of etiquette, mere conventions. There are, however, certain conditions which focus attention upon their importance and lift them to the level of conscious agencies. These conditions may be grouped under three heads. (1) The education of the younger, immature members of

10. Seebohm, *The Tribal System in Wales*, p. 59.

the group and their preparation for full membership. (2) The constraint and restraint of refractory members and the adjustment of conflicting interests. (3) Occasions which involve some notable danger or crisis and therefore call for the especial care to secure the favor of the gods and avert disaster.

1. Among the most striking educational customs are the initiation ceremonies which are so widely observed among primitive peoples. They are held with the purpose of inducting boys into the privileges of manhood and into the full life of the group. They are calculated at every step to impress upon the initiate his own ignorance and helplessness in contrast with the wisdom and power of the group; and as the mystery with which they are conducted imposes reverence for the elders and the authorities of the group, so the recital of the traditions and performances of the tribe, the long series of ritual acts, common participation in the mystic dance and song and decorations, serve to reenforce the ties that bind the tribe.

Initiation into the full privileges of manhood among the tribes of Central Australia, for instance, includes three sets of ceremonies which occupy weeks, and even months, for their completion. The first set, called "throwing up in the air," is performed for the boy when he has reached the age of from ten to twelve. In connection with being thrown up in the air by certain prescribed members of his tribe, he is decorated with various totem emblems and afterward the septum of his nose is bored for the insertion of the nose-bone. At a period some three or four years later a larger and more formidable series of ceremonies is undertaken, lasting for ten days. A screen of bushes is built, behind which the boy is kept during the whole period, unless he is brought out on the ceremonial ground to witness some performance. During this whole period of ten days, he is forbidden to speak except in answer to questions. He is decorated with various totem emblems, for which every detail is prescribed by the council of the tribal fathers and tribal elder brothers. He is charged to obey every command and never to tell any woman or boy what he may see. The sense that something out of the ordinary is to happen to him helps to impress him strongly with a feeling of the deep importance of compliance with the tribal rules, and further still, with a strong sense of the superiority of the older men who know and are familiar with the mysterious rites of which he is about to learn the meaning for the first time. At intervals he watches symbolic performances of men decorated like various totem animals, who represent the doings of the animal ancestors of the clan; he hears mysterious sounds of the so-called bull-roarers, which are supposed by the women and uninitiated to be due to unseen spirits; and the whole ends with the operation which symbolizes his induction into young manhood.

But even these ceremonies are not all; when the young man has reached the age of discretion, when it is felt that he can fully comprehend the traditions of the tribe, at the age of from twenty to twenty-five, a still more impressive series of ceremonies is conducted, which in the instance reported lasted from September to January. This period was filled up with dances, "corroborees," and inspection of the churinga or sacred emblems—stones or sticks which were supposed to be the dwellings of ancestral spirits and which are carefully preserved in the tribe, guarded from the sight of women and boys, but known individually to the elders as the sacred dwelling-place of father or grandfather. As these were shown and passed around, great solemnity was manifest and the relatives sometimes wept at the sight of the sacred object. Ceremonies imitating various totem animals, frequently of the most elaborate sort, were also performed. The young men were told the traditions of the past history of the tribe, and at the close of the recital they felt added reverence for the old men who had been their instructors, a sense of pride in the possession of this mysterious knowledge, and a deeper unity because of what they now have in common. One is at a loss whether to wonder most at the possibility of the whole tribe devoting itself for three months to these elaborate functions of initiation, or at the marvelous adaptability of such ceremonies to train the young into an attitude of docility and reverence. A tribe that can enforce such a process is not likely to be wanting in one side, at least, of the moral consciousness, namely, reverence for authority and regard for the social welfare.[11]

2. The occasions for some control over refractory members will constantly arise, even though the conflict between group and individual may need no physical sanctions to enforce the au-

11. The account is based on Spencer and Gillen, *The Native Tribes of Central Australia*, chs. vii.–ix.

thority of the group over its members. The economic motive frequently prompts an individual to leave the tribe or the joint family. There was a constant tendency, Eastman states, among his people, when on a hunting expedition in the enemy's country, to break up into smaller parties to obtain food more easily and freely. The police did all they could to keep in check those parties who were intent on stealing away. Another illustration of the same tendency is stated by Maine with reference to the joint families of the South Slavonians:

> The adventurous and energetic member of the brotherhood is always rebelling against its natural communism. He goes abroad and makes his fortune, and as strenuously resists the demands of his relatives to bring it into the common account. Or perhaps he thinks that his share of the common stock would be more profitably employed by him as capital in a mercantile venture. In either case he becomes a dissatisfied member or a declared enemy of the brotherhood.[12]

Or covetousness might lead to violation of the ban, as with Achan. Sex impulse may lead a man to seek for his wife a woman not in the lawful group. Or, as one of the most dangerous offenses possible, a member of the group may be supposed to practice witchcraft. This is to use invisible powers in a selfish manner, and has been feared and punished by almost all peoples.

In all these cases it is of course no abstract theory of crime which leads the community to react; it is self-preservation. The tribe must be kept together for protection against enemies. Achan's sin is felt to be the cause of defeat. The violation of sex taboos may ruin the clan. The sorcerer may cause disease, or inflict torture and death, or bring a pestilence or famine upon the whole group. None the less all such cases bring to consciousness one aspect of moral authority, the social control over the individual.

And it is a *social* control—not an exercise of brute force or a mere terrorizing by ghosts. For the chief or judge generally wins his authority by his powerful service to his tribesmen. A Gideon or Barak or Ehud or Jephthah judged Israel because he had delivered them. "Three things, if possessed by a man, make him fit

12. Maine, *Early Law and Custom*, p. 264.

to be a chief of kindred: That he should speak on behalf of his kin and be listened to, that he should fight on behalf of his kin and be feared, and that he should be security on behalf of his kin and be accepted." [13] If, as is often the case, the king or judge or chief regards himself as acting by divine right, the authority is still *within the group*. It is the group judging itself.

In its *standards* this primitive court is naturally on the level of customary morality, of which it is an agent. There is usually neither the conception of a general principle of justice (our Common Law), nor of a positive law enacted as the express will of the people. At first the judge or ruler may not act by any fixed law except that of upholding the customs. Each decision is then a special case. A step in advance is found when the heads or elders or priests of the tribe decide cases, not independently of all others, but in accordance with certain precedents or customs. A legal tradition is thus established, which, however imperfect, is likely to be more impartial than the arbitrary caprice of the moment, influenced as such special decisions are likely to be by the rank or power of the parties concerned. [14] A law of precedents or tradition is thus the normal method at this level. The progress toward a more rational standard belongs under the next chapter, but it is interesting to note that even at an early age the myths show a conception of a divine judge who is righteous, and a divine judgment which is ideal. Rhadamanthus is an embodiment of the demand for justice which human collisions and decisions awakened.

The conscious authority of the group is also evoked in the case of feuds or disputes between its members. The case of the blood feud, indeed, might well be treated as belonging under war and international law rather than as a case of private conflict. For so far as the members of the victim's clan are concerned, it is a case of war. It is a patriotic duty of every kinsman to avenge the shed blood. The groups concerned were smaller than modern nations which go to war for similar reasons, but the principle is the same. The chief difference in favor of modern international wars is that since the groups are larger they do not fight so often and require a more serious consideration of the possibility of peaceable adjustment. Orestes and Hamlet feel it a sacred duty to avenge their fathers' murders.

13. *Welsh Triads*, cited by Seebohm, *op. cit.*, p. 72.
14. Post, *Grundlagen des Rechts*, pp. 45 ff.

But the case is not simply that of clan against clan. For the smaller group of kin, who are bound to avenge, are nearly always part of a larger group. And the larger group may at once recognize the duty of vengeance and also the need of keeping it within bounds, or of substituting other practices. The larger group may see in the murder a pollution, dangerous to all;[15] the blood which "cries from the ground"[16] renders the ground "unclean" and the curse of gods or the spirits of the dead may work woe upon the whole region. But an unending blood feud is likewise an evil. And if the injured kin can be appeased by less than blood in return, so much the better. Hence the wergeld, or indemnity, a custom which persisted among the Irish until late, and seemed to the English judges a scandalous procedure.

For lesser offenses a sort of regulated duel is sometimes allowed. For example, among the Australians the incident is related of the treatment of a man who had eloped with his neighbor's wife. When the recreant parties returned the old men considered what should be done, and finally arranged the following penalty. The offender stood and called out to the injured husband, "I stole your woman; come and growl." The husband then proceeded to throw a spear at him from a distance, and afterwards to attack him with a knife, although he did not attempt to wound him in a vital part. The offender was allowed to evade injury, though not to resent the attack. Finally the old men said, "Enough." A curious form of private agencies for securing justice is also found in the Japanese custom of hara-kiri, according to which an injured man kills himself before the door of his offender, in order that he may bring public odium upon the man who has injured him. An Indian custom of Dharna is of similar significance, though less violent. The creditor fasts before the door of the debtor until he either is paid, or dies of starvation. It may be that he thinks that his double or spirit will haunt the cruel debtor who has thus permitted him to starve to death, but it also has the effect of bringing public opinion to bear.[17]

3. Certain occasions call for especial attention in order to secure success or avoid disaster. Under this head we note as typical

---

15. Deuteronomy 21:1–9; Numbers 35:33, 34.
16. Genesis 4:10–12; Job 16:18.
17. On the subject of early justice Westermarck, *The Origin and Development of Moral Ideas*, ch. vii. ff.; Hobhouse, *Morals in Evolution*, Part I., ch. ii.; Pollock and Maitland, *History of English Law*.

(1) birth, marriage, death; (2) seed time and harvest, or other seasons important for the maintenance of the group; (3) war; (4) hospitality.

1. The entrance of a new life into the world and the disappearance of the animating breath (*spiritus, anima, psyche*), might well impress man with the mysteries of his world. Whether the newborn infant is regarded as a reincarnation of an ancestral spirit as with the Australians, or as a new creation from the spirit world as with the Kafirs, it is a time of danger. The mother must be "purified,"[18] the child, and in some cases the father, must be carefully guarded. The elaborate customs show the group judgment of the importance of the occasion. And the rites for the dead are yet more impressive. For as a rule the savage has no thought of an entire extinction of the person. The dead lives on in some mode, shadowy and vague, perhaps, but he is still potent, still a member of the group, present at the tomb or the hearth. The preparation of the body for burial or other disposition, the ceremonies of interment or of the pyre, the wailing, the mourning costumes, the provision of food and weapons, or of the favorite horse or wife, to be with the dead in the unseen world, the perpetual homage paid—all these are eloquent. The event, as often as it occurs, appeals by both sympathy and awe to the common feeling, and brings to consciousness the unity of the group and the control exercised by its judgments.

The regulations for marriage are scarcely less important; indeed, they are often seemingly the most important of the customs. The phrases "marriage by capture" and "marriage by purchase," are quite misleading if they give the impression that in early culture any man may have any woman. It is an almost universal part of the clan system that the man must marry out of his own clan or totem (exogamy), and it is frequently specified exactly into what other clan he must marry. Among some tribes the regulations prescribe minutely from which of the age classes, and from which of the kin groups, a man of a specific group must choose. The courtship may follow different rules from ours, and the relation of the sexes in certain respects may seem so loose as to shock the student, but the regulation is in many respects stricter than with us, and punishment of its violation often se-

18. Leviticus, xii.

verer. There can be no doubt of the meaning of the control, however mistaken some of its features. Whether the regulations for exogamy, which provide so effectually for avoiding incest, are reenforced by an instinctive element of aversion to sex relations with intimates, is uncertain; in any case, they are enforced by the strongest taboos. Nor does primitive society stop with the negative side. The actual marriage is invested with the social values and religious sanctions which raise the relation to a higher level. Art, in garments and ornament, in dance and epithalamium, lends ideal values. The sacred meal at the encircled hearth secures the participation of the kindred gods.

2. Seed time and harvest, the winter and summer solstices, the return of spring, are of the highest importance to agricultural and pastoral peoples, and are widely observed with rites. Where the rain is the centre of anxiety, a whole ritual may arise in connection with it, as among the Zuñi Indians. Ceremonies lasting days, involving the preparation of special symbols of clouds and lightning, and the participation of numerous secret fraternities, constrain the attention of all. Moreover, this constraint of need, working through the conception of what the gods require, enforces some very positive moral attitudes:

A Zuñi must speak with one tongue (sincerely) in order to have his prayers received by the gods, and unless his prayers are accepted no rains will come, which means starvation. He must be gentle, and he must speak and act with kindness to all, for the gods care not for those whose lips speak harshly. He must observe continence four days previous to, and four days following, the sending of breath prayers through the spiritual essence of plume offerings, and thus their passions are brought under control.[19]

Phases of the moon give other sacred days. Sabbaths which originally are negative—the forbidding of labor—may become later the bearers of positive social and spiritual value. In any case, all these festivals bring the group authority to consciousness, and by their ritual promote the intimate group sympathy and consciousness of a common end.

3. War as a special crisis always brings out the significance and

19. Mrs. M. C. Stevenson in 23d Report, Bureau of Ethnology.

importance of certain customs. The deliberations, the magic, the war paint which precede, the obedience compelled to chiefs, the extraordinary powers exercised by the chief or heads at such crises, the sense of danger which strains the attention, all insure attention. No carelessness is permitted. Defeat is interpreted as a symbol of divine anger because of a violated law or custom. Victory brings all together to celebrate the glory of the clan and to mourn in common the warriors slain in the common cause. Excellence here may be so conspicuous in its service, or in the admiration it calls out, as to become a general term for what the group approves. So the *aretē* of the Greeks became their general term, and the Latin *virtus*, if not so clearly military, was yet largely military in its early coloring. The "spirit of Jehovah," the symbol of divine approval and so of group approval, was believed to be with Samson and Jephthah in their deeds of prowess in Israel's behalf.

4. To the modern man who travels without fear and receives guests as a matter of almost daily practice, it may seem strained to include hospitality along with unusual or critical events. But the ceremonies observed and the importance attached to its rites, show that hospitality was a matter of great significance; its customs were among the most sacred.

"But as for us," says Ulysses to the Cyclops, "we have lighted here, and come to these thy knees, if perchance they will give us a stranger's gift, or make any present, as is the due of strangers. Nay, lord, have regard to the gods, for we are thy suppliants, and Zeus is the avenger of suppliants and sojourners, Zeus, the god of the stranger, who fareth in the company of reverend strangers."

The duty of hospitality is one of the most widely recognized. Westermarck has brought together a series of maxims from a great variety of races which show this forcibly.[20] Indians, Kalmucks, Greeks, Romans, Teutons, Arabs, Africans, Ainos, and other peoples are contributors and tell the same story. The stranger is to be respected sacredly. His person must be guarded from insult even if the honor of the daughter of the house must

---

20. "The Influence of Magic on Social Relationships" in *Sociological Papers*, II., 1905. *Cf.* also Morgan, *House-Life.*

be sacrificed.[21] "Jehovah preserveth the sojourners," and they are grouped with the fatherless and the widow in Israel's law.[22] The Romans had their *dii hospitales* and the "duties toward a guest were even more stringent than those toward a relative"—*primum tutelae, deinde hospiti, deinde clienti, tum cognato, postea affini*.[23] "He who has a spark of caution in him," says Plato, "will do his best to pass through life without sinning against the stranger." And there is no doubt that this sanctity of the guest's person was not due to pure kindness. The whole conduct of group life is opposed to a general spirit of consideration for those outside. The word "guest" is akin to *hostis*, from which comes "hostile." The stranger or the guest was looked upon rather as a being who was specially potent. He was a "live wire." He might be a medium of blessing, or he might be a medium of hurt. But it was highly important to fail in no duty toward him. The definite possibility of entertaining angels unawares might not be always present to consciousness, but there seems reason to believe that the possibility of good luck or bad luck as attending on a visitor was generally believed in. It is also plausible that the importance attached to sharing a meal, or to bodily contact, is based on magical ideas of the way in which blessing or curse may be communicated. To cross a threshold or touch a tent-rope or to eat "salt," gives a sacred claim. In the right of asylum, the refugee takes advantage of his contact with the god. He lays hold of the altar and assumes that the god will protect him. The whole practice of hospitality is thus the converse of the custom of blood revenge. They are alike sacred—or rather the duty of hospitality may protect even the man whom the host is bound to pursue. But, whereas the one makes for group solidarity by acts of exclusive and hostile character, the other tends to set aside temporarily the division between the "we-group" and the "others-group." Under the sanction of religion it keeps open a way of communication which trade and other social interchange will widen. It adds to family and the men's house a powerful agency in maintaining at least the possibility of humaneness and sympathy.

21. Genesis 19:8; Judges 19:23, 24.
22. Psalms 146:9; Deuteronomy 24:14–22.
23. Gellius, in Westermarck, *op. cit.*, p. 155.

§ 4. Values and Defects of Customary Morality

These have been suggested, in the main, in the description of the nature of custom and its regulation of conduct. We may, however, summarize them as a preparation for the next stage of morality.

In so far as custom and mores are based on recognition of the actual relations of mutual or reciprocal interdependence they are setting standards for what is held to be "right" behavior, however much these may need criticism and reflection before they reach the highest levels of justice. In so far as customs and mores rest on rational conceptions of welfare they are pointing out what is to be regarded as "good." In so far as they provide approvals and disapprovals by the group they are preparing the way for conceptions of excellence and "virtue." Morality is thus guiding and controlling life even though it be defective in intelligence and flexibility.

The standards and valuations of custom are, however, only partly rational. Many customs are irrational; some are injurious. But in them all the habitual is a large, if not the largest, factor. And this is often strong enough to resist any attempt at rational testing. Dr. Arthur Smith tells us of the advantage it would be in certain parts of China to build a door on the south side of the house in order to get the breeze in hot weather. The simple and sufficient answer to such a suggestion is, "We don't build doors on the south side."

An additional weakness in the character of such irrational, or partly rational standards, is the misplaced energy they involve. What is merely trivial is made as important and impressive as what has real significance. Tithing mint, anise, and cummin is quite likely to involve neglect of the weightier matters of the law. Moral life requires men to estimate the value of acts. If the irrelevant or the petty is made important, it not only prevents a high level of value for the really important act, it loads up conduct with burdens which keep it back; it introduces elements which must be got rid of later, often with heavy loss of what is genuinely valuable.

In modern law the emphasis is chiefly upon what a man does, but in estimating a man's character we like to know also why he does it. The morality of custom makes use of two motives which we do not consider desirable except under carefully defined conditions, namely, fear in avoiding taboos, and resentment in its blood feuds. This fear is grounded in ignorance, and resentment is opposed to the friendly feeling which ought to prevail between man and man. It of course is obvious that our war morality of today also violates this friendly relation, but war morality is still largely of a primitive type, and presupposes broken human relations. Yet primitive blood revenge has one element by which it differs from mere animal passion. It is in most cases not a personal but a group affair. It is undertaken for a common interest. It is thus a *sympathetic* resentment, and such resentment is regarded by Westermarck as one of the fundamental elements in the beginnings of morality. Aside from the passions of fear and resentment, however, there is a wide range of motives enlisted. Filial and parental affection, some degree of affection between the sexes over and above sex passion, respect for the aged and the beings who embody ideals however crude, loyalty to fellow clansmen,—all these are not only fostered but actually secured by the primitive group. But the motives which imply reflection— reverence for duty as the imperious law of a larger life, sincere love of what is good for its own sake—cannot be brought to full consciousness until there is a more definite conception of a moral authority, a more definite contrast between the one great good and the partial or temporary satisfactions. The development of these conceptions requires a growth in individuality; it requires conflicts between authority and liberty, and those collisions between private interests and the public welfare which a higher civilization affords.

In the organization of stable character the morality of custom is strong on one side. The group trains its members to act in the ways it approves and afterwards holds them by all the agencies in its power. It forms habits and enforces them. Its weakness is that the element of habit is so large, that of freedom so small. It holds up the average man; it holds back the man who might forge ahead. It is an anchor, and a drag.

If next we ask, What are the actual, concrete effects of customary morality? Does it secure peace and harmony in society? Do men respect life, property, and the rights of others? Are women, children, and the aged well treated? Is there interest in nature and the arts or are people content with eating and drinking and fighting? we have to bear in mind two things. (1) Some of the conditions in question depend, not upon morality considered in isolation from all other factors in progress such as race, climate, commerce, invention, religion, but upon the general level of culture attained. (2) We do not need to look for our answers exclusively to peoples in a supposedly lower stage of culture, for a great part of our own morality is customary morality. The attitude of most of us toward men of other race or color is almost entirely that of our mores, depending largely on where we were born and grew up; our standards of living are set for us by the group we aspire to move in; our standard of honor by our family tradition or club or social circle; our attitude toward property by our occupation group and business associates; our patriotic allegiance by birth. Among many peoples who are backward in certain respects, life is safe, order is maintained, all share in the goods which are available, there are no professional criminals, there is much kindness. Evidently we can make no sweeping statements at this point of our study. For the mores themselves may be at a high level or a low level. How certain peoples have raised or changed their standards and given a larger place to reflection and to individual freedom and responsibility will occupy us for the remainder of this Part of the book, after a brief statement of some of the general factors involved in these changes.

Literature

Much of the literature at the close of Chapters 2 and 3, particularly the works of Spencer and Gillen and Schurtz, belongs here also. Schoolcraft, *Indian Tribes*, 1851–57; Eastman, *Indian Boyhood*, 1902. Papers on various cults of North American Indians in reports of the *Bureau of Ethnology*, by Stevenson, 8th, 1886–87, Dorsey, 11th, 1889–90, Fewkes, 15th, 1893–94, 21st, 1899–1900, Fletcher, 22nd, 1900–01, Stevenson, 23rd, 1901–02; Kidd, *Savage Childhood*, 1906, *The Essential Kafir*, 1904; Skeat, *Malay Magic*, 1900; N. W. Thomas, general editor of Series, *The Native Races of the British Empire*, 1907–; Barton, *A Sketch of Semitic Origins*, 1902; Harrison, *Prolegomena to the Study of Greek Religion*, 1903; Reinach, *Cultes, Mythes et Religions*, 3 vols., 1905; Frazer, *The Golden Bough*, 3 vols., 1900; Marett, "Is Taboo a Negative Magic?" in *Anthropological Essays*, presented to E. B. Tylor, 1907; Crawley, *The Mystic Rose*, 1902; Spencer, *Sociology*, 1876–96;

Clifford, "On the Scientific Basis of Morals" in *Lectures and Essays*, 1886; Maine, *Early History of Institutions*, 1888, *Early Law and Custom*, 1886; Post, *Die Grundlagen des Rechts und die Grundzüge seiner Entwicklungsgeschichte*, 1884, *Ethnologische Jurisprudenz*, 1894–95; Pollock and Maitland, *History of English Law*, 1899; Steinmetz, *Ethnologische Studien zur ersten Entwicklung der Strafe*, 1894; Malinowski, *Crime and Custom in Savage Society*, 1926; Vinogradoff, *Outlines of Historical Jurisprudence*, Vol. I., *Tribal Law*, 1920.

From Custom to Conscience; From
Group Morality to Personal Morality

§ 1. Contrast and Collision

Complete morality is reached only when the individual
recognizes the right or chooses the good freely, devotes himself
heartily to its fulfillment, and seeks a progressive social development in which every member of society shall share. Group morality with its agencies of custom set up a standard, but one that
was corporate rather than personal. It approved and disapproved,
that is, it had an idea of good, but this did not mean a good that
was personally valued. It enlisted its members, but it was by drill,
by pleasure and pain, and by habit, rather than by fully voluntary action. It secured steadiness by habit and social pressure,
rather than by choices built into character. It maintained community of feeling and action, but of the unconscious rather than
the definitely social type. Finally it was rather fitted to maintain a
fixed order than to promote and safeguard progress. Advance
then must (1) substitute some rational method of setting up standards and forming values, in place of habitual passive acceptance; (2) secure voluntary and personal choice and interest, instead of unconscious identification with the group welfare, or
instinctive and habitual response to group needs; (3) encourage
at the same time individual development and the demand that all
shall share in this development—the worth and happiness of the
person and of *every* person.

Such an advance brings to consciousness two collisions. The
oppositions were there before, but they were not felt as oppositions. So long as the man was fully with his group, or satisfied
with the custom, he would make no revolt. When the movement
begins the collisions are felt. These collisions are:

(1) The collision between the authority and interests of the
group, and the independence and private interests of the
individual.

(2) The collision between order and progress, between habit and reconstruction or reformation.

It is evident that there is a close connection between these two collisions; in fact, the second becomes in practice a form of the first. For we saw in the last chapter that custom is really backed and enforced by the group, and its merely habitual parts are as strongly supported as those parts which have a more rational basis. It would perhaps be conceivable that a people should move on all together, working out a higher civilization in which free thought should keep full reverence for social values, in which political liberty should keep even pace with the development of government, in which self-interest should be accompanied by regard for the welfare of others, just as it may be possible for a child to grow into full morality without a period of "storm and stress." But this is not usual. Progress has generally cost struggle. And the first phase of this struggle is opposition between the individual and the group. The self-assertive impulses and desires were present in group life, but they were in part undeveloped because they had not enough stimulus to call them out. A man could not develop his impulse for possession to its full extent if there was little or nothing for him to possess. In part they were not developed because the group held them back, and the conditions of living and fighting favored those groups which did keep them back. Nevertheless they were present in some degree, always contending against the more social forces. Indeed what makes the opposition between group and individual so strong and so continuous is that both the social and the individual are rooted in human nature. They constitute what Kant calls the *unsocial sociableness* of man. "Man cannot get on with his fellows and he cannot do without them."

The distinctive character and quality by which one man differs from his fellows or stands out from the mass or group pattern is known as *individuality*. It is that by which a man is himself and not another. One type of individuality is seen in the genius, another in the man who is able to wield power over his fellows, another in the prophet, another in a man or woman of broad human sympathy, and still another in a daring criminal. Individuality is therefore neutral morally, although it may be a power for good or a power for evil, and in either case is likely to lead to independence of group and customary standards. Action tends to become personal and voluntary.

The term *individualism*, on the contrary, although sometimes used as a synonym of individuality, ordinarily means either selfishness, exclusiveness, or refers to a definite theory or policy having primary regard for individual rights as contrasted with public or community interests. In its meaning of exclusiveness or selfishness it supposes that the individual's private interest may be set over against the interest of the group or community and deliberately chosen. Or at least that the individual is so taken up with his own interests that he does not concern himself with those of others or of the community. It is every man for himself. In its reference to a definite theory of government and economics it does not concern us at this point, but will be considered later.

It is evident that the growth of a child to manhood implies in any normal person a development of individuality. More and more he makes decisions and takes responsibility. He is likely to differ from the ways of family and school in certain respects. It is likewise apparent that growth of civilization favors growth of individuality. Whether there is or is not a similar development of individualism, it can readily be seen that there will often be favorable opportunities offered for selfish tendencies to assert themselves. When old restraints of custom and group control are thrown off the strong or crafty individual comes to the front and exploits his fellows. In varying degrees and proportions development of individuality and development of individualism combined in such times and movements as the age of the Sophists in Greece, of the Renaissance in Italy, of the Enlightenment and Romantic movement in Western Europe, and of the industrial revolution. Such critical movements bring both good and evil. To appraise the moral value of growth in individuality, however, we need to know what kind of qualities are coming to assert power and find expression. And even so priceless a value as liberty may at times tend to pass over into impatience of any social restraints or obligations, and in the selfish form of individualism become an enemy to the general good.

§ 2. Sociological Agencies in the Transition

The agencies which bring about the change from customary and group morality to conscious and personal morality are varied. Just as character is developed in the child and young man by various means, sometimes by success, sometimes by adversity or loss of a parent, sometimes by slow increase in knowledge, and sometimes by a sudden right-about-face with a strong emotional basis, so it is with peoples. We note four typical agencies which are usually more or less active.

1. The action of *economic forces* in breaking up the early kinship group or joint family may be noticed in the history of many peoples. The clan flourishes in such conditions of hunting life or of simple agriculture as were found among Australians and Indians, or among the Celts in Ireland and the Scottish Highlands. It cannot survive when a more advanced state of agriculture prevails. A certain amount of individualism will appear wherever the advantage for the individual lies in separate industry and private ownership. If buffalo was to be hunted it was better to pool issues, but for smaller game the skilful or persistent huntsman or shepherd will think he can gain more by working for himself. This is intensified when agriculture and commerce take the place of earlier modes of life. The farmer has to work so hard and long, his goal is so far in the future, that differences of character show themselves much more strongly. Hunting and fishing are so exciting, and the reward is so near, that even a man who is not very industrious will do his part. But in agriculture only the hard and patient worker gets a reward and he does not like to share it with the lazy, or even with the weaker. Commerce, bargaining, likewise put a great premium on individual shrewdness. Moreover commerce leads to the comparison of custom, and to interchange of ideas as well as goods. This tends to break down the sanctity of customs peculiar to a given group. The trader as well as the guest may overstep the barriers set up by kin. The early Greek colonists, among whom a great individualistic movement began, were the traders of their day. The parts of Europe where most survives of primitive group life are those little touched by modern commerce.

But we get a broader view of economic influences if we consider the methods of organizing industry which have successively prevailed. In early society, and likewise in the earlier period of modern civilization, the family was a great economic unit. Many or most of the industries could be advantageously carried on in the household. As in the cases cited above (p. 57) the stronger or adventurous member would be constantly trying to strike out for himself. This process of constant readjustment is, however, far less thoroughgoing in its effects on mores than the three great methods of securing a broader organization of industry. In primitive society large enterprises had to be carried on by the cooperation of the group. Forced labor as used by the Oriental civilizations substituted a method by which greater works like the pyramids or temples could be built, but it brought with it the overthrow of much of the old group sympathies and mutual aid. In Greece and Rome slavery did the drudgery and left the citizens free to cultivate art, letters, and government. It gave opportunity and scope for the few. Men of power and genius arose, and at the same time all the negative forces of individualism asserted themselves. In modern times capitalism is the method for organizing industry and trade. It proves more effective than forced labor or slavery in securing combination of forces and in exploiting natural resources. It likewise gives extraordinary opportunities for the rise of men of organizing genius. The careers of captains of industry are more fascinating than those of old-time conquerors because they involve more complex situations, and can utilize the discoveries and labors of more men. But modern capitalism has been as destructive to the morality of the Middle Ages, or even to that of a hundred years ago, as were forced labor and slavery to the group life and mores which they destroyed.

2. The effect of the progress of *science* and intelligence upon the mores is direct. Comparisons of the customs of one people with those of another bring out differences, and arouse questions as to the reasons for such diversity. And we have seen that there is more or less in the customs for which no reason can be given. Even if there was one originally it has been forgotten. Or again, increasing knowledge of weather and seasons, of plants and animals, of sickness and disease, discredits many of the taboos and ceremonials which the cruder beliefs had regarded as essential to welfare. Certain elements of ritual may survive under the protection of "mysteries," but the more enlightened portion of the community keeps aloof. Instead of the mores with their large infusion of accidental, habitual, and impulsive elements, increasing intelligence demands some rational rule of life.

Science joins with the various industrial and fine *arts* to create a new set of interests for the individual. The division of labor, begin in group life, is carried further. Craftsmen and artists develop increasing individuality as they construct temples or palaces, fashion statues or pottery, or sing of gods and heroes. Their minds grow with what they do. Side by side with the aspect of art which makes it a bond of society is the aspect which so frequently makes the skilled workman the critic, and the artist a law to himself. In the next place note the effect on those who can use and enjoy the products of the arts. A new world of satisfaction and happiness is opened which each person can enter for himself. In cruder conditions there was not much out of which to build up happiness. Food, labor, rest, the thrill of hunt or contest, the passion of sex, pride in children—these made up the interests of primitive life. Further means of enjoyment were found chiefly in society of the kin, or in the men's house. But as the arts advanced the individual could have made for him a fine house and elaborate clothing. Metal, wood, and clay minister to increasing wants. A permanent and stately tomb makes the future more definite. The ability to hand down wealth in durable form places a premium on its acquirement. Ambition has more stuff to work with. A more definite, assertive self is gradually built up. "Good" comes to have added meaning with every new want that awakes. The individual is not satisfied any longer to take the group's valuation. He wants to get his own good in his own way. And it will often seem to him that he can get his own good most easily and surely either by keeping out of the common life or by using his fellow men to his own advantage. Men of culture have frequently shown their selfishness in the first way; men of wealth in the second. An aristocracy of culture, or birth, or wealth may come to regard the whole process of civilization as properly ministering to the wants of the select few. Nearly every people which has developed the arts and sciences has developed also an aristocracy. In the ancient world slavery was a part of the process. In modern times other forms of exploitation may serve the purpose better. Individualism, released from the ties which bound up the good of one with the good of all, tends to become exclusive and selfish; civilization with all its opportunities for increasing happiness and increasing life has its moral risks and indirectly, at least, its moral evils.

These evils may appear as gratification of sense and appetite and thus may be opposed to a simpler, yet higher life of the spirit. Or they may appear as rooted in selfishness, in the desire for gratifying the exclusive self of material interests or ambition, as over against sympathy, justice, and kindness, which mark a broadly human and social life. In both cases serious men have sought to overcome by some form of self-discipline the evils that attend on civilization, even if they are not due to it.[1]

3. The kinship group is a protection so long as it has to contend only with similar groups. The headlong valor and tribal loyalty of German or Scottish clans may even win conflicts with more disciplined troops of Rome or England. But permanent success demands *higher organization* than the old clans and tribes permitted. Organization means authority, and a single directing, controlling commander or king. As Egypt, Assyria, Phoenicia show their strength the clans of Israel cry, "Nay, but we will have a king over us; that we may also be like all the nations; and that our king may judge us, and go out before us, and fight our battles."[2] Wars afford the opportunity for the strong and unscrupulous leader to assert himself. Like commerce they may tend also to spread culture and thus break down barriers of ancient custom. The conquests of Babylon and Alexander, the Crusades and the French Revolution, are instances of the power of military forces to destroy old customs and give individualism new scope. In most cases, it is true, it is only the leader or "tyrant" who gets the advantage. He uses the whole machinery of society for his own elevation. Nevertheless custom and group unity are broken for all. Respect for law must be built anew from the foundation.

4. While in general religion is a conservative agency, it is also true that a *new religion* or a new departure in religion has often exercised a powerful influence on moral development. The very fact that religion is so intimately bound up with all the group mores and ideals, makes a change in religion bear directly on old standards of life. The collision between old and new is likely to be fundamental and sharp. A conception of God may carry with it a view of what conduct is pleasing to him. A doctrine as to the future may require a certain mode of life. A cultus may approve or condemn certain relations between the sexes. Conflicting reli-

---

1. Walter Lippmann, *A Preface to Morals*, pp. 156 ff.
2. 1 Sam. 8:19, 20.

gions may then force a moral attitude in weighing their claims. The contests between Yahweh and Baal, between Orphic cults and the public Greek religion, between Judaism and Christianity, Christianity and Roman civilization, Christianity and Germanic religion, Catholicism and Protestantism, have brought out moral issues. We shall notice this factor especially in Chapters 6 and 9.

§ 3. The Psychological Agencies

The psychological forces underlying individuality and individualism have been stated to be self-assertive impulses and desires. They are all variations of the effort of the living being first to preserve itself and then to rise to more complicated life by entering into more complex relations and mastering its environment. Spinoza's "*sui esse conservare*," Schopenhauer's "will to live," Nietzsche's "will to power," the Hebrew's passionate ideal of "life," and Tennyson's "More life, and fuller" express in varying degree the meaning of this elemental bent and process. Growing intelligence adds to its strength by giving greater capacity to control. Starting with organic needs, this developing life process may find satisfactions in the physical world in the increasing power and mastery over nature gained by the explorer or the hunter, the discoverer, the craftsman, or the artist. In the world of persons it displays a peculiar intensity. We note four tendencies toward self-assertion.

1. The sex impulse and emotion occupies a peculiar position in this respect. On the one hand it is to some extent a socializing agency. It brings the sexes together and is thus fundamental to the family. But on the other hand it is constantly rebelling against the limits and conventions established by the social group for its regulation. The statutes against illicit relations, from the codes of Hammurabi and Moses to those of modern times, attest the collision between the individual's inclination and the will of the group. Repeatedly some passion of sex has broken over all social, legal, and religious sanctions. It has thus been a favorite theme of tragedy from the Greeks to O'Neill. Its value and proper regulation were points at issue in that wide-reaching change of mores attendant upon the Reformation, and apparently equilibrium has not yet been reached.

2. In the primitive group we have seen that there might be private property in tools or weapons, in cattle or slaves. There was little private property in land under the maternal clan; and indeed in any case, so long as the arts were undeveloped, private property had necessary limits. The demand for private property is a natural attendant upon individual modes of industry. As we have said, it was a common principle that what the group produced was owned by the group, and what the individual made or captured was treated as his. When individual industry came to count for more, the individual claimed more and more as private possession.

The change from the maternal clan to the paternal family or household was a reenforcement to the individual control of property. The father could hand down his cattle or his house to his son. The joint family of India is indeed a type of a paternal system. Nevertheless the tendency is much stronger to insist on individual property where the father's goods pass to his son than where they go to his sister's children.

The chiefs or rulers were likely to gain the right of private property first. Among certain families of the South Slavs today, the head has his individual eating utensils, the rest share. Among many people the chiefs have cattle which they can dispose of as they will; the rest have simply their share of the kin's goods. The old Brehon laws of Ireland show this stage.

But however it comes about, the very meaning of property is, in the first place, exclusion of others from some thing which I have. It is therefore in so far necessarily opposed to any such simple solidarity of life as we find in group morality.

3. Struggles for mastery or liberty make for a stronger individual. In most cases these cannot be separated from economic struggles. Masters and slaves were in economic as well as personal relations, and nearly all class contests on a large scale have had at least one economic root, whatever their other sources. But the economic is not their only root. There have been wars for glory or for liberty as well as for territory or booty or slaves. As the struggle for existence has bred into the race the impulse to self-defense with its emotion of anger, the zest for rivalry and mastery, and the corresponding aversion to being ruled, so the progress of society shows trials of strength between man and man, kin and kin, tribe and tribe. And while, as stated in the pre-

ceding chapter, the cooperation made necessary in war or feud is a uniting force, there is another side to the story. Contests between individuals show who is master; contests between groups tend to bring forward leaders. And while such masterful men may serve the group they are quite as likely to find an interest in opposing group customs. They assert an independence of the group, or a mastery over it, quite incompatible with the solidarity of the kinship clan, although the patriarchal type of household under a strong head may be quite possible. There comes to be one code for rich and another for poor, one for Patricians and another for Plebs, one for baron and another for peasant, one for gentry and another for the common folk. For a time this may be accepted patiently. But when once the rich become arrogant, the feudal lord insolent, customs of an earlier day seem unjust; they no longer hold. Old ties are cast off, the demand for freedom and equality rises, and the collision between authority and liberty is on.

Or the contest may be for intellectual liberty—for free thought and free speech. It is sometimes considered that such liberty meets its strongest opponent in the religious or ecclesiastical organization. There is no doubt a conservative tendency in religion. As we have pointed out, religion is the great conservator of group values and group standards. Intellectual criticism tends to undermine what is outgrown or merely habitual here as elsewhere. Rationalism or free thought has set itself in frequent opposition likewise to what has been claimed to be "above reason." Nevertheless it would be absurd to attribute all the innovation to science and all the conservatism to religion. Scientific dogmas and "idols" are hard to displace. Schools are about as conservative as churches. And on the other hand the struggle for religious liberty has usually been carried on not by the irreligious but by the religious. The history of the noble army of martyrs is a record of appeal to individual conscience, or to an immediate personal relation to God, as over against the formal, the traditional, the organized religious customs and doctrines of their age. The struggle for religious toleration and religious liberty takes its place side by side with the struggles for intellectual and political liberty in the chapters of growing individuality.

4. Desire for honor and social esteem may develop the individual. James, in his psychology of the self, calls the recognition

which a man gets from his mates his "social self." "We are not only gregarious animals, liking to be in sight of our fellows, but we have an innate propensity to get ourselves noticed, and noticed favorably by our kind. No more fiendish punishment could be devised, were such a thing physically possible, than that one should be turned loose in society and remain absolutely unnoticed by all the members thereof."[3] From such a punishment "the cruelest bodily tortures would be a relief; for this would make us feel that however bad might be our plight, we had not sunk to such depth as to be unworthy of attention at all."[4] Honor or fame is a name for one of the various "social selves" which a man may build up. It stands for what those of a given group may think or say of him. It has a place and a large place in group life. Precedence, salutations, decorations in costume and bodily ornament, praises in song for the brave, the strong, the cunning, the powerful, with ridicule for the coward or the weakling are all at work. But with the primitive group the difference between men of the group is kept within bounds. When more definite organization of groups for military or civil purposes begins, when the feudal chief gathers his retainers and begins to rise above the rest of the community in strength, finally when the progress of the arts gives greater means for display, the desire for recognition has immensely greater scope. It is increased by the urge of emulation; it often results in envy and jealousies. It becomes then a powerful factor in stimulating individuality, if not individualism.

When the group whose approval is sought is small, we have class standards, with all the provincialism, narrowness, and prejudice that belong to them. As the honor-seeker is merely after the opinion of his class, he is bound to be only partly social. So long as he is with his kin, or his set, or his "gang," or his "party," or his "union," or his "country"—regardless of any wider appeal—he is bound to be imperfectly rational and social in his conduct. The great possibilities of the desire for honor, and of the desire to be worthy of honor, lie then in the constant extension of the range. The martyr, the seeker for truth, the reformer, the neglected artist, looks for honor from posterity; if misjudged or neglected, he appeals to mankind. He is thus form-

3. *Psychology*, I., ch. x.
4. *Ibid.*, pp. 293 f.

ing for himself an ideal standard. And if he embodies this ideal standard in a personal, highest possible judging companion, his desire to be worthy of approval takes a religious form. He seeks "the honor that is from God." Though "the innermost of the empirical selves of a man is a self of the *social* sort, it yet can find its only adequate *socius* in an ideal world."[5]

The moral value of these forces was finely stated by Kant:

> The means which nature uses to bring about the development of all the capacities she has given man is their *antagonism* in society, in so far as this antagonism becomes in the end a cause of social order. Men have an inclination to *associate* themselves, for in a social state they feel themselves more completely men: i.e., they are conscious of the development of their natural capacities. But they have also a great propensity to *isolate* themselves, for they find in themselves at the same time this unsocial characteristic: each wishes to direct everything solely according to his own notion, and hence expects resistance, just as he knows that he is inclined to resist others. It is just this resistance which awakens all man's powers; this brings him to overcome his propensity to indolence, and drives him through the lust for honor, power, or wealth to win for himself a rank among his fellowmen. Man's will is for concord, but nature knows better what is good for the species, and she wills discord. He would like a life of comfort and pleasure; nature wills that he be dragged out of idleness and inactive content, and plunged into labor and trouble in order that he may find out the means of extricating himself from his difficulties. The natural impulses which prompt this effort, the sources of unsociableness and of the mutual conflict from which so many evils spring, are then spurs to a more complete development of man's powers.[6]

We have spoken of the "forces" which tend to break down the old unity of the group and bring about new organization. But of course these forces are not impersonal. Sometimes they seem to act like the ocean tide, pushing silently in, and only now and

5. James, *Psychology*, I., 316.
6. "Idea of a Universal Cosmopolitical History."

then sending a wave a little higher than its fellows. Frequently, however, some great personality stands out preeminent, either as critic of the old or builder of the new. The prophets were stoned because they condemned the present; the next generation was ready to build their sepulchers. Socrates is the classic example of the great man who perishes in seeking to find a rational basis to replace that of custom. Indeed, this conflict—on the one hand, the rigid system of tradition and corporate union hallowed by all the sanctions of religion and public opinion; upon the other, the individual making appeal to reason, or to his conscience, or to a "higher law"—is the tragedy of history.

§ 4. Positive Reconstruction

It must not be supposed that the moral process stops at the points indicated under the several divisions of this last section. As already stated, if a people really works out a higher type of conscious and personal morality, it means not only a more powerful individual, but a reconstructed individual and a reconstructed society. It means not only the disintegration of the old kinship or family group, which is as well an economic, political, and religious unity. It means the construction of a new basis for the family; new moral principles for business; a distinct political state with new means for government, new conceptions of authority and liberty; finally, a national or universal religion. And the individual on this higher level takes a more voluntary attitude toward these institutions. In the presence of new conflicting ends, he sets up or adopts a standard for himself. He thinks definitely of what is "good" and "right." As he recognizes its claim, he is responsible as well as free. As he identifies himself heartily with it, he becomes sincerely and genuinely moral. Reverence, duty, and love for what is good become the quickening emotions. Thoughtfulness, self-control, aspiration toward an ideal, courageous venturing in its achievement, kindness and justice, are recognized as the temper that should be dominant. The conception of moral character and moral personality is brought to consciousness. The development of the Hebrews and Greeks will show how these positive values emerge.

Literature

Kant's Principles of Politics, tr. by Hastie, 1891, especially the essay "The Idea of a Universal Cosmopolitical History"; Hegel, *Philosophy of History*, tr. by Sibree, 1881; Darwin, *The Descent of Man*, 1871, 1882–87; Schurman, *The Ethical Import of Darwinism*, 1888; Seth, "The Evolution of Morality," *Mind*, XIV., 1889, pp. 27–49; Williams, *A Review of Systems of Ethics Founded on the Theory of Evolution*, 1893; Harris, *Moral Evolution*, 1895; Tufts, "On Moral Evolution," in *Studies in Philosophy and Psychology (Garman Commemorative Volume)*, 1906; Ihering, *Der Kampf ums Recht*; Simcox, *Natural Law*, 1877; Sorley, *Ethics of Naturalism*, 1885.

6. The Hebrew Development

§ 1. Problem and Background

The problem of Hebrew moral and religious development is this: How can we explain the fact that the Hebrews, who according to their own early records and traditions, were, at the time of their entry into the land of Canaan, no better than other nomads and barbarians, should have reached such a high moral and spiritual level as we find evidenced in their later literature and in the New Testament? Their religion is said to have been a factor. Yet their god, Yahweh, as conceived by early tradition and in early documents was represented as cruel, vengeful, deceitful, an intensely partisan tribal deity, merciless toward other tribes that were regarded as enemies, and visiting the iniquities of the fathers upon the children. How could such a deity become a power for right and justice, a symbol of truth, fidelity, mercy, and lovingkindness, a Father of mankind? If, for the moment, we separate religion from morals, did their religion raise their morals, or did their morals transform their religion?

We suggest a third possibility. Moral problems were *set* by actual human relations and situations—in the family; in conflicts between standards from the desert clan and commercial standards of the city, or between rich and poor; in the administration of justice between man and man; in adjustments with other races and nations. These conflicts of interest forced reflection upon what was just and good. In religious minds such reflection took the form, What does God require? What does he value highest? Reflection upon family love prompted the, "Like as a father pitieth his children, so the Lord pitieth them that fear him." Oppression and favoritism gave the incentive to conceive a just judge. To the shepherd dweller upon the mountain the license in the cultus of the god of fertility and the luxury of the city seemed unworthy of the austere god of Sinai. But every moral aspiration or ideal thus transferred to God came back heightened and reenforced as a divine quality, or a divine command. Even such a peculiarly divine attribute as "holy," which early belonged to the essence of God as contrasted with man, and prohibited with fiery destruction any contact or look from man, was so far brought into contact with human feeling and emotion as to signify abhorrence of iniquity and injustice. A vision of the Lord as the holy One served to inspire the young Isaiah as a preacher of righteousness and purity.

Who were the chief agents in this moralizing of religion and transformation of moral judgments into divine qualities or commands? Undoubtedly the prophets. From Amos to Jesus, in the phrase of Professor Smith,[1] they "set themselves the task of interpreting the history of their times in terms of God." Law and ritual might stabilize, sages might warn against the seductions of wine or the strange woman, psalmists might voice the intimate fervor of praise and worship; it was the prophets who supplied the dynamic force that produced growth. They seldom prophesied "smooth things"; they denounced evils unsparingly and feared neither king nor popular rage. But they looked forward as well as at the here and now, and gave their people, and the world, a larger hope of a reign of justice, right, and peace.

When the Hebrews entered the land of Canaan, now Palestine, they came as clans and tribes of nomads, with flocks and herds. They found the country occupied by people of more advanced civilization, who practiced agriculture and had walled cities. The Hebrews brought tribal morality,[2] and the long contest for control strengthened the fierce hostility to other races which belongs to warring tribes. To kill the men and enslave the women was not only common practice, it was supposed to be strictly enjoined by Yahweh. Blood revenge was sacred duty; Yahweh enforced its execution by sending a famine upon the land, and was appeased only by vengeance exacted upon children and grandchildren of the original offender. Vows must be kept, but if a vow to Yahweh required the death of a daughter, Jephthah did not think the obligation could be avoided. Sacrifice of the first-born was de-

1. J. M. P. Smith, *The Prophets and Their Times*, p. 263.
2. J. M. P. Smith, *The Moral Life of the Hebrews*, Part I.

manded, and not uncommon, but a milder tradition sanctioned the substitution of a ram for a son. Yahweh could be a consuming fire; he would strike dead a man who innocently attempted to prevent the fall of the sacred ark, and send a destroying pestilence upon the whole people because King David presumed to make a census. Jacob won his contests with Esau and Laban by sharp practice, and Yahweh likewise used deceit, especially toward those of other peoples than Israel. Polygamy was common. On the other hand passionate desire for children was matched by such affection as that of Jacob for Joseph and Benjamin, and for Rachel their mother. "And Jacob served seven years for Rachel; and they seemed unto him but a few days for the love he had to her." Deborah the prophetess was honored, and her song which praises the loyal tribes and scourges the cowards is one of the best sources of tribal ideals, and of the early conception of Yahweh the defender, marching from Edom in the storm while "the earth trembled, and the heavens dropped, the clouds also dropped water."

After two or more centuries of struggle with varying fortunes under "judges" the people demanded a king "that we also may be like all the nations; and that our king may judge us, and go out before us and fight our battles." Saul, David, and Solomon built a kingdom, warred against neighboring peoples successfully, and began commerce which under their successors led to increasing wealth, to the growth of cities, and to a separation between rich and poor. This mocked the old tribal morality of a common solidarity. An Elijah from the desert confronted King Ahab, who had taken from Naboth the ancestral vineyard, with the indignant, "Hast thou killed, and hast thou taken possession?" A century later, Amos, from the mountains, denounced the luxury and oppression of the rich city-dwellers. The preaching of social justice had begun.

The fall of Samaria in the North, in 721 B.C. and of Jerusalem in the South, 586 B.C. followed by exile and captivity of prominent Jews in Babylon, came as a crushing calamity. It set a crucial problem for both morals and religion. Hitherto Law and Prophecy had held and taught that prosperity followed faithful obedience to Yahweh, and that defeat was a sign of his displeasure. But now the faithful were scattered and captive, and the holy city was wasted. Was the arm of Yahweh shortened that he could not save? We shall note later the struggles of prophets and sages with these problems. The return of the exiles, their rebuilding of the Temple, their patriotic resistance under the Maccabees to the abolition of their religion by Antiochus were evidences of the devotion of the remnant. The fall of Jerusalem at the hands of Titus and the Romans, A.D. 70, saw the destruction of the Temple, the end of sacrifices, and of the Jews as a nation. They still cherished their law and their sacred writings. But the moral ideals of their prophets and their vision of a better world-order of justice and peace lived on also in the world religion founded by the prophet of Nazareth, who came not to destroy but to fulfill.

§ 2. Religious Agencies

As already stated, the prophets were the great moralizing agency. But there were also other agencies which contributed to moral progress: the personal relation to Yahweh, as both friend and lawgiver; the cultus; the kingdom with its administration of justice; the sage.

1. As has been brought out several times in our study, the fundamental source of moral conceptions of right and justice is that men and women live in society, in a community of some sort. Religion regards God as a member of such a community. This implies fidelity; it implies that God and people have their respective parts to perform in order that the community may continue and prosper. In a national religion this relation is narrowly conceived; the people is to have no other god, Yahweh is to have (according to earlier views) no other people. Yet this makes for a certain intimacy, which may be a useful stage in fostering the feeling of dependence and reliance upon a divine helper. It may also be that the covenant relation between Yahweh and Israel which plays so important a role in the Ten Words and the teachings of Deuteronomy, contributed to emphasize the voluntary character of the relation, and the sacredness of a solemn promise. On the other hand the thought of Yahweh as father, or husband of his people evidently sought to carry over to God the close ties of family care and affection.

The conception of Yahweh as personal lawgiver came, of course, from the functions of a ruler in the community. This had an important influence in changing the attitude toward customs. Yahweh's law compelled obedience or rebellion. Customs were either forbidden or enjoined. In either case they ceased to be merely customs. In the law of Israel the whole body of observances in private life, in ceremonial, and in legal forms, is introduced with a "Thus saith the Lord." We know that other Semitic people observed the Sabbath, practiced circumcision, distinguished clean from unclean beasts, and respected the taboos of birth and death. Whether in Israel all these observances were old customs given new authority by statute, or were customs taken from other peoples under the authority of the laws of Yahweh, is immaterial. The ethical significance of the law is that these various observances, instead of being treated merely as customs, are regarded as personal commands of a personal deity.

This makes a vital difference in the view taken of the violation of these observances. When a man violates a custom he fails to do the correct thing. He misses the mark.[3] But when the observance is a personal command, its violation is a personal disobedience; it is rebellion; it is an act of will. The evil which follows is no longer bad luck; it is punishment. Now punishment must be either right or wrong, moral or immoral. It can never be merely non-moral. Hence the very conception of sin as a personal offense, and of ill as a personal punishment, forces a moral judgment. In its crudest form this may take the god's commands as right simply because he utters them, and assume that the sufferer is guilty merely because he suffers.

But side by side with the conception that the laws of Yahweh must be obeyed because they were his commands, there was another doctrine which was but an extension of the theory that the people had freely accepted their ruler. This was that Yahweh's commands were not arbitrary. They were right; they could be placed before the people for their approval; they were "life"; "the judge of all the earth" would "do right." We have here a striking illustration of the principle that moral standards, at first embodied in persons, slowly work free, so that persons are judged by them.

2. The elaborate cultus carried on by the priests, symbolized, however imperfectly, certain moral ideas. The solicitous care for

3. The Hebrew and Greek words for sin both mean "to miss."

ceremonial "purity" might have no direct moral value; the contamination from contact with birth or death or certain animals might be a very external sort of "uncleanness." Nevertheless, they symbolized control by a law. The "holiness" of the priests, as set apart to special service of Yahweh, emphasized the seriousness of their work; and further, it contributed to a distinction between spiritual and material. Moreover, while part of this value inheres in all ritual, the contrast between Yahweh's worship and that of other deities challenged moral attention. The gods of the land, the various Baals, were worshipped "upon every high hill and under every green tree." As gods of fertility, they were symbolized by the emblems of sex, and great freedom prevailed at their festivals. At certain shrines men and women gave themselves for the service of the god. Even first-born children were not infrequently sacrificed. These festivals and shrines seem to have been adopted more or less fully by Israel from the Canaanites, but the prophets have an utterly different idea of Yahweh worship. The god of Sinai rejects utterly such practices. License and drunkenness are not, as the cultus of Baal and Astarte implied, the proper symbols of life and deity.

Moreoever, one part of the cultus, the "sin offering," directly implied transgression and the need of forgiveness. The "sins" might themselves be ceremonial rather than moral, and the method of removing them might be external—especially the process of putting the sins upon a scapegoat which should "bear upon him all their iniquities into a solitary land,"—nevertheless, the solemn confession, and the shedding of the blood which was the "life," could not but remind of responsibility and deepen reflection. The need of atonement and reconciliation, thus impressed, symbolized the moral process of reconstructing, of putting away a lower past, and readjusting life to meet an ideal.

3. The ecstatic trances in which the prophets were believed to see visions, or become entrusted with divine messages, gave them prestige among their people, but did not prevent them from keeping keen and wide-open eyes upon the events and conditions before them. They made kings, and watched the armies of Assyria and Egypt. They saw the dress of rich women and heard the cry of the oppressed poor. As they mused on threatened invasion or flagrant injustice the fire burned within. The invasion must be in God's plan; the injustice must bring down divine

wrath. From trance or vision or meditation they came with a "Thus saith the Lord." They brought a message from a living source of authority, intended for the immediate situation. They brought a present command for a present duty. "Thou art the man," of Nathan to David, "Hast thou killed, and also taken possession?" of Elijah to Ahab, were personal rebukes. But the great sermons of Amos, Isaiah, Jeremiah, were no less for the hour. A licentious festival, an Assyrian invasion, an Egyptian embassy, a plague of locusts, an impending captivity—these inspire demand for repentance, warnings of destruction, promises of salvation. The prophet was thus the "living fountain." The divine will as coming through him "was still, so to speak, fluid, and not congealed into institutions."

In the second place, the prophets seized upon the inward purpose and social conduct of man as the all-important issues; cultus, sacrifice, are unimportant. "I hate, I despise your feasts, and I will take no delight in your solemn assemblies," cries Amos in Yahweh's name, "But let justice roll down as waters and righteousness as a mighty stream." "I have had enough of the burnt offerings of rams, and the fat of fed beasts," proclaims Isaiah, "new moons, and sabbaths, the calling of assemblies,—I cannot away with iniquity and the solemn meeting." You need not ceremonial, but moral, purity. "Wash you, make you clean; put away the evil of your doings;—seek justice, relieve the oppressed, judge the fatherless, plead for the widow." Micah's "Shall I give my first-born for my transgression, the fruit of my body for the sin of my soul?" seized upon the difference once for all between the physical and the moral; a completely ethical standpoint is gained in his summary of religious duty:. "What doth God require of thee, but to do justly, and to love mercy, and to walk humbly with thy God?" And the New Testament analogue marks the true ethical valuation of all the external religious manifestations, even of the cruder forms of prophecy itself. Gifts, mysteries, knowledge, or the "body to be burned"—there is a more excellent way than these. For all these are "in part." Their value is but temporary and relative. The values that abide, that stand criticism, are that staking of oneself upon the truth and worth of one's ideal which is faith; that aspiration and forward look which is hope; that sum of all social charity, sympathy, justice, and active helpfulness, which is love. "But the greatest of these is love."

4. Yahweh was the real king of Israel. The human ruler in Jerusalem was his representative. The expansion and glory of the kingdom under Solomon showed the divine favor. Division and calamity were not mere misfortunes, or the victory of greater armies; they were divine rebukes. Only in righteousness and justice could the nation survive. On the other hand, the confidence in Yahweh's love for Israel guaranteed that he would never forsake his people. He would purify them and redeem them even from the grave. He would establish a kingdom of law and peace, "an everlasting kingdom that should not be destroyed." Politics in Israel had a moral goal.

5. Sage and prophet gave to *suffering* a deeper significance. The Greek treatment of the problem of evil is found in the great tragedies. An ancestral curse follows down successive generations, dealing woe to all the unhappy house. For the victims there seems to be nothing but to suffer. The necessity of destiny makes the catastrophe sublime, but also hopeless. Ibsen's *Ghosts* is conceived in a similar spirit. There is a tremendous moral lesson in it for the fathers, but for the children only horror. The Greek and the Scandinavian are doubtless interpreting one phase of human life—its continuity and dependence upon cosmical nature. But the Hebrew was not content with this. His confidence in a divine government of the world forced him to seek some moral value, some purpose in the event. The search led along one path to a readjustment of values, it led by another path to a new view of social interdependence.

The book of Job gives the deepest study of the first of these problems. The old view had been that virtue and happiness always went together. Prosperity meant divine favor, and therefore it must be good. Adversity meant divine punishment; it showed wrongdoing and was itself an evil. When calamity comes upon Job, his friends assume it to be a sure proof of his wickedness. He had himself held the same view, and since he refuses to admit his wickedness and "holds fast to his integrity," it confounds all his philosophy of life and of God. It compels a reversal and revaluation of all values. If he could only meet God face to face and have it out with him he believes there would be some solution. But come what may, he will not sell his soul for happiness. To "repent," as his friends urge, in order that he may be again on good terms with God, would mean for him to call sin what he believes to be righteousness. And he will not lie in this way. God is doubtless stronger, and if he pursues his victim relentlessly, may convict him. But be this as it may, Job will not let go his fundamental consciousness of right and wrong. His "moral self" is the one anchor that holds, is the supreme value of life.

> As God liveth, who hath taken away my right,
> And the Almighty who hath vexed my soul;
> Surely my lips shall not speak unrighteousness.
> Till I die, I will not put away my integrity from me,
> My righteousness I hold fast, and will not let it go.[4]

Another suggestion of the book is that evil comes to prove man's sincerity: "Does Job serve God for naught?" and from that standpoint the answer is, Yes; he does. "There is a disinterested love of God."[5] In this setting, also, the experience of suffering produces a shifting of values from the extrinsic to the internal.

The other treatment of the problem of suffering is found in the latter half of Isaiah. It finds an interpretation of the problem by a deeper view of social interdependence, in which the old tribal solidarity is given, as it were, a transfigured meaning. The individualistic interpretation of suffering was that it meant personal guilt. "We did esteem him stricken of God." This breaks down. The suffering servant is not wicked. He is suffering for others— in some sense. "He hath borne our griefs and carried our sorrows." The conception here reached of an interrelation which implies that the good may suffer because of the sin or the suffering of others, and that the assuming of this burden marks the higher type of ethical relation, is one of the finest products of Israel's religion. As made central in the Christian conception of the Cross, it has furnished one of the great elements in the modern social consciousness.

§ 3. The Moral Conceptions Attained

1. *Righteousness and sin* were not exact or contradictory opposites. The righteous man was not necessarily sinless. Nevertheless, the consciousness of sin, like a dark background, brought out more emphatically the conception of righteousness.

4. Job 27:1–6.
5. Genung, *Job, The Epic of the Inner Life.*

This conception had its two aspects, derived from the civil and the religious spheres of life—spheres which were not separate for the Hebrew. On the one hand, the just or righteous respected the moral order in human society. The unrighteous was unjust, extortionate, cruel. He did not respect the rights of others. On the other hand, the righteous man was in "right" relation to God. This right relation might be tested by the divine law; but as God was conceived as a living person, loving his people, "forgiving iniquity, transgression, and sin," it might also be measured by an essential harmony of spirit with the divine will. There was the "righteousness of the law," and the "righteousness of faith." The first implies complete obedience; the second implies that in spite of transgressions there is room for atonement[6] or reconciliation. As the first means ethically the testing of conduct by a moral standard, a "moral law," so the second stands for the thought that character is rather a matter of spirit and of constant reconstruction than of exact conformity, once for all, to a hard and fast rule. Specific acts may fail to conform, but life is more than a series of specific acts. The measurement of conduct by the law has value in quickening a sense of shortcoming, but alone it may also lead either to self-righteous complacency or to despair. The possibility of new adjustment, of renewal, of "a new birth," means liberation and life. As such it may be contrasted with the Buddhist doctrine of Karma, the causality from which there is no escape but by the extinction of desire.

"Sin" had likewise its various aspects. It stood for missing the mark, for violating the rules of clean and unclean; but it stood also for personal disobedience to the divine will, for violation of the moral order of Israel. In this latter sense, as identified by the prophets with social unrighteousness, it is a significant ethical conception. It brings out the point that evil and wrongdoing are not merely individual matters, not merely failures; they are offences against a law which is above the private self, against a moral order which has its rightful demands upon us.

2. The transition from group to individual responsibility was thoroughly worked out by the prophets, even if they were not able to carry full popular assent. In early days the whole kin was treated as guilty for the offense of the kinsman. Achan's case has already been cited; and in the case of Korah, Dathan, and Abiram,

6. See Charles A. Dinsmore, *Atonement in Literature and Life*, Boston, 1906.

"Their wives and their sons and their little ones" were all treated alike.[7] In like manner, the family of the righteous man shared in the divine favor. The later prophets pronounced a radical change. The proverb, "The fathers have eaten sour grapes and the children's teeth are set on edge," is no more to be used, declares Ezekiel, speaking for Yahweh. "The soul that sinneth, it shall die; the son shall not bear the iniquity of the father, neither shall the father bear the iniquity of the son"; and it is especially interesting to note that the Lord is represented as pleading with the people that this is fair, while the people say, "Wherefore doth not the son bear the iniquity of the father?" The solidarity of the family resisted the individualism of the prophetic conception, and five hundred years after Ezekiel the traces of the older conception still lingered in the question, "Who did sin, this man or his parents, that he was born blind?"[8] For another aspect of responsibility, viz., intent, as distinct from accidental action,[9] we have certain transitional steps shown in the interesting "cities of refuge"[10] for the accidental homicide in which he might be safe from the avenger of blood, provided he was swift enough of foot to reach a city of refuge before he was caught. But the fullest development in the ethics of responsibility along this line seemed to take the form described under the next head.

3. Sincerity and purity of heart came to be essential qualities. The Hebrew had a philosophy of conduct which made it chiefly a matter of "wisdom" and "folly," but the favorite term of prophet and psalmist to symbolize the central principle was rather "the heart." This term stood for the voluntary disposition, especially in its inner springs of emotions and sentiments, affections and passions. The Greek was inclined to look askance at this side of life, to regard the emotions as perturbations of the soul, and to seek their control by reason, or even their repression

7. Numbers 16; Joshua 7.
8. John 9:2.
9. Hammurabi's code showed a disregard of intent which would make surgery a dangerous profession: "If a physician operate on a man for a severe wound with a bronze lancet and cause the man's death; or open an abscess [in the eye] of a man with a bronze lancet and destroy the man's eye, they shall cut off his fingers." Early German and English law is just as naïve. If a weapon was left to be repaired at a smith's and was then caught up or stolen and used to do harm, the original owner was held responsible.
10. Numbers 35; Deuteronomy 19; Joshua 20.

or elimination. The Hebrew found a more positive value in the emotional side of conduct, and at the same time worked out the conception of a sincere and thoroughgoing interest as lying at the very root of all right life. The religious influence was as elsewhere the important agency. "Man looketh on the outward appearance, but the Lord looketh on the heart," "If I regard iniquity in my heart, the Lord will not hear me," are characteristic expressions. A divine vision, which penetrates to the deepest springs of purpose and feeling, will not tolerate pretense. Nor will it be satisfied with anything less than entire devotion: the Israelite must serve Yahweh with all his heart. Outer conformity is not enough: "Rend your heart and not your garments." It is the "pure in heart" who have the beatific vision. Not external contacts, or ceremonial "uncleanness," on which earlier ritual had insisted, defile the man, but rather what proceeds from the heart. For the heart is the source of evil thoughts and evil deeds.[11] And conversely, the interests, the emotions, and enthusiasms which make up the man's deepest self do not spring forth in a vacuum; they go with the steadfast purpose and bent, with the self of achievement. "Where your treasure is, there will your heart be also."

Purity of motive in a full moral consciousness means not only (formal) sincerity, but sincere love of good and right. This was not stated by the Hebrew in abstract terms, but in the personal language of love to God. In early days there had been more or less of external motives in the appeals of the law and the prophets. Fear of punishment, hope of reward, blessings in basket and store, curses in land and field, were used to induce fidelity. But some of the prophets sought a deeper view, which seems to have been reached in the bitterness of human experience. Hosea's wife had forsaken him, and should not the love of people to Yahweh be as personal and sincere as that of wife to husband? She had said, "I will go after my lovers *that give me my bread and my water, my wool and my flax, my oil and my drink.*"[12] Is not serving God for hire a form of prostitution?[13] The calamities of the nation tested the disinterestedness of its fidelity. They were the challenge of the Adversary, "Doth Job fear God for naught?"

11. Mark 7:1–23.
12. Hosea 2:5.
13. H. P. Smith, *Old Testament History*, p. 222.

And a remnant at least attested that fidelity did not depend on rewards. The moral maxim that virtue is its own reward is put in personal terms by the prophet after the exile:

> For though the fig tree shall not blossom, neither shall fruit be in the vines; the labor of the olive shall fail, and the fields shall yield no meat; the flock shall be cut off from the fold, and there shall be no herd in the stalls: Yet I will rejoice in the Lord, I will joy in the God of my salvation.[14]

4. The content of Israel's moral ideal on its individual side was expressed by the term "Life." All the blessings that the leader of Israel could offer his people were summarized in the phrase, "I have set before you life and death; wherefore choose life." The same final standard of value appears in the question of Jesus, "What shall it profit a man to gain the whole world and lose his own life?" When we inquire what life meant, we must infer so far as the early sources give us data for judgment, that it was measured largely in terms of material comfort and prosperity, accompanied by the satisfaction of standing in right relations to the god and ruler. The latter element was so closely united with the first that it was practically identical with it. If the people were prosperous they might assume that they were right; if they suffered they were surely wrong. Good and evil were, therefore, in this stage, measured largely in terms of pleasure and pain. The end to be sought and the ideal to be kept in mind was that of long and prosperous life—"in her right hand length of days, in her left hand riches and honor." Intellectual and esthetic interests were not prized as such. The knowledge which was valued was the wisdom for the conduct of life, of which the beginning and crown was "the fear of the Lord." The art which was valued was sacred song or poetry. But the ideal values which came to bulk most in the expanding conception of "life" were those of personal relation. Family ties, always strong among Oriental peoples, gained in purity. Love between the sexes was refined and idealized.[15] National feeling took on added dignity, because of the consciousness of a divine mission. Above all, personal union with God, as voiced in the psalms and prophets, became the de-

14. Habakkuk 3:17, 18.
15. The Song of Songs.

sire. He, and not his gifts, was the supreme good. He was the "fountain of life." His likeness would satisfy. In his light the faithful would see light.

But even more significant than any specific content put into the term "life," was *what was involved in the idea itself*. The legalists had attempted to define conduct by a code, but there was an inherent vitality in the ideal of life, which refused to be measured or bounded. The "words of eternal life," which began the new moral movement of Christianity, had perhaps little definite content to the fishermen, and it is not easy to say just what they meant in moral terms to the writer of the Fourth Gospel who uses the phrase so often. With Paul, life as the realm of the spirit gets definition as it stands over against the "death" of sin and lust. But with all writers of Old or New Testament, whatever content it had, life meant above all the suggestion of something beyond, the gleam and dynamic power of a future not yet understood. It meant to Paul a progress which was governed not by law or "rudiments," but by freedom. Such a life would set itself new and higher standards; the laws and customs that had obtained were felt to be outgrown. The significance of early Christianity as a moral movement, aside from its elements of personal devotion and social unity to be noticed, was the spirit of movement, the sense of newly forming horizons beyond the old, the conviction that as sons of God its followers had boundless possibilities, that they were not the children of the bondwoman, but of the free.

5. The social ideal of a community in which justice, peace, and love should be controlling principles, was a crowning achievement of Hebrew-Christian religion and morality. We have seen how this ideal was framed in the setting of a kingdom of God. At first national, it became universal, and with a fraternity which the world is far from having realized, it was to know "neither Jew nor Greek, bond nor free." At first military, it took on with seer and psalmist the form of a reign of peace and justice. After the fierce and crude powers typified by the lion and the bear and the leopard had passed, the seer saw a kingdom represented by a human form. Such a kingdom it was that should not pass away. Such was the kingdom "not of this world" which Jesus presented as his message. Membership in this moral kingdom was for the poor in spirit, the pure in heart, the merciful, the peace-makers,

the hungerers after righteousness. Greatness in this moral community was to depend on service, not on power. The king should not fail till he had "set justice in the earth." He should "deliver the needy, and the poor."

Certain features of this ideal order have since found embodiment in social and political structures; certain features remain for the future. Certain periods in history have transferred the ideal entirely to another world, regarding human society as hopelessly given over to evil. Such theories find a morality possible only by renouncing society. The Hebrews presented rather the ideal of a moral order on earth, of a control of all life by right, of a realization of good, and of a completeness of life. It was an ideal not dreamed out in ecstatic visions of pure fancy, but worked out in struggle and suffering, in confidence that moral efforts are not hopeless or destined to defeat. The ideal order is to be made real. The divine kingdom is to come, the divine will to be done "*on earth* as it is in heaven."

Literature

The works of W. R. Smith (*Religion of the Semites*) and Barton (*A Sketch of Semitic Origins*) already mentioned. J. M. P. Smith, *The Moral Life of the Hebrews*, 1923; Johns, *The Oldest Code of Laws in the World* (Hammurabi), 1911; Schultz, *Old Testament Theology*, tr. 1892; Marti, *Religion of the Old Testament*, tr. 1907; Budde, *Religion of Israel to the Exile*, 1899; H. P. Smith, *Old Testament History*, 1903, *The Religion of Israel*, 1914; W. R. Smith, *The Prophets of Israel*, 1895; J. M. P. Smith, *The Prophets and Their Times*, 1925; Bruce, *Ethics of the Old Testament*, 1895; Peake, *Problem of Suffering in the Old Testament*, 1904; Royce, "The Problem of Job" in *Studies of Good and Evil*, 1898; Pratt, *The Psychology of Religious Belief*, 1907, ch. v.; Harnack, *What Is Christianity?* tr. 1901; Cone, *Rich and Poor in the New Testament*, 1902; Pfleiderer, *Primitive Christianity*, tr. 1906; Matthews, *The Social Teaching of Jesus*, 1897; Wendt, *The Teaching of Jesus*, 1899; Pfleiderer, *Paulinism*, 1891; Cone, *Paul, The Man, the Missionary, and the Teacher*, 1898; Beyschlag, *New Testament Theology*, tr. 1895; *Encyclopedia Biblica*, *Jewish Encyclopedia*, and Hastings' *Dictionary*, have numerous valuable articles.

The Moral Development of the Greeks

§ 1. The Fundamental Notes

The Hebrew moral life was developed under the relation, first of the people, then of the individuals, to God—a relation at once of union and of conflict. It was out of the relation of the individual to social traditions and political order that the Greek came to full consciousness of moral law on the one hand, and a moral personality on the other. And just as in Jewish life the law and the prophets (or, later, the "law and the gospel") stood for the conflicting forces, so in Greek life the opposition between the authority of the group, embodied in custom and institutions, on the one hand, and the urgent claims of developing personality, manifest in both intelligence and desire, on the other, found expression in contrasted terms. The authority of the group embodied in customs and institutions, came to be regarded by the radicals as relatively external, artificial, and rigid. It was dubbed "convention," or "institution" (*thesis*, what is set up). The rapidly developing intelligence challenged the merely customary and traditional; the increasing individuality challenged the superior authority of the group, especially when this manifested itself apparently in a government of force. Personal intelligence and personal feeling asserted a more elemental claim, as if they were rooted in a more original source; this source was called "nature" (*physis*). Social tradition and authority, individual reason and feeling, thus confronted each other as "convention" and "nature." It was a struggle which has its analogy in the development of many a young man or young woman who is emerging from parental control to self-direction. But in Greek life more distinctly than elsewhere we see the steps of the process as a civic and not merely an individual development. Aeschylus, Sophocles, and Euripides presented this conflict of the individual with law or destiny as the great, oft-repeated tragedy of human

life. Aristophanes mocked with bitter satire the "new" views. Socrates, Plato, Aristotle, Cynics, Cyrenaics, Epicureans, and Stoics
took part in the theoretical discussions.

The fundamental note of all Greek life, before, during, and
after this development, was *Measure, Order, Proportion*. This
note found expression in religion, science, art, and conduct.
Among their gods, the Greeks set Moira, "Destiny," and Themis,
"Custom," "Law," "Right." They found order in the universe,
which on this account they called the "cosmos." They expressed
it in their arts, especially in architecture, sculpture, the choral
dance, and the more highly developed tragedy or lyric:

"And all life is full of them [of form and measure]," says
Plato, "as well as every constructive and creative art. And
surely the art of the painter and every other creative and
constructive art are full of them—weaving, embroidery, architecture, and every kind of manufacture; also nature, animal and vegetable—in all of them there is grace or the
absence of grace; and if our youth are to do their work in
life, must they not make these graces and harmonies their
perpetual aim?"

The best people, the "gentlemen," were styled *kaloikagathoi*—
"fair and good." The motto at the Delphic shrine was, "Nothing
in excess." Insolent disregard of propriety, *hybris*, was the quality most denounced by the early moralizing poets. Tityus,
Tantalus, and Sisyphus, the three special subjects of divine punishment, suffered the penalty of insatiate desire, or limits over-
stepped. And after criticism and individualism had done their
work, Plato's conception of justice, Aristotle's doctrine of the
"mean," the Stoic maxim of "life according to nature," have but
discovered a deeper significance for the fundamental law of
Greek life.

The conceptions of the Good and the Just are developed from
the two notes just presented. The motive for challenge to established institutions was the awakening desire of the individual to
seek his own good and to live his own life. Commerce was bringing a great variety of rewards to the shrewd merchant and a great
variety of goods to evoke and gratify wants. Slavery set free the
citizen from the need of manual labor and gave him leisure to
cultivate his tastes. The forces of individuality, described in

THE MORAL DEVELOPMENT OF THE GREEKS   99

Chapter 5, were all at work to bring the process and object of desire to consciousness. Moreover, the term "good" was also in use to mark the popular ideal. It was applied to what we should call the "successful" men of the day. In present life our term "good" has become so definitely moral that probably most young persons would hesitate to say that they have it as their ideal to become good, although few would hesitate to say that they wish to be capable and successful. For social and political recognition seems to be based rather on achievement of striking results than upon what is technically called "goodness." But in Greece moral goodness was not used to designate "character" as contrasted with "results." The "good man" was like the "good lawyer" or "good athlete" or "good soldier," the man who was efficient and conspicuous. It was in the process which we are to trace that the ambiguities and deeper meanings of the term came to definition.

The terms Just and Justice were not of course merely synonyms for order and measure. They had likewise the social significance coming from the courts and the assembly. They stood for the control side of life, as Good stood for its aspect of valuation and desire. But as compared with the Hebrew conception of righteousness, they meant much less a conformity to a law divine or human which had been already set up as standard, and much more, an ordering, a regulating, a harmonizing. The rational element of measure or order was more prominent than the personal note of authority. Hence we shall find Plato passing easily back and forth between justice or order in the individual and justice or order in the State. On the other hand, the radicals of the day could seize upon the legal usage and declare that justice or the law was purely a matter of self-interest or class interest.

§ 2. Intellectual Forces of Individuality and Individualism

The older standards were embodied in religious and political ideas and institutions; the agency which was to disentangle and bring into clear consciousness the standards *as such*, was the *scientific spirit*, the knowledge and reflection of an intellectual people at a period of extraordinarily rapid development. The commercial life, the free intercourse with other peoples and civilizations, especially in the colonies, the absence of any generally dominant political authority, the architectural problems suggested by a beauty-loving people—all promoted alertness and flexibility of mind.

In a concrete form, this rational character had already found expression in the quality of Greek art. Reference has already been made to the formal side of Greek art, with its embodiment of rhythm and measure; the subject-matter shows the same element. The Greek world, as contrasted with the barbarian world, was conceived by the Greek as the realm of light contrasted with darkness; the national God, Apollo, embodied this ideal of light and reason, and his fitting symbol was the sun. The great Pan-Athenaic procession, as reproduced in the Parthenon frieze, celebrated the triumph of Greek light and intelligence over barbarian darkness. Athena, goddess of wisdom, was a fitting guardian of the most Greek of all Greek cities. Greek tragedy, beginning in hymns of worship, soon passed over into a portrayal of the all-controlling laws of life, as these were brought into stronger relief by a tragic collision with human agents.

It was, however, in the realm of science that this intellectual genius found field for expression in a clearly conscious manner. Almost all our sciences were originated by the Greeks, and they were particularly successful in those which called for abstract thinking in the highest degree. Euclid's geometry and Aristotle's logic are conspicuous illustrations of this ability. The most general conceptions of natural science: e.g., the conception of the atom and the whole materialistic theory of the universe; the conception of evolution, meaning by this the process of change according to an all-controlling law; the conception of natural selection, according to which those organisms survive which are fitted for their environment—all these were the product of the keen intelligence of the Greeks. Nor was their scientific ability expended upon external nature alone. The conception of history as more than a series of events, the comparative method in the study of political systems, the analysis of literary and artistic effects, attest the same clarity of mind and the same eager search for the most general laws of every aspect of experience.

When this scientific mind began to consider the practical guidance of life, the older political and religious controls presented serious difficulty. The gods were supposed to reward the good and punish the evil,[1] but how could this be reconciled with their practices? Aeschylus attempted a purifying and elevating of the divine ideal, similar to that which Israel's conception underwent in the work of the prophets. He magnified the dignity and providential government of Zeus, which, though dark, is yet just and certain. But the great obstacle was that the earlier and cruder conceptions of the gods had been fixed in literary form; the tales of Cronos' impiety to Uranus, of Zeus' deceitful messenger and marital unfaithfulness, of Aphrodite's amours, and Hermes' gift of theft, were all written in Hesiod and Homer. The cruder conceptions of the gods had thus become too firmly fixed in the popular imagination to be capable of becoming the bearers of advancing ethical ideals, and so not merely the irreverent scoffer, but the serious tragedian, Euripides, and the religious idealist, Plato, do not hesitate to challenge boldly the older conceptions, or to demand a revision of all this literature before it comes into the hands of the young.

The social standards of propriety and honorable conduct were likewise brought in question by advancing intelligence. The word which summed up the early Greek idea of the best type was *Kalokagathos*. This word was very nearly the equivalent of our English word "gentleman." It combined the elements of birth, ability, and refinement, but in the earlier usage the emphasis was upon the fact of birth, even as our terms "generous," "noble," "gentle," originally referred to membership in a "gens." Socrates investigated the current estimates and found that the people who were generally regarded as the "respectable," or, as we should say, the "best" people of Athens, were not necessarily either "fine" or "good" in person or character; the term had come to be one of "convention," without basis in reason. Plato goes still further and with a direct application of the rational standard to the current estimates, pokes fun at the conventional judgment of what constitutes the respectable gentleman.

1. *Cf.*, Xenophon's account of the impressive appeal of Clearchus: "For, first and greatest, the oaths which we have sworn by the gods forbid us to be enemies to each other. Whoever is conscious of having transgressed these,—him I could never deem happy. For if one were at war with the gods, I know not with what swiftness he might flee so as to escape, or into what darkness he might run, or into what stronghold he might retreat and find refuge. For all things are everywhere subject to the gods, and the gods rule all everywhere with equity."— *Anabasis*, II., v.

When they sing the praises of family and say that some
one is a gentleman because he has had seven generations of
wealthy ancestors, he [the philosopher] thinks that their sentiments only betray the dullness and narrowness of vision of
those who utter them, and who are not educated enough to
look at the whole, nor to consider that every man has had
thousands and thousands of progenitors, and among them
have been rich and poor, kings and slaves, Hellenes and
barbarians, many times over. And when some one boasts
of a catalogue of twenty-five ancestors, and goes back to
Heracles, the son of Amphitryon, he cannot understand his
poverty of ideas. Why is he unable to calculate that
Amphitryon had a twenty-fifth ancestor, who might have
been anybody, and was such as fortune made him, and he
had a fiftieth, and so on? He is amused at the notion that he
cannot do a sum, and thinks that a little arithmetic would
have got rid of his senseless vanity.[2]

The type of life that is really noble or fine and good is to
be found in the seeker for true beauty and goodness. External
beauty of form and appearance has its value in kindling the desire for the higher forms of beauty—beauty of mind, of institutions and laws, of science—until finally the conception of true
beauty is reached. This true beauty, as distinct from particular
beauties, and true good, as distinct from seeming or partial good,
are discovered only by the "philosopher," the seeker for wisdom.

Nor did the more positively recognized types of moral excellence fare better. As recognized in common life, they were courage, prudence or moderation, holiness or a certain respect for the
serious things of life, and justice; but none of these, Plato argues,
is really an independent excellence, apart from conscious and intelligent action. Courage, for example, is not really courage unless one knows and foresees the danger in all its strength; otherwise there is merely reckless bravery. Prudence or moderation, to
be really excellent, must be measured by wisdom. Even justice
cannot be regarded as at bottom distinct from wisdom, the true
measure of all the relations of life.

2. *Theaetetus*, 174–175.

The political control was likewise involved in question by the same forces of intelligence which had challenged the religious authority. The frequent changes of government, and the more or less arbitrary measures that were oftentimes adopted, were adapted to awaken doubt as to the absolute right and authority of the laws. The despot who gained control in many a Greek city was not bound by ties of blood to all members of the community, nor did he govern in accordance with the ancestral traditions of the tribe. The political authority frequently clashed with the instincts and traditions of family and kinship. Under such circumstances, the political authority was likely to be challenged and its constraining power stretched to the breaking point. So in the *Antigone* of Sophocles, the command of the ruler is opposed to the "higher law" of kinship and nature. Law of man is not law of nature or of God. Disobedience to this conventional law of man may be commission of "holiest crime." The old standards, both of religion and of political life, crumbled before the analysis of the developing intelligence, and the demand for some standard could be met only by the intelligence itself. To question the old must inevitably seem irreverent and anarchical. Some questioned merely to doubt; others, and of these Socrates was the leader, questioned in order to find a firmer basis, a more authoritative standard. But naturally the popular mind did not distinguish between these two classes of questioners, and so Socrates perished, not merely as the victim of unjust popular calumny, but as the victim of the tragedy of moral progress, of the change from the established to the new.

§ 3. Commercial and Political Individualism

A further line of development joined forces with this growth of intelligence, to emphasize the problem of moral control, and to set the individual with his standards over against the objective standards of society. This was the rapidly growing consciousness of individual goods and interests. The commercial life, with its possibilities of individual property, the rapid changes of political life, with the rise of individuals to power and privilege, the increasing opportunities which a high civilization brought both men and women for personal enjoyment and gratification of rapidly increasing wants, all tended to make the individual seek his own good, and to shift the emphasis of life from the question, What is proper, or honorable? to the question, What is *good*—good for *me*?

The conviction that the authority of government and law was largely dictated by the very considerations of private interests which they were supposed to overrule and eliminate, made the situation more acute. For the Greek States were no longer groups with common interests. The growth of capital, the corresponding eagerness for gain, the formation of distinct classes, each intent on its interests, supplanted the older, more homogeneous State. "The whole development of the political life of the Hellenic republics depended ultimately on the decision of the question, which of the different social classes—the capitalistic minority, the middle class, or the poor—should obtain the dominant place." Aristotle defines an oligarchy as a State governed in the interest of the rich; a democracy, as a State governed in the interest of the poor. Another contemporary writer explains a democracy as consulting the interests of the democrats, the "lower classes," and considers this a matter of course, "for if the rich had the say, they would do what was good for themselves but not for the multitude." Naturally such dominance by classes called out vigorous criticisms upon the laws and standards so established. The aristocratic minority inveighed against "custom" or conventions which would tame the strong to the level of the weak. Nature demands rather the "survival of the fittest," i.e., of the strong. The enlightened spectator of the game of government, on the other hand, declares that all laws are made in the interest of ruling classes. The reader of current criticisms on laws and courts will see how close is the parallel to present complaints. We have today the same two classes: One inveighs against governmental interference with the right to combine, to contract, and in general to get from the earth or from men, women, and children all that superior power and shrewdness can possibly extract. The other complains that legislatures are owned by wealth, that judges are appointed from corporation lawyers, that common law is a survival of ancient aristocratic status, and that for these reasons labor can get no justice.

Let us first hear the plea for inequality:

Custom and nature are generally at variance with one another; . . . for by the rule of nature, that only is the more
disgraceful which is the greater evil; as, for example, to suffer
injustice; but by the rule of custom, to do evil is the more
disgraceful. For this suffering of injustice is not the part of a
man, but of a slave, who indeed had better die than live; for
when he is wronged and trampled upon, he is unable to help
himself or any other about whom he cares. The reason, as I
conceive, is that the makers of laws are the many weak; and
they make laws and distribute praises and censures with a
view to themselves and their own interests; and they terrify
the mightier sort of men, and those who are able to get the
better of them, in order that they may not get the better of
them; and they say that dishonesty is shameful and unjust;
meanwhile, when they speak of injustice, they desire to have
more than their neighbors, for knowing their own inferiority,
they are only too glad of equality. And therefore, this seeking
to have more than the many is conventionally said to be
shameful and unjust, and is called injustice, whereas nature
herself intimates that it is just for the better to have more
than the worse, the more powerful than the weaker; and in
many ways she shows, among men as well as among animals,
and indeed among whole cities and races, that justice consists
in the superior ruling over and having more than the inferior.
For on what principle of justice did Xerxes invade Hellas, or
his father the Scythians (not to speak of numberless other
examples)? They, I conceive, act according to nature; yes,
and according to the law of nature; not perhaps, according
to that artificial law which we frame and fashion, taking the
best and strongest of us from their youth upwards, and
taming them like young lions, and charming them with the
sound of the voice, saying to them that with equality they
must be content, and that this is the honorable and the just.
But if there were a man who had sufficient force, he would
shake off and break through and escape from all this; he
would trample under foot all our formulas and spells and
charms, and all our laws, sinning against nature; the slave
would rise in rebellion and be lord over us, and the light of
natural justice would shine forth. And this I take to be the
lesson of Pindar, in the poem in which he says that

"Law is the King of all, mortals as well as immortals!"

This, as he says:

"Makes might to be right, and does violence with exalted hand; as I infer from the deeds of Heracles, for without buying them—"

I do not remember the exact words, but the meaning is, that he carried off the oxen of Geryon without buying them, and without their being given to him by Geryon, according to the law of natural right, and that the oxen and other possessions of the weaker and inferior properly belong to the stronger and superior.[3]

The essence of this view is, therefore, that might is right, and that no legislation or conventional code ought to stand in the way of the free assertion of genius and power. It is similar to the teaching of Nietzsche in recent times.

But the other side had its complaint also. The laws are made by the "shepherds" of the people, as Homer called them. But who is now so simple as to suppose that the shepherds fatten or tend the sheep with a view to the good of the sheep, and not to their own good? All laws and governments really exist for the interest of the ruling class.[4] They rest upon convention or "institution," not upon "nature."

And if laws and social codes are but class legislation, conventional, why obey them? The older Greek life had felt the motives described in Chapter 4, though it had embodied them in symbolism and imagery. The Nemesis that followed the guilty, the Erinnys, or avenging goddesses, were the personified wrath of outraged law; *aidōs*, respect or reverence, *aischyne*, regard for public opinion, were the inner feelings. But with the advancing tide of intellectual criticism and individual interest, these sanctions were discredited; feelings of personal enjoyment demanded recognition, and the moralists at first appealed to this. "Parents and tutors are always telling their sons and their wards that they are to be just; but only not for the sake of justice, but for the sake of character and reputation." But if the only reason for jus-

3. Plato, *Gorgias*, 482–484.
4. *Republic*, I., 343.

tice is reputation, there might seem to be no sufficient reason for taking the thorny path, if there be an easier. Will not the youth say, in the words of Pindar:

> Can I by justice, or by crooked ways of deceit, ascend a loftier tower which may be a fortress to me all my days?[5]

And if I decide that the crooked way is the easier, why shall I not follow it? My party, or my "gang," or my lawyer will stand by and see me through:

> But I hear some one exclaiming that the concealment of wickedness is often difficult; to which I answer, Nothing great is easy. Nevertheless, the argument indicates this, if we would be happy, to be the path along which we should proceed. With a view to concealment we will establish secret brotherhoods and political clubs. And there are professors of rhetoric who teach the art of persuading courts and assemblies; and so, partly by persuasion and partly by force, I shall make unlawful gains and not be punished. Still I hear a voice saying that the gods cannot be deceived, neither can they be compelled. But what if there are no gods? or, suppose them to have no care of human things, why in either case should we mind about concealment?[6]

Besides, the greatest prizes, not only in material goods, but even in the line of reputation, seemed to fall to the individualist if he could only act on a sufficiently large scale. He could then be both prosperous and "respectable." If he could steal the government, or, in modern phrase, secure public lands, or a tariff from the Congress, bribe a legislature, control a utilities commission, obtain a valuable franchise or other "honest graft," he could not merely escape punishment, but be honored by his fellows.

I am speaking of injustice on a large scale, in which the advantage of the unjust is most apparent, and my meaning will be most clearly seen in the highest form of injustice, the perpetrator of which is the happiest of men, as the sufferers of these who refuse to do injustice are the most miserable—I

5. *Republic*, II., 365.
6. *Ibid.*

mean tyranny which by fraud and force takes away the property of others, not retail but wholesale; comprehending in
one things sacred as well as profane, private and public, for
any of which acts of wrong, if he were detected perpetrating
them singly, he would be punished and incur great dishonor;
for they who are guilty of any of these crimes in single instances are called robbers of temples and man-stealers and
burglars and swindlers and thieves. But when a man has
taken away the money of the citizens and made slaves of
them, then instead of these dishonorable names, he is called
happy and blessed, not only by the citizens but by all who
hear of his having achieved the consummation of injustice.
For injustice is censured because the censurers are afraid of
suffering, and not from any fear which they have of doing
injustice. And thus, as I have shown, Socrates, injustice,
when on a sufficient scale, has more strength and freedom
and mastery than justice; and, as I said at first, justice is the
interest of the stronger, whereas injustice is a man's own
profit and interest.[7]

§ 4. The Individual and Ethical Theory

The outcome of this first movement was thus twofold:
(a) It forced the questions, "What is just?" "What is good?" into
clear and definite consciousness. The necessity of comparison
and of getting a *general standard*, forced the inquirer to disentangle the concepts previously embodied in customs and laws.
But when the essence was thus found and freed, or disembodied,
as it were, the custom seemed lifeless, merely convention, and
the essence often quite opposed to the form. (b) It emphasized
the *personal interest*, the affective or emotional side of conduct,
and made the moral problem take the form, "What is the good?"
Furthermore, two positive theses have been established by the
very forces which have been active in disintegrating the old status. If custom no longer suffices, then reason must set the standard; if society cannot prescribe the good to the individual, then

7. *Republic*, I., 343 f.

the individual must find some method of defining and seeking it for himself unless he is to make shipwreck of his whole venture.

We may bring both aspects of the problem under the conception of "nature," as opposed to convention or institution. Convention is indeed outgrown, nature is the imperious authority. But granting that nature is rightful master, is nature to be sought in the primitive beginnings, or in the fullest development? in a life of isolation, or in a life of society? in the desires and passions, or in reason and a harmonious life?

Or, stating the same problem otherwise: granting that reason must fix the measure, that the individual must define and seek the good for himself, is the good to be found in isolation, or is it to be sought in human society with its bonds of family, friendship, and justice? Is the end to be pleasure, found in the gratification of desires, irrespective of their quality, and is it the business of reason merely to measure one gratification with another and get the most? or is wisdom itself a good, and is it better to satisfy certain impulses rather than others? i.e., shall reason form the standard as well as apply it?

These contrasting solutions of the problem of life may be stated then under the two pairs of antitheses: (1) The Individual *versus* the Social; (2) Immediate Satisfaction *versus* an Ideal Standard, at once higher and more permanent.

Poets, radicals, sensualists, individualists of no philosophic school, as well as the historic philosophic schools, contributed to the discussion and solution of these problems. All sought the "natural" life; but it is noteworthy that all the philosophic schools claimed Socrates as their master, and all sought to justify their answers by reason, all made the wise man the ideal. The Cynics and Cyrenaics, Stoics and Epicureans, Plato and Aristotle represent the various philosophic answers to these alternatives. Cynics and Cyrenaics both answer (1) by individualism, but diverge on (2), the Cynics placing emphasis on independence from wants, the Cyrenaics on gratification of wants. Stoics and Epicureans represent broader and more social development of the same principles, the Stoics seeking a cosmopolitan State, the Epicureans a community of friends; the Stoics emphasizing reason or wisdom as the only good; the Epicureans finding for wisdom a field in the selection of refined pleasures. Plato and Aristotle, with varying emphasis but essential agreement, insist (1) that the good of man is found in fulfilling completely his highest possible functions, which is possible only in society; (2) that wisdom is not merely to apply a standard but to form one; that while neither reason alone nor feeling alone is enough for life, yet that pleasure is rather for life than life for pleasure. Finally, Plato, Aristotle, and the Stoics, as well as the tragic poets, contribute successively to the formation of an ideal of responsible character.

Cynics and Cyrenaics were alike individualists. Society, they held, is artificial. Its so-called goods, on the one hand, and its restrictions on the other, are to be rejected unless they favor the individual's happiness. Independence was the mark of wisdom among the Cynics; Antisthenes, proud of the holes in his garment; Diogenes, dwelling in his tent or sleeping in the street, scoffing at the current "conventions" of decency, asking from Alexander only that he would get out of his sunshine—are the characteristic figures. The "state of nature" was opposed to the State. Only the primitive wants were recognized as natural. "Art and science, family and native land, were indifferent. Wealth and refinement, fame and honor, seemed as superfluous as those enjoyments of the senses which went beyond the satisfaction of the natural wants of hunger and sex."[8]

The Cyrenaics, or hedonists (*hēdonē*, pleasure), gave a different turn to wisdom. The good is pleasure, and wisdom is found in that prudence which selects the purest and most intense. Hence, if this is the good, why should a man trouble himself about social standards or social obligations? "The hedonists gladly shared the refinement of enjoyment which civilization brought with it; they found it convenient and permissible that the intelligent man should enjoy the honey which others prepared; but no feeling of duty or thankfulness bound them to the civilization whose fruits they enjoyed. Sacrifice for others, patriotism, and devotion to a general object, Theodorus declared to be a form of foolishness which it did not become the wise man to share."[9]

8. Windelband, *History of Philosophy*, p. 84.
9. *Ibid.*, p. 86.

§ 5. The Deeper View of Nature and the Good; of the Individual and the Social Order

Plato and Aristotle take up boldly the challenge of individualism. It may indeed be granted that existing States are too often ruled by classes. There are oligarchies in which the soldier or the rich control for their own interests; there are tyrannies in which the despot is greed and force personified; there are democracies (Plato was an aristocrat) in which the mob bears rule, and those who flatter and feed its passions are in authority. But all these do but serve to bring out more clearly the conception of a true State, in which the rule is by the wisest and best and is not for the interest of a class, but for the welfare of all. Even as it was, the State of Athens in Plato's day—except when it condemned a Socrates—meant completeness and freedom of life. It represented not merely a police force to protect the individual, but stood for the complete organization of all the life which needs cooperation and mutual support. The State provided instruction for the mind and training for the body. It surrounded the citizen with an atmosphere of beauty and provided in the tragedy and comedy opportunities for every citizen to consider the larger significance of life or to join in the contagious sympathy of mirth. In festivals and solemn processions it brought the citizen into unity of religious feeling. To be an Athenian citizen meant to share in all the higher possibilities which life afforded. Interpreting this life, Aristotle proclaims that it is not in isolation, but in the State, that "the goal of full independence may be said to be first attained."

Aristotle goes directly to the heart of the problem as to what is natural by asserting that nature is not to be found in the crude beginning, but rather in the complete development. "The nature of anything, e.g., of a man, a horse, or a house, may be defined to be its condition when the process of production is complete." Hence the State "in which alone completeness of life is attained" is in the highest sense natural:

> "The object proposed or the complete development of a thing is its highest good; but independence which is first attained in the State is a complete development or the highest

good and is therefore natural." "For as the State was formed to make life possible, so it exists to make life good."

"Thus we see that the State is a natural institution, that man is naturally a political animal and that one who is not a citizen of any State, if the cause of his isolation be natural and not accidental, is either a superhuman being or low in the scale of human civilization, as he stands alone like a 'blot' on the backgammon board. The 'clanless, lawless, hearthless man,' so bitterly described by Homer, is a case in point, for he is naturally a citizen of no state and a lover of war." [10]

Nor does Aristotle stop here. With a profound insight into the relation of man to society, and the dependence of the individual upon the social body, a relation which modern social psychology has worked out in greater detail, Aristotle asserts that the State is not merely the goal of the individual's development, but the source of his life.

Again in the order of nature the State is prior to the household or individual. For the whole must needs be prior to its part. For instance, if you take away the body which is the whole, there will not remain any such thing as a hand or foot, unless we use the same word in a different sense, as when we speak of a stone hand as a hand. For a hand separated from the body will be a disabled hand; whereas it is the faculty or function of a thing which makes it what it is, and therefore when things lose their function or faculty, it is not correct to call them the same things, but rather homonymous, i.e., different things having the same name. We see, then, the State is a natural institution, and also that it is prior to the individual. For if the individual as a separate unit is not independent, he must be a part and must bear the same relation to the State as the other parts to their wholes; and one who is incapable of association with others or is independent and has no need of such association, is no member of a State; in other words, he is either a brute or a god. [11]

10. *Politics*, I., ii. Welldon's translation.
11. *Ibid.*

And, moreover, when we look into the nature of the individual, we do not find him a being devoid of the sympathies and qualities which find their natural expression not only in the State, but in various social and friendly relations. There is "an impulse toward the life in common" (φιλία) which expresses itself in friendship, but which is also so essential to that recognition of others called justice that we may say "it is the most just of all just things." There is also a unity of disposition and purpose (ὁμόνοια) which may be called "political friendship." [12]

How then is the State constituted and governed which is to provide for man's full development, his complete good? Evidently two principles must control. In the first place, it must be so constituted that every man may develop in it the full capacities of his nature, and thereby serve at once the perfection of the State and his own completeness; and in the second place, the State or social whole must be ruled by those best fitted for this work. Not the soldier, nor the plutocrat, nor the artisan, but the man who knows, is the suitable ruler for our ideal community. The soldier may defend, the artisan may support, but the scientific or intelligent man should rule. And it is evident that in settling this principle, we have also answered our first problem; for the soldier and the artisan will find his full development by doing the work which he can do well, not by meddling with a task in which he must necessarily fail. In order to guard against the greed which was so characteristic of the governments of his day, Plato would provide that the rulers and warriors should have no private property, and not even private families. Their eye should be single to the good of the whole. When asked as to the practicability of a State governed by such disinterested rulers, and with such wisdom, he admits indeed its difficulty, but he stoutly demands its necessity:

> Until philosophers are kings, or the kings and princes of this world have the spirit and power of philosophy, and political greatness and wisdom meet in one, and those commoner natures who pursue either to the exclusion of the other are compelled to stand aside, cities will never have rest from their evils—no, nor the human race, as I believe—and

12. *Ethics*, VIII., i.; IX., vi.

then only will this our State have a possibility of life and behold the light of day.[13]

And yet the question of the actual existence of a perfect State is not the question of supreme importance. For Plato has grasped the thought that man is controlled not only by what he sees, but by what he images as desirable. And if a man has once formed the image of an ideal State or city of this kind, in which justice prevails, and life reaches fuller and higher possibilities than it has yet attained, this is the main thing:

> In heaven, there is laid up a pattern of it, methinks, which he who desires may behold, and beholding, may set his own house in order. But whether such an one exists, or ever will exist in fact, is no matter: for he will live after the manner of that city, having nothing to do with any other.[14]

The social nature of man, thus vindicated by Plato and Aristotle, remained as the permanent possession of Greek thought. Even the Epicureans, who developed further the hedonistic theory of life, emphasized the values of friendship as among the choicest and most refined sources of pleasure. The Stoics, who in their independence of wants took up the tradition of the Cynics, were yet far from interpreting this as an independence of society. The disintegration of the Greek States made it impossible to find the social body in the old city-state, and so we find with the Stoics a certain cosmopolitanism. It is the highest glory of man to be a citizen not of Athens but of the universe—not of the city of Cecrops, but of the city of Zeus. And through this conception the social nature of man was made the basis of a "natural law," which found its expression in the principles of Roman and modern jurisprudence.

In answering the question as to the true nature of man, Plato and Aristotle found the suggestions likewise for the problem of individual good. For if the soldier as the seeker for fame and honor, the avaricious man embodying the desire for wealth, and still more, the tyrant personifying the unbridled expression of every lust and passion, are abhorrent, is it not easy to see that an orderly and harmonious development of impulses under the

13. *Republic*, V., 473.
14. *Ibid.*, IX., 592.

guidance and control of reason, is far better than that uncramped expression of desires and cravings for which some of the radical individualists and sensualists of the day were clamoring? As representative of this class, hear Callicles:

> "I plainly assert that he who would truly live ought to allow his desires to wax to the uttermost, and not to chastise them; but when they have grown to their greatest, he should have courage and intelligence to minister to them and to satisfy all his longings. And this I affirm to be natural justice and nobility." The temperate man is a fool. It is only in hungering and eating, in thirsting and drinking, in having all his desires about him, and gratifying every possible desire, that man lives happily.[15]

But even Callicles himself admits that there are certain men, the creatures of degraded desire, whose lives are not ideal, and hence that there must be some choice of pleasure. And carrying out in the individual life the thought above suggested by the State, Plato raises the question as to whether man, a complex being, with both noble and ignoble impulses, and with the capacity of controlling reason, can be said to make a wise choice if he lets the passions run riot and choke out wholly his rational nature:

> Is not the noble that which subjects the beast to the man, or rather to the god in man; and the ignoble that which subjects the man to the beast? He can hardly avoid admitting this—can he now? Not if he has any regard for my opinion. But, if he admits this, we may ask him another question: How would a man profit if he received gold and silver on the condition that he was to enslave the noblest part of him to the worst? Who can imagine that a man who sold his son or daughter into slavery for money, especially if he sold them into the hands of fierce and evil men, would be the gainer, however large might be the sum which he received? And will any one say that he is not a miserable caitiff who sells his own divine being to that which is most atheistical and detestable and has no pity? Eriphyle took the necklace as the price

15. *Gorgias*, 491 ff.

of her husband's life, but he is taking a bribe in order to compass a worse ruin.[16]

If, for the moment, we rule out the question of what is noble or *kalon*, and admit that the aim of life is to live pleasantly, or if, in other words, it is urged as above that justice is not profitable and that hence he who would seek the highest good will seek it by some other than the thorny path, we must recognize that the decision as to which kind of pleasure is preferable will depend on the character of the man who judges:

> Then we may assume that there are three classes of men,— lovers of wisdom, lovers of ambition, lovers of gain? Exactly. And there are three kinds of pleasure, which are their several objects? Very true. Now, if you examine the three classes and ask of them in turn which of their lives is pleasantest, each of them will be found praising his own and depreciating that of others; the money-maker will contrast the vanity of honor or of learning with the solid advantages of gold and silver? True, he said. And the lover of honor—what will be his opinion? Will he not think that the pleasure of riches is vulgar, while the pleasure of learning, which has no meed of honor, he regards as all smoke and nonsense? True, he said. But may we not suppose, I said, that philosophy estimates other pleasures as nothing in comparison with knowing the truth, and in that abiding, ever learning, in the pursuit of truth, not far indeed from the heaven of pleasure? The other pleasures the philosopher disparages by calling them neces- sary, meaning that if there were no necessity for them, he would not have them. There ought to be no doubt about that, he replied. Since, then, the pleasure of each class and the life of each is in dispute, and the question is not which life is more or less honorable, or better or worse, but which is the more pleasant or painless—how shall we know? I cannot tell, he said. Well, but what ought to be the criterion? Is any better than experience and wisdom and reason? There can- not be a better, he said. If wealth and gain were the criterion, then what the lover of gain praised and blamed would surely be the truest? Assuredly. Or if honor or victory or courage, in

16. *Republic*, IX., 589 f.

that case the ambitious or contentious would decide best? Clearly. But since experience and wisdom and reason are the judges, the inference of course is, that the truest pleasures are those which are approved by the lover of wisdom and reason.[17]

It is thus evident that even if we start out to find the good in pleasure, we need some kind of measuring art. We need a "standard for pleasure," and this standard can be found only in wisdom. And this forces us to maintain that wisdom is after all *the* good. Not merely intellectual attainment—a life of intellect without feeling would be just as little a true human life as would the life of an oyster, which has feeling with no intelligence. A life which includes sciences and arts, and the pure pleasures of beauty, presided over by wisdom and measure and symmetry— this is Plato's vision of the life of the individual, viewed from within.

Aristotle's conception of the good is fundamentally the same. It is a full development of man's capacities, culminating in a rational and harmonious life. If, says Aristotle, we are to find the ultimate good, we must try to find, if possible, some one end which is pursued as an end in itself, and never as a means to something else, and the most general term for this final end is *eudaimonia*, or well-being, "for we also choose it for itself and never for the sake of something else." What is the essence of well-being? This, according to Aristotle, is to be found by asking what is the function of man. The life of nutrition and growth man has in common with the plants; the life of sense in common with the animal. It is in the life of his rational nature that we must find his especial function. "The good of man is exercise of his faculties in accordance with their appropriate excellence." External goods are valuable because they may be instruments toward such full activity. Pleasure is to be valued because it "perfects the activities, and therefore perfects life, which is the aim of human desire"—rather than valued as an end in itself. No one would choose to live on condition of having a child's intellect all his life, though he were to enjoy in the highest possible degree all the pleasures of a child.[18]

17. *Republic*, IX., 581 f.
18. *Ethics*, I., vii.; X., ii.–iv.

The crowning importance of wisdom as the rational measure of the ideal life and its intimate connection with the Greek tradition of proportion and beauty are also illustrated in Aristotle's theory of excellence (or virtue) as a "mean." This phrase is somewhat ambiguous, for some passages would seem to indicate that it is merely striking an average between two kinds of excesses, and finding, as it were, a moderate amount of feeling or action; but there is evidently involved here just the old thought of measure. Measure, on the one hand implies, as with Plato, valuation in terms of what is fitting, noble, fair (*kalon*), and on the other, the more analytic activity of intelligence: "the mean is what right reason prescribes." It is not every one who can find the mean, but only he who has the requisite knowledge. The supreme excellence or virtue is, therefore, the wisdom which can find the true standard for action.[19]

Finally the conception of virtue as wisdom is illustrated in the ideals of the three prominent schools in later Greek thought—the Sceptics, Epicureans, and Stoics. The wise man among Sceptics is he who suspends judgment where it is impossible to be certain. The wise man among Epicureans is he who chooses the finest and surest and most lasting pleasures. The wise man among Stoics is he who overcomes his emotions. But in every case the ideal is expressed in the same phrase, "the wise man."

We see thus how Greek thought, starting out to challenge all society's laws and standards and bring them to the bar of knowledge, has found a deeper value and higher validity in the true so-

19. Among the various types of excellence which Aristotle enumerates as exemplifying this principle, the quality of high-mindedness (μεγαλοψυχία) is preeminent, and may be taken as embodying the trait most prized in an Athenian gentleman. The high-minded man claims much and deserves much; lofty in his standard of honor and excellence he accepts tributes from good men as his just desert, but despises honor from ordinary men or on trivial grounds; good and evil fortune are alike of relatively small importance. He neither seeks nor fears danger; he is ready to confer favors and forget injuries, slow to ask favors or cry for help; fearless in his love and hatred, in his truth and his independence of conduct; "not easily moved to admiration, for nothing is great to him. He loves to possess beautiful things that bring no profit, rather than useful things that pay; for this is characteristic of the man whose resources are in himself. Further, the character of the high-minded man seems to require that his gait should be slow, his voice deep, his speech measured; for a man is not likely to be in a hurry when there are few things in which he is deeply interested, nor excited when he holds nothing to be of very great importance; and these are the causes of a high voice and rapid movements."
—*Ethics*, IV., iii.

cial and moral order. The appeal was to the Caesar of reason, and reason taken in its full significance carries us beyond the immediate and transient to the broader and more permanent good. Nor can reason in its search for good be content, urges Plato, with the superficial facts of life and society. He who would find and achieve his complete function, his full development, must broaden his horizon still further. As his own particular life is but a part of the ongoing of the larger world, whose forces act upon him, limit him, and determine his possibilities, it becomes absolutely necessary to study not merely his own end and purpose, but the end and purpose of the universe. Human good requires us to know the larger good, *the* Good, in the full and complete sense. And this perfect Good which is, in truth, the very essence of the universe, is but another term for God, and Plato often uses the two as interchangeable terms.

So the "nature" which Greek life was seeking gets its deepest significance and reinterprets the old religious demand for unity of the life of man with the forces of the unseen. And the Stoic later, in his maxim "Follow nature," gives more explicit recognition to the return of the circle. For the great work of Greek science had brought out into complete clearness the idea of nature as a system of law. The universe is a rational universe, a cosmos, and man, as above all else a rational being, finds thus his kinship to the universe. To follow nature, therefore, means to know the all-pervading law of nature and submit to it in calm acceptance or resignation.

"All is harmonious to me that is harmonious to thee, O universe; all is fruit to me which thy seasons bring." [20]

§ 6. The Conception of the Ideal

The two stages of Greek thought which we have sketched did more than to readjust Greek life to deeper views of the State and the individual; of the good and of nature. The challenge and process brought into explicit consciousness a new feature of the moral life, which is fundamental to true moral consciousness, viz., the factor of contrast between the actual and the ideal. We

20. Marcus Aurelius, *Thoughts*, IV., 23.

have seen that the clash of one-sided interests and political institutions and, in the case of Plato, the tragic execution of Socrates, obliged Plato and Aristotle to admit that the actual State did not subserve the real purpose which they were forced to seek in social organization. Both Plato and Aristotle, therefore, draw the picture of a State that should serve the complete purposes of human development. And again, in the individual life, both the conception of the development of man's highest possibilities and the conception of a measure or standard for the conflicting desires and purposes lead on to a conception which shall embody not merely the existing status but the goal of yet unrealized purpose.

Various qualities and aspirations are embodied by Plato in this conception, and with characteristic Greek genius he has given to this conception of the ideal almost as concrete and definite a form as the Greek sculptor of Apollo gave to his ideal of light and clarity, or the sculptor of Aphrodite to the conception of grace. As contrasted with the flux of transient emotions, or the uncertain play of half-comprehended or futile goods, this ideal good is conceived as eternal, unchanging, ever the same. It is superhuman and divine. As contrasted with various particular and partial goods on which the sons of men fix their affections, it is the one universal good which is valid for all men everywhere and forever. In his effort to find suitable imagery for this conception, Plato was aided by the religious conceptions of the Orphic and Pythagorean societies, which had emphasized the preexistence and future existence of the soul, and its distinction from the body. In its previous life, said Plato, the soul has had visions of a beauty, a truth, and a goodness of which this life affords no adequate examples. And with this memory within it of what it has looked upon before, it judges the imperfect and finite goods of this present world and longs to fly away again and be with God. This thought of contrast between ideal and actual, to which Plato in some of his writings gave the turn of a contrast between soul and body, passed on with increased emphasis into Stoic and later Platonist schools, and furnished a philosophic basis for the dualism and asceticism which is found in Hellenistic and medieval morality.

While the true ethical contrast between the actual and the ideal was thus shifted over into a metaphysical contrast between soul and body, or between what is fixed and what is changing, the fundamental thought is highly significant, for it merely symbolizes in objective form the characteristic of every moral judgment, viz., the testing and valuing of an act by some standard, and what is even more important, the forming of a standard by which to do the testing. Even Aristotle, who is frequently regarded as the mere describer of what is, rather than the idealistic portrayer of what ought to be, is no less insistent upon the significance of the ideal. In fact his isolation of reflection or *theoria* from the civic virtues was used by the medieval church in its idealization of the "contemplative life." Like Plato, he conceives the ideal as a divine element in human nature:

Nevertheless, instead of listening to those who advise us as men and mortals not to lift our thoughts above what is human and mortal, we ought rather, as far as possible, to put off our mortality and make every effort to live in the exercise of the highest of our faculties; for though it be but a small part of us, yet in power and value it far surpasses all the rest.[21]

§ 7. The Conception of the Self; of Character and Responsibility

Out of the fierce competition of individual desires, the clashing of individual ambitions, the conflict between the individual and the State, and the deepening of the conception of the individual's "nature," emerged also another conception of fundamental importance for the more highly developed reflective moral life, viz., that of the moral personality, its character and its responsibility. We may trace the development of this conception through the poets, as well as in the philosophers. Aeschylus set man over against the gods, subject to their divine laws, but gave little play to human character or conscious self-direction. With Sophocles, the tragic situation was brought more directly into the field of human character, although the conception of destiny and the limitations marked thereby were still the dominant note.

21. *Ethics*, X., vii.

With Euripides, human emotions and character are brought into the foreground. Stout-heartedness, the high spirit that can endure in suffering or triumph in death, which shows not merely in his heroes but in the women, Polyxena and Medea, Phaedra and Iphigenia, evinces the growing consciousness of the self—a consciousness which will find further development in the proud and self-sufficient endurance of the Stoic. In more directly ethical lines, we find increasing recognition of the self in the motives which are set up for human action, and in the view which is formed of human character. Conscience in the earlier poets and moralists, was largely a compound of Nemesis, the external symbol and messenger of divine penalty, on the one hand, and Aidos, the sense of respect or reverence for public opinion and for the higher authority of the gods, on the other. But already in the tragedians we find suggestions of a more intimate and personal conception. Pains sent by Zeus in dreams may lead the individual to meditate, and thus to better life. Neoptolemus, in Sophocles, says,

> All things are noisome when a man deserts
> His own true self and does what is not meet.

and Philoctetes replies

> Have mercy on me, boy, by all the gods,
> And do not shame thyself by tricking me.

The whole *Antigone* of Sophocles is the struggle between obedience to the political rulers and obedience to the higher laws which as "laws of reverence" become virtually inner laws of duty:

> I know I please the souls I ought to please.

Here, as in the formulation of his conception of the ideal, religious imagery helped Plato to find a more objective statement for the conception of a moral judgment and a moral character. In the final judgment of the soul after death, Plato sees the real self stripped bare of all external adornments of beauty, rank, power, or wealth, and standing as naked soul before the naked judge, to receive his just reward. And the very nature of this reward or penalty shows the deepening conception of the self, and of the intrinsic nature of moral character. The true penalty of injustice is not to be found in anything external, but in the very fact that the evildoers become base and wicked:

Soc. They do not know the penalty of injustice, which above all things they ought to know—not stripes and death, as they suppose, which evil doers often escape, but a penalty which cannot be escaped.

THEOD. What is that?

Soc. There are two patterns set before them in nature; the one blessed and divine, the other godless and wretched; and they do not see, in their utter folly and infatuation, that they are growing like the one and unlike the other, by reason of their evil deeds; and the penalty is that they lead a life answering to the pattern which they resemble.[22]

It is, however, in the Stoics that we find the conception of inner reflection reaching clearest expression. Seneca and Epictetus repeat again and again the thought that the conscience is of higher importance than any external judgment—that its judgment is inevitable. In these various conceptions, we see attained the third stage of Adam Smith's description of the formation of conscience.[23] Man who read his duty at first in the judgments of his fellows, in the customs and laws and codes of honor, and in the religious precepts of the gods, has again come to find in gods and laws, in custom and authority, the true rational law of life; but it is now a law of self. Not a particular, or individual self, but a self which embraces within it at once the human and the divine. The individual has become social and has recognized himself as such. The religious, social, and political judgments have become the judgments of man upon himself. "Duty," what is binding or necessary, takes its place as a definite moral conception.

Literature

Besides the writings of Plato (especially, the *Apology, Crito, Protagoras, Gorgias,* and *Republic*), Xenophon (*Memorabilia*), Aristotle (*Ethics, Politics*), Cicero (*On Ends, Laws, Duties; On the Nature of the*

---

22. *Theaetetus,* 176 f.
23. Smith held that we (1) approve or disapprove the conduct of others; (2) see ourselves as others see us, judging ourselves from their standpoint; (3) finally, form a true social standard, that of the "impartial spectator." This is an inner standard—conscience.

Gods), Epictetus, Seneca, M. Aurelius, Plutarch, and the fragments of various Stoics, Epicureans, and Sceptics, the tragedies of Aeschylus, Sophocles, and Euripides, and the comedies of Aristophanes (especially the *Clouds*) afford valuable material.

All the histories of philosophy treat the theoretical side; among them may be mentioned Gomperz (*Greek Thinkers*, 1900–05), Zeller (*Socrates*; *Plato*; *Aristotle*; *Stoics, Epicureans and Sceptics*), Windelband; Benn (*Philosophy of Greece*, 1898, chs. i., v.).

ON THE MORAL CONSCIOUSNESS: Jones, *Greek Morality*; Schmidt, *Ethik der alten Griechen*, 1882. On the social conditions and theories: Pöhlmann, *Geschichte des antiken Kommunismus und Sozialismus*, 1893–1901; Döring, *Die Lehre des Sokrates als sociales Reformsystem*, 1895. On the religion: Farnell, *Cults of the Greek States*, 3 vols., 1896; Rohde, *Psyche*, 1894.

ON POLITICAL CONDITIONS AND THEORY: Newman, Introd. to *Politics of Aristotle*, 1887; Bradley, "Aristotle's Conception of the State" in *Hellenica*; Wilamowitz-Möllendorff, *Aristoteles und Athen*, 1893; Barker, *Greek Political Theory*, 1918.

ON NATURE AND LAW OF NATURE: Ritchie, *Natural Rights*, 1895; Burnet, *Int. Journal of Ethics*, VII., 1897, pp. 328–333; Hardy, *Begriff der Physis*, 1884; Voigt, *Die Lehre vom jus naturale*, 1856–75.

GENERAL: Taylor, *Plato, the Man and His Work*, 1926; Ross, *Aristotle*, 1923; Murray and Others, *The Legacy of Greece*, 1924; Vinogradoff, *Outlines of Historical Jurisprudence*, Vol. 2, *Jurisprudence of the Greek City*, 1922; Bonner and Smith, *Administration of Justice from Homer to Aristotle*, 1930; Denis, *Histoire des Théories et des Idées Morales dans l'Antiquité*, 1879; Taylor, *Ancient Ideals*, 1900; Caird, *Evolution of Theology in the Greek Philosophers*, 1904; Janet, *Histoire de la Science Politique dans ses Rapports avec la Morale*, 1887; Grote, *History of Greece*, 4th ed., 1872, *Plato, and the Other Companions of Sokrates*, 1888; Max Wundt, *Geschichte d. griechischen Ethik*, 1908.

8. The Roman Contribution to the Modern Moral Consciousness

If the modern world owes to the Hebrews its religion with the moral emphasis upon inner motives and the ideal of a kingdom of God, and if Greece gave us methods of scientific search for the good, it is to Rome that we are largely indebted for a third factor in the moral consciousness—the law, and the conceptions derived from it. If we today so frequently speak of the moral law, of justice, equity, honesty, fidelity, charity, reasonable standards, it is because the Roman either originated these or in adopting them from the Greek gave them the color of the Latin speech and mind, and to some extent embodied them in permanent institutions.

§ 1. Roman Society

Three characteristics of Roman society may be noted as significant for our purpose: (1) It was preeminently a political, i.e., a governing society. Problems of authority and power were foremost. (2) It was a society in which class distinctions on the one hand, and far-reaching, world-wide rule on the other, were present side by side. Patrician power and slavery found extreme expression; so likewise did widespread toleration and a leveling of such cultural barriers as those which separated Greeks from barbarians, and such religious barriers as separated Jews from Gentiles. (3) It was a society in which wealth took its place side by side with political power. In neither Greece nor Judaea had there been any such enormous fortunes. Nor on the other hand had there been such opening up of the world through trade and such a developed law of business and property.

These outstanding traits of Roman purpose and character are expressed or suggested by their art and literature, and especially by their architecture. The highest art of the Hebrews was their lyric or prophetic poetry on the one hand, and their dramatic statement of the problem of evil upon the other. The Greek found expression for his sense of beauty through the whole range of the arts, but in his architecture and sculpture it was beauty as contrasted with grandeur that was dominant. It was enlisted in the service of a religion not too awe-inspiring or remote from human life, or in the service of such patriotic subjects as the victors in the Olympian games. The subjects of Roman architecture include indeed temples for the gods, constructed for the most part from Grecian models, but their most characteristic structures are for public use such as bridges, aqueducts, fora, or as monumental tributes to glory and conquest, such as the magnificent triumphal arches, or finally as structures for luxury and public spectacles, such as the baths, the theaters, the circuses, of which latter the Colosseum early took its place among the seven wonders of the world. In letters, the work through which most students are introduced to the study of Latin is a compressed record of conquest by the Romans under the command of Caesar. This is usually followed by examples of oratory called out by a political crisis. The strongest department of Roman literature is, however, generally considered to be its satire, in which the luxuries, vices, and political problems of the time afford rich material.

1. We know too little as yet about the characteristics of different races and the extent to which these depend upon physical and physiological causes on the one hand, or upon geographic and other environmental conditions on the other, to speak with any confidence as to why the Romans early showed ability in an unusual degree to play the part of a governing people. So far as the stock from which they sprang was concerned, it seems to have been in general that from which other European groups— Greeks, Celts, Germans—came. The beginnings, so far as we can gather them, were small enough. A little group of sturdy warriors in which the clan or patriarchal household was strongly developed had conflict after conflict with adjacent tribes, sometimes conquering, sometimes uniting on terms of mutual adjustment, seldom showing the disposition to exterminate, until it was strong enough to challenge and overcome the leading commercial rival, Carthage. Thenceforth Rome moved on with the

resistless power of a machine, not merely conquering, but organizing the districts and peoples that were conquered, until the Mediterranean became a Roman lake, and the Empire extended from the northern regions of Britain to the borders of India, including within its bounds the territories of the earlier empires of Egypt, Assyria, Persia, and Macedonia. Trade routes were secured, roads penetrated and united distant regions, a common language made Europe capable of unity in its culture and civilization, even though it was not able to displace Greek in the eastern regions of the Empire.

To govern and administer this great territory of different races and cultures required the development of government on a far greater scale than had existed before. The Senate, representing the older patrician families, was enlarged by new blood. New officers were selected from time to time. A system of law for citizens, and another system for the various residents of Rome and of the outlying regions who were not citizens, were developed. Able young men saw the pathway to glory to lie through government. Those who were rich spent huge sums to be elected to office, and even those who had no ancestral wealth on which to depend seemed able to borrow large amounts. The expectation was that after holding office for a term of years at Rome, the successful candidate would then in due course be entrusted with the government of a province. This would give opportunity to pay off debts incurred and to amass a fortune besides.

Our opinion of the government of Rome under the Empire is probably colored strongly by the evil reputations of some of its worst rulers. Nero is more widely known than Marcus Aurelius. But in considering the Roman ability for government, we have to remember that, although in Western Europe the Empire finally succumbed to the invasions of the barbarians, it yet continued for more than four centuries after the time of Augustus; that even when Romans by birth no longer wielded its authority the pattern lived on for other centuries; that its forms and structures and much of the law which the Romans developed are still a power in Europe and in lesser degree in America.

2. From early times the old families, the patricians, who were descended from the conquering group, held themselves above their vassals or clients, and above the conquered groups that were allowed to carry on agriculture and various crafts under the

rule of the conquerors. These subordinate groups, the plebeians, struggled with more or less success for a share in power. The Romans were on the whole liberal in admitting to citizenship various tribes and peoples whom they conquered or with whom they united on terms of mutual adjustment. But the aristocratic great families of the patricians were very skilful in keeping the main power in their own hands, and even after the Senate, composed originally of patricians, lost the controlling power the social distinction remained. That the Senate was able to maintain itself so long was due in part to the fact that, although grudgingly, it did admit a rather constant stream of new blood from the more ambitious of the lower orders, especially from the great business class, usually called knights.

At the bottom were the slaves. Early Roman citizens were largely farmers with small holdings who worked with their own hands side by side with their servants. As the result of successful wars great numbers of conquered peoples were enslaved, and in many cases treated with severity. The elder Cato taught that they should be kept at work when not asleep, worked as hard as possible, and sold or left to perish when too old to work longer. They had become so numerous in 74 B.C. as to attempt a revolt under Spartacus, the Gladiator, and when they had been defeated six thousand were crucified along the road from Capua to Rome. Some slaves were educated men. The philosopher Epictetus was of this type. Many slaves gained their liberty in one way or another and were called freedmen. These might enter trades and retail business which the older citizen was taught to despise. Masters were later deprived of the power of life and death over their slaves. But the institution of slavery remained as a corner stone of Roman industry and a factor in Roman society.

Yet despite this sharp distinction between classes Rome became a powerful agency for the leveling of barriers between racial and language groups. So far as language and commerce were concerned the Romans were but carrying further the influences already set in motion by the Greeks in the Macedonian Empire. But as the Roman administration continued for generation after generation, the numerous tribal groups of Italy, of Gaul, of Spain, gradually forgot their ancient feuds and became members, as citizens, or subjects, of a great commonwealth. The *pax Romana*, even though enforced by power, was a uniting and harmonizing atmosphere. The basis was prepared for the remarkable declarations of the unity and equality of mankind which will be cited under Section 2 from Cicero and the Roman jurists.

3. The conquests of Rome brought in vast wealth to certain classes of citizens. On the one hand, governors of provinces, on the other, business men who acted as farmers of taxes, found the provinces of Sicily and Asia Minor a gold mine. The governor counted upon his haul to pay off enormous debts, and to amass resources for future needs. For to gain and keep office was expensive. The candidate might spend huge sums in distributing bread and entertainment—*panem et circenses*—for the multitude. Wealthy citizens also lavished money upon estates, villas, luxurious baths, works of art, upon feasts and all the sources of pleasure for body or mind which the age could provide. At Rome one saw, not only, as at Athens, the splendor of public buildings, but also the luxuries of private dwellings upon a scale surpassing anything the world had seen before. The satirists have portrayed the extravagant excesses of the feasts, and complain of the deterioration of character which these implied.

But along with evil effects from wealth came also certain goods. One was the indirect aid which the possession of property gave to improving the status of woman, and especially of married women. In the earlier patrician, patriarchal household the woman at marriage passed from the *manus* of the father to that of the husband. The matron held a position of dignity, but she was not a "person" before the law. In the words of Bryce, "One can hardly imagine a more absolute subjection to one person of another person who was nevertheless not only free but respected and influential, as we know that the wife in old Rome was." As wealth and property increased the father naturally grew disinclined to see his daughter's dowry pass out of his family into that of the husband. Other forms of marriage than that of *manus*, which allowed greater freedom and independence to the wife, gradually superseded the older type. "The Roman matron of the Empire," says Hobhouse, "was more fully her own mistress than the married woman of any earlier civilization, with the possible exception of a certain period of Egyptian history, and it must be added, than the wife of any later civilization down to our own generation." Ulpian, the jurist, held that the consent of the parties, as well as that of the guardians, was essential to marriage. Doubtless other factors contributed to the liberalizing of woman's status, but the possession of wealth and property was influential.

§ 2. Moral Ideas

The important moral ideas in such a society as that of Rome would naturally be closely connected with problems of government, or of business. Besides these spheres of action, it would be expected that the family would be affected by the growth of wealth, and that in their private life wealthy citizens would be inclined to a philosophy which would justify their luxurious tastes. To find guiding ideas with which to meet their problems, the Romans went to the Greeks. They were not themselves philosophical by nature. They had, of course, as every coherent group of strong character must have, their own mores. The family was of the patriarchal type; the husband and father had great authority over the whole household, including even, in the earlier years, power of life and death over children, and slaves. They were strictly monogamous, and in the earlier years there was little divorce. But the most interesting and important ideas for our purpose were those which grew out of their political and business activities, and these ideas were based to a great extent upon Stoic doctrines. The more important of these doctrines which found expression in Roman law and thereby were handed down to modern times as elements not only of our law, but of our morals, are (1) the conception of nature as a source of universal law; (2) the conception of Reason as the essential principle of nature; (3) the conception that all men share in reason, and therefore are equal; (4) the conception that justice is the rightful test of government; (5) the conception of duty.

1. We have seen in the preceding chapter that the Greeks debated whether governments and laws were natural or conventional, and that Aristotle pointed out the twofold meaning of the word "natural" as signifying on the one hand what is original, and on the other what characterizes full development or perfection. From this second point of view, Aristotle argued, the State is natural because in it man reaches full development. The Greek was likely to think of Athens or some other Greek city when

considering the State. The conquests of Alexander did much to break down local feeling, and the Greek Stoics declared themselves not citizens of Athens, but citizens of the world. But when the Romans had actually brought the world under one sway, the conception of universal law, governing everywhere, gained a concrete expression. Instead of a patchwork of tribes and peoples with their own laws and customs, the consciousness of something like a common humanity found expression not only in the *homo sum*; *humani nihil a me alienum puto* of the dramatist Terence, but in the philosophical writings of Cicero, Seneca, and the jurists. To find the source of authority that should be adequate for a law binding the whole world, the Roman philosophers adopted the Greek conception of nature as the all-inclusive essence or order of the universe, more fundamental, if possible, than even the gods themselves, although at other times it is spoken of as the "divine law of eternal and immutable morality."

2. Nature in this sense was by the Stoics regarded as through and through rational. The law of nature is therefore rational and universal.

> True law is indeed right reason, conformable to Nature, pervading all things, constant, eternal; . . . It is not lawful to alter this law, to derogate from it, or to repeal it. . . . Nor will it be one law for Rome and another for Athens; one thing to-day and another to-morrow; but it is a law eternal and unchangeable for all people and in every age; and it becomes as it were the one common god, master, and governor of all.[1]

This conception of a universal law governing all men was given a more concrete setting by the actual legal development at Rome. The early customs and law of the city were naturally those of the tribes which made up the ruling class. These continued to be known as the law of the citizens, or as the *lex civilis*. But there were many dwelling at Rome who were not citizens, and there were, besides, the inhabitants of outlying regions, who were constantly having relations of trade or seeking decisions from the Roman government in their contesting claims. For all these classes of persons the Romans gradually developed what they

1. Cicero, *Republic*, III., 22.

called a law of tribes or peoples (*ius gentium*). To introduce some sort of consistency into this law, the judges would naturally rely on what might be called "reason." As time went on, under the influence of the Stoic philosophy they worked out certain principles which they regarded as prescribed by reason, such as "good faith," and in general they distinguished between "strict law," and what was fair and good or humane (*ius aequum et bonum*). This latter as the law of reason was also the law of nature. Here, then, was a great conception, scarcely possible when mankind was split up into local groups, which was handed down through the Middle Ages as a permanent possession for all who came under the influence of the Roman civilization. As embodied in the famous Code of Justinian it became the law for the Eastern Empire as well.

3. Aristotle in the *Politics* held that men belong to two types, one capable of directing, the other needing to be directed and controlled; hence the reason for slavery. A remarkable change is found in the writings of Cicero and Seneca. As already suggested, the Stoic conception of nature was that it was but another word for reason. Gods and men share in reason, which makes them

> fellow citizens of one city and commonwealth. . . . Man is born for justice. . . . There is no one thing more like to another, a more homogeneous and analogous, than man is to man. And if the corruption of customs, and the variation of opinions, had not induced an imbecility of minds, and turned them aside from the course of nature, no one would more nearly resemble himself than all men would resemble all men. Therefore whatever definition we give of man, it must include the whole human race.[2]

So too Seneca: "We are all descended from one common parent, the world. It is fortune that makes a man a slave." Slavery is only external, only affects the body of a man. The body may belong to a master, the mind is its own. The lawyers had to recognize slavery as a fact, and although its conditions were from time to time somewhat ameliorated by restricting the powers of the master, no one thought of abolishing it. Nevertheless, they recognized

2. Cicero, *De Legibus*.

that slavery was contrary to nature. One of them, Ulpian, says that, so far as concerns the civil law, slaves are held as if not counting (*pro nullis*); but this is not so by natural law, because as regards natural law, all men are equal. And another jurist, using words which later had power to thrill the men of the American and French Revolutions, wrote, "By natural law, from the beginning all men were born free." Sometimes ideas are uttered by prophets and thinkers which are destined to wait years or centuries for their fulfillment. Such were the ideas of natural liberty and equality of all men. But it is to the glory of these Roman thinkers that they framed words which could later become the watchwords of great movements for human liberation.

4. As law is the fundamental principle of nature and of the universe, so law and justice (which is only another name for that law which is the true law of nature) form the basis of that association of men which we call a commonwealth. The commonwealth, says Cicero, is the affair of the people, but the people is not every sort of aggregation of men, but an association united by a compact of law, and by participation in common utility. Like the sentiments concerning equality and liberty in the preceding paragraph, this definition of a commonwealth might be regarded as an ideal rather than as corresponding precisely to the actual conditions in the Empire. Nevertheless, in the two hundred years of peace which followed the reign of Augustus, there was a large measure of justice in the imperial law, and the common well-being which made property and commerce and industry reasonably secure was measurably realized. And like the doctrines of equality and liberty, this conception of law and justice as the true test of authority found a very real application in later times. We can trace its influence in the doctrine that law is a higher authority than the king himself—the *lex facit regem* of the English lawyer Bracton—and in the conception of a fundamental law superior to the will of kings or legislatures, which has played so great a part in recent times.

5. Finally, the Stoic conception of *duty* found congenial soil in the Roman morale. Duty was, indeed, the inner correlate of a social and political system that made law and government supreme. As rational, Cicero held, man ought to recognize the law of reason. As human, he is endowed by nature with a sense of order, decency, and propriety; he should therefore conform to

the law of nature and respond to the intrinsic worth of what is honorable—*honestum,* the nearest Roman equivalent of the Greek *kalon.* As a member of society, a status which is deeply rooted in nature, he ought not to injure his fellow, or do anything to disrupt the social bond. In short, duty is our response to the law of our being.

Literature

Cicero, *Laws, Republic, Offices;* Carlyle, *Mediaeval Political Theory in the West,* Vol. I., 191; Voigt, *Das jus naturale, aequum et bonum und jus gentium der Römer,* 1856–75.

9. Factors and Trends in the Modern Moral Consciousness

§ 1. The Medieval Period—Authority and Unity

When the Roman Empire of the West yielded to the assaults of the barbarians, Christianity had already been for a century and a half the official religion. The bishops of Rome had already claimed a primacy, and St. Augustine in his *Civitas Dei* had presented the City of God as superior to the earthly realm which was crumbling from inner disintegration and outer attacks. For a thousand years the church asserted and maintained increasing sway over Europe. The Bishop of Rome had come to be recognized as the Vicar of Christ. As God was Creator and Ruler, whose will was law, and whose being was perfect goodness, so his representative was entitled to the obedience of all people. It was not the rule of a cruel or unreasonable sovereign— God was love as well as justice. His grace provided salvation for men. The church with its sacraments was the institution through which this grace came. It brought the newly born into its care, consecrated his marriage, reproved his faults, absolved his sins, gave comfort in the hour of death and promised a future of blessedness to the faithful. The church included all men—not merely the saints. Some, like beginners in a school, were regarded as less advanced than others, but all were conceived to be within its care. So the church claimed to be universal not only in its rule over all but in its inclusion of all within its ministrations. It symbolized the unity of mankind, as all men were the creatures and rightful subjects of God.

There was a graded succession in the clergy through whom the divine grace descended. From pope to bishop, and bishop to priest who administered the sacraments. In a similar way the member owed obedience to the priest and priest to bishop, and bishop to pope, and pope to God.

The church attempted and to a considerable degree exercised a restraining power over the two great spheres of politics and economics which later claimed independence of at least the then prevalent moral standards. The family, on the other hand, felt the support of the religious community so desirable that even in Protestant countries marriages continued largely to be performed by the clergy who for this purpose served as officers of the civil government.

In the field of *government* the church had to oppose the turbulent tribal chiefs and feudal lords who not only had frequent occasions for quarrels in the absence of recognized authority, but also considered arms the only manly profession and prized military glory as the highest honor. Against such frequent truculence and almost continuous wars the church inherited on the one hand the spirit of the prophet and of Jesus which called for peace. It inherited also the ideal of a beloved community in which the love of the Master for his followers should be imitated in the love of each for the brethren. It enacted in various councils decrees for a "peace of God" which, if not forbidding war entirely, aimed to limit its cruelties and burdens by forbidding under pain of excommunication every act of private warfare or violence against ecclesiastical buildings and against clerics, pilgrims, merchants, women, and peasants. The truce of God (*treuga Dei*), at first prohibited every act of private warfare from Saturday noon until Monday morning; by the middle of the eleventh century it extended from Wednesday evening to Monday morning, and also in most places included Lent and Advent. It spread through France, Italy, and the Empire. When it reached its limits three quarters of the days of the year were covered by it. The Crusades showed the conflicts between the unifying purpose under which the kings were marshaled and the jealousies which rendered the expeditions futile.

In the *economic* field the church aimed to govern the excessive greed of gain. In particular it condemned usury. At that time men did not ordinarily borrow money in order to invest it in profitable enterprise. The borrower was usually a man caught in some misfortune. To take advantage of his necessity was not fair. Prices in trade were to be "just," and reasonable. Every product was held to have intrinsic value, so that it was not considered ethical to make money by exchanges of goods, by buying cheap and selling dear. Consumption ought to be measured by the natural end of maintaining life and by a regard for the needs of others. Wealth according to the parable of the rich man was a danger to the soul. Private property according to the Fathers of the early Christian centuries was not according to God's original plan. It was the will of God, said St. Ambrose, that the earth should be the common possession of all men, and should furnish its fruits to all; it was avarice which created the rights of property. Gratian, the compiler of the Canon Law in the twelfth century, draws on the Stoic-Roman conception of the law of nature for a similar view. By the law of nature all things are common to all men—it is only by the law of custom or of positive law that this is mine and that is another's—almsgiving to those in need was then consistently held to be an act of justice, not of mercy. St. Thomas, indeed, distinguishes property, as a right to acquire and distribute, from the right to use for oneself. The first is legitimate and necessary; the second not, for a man must hold his goods for common use.

It added to the prestige of the clergy that they were the learned class. They could read and write. They were the custodians of what survived of the culture of Greece and Rome as well as of the sacred books of the Christian religion.

To enforce its decrees and decisions the church relied principally on the respect and awe which it received in the Ages of Faith as being God's representative. For lesser offenses it employed confession, admonition, and penance; for the bolder and graver sins, excommunication, which none would lightly incur. But the significant thing was that the *moral life was clearly defined by the guidance of the church   the moral law was the law of God.*

§ 2. The Renaissance and Reformation to the Revolutions

This period saw the rise of nationalism and of civil and religious liberty, the growth of a middle class and of capitalism, the discovery of the New World and the settlement of it, the birth of modern science, the flowering of the arts of painting, music, and poetry. All these affected morality. They tended to loosen the bonds of custom and authority, to give greater freedom of choice and action and greater responsibility to the individual. They broadened the goods that life offers.

1. Largely by force of arms—by blood and iron—the lesser dukedoms and fiefs of the Empire were consolidated under warrior kings into national States. England, France, Spain led; Germany and Italy did not achieve this status until the nineteenth century. Some of the present moral values and evils of nationalism will be discussed in Part III. Here we need only point out that the formation of national States tended to strengthen the sovereignty of such governments in opposition to the unity of Europe for which church and pope had stood. It was a breaking away from the rule of Rome. The act of Henry VIII in proclaiming himself Head of the English Church was a dramatic expression. It tended to substitute patriotism for religion as supreme authority. But perhaps the most significant influence for morality was the consequence drawn by Machiavelli and by rulers of States, that politics is politics—not morals. Machiavelli conceived the deliverance of Italy from foreign power to be so important that a prince who had this aim would be justified in any policies or measures necessary in order to gain and keep power. This had been a working theory with many who had not so frankly avowed it as did Machiavelli. In the United States it is still frequently accepted as a principle in the practices of political parties. In Europe it has been used in justification of wars.

2. A middle class—merchants, yeomen, craftsmen—emerged, which led in a struggle for civil and political liberty. In the Middle Ages men from various orders of society might enter the clergy and rise to high position in the church. But the great mass of the population were of the two classes, landholders and serfs, or villeins. In England at the time of Domesday Book—a census made for William the Conqueror in 1086—Gentry and Clergy numbered 9,300; Freeholders and Yeomen, 35,000; Half-free or Unfree, Villeins, Cottars, and Bordars, 259,000; Slaves 25,000. The proportion of free to unfree was then about one to six, and the six had few rights against the one. In the early English law 107 paragraphs have been counted which were dictated by the purpose of distinguishing between classes. But in the fourteenth and fifteenth centuries the shift from the old method of service in exchange for the use of land to money payments of wages, to-

gether with the Black Death in the middle of the fourteenth century, and numerous other changes, broke down the feudal system of land tenure and the villeins became free. The growth of free cities was a parallel development which marked the increase and growing power of merchants and craftsmen. The new trade routes opened by the Portuguese, Spanish, Dutch, and English navigators added to the prosperity of the cities which were seaports. Freemen were entitled to rights, and wealth was a powerful support to their claims. Yeomen and London were the main supports of the Parliamentary cause in the struggle with the Stuarts; the country districts generally supported the King.

Meanwhile out of the older local and tribal customs the king's judges in England were gradually building a "common law" of the realm, which at first was no doubt based on the distinction in class which we have noted, but which, largely because it was "common," came to be more uniform, not only for all parts of the realm, but for all persons, and to be regarded as an agent of protection, even against the arbitrary acts of the king himself. By the seventeenth century civil rights had been so recognized and defined that even the overthrow and execution of a king could be regarded as a legal procedure made necessary to maintain the liberties of the people of England.

Milton and Locke were eloquent defenders of liberty. They drew on both the old Stoic-Roman conception of natural law and the Christian conception of God-given law. But to use these conceptions in defense of liberty, men of the seventeenth and eighteenth centuries shifted the emphasis from law to rights. The doctrine of natural rights became a symbol of the growing strength of the individual, asserting itself as over against the formerly claimed divine right of monarchs.

"All men naturally were born free," wrote Milton. "To understand political power right," wrote Locke, "and derive it from the original, we must consider what state all men are naturally in, and that is a state of perfect freedom to order their actions and dispose of their possessions and persons, as they think fit within the bounds of the law of nature; without asking leave or depending upon the will of any other man. A state also of equality, wherein all the power and jurisdiction is reciprocal." These doctrines of natural liberty and natural rights found eloquent portrayal in Rousseau; they challenged the old order in the bold declarations of American independence in 1776, and of the French Revolution in 1789. For they declared that governments were established to secure these rights, and derived their just powers from the consent of the governed.

The effect of such assertion of rights upon the moral consciousness was obviously to make it less willing to accept any authority in morals that could not justify itself to reason and conscience.

3. The great *religious* event of the period was the Reformation. Instead of the unity of Christendom which the medieval church had sought, fierce contests became general between princes, vigorous arguments between divines. Besides the reforms of the church which Luther and Calvin urged, another theory of Christianity and Christian community came forward. Even from the beginning there were two interpretations of the spirit of Christianity. The Catholic church conceived itself as the agency of divine grace and salvation for a sinful world. Its sacraments were the channels of this grace. It aimed to include all from birth to death in care, instruction, reproof, and remission.

On the other hand some believers had cherished the more personal and individual aspects of the Founder's life and teaching. The Sermon on the Mount seemed to lend little support for imposing hierarchy and temporal power. Instead of a universal church, including all, these believers held that the church should consist of those only who had been converted, and were sincerely seeking to follow the Master. The beloved community was for them to include those who loved the Master and each other. They would keep aloof from the World, not in the ascetic temper of the monk, not to mortify the flesh, but to pursue a radically different type of life from that dominated by ambition, wealth, or lust. They regarded the sacrament of the Eucharist as a commemoration by the faithful instead of as a sacrifice reenacted in the Mass. In the medieval period the Waldenses had declared for such a conception of a voluntary community of believers; the Franciscans aimed in the spirit of Matthew, ch. 10, to imitate Christ, in poverty and ministry to the poor, although they remained within the Catholic church. In the fourteenth century Wycliffe (1320–84) had sent out "poor" or "simple" priests to preach to the common people, and with his followers had translated the Bible into English. He attacked the right of the clergy to hold property, and opposed to the political conception of the church organization the simpler pattern set by Christ, and the first disciples. He not only appealed to the authority of the Scripture as superior to that of the church but by his translation appealed also to the common man to test his position. John Huss of Bohemia held similar doctrines. The Lollards continued the Wycliffe tradition. Mennonites, Baptists, the Scrooby group of Separatists who crossed to Holland, and later to Plymouth, Massachusetts, as "Pilgrims," all held to the view of the church as a company of believers. The Friends or Quakers appealed to an inner light as authority. In all these groups, even more decisively than in the Reforming groups of Lutherans, Calvinists, and Puritans within the church of England, the rejection of the rule of the church forced an effort to justify this rejection. At first the authority of the Scriptures was often the court of appeal. The invention of printing was of great importance in making the individual the interpreter of the Scriptures. The emphasis upon the individual's own belief and his voluntary choice of membership in the Christian community made for moral reflection and individual responsibility.

All these dissenting groups sought liberty for themselves—for what they regarded as the true teaching. Few conceived of toleration or regarded religious liberty as permissible. The Baptists were pioneers in religious liberty; in England, John Locke's powerful *Essay* (1667) and four *Letters on Toleration* were among the strongest influences in its advance. Thomas Jefferson linked his own service in this field with that in the cause of civil and political liberty, and in education, in the epitaph which he selected: "Author of the American Declaration of Independence, of the statute of Virginia for religious freedom, and father of the University of Virginia."

4. The *economic development* in this period saw the change from the feudal system of service to the system of money payment. This was a step toward greater economic liberty. The discoveries of new trade routes to the Far East, and of the New World, tended to increase the wealth of merchants and to some extent of other classes. When men gained wealth, they gained power. The palaces and dwellings of Venice, of the old Flemish ports, and of many another European city show the early manifestations of this new power. They show also the new interests in

making fine and beautiful the abodes of secular life, whereas in the Middle Ages the skill of craftsmen as well as the resources of the people had gone into cathedrals that so well represent what was most prized when Chartres, Rheims, Canterbury, and Lincoln were building.

Along with the growth of commerce and industry came a new theory as to the place of trade in national life, and as to the method of regulating economic affairs. A policy of economic liberty gradually took shape, which was the natural analogue of civil and religious liberty. In the Middle Ages, trade was controlled. Certain customs and standards which were at first not included within the common law, were administered by courts of merchants. Gilds were in some cases responsible for honest dealing. The very word "honesty," which in Rome meant rather what was honorable, came to refer particularly to the maintenance of good faith and fair dealing in trade or financial transactions. Society attempted to set a moral standard and to control business and industry by it. It aimed to find out by some means what was a reasonable price. In the case of manufactured goods, this could be sometimes fixed by the opinion of fellow craftsmen. Where buyers and sellers met and bargained in an open market, a "common estimation" could be trusted to give a fair value. A maximum limit, however, was set for victuals in towns. Or again, custom prescribed what should be the money equivalent for payments formerly made in kind or in personal service. One type of regulation has survived to the present day in the form of usury laws.

The distinctive feature of modern economic life has been the tendency to abandon all restriction imposed by an outside moral standard, and to substitute a system of free bargaining, free contract. This is one aspect of the complex system called capitalism, although the full development of capitalism was not reached in this period.

To prevent extortionate prices on the one hand, or unduly low prices on the other, the reliance of capitalism has been on competition and the general principle of supply and demand. If a baker charges too high for his bread, others will set up shops and sell cheaper. If a money lender asks too high interest, men will not borrow or will find a loan elsewhere. If a wage is too low, labor will go elsewhere; if too high, capital will not be able to find a profit and so will not employ labor—so runs the theory.

Without analyzing the moral value of the theory at this point, we notice that, in so far as it assumes to secure fair bargains and a just distribution, it assumes the parties to the free contract to be really free. This implies that they are upon nearly equal footing. In the days of hand work and small industries, that is, until the industrial revolution, this was a plausible assumption.

This theory of free bargaining fitted in well with the doctrine of natural rights which flourished in the eighteenth century. It is an interesting coincidence that Adam Smith's *Wealth of Nations* which advocated freedom from various restrictions of former times in commerce and industry appeared in the same year with the American Declaration of Independence, in 1776. Adam Smith went further: he held that although the rich man might be seeking only his own gain with no thought of public benefit, he would be led "as if by an invisible hand to contribute to the general good." If this was true, why worry over the morality of the selfish pursuit of gain? This of course did not mean that there were no moral principles observed in business. On the contrary, business worked out certain rules which were absolutely essential to maintenance of business relations, such as the payment of debts, the observance of all contracts, and of good faith in certain respects at least. But the full force of the moral problems of capitalism did not develop until after the industrial revolution.

So far as industry was concerned, this rise of a new middle class, made up of those who were in part workers with their hands, resulted in a changed attitude toward manual labor. The class ideal of the warrior and his descendant, the gentleman, was distinctly opposed to manual labor. "Arms," or the Court, or the Church, was the proper profession; hunting, or fishing, or sport, was the appropriate recreation. This view was more or less bound up with the fact that in primitive conditions, labor was mainly performed by women or by slaves. It was the business, the "virtue" of men to fight, or govern. Ancient culture strengthened this prejudice. The church, on the other hand, had maintained both the dignity and the moral value of labor. Not only the example of the Founder of Christianity and his early disciples, who were for the most part of the humbler classes of society, but the intrinsic moral value of work entered into appraisal. The Puritans especially, who had a wide-reaching influence upon the northern and western portions of America, were insistent upon industry, not merely for the sake of its products—they were frugal in their consumption—but as expressing a type of character. Idleness and "shiftlessness" were not merely ineffective, they were sinful. "If any will not work, neither let him eat," commended itself thoroughly to this class ideal. Further as good Calvinists who believed in the doctrine of divine election, the Puritans laid stress upon the idea that every man—not the clergy only—had a "calling," a part to perform, in God's plan of the work of the world.

That the laborer brought something to the common weal, while the idler had to be supported was a further reenforcement. As the middle and lower classes became increasingly influential, the very fact that they were themselves laborers and traders added a class motive. It was natural that a laboring class should regard labor as "honest" (i.e., honorable), though at an earlier time such a collocation of terms as "honest labor" would have sounded as absurd as "honest villain" (villein). A further influence effective in America was the fluidity of class distinctions in a new country. The man who was honored on the frontier was the man who could shoot straight, fell his trees, and subdue the soil. The influence of the frontier was largely on the side of the value of work, and the reprobation of idleness.

5. The Renaissance saw the dawn of modern science; the eighteenth century witnessed a further emancipation of thought. It would be giving a wrong impression to imply that there was no inquiry, no use of reason in the medieval world. The problems set by the inheritance of Old-World religion and politics, forced themselves upon the builders of castles and cathedrals, of law and of dogma. The universities were centres of discussion in which brilliant minds often challenged received opinions. Men like Roger Bacon sought to discover nature's secrets, and the great scholastics mastered Greek philosophy in the interest of defending the faith. But theological interest limited freedom and choice of theme. It was not until the expansion of the individual—in political freedom, in the use of the arts, in the development of commerce—that the purely intellectual interest such as had once characterized Greece awoke. A new world of possibilities seemed dawning upon the Italian, Galileo, the Frenchman, Descartes, the Englishman, Francis Bacon. The instruments of thought had been sharpened by the dialectics of the schools; now let them be used to analyze the world in which we live. In-

stead of merely observing nature Galileo applied the experimental method, putting definite questions to nature and thus preparing the way for a progress step by step toward a positive knowledge of nature's laws. Descartes found in mathematics a method of analysis which had never been appreciated before. What seemed the mysterious path of bodies in curved lines could be given a simple statement in his analytic geometry. Leibniz and Newton carried this method to triumphant results in the analysis of forces. Reason appeared able to discover and frame the laws of the universe—the "principles" of nature. Bacon, with less of positive contribution in method, sounded another note which was equally significant. The human mind is liable to be clouded and hindered in its activities by certain inveterate sources of error. Like deceitful images or obsessions the "idols" of the tribe, of the cave, of the market, and of the theater—due to instinct or habit, to language or tradition—prevent the reason from doing its best work. It needs vigorous effort to free the mind from these idols. But this can be done. Let man turn from metaphysics and theology to nature and life; let him follow reason instead of instinct or prejudice. "Knowledge is power." Through it may rise above the kingdom of nature the "kingdom of man." In his *New Atlantis*, Bacon foresees a human society in which skill and invention and government shall all contribute to human welfare. These three notes, the experimental method, the power of rational analysis through mathematics and the possibility of controlling nature in the interests of man, were characteristic of the period.

A conflict of reason with authority went on side by side with the progress of science. Humanists and scientists had often set themselves against dogma and tradition. The Reformation was not in form an appeal to reason, but the clash of authorities stimulated men to reasoning upon the respective claims of Catholic and Protestant. And in the eighteenth century, under the favoring influence of a broad toleration and a general growth of intelligence, the conflict of reason with dogma reached its culmination. The French call the period *l'Illumination*—the illumination of life and experience by the light of reason. The Germans call it the *Aufklärung*, "the clearing-up." What was to be cleared up? First, ignorance, which limits the range of man's power and infects him with fear of the unknown; then superstition, which is ignorance consecrated by wont and emotion; finally, dogma, which usually embodies irrational elements and seeks to force them upon the mind by the power of authority, not of truth. Nor was it merely a question of intellectual criticism. Voltaire saw that dogma was often responsible for cruelty. Ignorance meant belief in witchcraft and magic. From the dawn of civilization this had beset man's progress and quenched many of the brightest geniuses of the past. It was time to put an end once for all to the remnants of primitive credulity; it was time to be guided by the light of reason. The movement was not all negative. Using the same appeal to "nature," which had served so well as a rallying cry in the development of political rights, the protagonists of the movement spoke of a "natural light" which God had placed in man for his guidance—"the candle of the Lord set up by himself in men's minds, which it is impossible for the breath or power of man wholly to extinguish." A natural and rational religion should take the place of supposed revelation.

But the great achievement of the eighteenth century in the intellectual development of the individual was that the human mind came to realize the part it was itself playing in the whole realm of science and conduct. Man began to look within. Whether he called his work an *Essay concerning Human Understanding,* or a *Treatise of Human Nature,* or a *Theory of Moral Sentiments,* or a *Critique of Pure Reason,* the aim was to study human experience. For of a sudden it was dawning upon man that, if he was then living upon a higher level of knowledge and conduct than the animal or the savage, this must be due to the activity of the mind. It appeared that man, not satisfied with "nature," had gone on to build a new world with institutions and morality, with art and science. This was no creation of instinct or habit; nor could it be explained in terms of sense, or feeling, or impulse alone; it was the work of that more active, universal, and creative type of intelligence which we call reason. Man, as capable of such achievements in science and conduct, must be regarded with new respect. As having political rights, freedom, and responsibility, man has the dignity of a citizen, sovereign as well as subject. As guiding and controlling his own life and that of others by the power of ideas, not of force, he has the dignity of a moral person, a moral sovereignty. He does not merely take what nature brings; he sets up ends of his own and gives them worth. In this, Kant saw the supreme dignity of the human spirit.

6. Art and letters revealed and ministered to growing individuality. The Middle Ages found appropriate expression for its spirit in the cathedrals erected to the service of God, in which the community came together to bow before a supreme authority, and to feel their common membership in the City of God. The modern world, if it has found no art so expressive of reverence and community, has developed many arts that have disclosed the aspirations, the wide-ranging interests, the delight in adventure, the urgent passions, and the broadening sympathies of modern life. The Crusades, contact, through them and later through commerce, with Arabian civilization, growing acquaintance with the literature and art of Greece and Rome, were effective agencies in the beginnings. The Renaissance, or rebirth of interest and joy in the secular life, showed itself in Italy in painting, sculpture, and romance; in England, in the drama of Shakspere. These were followed by the painting of the Low Countries and of Spain, the drama of France, the music of Germany. And finally fiction, a form of art peculiarly adapted to the portrayal of individual character spread through the whole modern world.

This rich development of artistic and literary expression claimed independence from such moral control of subject and treatment as was characteristic of the Middle Ages. The Renaissance led with its portraiture of powerful personalities. The Restoration drama reacted against Puritanism. The Storm and Stress movement revolted not only against literary tradition, but also against institutions and customs which were felt to be constraints of the individual.

One other influence of art and letters was of a more positive nature. The increase of humanitarianism during the period had many sources, but art both expressed and contributed to wider sympathies. Art communicates feeling. Drama and fiction take us into the lives of other people. During the Renaissance it was largely the upper class that provided most of the heroes and heroines, but as time went on the middle class also claimed attention. A Rembrandt found lines of character in an old man or woman, and the portrait did not suggest any query as to whether the subject were prince or peasant. Velasquez painted kings and

topers with the same merciless and unflinching search for character. Burns, the farmer, looked forward to a day

> When man to man the warld o'er
> Shall brithers be for a' that.

§ 3. Since the Revolutions

1. The American and French Revolutions marked a crisis in government; the industrial revolution brought about an
even more far-reaching change in the life of the average man in
Europe and America. The American and French Revolutions
carried one step farther a movement in the interest of liberty
which had its beginnings in the freeing of villeins and rise of a
middle class. The English had already achieved Parliamentary
government in their civil war and in 1688. They took a further
step in 1832 in their reform of abuses and extension of the franchise. What made the American Revolution more striking was
its clear declaration of liberty and its result in the formation
of a new nation. The French Revolution was more spectacular
than the American because of its more radical character. It affected the ideas of Europeans more profoundly, because for one
reason it was nearer home. It was echoed in the literature of the
time. The American and French Revolutions both emphasized
democracy not only in its aspect of liberty and self-government,
but in its other meaning of equality. They contributed powerfully
to level the distinctions fixed by birth between classes. The American nation was in Lincoln's words, "conceived in liberty and
dedicated to the proposition that all men are created equal." The
French made Liberty, Equality, Fraternity their motto.

In continuation of these Revolutions, *Democracy* in both aspects has become the generally accepted theory of government
and in a great degree a standard of social life. James, Viscount
Bryce, in his *Modern Democracies* published in 1921, com-
mented on the change which had taken place in the past century.
One hundred years before there was in the Old World one tiny
spot (some of the Swiss cantons) under democratic government.
By 1921 there were "more than one hundred representative assemblies at work all over the earth legislating for self-governing

communities." Not only so but in the United States, Canada, and Northern Europe, women have been admitted to the franchise. Not less significant, in Lord Bryce's opinion is the change of general attitude. "Seventy years ago—the word Democracy awakened dislike or fear. Now it is a word of praise." The spread of self-government and of equality has had a fundamental influence upon morals, as regards the general attitude toward authority. When people make their own laws they do not readily accept any moral standard or law which rests on authority of a ruling class, or of elders, or of church, or of school—unless it can justify itself by some other test.

In the train of political democracy has followed enlarged educational opportunity. This has appealed to general sentiment both as a necessity for intelligent voting and as a right of every child to share in at least the rudiments of the general inheritance. Education makes possible the reading of news and the participation in discussion. It is another influence making for reflective morality.

The growth of political democracy and the widening of educational opportunity have made for a deepening and broadening of moral consciousness. Another political development has added rather to its perplexities. The power of nationalism has increased. Cultural tradition, economic advantage, pride in national strength, fear of other nations, military armaments on a vast scale, constant pressure from military personnel, imperial expansion of the great powers—all have contributed to a war spirit which culminated in the Great War, and still threatens the peace of the world and the existence of civilization. No issue of our time has evoked such bitter conflicts of moral judgments. Some aspects of these will be considered in Part III.

2. Unlike the American and French Revolutions, the *industrial revolution* cannot be assigned to exact years. It began with the introduction on a large scale of machinery driven by water or steam power. It is still going on in new devices for mass production. It has been accompanied by enormous activity in invention, and in the discovery and use of new forces of nature. It has had as a counterpart the organization of corporate ownership and control of industry. It has been aided in its command of vast resources in money and credit by the expansion of banking and other financial agencies. It has shifted the mass of population

from country to city. It has divested the family and home of many of their former functions. It has changed America from a nation of independent farmers and craftsmen to a nation composed in large measure of men and women working for employers. It has produced enormous wealth. In America it has made possible the rapid exploitation of natural resources, and the administration of such a widespread area under a single Federal government.

By improved methods of communication and transportation it is breaking down barriers of language, tradition, and political isolation between peoples, and bringing back in another form something of the unity which the medieval church sought. It has made possible the political unification of the widely distant parts of the United States which today read the same news in the morning newspaper or hear it over the radio. It has contributed to the progress of democracy in government, while it has brought back autocracy in industry. It has brought about a shift in men's scale of values and a shift in the relative power and prestige of institutions. In the Middle Ages, the church and the glory of God; in the fifteenth to the eighteenth centuries, national power and the liberty of the individual; since the Revolutions, democracy and wealth, have been the notes which have stirred men's hearts and enlisted their devotion.

Space admits of but the bare mention of three outstanding effects of the industrial revolution which set moral problems for present and future, viz., the new alignment of classes, the autocratic or oligarchic organization of the economic system, and the unequal distribution of the vast wealth produced. More subtle and perhaps more fundamental than any of these have been the changes in valuation of goods, in the meaning of a good life, of success and excellence, which the direction of our energies toward the hitherto unexpected resources of nature has brought about. These problems will be considered in Part III.

3. The third principal aspect of the period which has affected morals and its problems is *the progress of natural and social science*. Chemistry, biology, anthropology, sociology, have come into being. Physics, psychology, physiology, medicine, economics, political science have developed new methods. Applications of the physical sciences have increased comforts and luxuries and made them more generally available. Production of all kinds

of goods has vastly increased and this has raised questions of just distribution. But a more direct influence of science upon morals has come from the general spirit and method of scientific inquiry, and in particular from the doctrine of evolution as presented by Darwin and Spencer, and since employed as a method in many fields. For the general spirit of inquiry has led to questioning of many dogmas; the experimental method has not only led to widening of knowledge but in its combination of reasoning and observation—of putting questions to nature—it has set up a test of truth which has wide application; the conception of evolution places the morals of any given time or people in a perspective which renders them less absolute, while it compares them with those of other times and other peoples.

§ 4. Sources of Present-Day Moral Conceptions

Our conceptions for the moral fact are nearly all taken from the group relations or from the jural and religious aspects, as these have been gradually brought to clearer consciousness. As already noted, the Greek term "ethical," the Latin "moral," the German *sittlich*, suggest this—*ethos* meant the "sum of the characteristic usages, ideas, standards, and codes by which a group was differentiated and individualized in character from other groups."[1]

Some specific moral terms come directly from group relations. The "kind" man acts as one of the kin. When the ruling or privileged group is contrasted with the man of no family or of inferior birth, we get a large number of terms implying "superiority" or "inferiority" in birth, and so of general value. This may or may not be due to some inherent superiority of the upper class, but it means at least that the upper class has been most effectual in shaping language and standards of approval. So "noble" and "gentle" referred to birth before they had moral value; "duty" in modern usage seems to have been principally what was due to a superior. Many words for moral disapproval are very significant of class feeling. The "caitiff" was a captive, and the Italians have their general term for morally bad, "*cattivo*," from the same

1. Sumner, *Folkways*, p. 36.

idea. The "villain" was a feudal tenant, the "blackguard" looked after the kettles, the "rascal" was one of the common herd, the "knave" was the servant, the "base" and "mean" were opposed to the gentle and noble. "Lewd" meant, characteristic of the laity as contrasted with the clergy.

Another set of conceptions reflects the old group *approvals* or combines these with conceptions of birth. We have noted the twofold root of *kalokagathia* in Greek. "Honor" and "honesty" were what the group admired, and conversely "*aischros*" and "*turpe*" in Greek and Latin, like the English "disgraceful" or "shameful," were what the group condemned. "Virtue" was the manly excellence which called out the praise of a warlike time, while one of the Greek terms for morally bad originally meant cowardly, and our "scoundrel" has possibly the same origin. The "bad" was probably the weak or the womanish. The economic appears in "merit," what I have earned, and likewise in "duty" and "ought," what is due or owed—though duty seems to have made itself felt especially, as noted above, toward a superior. Forethought and skill in practical affairs provided the conception of "wisdom," which was highest of the virtues for the Greeks, and as "prudence" stood high in medieval systems. The conception of valuing and thus of forming some permanent standard of a better and a worse, is also aided, if not created, by economic exchange. It appears in almost identical terms in Plato and the New Testament in the challenge, "What shall it profit a man if he gain the whole world and lose his own life?" [2] From the processes of fine or useful arts came probably the conceptions of measure, order, and harmony. A whole mode of considering the moral life is jural. "Moral law," "authority," "obligation," "responsibility," "justice," "righteousness," bring with them the associations of group control and of the more definitely organized government and law. Finally the last named terms bear also a religious imprint, and numerous conceptions of the moral come from that sphere or get their specific flavor from religious usage. The conceptions of the "soul" have contributed to the ideal of a good which is permanent, and which is made rather by personal companionship, than by sensuous gratification. "Purity" began as a magical and religious idea; it came to symbolize not only free-

2. Plato's wording is given on p. 115.

dom from contamination but singleness of purpose. "Chastity" lends a religious sacredness to a virtue which had its roots largely in the conception of property. "Wicked" is from witch. We have indeed certain conceptions drawn from individual experiences of impulse, or reflection. From the sense recoil from what was disgusting came such conceptions as "foul," and from kindred imagery of what suits eye or muscular sense came "straightforward," "upright," "steady." From the thinking process itself we have "conscience." This word in Greek and Latin was a general term for consciousness and suggests one of the distinctive, perhaps the most distinctive characteristic of the moral. For it implies a "conscious" thoughtful attitude, which operates not only in forming purposes, but in measuring and valuing action by the standards it approves. But it is evident that by far the larger part of our ethical terms are derived from social relations in the broad sense.

§ 5. Interpretations of Modern Trends by Ethical Systems

It is clear that if ethical systems were to interpret the modern development of the individual along these various lines, they must seek some new basis for the authority of the moral life if the moral life were to have any authority, and must do justice on the one hand to the individual's personal interests, and on the other to his increasing contacts with his fellows, and the growing democracy due to the rise of new classes to the level of consideration and democratic regard. Four such systems had appeared previously to the great change in thought brought about by the work of Darwin and the doctrine of evolution in the middle of the last century: the Selfish System, the Moral Sense theory, the Kantian theory, and the theory of Utilitarianism.

1. The *selfish system* so called was the simplest formulation of the early individualism, particularly as it expressed itself in wars for ambition and plunder, or sought protection for private interests under the authority of the State. Its most famous expounder was the Englishman, Thomas Hobbes (1588–1679), whose great work the *Leviathan* or *The Matter, Form and Power of a Common-wealth* appeared in 1651 just following the Thirty

Years' War on the continent and the civil war in England which ended with the execution of Charles I. Self-preservation is according to Hobbes the first law of nature; all society is "for gain or for glory." Instead of the natural law of Rome and of Grotius, Hobbes could see only a natural "right" of each man to protect himself by any means in his power, and a natural law of prudence. This leads him to combine with others to set up an authority or sovereign that can keep the peace and make it practicable for each man to keep his contracts and abstain from warfare and plots against his fellows. We may regard it from one point of view as an attempt to show that even if we set aside all laws of God and all the standards that tradition has built up, we are nevertheless forced, if we wish to preserve life at all, to find a new basis for morals. If we strip off everything else and come down to the last ultimate fact of self-preservation, we find that we must create a moral system to protect ourselves.

2. This selfish system seemed shocking in its naked reduction of human life to the single bare struggle for self-preservation. Is humanity so simple, so egoistic as this? The *Moral Sense* writers (Shaftesbury, 1671–1713; Hutcheson, 1694–1747; Hume, 1711–76; Adam Smith, 1723–90) answered, No. Man has other impulses than merely to preserve himself; he has a "herding instinct" which leads him to seek the company of his fellows. He has kindly impulses and affections, and is made happy when he gratifies these in generous activities. And further he is pleased and delights in observing kindly and generous behavior in others. He does not first have to calculate whether a noble and generous deed will benefit him personally; he approves it at once. He sympathizes with the one who is aided; he sympathizes no less with the generous actor. His approval of what is noble and generous and right, and his resentment at what is cruel, injurious, mean, and wrong are thus so direct and immediate that we may properly call their source a "sense"—a moral sense. Even if man denies any authority above him, he cannot get rid of his own feelings. The individual is thus moral because he has these moral feelings and sentiments as an ineradicable part of his own nature.

3. The *Kantian* theory took its stand on a different part of human nature, which Kant believed to be as fundamental as the sentiments but more adequate to account for the authority which morality seems to possess. The author of the theory, Immanuel

Kant, of Königsberg (1724–1804) published his most important ethical writings in 1785 and 1788. He was tremendously impressed by the whole movement toward freedom in political life, in religion, and in the intellectual sphere. At the same time he was as thoroughly convinced of the necessity of order and law. The central fact of morals appeared to him to be the voice of duty, "I ought." How can we do justice to this fact and also to the freedom and independence of the individual? On the one hand, the more we consider the essence of morality the more we see that it presupposes something binding upon all of us, and (as against the selfish system) something that shall bring about harmony in human life. The Moral Sense system is weak on the first demand, for the objector may urge, "I have no such feelings as you describe and therefore I don't feel any compulsion to be just or generous." The selfish system is weak on the second point, because if each man is looking out for himself the result is a selfish scramble and discord rather than harmony. The only agreement reached on this basis is that of the married couple who agreed perfectly in that each wanted his own way. The source of morality and of the law that shall control and harmonize life must be sought not in interest or feelings but (as by the ancient Stoics) in reason. And this gives us a clue to the problem of uniting authority with liberty. For in obeying the law of reason man is not obeying an outside authority; he is obeying a law imposed by himself. Autonomy, i.e., a law which is self given, is the same as freedom. In this statement, Kant is putting into different terms Rousseau's formulation of the basis of rightful government, namely, a government which men establish by their own will. Finally, Kant gave his finest and most influential interpretation of the essence of morality in the conception that every human being is an end in himself, that he has intrinsic worth—"So treat humanity whether in thine own person or that of another always as an end, never as means only."

4. The fourth system, *Utilitarianism*, like the first two, had its seat in England. It included writers of both the eighteenth and nineteenth centuries, but the most famous were Bentham (1748–1832; *Introduction to the Principles of Morals and Legislation*, 1789); Paley (1743–1805; *Moral and Political Philosophy*, 1785); John Stuart Mill (1806–1873; *On Liberty*, 1859; *Utilitarianism*, 1863). The Utilitarians were primarily interested,

not so much in finding a new basis for authority as in finding some working standard for testing existing claims to authority on the part of laws and institutions. They felt that moral sense was likely to be arbitrary; persons become strongly attached to certain habits and ways of looking at things, and come to feel that these are the only right ways. And on the other hand the Utilitarians were suspicious of "reason"; for they held that men are likely to claim that reason sanctions this or forbids that, when it is really some prejudice or old established habit that asserts itself. They suspected therefore what they called the *a priori* method, and believed it to be more in accordance with the modern spirit of science to look to human observation and experience in order to find what men value. Instead of judging conduct by feelings or intuition, they would judge its *consequences*. The particular kind of consequences which they thought most important were again another outcome of certain aspects of this modern development. Each individual, they held, is really seeking his happiness above everything else. If then we are to find a moral standard in what men actually value, we must find it not in the heavens above, but in human happiness. But—and here come in the revolt against the special privilege of an upper class, and the democratic sympathetic regard for all sorts and conditions of men—when we take happiness as our standard, it must be the happiness of the greatest number, "every man to count as one."

Just as Plato and Aristotle interpreted the measure, order, and community spirit of an aristocratic Greek society, as the law of nature interpreted the underlying spirit of imperial Rome, as the church of the Middle Ages voiced the life of an age bowing to authority of a divine law, and reverencing the values of another world, so these four systems interpreted the spirit of the modern world, seeking to be free to live out its own life through new forms of expression, yet recognizing the necessity and importance of directing its development, of examining its life.

Literature

J. H. Randall, Jr., *The Making of the Modern Mind*, has extended references to the literature of this period.

The histories of philosophy and of ethics give the theoretical side. In addition to those previously mentioned the works of Höffding, Falckenberg, and Fischer may be named. Stephen, *English Thought in the Eighteenth Century*, and *The Utilitarians*; Fichte, *Characteristics of the Present Age* (in *Popular Works*, tr. by Smith); Stein, *Die sociale Frage im Lichte der Philosophie*, 1897; Comte, *Positive Philosophy*, tr. by Martineau, 1875, Book VI.; Dewey, *Reconstruction in Philosophy*, 1921; E. Troeltsch, *Die Soziallehren der christlichen Kirchen und Gruppen*, 1913, Eng. tr., *Social Teaching of the Christian Churches*, by Wyon, 1931; Merz, *History of European Thought in the 19th Century*, 1904; Robertson, *A Short History of Free Thought*, 1899; Bonar, *Philosophy and Political Economy in Some of Their Historical Relations*, 1893; Bury, *History of Freedom of Thought*, 1913; Schneider, *The Puritan Mind*, 1930.

On the Medieval and Renaissance Attitude: Taylor, *The Mediaeval Mind*, 1914; Stawell and Marvin, *The Making of the Western Mind*, 1923; Grandgent, *Dante*, 1916; Lecky, *History of European Morals*, 3rd ed., 1877; Adams, *Civilization during the Middle Ages*, 1895; Rashdall, *The Universities of Europe in the Middle Ages*, 1895; Eicken, *Geschichte und System der mittelalterlichen Weltanschauung*, 1887; Burckhardt, *The Civilisation of the Renaissance in Italy*, 1892; Draper, *History of the Intellectual Development of Europe*, 1876.

On the Industrial and Social Side: Tawney, *Religion and the Rise of Capitalism*, 1926; Weber, *The Protestant Ethic and the Spirit of Capitalism*, tr. by Parsons, 1930; Hall, *Religious Background of American Culture*, 1930; Ashley, *English Economic History*, 1888–93; Cunningham, *Western Civilization in Its Economic Aspects*, 1900, and *Growth of English Industry and Commerce*, 3rd ed., 1896–1903; Hobson, *The Evolution of Modern Capitalism*, 1894; Traill, *Social England*, 1894; Rambaud, *Histoire de Civilisation Française*, 1897; Held, *Zwei Bücher zur socialen Geschichte Englands*, 1881; Carlyle, *Past and Present*; Ziegler, *Die Geistigen und socialen Strömungen des neunzehnten Jahrhunderts*, 1901.

On the Political and Jural Development: Hadley, *Freedom and Responsibility in the Evolution of Democratic Government*, 1903; Pollock, *The Expansion of the Common Law*, 1904; Ritchie, *Natural Rights*, 1895, *Darwin and Hegel*, 1893, ch. vii.; Dicey, *Lectures on the Relation between Law and Public Opinion in England during the Nineteenth Century*, 1905; Bryce, *Modern Democracies*, 1921.

On the Literary Side: Brandes, *Main Currents in Nineteenth Century Literature*, 1905; Francke, *Social Forces in German Literature*, 1896; Carriere, *Die Kunst im Zusammenhang der Culturentwickelung und die Ideale der Menschheit*, 3rd ed., 1877–86; Parrington, *Main Currents in American Thought*, 1927–31.

Part II

Theory of the Moral Life

General Literature for Part II

Among the works which have had the most influence upon the development of the theory of morals are: Plato, dialogues entitled *Republic, Laws, Protagoras* and *Gorgias*; Aristotle, *Ethics*; Cicero, *De Finibus* and *De Officiis*; Marcus Aurelius, *Meditations*; Epictetus, *Conversations*; Lucretius, *De Rerum Natura*; St. Thomas Aquinas (selected and translated by Rickaby under title of *Aquinas Ethicus*); Hobbes, *Leviathan*; Spinoza, *Ethics*; Shaftesbury, *Characteristics*, and *Inquiry concerning Virtue*; Hutcheson, *System of Moral Philosophy*; Butler, *Sermons*; Hume, *Essays, Principles of Morals*; Adam Smith, *Theory of Moral Sentiments*; Bentham, *Principles of Morals and Legislation*; Kant, *Critique of Practical Reason*, and *Fundamental Principles of the Metaphysics of Ethics*; Comte, "Social Physics" (in his *Course of Positive Philosophy*); Mill, *Utilitarianism*; Spencer, *Principles of Ethics*; Green, *Prolegomena to Ethics*; Sidgwick, *Methods of Ethics*; Selby-Bigge, *British Moralists*, 2 vols. (a convenient collection of selections). For contemporary treatises and histories consult the literature referred to in ch. 1 of Part I.

10. The Nature of Moral Theory

§ 1. Reflective Morality and Ethical Theory

The intellectual distinction between customary and reflective morality is clearly marked. The former places the standard and rules of conduct in ancestral habit; the latter appeals to conscience, reason, or to some principle which includes thought. The distinction is as important as it is definite, for it shifts the centre of gravity in morality. Nevertheless the distinction is relative rather than absolute. Some degree of reflective thought must have entered occasionally into systems which in the main were founded on social wont and use, while in contemporary morals, even when the need of critical judgment is most recognized, there is an immense amount of conduct that is merely accommodated to social usage. In what follows we shall, accordingly, emphasize the difference in *principle* between customary and reflective morals rather than try to describe different historic and social epochs. In principle a revolution was wrought when Hebrew prophets and Greek seers asserted that conduct is not truly conduct unless it springs from the heart, from personal desires and affections, or from personal insight and rational choice.

The change was revolutionary not only because it displaced custom from the supreme position, but even more because it entailed the necessity of criticizing existing customs and institutions from a new point of view. Standards which were regarded by the followers of tradition as the basis of duty and responsibility were denounced by prophet and philosopher as the source of moral corruption. These proclaimed the hollowness of outer conformity and insisted upon the cleansing of the heart and the clarifying of the mind as preconditions of any genuinely good conduct.

One great source of the abiding interest which Greek thought has for the western world is that it records so clearly the struggle to make the transition from customary to reflective conduct. In the Platonic dialogues for example Socrates is represented as constantly raising the question of whether morals can be taught. Some other thinker (like Protagoras in the dialogue of that name) is brought in who points out that habituation to existing moral traditions is actually taught. Parents and teachers constantly admonish the young "pointing out that one act is just, another unjust; one honorable and another dishonorable; one holy and another unholy." When a youth emerges from parental tutelage, the State takes up the task, for "the community compels them to learn laws and to live after the pattern of the laws and not according to their own fancies."

In reply, Socrates raises the question of the foundations of such teaching, of its right to be termed a genuine teaching of virtue, and in effect points out the need of a morality which shall be stable and secure because based upon constant and universal principles. Parents and teachers differ in their injunctions and prohibitions; different communities have different laws; the same community changes its habits with time and with transformations of government. How shall we know who among the teachers, whether individuals or States, is right? Is there no basis for morals except this fluctuating one? It is not enough to praise and blame, reward and punish, enjoin and prohibit. The essence of morals, it is implied, is to know the reason for these customary instructions; to ascertain the criterion which insures their being just. And in other dialogues, it is frequently asserted that even if the mass must follow custom and law without insight, those who make laws and fix customs should have sure insight into enduring principles, or else the blind will be leading the blind.

No fundamental difference exists between systematic moral theory—the general theme of this Second Part of our study—and the reflection an individual engages in when he attempts to find general principles which shall direct and justify his conduct. Moral theory begins, in germ, when any one asks "Why should I act thus and not otherwise? Why is this right and that wrong? What right has any one to frown upon this way of acting and impose that other way?" Children make at least a start upon the road of theory when they assert that the injunctions of elders are arbitrary, being simply a matter of superior position. Any adult enters the road when, in the presence of moral perplexity, of doubt as to what it is right or best to do, he attempts to find his way out through reflection which will lead him to some principle he regards as dependable.

Moral theory cannot emerge when there is positive belief as to what is right and what is wrong, for then there is no occasion for reflection. It emerges when men are confronted with situations in which different desires promise opposed goods and in which incompatible courses of action seem to be morally justified. Only such a conflict of good ends and of standards and rules of right and wrong calls forth personal inquiry into the bases of morals. A critical juncture may occur when a person, for example, goes from a protected home life into the stress of competitive business, and finds that moral standards which apply in one do not hold in the other. Unless he merely drifts, accommodating himself to whatever social pressure is uppermost, he will feel the conflict. If he tries to face it in thought, he will search for a reasonable principle by which to decide where the right really lies. In so doing he enters into the domain of moral theory, even if he does so unwittingly.

For what is called moral theory is but a more conscious and systematic raising of the question which occupies the mind of any one who in the face of moral conflict and doubt seeks a way out through reflection. In short, moral theory is but an extension of what is involved in all reflective morality. There are two kinds of moral struggle. One kind, and that the most emphasized in moral writings and lectures, is the conflict which takes place when an individual is tempted to do something which he is convinced is wrong. Such instances are important practically in the life of an individual, but they are not the occasion of moral theory. The employee of a bank who is tempted to embezzle funds may indeed try to argue himself into finding reasons why it would not be wrong for him to do it. But in such a case, he is not really thinking, but merely permitting his desire to govern his beliefs. There is no sincere doubt in his mind as to what he should do when he seeks to find some justification for what he has made up his mind to do.

Take, on the other hand, the case of a citizen of a nation which has just declared war on another country. He is deeply attached to his own State. He has formed habits of loyalty and of abiding by its laws, and now one of its decrees is that he shall support war. He feels in addition gratitude and affection for the country which has sheltered and nurtured him. But he believes that this war is unjust, or perhaps he has a conviction that all war is a form of murder and hence wrong. One side of his nature, one set of convictions and habits, leads him to acquiesce in war; another deep part of his being protests. He is torn between two duties: he experiences a conflict between the incompatible values presented to him by his habits of citizenship and by his religious beliefs respectively. Up to this time, he has never experienced a struggle between the two; they have coincided and reenforced one another. Now he has to make a choice between competing moral loyalties and convictions. The struggle is not between a good which is clear to him and something else which attracts him but which he knows to be wrong. It is between values each of which is an undoubted good in its place but which now get in each other's way. He is forced to reflect in order to come to a decision. Moral theory is a generalized extension of the kind of thinking in which he now engages.

There are periods in history when a whole community or a group in a community finds itself in the presence of new issues which its old customs do not adequately meet. The habits and beliefs which were formed in the past do not fit into the opportunities and requirements of contemporary life. The age in Greece following the time of Pericles was of this sort; that of the Jews after their captivity; that following the Middle Ages when secular interests on a large scale were introduced into previous religious and ecclesiastic interests; the present is preeminently a period of this sort with the vast social changes which have followed the industrial expansion of the machine age.

Realization that the need for reflective morality and for moral theories grows out of conflict between ends, responsibilities, rights, and duties defines the service which moral theory may render, and also protects the student from false conceptions of its nature. The difference between customary and reflective morality is precisely that definite precepts, rules, definitive injunctions and prohibitions issue from the former, while they cannot proceed from the latter. Confusion ensues when appeal to rational principles is treated as if it were merely a substitute for custom, transferring the authority of moral commands from one source to another. Moral theory can (i) generalize the types of moral conflicts which arise, thus enabling a perplexed and doubtful individual to clarify his own particular problem by placing it in a larger context; it can (ii) state the leading ways in which such problems have been intellectually dealt with by those who have thought upon such matters; it can (iii) render personal reflection more systematic and enlightened, suggesting alternatives that might otherwise be overlooked, and stimulating greater consistency in judgment. But it does not offer a table of commandments in a catechism in which answers are as definite as are the questions which are asked. It can render personal choice more intelligent, but it cannot take the place of personal decision, which must be made in every case of moral perplexity. Such at least is the standpoint of the discussions which follow; the student who expects more from moral theory will be disappointed. The conclusion follows from the very nature of reflective morality; the attempt to set up ready-made conclusions contradicts the very nature of reflective morality.

§ 2. The Nature of a Moral Act

Since the change from customary to reflective morality shifts emphasis from conformity to prevailing modes of action over to personal disposition and attitudes, the first business of moral theory is to obtain in outline an idea of the factors which constitute personal disposition. In its general features, the traits of a reflective moral situation have long been clear; doubts and disputes arise chiefly as to the relation which they bear to one another. The formula was well stated by Aristotle. The doer of the moral deed must have a certain "state of mind" in doing it. First, he must *know* what he is doing; secondly, he must *choose* it, and choose it for itself, and thirdly, the act must be the expression of a formed and stable *character*. In other words, the act must be *voluntary*; that is, it must manifest a choice, and for full morality at least, the choice must be an expression of the general tenor and set of personality. It must involve awareness of what one is about; a fact which in the concrete signifies that there must be a purpose, an aim, an end in view, something for the sake of which the particular act is done. The acts of infants, imbeciles, insane persons in some cases, have no moral quality; they do not know what they are about. Children learn early in life to appeal to accident, that is, absence of intention and purpose on their part, as an excuse for deeds that have bad consequences. When they exculpate themselves on the ground that they did not "mean" to do something they show a realization that intent is a normal part of a moral situation. Again, there is no choice, no implication of personal disposition, when one is coerced by superior physical power. Even when force takes the form of threats, rather than of immediate exercise of it, "duress" is at least a mitigating circumstance. It is recognized that fear of extreme harm to life and limb will overpower choice in all but those of heroic make-up.

An act must be the expression of a formed and stable character. But stability of character is an affair of degrees, and is not to be taken absolutely. No human being, however mature, has a completely formed character, while any child in the degree in which he has acquired attitudes and habits has a stable character to that extent. The point of including this qualification is that it suggests a kind of running scale of acts, some of which proceed from greater depths of the self, while others are more casual, more due to accidental and variable circumstances. We overlook acts performed under conditions of great stress or of physical weakness on the ground that the doer was "not himself" at the time. Yet we should not overdo this interpretation. Conduct may be eccentric and erratic just because a person in the past has formed that kind of disposition. An unstable character may be the product of acts deliberately chosen aforetime. A man is not himself in a state of intoxication. But a difference will be made between the case in which a usually temperate man is overcome by drink, and the case in which intoxication is so habitual as to be a sign of a habit formed by choice and of character.

May acts be voluntary, that is, be expressions of desire, intent, choice, and habitual disposition, and yet be morally neutral, indifferent? To all appearances the answer must be in the affirmative. We rise in the morning, dress, eat, and go about our usual business without attaching moral significance to what we are doing. These are the regular and normal things to do, and the acts, while many of them are performed intentionally and with a knowledge of what we are doing, are a matter of course. So with the student's, merchant's, engineer's, lawyer's, or doctor's daily round of affairs. We feel that it would be rather morbid if a moral issue were raised in connection with each act; we should probably suspect some mental disorder if it were, at least some weakness in power of decision. On the other hand, we speak of the persons in question going about their daily round of *duties*. If we omitted from our estimate of moral character all the deeds done in the performance of daily tasks, satisfaction of recurrent needs, meeting of responsibilities, each slight perhaps in itself but enormous in mass, morality would be a weak and sickly thing indeed.

The inconsistency between these two points of view is only apparent. Many acts are done not only without thought of their *moral* quality but with practically no thought of any kind. Yet these acts are preconditions of other acts having significant value. A criminal on his way to commit a crime and a benevolent person on his way to a deed of mercy both have to walk or ride. Such acts, non-moral in isolation, derive moral significance from the ends to which they lead. If a man who had an important engagement to keep declined to get out of bed in the morning from sheer laziness, the indirect moral quality of a seemingly automatic act would be apparent. A vast number of acts are performed which seem to be trivial in themselves but which in reality are the supports and buttresses of acts in which definite moral considerations are present. The person who completely ignored the connection of the great number of more or less routine acts with the small number in which there is a clear moral issue would be an utterly independable person.

§ 3. Conduct and Character

These facts are implicitly recognized in common speech by the use of the word *conduct*. The word expresses continuity of action, an idea which we have already met in the conception of a stable and formed character. Where there is conduct there is not simply a succession of disconnected acts but each thing done carries forward an underlying tendency and intent, *conducting*, leading up, to further acts and to a final fulfillment or consummation. Moral development, in the training given by others and in the education one secures for oneself, consists in becoming aware that our acts are connected with one another; thereby an ideal of *conduct* is substituted for the blind and thoughtless performance of isolated acts. Even when a person has attained a certain degree of moral stability, his temptations usually take the form of fancying that this particular act will not count, that it is an exception, that for this just one occasion it will not do any harm. His "temptation" is to disregard that continuity of sequence in which one act leads on to others and to a cumulative result.

We commence life under the influence of appetites and impulses, and of direct response to immediate stimuli of heat and cold, comfort and pain, light, noise, etc. The hungry child snatches at food. To him the act is innocent and natural. But he brings down reproach upon himself; he is told that he is unmannerly, inconsiderate, greedy; that he should wait till he is served, till his turn comes. He is made aware that his act has other connections than the one he had assigned to it: the immediate satisfaction of hunger. He learns to look at single acts not as single but as related links in a chain. Thus the idea of a *series*, an idea which is the essence of conduct, gradually takes the place of a mere succession of disconnected acts.

This idea of conduct as a serial whole solves the problem of morally indifferent acts. Every act has *potential* moral significance, because it is, through its consequences, part of a larger whole of behavior. A person starts to open a window because he feels the need of air—no act could be more "natural," more morally indifferent in appearance. But he remembers that his associate is an invalid and sensitive to drafts. He now sees his act in two different lights, possessed of two different values, and he has to make a choice. The potential moral import of a seemingly insignificant act has come home to him. Or, wishing to take exercise, there are two routes open to him. Ordinarily it would be a mere matter of personal taste which he would choose. But he recalls that the more pleasing of the two is longer, and that if he went that way he might be unable to keep an appointment of importance. He now has to place his act in a larger context of continuity and determine which ulterior consequence he prizes most: personal pleasure or meeting the needs of another. Thus while there is no single act which *must* under all circumstances have conscious moral quality, there is no act, since it is a part of conduct, which *may* not have definitive moral significance. There is no hard and fast line between the morally indifferent and the morally significant. Matthew Arnold expressed a prevailing idea when he said that conduct—in the moral sense—is three-fourths of life. Although he probably assigned it a higher ratio than most persons would, the statement expresses a widely shared idea, namely, that morality has to do with a clearly marked out portion of our life, leaving other things indifferent. Our conclusion is different. It is that *potentially* conduct is one hundred per cent of our conscious life. For all acts are so tied together that any one of them may have to be judged as an expression of character. On the other hand, there is no act which may not, under some circumstances, be morally indifferent, for at the time there may be no need for consideration of its relation to character. There is no better evidence of a well formed moral character than knowledge of when to raise the moral issue and when not. It implies a sensitiveness to values which is the token of a balanced personality. Undoubtedly many persons are so callous or so careless that they do not raise the moral issue often enough. But there are others so unbalanced that they hamper and paralyze conduct by indulging in what approaches a mania of doubt.

It is not enough to show that the binding together of acts so that they lead up to and carry one another forward constitutes conduct. We have also to consider why and how it is that they are thus bound together into a whole, instead of forming, as in the case of physical events, a mere succession. The answer is contained in rendering explicit the allusions which have been made to disposition and character. If an act were connected with other acts merely in the way in which the flame of a match is connected with an explosion of gunpowder, there would be action, but not conduct. But our actions not only lead up to other actions which follow as their effects but they also leave an enduring impress on the one who performs them, strengthening and weakening permanent tendencies to act. This fact is familiar to us in the existence of *habit*.

We are, however, likely to have a conception of habit which needs to be deepened and extended. For we are given to thinking of a habit as simply a recurrent external mode of action, like smoking or swearing, being neat or negligent in clothes and person, taking exercise, or playing games. But habit reaches even more significantly down into the very structure of the self; it signifies a building up and solidifying of certain desires; an increased sensitiveness and responsiveness to certain stimuli, a confirmed or an impaired capacity to attend to and think about certain things. Habit covers in other words the very make-up of desire, intent, choice, disposition which gives an act its voluntary quality. And this aspect of habit is much more important than that which is suggested merely by the tendency to repeated outer action, for the significance of the latter lies in the permanence of the personal disposition which is the real cause of the outer acts and of their resemblance to one another. Acts are not linked up together to form conduct in and of themselves, but because of their common relation to an enduring and single condition— the self or character as the abiding unity in which different acts leave their lasting traces. If one surrenders to a momentary impulse, the significant thing is not the particular act which follows, but the strengthening of the power of that impulse—this strengthening is the reality of that which we call habit. In giving way, the person in so far commits himself not just to *that* isolated act but to a *course* of action, to a *line* of behavior.

Sometimes a juncture is so critical that a person, in deciding upon what course he will take, feels that his future, his very being, is at stake. Such cases are obviously of great practical importance for the person concerned. They are of importance for theory, because some degree of what is conspicuous in these momentous cases is found in *every* voluntary decision. Indeed, also it belongs to acts performed impulsively without deliberate choice. In such cases, it is later experience which makes us aware of the serious commitment implied in an earlier act. We find ourselves involved in embarrassing complications and on reflection we trace the cause of our embarrassment to a deed which we performed casually, without reflection and deliberate intent. Then we reflect upon the value of the entire class of actions. We realize the difference which exists between the thought of an act before it is done and as it is experienced afterwards. As Goldsmith so truly said "In the first place, we cook the dish to our own appetite; in the latter, Nature cooks it for us." We plunge at first into action pushed by impulse, drawn by appetite. After we have acted and consequences which are unexpected and undesired show themselves, we begin to reflect. We review the wisdom or the rightness of the course which we engaged in with little or no thought. Our judgment turns backward for its material; something has turned out differently than we anticipated, and so we think back to discover what was the matter. But while the material of the judgment comes to us from the past, what really concerns us is what we shall do the next time; the function of reflection is prospective. We wish to decide whether to continue in the course of action entered upon or to shift to another. The person who reflects on his past action in order to get light on his future behavior is the conscientious person. There is always a temptation to seek for something external to the self on which to lay the blame when things go wrong; we dislike to trace the cause back to something in ourselves. When this temptation is yielded to, a person becomes irresponsible; he neither pins himself nor can be pinned down by others to any consistent course of action, for he will not institute any connection of cause and effect between his character and his deeds.

The conclusion is that conduct and character are strictly correlative. Continuity, consistency, throughout a series of acts is the expression of the enduring unity of attitudes and habits. Deeds hang together because they proceed from a single and stable self. Customary morality tends to neglect or blur the connection between character and action; the essence of reflective morals is that it is conscious of the existence of a persistent self and of the part it plays in what is externally done. Leslie Stephen has expressed this principle as follows:

> The clear enunciation of one principle seems to be a characteristic of all great moral revolutions. The recognition amounts almost to a discovery, and may be said to mark the point at which the *moral* code first becomes distinctly separated from other codes. It may be briefly expressed in the phrase that morality is internal. The *moral* law, we may say, has to be expressed in the form, "be this," not in the form, "do this." The possibility of expressing any rule in this form may be regarded as deciding whether it can or cannot have a distinctively moral character. Christianity gave prominence to the doctrine that the true moral law says "hate not," instead of "kill not." The men of old time had forbidden adul-

tery; the new moral teacher forbade lust; and his greatness as a moral teacher was manifested in nothing more than in the clearness with which he gave utterance to this doctrine. It would be easy to show how profoundly the same doctrine, in various forms, has been bound up with other moral and religious reformations in many ages of the world.[1]

§ 4. Motive and Consequences

In reaching the conclusion that conduct and character are morally one and the same thing, first taken as effect and then as causal and productive factor, we have virtually disposed of one outstanding point of controversy in moral theory. The issue in question is that between those who hold that *motives* are the only thing which count morally and those who hold that *consequences* are alone of moral import. On one side stand those who, like Kant, say that results actually attained are of no importance morally speaking, because they do not depend upon the will alone; that only the will can be good or bad in the moral sense. On the other side, are those who, like Bentham, say that morality consists in producing consequences which contribute to the general welfare, and that motives do not count at all save as they happen to influence the consequences one way or another. One theory puts sole emphasis upon *attitude*, upon *how* the chosen act is conceived and inspired; the other theory lays stress solely upon *what* is actually done, upon the objective *content* of the deed in the way of its effect upon others. Our analysis shows that both views are one-sided. At whichever end we begin we find ourselves intellectually compelled to consider the other end. We are dealing not with two different things but with two poles of the same thing. The school of Bentham, for example, does not hold that *every* consequence is of importance in judging an act morally. It would not say that the act of a surgeon is necessarily to be condemned because an operation results in the death of a patient. It limits the theory to *foreseen* and desired consequences. The intended consequence, the intention, of the surgeon was to save life; morally his act was beneficent, although unsuccessful

1. *Science of Ethics*, p. 155.

from causes which he could not control. They say if his *intent* was right, it makes no difference what his *motive* was; whether he was moved by kindly feeling, by desire for professional standing, by a wish to show his skill, or to gain a fee, is immaterial. The only thing that counts morally is that he intended to effect certain consequences.

The protest contained in this position against locating morals in the conscious feeling which attends the doing of an act is valuable and valid. Persons, children and grown-ups alike, often say in justification for some act that turned out badly that they meant well; they allege some innocent or amiable feeling as the "motive" of the act. The real fact in all probability was that they took next to no pains to think out the consequences of what they proposed to do. They kept their minds upon any favorable results that might be fancied to follow, and glossed over or kept from view its undesirable consequences. If "motive" signified the emotional state which happens to exist in consciousness at the time of acting, Bentham's position would be entirely sound. Since that conception of motives is more or less prevalent, he was not setting up a man of straw to hit, but was attacking a doctrine which is morally dangerous. For it encourages men to neglect the purpose and bearing of their actions, and to justify what they feel inclined to do on the ground that their feelings when doing it were innocent and amiable.

The underlying identification of motive with personal feeling is, however, erroneous. What moves a man is not a feeling but the set disposition, of which a feeling is at best but a dubious indication. An emotion, as the word suggests, moves us, but an emotion is a good deal more than a bare "feeling"; anger is not so much a state of conscious feeling as it is a tendency to act in a destructive way towards whatever arouses it. It is doubtful if a miserly person is conscious of feelings of stinginess; he rather prizes that which he hoards and is moved to keep up and conserve that which he prizes. Just as an angry person may deny, quite honestly, that he is angry, so an ambitious man is likely to be quite devoid of any *feeling* of ambition. There are objects and ends which arouse his energy and into the attaining of which he throws himself with whole-heartedness. If he were to interpret his own conduct he would say that he acts as he does not because of personal ambition, but because the objects in question are so important.

When it is recognized that "motive" is but an abbreviated name for the attitude and predisposition toward ends which is embodied in action, all ground for making a sharp separation between motive and intention—foresight of consequences—falls away. Mere foresight of results may be coldly intellectual, like a prediction of an eclipse. It moves to action only when it is accompanied with desire for that sort of result. On the other hand, a set and disposition of character leads to anticipation of certain kinds of consequences and to passing over other effects of action without notice. A careless man will not be aware of consequences that occur to a prudent man; if they do present themselves to thought, he will not attach the force to them which the careful man does. A crafty character will foresee consequences which will not occur to a frank and open man; if they should happen to come to the mind of the latter, he will be repelled by the very considerations that would attract the sly and intriguing person. Othello and Iago foresee different consequences because they have different kinds of characters. Thus the formation of intention, of purpose, is a function of the forces of human nature which lead to action, and the foreseen consequences move to action only as they are also prized and desired. The distinction between motive and intent is not found in the facts themselves, but is simply a result of our own analysis, according as we emphasize either the emotional or the intellectual aspect of an action. The theoretical value of the utilitarian position consists in the fact that it warns us against overlooking the essential place of the intellectual factor, namely, foresight of consequences. The practical value of the theory which lays stress on motive is that it calls attention to the part played by character, by personal disposition and attitude, in determining the direction which the intellectual factor takes.

But in its extreme form it suffers from the same one-sidedness as does the Benthamite theory of intention, although in the opposite direction. It is possible to make good sense of the proposition that it is the "will" which counts morally, rather than consequences. But only so, if we recognize that *will* signifies an active tendency to foresee consequences, to form resolute purposes, and to use all the efforts at command to produce the intended consequences in fact. The idea that consequences are morally irrelevant is true only in the sense that any act is always likely to have some consequences which could not have been foreseen, even with the best will in the world. We always build better or worse than we know, and the best laid plans of men as of mice are more or less at the mercy of uncontrollable contingent circumstances when it comes to actual consequences. But this fact of the limitation of intention cannot be converted into the doctrine that there is such a thing as motive and will apart from projection of consequences and from effort to bring them to pass. "Will," in the sense of unity of impulse, desire, and thought which anticipates and plans, is central in morals just because by its very nature it is the most constant and effectual factor in control of consequences.

This emphasis upon character is not peculiar to any special type of moral theory. Our dominating interest is the manifestation and interaction of personalities. It is the same interest which shows itself in the drama where the colorful display of incidents is, save in the melodramatic and sentimental, a display of the outworking of character. Political thought tends to be too much rather than too little concerned with personality at the expense of issues and principles. What Hamlet, Macbeth, Nora, Tartuffe are to the theater, Roosevelt, Wilson, Lloyd George, Mussolini are to politics. For practical reasons we must be concerned with character in our daily affairs. Whether we buy or sell goods, lend money or invest in securities, call a physician or consult a lawyer, take or refuse advice from a friend, fall in love and marry, the ultimate outcome depends upon the characters which are involved.

§ 5. Present Need of Theory

We have already noted in passing that the present time is one which is in peculiar need of reflective morals and of a working theory of morals. The scientific outlook on the world and on life has undergone and is still undergoing radical change. Methods of industry, of the production, and distribution of goods have been completely transformed. The basic conditions on which men meet and associate, in work and amusement, have been altered. There has been a vast dislocation of older habits and traditions. Travel and migration are as common as they were once unusual. The masses are educated enough to read and a prolific press exists which supplies cheap reading matter. Schooling has ceased to be the privilege of the few and has become the right and even the enforced duty of the many. The stratification of society into classes each fairly homogeneous in itself has been broken into. The area of contacts with persons and populations alien to our bringing up and traditions has enormously extended. A ward of a large city in the United States may have persons of from a score to fifty racial origins. The walls and barriers that once separated nations have become less important because of the railway, steamship, telegraph, telephone, and radio.

Only a few of the more obvious changes in social conditions and interests have been mentioned. Each one of them has created new problems and issues that contain moral values which are uncertain and disputed. Nationalism and internationalism, capital and labor, war and peace, science and religious tradition, competition and cooperation, *laissez faire* and State planning in industry, democracy and dictatorship in government, rural and city life, personal work and control *versus* investment and vicarious riches through stocks and bonds, native born and alien, contact of Jew and Gentile, of white and colored, of Catholic and Protestant, and those of new religions: a multitude of such relationships have brought to the fore new moral problems with which neither old customs nor beliefs are competent to cope. In addition, the rapidity with which social changes occur brings moral unsettlement and tends to destroy many ties which were the chief safeguards of the morals of custom. There was never a time in the history of the world when human relationships and their accompanying rights and duties, opportunities and demands, needed the unremitting and systematic attention of intelligent thought as they do at present.

There are those who tend to minimize the importance of reflection in moral issues. They hold that men already know more morally than they practice and that there is general agreement among men on all moral fundamentals. Usually such persons will be found to adhere to some especial tradition in whose dogmas they find final and complete authority. But in fact the agreement exists to a large extent only with reference to concepts that are taken vaguely and apart from practical application. Justice: to be sure; give to each that which is his due. But is individualistic competitive capitalism a just system? or socialism? or communism? Is inheritance of large fortunes, without rendering of personal service to society, just? What system of taxation is just? What are the moral claims of free-trade and protection? What would constitute a just system of the distribution of national income? Few would question the desirability of chastity, but there are a multitude of interpretations of its meaning. Does it mean that celibacy is more pleasing to God than marriage? This idea is not generally held today, but its former vogue still affects the beliefs and practices of men and women. What is the relation of chastity as a moral idea to divorce, birth control, state censorship of literature? Human life is sacred. But what about many of the health-destroying practices and accident-inducing practices of modern industry? What about war, preparation for which absorbs the chief part of the revenue of modern States?

And so we could go down the list of all the time-honored virtues and duties, and show that changes in conditions have made what they signify for human action a matter of uncertainty and controversy. The ultimate difference, for example, between the employing and the employed in industry is one of moral criteria and outlook. They envisage different values as having a superior claim. The same is evidently even more true of the convinced nationalist and internationalist, pacifist and militarist, secularist and devotee of authoritatively revealed religion. Now it is not held for a moment that moral theory can give direct and final answers to these questions. But it is held that they cannot be dealt with by adherence to mere tradition nor by trusting to casual impulse and momentary inspiration. Even if all men agreed sincerely to act upon the principle of the Golden Rule as the supreme law of conduct, we should still need inquiry and thought to arrive at even a passable conception of what the Rule means in terms of concrete practice under mixed and changing social conditions. Universal agreement upon the abstract principle even if it existed would be of value only as a preliminary to cooperative undertaking of investigation and thoughtful planning; as a preparation, in other words, for systematic and consistent reflection.

§ 6. Sources of Moral Theory

No theory can operate in a vacuum. Moral as well as physical theory requires a body of dependable data, and a set of intelligible working hypotheses. Where shall moral theory find the material with which to satisfy these needs?

1. While all that has been said about the extent of change in all conditions of life is true, nevertheless there has been no complete breach of continuity. From the beginning of human life, men have arrived at some conclusions regarding what is proper and fair in human relationships, and have engaged in working out codes of conduct. The dogmatist, whether made so by tradition or through some special insight which he claims as his own, will pick out from the many conflicting codes that one which agrees the most closely with his own education and taste. A genuinely reflective morals will look upon all the codes as possible *data*; it will consider the conditions under which they arose; the methods which consciously or unconsciously determined their formation and acceptance; it will inquire into their applicability in present conditions. It will neither insist dogmatically upon some of them, nor idly throw them all away as of no significance. It will treat them as a storehouse of information and possible indications of what is now right and good.

2. Closely connected with this body of material in codes and convictions, is the more consciously elaborated material of legal history, judicial decisions, and legislative activity. Here we have a long experimentation in working out principles for direction of human beings in their conduct. Something of the same kind is true of the workings of all great human institutions. The history of the family, of industry, of property systems, of government and the state, of education and art, is full of instructions about modes of human conduct and the consequences of adopting this or that mode of conduct. Informal material of the same sort abounds in biographies, especially of those who have been selected as the great moral teachers of the race.

3. A resource which mankind was late in utilizing and which it has hardly as yet begun to draw upon adequately is found in the various sciences, especially those closest to man, such as biology, physiology, hygiene and medicine, psychology and psychiatry, as well as statistics, sociology, economics, and politics. The latter upon the whole present problems rather than solutions. But it is well to get problems more clearly in mind, and the very fact that these social disciplines usually approach their material independently of consideration of moral values has a certain intellectual advantage for the moralist. For although he still has to translate economic and political statement over into moral terms, there is some guarantee of intellectual objectivity and impartiality in the

fact that these sciences approach their subject-matter in greater detachment from preformed and set moral convictions, since the latter may be only the prejudices of tradition or temperament. From the biological and psychological sciences, there are derivable highly valuable techniques for study of human and social problems and the opening of new vistas. For example, the discovery of the conditions and the consequences of health of body, personal and public, which these sciences have already effected, opens the way to a relatively new body of moral interests and responsibilities. It is impossible any longer to regard health and the conditions which affect it as a merely technical or physical matter. Its ramifications with moral order and disorder have been clearly demonstrated.

4. Then there is the body of definitely theoretical methods and conclusions which characterize European history for the last two thousand years, to say nothing of the doctrines of Asiatic thinkers for a still longer period. Keen intellects have been engaged in analysis and in the development of directive principles on a rational basis. Alternative positions and their implications have been explored and systematically developed. At first sight, the variety of logically incompatible positions which have been taken by theorists may seem to the student to indicate simply a scene of confusion and conflict. But when studied more closely they reveal the complexity of moral situations, a complexity so great that while every theory may be found to ignore factors and relations which ought to be taken into account, each one will also be found to bring to light some phase of the moral life demanding reflective attention, and which, save for it, might have remained hidden. The proper inference to be drawn is not that we should make a mechanical compromise or an eclectic combination of the different theories, but that each great system of moral thought brings to light some point of view from which the facts of our own situations are to be looked at and studied. Theories afford us at least a set of questions with which we may approach and challenge present conditions.

§ 7. Classification of Problems

For the remaining portion of this Second Part we shall be occupied mainly with a consideration of some of the chief classic theories about morals which have left a moral impress on civilization. A survey of these theories brings out certain underlying differences of emphasis and resulting intellectual problems, which the student will be put in possession of, before taking up the conceptions themselves. Roughly speaking, theories will be found to vary primarily because some of them attach chief importance to purposes and ends, leading to the concept of the *Good* as ultimate; while some others are impressed by the importance of law and regulation, leading up to the supremacy of the concepts of *Duty* and the *Right*; while a third set regards approbation and disapprobation, praise and blame as the primary moral fact, thus terminating with making the concepts of *Virtue* and *Vice* central. Within each tendency, there are further differences of opinion as to what is the Good, the nature of Duty, Law, and the Right, and the relative standing of different virtues.

1. That men form purposes, strive for the realization of ends, is an established fact. If it is asked why they do so, the only answer to the question, aside from saying that they do so unreasonably from mere blind custom, is that they strive to attain certain goals because they believe that these ends have an intrinsic value of their own; they are *good*, satisfactory. The chief province of reason in practical matters is to discriminate between ends that merely seem good and those which are really so—between specious, deceptive goods, and lasting true goods. Men have desires; immediately and apart from reflection they want this and that thing, food, a companion, money, fame and repute, health, distinction among their fellows, power, the love of friends, the admiration of rivals, etc. But why do they want these things? Because value is attributed to them; because they are thought to be good. As the scholastics said, we desire *sub specie boni*; beneath all the special ends striven for is the common idea of the Good, the Satisfying. Theories which regard *ends* as the important thing in morals accordingly make the conception of Good central in theory. Since men often take things to be good in anticipatory judgment which are not so in fact, the problem of this group of theories is to determine the *real* good as distinct from the things that merely *seem* to be so, or, what is the same thing, the permanent good from transitory and fleeting goods. From the side of attitude and disposition, the fundamental matter is therefore the *insight and wisdom* which is able to discriminate between ends that deceptively promise satisfaction and the ends

which truly constitute it. The great problem of morals on this score is the attainment of right knowledge.

2. To other observers of human life, the *control* of desire and appetite has seemed much more fundamental than their satisfaction. Many of them are suspicious of the very principle of desire and of the ends which are connected with it. Desire seems to them so personal and so bent on its own satisfaction as to be the source of temptation, to be the cause which leads men to deviate from the lawful course of action. Empirically, these thinkers are struck by the role played in human government by commands, prohibitions, and all the devices that regulate the play of passions and desires. To them, the great problem is to discover some underlying authority which shall control the formation of aims and purposes. The lower animals follow desire and appetite because they have no conception of regulative law; men have the consciousness of being *bound* by a principle superior to impulse and want. The morally *right* and the naturally satisfying are often in conflict and the heart of the moral struggle is to subordinate good to the demands of *duty*. The theory that makes ends supreme has been called the *teleological* (from the Greek, τέλος, end); the theory which makes law and duty supreme, the *jural*.

3. There is another group of thinkers who feel that the principle of ends and rational insight places altogether too much emphasis upon the intellectual factor in human nature, and that the theory of law and duty is too legal, external, and stringent. They are struck by the enormous part played in human life by facts of approbation and condemnation, praise and blame, reward and punishment, encouragement of some courses of action, resentment at others, and pressure to keep persons from adopting those courses which are frowned upon. They find in human nature a spontaneous tendency to favor some lines of conduct, and to censure and penalize other modes of action, a tendency which in time is extended from acts to the dispositions from which the acts flow. Out of the mass of approbations arise the ideas of virtue and vice; the dispositions which are socially commended and encouraged constituting the excellencies of character which are to be cultivated, vices and defects being those traits which are condemned. Those who hold to this theory have no difficulty in demonstrating the great role of commendation and disfavor in customary morality. The problem of reflective morality and hence of

theory is to lay bare the standard or criterion implicit in current social approbation and reproach. In general, they agree that what men like and praise are acts and motives that tend to serve others, while those acts and motives which are condemned are those which bring harm instead of benefit to others. Reflective morality makes this principle of popular moral judgments conscious, and one to be *rationally* adopted and exercised.

In our succeeding chapters we shall consider these three types of theory and the various subdivisions into which they have evolved. Our aim will be not so much to determine which is true and which false as to see what factors of permanent value each group contributes to the clarification and direction of reflective morality.

Literature

In addition to references at the end of Chapter 1 of Part I. see Sharp, *Ethics*, 1928, ch. i.; Martineau, *Types of Ethical Theory*, 1891, Vol. I., Introduction; Sorley, *Recent Tendencies in Ethics*, 1904; Moore, *Philosophical Studies*, 1922, essay on "The Nature of Moral Philosophy"; Broad, *Five Types of Ethical Theory*, 1930; Fite, *Moral Philosophy*, 1925, ch. i.; James, "The Moral Philosopher and the Moral Life," in *The Will to Believe*, 1912; Otto, *Things and Ideals*, 1924, ch. v.; Lévy-Bruhl, *Ethics and Moral Science*, trans. 1905; Everett, *Moral Values*, 1918, ch. i.

On CONDUCT AND CHARACTER in general, see Paulsen, *System of Ethics*, 1899, pp. 468–472; Mackenzie, *Manual of Ethics*, 1901, Book I., ch. iii.; Spencer, *Principles of Ethics*, Part I., chs. ii.–viii.; Green, *Prolegomena to Ethics*, 1890, pp. 110–117, 152–159; Alexander, *Moral Order and Progress*, pp. 48–52; Stephen, *Science of Ethics*, 1882, ch. ii.; Mezes, *Ethics*, 1901, ch. iv.; Seth, *Ethical Principles*, 1898, ch. iii.; Dewey, *Human Nature and Conduct*, 1922.

Upon MOTIVE AND INTENTION consult Bentham, *Principles of Morals and Legislation*, chs. viii. and x.; Mill, *Analysis of Human Mind*, Vol. II., chs. xxii., and xxv.; Austin, *Jurisprudence*, Vol. I., chs. viii.–xx.; Green, *Prolegomena*, 1890, pp. 315–325; Alexander, *Moral Order and Progress*, pp. 36–47; Westermarck, *Origin and Development of the Moral Ideas*, 1906, chs. viii., xi., and xiii.; Ritchie, *International Journal of Ethics*, Vol. IV., pp. 89–94, and 229–238, where further references are given; Dewey, *Human Nature and Conduct*, 1922, pp. 118–122.

Ends, the Good and Wisdom

§ 1. Reflection and Ends

The question of what ends a man should live for does not arise as a general problem in customary morality. It is forestalled by the habits and institutions which a person finds existing all about him. What others, especially elders, are doing provides the ends for which one should act. These ends are sanctioned by tradition; they are hallowed by the semi-divine character of the ancestors who instituted the customs; they are set forth by the wise elders, and are enforced by the rulers. Individuals trespass, deviating from these established purposes, but they do so with the conviction that thereby social condemnation, reenforced by supernatural penalties inflicted by divine beings, ensues. There are today multitudes of men and women who take their aims from what they observe to be going on around them. They accept the aims provided by religious teachers, by political authorities, by persons in the community who have prestige. Failure to adopt such a course would seem to many persons to be a kind of moral rebellion or anarchy. Many other persons find their ends practically forced upon them. Because of lack of education and because of economic stress they for the most part do just what they have to do. In the absence of the possibility of real choice, such a thing as reflection upon purposes and the attempt to frame a general theory of ends and of the good would seem to be idle luxuries.

There can, however, be no such thing as reflective morality except where men seriously ask by what purposes they should direct their conduct and why they should do so; what it is which makes their purposes good. This intellectual search for ends is bound to arise when customs fail to give required guidance. And this failure happens when old institutions break down; when invasions from without and inventions and innovations from within radically alter the course of life.

If habit fails, the sole alternative to caprice and random action is reflection. And reflection upon what one shall do is identical with formation of ends. Moreover, when social change is great, and a great variety of conflicting aims are suggested, reflection cannot be limited to the selection of one end out of a number which are suggested by conditions. Thinking has to operate creatively to form new ends.

Every habit introduces continuity into activity; it furnishes a permanent thread or axis. When custom breaks down, the only thing which can link together the succession of various acts is a common purpose running through separate acts. An end-in-view gives unity and continuity, whether it be the securing of an education, the carrying on of a military campaign, or the building of a house. The more inclusive the aim in question the broader is the unification which is attained. Comprehensive ends may connect together acts performed during a long span of years. To the common soldier or even to the general in command, winning the campaign may be a sufficiently comprehensive aim to unify acts into conduct. But some one is bound to ask: What then? To what uses shall victory when achieved be put? At least that question is bound to be asked, provided men are intelligently interested in their behavior and are not governed by chance and the pressure of the passing moment. *The development of inclusive and enduring aims is the necessary condition of the application of reflection in conduct; indeed, they are two names for the same fact.* There can be no such thing as reflective morality where there is not solicitude for the ends to which action is directed.

Habit and impulse have consequences, just as every occurrence has effects. But merely as habit, impulse, and appetite they do not lead to foresight of what will happen as a consequence of their operation. An animal is moved by hunger and the outcome is satisfaction of appetite and the nourishment of the body. In the case of a human being, having mature experience upon which to fall back, obstacles in the way of satisfaction of hunger, difficulties encountered in the pursuit of food, will make a man aware of *what* he wants:—the outcome will be anticipated as an end-in-view, as something desired and striven for. Behavior has ends in the sense of results which *put an end* to that particular

activity, while an *end-in-view* arises when a particular consequence is foreseen and being foreseen is consciously adopted by
desire and deliberately made the directive purpose of action.
A purpose or aim represents a craving, an urge, translated into
the idea of an object, as blind hunger is transformed into a purpose through the thought of a food which is wanted, say flour,
which then develops into the thought of grain to be sown and
land to be cultivated:—a whole series of activities to be intelligently carried on.

An end-in-view thus differs on one side from a mere anticipation or prediction of an outcome, and on the other side from the
propulsive force of mere habit and appetite. In distinction from
the first, it involves a want, an impulsive urge and forward drive;
in distinction from the second, it involves an intellectual factor,
the thought of an object which gives meaning and direction to
the urge. This connection between purpose and desire is the
source of one whole class of moral problems. Attainment of
learning, professional skill, wealth, power, would not be animating purposes unless the thought of some result were unified
with some intense need of the self, for it takes *thought* to convert
an impulse into a desire centered in an object. But on the other
end, a strong craving tends to exclude thought. It is in haste for
its own speedy realization. An intense appetite, say thirst, impels
to immediate action without thought of its consequences, as a
very thirsty man at sea tends to drink salt water without regard
to objective results. Deliberation and inquiry, on the other hand,
take time; they demand delay, the deferring of immediate action.
Craving does not look beyond the moment, but it is of the very
nature of thought to look toward a remote end.

§ 2. Ends and the Good: The Union of Desire and Thought

There is accordingly a conflict brought about within the
self. The impetus of reflection when it is aroused is to look
ahead; to hunt out and to give weight to remoter consequences.
But the force of craving, the impulsion of immediate need, call
thought back to some near-by object in which want will find its

immediate and direct satisfaction. The wavering and conflict which result are the ground for the theory which holds that there is an inherent warfare in the moral life between desire and reason; the theory that appetite and desire tend to delude us with deceptive goods, leading us away from the true end that reason holds up to view. In consequence, some moralists have gone so far as to hold that appetite and impulse are inherently evil, being expressions of the lust of the flesh, a power which pulls men away from the ends which reason approves. This view, however, is impossible. No idea or object could operate as an end and become a purpose unless it were connected with some need; otherwise it would be a mere idea without any moving and impelling power.

In short, while there is conflict, it is not between desire and reason, but between a desire which wants a near-by object and a desire which wants an object which is seen by thought to occur in consequence of an intervening series of conditions, or in the "long run"; it is a conflict between two objects presented in thought, one corresponding to a want or appetite just as it presents itself in isolation, the other corresponding to the want thought of in relation to other wants. Fear may suggest flight or lying to a man as ends to be sought; further thought may bring a man to a conviction that steadfastness and truthfulness will insure a much larger and more enduring good. There is an idea in each case, in the first case, an idea of personal safety, in the second instance, an idea of, say, the safety of others to be achieved by remaining at a post. In each case also there is desire; in the first instance a desire which lies close to natural impulse and instinct; in the second instance, a desire which would not be aroused were it not that *thought* brings into view remote consequences. *In one case, original impulse dictates the thought of the object; in the other case, this original impulse is transformed into a different desire because of objects which thought holds up to view.* But no matter how elaborate and how rational is the object of thought, it is impotent unless it arouses desire.

In other words, there is nothing intrinsically bad about raw impulse and desire. They *become* evil in contrast with another desire whose object includes more inclusive and more enduring consequences. What is morally dangerous in the desire as it first

shows itself is its tendency to confine attention to its own immediate object and to shut out the thought of a larger whole of
conduct.
William James has truly described the situation.

What constitutes the difficulty for a man laboring under an
unwise passion to act as if the passion were unwise? . . . The
difficulty is mental; it is that of getting the idea of the wise
action to stay before the mind at all. Whenever any strong
emotional state is upon us, the tendency is for no images but
those which are congruous with it to come up. If others by
chance offer themselves, they are instantly smothered and
crowded out. . . . By a sort of self-preserving instinct which
our passion has, it feels that these chill objects if they once
but gain a lodgment will work and work till they have frozen
the very vital spark from out of all our mood. Passion's cue
accordingly is always and everywhere to prevent the still
small voice from being heard at all.[1]

The conclusion that the conflict is not between impulse and
want on the one hand, and a rational end on the other, but between two desires and two ends present in thought, agrees with
our practical experience. Sometimes persons who have been subjected to one-sided moral training feel shame and remorse because some malicious or foul idea has come into their minds,
even though they have not acted upon it but have speedily dismissed it. Momentary impulses enter our minds by all sorts of
channels. Unless a person is responsible for having previously
cultivated habits which excite and strengthen them, he has no
ground for moral blame of himself, merely because the idea of a
certain end has "popped into his head." His moral condition depends upon what he does with the idea *after* it has presented itself. That is to say, the real object of moral judgment is a union
between thought and purposeful desire. There is also a temptation to indulge freely in purely imaginative satisfactions of desires known to be unworthy, on the ground that no harm is done
as long as the desires are kept within the realm of fancy and do
not pass into overt conduct. This view of things overlooks the

1. *Principles of Psychology*, Vol. II., pp. 562–563. The entire passage, pp. 561–
569, should be consulted. What is said in Vol. I., pp. 284–290, on the selective
operation of feeling should also be consulted.

fact that giving way to *thoughts* of the pleasurable satisfaction of desires actually strengthens the force of a desire and adds to its power to eventuate in overt action on some future occasion. There can be no separation morally of desire and thought because the union of thought and desire is just what makes an act voluntary.

The same result is reached when we consider inhibition of desire *versus* free surrender to it. There are different kinds of inhibition, and they have very different moral values and consequences. One sort is a deliberate exclusion of the appetite and impulse from the field of thinking and observation; there is then a suppression which simply drives the desire into underground channels. In this case there is no weakening of its power, but only a shift so that it exercises its power indirectly. On the other hand, all thinking exercises by its very nature an inhibitory effect. It delays the operation of desire, and tends to call up new considerations which alter the nature of the action to which one felt originally impelled. This inhibitory action does not consist in smothering or suppressing desire but in transforming a desire into a form which is more intelligent because more cognizant of relations and bearings.

A third confirmation in practical experience is found in the issue of sacrifice *versus* indulgence. Here too we find that the true solution of the problem lies in bringing thought and desire together instead of pitting them against each other. Sometimes sacrifice is made an end in itself. This is equivalent to treating an impulse as evil in and of itself. Sacrifice of this sort ends in maiming life, curtailing power, and narrowing the horizon of opportunities for action. But there is another kind of renunciation which takes place when some end is perceived which is judged to be more worthy, and desire is attached to this better end which thought discloses. No one can have everything he wants; our powers are too limited and our environment too unyielding to permit of any such state of affairs. In consequence we must give up, sacrifice, some objects which desire places before us. Unwillingness to make *any* sacrifice merely indicates immaturity of character, like that of a young child who supposes he can compass all the objects of his heart's desire. Reflection has its normal function in placing the objects of desire in a perspective of relative values, so that when we give up one good we do it because we see another which is of greater worth and which evokes a more inclusive and a more enduring desire. We then escape from that kind of renunciation which Goethe called blasphemous, as well as from that which makes it a good in and of itself. For as Goethe pointed out, renunciation tends to be thoughtless. "We renounce particular things at each moment by sheer levity, if only we can grasp something else the next moment. We merely put one passion in place of another: business, inclinations, amusements, hobbies. We try them all, one after another, only to cry out in the end that 'all is vanity.'" Once more, thoughtful desire is the alternative both to suppression of desire and to yielding to a desire just as it first presents itself.

An understanding of the relationship between the propulsive, urging force of desire and the widening scope of thought enables us to understand what is meant by *will*, especially by the term a "strong will." Sometimes the latter is confused with mere stiff-necked obstinacy—a blind refusal to alter one's purpose no matter what new considerations thinking can produce. Sometimes it is confused with an intense although brief display of spasmodic external energy, even though the forceful manifestation is nothing better than a great ado about nothing. In reality "strength of will" (or, to speak more advisedly, of character) consists of an abiding identification of impulse with thought, in which impulse provides the drive while thought supplies consecutiveness, patience, and persistence, leading to a unified course of conduct. It is not the same as obstinacy because instead of insisting on repetition of the same act, it is observant of changes of conditions and is flexible in making new adjustments. It is *thinking* which is persisted in, even though special ends in view change, while the obstinate person insists upon the same act even when thinking would disclose a wiser course. In the passage quoted, James says that the difficulty in holding to a resolution when a strong passion is upon us is *mental*. It consists in the difficulty of maintaining an idea, in keeping attention alert and continuous. But at the same time, *mere* thinking would not lead to action; thinking must be taken up into vital impulse and desire in order to have body and weight in action.

From the peculiar union of desire and thought in voluntary action, it follows that every moral theory which tries to determine the *end* of conduct has a double aspect. In its relation to *desire*, it requires a theory of the *Good*: the Good is that which satisfies want, craving, which fulfills or makes complete the need which stirs to action. In its relation to *thought*, or as an *idea* of an object to be attained, it imposes upon those about to act the necessity for rational insight, or moral *wisdom*. For experience shows, as we have seen, that not every satisfaction of appetite and craving turns out to be a good; many ends *seem* good while we are under the influence of strong passion which in actual experience and in such thought as might have occurred in a cool moment are actually bad. The task of moral theory is thus to frame a theory of Good as the end or objective of desire, and also to frame a theory of the true, as distinct from the specious, good. In effect this latter need signifies the discovery of ends which will meet the demands of impartial and far-sighted thought as well as satisfy the urgencies of desire.

This double aspect of ends gives a clew to the consideration of the different theories which have been advanced, and also a criterion for judging their worth. A theory may appear, superficially, to offer a conception of the Good that connects it in a satisfactory way with desire and yet fail to provide the conditions which alone would enable the end to afford intelligent direction to conduct. This is especially true of the first theory which we shall now take up.

§ 3. Pleasure as the Good and the End

To many minds it has seemed not only plausible but practically self-evident that what makes any object of desire and of attainment good is the pleasure which it gives to the one who has the experience. We find mankind seeking for many and for diverse objects. But why? What is the common quality which renders all these different things desirable? According to the theory under discussion (called *Hedonism*, from the Greek ἡδονή, signifying pleasure) this common quality is pleasure. The evidence for the theory is asserted to be found in experience itself. Why does and why should any one seek for any object unless he believes it will be enjoyed? Why should any one avoid any object as evil unless he believes its experience will be painful? The words of Bain and of John Stuart Mill are typical. The former said: "There can be no proof offered for the position that Happiness is the proper end of all human procedures. . . . It is an ultimate or final assumption to be tested by reference to the individual judgments of mankind." The latter said: "The only proof capable of being given that an object is visible is that people actually see it. In like manner the sole proof it is possible to produce that any thing is desirable is that people do actually desire it."

Without going into detail at this point, we may anticipate the discussion which follows to the extent of saying that such statements suffer from a fatal ambiguity. Happiness may be the Good and yet happiness not be the same thing as pleasure. Again, the ending "able" has two meanings in different words. It signifies "*capable* of being seen," when it occurs in the word "visible." But in other words, it signifies that which is fit, proper, as in the words "enjoyable," "lovable." "Desirable" signifies not that which is capable of being desired (experience shows that about everything has been desired by some one at some time) but that which in the eye of impartial thought *should* be desired. It is true, of course, that it would be foolish to set up anything as the end of desire, or as desirable, which is not actually desired or capable of being desired. But it would be equally stupid to assume that what *should* be desired can be determined by a mere examination of what men do desire, until a critical examination of the *reasonableness* of things desired has taken place. So there is a distinction between the enjoy*ed* and the enjoy*able*.

We have then to examine the hedonistic theory both as a theory of desire and as a theory of practical wisdom or prudence in the choice of ends to be pursued. The very idea of an *end* implies something more or less distant, remote; it implies the need of looking ahead, of judging. The advice which it gives to desire is: *Respice finem*. Consider how you will come out if you act upon the desire you now feel; count the cost. Calculate consequences over a period of time. Circumspection, prudent estimate of the whole course of consequences set in train, is the precondition of attaining satisfaction or the Good. All folly and stupidity consist in failure to consider the remote, the long run, because of the engrossing and blinding power exercised by some present intense desire.

Our first criticism is devoted to showing that if pleasure be taken as the end, no such cool and far-seeing judgment of consequences as the theory calls for is possible; in other words, it defeats itself. For consequences in the way of pleasures and pains are just the things in the way of consequences which it is most difficult to estimate. The prudent course *is* to consider the end, count the cost, before adopting the course that desire suggests. But pleasures are so externally and accidentally connected with the performance of a deed, that attempt to foresee them is probably the stupidest course which could be taken in order to secure guidance for action. Suppose a man has a desire to visit a sick friend, and tries to determine the good by calculation of pleasures and pains. Suppose he is especially sensitive to the sight of suffering; suppose a disagreeable difference of opinion on some topic comes up in the course of the interview; suppose some bore turns up during the visit:—consider in short the multitude of accidental features of pleasure and pain which are wholly irrelevant to making a wise judgment as to what should be done. An indefinite number of extraneous circumstances affect the pleasures and pains which follow from an act, and have results which are quite foreign to the intrinsic and foreseeable consequences of the act.

We may, however, modify the line of reasoning somewhat, and confine the scope of the theory to pleasures and pains which so intrinsically accompany the nature of an act that they may be calculated. All of us get some pleasure by performing the acts which are congenial to our dispositions; such acts are, by conception, agreeable; they agree with, suit, our own tendencies. An expert in tennis likes to play tennis; an artist likes to paint pictures; a scientific man to investigate; a philosopher to speculate; a benevolent man to do kindly deeds; a brave man seeks out scenes in which endurance and loyalty may be exercised, etc. In such cases, given a certain structure of character and trend of aptitudes, there is an intrinsic basis for foreseeing pleasures and pains, and we may limit the theory to such consequences, excluding purely accidental ones.

But in modifying the theory in this way we have really set up the man's existing character as the criterion. A crafty, unscrupulous man, will get pleasure out of his sheer wiliness. When *he* thinks of an act which would bring pain in the experience of a generous frank person, he will find the thought a source of pleasure, and (so by the theory) a good act to perform. The same sort of thing will be true of the cruel, the dissolute, the malicious, person. The pleasures and pains each will foresee will be those which are in accord with his present character. Imagine two men who momentarily are taken by the idea of a harsh revenge upon a man who has inflicted ill treatment. For the moment both of them will get at least a passing pleasure from the image of the other man as overthrown and suffering. But the one who is kind-hearted will soon find himself pained at the thought of the harm the other man is experiencing; the cruel and revengeful person will glow with more and more pleasure the longer he dwells upon the distress of his enemy—if pleasure be a sign of goodness, the act will indeed be good to him.

There is thus a double misconception in the theory. Unconsciously, it slips in the criterion of the kind of pleasures which would be enjoyed by a man already good; the sort of pleasures which are taken to be normal. Other things being equal, pleasures are certainly a good to be enjoyed, not an evil to be shunned. But the phrase "other things being equal" covers a good deal of ground. One does not think of the pleasures of the dissolute, the dishonest, the mean and stingy, person, but of the pleasure of esthetic enjoyment, of friendship and good companionship, of knowledge, and so on. But there is no denying that characters we morally contemn get actual pleasure from *their* lines of conduct. We may think, and quite properly so, that they *ought* not to, but nevertheless they do. There are certain kinds of happiness which the good man enjoys which the evil-minded man does not—but the reverse is true. And this fact is fatal to the theory that pleasures constitute the good because of which a given object is entitled to be the end of action.

The other misconception consists in confusion of anticipated, prospective pleasure with the enjoyment immediately experienced in the thought of an end. Whenever a future object is thought of as an end, the thought arouses a *present* pleasure or discomfort. And any *present* enjoyment or disagreeableness strengthens or weakens the hold of its particular object upon our attention. It intensifies or reduces the *moving* force of the object thought of. A desire may be inflamed to a practically uncontrollable degree by dwelling upon the pleasures which the imagination of it *now* excites in me. But this increase of the dynamic motive power of the object has nothing to do with judgment, or foresight of the goodness of the consequences which *will* ensue if we take that object to be our end. Indeed, in many cases it is positively hostile to sound judgment of future consequences. The most which can be said is that after a man has judged that some end is good to attain, it is a wise act on his part to foster its pleasurable associations. In this way his resolution will be confirmed against distractions. A student who has decided to spend his evening in study will find his determination weakened if he continually permits his mind to dwell on the enjoyments he might have had by doing something else.

Hazlitt said that "pleasure is that which is so in itself. Good is that which approves itself on reflection, or the *idea* of which is a source of satisfaction. All pleasure is not therefore, morally speaking, equally a good; for all pleasure does not equally bear reflecting upon."

It is true that there is nothing good to us which does not include an element of enjoyment and nothing bad which does not contain an element of the disagreeable and repulsive. Otherwise the act or object is merely indifferent; it is passed by. But the statement that all good has enjoyment as an ingredient is not equivalent to the statement that all pleasure is a good. The quotation from Hazlitt points out the difference. If we judge, we often find that we cannot *approve* an enjoyment. This is not because the pleasure is itself evil but because judgment brings to light relations of the pleasure-giving act and object which we shrink from morally, or are ashamed of. An act appeals to us as pleasurable. If we stop to think we may find that the pleasure is due to something in ourselves which we feel to be unworthy, as to a mean or yellow streak. Or when we judge, we approve the enjoyment; not because it is in its isolation a good, but because upon examination we find that we are willing to stand by the conditions and the effects with which the pleasure is connected. Things give us pleasure because they are agreeable to (agree with or suit) something in our own make-up. When we reflect, we become aware of this connection: thus in the judgment to the moral value of an enjoyment we are really judging our own character and disposition. If you know what sort of things a man finds enjoyable and disagreeable you have a sure clew to his nature—and the principle applies to ourselves as well as to others.

The prudence or insight which constitutes, from the side of the goodness and badness of ends, the chief virtue is thus that which is exercised by an impartial and undisturbed spectator; by a man, not when he is undergoing the urge of a strong desire, but in a moment of calm reflection. In the latter case he judges the desire and its satisfaction as elements in a larger whole of conduct and character. There may well be as much difference in these two attitudes as there is between a man pushed by intense desire to the performance of a criminal act and the judge who passes upon his act. The important truth conveyed by the relation which exists between enjoyment and good is that we should integrate the office of the judge—of reflection—into the formation of our very desires and thus learn to take pleasure in the ends which reflection approves.

The conclusion we have arrived at is that there is important difference in the intrinsic quality of enjoyments, that a pleasure which does not "bear reflecting upon" is different in kind from one which does bear reflecting upon. While most hedonists have held that pleasures are alike, differing only in intensity and duration, John Stuart Mill introduced the idea of difference in quality. He said, "Human beings have faculties more elevated than animal appetites, and when once made conscious of them, do not regard any thing as happiness that does not include their gratification."

> Few human creatures would consent to be changed into any of the lower animals, for a promise of the fullest allowance of a beast's pleasure; no intelligent human being would consent to be a fool, no instructed person would be an ignoramus, no person of feeling and conscience would be selfish and base, even though they should be persuaded that the fool, the dunce or the rascal is better satisfied with his lot than they are with theirs. . . . It is indisputable that the being whose capacities of enjoyment are low has the greatest chance of having them fully satisfied; and a highly endowed being will always feel that any happiness which he can look for, as the world is constituted, is imperfect. . . . It is better to be a human being dissatisfied than a pig satisfied; better to be a Socrates dissatisfied than a fool satisfied. And if the fool or the pig is of a different opinion, it is because he only knows his own side of the question. The other party to the comparison knows both sides.

Such a passage wins ready assent from moral common-sense. Yet its meaning is not wholly clear. There are persons who have "known" both higher and lower enjoyments who still choose the latter; they prefer, we may truly say, to be pigs. It is often easier to be a pig than to judge and act like a Socrates—and Socrates, one may remind oneself, came to death as a consequence of his "wisdom." In order that Mill's statement may be acceptable we must include *understanding* as part of the meaning of "knowing." In isolation, one enjoyment cannot be said to be higher or lower than another. There is nothing intrinsically higher in the enjoyment of a picture or an instructive book than there is in that of food—that is, when the satisfaction is taken apart from the bearings and relationships of the object in life as a connected whole. There are times when the satisfaction of hunger takes precedence of other satisfactions; it is at that time—for the time being—"higher." We conclude that the truth contained in Mill's statement is not that one "faculty" is inherently higher than another, but that a satisfaction which is seen, by reflection based on large experience, to unify in a harmonious way his whole system of desires is higher in quality than a good which is such only in relation to a particular want in isolation. The entire implication of Mill's statement is that the satisfaction of the whole self in any end and object is a very different *sort* of thing from the satisfaction of a single and independent appetite. It is doing no violence to ordinary speech to say that the former kind of satisfaction is denoted by the term "happiness," and the latter kind by the term "pleasure," so that Mill's argument points not so much to a different quality in different pleasures, as it does to a difference in quality between an enduring satisfaction of the whole self and a transient satisfaction of some isolated element in the self.

We therefore not only may but must, in accordance with facts, make a distinction between pleasures and happiness, well-being, what Aristotle called *eudaimonia*. There is no such thing strictly speaking as *a* pleasure; pleasure is pleasant*ness*, an abstract noun designating objects that are pleasant, agreeable. And any state of affairs is pleasant or agreeable which is congenial to the existing state of a person whatever that may be.

What is agreeable at one time disagrees at another; what pleases in health is distasteful in fatigue or illness; what annoys or disgusts in a state of repletion is gratifying when one is hungry and eager. And on a higher scale, that which is pleasant to a man of generous disposition arouses aversion in a mean and stingy person. What is pleasant to a child may bore an adult; the objects that gratify a scholar are repulsive to a boor. Pleasantness and unpleasantness are accordingly signs and symptoms of the things which at a particular time are congenial to a particular make-up of the organism and character. And there is nothing in a symptom of the quality of an existing character which fits it to be a desirable end, however much it may serve as a guide or a warning.

There is something accidental in the merely agreeable and gratifying. They *happen* to us. A man may get pleasure by finding a sum of money on the street, eating a good dinner, running unexpectedly across an old friend. Or a man stumbles and falls, hurts himself and suffers pain; or, through no fault of his own he experiences an intensely disagreeable disappointment. It would be absurd to attribute goodness or badness in any moral sense to these things which have no intrinsic connection with deliberate action. There is nothing more productive of suffering than the loss of a dear friend, but no one thinks of the man who suffers the loss as thereby injured in character. A "lucky" man experiences pleasant objects to an unusual degree, but he may only be rendered obtuse, thoughtless and conceited because of that fact.

Happiness, on the contrary, is a stable condition, because it is dependent not upon what transiently happens to us but upon the standing disposition of the self. One may find happiness in the midst of annoyances; be contented and cheerful in spite of a succession of disagreeable experiences, if one has braveness and equanimity of soul. Agreeableness depends upon the way a particular event touches us; it tends to focus attention on the self, so that a love of pleasures as such tends to render one selfish or greedy. Happiness is a matter of the disposition we actively bring with us to meet situations, the qualities of mind and heart with which we greet and interpret situations. Even so it is not directly an *end* of desire and effort, in the sense of an end-in-view purposely sought for, but is rather an end-product, a necessary accompaniment, of the character which is interested in objects that are enduring and intrinsically related to an outgoing and expansive nature. As George Eliot remarked in her novel,

Romola, "It is only a poor sort of happiness that could ever come by caring very much about our own narrow pleasures. We can only have the highest happiness, such as goes along with being a great man, by having wide thought and much feeling for the rest of the world as well as ourselves; and this sort of happiness often brings so much pain with it, that we can only tell it from pain by its being what we would choose before everything else, because our souls see it is good."[2]

Happiness as distinct from pleasure is a condition of the self. There is a difference between a tranquil pleasure and tranquillity of mind; there is contentment with external circumstances because they cater to our immediate enjoyment, and there is contentment of character and spirit which is maintained in adverse circumstances. A criterion can be given for marking off mere transient gratification from true happiness. The latter issues from objects which are enjoyable in themselves but which also reenforce and enlarge the other desires and tendencies which are sources of happiness; in a pleasure there is no such harmonizing and expanding tendency. There are powers within us whose exercise creates and strengthens objects that are enduring and stable while it excludes objects which occasion those merely transient gratifications that produce restlessness and peevishness. Harmony and readiness to expand into union with other values is a mark of happiness. Isolation and liability to conflict and interference are marks of those states which are exhausted in being pleasurable.

§ 4. The Epicurean Theory of Good and Wisdom

We now pass on to another theory of the proper end of desire and thought—that known as the Epicurean. The versions we have been dealing with are occupied with *future* ends, the thought of which should regulate present desire and effort. But future enjoyments and sufferings are notoriously uncertain. They

2. That "happiness," so conceived, forms a *standard of judgment* rather than an *end of desire* is a fact which is taken up in the Chapter on Approbation. See pp. 245–248.

are contingent upon all sorts of external circumstances, of which even the most fundamental, the persistence of life itself, is highly precarious. Reflection upon the vicissitudes of life led therefore some observers to regard solicitude for the future as a source of worry and anxiety, rather than as a condition of attaining the good. There is no wisdom in finding good in what is exposed to circumstances beyond our control; such conduct is rather a manifestation of folly. The part of wisdom is then to cultivate the present moment as it passes, to extract from it all the enjoyment which it is capable of yielding. *Carpe diem.* The idea is poetically expressed in the lines of Edna St. Vincent Millay:

> I burn my candle at both ends,
> It will not last the night;
> But ah, my foes, and oh, my friends
> It gives a lovely light—

It is grossly expressed in the saying "Eat, drink and be merry, for tomorrow we die."

There is nevertheless on this theory great difference between a thoughtless grasping at the pleasures of the moment, and a reflectively regulated procedure. Experience teaches that some enjoyments are extremely fleeting and are also likely to be followed by reactions of discomfort and suffering. Such is the case with all extreme and violent pleasures. Indulgence in intense pleasure rarely pays; it is a liability rather than an asset. For experience shows that such a pleasure usually plunges us into situations that are attended with inconvenience and suffering. Those enjoyments which turn out to be *good* are calm and equable pleasures; experience discloses that these spring from intellectual and esthetic sources which, being within us, are within our control. Pleasures of the appetites, like sex, may be more intense, but they are not so enduring nor so likely to give rise to future occasions of enjoyment as those which come from books, friendship, the fostering of esthetic delight. Our senses and appetites are concerned with external things, and hence commit us to situations we cannot control. Of the delights of the senses, however, those of the eye and ear are better worth cultivating than those of taste and smell. For the former are more closely associated with intellectual pleasures, and also with conditions more common, more widely spread, in nature. Enjoyment of sunlight, moving waters, fresh air, is tranquil and easily obtainable. To entrust one's gratifications to objects of luxury is to commit one's self to troublesome search and probable disappointment. The simple life is the good life because it is the one most assured of present enjoyment. Private friendship is better than public life. For friends gather together naturally and foster harmony. To engage in public life is to put one's fortunes at the disposal of things beyond control, and to involve oneself in violent changes or at least continual vicissitudes.

This theory constitutes Epicureanism in its original form—a doctrine far removed from that surrender to voluptuous pleasures often associated with the name. Its maxim is to cherish those elements of enjoyment in the present which are most assured, and to avoid entanglement in external circumstances. This emphasis upon the conditions of security of *present* enjoyment is at once the strong and the weak point in the Epicurean doctrine.

The theory avoids the difficulties about foresight and calculation of future pleasures and pains which nullify the type of theory previously considered. It is a matter of experience, personal and social, that gentle and equable enjoyment is safer and more lasting than the vehement gratifications of excessive excitement. The person cultivated in books, intellectual pursuits, apt in friendly companionship, has sources of satisfaction more wholly within himself than has the person given to sensual pleasures or to the pursuit of money and fame. There is obviously sound sense in the maxim as far as it goes. The lesson is particularly needed in periods of bustle, hurry, and luxury, when men are carried away by interest in external and passing things, preoccupied with the material consequences of machinery and business and lose possession of themselves.

On the other hand, the doctrine is fundamentally one of withdrawal and restriction, even if it take the form of a high intellectual "disinterestedness," aloof from the ado and mêlée of practical affairs. If it were possible to isolate the present from the future, perhaps no better working rule for attaining happiness could be found. But the quality of selfish engrossment in one's own enjoyment which seems to cling to the doctrine is a necessary product of the attempt to exclude concern for the future. The doctrine is, ultimately, one of seclusion and passivity. It not only omits the enjoyment which comes from struggle against adverse conditions, with effort to achieve the difficult, but it is a doctrine of retreat from the scene of struggle in which the mass of men are perforce engaged. It is a doctrine which can appeal only to those who are already advantageously situated. It presupposes that there are others who are doing the hard, rough work of the world, so that the few can live a life of tranquil refinement. It is selfish because of what it excludes. It is a doctrine which will always flourish, though probably under some other name than Epicureanism, when social conditions are troubled and harsh, so that men of cultivation tend to withdraw into themselves and devote themselves to intellectual and esthetic refinement.

§ 5. Success as the End

A third variant of the theory that the chief moral demand is for wisdom in choice of ends is the doctrine of "success," understood in the sense of enlightened self-interest. This theory is not committed to any particular doctrine about pleasures and pains, and has rarely been formulated with the intellectual precision of the other principles. But it is widely acted upon in practice. It is hinted at in the saying that "honesty is the best policy." It tends to prevail in what are called practical affairs; business, politics, administration, wherever achievement and failure can be measured in terms of external power, repute, making money, and attainment of social status. The doctrine puts a high estimate on efficiency, on getting things done; it admires thrift, shrewdness, industriousness, and condemns laziness and stupidity. It is suspicious of art, save as an embellishment of practical success, and is distrustful of distinctively intellectual pursuits save when they bear tangible practical fruit.

In spite of the fact that moralists generally take a disparaging attitude toward this view of life, there is something to be said for it. Enlightened self-interest, planning and calculation for success, do not seem to rank very high as motives. But when one considers the amount of harm done by sheer ignorance, folly, carelessness, by surrender to momentary whim and impulse, one may safely conclude that the state of things would be better than it is if more persons were moved by intelligent interest in external achievement. And when we consider how much that has prided itself upon being moral has been content with mere "meaning well," with good intentions (which according to the saying help to "pave hell"), that are devoid of energy in action and efficiency in execution, one cannot withhold a modicum of respect for a doctrine that lays stress upon accomplishment, even if its standard of accomplishment is not high. Moreover there are comparatively few who can afford to despise reference to success in achievement. Students, engineers, professional men are likely to be steadied in their callings by regard for success. The maxim of prudence, interpreted to signify expediency in respect to achievement, at least tends to hold men to their work, and to protect them from distraction and waste of time and energy.

When all allowances are made, however, the defects of the doctrine are sufficiently obvious. It hardly rises above the more external aspects of life; it encourages the idea of "rising," of "getting on," of "making a go," while it accepts without question current estimates of what these things consist in. It does not criticize the scheme of values which happens to be current, say, in an age when men are devoted to pecuniary gain. It encourages conceiving of gain and loss in tangible material terms. The idea of success in the general sense of *achievement* is a necessary part of all morality that is not futile and confined to mere states of inner feeling. But the theory in question commits itself to a superficial, conventional, and unexamined conception of what constitutes achievement. It pins its faith to certain values at the expense of others more human and more significant. Morality must be "worldly" enough to take account of the fact that we live in a world where things have to be done. But that does not signify that achievement should be understood in a worldly-minded way.

§ 6. Asceticism as the End

Another interpretation of the nature of wisdom in the formation of ends and judgment of the good was put forth in Greece by the Cynic school. As we have seen the great problem concerning ends is to discriminate between those which are "good" in a near-by and partial view, and those which are enduringly and inclusively good. The former are more obvious; the latter depend upon the exercise of reflection and often can be discovered and sustained in thought only by reflection which is patient and thorough. Even so, it is notorious that things which are simply *judged* to be good are pallid and without power to move us compared with warmer and nearer goods which make a direct appeal to those impulses and desires that are already urgent. Hence, the Cynic school thought it the part of moral wisdom to treat practical exercises which form stable habits as the important thing. Artisans and craftsmen are skilful and persistent in pursuit of aims not in virtue of reflection and theory, but because of habits formed by exercise. Why not carry the principle over into morals generally? The great thing is to attain command over immediate appetite and desire. Thinking is comparatively impotent in giving this command; trained habit is potent. The moral maxim is then to *practice* the right act till habit is firm.

In the precise form in which the theory was advanced by the Cynic school it has not had great influence. But the underlying conception that wisdom consists in subjection and discipline of desire, and that this subordination is obtained by deliberate exercise rather than by reflection, has become an important part of all those moral ideas which have a Puritanical color. In the extreme form, the principle is called Asceticism (from the Greek, ἄσκησις, exercise, discipline). Popularly, the view is presumed to be opposed to the very idea of happiness and satisfaction. It does look with suspicion upon all ordinary forms of gratification as morally dangerous. But it does so in the interest of a final satisfaction of a different type—as a martyr endures suffering in this world in the hope of eternal happiness in another world, or if not that, then because of the satisfaction he obtains through being faithful to his principles. Ordinary pleasures are deceptive; they mislead judgment and action. Their deceptive quality is what stands between us and the wisdom that lays hold of the true good. The pleasures of ordinary desire are so strong that the latter have to be subdued if we are to be loyal to real satisfaction. The way to subdue them is to engage systematically in exercises which are naturally uncongenial; then we harden ourselves to pain and steel ourselves against the seductions of desire. Repeated exercise moreover weakens the intensity of desire.

John Locke was no ascetic. Yet there is an ascetic element contained in his statement that "It seems plain to me that the principle of all virtue and excellency lies in a power of denying ourselves the satisfaction of our desires when reason does not authorise them." And he goes on to add, "This power is got by custom, made easy and familiar by an early practice. If therefore I might be heard I would urge that contrary to the ordinary way, children should be used to submit their desires and go without their longings even from their very cradles."[3] Nor was William James an ascetic. Yet in his discussion of Habit he says, "Keep the faculty of effort alive in yourself by a little gratuitous exercise every day. That is, be systematically ascetic or heroic in unnecessary points. Do every day or two something for no other reason than that you would rather not do it, so that when the hour of dire need draws nigh it may not find you unnerved and untrained to stand the test."[4]

It is impossible not to recognize an element of truth in such advice. Ends contemplated only in thought are weak in comparison with the urgencies of passion. Our reflective judgment of the good needs an ally outside of reflection. Habit is such an ally. And habits are not maintained save by exercise; they are not self-generated. They are produced only by a course of action which is persisted in, and the required persistence cannot be left to chance. It is not necessary to go to the extreme of ascetic doctrine and hold that there is something inherently beneficial in enduring pain and suppressing enjoyment. But it is a fact that some degree of unpleasantness is almost sure to attend the first performance of deeds that are done for the sake of forming a strong habit. "Discipline" is proverbially hard to undergo.

The criticism of this theory is in principle similar to that directed against both Epicureanism and the doctrine of successful policy. There is an element of truth in the idea that exercise is necessary to form habits strong enough to resist the solicitations of passion. But as in the case of cultivating immediate gentle pleasures and of aiming at achievement, this element of truth should be stated positively, not negatively. Instead of making the subjugation of desire an end in itself, it should be treated as a

3. *Of Education*, sec. 38.
4. *Principles of Psychology*, I., p. 125.

necessary function in the development of a desire which will bring about a more inclusive and enduring good. Few indeed at present go to the extremes of the early ascetics who looked with suspicion upon the family, state, art, and science since these may cater to sexual appetite, earthly ambition for power, or indulge the lust of the eye and the pride of intellect. But professed moralists still sometimes repel others, especially the young, from all morals by identifying morality with the negative for the sake of the negative, with restraint as itself an end.

There is not much danger in most circles in modern society that the ascetic principle will be taken seriously; there is, however, a real danger that it will affect the teaching of morals in some quarters to such a degree as to throw those taught over to the opposite extreme, and thus instigate them to take up with the doctrine that all inhibition is dangerous, and that every impulse should be "expressed" and every desire indulged. What is dangerous is not inhibition but those methods of trying to accomplish it which do not in fact inhibit or control, but which merely cover the desire up from consciousness, force it below observation and thought, and thus encourage it to work in indirect and morbid channels. All thought involves inhibition, if only that of delay until the worth of a desire has been inquired into; usually it involves a further control in which the original desire is subordinated by being taken up into a larger purpose.

The error of the ascetic and the "free-expression" theories is the same. It is the failure to see that the negative element of restraint is valuable as a factor in the formation of a *new* end and the construction of a new good. The important thing is the realization of this new good, something to be attained by positive means not by sheer endeavor to stamp out contrary impulses. The larger good when dwelt upon alone has the power to attenuate the force of opposed tendencies. The real danger lies in dallying, in toying, with the immediately urgent impulse, postponing decisive action in behalf of the approved end. As James says, "No matter how full a reservoir of maxims one may possess . . . if one has not taken advantage of every concrete opportunity to *act*, one's character may remain entirely unaffected for the better. . . . Let the expression be the least thing in the world— speaking genially to one's aunt, or giving up one's seat in a horse-car, if nothing more heroic offers—but let it not fail to take place." What Milton calls "fugitive and cloistered virtue" is fugitive because it is cloistered, because it is not decisively acted upon when the occasion presents itself. Genuine power is gained not by exercises performed for their own sake, especially not by acts of mere repression, but by exercise in the fields where power is positively needed in order to accomplish results.

In its extreme and logical form the conception of ends which dominates the theory under discussion has no great present vogue. Discussion of it is still important, however, because its underlying idea is perpetuated in the tendency to regard morals as a set of special and separate dispositions. Moral goodness is quite commonly divided off from interest in all the objects which make life fuller, and is confined to a narrow set of aims, which are prized too often merely because they involve inhibition and repression. Experience shows that the effect of this attitude is to keep attention fixed upon the things which are thought to be evil. The mind becomes obsessed with guilt and how to avoid it. In consequence, a sour and morose disposition is fostered. An individual affected in this way is given to condemnation of others and to looking for evil in them. The generosity of mind which is rooted in faith in human nature is stifled. Meanwhile, the positive interest in ends which is the source of abundant power grows weak. Normally, discipline comes about as a fruit of steady devotion to ends that are of positive value. The person thoroughly interested in an end—whether it be that of an art or a profession or calling—will endure hardship and repellant conditions because they are incidents of the pursuit of what is good. He will find in the course of his pursuit sufficient opportunity for exercise of the harder virtues. The man who can make a sport out of his endeavor to break a bad habit will succeed, while failure will await the person who concentrates his effort upon the negative idea of mere abstinence. There is a contrast between the natural goods—those which appeal to immediate desire—and the moral good, that which is approved after reflection. But the difference is not absolute and inherent. The moral good is some natural good which is sustained and developed through consideration of it in its relations; the natural enjoyment which conflicts with the moral good is that which accompanies some desire which persists because it is allowed to sway action by itself, apart from the connections which reflection would bring to light.

§ 7. Conclusion: Cultivation of Interests as the End

We have seen that the idea of Ends and the Good is the counterpart of the *intellectual* aspect of character and conduct. The difficulty in the way of attaining and maintaining practical wisdom is the urgency of immediate impulse and desire which swell and swell until they crowd out all thought of remote and comprehensive goods. The conflict is a real one and is at the heart of many of our serious moral struggles and lapses. In the main, solution is found in utilizing all possible occasions, when we are not in the presence of conflicting desires, to cultivate interest in those goods which we do approve in our calm moments of reflection. John Stuart Mill remarked that "the cultivated mind . . . finds sources of inexhaustible interest in all that surrounds it; in the objects of nature, the achievements of art, the imaginations of poetry, the incidents of history, the ways of mankind, past, present and their prospects in the future." There are many times when the cultivation of these interests meets with no strong obstacle. The habits which are built up and reenforced under such conditions are the best bulwarks against weakness and surrender in the moments when the reflective or "true" good conflicts with that set up by temporary and intense desire. The proper course of action is, then, to multiply occasions for the enjoyment of these ends, to prolong and deepen the experiences connected with them. Morality then becomes positive instead of a struggle carried against the seductive force of lesser goods. This course of action gives no guarantee against occurrence of situations of conflict and of possible failure to maintain the greater good. But *reflective* attachment to the ends which reason presents is enormously increased when these ends have themselves been, on earlier occasions, *natural* goods enjoyed in the normal course of life. Ideal ends, those sustained by thought, do not lose their ideal character when they are directly appreciated; in the degree in which they become objects of positive interest their power to control and move conduct in times of stress is reenforced.

This fact brings out the common element found in the criticism of the various points of view discussed in this chapter. The truth hinted at in the hedonistic view of moral wisdom, (that it consists in foresight and calculation of future enjoyments and sufferings) is that *present* enjoyment may accompany the thought of remote objects when they are held before the mind. Its error lies in supposing that in reflection our ideas go out to future pleasures instead of to future objects. A man in order to cultivate good health does not think of the pleasures it will bring to him: in thinking of the various objects and acts which will follow from good health he experiences a *present* enjoyment, and this enjoyment strengthens his effort to attain it. As Plato and Aristotle said over two thousand years ago, the aim of moral education is to develop a character which finds pleasure in right objects and pain in wrong ends.

Something similar is to be said of wisdom or prudence viewed as a judgment of ends which are expedient or that mark "good policy." As far as the maxim emphasizes means and conditions that are necessary to achievement, thus taking morals out of the region of sentimental vaporing and fantasies, miscalled idealism, the principle is sound. Error lies in restriction of the domains of value in which achievement is desirable. It is folly rather than wisdom to include in the concept of success only tangible material goods and to exclude those of culture, art, science, sympathetic relations with others. Once a man has experienced certain kinds of good in a concrete and intimate way, he would rather fail in external achievement than forego striving for them. The zest of endeavor is itself an enjoyment to be fostered, and life is poor without it. As John Stuart Mill said "some things called expedient are not useful but in reality are one branch of the harmful." To due reflection, things sometimes regarded as "practical" are in truth highly impolitic and shortsighted. But the way to eliminate preference for narrow and shortsighted expediences is not to condemn the practical as low and mercenary in comparison with spiritual ideals, but to cultivate all possible opportunities for the actual enjoyment of the reflective values and to engage in the activity, the practice, which extends their scope.

The morally wise, accordingly, appreciate the necessity of doing, of "exercise." They realize the importance of habit as a protection against beguilement by the goods proposed by immediate desire and urgent passion. But they also apprehend that abstinence for the sake of abstinence, mortification of the flesh for the sake of mortification, is not a rational end. The important ally to doing is sense of power, and this sense of power is the accompaniment of progress in actual achievement of a positive good. Next, if not equal in importance (in some temperaments, superior), is the esthetic factor. A golfer or tennis player may enjoy his exercises because he appreciates the value of "form." Emerson speaks of the *elegance* of abstinence. Moderation is the associate of proportion, and there is no art without measure. The restraint that ensues from a sense of the fitness of proportion is very different in quality from that which is exercised for its own sake. To find excess disgusting is more efficacious than finding it wrong although attractive.

Finally, the underlying truth of what is called Epicureanism contains an element upon which we have insisted: the importance of nurturing the *present* enjoyment of things worth while, instead of sacrificing present value to an unknown and uncertain future. If this course is popularly thought of as mere self-indulgence, as selfish and destructive of consecutive striving for remote ends, it is because emphasis is laid upon the bare fact of enjoyment instead of upon the *values* enjoyed. Here as with the other principles discussed, the conclusion is the need of fostering at every opportunity direct enjoyment of the kind of goods reflection approves. To deny direct satisfaction any place in morals is simply to weaken the moving force of the goods approved by thought.

Our discussion has centered on the goods which approve themselves to the thoughtful, or morally "wise," person in their relation to the satisfactions which suggest themselves because of immediate and intense desire, impulse, and appetite. The office of reflection we have seen to be the formation of a judgment of value in which particular satisfactions are placed as integral parts of conduct as a consistent harmonious whole. If values did not get in one another's way, if, that is, the realization of one desire were not incompatible with that of another, there would be no need of reflection. We should grasp and enjoy each thing as it comes along. Wisdom, or as it is called on the ordinary plane, prudence, sound judgment, is the ability to foresee consequences in such a way that we form ends which grow into one another and reenforce one another. Moral folly is the surrender of the greater good for the lesser; it is snatching at one satisfaction in a way which prevents us from having others and which gets us subsequently into trouble and dissatisfaction.

Up to this point we have passed over the social conditions which affect the development of wise and prudent attitudes of mind. But it is clear that the education which one receives, not so much the formal schooling as the influence of the traditions and institutions of the community in which one lives, and the habits of one's associates, are a profound influence. The simplest illustration is that of a spoiled child. The person who is encouraged to yield to every desire as it arises, the one who receives constantly the help of others in getting what he wants when he wants it, will have to possess extraordinary intellectual powers if he develops a habit of reflective valuation. What is true on this personal scale is true on a wide social scale. The general social order may be such as to put a premium upon the kind of satisfaction which is coarse, gross, "materialistic," and upon attitudes which are in impatient haste to grab any seeming near-by good. This state of affairs is characteristic of many phases of American life today. Love of power over others, of display and luxury, of pecuniary wealth, is fostered by our economic régime. Goods that are more ideal, esthetic, intellectual values, those of friendship which is more than a superficial comradeship, are forced into subordination. The need of fostering the reflective and contemplative attitudes of character is therefore the greater. Above all, there is the need to remake social conditions so that they will almost automatically support fuller and more enduring values and will reduce those social habits which favor the free play of impulse unordered by thought, or which make men satisfied to fall into mere routine and convention. The great bulwark of wisdom in judging values is a just and noble social order. Said Santayana,

> Could a better system prevail in our lives a better order
> would establish itself in our thinking. It has not been for
> want of keen senses, or personal genius, or a constant order
> in the outer world, that mankind have fallen back repeatedly
> into barbarism and superstition. It has been for want of good
> character, good example, and good government. There is a
> pathetic capacity in men to live nobly if only they would give

one another the chance. The ideal of political perfection, vague and remote as it yet is, is certainly approachable, for it is as definite and constant as human nature.[5]

In conclusion, we point out that the discussion enables us to give an empirically verifiable meaning to the conception of *ideal* values in contrast with *material* values. The distinction is one between goods which, when they present themselves to imagination, are approved by reflection after wide examination of their relations, and the goods which are such only because their wider connections are not looked into. We cannot draw up a catalogue and say that such and such goods are intrinsically and always ideal, and such and such other ones inherently base because material. There are circumstances under which enjoyment of a value called spiritual because it is associated with religion is mere indulgence; when its good, in other words, becomes one of mere sensuous emotion. There are occasions when attention to the material environment constitutes the ideal good because that is the act which thoroughgoing inquiry would approve. In a general way, of course, we can safely point out that certain goods are ideal in character: those of art, science, culture, interchange of knowledge and ideas, etc. But that is because past experience has shown that they are the *kind* of values which are likely to be approved upon searching reflection. Hence a *presumption* exists in their favor, but in concrete cases only a presumption. To suppose that the higher ideal value inheres in them *per se* would result in fostering the life of a dilettante and mere esthete, and would relegate all goods experienced in the natural course of life to a nonmoral or anti-moral plane. There is in fact a place and time—that is, there are relationships—in which the satisfactions of the normal appetites, usually called physical and sensuous, have an ideal quality. Were it not so, some form of asceticism would be the only moral course. The business of reflection in determining the true good cannot be done once for all, as, for instance, making out a table of values arranged in a hierarchical order of higher and lower. It needs to be done, and done over and over and over again, in terms of the conditions of concrete situations as they arise. In short, the need for reflection and insight is perpetually recurring.

5. *Reason in Science*, p. 320.

Literature

Regarding the GOOD AND HAPPINESS, see Aristotle, *Ethics*, trans. by Peters, 1884, Book I. and Book X., chs. vi.–ix.; Paulsen, *System of Ethics*, 1899, pp. 268–286; Rickaby, *Aquinas Ethicus*, Vol. I., pp. 6–39; Rashdall, *The Theory of Good and Evil*, 1907; Eaton, *The Austrian Philosophy of Values*, 1930, ch. iv.; Perry, *The Moral Economy*, 1909, and *General Theory of Value*, 1926, especially chs. i.–iv., xx., xxi.; Hastings' *Encyclopaedia of Religion and Ethics*, 1922, article on Summum Bonum by Shorey; Hobhouse, *The Rational Good*, 1921; Russell, *The Right to Be Happy*, 1927; Sturt, *Human Value*, 1923; Palmer, *The Nature of Goodness*, 1903; Sharp, *Ethics*, 1928, Book II. on the Good, and chs. xxii. and xxiii. on Self-sacrifice; references on Happiness in III. of Baldwin's *Dictionary of Philosophy and Psychology*, 1905.

Regarding HEDONISM, see for historical material, Watson, *Hedonistic Theories from Aristippus to Spencer*, 1895; Wallace, *Epicureanism*; Pater, *Marius the Epicurean*; Sidgwick, *History of Ethics*, chs. ii. and iv. For criticism and exposition of Hedonism, see Green, *Prolegomena to Ethics*, 1890, pp. 163–167, 226–240, 374–388; James, *Principles of Psychology*, 1890, II., pp. 549–559; Sidgwick, *Methods of Ethics*, 1901, pp. 34–47, Book II. and chs. xiii. and xiv. of Book III.; Bain, *Emotions and Will*, Part II., ch. viii.; Calkins, *The Good Man and the Good*, 1918, ch. v.; Everett, *Moral Values*, 1918, ch. iii.; Stapledon, *A Modern Theory of Ethics*, 1929, ch. iv.

An effective statement of the truth in EPICUREANISM is found in Fite, *Moral Philosophy*, 1925, ch. xiii. For asceticism, see Lecky, *History of European Morals*, 3rd ed., 1916; Lippmann, *A Preface to Morals*, 1929, ch. ix. For the ethics of success, see Plato, *Gorgias* and Book I. of the *Republic*; Sumner, *Folkways*, 1907, ch. xx.; Nietzsche, *The Will to Power*.

12.   Right, Duty, and Loyalty

§ 1. The Idea of the Right

The theories discussed in the last chapter differ among themselves. But they agree in regarding Good as the central fact in morals and in believing the great problem of morals to be determination of those ends of desire and action which are truly or rationally good. There are, however, factors in morality which seem to be independent of any form of satisfaction. Children, for example, are constantly told to do right because it is right. Adults find themselves under obligations which are imperative and which nevertheless prevent the satisfaction of their desires. We find ourselves subject to authority, under law, bearers of responsibilities which we did not choose and which we must meet. There is a strain of authority and obligation in morality which is not, on its face at least, reducible to the conception of the good as satisfaction, even reasonable satisfaction, of desire. On a large scale, we are taught that the claims of law are superior to the solicitations of desire, and that it is an immoral principle, that of selfishness, which leads us to put happiness ahead of loyalty to these claims.

Since these factors are so prominent in conduct, there is, as we might expect, a type of theory which centres in them. Upholders of this type do not exclude reference to the Good, but they give Good a radically different meaning from the theories previously considered. They admit the existence of *a* good which consists in the satisfaction of desires, but they regard this as a non-moral good; in extreme forms of the theory as even an *anti*-moral satisfaction. The moral Good, according to them, is that which is Right, that which accords with law and the commands of duty. Men *ought* to find satisfaction in heeding the dictates of the right. But such satisfaction is different in kind from that which springs from gratification of natural impulses and affections.

The conflict between the good and the right is acutely apparent in the cases in which social demands run counter to desire. A child wants to run on the grass; he is told that the lawn belongs to another and that he must not trespass. Flowers attract his notice and he wishes to pick them. He is told that they are the property of another, and that he must not steal. Such instances are of daily occurrence. The institutions and legal regulations of the community stand over against the wishes and satisfactions of an individual, imposing injunctions and bans upon him.

In everyday experience, this conflict between law and the duties it imposes occasions more conflicts than proceed from the disparity between the good of immediate craving and the good determined by reflection, such as was discussed in the last chapter. Obedience to parents and teachers is, for example, constantly demanded of the young. They find themselves under authority, personal, and that of rules. The principles of morality come home to them, not so much as the purposes and aims which wise foresight sets forth, as prohibitions and injunctions which claim authority in the name of right, law, and duty. The morally good to them is what is permissible, allowed, *licit*; the morally bad is that which is forbidden, illegitimate. The dominant aim and purpose which morals sets up is to obey rules, to respect authority, to be loyal to the right.

Now theorists who uphold the primacy of the concept of Ends, Good, and Insight, may reasonably object to this type of morals in its cruder forms; they may contend that it has no place in reflective morals, since it represents simply the power given by custom to some persons to direct the conduct of others. We shall assume without argument that the retort is valid against much of the use which is currently made of authority and obedience. But the underlying principle cannot be so readily disposed of. It is asserted by some that "right" signifies merely the road or path which leads to good.

Its authority is said to be borrowed from the good which the right course serves. Or it is asserted that the conflict is not between good and right, but between the lesser and the greater good, since laws represent a social good which is superior to private good, so that the problem is one of making persons see that the social good is their *own true* good. The first version, that the right is the way to the good, is in agreement with forms of speech which identify the right with the proper and suitable; we have to use means to attain ends, and some means are adapted to the end and others are not. The first are proper, fit, right; the second are wrong, improper, unsuitable. The other version of the primacy of Good emphasizes the fact that all human experience shows the inability of individuals to judge what is good without the experience of mankind embodied in laws and institutions. The experience of the individual is narrow; that of the race is wide. Laws in the main express the sober and considered judgment of the community as to what is really good for individuals; the authority of law is on this basis the authority of comprehensive and reflectively approved good.

Regarding the notion that the right is the means to the good, it may be said that it is certainly *desirable* that acts which are deemed right should in fact be contributory to good. But this consideration does not do away with the fact that the *concept of Rightness*, in many cases, is independent of the concept of satisfaction and good. When a parent says "this is right and therefore you should do it," it is to be hoped that the performance of the act will actually conduce to some good. But as an idea, "right" introduces an element which is quite outside that of the good. This element is that of *exaction, demand*. A direct road means the straight, the best, course; but it also signifies the regulated and ordered course. A person may admit, intellectually, that a certain act is foolish, in that it involves a sacrifice of a greater ultimate good to a lesser near-by one. But he may then ask: why not be foolish if I want to be? The idea of wrong introduces an independent factor: that the act is from the standpoint of moral authority a refusal to meet a legitimate demand. There has to be an idea of the authoritative claim of what is reasonable in order to convert the Good into the Right.

Much the same thing is to be said when it is urged that the seeming conflict is between the social good and the private good, or between a large and comprehensive good and a smaller good, where it is reasonable to choose the greater satisfaction instead of the lesser. The real difficulty is that the person involved in the conflict does not realize that the social good is a good, in any sense, for *him*. In order that he may do so, he must first recognize it as having an independent and authoritative claim upon his attention. The Good is that which attracts; the Right is that which asserts that we *ought* to be drawn by some object whether we are naturally attracted to it or not.

A type of theory, contrasting with that based upon desire and satisfaction, reverses, accordingly, the order of ideas characteristic of the latter. It often makes much, for example, of Reason and Rational Ideas. But the significance attached to the terms in the two theories differs radically. "Reason" is now thought of not as intelligent insight into complete and remote consequences of desire, but as a power which is opposed to desire and which imposes restrictions on its exercise through issuing commands. Moral judgment ceases to be an exercise of prudence and circumspection and becomes a faculty, usually termed conscience, which makes us aware of the Right and the claims of duty. Many theories of this type have not been content to proclaim that the concept of the Right is independent of that of Good, but have asserted that the Right as the Moral Good is something completely isolated from all natural desires and satisfactions. They fall, accordingly, under the strictures already passed (p. 207) on conceptions which divide conduct into two isolated spheres, one moral and one not, and which look with suspicion upon all the natural affections and impulses. Our discussion will accordingly be directed to showing that it is possible to maintain the distinctness of the concept of right without separating it from the ends and the values which spring from those desires and affections that belong inherently to human nature.

§ 2. The Origin of Moral Claims

Can we find a place for the moral authority of the demands to which we are subject, a place which is distinct, on the one hand, from mere coercion, from physical and mental pressure, and which, on the other hand, does not set up a law of duty and right that has nothing to do with the natural desires and tendencies of our human constitution? Such is the problem that confronts us. For, on the one hand, mere compulsion has no moral standing. Persons may and do yield to the demands of arbitrary force simply because they will suffer if they do not. But such yielding develops a slavish weakness in them and an arrogant disregard of the rights of others in those who have power. On the other hand, we split man into two disconnected parts if we say that there is a law and principle of Duty which has nothing to do with our normal impulses and purposes and which yet is supreme over them.

The way out is found by recognizing that the exercise of claims is as natural as anything else in a world in which persons are not isolated from one another but live in constant association and interaction. A child may be subject to demands from a parent which express nothing but the arbitrary wish of the latter, plus a power to make the child suffer if he does not conform. But the claims and demands to which the child is subject *need* not proceed from arbitrary will; they may issue from the very nature of family life in the relation which exists between parent and offspring. Then they do not come to the child as an external and despotic power, but as expressions of a whole to which he himself belongs. He is moved to respond by his affection for his parents, by his respect for their judgment; even when the demand runs contrary to his uppermost desire he still responds to it as to something not wholly alien. Because of inherent relationships persons sustain to one another, they are exposed to the expectations of others and to the demands in which these expectations are made manifest.

The case is perhaps even clearer if we consider the parent as one who is also subject to claims. These need not be voiced in explicit form by the child; they do not proceed consciously from him. But the parent who is conscientious feels that they are involved in the *parental relation*. Because of this human relationship, something is owed to the child even though (perhaps even more because) the latter is not able to formulate that claim in any express demand. So friends owe something to one another because of the very nature of the friendly relation. Citizens in a just state respond at their personal inconvenience to the demands of the state, not because the latter may bring physical pressure or mental coercion to bear upon them, but because they are members of organized society: members in such an intimate sense that the demands are not external impositions even when they run counter to the good which a present desire calls for. The claims of friendship are not always agreeable; sometimes they may be extremely irksome. But we should not hesitate to say that one who refused to meet them merely because they were troublesome was no true friend. If we generalize such instances, we reach the conclusion that Right, law, duty, arise from the relations which human beings intimately sustain to one another, and that their authoritative force springs from the very nature of the relation that binds people together.

This conclusion will be strengthened if we consider in some detail the theories which explain moral authority and rightfulness on other grounds. Some of these conceptions make the will of God the *locus* of authority; others (like that of Thomas Hobbes) transfer it from God to the political State; Kant, in reaction against any external source, found it in a law of practical reason resident in man but having an entirely different origin and constitution from his impulses and affections. A popular version of the same underlying idea is that man has a double nature, being both spiritual and carnal, and that the flesh is rightfully subject to the law of the spirit. From the standpoint of history, it is worth noting that while the Greeks developed the idea of the Good and of moral insight, it was the Romans, with their strong legal and administrative talents, who made central the idea of authorization by law. The three maxims in which Roman moralists and jurists summed up the moral code all take the form of duties. Render to every other man that which is his due. So use what is your own as not to injure others. *Vivere honestum*: that is, live so as to deserve good repute from others. These maxims were said to be the essentials of the "law of nature," from accord with which the rightfulness of human institutions and laws is derived.

§ 3. The Kantian Theory

Undoubtedly the most logically extreme formulation of the belief that authority and law come first, and that the conception of the good, in a moral sense, is secondary, is that of Kant. The subordination of Good to the Right is summed up in the words "the concept of good and evil must not be determined before the moral law, but only after it and by means of it." Nor does Kant stop here. He carries to its logical extreme that notion of the opposition between all the values which satisfy desires and the true moral good referred to in the previous chapter (p. 186). He accepts the hedonistic psychology with respect to desires. From the standpoint of desire, all good is a pleasure which is personal and private. The man who allows desires, even those of affection for others, to direct his conduct is, in final account, only seeking his *own* good, that is, his own pleasure. The ruling principle of all desires is Self-love, a development of the instinct for self-preservation which according to him governs all appetite and impulse. Thus the moral good is not only different from the natural goods which man experiences in the regular course of living but is *opposed* to them. The essence of the moral struggle is to put regard for moral law in the place of desire for satisfaction as the dominant maxim and motive of conduct. Morality is a struggle just because men in their native make-up and capacity naturally seek to satisfy their desires, while their higher nature imposes a complete check on this tendency.

Kant expressed the idea of the supreme authority of the concepts of law and duty so logically that his views are worthy of particular attention by means of a few examples. Natural impulse suggests to a mother care of her infant; but to be *morally good*, the motive of her conduct must be reverence for the moral law which makes it her bounden duty to care for the child. The view has been caricatured by saying that to be truly moral, the mother must suppress her natural affection. This extreme result is not implied. But it is no caricature to say that, according to Kant, the parent must suppress the tendency of natural affection to become the *motive* for performance of acts of attention to offspring. She must bring, as far as the moving spring of her actions is concerned, her affection *under* a deliberate appreciation of the *obligatory* nature of what she does. Her act is not morally good because it flows from affection, nor because it promotes the welfare of the young as its consequence. Again, a man engaged in service of a client is moved either by ambition for professional success or by acquired professional habits to do the best he can for the affairs of clients entrusted to his charge. But his acts are morally good—are *right* as distinct from satisfactory—only when such motives as affect his conduct, including even the wish to be of service to others, are subordinated to reverence for the moral law. Again, a merchant may supply customers with proper commodities, give honest change, serve them zealously, just because he thinks it good policy. He is only looking out for number one, while he *ought* to be doing what he does because it is a moral duty to act in that way.

One aspect of Kant's theory has been incidentally touched upon before (p. 173); namely, the contrast which is set up between will, defined as motive, and consequences; together with the attribution of moral goodness to the former alone. We shall here confine ourselves accordingly to that one element which is peculiar to his position; namely, the conception of reverence for law and duty as the only *justifying* motive. The law according to Kant is imperative; and the imperative command is absolute, unconditioned—the "categorical imperative," he calls it, in order to distinguish it from requirements of prudence and skill which are only hypothetical. The latter take the form: *If* you wish good health, or success in your calling, you *must* do so and so. The moral command says, You *must* act from the motive of duty, anyway. The extreme and logical form in which Kant states the principle of Right as distinct from the Good, of Law and Duty, brings out the difficulty in all theories which separate the right entirely from satisfaction of desires and affections. Ignoring technicalities in the Kantian theory, the difficulty is this: When all regard for consequences and for all ends which desire sets before us is excluded, what concrete material is left to be included within the idea of duty? Why may not a man go ahead in any line of conduct provided he is persuaded that his duty lies there? What saves him from self-deceit, from fanaticism, from cruel disregard of the interest of others, once he decides, apart from consideration of consequences, that something is his duty and is commanded by the moral law? Putting the question in its precise form, how shall a man go from the idea of duty in general to that of some particular act or mode of conduct as dutiful?

Kant recognizes the difficulty, and fancies he has an adequate answer to it. He does not blink the fact that the idea of Duty in general is without any particular content of its own. We are not aware, according to him, that any particular act is obligatory; we are only aware that it is our imperative duty to make the law of duty supreme in conduct. In itself this law of Duty is, he claims rather than merely admits, formal and empty. For all particular ends have to do with consequences and are linked up with desires. Where then is there any road from Duty in general to the knowledge that it is our duty to pursue some actual concrete end?

His answer takes the following form: The consciousness of duty is imposed upon us by our moral reason. We are not mere creatures of appetite and desire, of sense and nature, but there is within us a rational faculty which rises above desire and nature. It is the essence of Reason to express itself in universal and necessary terms. This trait implies that it is wholly self-consistent or universal. It does not say one thing at one time and another at another time; it does not vary with circumstances. So all that is required to know our duty in a particular case is to ask ourselves if the motive of that act can be made universal without falling into self-contradiction. For example:

> May I, when in distress, make a promise with the intention not to keep it? . . . The shortest way, and an unerring one to discover the answer to the question whether a lying promise is consistent with duty, is to ask myself, Should I be content that my maxim (to extricate myself from trouble by a false promise) should hold good as a universal law, for myself as well as for others? And should I be able to say to myself, every one may make a deceitful promise when he finds himself in a difficulty from which he cannot otherwise extricate himself? Then I personally become aware that while I can will the lie, I can by no means will that lying should be a universal law. For with such a law there would be no such thing as a promise. No one should have any faith in the proffered intention, or, if they do so over-hastily, would pay one back in one's own coin at the first opportunity.

The principle if made universal simply contradicts itself, and thus reveals that it is no principle at all, not rational. Summing this up in a formula, we get as our standard of right action the principle: "Act as if the maxim of thy action were to become by thy will a universal law of nature."

It is not easy to do justice to Kant's formula without going into a consideration of the place which "Reason" occupies in his whole system. But it can be pointed out that in passing from the general and formal command of Reason over to judgment on the rightfulness or dutifulness of the particular case, there is an unconscious and yet complete shift in the conception of the work of reason. It is perfectly true that if a person considers the purpose or motive of his act in isolation, as if it were not a member of *Conduct* as a linked series of actions (p. 169), there is no rationality or reasonableness in his act. There is no principle or law because there is nothing which binds different acts together. Each act is a complete law unto itself, which is the same as no law at all. It *is* the part of reason to lead us to judge: Would I be willing to act for this end always and under all circumstances? Would I be willing to have others treat me according to it under similar circumstances? In Kant's language: Am I willing to have it made "universal," or am I seeking some special exception for myself under particular circumstances?

But this method instead of excluding all reference to consequences is but a way of securing impartial and general consideration *of* consequences. It does not say: Ignore consequences and do your duty because moral law, through the voice of reason, commands it. It says: Consider as widely as possible the consequences of acting in this way; imagine the results if you and others always acted upon such a purpose as you are tempted to make your end, and see whether you would then be willing to stand by it. If you proceed in this manner, you will get light upon the real character of your particular purpose at the moment. You will be aided in finding where your duty lies. And if a man discovers upon reflection that he would not like to be "paid back in his own coin," in as far as he is fair-minded (and in popular usage, fair-mindedness and rationality of judgment are synonymous terms) he will perceive the wrongness of his proposed act.

That in reality, although not in formal theory, Kant's universality signifies regard for social consequences instead of disregard of all consequences appears in another formula of the moral law which he sets forth. According to his view, the moral or rational will is an end in itself, not a means to something else. Now *every* person is equally an end in himself. Indeed, this is the very quality which marks off a person from a mere thing. Things we use as means; we subordinate physical objects and energies to our own special purposes; stones, timber, heat, electricity. But when we make another person a means to our ends, we violate his very being; we treat him as a slave and reduce him to the status of a merely physical object, or of a domestic animal, a horse or cow. Hence the moral law may be stated in the following form: "So act as to treat humanity, whether in thine own person or in that of any other, as an end, never as a means only." The person who makes a lying promise to another uses that other person as a means to his own profit. The man who proposes suicide treats personality in himself as merely a means to avoiding discomfort and trouble. This second formula is equivalent to a third and final principle: Since all human beings are equally persons and of equal claim upon the conduct of all, the ideal of rational conduct in observance of duty leads to the idea of a kingdom of ends. The moral law demands "the union of different rational beings in a system by common laws."

If we bear this outcome in mind, and think of the claims of others to whom we are bound in social relations, we are enabled to see in what respect the idea of Right and Duty is distinct from that of the Good, and yet how the two are connected.

In case of conflict of personal good with the good of others, most persons have a strong tendency to estimate their own satisfaction as having the higher value. There is no doubt that serious moral problems arise when that which we judge to be good because it is agreeable to our own desires comes into conflict with that which, if our own interests were not deeply involved, we should see to be the good of others. To regard oneself as one among others and not as the "only pebble on the beach," and to carry out this estimate in practice is perhaps the most difficult lesson we have to learn. If others did not put forth their claims and if these general claims were not embodied in a system of general social expectations, demands, and laws, he would be an exceptional individual indeed who should give only the same weight to his own good, as dictated by his own wants and purposes, as he gives to that of others. The urgency, intimate and close-by character of our own good operate strongly against our giving due heed to the welfare of others; in comparison, this seems to him pale, remote, negligible.

But the supposition of complete isolation is contrary to fact. Others do not leave us alone. They actively express their estimates of good in demands made upon each one of us. They accompany them with virtual promise of aid and support if their expectations are met, and with virtual threats of withdrawal of help, and of positive infliction of penalty, if we do not then take them into account in forming the purposes which control our own conduct. And these demands of others are not just so many special demands of so many different individuals. They are generalized into laws; they are formulated as standing claims of "society" in distinction from those of individuals in their isolated severalty. When considered as claims and expectations, they constitute the Right in distinction from the Good. But their ultimate function and effect is to lead the individual to broaden his conception of the Good; they operate to induce the individual to feel that nothing is good for himself which is not also a good for others. They are stimuli to a widening of the area of consequences to be taken into account in forming ends and deciding what is Good.

This conclusion confers an independent standing upon the conception of Right, and yet makes clear its ultimate moral connection with the conception of the Good. It preserves Right from being arbitrary and formal and Good from being narrow and private. But the whole problem is not yet disposed of. Reflective morality asks: What about the rightfulness of specific claims and demands that are put forth by society, especially by those in authority? Are they, in the concrete forms in which they are put forth, claims and expectations which *should* be exercised? What is the connection, for example, between a particular injunction or prohibition of parent or governmental official and the general notion of right which it claims to embody? What is *its* moral justification?

§ 4. The Justification of a Claim

The question is not a purely speculative one. Children in the family, citizens and groups in the State, may feel that the demands to which they are socially subject are arbitrary and lacking in genuine moral authority. They may feel that current laws spring from past customs which are outworn, or that they represent the *force* of those in power rather than a moral ideal. A parent's, teacher's, ruler's injunction "Do this" may turn out on reflection to be the expression of *his* impulse, or a manifestation of his personal interest in his *own* power and privilege, a manifestation backed up by his superior position rather than by ethical principle. Obedience is often procured by the use of rewards and penalties, promises and threats: by what in moral theory have come to be called "sanctions." And if the ultimate "reason" for observance of law and respect for duty lies in the hope of reward and fear of penalty, then the "right" is nothing but a round-about means to the hedonistic end of private satisfaction. Morality becomes servile; a condition of apparent obedience may signify in fact nothing but a state of fear. Moreover, the situation leads to a kind of clever hypocrisy. An individual may be clever enough to get his own way, while so covering up his tracks that he seems loyal to constituted authority.

The same point comes out when the situation is viewed in reverse. A shrewd observer of political life remarked that power is poison. It is difficult for a person in a place of authoritative power to avoid supposing that what he wants is right as long as he has power to enforce his demand. And even with the best will in the world, he is likely to be isolated from the real needs of others, and the perils of ignorance are added to those of self-ishness. History reveals the tendency to confusion of private privilege with official status. The history of the struggle for political liberty is largely a record of attempt to get free from oppressions which were exercised in the name of law and authority, but which in effect identified loyalty with enslavement. With the concentration of alleged moral authority in the few, there is a corresponding weakening of judgment and the power to accept responsibility on the part of the many. "Morality" gets reduced to carrying out orders.

The discussion brings to light an underlying problem. What is the ultimate nature of moral authority? What differentiates it from habitual custom or from command of power? The problem as we have seen is not merely theoretical; it has its practical side. Men of affairs, those in position of power, executives and administrators, are constantly under the temptation to view laws as ends in themselves, and to think that the Right is made secure through the issuing of rules and regulations and by securing conformity to them. Even when the ruler is the mass of the people, as in a democracy, the danger remains. Is there not a saying, "*Vox populi, vox dei*"? That law exists for man and not man for law is not an easy lesson to learn, nor is the difficulty lessened when in reaction against authority which seems repressive and arbitrary, there is recourse to the anarchy of individual appetite and impulse.

In short, while Right as an idea is an independent moral conception or "category," this fact does not solve the question of *what* is right in particular. Law and lawfulness are not all one with *a* law. Law is necessary because men are born and live in social relationships; *a* law is always questionable, for it is but a special means of realizing the function of law in general, namely, the institution of those relations among men which conduce to the welfare and freedom of all.

Individuals are interdependent. No one is born except in dependence on others. Without aid and nurture from others, he would miserably perish. The material of his intellectual subsistence, as well as of his physical, comes to him from others. As he matures, he becomes more physically and economically independent; but he can carry on his calling only through cooperation and competition with others; he has needs which are satisfied only through exchange of services and commodities. His recreations as well as his achievements are dependent upon sharing with others. The idea that individuals are born separate and isolated and are brought into society only through some artificial device is a pure myth. Social ties and connections are as natural and inevitable as are physical. Even when a person is alone he thinks with language that is derived from association with others, and thinks about questions and issues that have been born in intercourse. Independence of character and judgment is to be prized. But it is an independence which does not signify separateness; it is something displayed in relation to others. There is no one, for example, of whom independent inquiry, reflection, and insight are more characteristic than the genuine scientific and philosophic thinker. But his independence is a futile eccentricity unless he thinks upon problems which have originated in a long tradition, and unless he intends to share his conclusions with others, so as to win their assent or elicit their corrections. Such facts are familiar and commonplace. Their meaning is not always so definitely recognized:—namely, that the human being is an individual because of and in relations with others. Otherwise, he is an individual only as a stick of wood is, namely, as spatially and numerically separate.

Many of these relations are enduring, or recur frequently. The relation of child and parent, for example, lasts for a number of years, giving rise to claims for protection and nurture, and for attention, respect, and affection. The duties which express these relations are intrinsic to the situation, not enforced from without. The one who becomes a parent assumes by that very fact certain responsibilities. Even if he feels these to be a burden and seeks to escape from them, he flees from something which is part of himself and not from something imposed by external force. Many of the duties recognized in our system of common law arose out of relations which recur pretty constantly in the economic relations of men, as, for example, those of landlord and tenant, vendor and purchaser, master and servant, trustee and beneficiary. It does not follow from this fact that the duties expressing the relation have always been just what they should be; the relation may have been one-sided rather than reciprocal. But the remedy lies not in the abolition of all duties but in a change in the character of the relationship.

While particular rights and duties may, then, be arbitrary there is nothing arbitrary or forced in the existence of right and obligation. The Romans spoke of duties as *offices*. An office is a function which has a representative value; that is, it stands for something beyond itself. It is as a parent, not just as an isolated individual, that a man or woman imposes obligations on children; these grow out of the office or function the parent sustains, not out of mere personal will. When they express merely one will in opposition to another, instead of proceeding from the tie which binds persons together, they violate their own basis. In the case of those persons who are usually called officers the point is even clearer. The legislator, judge, assessor, sheriff, does not exercise authority as his private possession, but as the representative of relations in which many share. He is an organ of a community of interests and purposes. In principle, therefore, Right expresses the way in which the good of a number of persons, held together by intrinsic ties, becomes efficacious in the regulation of the members of a community.

The fact that the idea or principle of Right has such a natural basis and inevitable role does not, however, signify that it will not conflict with what an individual judges to be his good and his end, nor does it guarantee the rightfulness of all claims and demands that are put forth in its name. On the contrary, one may use the power and prestige which a representative capacity confers to advance one's personal interests, add to one's individual enjoyments, and enhance one's private gains. A parent may degrade the parental office into a means of increasing his own comfort and displaying his own whims, satisfying his love of power over others. And so with civic and political officials. Such conduct is *faithlessness*, but such betrayal is unfortunately a common event. The evil extends; it provokes resentment against all authority, and the feeling grows that all duties are limitations of personal freedom and arbitrary impositions of superior power. The conflict affects the interpretation of the meaning of law. On one hand, it is regarded as the expression of a superior will in reference to the wills of those whose wills are inferior and subject. On the other hand, it is erected into an impersonal and independent entity, above all human wills. Kant virtually defined the moral law in this fashion, although he did so in the professed name of a rational will. Undoubtedly the tendency to treat law as something in itself, over and above of all human relations instead of as an expression of the end and good which these relations should serve, has arisen in part at least because of a feeling that human relations fluctuate, and from the desire to find something stable and constant. This motive is implicit when the "majesty" and "sublimity" of law are spoken of. But the logical consequence and the practical effect, if the belief is acted upon, is to render morals harsh, because of neglect of the relation between law and obligation and the attainment of Good. It subjects the mass of men to the desires of those who have it in their power to declare and enforce what they take to be law.

The outcome of the discussion is that while Right in general has an independent status because of the social claims which attend human relations, any *particular* claim is open to examination and criticism. Is it entitled to claim the authority of right for itself? Is it truly rightful? To answer such questions and to guide judgment in criticism a criterion for the rightfulness of particular laws and obligations has to be found. The essence of the claim which Right puts forth is that even if the thing exacted does not appeal as his good to the one to whom it is addressed, he *should* voluntarily take it to be a good; that, in short, it should *become* his good, even if he does not so judge it at the time. This element of the "should" or "ought" is what differentiates the idea of Right from that of Good. But it does not cut the idea wholly loose from that of Good, for what "should be" is that an individual should *find* the required conduct good. The solution of the apparent contradiction between that which is not now judged good and yet *should* be judged good points the way to the criterion of which we are in search. Does the conduct alleged to be obligatory, alleged to have the authority of moral law behind it, actually contribute to a good in which the one from whom an act is demanded will *share?* The person upon whom the duty is laid himself makes claims upon others; he expects benefits from others; he holds others to the duties which they owe him, because of his ends and the values which he seeks to obtain. If the claim is, then, of the kind which he himself puts forth, if it serves a good which he prizes for himself, he must, in the degree in which he is fair-minded, acknowledge it to be a common good, and hence binding upon his judgment and action.

The point comes out perhaps most clearly if we ask what it is which makes an act wrong. Our theory commits us to the conclusion that a choice and deed are not wrong *merely* because they fail to conform with current laws and the customary code of duties. For these may be wrong, and an individual may have Right on his side in refusal to conform. Some persons persecuted as moral rebels in one period have been hailed as moral heroes at a later time; children build monuments to those whom their fathers stoned. Yet this fact does not commit us to the conclusion that there is no criterion of right and wrong except that personal subjective opinion sometimes improperly called private conscience. A man would not steal if there were no value placed by him on property; even a thief resents having what he has stolen taken from him. If there were no such thing as good faith, there could be no fraud. The wrongdoer counts upon good faith and honesty in others; otherwise there would be nothing beneficial to him in violating these ties. Wrong consists in faithlessness to that upon which the wrongdoer counts when he is judging and seeking for what is good to him. He betrays the principles upon which he depends; he turns to his personal advantage the very values which he refuses to acknowledge in his own conduct towards others. He contradicts, not as Kant would have it, some abstract law of reason, but the principle of reciprocity when he refuses to extend to others the goods which he seeks for himself. The justification of the moral non-conformist is that when he denies the rightfulness of a particular claim he is doing so not for the sake of private advantage, but for the sake of an object which will serve more amply and consistently the welfare of all. The burden of proof is upon him. In asserting the rightfulness of his own judgment of what is obligatory, he is implicitly putting forth a social claim, something therefore to be tested and confirmed by further trial by others. He therefore recognizes that when he protests he is liable to suffer the consequences that result from his protesting; he will strive with patience and cheerfulness to convince others.

If patience, cheerfulness, freedom from conceit, self-display, and self-pity are demanded of the moral non-conformist, there is a correlative duty imposed upon conformists: namely, the duty of toleration. History shows how much of moral progress has been due to those who in their own time were regarded as rebels and treated as criminals. The heart of reflective morality *is* reflection, and reflection is sure to result in criticism of some matters generally accepted and in proposals for variation of what is currently regarded as right. Toleration is thus not just an attitude of good-humored indifference. It is positive willingness to permit reflection and inquiry to go on in the faith that the truly right will be rendered more secure through questioning and discussion, while things which have endured merely from custom will be amended or done away with. Toleration of difference in moral judgment is a duty which those most insistent upon duty find it hardest to learn. As soon as one enemy of inquiry and public discussion is overcome, new enemies with new plausible reasons for exercising censorship and suppression of thought arise. And yet without freedom of thought and expression of ideas, moral progress can occur only accidentally and by stealth. Mankind still prefers upon the whole to rely upon force, not now exercised directly and physically as it was once, but upon covert and indirect force, rather than upon intelligence to discover and cling to what is right.

§ 5. The Sense of Duty

Corresponding to the generalized form in which demands are made there grows up a generalized sense of Duty—a sense of being bound by that which is right because of its rightfulness. At first, duties are connected with specific relations, like those of a child to his parents, to his brothers and sisters. But with increasing moral maturity, there develops a sense of obligation in distinction from any particular situation. While a general idea arises out of the recurrence of special situations, it is more than a mere extract from them. It constitutes also a new attitude toward further special situations. A person may use a variety of things in succession as if they were tables. When he has the general idea of a table, he is in possession of a *principle* of action. He can use his idea as an ideal, as something by which to criticize existing tables, and by which, under changed conditions, to invent a new table. One might warm himself by a fire a thousand times without having it occur to him to *make* a fire when he is cold. When he has the general idea of a fire, he has something which is emancipated from any given case and which may be employed to generate a fire when there is none in actual existence. So a person with a general conception of duty will have a new attitude; he will be on the lookout for situations in which the idea applies. He will have an ideal or standard to which he must bring up particular cases.

While general ideas are of utmost value in the direction and enlargement of conduct, they are also dangerous: they tend to be set up as fixed things in themselves, apart from reference to any particular case. Such is the case when there develops the idea of "duty for the sake of duty." Here the notion of duty is isolated from the demands of special situations and is made a fetish. Conformity to the letter of the law then takes the place of faithfulness to its spirit—to its usefulness in calling attention to the good which is wider than that of immediate convenience or strong appetite. Duty is made to take precedence of all human claims, instead of operating as a reminder to consider human claims in a large way. The proper function of a general sense of duty is to make us sensitive to the relations and claims involved in particular situations, and this sensitiveness is especially needed whenever some immediate solicitation of desire tends to blind us to everything but itself. A generalized sense of right is a support in times of temptation; it gives a reenforcing impetus in carrying us over a hard place in conduct. A mother is habitually attentive to the claims of her offspring. Nevertheless, cases arise when it is much easier for her to put her own comfort first. A generalized sense of right and obligation is a great protection; it makes the general habit consciously available. But such a general sense as this grows out of occasions when the mother was faithful because she was actuated by direct affection for the child and direct interest in his welfare. A sense of duty is a weak staff when it is not the outcome of a habit formed in whole-hearted recognition of the value of the ties involved in concrete cases.

A sense of a common value and interest binding persons together is therefore the normal support and guide. But we are all of us subject to conditions in which we tend to be insensitive to this value, and where the sense of what is due others is weak in comparison with the force of a contrary inclination. The claims of others then find a valuable ally in a generalized sense of right and obligation which has been growing up because of previous appreciations of concrete relations.

In the final part of our discussion of the Good and moral wisdom, we noted that different social environments operate very differently in building up the power of good practical judgment. The same thing is true, and perhaps in even a greater degree, of the relation of social institutions to fostering loyalty, faithfulness, to the Right. There are social institutions which promote rebellion or at least indifference. Some tend to produce a specious, a conventional, or even hypocritical, loyalty. This happens when fear of suffering if one does not conform, is the leading consideration. Some social conditions foster external acknowledgment of duty at the expense of personal and critical judgment of ends and values. Other conditions induce men to think about what is truly right, and to create new forms of obligation. At present, without doubt, the social scene is so complex and so subject to rapid change, that its effect is distracting. It is hard to find any compass which will give steady guidance to conduct. In consequence the demand for a truly reflective, a thoughtful, morality was never so great. This is almost the only alternative to either moral drifting or else to unreasoning and dogmatic insistence upon arbitrary, formal codes held up as obligatory for no reason except that custom and tradition have laid complete hold upon us.

There is perhaps always a tendency to overestimate the amount of strict adherence to moral standards in the past and to exaggerate the extent of contemporary laxity. Nevertheless, changes in domestic, economic, and political relations have brought about a serious loosening of the social ties which hold people together in definite and readily recognizable relations. The machine, for example, has come between the worker and the employer; distant markets intervene between producer and consumer; mobility and migration have invaded and often broken up local community bonds; industries once carried on in the home and serving as a focus for union in the household have gone to the factory with its impersonal methods, and the mother as well as the father has followed them; the share of the family in the education of the young has become less; the motor car, the telephone, and new modes of amusement have placed the centre of gravity in social matters in contacts that are shifting and superficial. In countless ways the customary loyalties that once held men together and made them aware of their reciprocal obligations have been sapped. Since the change is due to alteration of conditions, the new forms of lawlessness and the light and loose way in which duties are held cannot be met by direct and general appeal to a sense of duty or to the restraint of an inner law. The problem is to develop new stable relationships in society out of which duties and loyalties will naturally grow.

Literature

Kantian theory of Duty, *Theory of Ethics*, trans. by Abbott; *cf.* in Bradley, *Ethical Studies*, 1904, 1927, chapter on Duty for Duty's Sake; Clutton-Brock, *The Ultimate Belief*, and Otto, *Things and Ideals*, 1924, ch. iii.; Green, *Prolegomena to Ethics*, 1890, pp. 315–320, 381–388. For opposite view, Guyau, *Sketch of Morality Independent of Obligation or Sanction*.

For utilitarian interpretation of duty, see Bentham, *Principles of Morals and Legislation*; Bain, *Emotions and Will*; Spencer, *Principles of Ethics*, especially Vol. I., Part I., ch. vii.

GENERAL DISCUSSION: McGilvary, *Philosophical Review*, Vol. XI., pp. 333–352; Sharp, *Ethics*, 1928, Book I. on the Right, and *International Journal of Ethics*, Vol. II., pp. 500–513; Adler, *An Ethical Philosophy of Life*, 1918; Calkins, *The Good Man and the Good*, 1918, ch. i.; Driesch, *Ethical Principles in Theory and Practice*, trans. 1930, pp. 70–190; Everett, *Moral Values*, 1918, ch. ix. on Duty and ch. xi. on Law.

Approbation, the Standard and Virtue

§ 1. Approval and Disapproval as Original Facts

Conduct is complex. It is so complex that attempts to reduce it intellectually to a single principle have failed. We have already noted two leading considerations which cut across each other: ends which are judged to satisfy desire, and the claims of right and duty which inhibit desire.

Although different schools of theory have tried to derive one from the other, they remain in some respects independent variables. Still another school of moralists has been impressed by the universality in conduct of actions which manifest approval and disapproval, praise and blame, sympathetic encouragement and resentment. Theorists of this school have been struck with the spontaneity and directness of such actions, since it is "natural," in the most immediate sense of the word, for men to show favor or disfavor toward the conduct of others. This is done without conscious reflection, without reference to the ideas of either a Good end which is to be attained or of a Duty which is authoritative. In fact, according to this school, the ideas of Good and Duty are secondary; the Good is that which calls out approbation; duties are derived from the pressure of others expressed in the rewards and penalties, in the praise and blame, they spontaneously attach to acts.

Upon this view, the problem of reflective morality is to discover the basis upon which men unconsciously manifest approval and resentment. In making explicit what is implicit in the spontaneous and direct attitudes of praise and blame, reflection introduces consistency and system into the reactions which take place without thought. It is significant that in morals the word "judgment" has a double sense. In respect to knowledge, the word has an intellectual sense. To judge is to weigh pros and cons in thought and decide according to the balance of evidence. This signification is the only one recognized in logical theory. But in human relations, it has a definitely practical meaning. To "judge" is to condemn or approve, praise or blame. Such judgments are practical reactions, not coldly intellectual propositions. They manifest favor and disfavor, and on account of the sensitiveness of persons to the likes and dislikes of others exercise a positive influence on those judged. The injunction in the New Testament "Judge not" is a familiar instance of this usage of judgment; it also indicates that indulgence in such judgments is itself a moral matter. The desire on one side to escape censure has a counterpart, as a motive of conduct, in a tendency to exhibit superiority by indulging in condemnation of others.

There is nothing more spontaneous, more "instinctive," than praise and blame of others. Reflective morality notes the inconsistency and arbitrary variations in popular expressions of esteem and disapproval, and seeks to discover a rational principle by which they will be justified and rendered coherent. It notes especially that unreflective acclaim and reproof merely repeat and reflect the scheme of values which is embodied in the social habits of a particular group. Thus a militant community admires and extols all warlike achievements and traits; an industrialized community sets store by thrift, calculation, constancy of labor, and applauds those persons who exhibit these qualities. In one group "success" signifies prowess; in the other group, the amassing of property; and praise and blame are correspondingly awarded. In Greek life, the contrast between the system of acts and dispositions prized by the Athenian and Spartan respectively was a stock theme of moralists. Recently, an analogous opposition has been set up by some critics between "Americanism" and "Europeanism."

These differences inevitably lead in time to asking a question: What plan of commendation and reprobation is to be itself approved and adopted? The question is the more acute because of the great influence of the attitude of others in shaping disposition. Habitual attitudes of favor and disfavor, often expressed in overt punishment and tangible reward and almost always in ridicule and conferring of prestige, are the weapons of customary morality. Moreover they are so deeply engrained in human nature, that, according to one view, the whole business of reflective morality and of moral theory is to determine a rational principle as the basis for their operation. The point may be illustrated by reference to the conceptions of virtue and vice. The theory in question holds that the morally good, as distinct from the good of satisfying desire, is the same as the virtuous; it holds that the right is also the virtuous, while the morally bad and the wrong are one with what is vicious. But the virtuous at first signifies that which is approved; the vicious that which is condemned. In customary morality, acts and traits of character are not esteemed because they are virtuous; rather they are virtues because they are supported by social approval and admiration. So virtue means valor in a martial society, and denotes enterprise, thrift, industriousness in an industrialized community, while it may signify poverty, rags, ascetic habits, in a community in which devotion to supernatural things is prized as the highest good. Reflection tries to reverse the order: it wants to discover what *should* be esteemed so that approbation will follow what is decided to be *worth* approving, instead of designating virtues on the basis of what happens to be especially looked up to and rewarded in a particular society.

§ 2. The Nature of Standards and of Utilitarian Theory

The principle upon which the assignment of praise and blame rationally rests constitutes what is known as a *standard*. It is the foundation of judgment in its *practical* sense. In this type of theory the concept of Standard occupies the place held respectively by Good and Duty in the other theories already considered. The principle by which acclaim and reprehension should be regulated is made the dominant ethical "category," taking precedence of the good and the obligatory. For, on this theory, that which is morally good is that which is approved, while the right is that which should be approved. Duties pass from the mere *de facto* realm of things exacted by social pressure into the *de jure* realm of acts which are rightfully demanded only as they agree with the Standard of approval; otherwise they are coercive and are restrictive of freedom. The right is that which *deserves* commendation; the wrong is that which *merits* punishment, overt or attenuated to the form of censure.

It is significant that, upon the whole, the idea of approval or disapproval and its proper standard is characteristic of English moral theory, as that of Ends is of Greek and Duty of Roman ethical philosophy. It is implicit in Greek theory in the importance attached to measure and proportionateness in judging acts and in the tendency to identify *to agathon*, the good, with *to kalon*, the beautiful. But in English moral theorizing the manifestation of commendation and condemnation, and their influence upon the formation of character, are for the first time made central. It appears in Shaftesbury as an immediate intuition of moral sense, strictly comparable to "good taste" in esthetic matters; to Hume, approbation is identical with what "pleases on a *general* view," that is after reflective generalization in distinction from first and personal reaction; Adam Smith's conception that it is what satisfies the "*impartial* spectator" is a variant of the same notion.

To Bentham, most of the interpretations of his predecessors were still infected too much with "*ipse dixitism*," the vice, according to him, of all intuitional theories. He sought for a general and impersonal, an objective, principle which should control and justify the personal reactions of good taste or whatever. In Smith and especially in Hume he found implicit the concept that the usefulness of a deed or a trait of character to others is the ultimate ground of approval, while disservice, harmfulness, is the ground of condemnation and depreciation. Men spontaneously applaud acts which help them, which further their happiness; no explanation has to be sought for this fact. Sympathy is also an original trait of human nature. Because of sympathy we praise acts which assist others even when our own fortunes are not involved; we are moved sympathetically to indignation by wilful infliction of suffering on third parties. Sympathy instinctively transports us to their position, and we share their glow of liking and their fire of resentment as if we were personally concerned. Only the abnormally callous are untouched emotionally by heroic acts of devotion to the welfare of others or by deeds of base ingratitude and malicious spite.

There are, however, definite limitations to the spontaneous and customary exercise of sympathetic admiration and resentment. It rarely extends beyond those near to us, members of our own family and our friends. It rarely operates with reference to those out of sight or to strangers, certainly not to enemies. In the second place, unreflective admiration and disesteem are superficial. They take account of striking, conspicuous cases of help and injury, but not those of a more delicate and subtle sort; they take notice of consequences in the way of assistance and harm which show themselves in a short time, but not those which emerge later, even though the latter are in truth the more important. And, finally, when certain acts have become thoroughly habitual, they are taken for granted like phenomena of nature and are not judged at all. The beneficial and hurtful consequences of laws and institutions, for example, are not taken into account by customary morality.

Hence follow certain changes introduced by the utilitarian theory of the standard of approbation. When men recognize that contribution to universal happiness or welfare is the only ground for admiration and esteem, they eliminate the three limitations just mentioned. The standard is generalized; judgment must be passed upon consequences of weal and woe for *all* sentient creatures who are affected by an act. The same emphasis upon general or widespread consequences, brings to the fore the idea of *equality*, and does it in a way which transforms the customary award of praise and blame, sympathy and resentment. For the latter does not put the happiness of self and of others, of a member of the family and the outsider, of a fellow citizen and a stranger, of nobleman and commoner, of the lord and the peasant, of the man of distinction and the obscure person, of rich and poor, upon the same footing. But the utilitarian theory, in addition to its insistence upon taking into consideration the widest, most general range of consequences, insists that in estimating consequences in the way of help and harm, pleasure and suffering, each one shall count as one, irrespective of distinctions of birth, sex, race, social status, economic and political position. It is significant that the rise and chief influence of utilitarianism in England coincided socially with the manifestation of philanthropic sentiment on a large scale, and politically with the emergence of democratic ideals.[1] It is no accident that its chief practical influence was modification of the laws and institutions that sprang from and that fostered inequality.

§ 3. Confusion of Utilitarianism with Hedonism

So far we have passed by one important feature of utilitarianism. We have spoken in general terms of welfare, of benefit and injury, with no attempt to specify in just what they consist. Bentham, however, prided himself upon the fact that utilitarianism had a definite and measurable conception of their nature. They consist, according to him, of units of pleasure and pain, being merely their algebraic summation. Thus he reduced, according to his followers, the vague notion of welfare and happiness to a fact so precise as to be capable of quantitative statement.[2] This definition in terms of units of pleasure and pain had, however, another effect. It exposed utilitarianism to all the objections which can be brought against hedonism (see p. 192). Nor did the consequences of their identification stop at this point. It involved utilitarianism, as its critics promptly pointed out, in a peculiar contradiction. According to its conception of desire and of motive, the sole object and aim of all action is the obtaining of *personal* pleasure. The proper standard for judging the morality of action is, however, its contribution to the pleasure of *others*—the benefit conferred upon others than one's self. The utilitarians were thus faced by the problem of conflict between the strictly personal and selfish character of the motive of conduct, and the broadly social and philanthropic character of the standard of approval. Desire for private pleasure as the sole motive of action and universal benevolence as the principle of approval are at war with one another. The chief interest of

1. The life of Bentham fell between 1748 and 1832; his chief disciple, John Stuart Mill, lived from 1806 to 1873.
2. Thus Mill said: "He introduced into morals and politics those habits of thought, and modes of investigation, which are essential to the idea of science. . . . He, for the first time, introduced precision of thought in moral and political philosophy." *Autobiography*, pp. 65–67 of the London edition of 1874, and *Dissertations and Discussions*, "Essay on Bentham."

Bentham was in the standard of judgment, and his acceptance of hedonistic psychology was, in the broad sense, an historic accident. He failed to realize the inconsistency of the two principles because his own interest was in the inequitable effect of the laws and institutions of his time upon the general distribution of happiness and unhappiness. He realized the extent to which they expressed class interests and were animated by favoritism to special interests, bringing benefit to the privileged few and harm and suffering to the masses. Now laws and institutions could be viewed *impersonally*, with respect only to their consequences, since motives cannot be attributed to laws and institutions as such.

His follower, John Stuart Mill, while interested in social and political reforms, was also interested in personal morality in a way in which Bentham was not. Therefore he brought the question of personal *disposition*, of *character*, to the fore, and instituted a transformation in utilitarian morals, although he never formally surrendered the hedonistic psychology. Before considering Mill's contribution in particular, however, we shall state the problem of the relation of disposition to beneficial social consequences in its general form. Suppose we drop the hedonistic emphasis upon states of pleasure and pain and substitute the wider, if vaguer, idea of well-being, welfare, happiness, as the proper standard of approval. The problem of the relation of the standard to personal disposition still remains. The moral problem which confronts every person is how regard for general welfare, for happiness of others than himself, is to be made a regulative purpose in his conduct. It is difficult to make a regard for general happiness the standard of right and wrong, even in a purely theoretical estimate. For such a method of appraisal goes contrary to our natural tendency to put first our own happiness and that of persons near to us. This difficulty, however, is slight in comparison with that of making the intellectual estimate effective in action whenever it conflicts with our natural partiality in our own favor.

It is evident that only intimate personal disposition will enable us to solve these problems. The more importance we attach to objective consequences as the standard, the more we are compelled to fall back upon personal character as the only guarantee that this standard will operate, either intellectually in our estimates or practically in our behavior. The alleged precision for which Bentham was praised introduces an impossibility into actual conduct. One can make an estimate on the basis of experience of the general tendency of a proposed action upon welfare and suffering; no one can figure out in advance all the units of pleasure and pain (even admitting they can be reduced to unit quantities) which will follow. We are sure that the *attitude* of personal kindliness, of sincerity and fairness, will make our judgment of the effects of a proposed action on the good of others infinitely more likely to be correct than will those of hate, hypocrisy, and self-seeking. A man who trusted simply to details of external consequences might readily convince himself that the removal of a certain person by murder would contribute to general happiness. One cannot imagine an honest person convincing himself that a disposition of disregard for human life would have beneficial consequences. It is true, on one hand, that the ultimate standard for judgment of acts is their objective consequences; the outcome constitutes the meaning of an act. But it is equally true that the warrant for correctness of judgment and for power of judgment to operate as an influence in conduct lies in the intrinsic make-up of character; it would be safer to trust a man of a kind and honest disposition without much ability in calculation than it would a man having great power of foresight of the future who was malicious and insincere. When, on the other hand, we are judging the moral value of laws and institutions (that is to say, estimating them from the standpoint of their bearing upon the general welfare), impersonal and minute consideration of consequences is in order, since they, being impersonal, have no inner disposition one way or another.

Mill accordingly brought utilitarianism in closer accord with the unbiased moral sense of mankind when he said that "to do as you would be done by and to love your neighbor as yourself, constitute the ideal perfection of utilitarian morality." For such a statement puts disposition, character, first, and calculation of specific results second. Consequently on Mill's view we can say that "laws and social arrangements should place the happiness of every individual as nearly as possible in harmony with the interest of the whole, and that education and opinion, which have so vast a power over human character should so use that power as to establish in the mind of every individual an indissoluble association between his own happiness and the good of the whole." In short, we have a principle by which to judge the moral value of social arrangements: Do they tend to lead members of the community to find their happiness in the objects and purposes which bring happiness to others? There is also an ideal provided for the processes of education, formal and informal. Education should create an interest in all persons in furthering the general good, so that they will find their own happiness realized in what they can do to improve the conditions of others.

Emphasis upon personal disposition also appears in Mill's desire to see certain attitudes cultivated in and for themselves, *as if* they were ends in themselves without conscious thought of their external consequences. Intrinsically, and by our very make-up, apart from any calculation, we prize friendly relations with others. We naturally

"desire to be in unity with our fellow-creatures. . . . The social state is at once so natural, so necessary, and so habitual to man, that except in some unusual circumstances or by an effort of voluntary abstraction, *he never conceives himself otherwise than as a member of a body.* . . . Any condition, therefore, which is essential to a state of society becomes more and more an inseparable part of every person's conception of the state of things he is born into and which is the destiny of a human being." This strengthening of social ties leads the individual "to identify his *feelings* more and more with the good" of others. "He comes, as though instinctively, to be conscious of himself as a being, who, *of course,* pays regard to others. The good of others becomes to him a thing naturally and necessarily to be attended to, like any of the physical conditions of our existence." This social feeling, finally, however weak, does not present itself "as a superstition of education, or a law despotically imposed from without, but as an attribute which it would not be well to be without. . . . Few but those whose mind is a moral blank could *bear* to lay out their course of life on the line of paying no regard to others except so far as their own private interest compels."[3]

3. *Utilitarianism*, ch. iii., *passim.*

Even under the head of sympathy, Bentham's

"recognition does not extend to the more complex forms of the feeling—the love of *loving*, the need of a sympathising support, or of an object of admiration and reverence."[4] "Self-culture, the training by the human being himself of his affections and will . . . is a blank in Bentham's system. The other and co-equal part, the regulation of his outward actions, must be altogether halting and imperfect without the first; for how can we judge in what manner many an action will affect the worldly interests of ourselves or others unless we take in, as part of the question, its influence on the regulation of our or their affections and desires?"[5]

In other words, Mill saw that a weakness of Bentham's theory lay in his supposing that the factors which make up disposition are of value only as moving us to special acts which produce pleasure; to Mill they have a worth of their own as *direct* sources and ingredients of happiness. So Mill says:

I regard any considerable increase of human happiness, through mere changes in outward circumstances, unaccompanied by changes in the state of desires, as hopeless.[6]

And in his *Autobiography*, speaking of his first reaction against Benthamism, he says:

I, for the first time, gave its proper place, among the prime necessities of human well-being, to the internal culture of the individual. I ceased to attach almost exclusive importance to the ordering of outward circumstances. . . . The cultivation of the feelings became one of the cardinal points in my ethical and philosophical creed.[7]

The close connection between happiness and traits of character is also borne out by the fact that pleasures differ in *quality*, and not merely in quantity and intensity. Appreciation of poetry, of art, of science yields a kind of satisfaction which is not to be compared with that coming from purely sensuous sources. The

4. *Early Essays*, p. 354. (Reprint by Gibbs, London, 1897.)
5. *Ibid.*, p. 357.
6. *Ibid.*, p. 404.
7. *Autobiography*, London, 1874, p. 143.

extent to which the working standard is shifted by Mill from pleasures to character (since the quality of pleasure is ranked by the nature of the personal trait the pleasure accompanies) is obvious in the following quotation: "No intelligent person would consent to be a fool, no instructed person would be an ignoramus, no person of feeling and conscience would be selfish and base, even though they should be persuaded that the fool, the dunce or the rascal is better satisfied with his lot than they are. . . . It is better to be a human being dissatisfied than a pig satisfied."

We have devoted considerable space to a consideration of the shift from Bentham to Mill, not so much as a matter of historical contrast and information as because the position of the latter involves in fact, although Mill never quite acknowledges it in words, a surrender of the hedonistic element in utilitarianism. Since this hedonistic element is that which renders utilitarianism vulnerable in theory and unworkable in practice, it is significant to know that the conception of regard for social (that is widespread and impartially measured) welfare may be maintained as a standard of approbation in spite of historic utilitarianism's entanglement with an untenable hedonism. This revised version recognizes the great part played by factors internal to the self in creating a worthy happiness, while it also provides a standard for the moral appraisal of laws and institutions. For aside from the direct suffering which bad social arrangements occasion, they have a deteriorating effect upon those dispositions which conduce to an elevated and pure happiness.

Institutions are good not only because of their direct contribution to well-being but even more because they favor the development of the worthy dispositions from which issue noble enjoyments.

§ 4. The Relation of Ends and Standards

Purposes, aims, ends-in-view, are distinct from standards and yet are closely related to them; and *vice versa*. Ends-in-view are connected with desire; they look to the future, because they are projections of the objects in which desires would be satisfied. Standards, on the other hand, envisage acts already performed or viewed in imagination *as if* they had been performed. An object viewed as an end or fulfillment of desire is good in proportion as it is found to be a genuine satisfaction or realization of desire. From the standpoint of a standard, an act is good if it can evoke and sustain *approbation*. At the outset, the approbation in question is that proceeding from others. Will the group, or some particular influential member of the group, tolerate, abet, encourage, praise me if I act thus and so? The admiration and resentment of others is the mirror in which one beholds the moral quality of his act reflected back to him. Because of this reflection the agent can judge his act from a standpoint which is different from that of a satisfaction directly promised. He is led to widen and generalize his conception of his act when he takes into account the reaction of others; he views his act objectively when he takes the standpoint of standard; personally, when it is an end merely as such.

Later on, the thought of the reaction of favor or disfavor of a particular social group or a particular person tends to recede to the background. An *ideal* spectator is projected and the doer of the act looks at his proposed act through the eyes of this impartial and far-seeing objective judge. Although end and standard are two distinct conceptions having different meanings, yet it is the very nature of a standard to demand that what is approvable according to it shall *become* an end. In other words, it calls for the creation of a new end; or, in case the end suggested by desire is approved, for an end with a new quality, that of having received the stamp of approval. Unless the conception of standard arose from a different source and had a different meaning from that of ends, it could not exercise a controlling formative influence on the latter. The significance of the standard is that it involves a conception of the *way* in which ends that are adopted *should* be formed; namely, that they should be such as to merit approbation because their execution will conduce to the general well-being.

Recognition of this fact enables us to deal with a problem which is attended with a good deal of difficulty. The problem is illustrated in the so-called hedonistic paradox, that the way to attain pleasure is not to seek for it. And this saying may be paralleled by another paradox, namely, that the way to achieve virtue is not to aim directly at it. For the standard is not the same as the end of desire. Hence contribution to the general good may be the standard of reflective approval without its being the end-in-view. Indeed, it is hard to imagine its being made the end of desire; as a direct object to be aimed at, it would be so indeterminate and vague that it would only arouse a diffused sentimental state, without indicating just how and where conduct should be directed. Desire on the other hand points to a definite and concrete object at which to aim. After this end has occurred to the mind it is examined and tested from another point of view: Would the action which achieves it further the well-being of all concerned? The idea of happiness is originally derived from cases of fulfilled desire. It is a general term for the fact that while desires are different and the objects which satisfy them are different, there is one common quality in all of them: namely, the fact of being fulfillments. This is a formal trait. It is a mistake to suppose that there is homogeneity of material or content, just because there is the single name "happiness." One might as well suppose that all persons named Smith are just alike because they have the same name. No two concrete cases of happiness are just like each other in actual stuff and make-up. They are alike in being cases of fulfillment, of meeting the requirements set up by some desire. A miser finds satisfaction in storing up money, and a liberal person in spending it to give happiness to others. One man is happy when he gets ahead of others in some tangible way and another man is happy when he helps others out of some trouble. In material content, the two cases differ radically; in form they are alike, since both occupy the same status and play the same role—that of satisfying a desire.

The function of the standard then is to discriminate between the various material kinds of satisfaction so as to determine which kind of happiness is truly moral; that is, approvable. It says that among the different kinds that one is to be approved which at the same time brings satisfaction to others, or which at least harmonizes with their well-being in that it does not inflict suffering upon them. It does not tell what things should be specifically aimed at. It does tell us how to proceed in passing condemnation or giving approval to those ends and purposes which occur to the mind independently because of our desires. When this point is clearly recognized, we can appreciate the artificial nature of a problem which is often raised. It has been asserted that the crux of all moral theory is the relation between personal happiness and general happiness. It is asserted that morality as justice requires that there be a complete equation between the two; that we cannot be morally satisfied with a world in which the conduct which brings good to others brings suffering to the one who promotes the interests of others, or in which the conduct which makes others suffer yields happiness to the one who injures others. Much ingenuity has been spent in explaining away the frequent discrepancies. For it may even be argued that although extreme egoistic isolation is unfavorable to happiness, so also are great breadth and sensitiveness of affections; that the person who stands the best show of being happy is the one who exercises a prudent control over his sympathies, and so keeps from getting involved in the fortunes of other persons. If we once become aware of the difference between the standard and end, this problem of instituting an identity or equation between personal and general happiness is seen to be unreal. The standard says that we should desire those objects and find our satisfactions in the things which also bring good to those with whom we are associated, in friendship, comradeship, citizenship, the pursuit of science, art, and so on.

Many an individual solves the problem. He does so not by any theoretical demonstration that what gives others happiness will also make him happy, but by voluntary choice of those objects which do bring good to others. He gets a personal satisfaction or happiness because his desire is fulfilled, but his desire has first been made after a definite pattern. This enjoyment may be shorter in duration and less intense than those which he might have had some other way. But it has one mark which is unique and which for that individual may outweigh everything else. He has achieved a happiness which has *approved* itself to him, and this quality of being an approved happiness may render it invaluable, not to be compared with others. By personal choice among the ends suggested by desires of objects which are in agreement with the needs of social relations, an individual achieves a *kind* of happiness which is harmonious with the happiness of others. This is the only sense in which there is an equation between personal and general happiness. But it is also the only sense which is morally required.

§ 5. The Place of Justice and Benevolence in the Standard

When contribution to a shared good is taken to be the standard of approbation, a question comes up as to the relation of justice to the standard. At first sight, it seems as if benevolence were exalted to such a point that justice almost falls out of the moral picture. At all events, this conception of the nature of the standard has been attacked on the ground that justice is the supreme virtue and that the standard of general well-being subordinates justice, said to be self-sufficing in isolation, to something beyond itself in the way of consequences. Fundamentally, the issue here is that which we have considered previously in other guises: namely, the place of consequences in moral conduct. Those who regard consideration of consequences to be a degradation of morals take their stand on some abstract principle of justice. "*Fiat justitia, ruat coelum*" is the classic expression of this point of view. Let justice be done, be the consequences what they may, even to the collapse of the heavens. It is argued that regard for consequences, even such consequences as the common and shared good, reduces justice to a matter of expediency and abates its authority and majesty.

The reply to this objection is twofold. In the first place, elimination from the moral standard of the consequences of actions leaves us with only a formal principle; it sets up an abstraction and treats morality as mere conformity to an abstraction instead of as vital effort in behalf of a significant end. Experience shows that the subordination of human good to an external and formal rule tends in the direction of harshness and cruelty. The common saying that justice should be tempered with mercy is the popular way of stating recognition of the hard and ultimately *unjust* character of setting up a principle of action which is divorced from all consideration of human consequences. Justice as an end in itself is a case of making an idol out of a means at the expense of the end which the means serves. The second factor in the reply to the objection is that justice is not an external means to human welfare but a means which is organically integrated with the end it serves. There are means which are constituent parts of the consequences they bring into being, as tones are integral constituents of music as well as means to its production, and as food is an indispensable ingredient within the organism which it serves. On this account the character, the self, which has adopted fair play and equity into its own attitude will not only have the sense of humanity which protects it from harsh application of the principle, but will also be protected from any temptation to disregard the principle in order to obtain some short-term specific good. A rough analogy of what is here signified is that while rules of the hygiene of eating grow out of the service which foods render to the well-being of the organism, and are not abstract ends on their own account, yet nevertheless these rules, when once understood in their relation to the end they serve, save us from using food as a mere means to a temporary enjoyment. We can fall back on the rule in case of doubt.

There is moreover an inherent difficulty in the conception that justice can be separated from the effect of actions and attitudes upon human well-being. The separation leaves the practical meaning of standard arbitrary or open to different constructions. It is sometimes interpreted to signify strict retribution, an eye for an eye, a tooth for a tooth. Herbert Spencer gives another meaning to the principle, and employs this meaning to justify a thoroughgoing policy of *laissez faire* in social matters. He identifies the principle of justice with the relation of cause and effect in its biological meaning, that is with natural selection and the elimination of the unfit in the struggle for existence. It is "just" he asserts that the inferior should stand the consequences of their inferiority and that the superior should reap the rewards of their superiority. To interfere with the workings of natural selection is thus to violate the law of justice. In other words, Spencer uses the abstract principle of justice to warrant a policy of extreme individualism in letting the "natural" play of self-interest in a competitive society take its course. Examples of other interpretations of justice might be given. But the two instances cited should indicate the complete falsity of the common notion that justice carries its definite meaning. The truth lies on the other side. The meaning of justice in concrete cases is something to be determined by seeing what consequences will bring about human welfare in a fair and even way.

Another type of objection to social welfare as the standard of approval is that it elevates sentimentality to a supreme position in morals. Thus Carlyle condemned utilitarianism as "a universal syllabub of sentimental twaddle." It is true that there is a close relation between the standard of extensive well-being and the attitude of sympathy. But regard for consequences does not encourage giving away to every sentiment of pity and sympathy which is experienced. On the contrary, it says that we should restrain acting upon them until we have considered what the effect will be on human happiness if we give way to them. The emotion of sympathy is morally invaluable. But it functions properly when used as a principle of reflection and insight, rather than of direct action. Intelligent sympathy widens and deepens concern for consequences. To put ourselves in the place of another, to see things from the standpoint of his aims and values, to humble our estimate of our own pretensions to the level they assume in the eyes of an impartial observer, is the surest way to appreciate what justice demands in concrete cases. The real defect of sentimentalism is that it fails to consider the consequences of acting upon objective well-being; it makes the immediate indulgence of a dominant emotion more important than results.

The tendency, moreover, of adopting social well-being as a standard is to make us intellectually sensitive and critical about the effect of laws, social arrangements, and education upon human happiness and development. Historic utilitarianism, even with the handicap of its hedonistic psychology, did a great work in Great Britain in getting rid of inequalities in law and administration, and in making the mass of men conscious of the connection which exists between political oppression and corruption on one side and the suffering of the masses on the other.

The meaning to be given, from the moral point of view, to the idea of reform and the reformer furnishes a good test of the standard of approval. In one meaning, reform is almost synonymous with officious meddling; with an assumption that the would-be reformers know better than others what is good for them and can proceed to confer some great boon upon them. But the true significance of "the greatest good of the greatest number" is that social conditions should be such that all individuals can exercise their own initiative in a social medium which will develop their personal capacities and reward their efforts. That is, it is concerned with providing the objective political, economic, and social conditions which will enable the greatest possible number because of their *own* endeavors to have a full and generous share in the values of living. Of course direct help to others is needed in times of illness, physical incapacity, pecuniary distress, etc. But the chief application of the standard is concern for the influence of objective social conditions. Thus the standard saves endeavors at social change, made in its name, from the offensiveness of snobbery and personal interference. It accomplishes beneficent ends by the means of impersonal justice.

The opposition which is frequently instituted between beneficence and justice rests upon a narrow conception of the latter as well as upon a sentimental conception of the former. If beneficence is taken to signify acts which exceed the necessities of legal obligation, and justice to denote the strict letter of moral law there is, of course, a wide gap between them. But in reality the scope of justice is broad enough to cover all the conditions which make for social welfare, while a large part of what passes as charity and philanthropy is merely a makeshift to compensate for lack of just social conditions. The classic conception of justice is derived from Roman law, and shares its formal legalistic character. It is "rendering to another that which is his." According to the legal conception of what belongs to a man, the idea is limited to rather external matters, material property, repute and honor, esteem for good character, etc. But in its wide meaning the formula only raises a question, instead of affording a solution. What does belong to a man as man? How is what is morally due to a man to be measured? Can it be fixed by conventional considerations? Or is what is owed to a person anything less than opportunity to become all which he is capable of becoming? Suppose a man is detected in violation of the social code. Is what is owed him in the way of justice some retributive penalty, as exactly proportioned as possible to his offense, on the principle of an eye for an eye, a tooth for a tooth? or is it the treatment which will tend to evoke his own efforts at moral betterment? Is "justice" to be measured on the ground of existing social status, or on the ground of possibilities of development? Such questions suggest that social utilitarianism, when freed from its hedonistic handicap, makes justice to be a concern for the objective conditions of personal growth and achievement which cannot be distinguished from beneficence in its fundamental and objective sense.

§ 6. Praise and Blame as Moral Forces

It was noted earlier in passing (p. 182) that the concept of virtue is closely connected with the operation of approbation. It is not too much to say of primitive morals that in them traits of character are not approved because they are virtuous, but are virtuous because they are approved, while whatever is generally censured is *ipso facto*, regarded as vicious. Reflective morality reverses this attitude. It is concerned to discover what traits of character should be approved; it identifies virtue not with that which is *de facto* approved but that which is approv*able*, which *should* be approved. But, as we have often had occasion to note, a large strain of customary morality holds over in morality which is theoretically reflective. "Conventional morality" is precisely a morality of praise and blame based on the code of valuations which happens to be current at a particular time in a particular social group. Whatever conforms, at least outwardly, to current practices, especially those of an institutional sort, receives commendation or at least passes without censure; whatever deviates exposes one to censure. The practical effect is a negative morality; virtue is identified with "respectability," and respectability means such conduct as is exempt from overt reproach and censure rather than what is inherently *worthy* of respect. The moral ideal of multitudes of persons comes to be that sort of behavior which will pass without arousing adverse comment, just as a child too often identifies the "right" with whatever passes without a scolding.

Accordingly, this is a convenient place in which to consider the point we passed over at first, namely, the proper moral place and function of praise and blame.

At first sight, it might seem as if reflection on the customary use of approbation and condemnation would still leave praise and blame as primary factors, only giving them a standard by which to operate. Such is not the case, however. Reflection reacts to modify the character and use of praise and blame. The latter tend to fix the attention of the one commended or reprobated upon the way in which he can secure the one and avoid the other. Their effect therefore is to distract attention from the reasons and causes which make conduct praise*worthy* and blame*worthy*. Habitual exposure to praise and blame makes one think of how he may exculpate himself from accusation and may recommend himself to favor. Morality that makes much of blaming breeds a defensive and apologetic attitude; the person subjected to it thinks up excuses instead of thinking what objects are worthy to be pursued. Moreover, it distracts attention from thought of objective conditions and causes, because it tends to make one want to get even for being blamed by passing the blame on to others. One relieves himself from a charge by transferring it to some one else. In stronger natures, resentment is produced and to a point where the person blamed feels he is doing a brave thing in defying all authority. In others, it produces a feeling which put in words amounts to: "What is the use? It makes no difference what I do, since I get blamed anyway."

Reflective morality instead of leaving praise and blame where they were except for putting under them a rational basis tends to shift the emphasis to scrutiny of conduct in an objective way, that is with reference to its causes and results. What is desirable is that a person shall see for himself what he is doing and why he is doing it; shall be sensitive to results in fact and in anticipation, and shall be able to analyze the forces which make him act as he does act. Accordingly, approval and disapproval themselves are subjected to judgment by a standard instead of being taken as ultimate. On the whole, the prevalence of a morality based on praise and blame is evidence of the extent to which customary and conventional forces still influence a morality nominally reflective. The possession of a reflective standard checks and directs the use of praise and blame as it does the use of other human tendencies. It makes men realize that reward and punishment, commendation and condemnation are good or bad according to their consequences and that they may be used immorally as well as helpfully.

We have already noted the reflex origin of the traits regarded as virtuous and vicious. They are derived at the outset from the conceptions of merit and demerit, of deserts; and meritoriousness, deservingness, is measured by the reactions of others. It is others who, approving and disapproving, award honor, esteem, merit. For this reason, as has also been noted, virtues and vices in morals as far as dominated by custom are strictly correlative to the ruling institutions and habits of a given social group. Its members are trained to commend and admire whatever conforms to its established ways of life; hence the great divergence of schemes of valuation of conduct in different civilizations. Their common element is formal rather than material—namely, adherence to prevailing customs. *Nomos* is indeed "king of all," and especially of acts and traits of character deemed virtues and vices.

The attempt to discover a *standard* upon the basis of which approbation and disapprobation, esteem and disesteem, *should* be awarded has therefore nothing less than a revolutionary effect upon the whole concept of virtue and vice. For it involves *criticism* of prevailing habits of valuation. The very idea of a standard is *intellectual*; it implies something universally applicable. It does not eliminate the element of favor and hostility to certain modes of conduct. But it introduces the regulation of these manifestations by something beyond themselves. Customary morals naturally "make it hot" for those who transgress its code, and make it comfortable for those who conform. The reflective standard holds individuals to responsibility for the ways in which favor and dislike are expressed. It makes prominent the fact that in judging, in commending and condemning, we are judging ourselves, revealing our own tastes and desires. Approval and disapproval, the attitude of attributing vice and virtue, becomes itself a vice or a virtue according to the way in which it is administered.

§ 7. The Conception of Virtue in Reflective Morality

In customary morality it is possible to draw up a list or catalogue of vices and virtues. For the latter reflect some definite existing custom, and the former some deviation from or violation of custom. The acts approved and disapproved have therefore the same definiteness and fixity as belong to the customs to which they refer. In reflective morality, a list of virtues has a much more tentative status. Chastity, kindness, honesty, patriotism, modesty, toleration, bravery, etc., cannot be given a fixed meaning, because each expresses an interest in objects and institutions which are changing. In form, *as* interests, they may be permanent, since no community could endure in which there were not, say, fair dealing, public spirit, regard for life, faithfulness to others. But no two communities conceive the objects to which these qualities attach in quite identical ways. They can be defined, therefore, only on the basis of *qualities characteristic of interest*, not on the basis of permanent and uniform objects in which interest is taken. This is as true of, say, temperance and chastity as it is of regard for life, which in some communities does not extend to girl babies nor to the aged, and which in all historic communities is limited by war with hostile communities.

Accordingly we shall discuss virtue through enumeration of traits which must belong to an attitude if it is to be genuinely an interest, not by an enumeration of virtues as if they were separate entities. (1) *An interest must be wholehearted.* Virtue is integrity, vice is duplicity. Sincerity is another name for the same quality, for it signifies that devotion to an object is unmixed and undiluted. The quality has a much broader scope than might at first seem to be the case.

Conscious hypocrisy is rare. Divided and inconsistent interest is common. Devotion that is complete, knowing no reservations and exceptions, is extremely difficult to attain. We imagine we are whole-hearted when we throw ourselves into a line of action which is agreeable, failing to notice that we give up or act upon an incompatible interest when obstacles arise. Whole-heartedness is something quite different from immediate enthusiasm and ardor. It always has an emotional quality, but it is far from being identical with a succession of even intense emotional likings for a succession of things into each of which we eagerly throw ourselves. For it requires consistency, continuity, and community of purpose and effort. And this condition cannot be fulfilled except when the various objects and ends which succeed one another have been brought into order and unity by reflection upon the nature and bearing of each one. We cannot be genuinely whole-hearted unless we are single-minded.

Hence (2) the interest which constitutes a disposition virtuous must be continuous and *persistent*. One swallow does not make a summer nor does a passing right interest, no matter how strong, constitute a virtue. Fair weather "virtue" has a bad name because it indicates lack of stability. It demands character to stick it out when conditions are adverse, as they are when there is danger of incurring the ill-will of others, or when it requires more than ordinary energy to overcome obstacles. The *vitality* of interest in what is reflectively approved is attested by persistence under unfavorable conditions.

A complete interest must be (3) *impartial* as well as enduring. Interest, apart from a character formed and fortified through reflection, is partial, and in that sense divided and, though unconsciously, insincere. A person readily tends to evince interest in the well-being of friends and members of his family, and to be indifferent to those with whom he is not bound by ties of gratitude or affection. It is easy to have one scale for determining interest in those of one's own nation and a totally different one for the regard of those of another race, color, religion, or nationality. Complete universality of interest is, of course, impossible in the sense of equality of strength or force of quantity; that is, it would be mere pretense to suppose that one can be as *much* interested in those at a distance with whom one has little contact as in those with whom one is in constant communication. But equity, or impartiality, of interest is a matter of quality not of quantity as in-iquity is a matter not of more or less, but of using uneven measures of judgment. Equity demands that *when* one has to act in relation to others, no matter whether friends or strangers, fellow citizens or foreigners, one should have an equal and even measure of value as far as the interests of the others come into the reckoning. In an immediate or emotional sense it is not possible to love our enemies as we love our friends. But the maxim to love our enemies as we love ourselves signifies that in our conduct we should take into account their interests at the same rate of estimate as we rate our own. It is a principle for regulating judgment of the bearings of our acts on the happiness of others.

Single-mindedness of purpose would be narrow were it not united to breadth and impartiality of interest. The conception that virtue resides in fundamental and thoroughgoing interest in approved objects accomplishes more than merely saving us from the identification of virtues with whatever is conventionally and currently prized in a particular community or social set. For it protects us from an unreal separation of virtuous qualities from one another. The mere idea of a catalogue of different virtues commits us to the notion that virtues may be kept apart, pigeonholed in water-tight compartments. In fact virtuous traits interpenetrate one another; this unity is involved in the very idea of integrity of character. At one time persistence and endurance in

the face of obstacles is the most prominent feature; then the attitude is the excellence called courage. At another time, the trait
of impartiality and equity is uppermost, and we call it justice. At
other times, the necessity for subordinating immediate satisfaction of a strong appetite or desire to a comprehensive good is the
conspicuous feature. Then the disposition is denominated temperance, self-control. When the prominent phase is the need for
thoughtfulness, for consecutive and persistent attention, in order
that these other qualities may function, the interest receives the
name of moral wisdom, insight, conscientiousness. In each case
the difference is one of emphasis only.

This fact is of practical as well as theoretical import. The supposition that virtues are separated from one another leads, when
it is acted upon, to that narrowing and hardening of action
which induces many persons to conceive of all morality as negative and restrictive. When, for example, an independent thing is
made of temperance or self-control it becomes mere inhibition,
a sour constraint. But as one phase of an interpenetrated whole,
it is the positive harmony characteristic of integrated interest. Is
justice thought of as an isolated virtue? Then it takes on a mechanical and quantitative form, like the exact meting out of
praise and blame, reward and punishment. Or it is thought of as
vindication of abstract and impersonal law—an attitude which
always tends to make men vindictive and leads them to justify
their harshness as a virtue. To the notion of courage there still
adheres something of its original notion of fortitude in meeting
an enemy. The Greeks broadened the conception to include all
the disagreeable things which need to be borne but which one
would like to run away from. As soon as we recognize that there
can be no continuity in maintaining and executing a purpose
which does not at some time meet difficulties and obstacles that
are disagreeable, we also recognize that courage is no separate
thing. Its scope is as wide as the fullness of positive interest
which causes us in spite of difficulties to seek for the realization
of the object to which the interest is attached. Otherwise it
shrinks to mere stoical and negative resistance, a passive rather
than an active virtue.

Finally, conscientiousness is sometimes treated as if it were
mere morbid anxiety about the state of one's own virtue. It may
even become a kind of sublimated egoism, since the person con-

centrates his thoughts upon himself, none the less egoistic because concerned with personal "goodness" instead of with personal pleasure or profit. In other cases, it becomes a kind of anxious scrupulosity which is so fearful of going wrong that it abstains as much as possible from positive outgoing action. Concern for the good is reduced to a paralyzing solicitude to be preserved from falling into error. Energy that should go into action is absorbed in prying into motives. Conscience, moral thoughtfulness, makes us cowards as soon as it is isolated from courage.

Another bad consequence of treating virtues as if they were separate from one another and capable of being listed one by one is the attempt to cultivate each one by itself, instead of developing a rounded and positive character. There are, however, in traditional teachings many reminders of the wholeness of virtue. One such saying is that "love is the fulfilling of the law." For in its ethical sense, love signifies completeness of devotion to the objects esteemed good. Such an interest, or love, is marked by temperance because a comprehensive interest demands a harmony which can be attained only by subordination of particular impulses and passions. It involves courage because an active and genuine interest nerves us to meet and overcome the obstacles which stand in the way of its realization. It includes wisdom or thoughtfulness because sympathy, concern for the welfare of all affected by conduct, is the surest guarantee for the exercise of consideration, for examination of a proposed line of conduct in all its bearings. And such a complete interest is the only way in which justice can be assured. For it includes as part of itself impartial concern for all conditions which affect the common welfare, be they specific acts, laws, economic arrangements, political institutions, or whatever.

In the case of both the Good and Duty, we noted the moral effect of different social environments. The principle applies equally (and perhaps more obviously) to the use made of approval in determining standards as tests of conduct and the appraisal of virtues and vices. As we have had occasion to observe, each community tends to approve that which is in line with what it prizes in practice. Theoretical approvals that run counter to strong social tendencies tend to become purely nominal. In theory and in verbal instruction our present society is the heir of a great idealistic tradition. Through religion and from other sources, love of neighbor, exact equity, kindliness of action and judgment, are taught and in theory accepted. The structure of society, however, puts emphasis upon other qualities. "Business" absorbs a large part of the life of most persons and business is conducted upon the basis of ruthless competition for private gain. National life is organized on the basis of exclusiveness and tends to generate suspicion, fear, often hatred, of other peoples. The world is divided into classes and races, and, in spite of acceptance of an opposed theory, the standards of valuation are based on the class, race, color, with which one identifies oneself. The convictions that obtain in personal morality are negated on a large scale in collective conduct, and for this reason are weakened even in their strictly personal application. They cannot be made good in practice except as they are extended to include the remaking of the social environment, economic, political, international.

Literature

The literature on utilitarianism is voluminous. For its history, see Albee, *History of English Utilitarianism*, 1902; Stephen, *The English Utilitarians*, three vols., 1900; Halévy, *La Formation du Radicalisme philosophique*, Vols. I. and II.

Criticisms of it will be found in the references on hedonism at the close of Chapter 11. Expositions and criticisms are found also in Lecky, *History of European Morals*, 3rd ed., 1916; Stephen, *Science of Ethics*, 1882, chs. iv. and v.; Höffding, *Ethik*, 1888, ch. vii.; Grote, *Examination of the Utilitarian Philosophy*; Wilson and Fowler, *Principles of Morals*, Vol. I., pp. 98–112, Vol. II., pp. 262–273; Green, *Prolegomena to Ethics*, 1890, pp. 240–255, 399–415; Sidgwick, *The Ethics of T. H. Green, Herbert Spencer, and J. Martineau*, 1902. His *Methods of Ethics*, 1901, almost throughout a critical examination and exposition of utilitarianism; Sharp, *Ethics*, 1928, ch. xvii.; Everett, *Moral Values*, 1918, ch. v.

Upon the principle of virtue in general, see Plato, *Republic*, 427–443; Aristotle, *Ethics*, Books II. and IV.; Kant, *Theory of Ethics*, trans. by Abbott, pp. 164–182, 305, 316–322; Green, *Prolegomena*, pp. 256–314 (and for conscientiousness, pp. 323–337); Paulsen, *System of Ethics*, 1899, pp. 475–482; Alexander, *Moral Order and Progress*, pp. 242–253; Stephen, *Science of Ethics*, 1882, ch. v.; Spencer, *Principles of Ethics*, Vol. II., pp. 3–34 and 263–276; Sidgwick, *Methods of*

Ethics, 1901, pp. 2–5 and 9–10; Rickaby, *Aquinas Ethicus*, Vol. I., pp. 155–195; Fite, *Moral Philosophy*, 1925, ch. iii., contains a discussion of variations in popular standards.

For natural ability and virtue: Hume, *Treatise*, Book III., Part III., and *Inquiry*, Appendix IV.; Bonar, *Intellectual Virtues*.

For discussions of special virtues: Aristotle, *Ethics*, Book III., and Book VII., chs. i.–x.; for justice: Aristotle, *Ethics*, Book V.; Rickaby, *Moral Philosophy*, pp. 102–108, and *Aquinas Ethicus* (see Index); Paulsen, *System of Ethics*, 1899, pp. 599–637; Mill, *Utilitarianism*, ch. v.; Sidgwick, *Methods of Ethics*, 1901, Book III., ch. v., and see Index; also criticism of Spencer in his *Lectures on the Ethics of Green, Spencer, and Martineau*, 1902, pp. 272–302; Spencer, *Principles of Ethics*, Vol. II.; Stephen, *Science of Ethics*, 1882, ch. v.

For benevolence, see Aristotle, *Ethics*, Books VII.–IX. (on friendship); Rickaby, *Moral Philosophy*, pp. 237–244, and *Aquinas Ethicus* (see charity and almsgiving in Index); Paulsen, *System*, 1899, chs. viii. and x. of Part III.; Sidgwick, *Methods of Ethics*, 1901, Book II., ch. iv.; Spencer, *Principles of Ethics*, Vol. II.; see also the references under sympathy and altruism at end of Chapters 14 and 15.

On JUSTICE, Spencer, *Principles of Ethics*, Part IV.; Hobhouse, *The Elements of Social Justice*, 1922; Tufts, "Some Contributions of Psychology to the Conception of Justice," *Philosophical Review*, Vol. XV., p. 361; Calkins, *The Good Man and the Good*, 1918, ch. x.

14.   Moral Judgment and Knowledge

§ 1. Moral Judgments as Intuitive or Developed

That reflective morality, since it *is* reflective, involves thought and knowledge is a truism. The truism raises, however, important problems of theory. What is the nature of knowledge in its moral sense? What is its function? How does it originate and operate? To these questions, writers upon morals have given different answers. Those, for example, who have dwelt upon approval and resentment as the fundamental ethical factor have emphasized its spontaneous and "instinctive" character—that is, its non-reflective nature—and have assigned a subordinate position to the intellectual factor in morals. Those who, like Kant, have made the authority of duty supreme, have marked off Moral Reason from thought and reasoning as they show themselves in ordinary life and in science. They have erected a unique faculty whose sole office is to make us aware of duty and of its imperatively rightful authority over conduct. The moralists who have insisted upon the identity of the Good with ends of desire have, on the contrary, made knowledge, in the sense of insight into the ends which bring enduring satisfaction, the supreme thing in conduct; ignorance, as Plato said, is the root of all evil. And yet, according to Plato, this assured insight into the true End and Good implies a kind of rationality which is radically different from that involved in the ordinary affairs of life. It can be directly attained only by the few who are gifted with those peculiar qualities which enable them to rise to metaphysical understanding of the ultimate constitution of the universe; others must take it on faith or as it is embodied, in a derived way, in laws and institutions. Without going into all the recondite problems associated with the conflict of views, we may say that two significant questions emerge. First, are thought and knowledge mere servants and attendants of emotion, or do they exercise a positive and transforming influence? Secondly, are the thought and judgment employed in connection with moral matters the same that are used in ordinary practical affairs, or are they something separate, having an *exclusively* moral significance? Putting the question in the form which it assumed in discussion during the nineteenth century: Is conscience a faculty of intuition independent of human experience, or is it a product and expression of experience?

The questions are stated in a theoretical form. They have, however, an important practical bearing. They are connected, for example, with the question discussed in the last chapter. Are praise and blame, esteem and condemnation, not only original and spontaneous tendencies, but are they also *ultimate*, incapable of being modified by the critical and constructive work of thought? Again, if conscience is a unique and separate faculty it is incapable of education and modification; it can only be directly appealed to. Most important of all, practically, is that some theories, like the Kantian, make a sharp separation between conduct that is moral and everyday conduct which is morally indifferent and neutral.

It would be difficult to find a question more significant for actual behavior than just this one: Is the moral region isolated from the rest of human activity? Does only one special class of human aims and relations have moral value? This conclusion is a necessary result of the view that our moral consciousness and knowledge is unique in kind. But if moral consciousness is not separate, then no hard and fast line can be drawn within conduct shutting off a moral realm from a non-moral. Now our whole previous discussion is bound up with the latter view. For it has found moral good and excellence in objects and activities which develop out of natural desires and normal social relations in family, neighborhood, and community. We shall accordingly now proceed to make explicit the bearing of this idea upon the nature of moral insight, comparing our conclusions with those arrived at by some other typical theories.

Moral judgments, whatever else they are, are a species of judgments of *value*. They characterize acts and traits of character as having *worth*, positive or negative. Judgments of value are not confined to matters which are explicitly moral in significance.

Our estimates of poems, pictures, landscapes, from the stand-point of their esthetic quality, are value-judgments. Business men are rated with respect to their economic standing in giving of credit, etc. We do not content ourselves with a purely external statement about the weather as it is measured scientifically by the thermometer or barometer. We term it fine or nasty: epithets of value. Articles of furniture are judged useful, comfortable, or the reverse. Scientifically, the condition of the body and mind can be described in terms which neglect entirely the difference between health and disease, in terms, that is, of certain physical and chemical processes. When we pronounce the judgment, "well" or "ill" we estimate in value terms. When we judge the statements of others, whether made in casual conversation or in scientific discourse and pronounce them "true" or "false" we are making judgments of value. Indeed, the chief embarrassment in giving illustrations of value-judgments is that we are so con-stantly engaged in making them. In its popular sense, *all* judg-ment is estimation, appraisal, assigning value to something; a discrimination as to advantage, serviceability, fitness for a pur-pose, enjoyability, and so on.

There is a difference which must be noted between valuation as judgment (which involves thought in placing the thing judged in its relations and bearings) and valuing as a direct emotional and practical act. There is difference between esteem and estima-tion, between prizing and appraising. To esteem is to prize, hold dear, admire, approve; to estimate is to measure in intellectual fashion. One is direct, spontaneous; the other is reflex, reflective. We esteem before we estimate, and estimation comes in to con-sider whether and to what extent something is *worthy* of esteem. Is the object one which we *should* admire? Should we really prize it? Does it have the qualities which *justify* our holding it dear? All growth in maturity is attended with this change from a spontaneous to a reflective and critical attitude. First, our affec-tions go out to something in attraction or repulsion; we like and dislike. Then experience raises the question whether the ob-ject in question is what our esteem or disesteem took it to be, whether it is such as to justify our reaction to it.

The obvious difference between the two attitudes is that direct admiration and prizing are absorbed in the object, a person, act, natural scene, work of art or whatever, to the neglect of its place and effects, its connections with other things. That a lover does not see the beloved one as others do is notorious, and the principle is of universal application. For to think is to look at a thing in its *relations* with other things, and such judgment often modifies radically the original attitude of esteem and liking. A commonplace instance is the difference between natural liking for some object of food, and the recognition forced upon us by experience that it is not "good" for us, that it is not healthful. A child may like and prize candy inordinately; an adult tells him it is not good for him, that it will make him ill. "Good" to the child signifies that which tastes good; that which satisfies an immediate craving. "Good" from the standpoint of the more experienced person is that which serves certain ends, that which stands in certain connections with consequences. Judgment of value is the name of the act which searches for and takes into consideration these connections.

There is an evident unity between this point and what was said in the last chapter about approval and reprobation, praise and blame. A normal person will not witness an act of wanton cruelty without an immediate response of disfavor; resentment and indignation immediately ensue. A child will respond in this way when some person of whom he is fond is made to suffer by another. An adult, however, may recognize that the one inflicting the suffering is a physician who is doing what he does in the interest of a patient. The child takes the act for what is immediately present to him and finds it bad; the other interprets it as one element in a larger whole and finds it good in that connection. In this change is illustrated in a rudimentary way the processes through which, out of spontaneous acts of favor and disfavor, there develops the idea of a *standard* by which approval and disapproval should be regulated. The change explains the fact that judgments of value are not mere registrations (see p. 253) of previous attitudes of favor and disfavor, liking and aversion, but have a reconstructive and transforming effect upon them, by determining the objects that are worthy of esteem and approbation.

§ 2. The Immediate Sense of Value and Its Limitations

The distinction between direct *valuing*, in the sense of prizing and being absorbed in an object or person, and *valuation* as reflective judgment, based upon consideration of a comprehensive scheme, has an important bearing upon the controversy as to the *intuitive* character of moral judgments. Our immediate responses of approval and reprobation may well be termed intuitive. They are not based upon any thought-out reason or ground. We just admire and resent, are attracted and repelled. This attitude is not only original and primitive but it persists in acquired dispositions. The reaction of an expert in any field is, relatively at least, intuitive rather than reflective. An expert in real estate will, for example, "size up" pecuniary values of land and property with a promptness and exactness which are far beyond the capacity of a layman. A scientifically trained person will see the meaning and possibilities of some line of investigation, where the untrained person might require years of study to make anything out of it. Some persons are happily gifted in their direct appreciation of personal relations; they are noted for tact, not in the sense of a superficial amiability but of real insight into human needs and affections. The results of prior experience, including previous conscious thinking, get taken up into direct habits, and express themselves in direct appraisals of value. Most of our moral judgments are intuitive, but this fact is not a proof of the existence of a separate faculty of moral insight, but is the result of past experience funded into direct outlook upon the scene of life. As Aristotle remarked in effect a long time ago, the immediate judgments of good and evil of a good man are more to be trusted than many of the elaborately reasoned out estimates of the inexperienced.

The immediate character of moral judgments is reenforced by the lessons of childhood and youth. Children are surrounded by adults who constantly pass judgments of value on conduct. And these comments are not coldly intellectual; they are made under conditions of a strongly emotional nature. Pains are taken to stamp them in by impregnating the childish response with elements of awe and mystery, as well as ordinary reward and punishment. The attitudes remain when the circumstances of their origin are forgotten; they are made so much a part of the self that they seem to be inevitable and innate.

This fact, while it explains the intuitive character of reactions, also indicates a limitation of direct valuations. They are often the result of an education which was misdirected. If the conditions of their origin were intelligent, that is, if parents and friends who took part in their creation, were morally wise, they are likely to be intelligent. But arbitrary and irrelevant circumstances often enter in, and leave their impress as surely as do reasonable factors. The very fact of the early origin and now unconscious quality of the attendant intuitions is often distorting and limiting. It is almost impossible for later reflection to get at and correct that which has become unconsciously a part of the self. The warped and distorted will seem natural. Only the conventional and the fanatical are always immediately sure of right and wrong in conduct.

There is a permanent limit to the value of even the best of the intuitive appraisals of which we have been speaking. These are dependable in the degree in which conditions and objects of esteem are fairly uniform and recurrent. They do not work with equal sureness in the cases in which the new and unfamiliar enters in. "New occasions teach new duties." But they cannot teach them to those who suppose that they can trust without further reflection to estimates of the good and evil which are brought over from the past to the new occasion. Extreme intuitionalism and extreme conservatism often go together. Dislike to thoughtful consideration of the requirements of new situations is frequently a sign of fear that the result of examination will be a new insight which will entail the changing of settled habits and will compel departure from easy grooves in behavior—a process which is uncomfortable.

Taken in and of themselves, intuitions or immediate feelings of what is good and bad are of psychological rather than moral import. They are indications of formed habits rather than adequate evidence of what should be approved and disapproved. They afford at most, when habits already existing are of a good character, a *presumption* of correctness, and are guides, clews. But (a) nothing is more immediate and seemingly sure of itself than inveterate prejudice. The morals of a class, clique, or race when brought in contact with those of other races and peoples, are usually so sure of the rectitude of their own judgments of good and bad that they are narrow and give rise to misunderstanding and hostility. (b) A judgment which is adequate under ordinary circumstance may go far astray under changed conditions. It goes without saying that false ideas about values have to be emended; it is not so readily seen that ideas of good and evil which were once true have to be modified as social conditions change. Men become attached to their judgments as they cling to other possessions which familiarity has made dear. Especially in times like the present, when industrial, political, and scientific transformations are rapidly in process, a revision of old appraisals is especially needed. (c) The tendency of undiluted intuitional theory is in the direction of an unquestioning dogmatism, what Bentham called *ipse dixitism*. Every intuition, even the best, is likely to become perfunctory and second-hand unless revitalized by consideration of its meaning—that is, of the consequences which will accrue from acting upon it. There is no necessary connection between a conviction of right and good in general and *what* is right and good in particular. A man may have a strong conviction of duty without enlightenment as to just where his duty lies. When he assumes that because he is actuated by consciousness of duty in general, he can trust without reflective inquiry to his immediate ideas of the particular thing which is his duty, he is likely to become socially dangerous. If he is a person of strong will he will attempt to impose his judgments and standards upon others in a ruthless way, convinced that he is supported by the authority of Right and the Will of God.

§ 3. Sensitivity and Thoughtfulness

The permanent element of value in the intuitional theory lies in its implicit emphasis upon the importance of direct responsiveness to the qualities of situations and acts. A keen eye and a quick ear are not in themselves guarantees of correct knowledge of physical objects. But they are conditions without which such knowledge cannot arise. Nothing can make up for the absence of immediate sensitiveness; the insensitive person is callous, indifferent. Unless there is a direct, mainly unreflective appreciation of persons and deeds, the data for subsequent thought will be lacking or distorted. A person must *feel* the qualities of acts as one feels with the hands the qualities of roughness and smoothness in objects, before he has an inducement to deliberate or material with which to deliberate. Effective reflection must also terminate in a situation which is directly appreciated, if thought is to be effective in action. "Cold blooded" thought may reach a correct conclusion, but if a person remains anti-pathetic or indifferent to the considerations presented to him in a rational way, they will not stir him to act in accord with them (see p. 190).

This fact explains the element of truth in the theories which insist that in their root and essence moral judgments are emotional rather than intellectual. A moral judgment, however intellectual it may be, must at least be colored with feeling if it is to influence behavior. Resentment, ranging from fierce abhorrence through disgust to mild repugnance, is a necessary ingredient of knowledge of evil which is genuine knowledge. Affection, from intense love to mild favor, is an ingredient in all operative knowledge, all full apprehension, of the good. It is, however, going too far to say that such appreciation can dispense with every cognitive element. There may be no knowledge of *why* a given act calls out sympathy or antipathy, no knowledge of the grounds upon which it rests for justification. In fact a strong emotional appreciation seems at the time to be its own reason and justification. But there must at least be an idea of the object which is admired or despised, there must be some perceived cause, or person, that is cared for, and that solicits concern. Otherwise we have mere brute anger like the destructive rage of a beast, or mere immediate gratification like that of an animal in taking food.

Our sensory reactions, of eye, ear, hand, nose, and tongue supply material of our knowledge of qualities of physical things, sticks, stones, fruits, etc. It is sometimes argued that they afford also the material of our knowledge of persons; that, seeing certain shapes and colors, hearing certain sounds, etc., we infer by analogy that a particular physical body is inhabited by a sentient and emotional being such as we associate with the forms and contacts which compose our own body. The theory is absurd. *Emotional* reactions form the chief materials of our knowledge of ourselves and of others. Just as ideas of physical objects are constituted out of sensory material, so those of persons are framed out of emotional and affectional materials. The latter are as direct, as immediate as the former, and more interesting, with a greater hold on attention. The animism of primitive life, the tendency to personify natural events and things (which survives in poetry), is evidence of the original nature of perception of persons; it is inexplicable on the theory that we infer the existence of persons through a round-about use of analogy. Wherever we strongly hate or love, we tend to predicate directly a lovely and loving, a hateful and hating being. Without emotional behavior, all human beings would be for us only animated automatons. Consequently all actions which call out lively esteem or disfavor are perceived as acts *of* persons: we do not make a distinction in such cases between the doer and the deed. A noble act signifies a noble person; a mean act a mean person.

On this account, the reasonable act and the generous act lie close together. A person entirely lacking in sympathetic response might have a keen calculating intellect, but he would have no spontaneous sense of the claims of others for satisfaction of their desires. A person of narrow sympathy is of necessity a person of confined outlook upon the scene of human good. The only truly *general* thought is the *generous* thought. It is sympathy which carries thought out beyond the self and which extends its scope till it approaches the universal as its limit. It is sympathy which saves consideration of consequences from degenerating into mere calculation, by rendering vivid the interests of others and urging us to give them the same weight as those which touch our own honor, purse, and power. To put ourselves in the place of others, to see things from the standpoint of their purposes and values, to humble, contrariwise, our own pretensions and claims till they reach the level they would assume in the eye of an impartial sympathetic observer, is the surest way to attain objectivity of moral knowledge. Sympathy is the animating mold of moral judgment not because its dictates take precedence in action over those of other impulses (which they do not do), but because it furnishes the most efficacious *intellectual* standpoint. It is the tool, *par excellence*, for resolving complex situations. Then when it passes into active and overt conduct, it does so *fused* with other impulses and not in isolation and is thus protected from sentimentality. In this fusion there is broad and objective survey of all desires and projects because there is an expanded personality.

Through sympathy the cold calculation of utilitarianism and the formal law of Kant are transported into vital and moving realities. One of the earliest discoveries of morals was the similarity of judgment of good and bad in conduct with the recognition of beauty and ugliness in conduct. Feelings of the repulsiveness of vice and the attractiveness of virtuous acts root in esthetic sentiment. Emotions of admiration and of disgust are native; when they are turned upon conduct they form an element which furnishes the truth that lies in the theory of a moral *sense*. The sense of justice, moreover, has a strong ally in the sense of symmetry and proportion. The double meaning of the term "fair" is no accident. The Greek *sophrosyne* (of which our temperance, through the Latin *temperantia*, is a poor representation), a harmonious blending of affections into a beautiful whole, was essentially an artistic idea. Self-control was its inevitable *result*, but self-control as a deliberate cause would have seemed as abhorrent to the Athenian as would "control" in a building or statue where control signified anything other than the idea of the whole permeating all parts and bringing them into order and measured unity. The Greek emphasis upon *Kalokagathos*, the Aristotelian identification of virtue with the proportionate mean, are indications of an acute estimate of grace, rhythm, and harmony as dominant traits of good conduct (p. 98). The modern mind has been much less sensitive to esthetic values in general and to these values in conduct in particular. Much has been lost in direct responsiveness to right. The bleakness and harshness often associated with morals is a sign of this loss.

The direct valuing which accompanies immediate sensitive responsiveness to acts has its complement and expansion in valuations which are deliberate, reflective. As Aristotle pointed out, only the good man is a good judge of what is truly good; it takes a fine and well-grounded character to react immediately with the right approvals and condemnations. And to this statement must be added two qualifications. One is that even the good man can trust for enlightenment to his direct responses of values only in simpler situations, in those which are already upon the whole familiar. The better he is, the more likely he is to be perplexed as to what to do in novel, complicated situations. Then the only way out is through examination, inquiry, turning things over in his mind till something presents itself, perhaps after prolonged men-

tal fermentation, to which he can directly react. The other qualification is that there is no such thing as a good man—in an absolute sense. Immediate appreciation is liable to be warped by
many considerations which can be detected and uprooted only
through inquiry and criticism. To be completely good and an infallible judge of right a man would have had to live from infancy
in a thoroughly good social medium free from all limiting and
distorting influences. As it is, habits of liking and disliking are
formed early in life, prior to ability to use discriminating intelligence. Prejudices, unconscious biases, are generated; one is uneven in his distribution of esteem and admiration; he is unduly
sensitive to some values, relatively indifferent to others. He is
set in his ways, and his immediate appreciations travel in the
grooves laid down by his unconsciously formed habits. Hence
the spontaneous "intuitions" of value have to be entertained
subject to correction, to confirmation and revision, by personal
observation of consequences and cross-questioning of their quality and scope.

§ 4. Conscience and Deliberation

The usual name for this process is deliberation; the
name given moral deliberativeness when it is habitual is conscientiousness. This quality is constituted by scrupulous attentiveness to the potentialities of any act or proposed aim. Its possession is a characteristic of those who do not allow themselves
to be unduly swayed by immediate appetite and passion, nor to
fall into ruts of routine behavior. The "good" man who rests on
his oars, who permits himself to be propelled simply by the momentum of his attained right habits, loses alertness; he ceases to
be on the lookout. With that loss, his goodness drops away from
him. There is, indeed, a quality called "overconscientiousness,"
but it is not far from a vice. It signifies constant anxiety as to
whether one is really good or not, a moral "self-consciousness"
which spells embarrassment, constraint in action, morbid fear. It
is a caricature of genuine conscientiousness. For the latter is not
an anxious prying into motives, a fingering of the inner springs
of action to detect whether or not a "motive" is good. Genuine
conscientiousness has an objective outlook; it is intelligent atten-

tion and care to the quality of an act in view of its consequences for general happiness; it is not anxious solicitude for one's own virtuous state.

Perhaps the most striking difference between immediate sensitiveness, or "intuition," and "conscientiousness" as reflective interest, is that the former tends to rest upon the plane of achieved goods, while the latter is on the outlook for something *better*. The truly conscientious person not only uses a standard in judging, but is concerned to revise and improve his standard. He realizes that the value resident in acts goes beyond anything which he has already apprehended, and that therefore there must be something inadequate in any standard which has been definitely formulated. He is on the *lookout* for good not already achieved. Only by thoughtfulness does one become sensitive to the far-reaching implications of an act; apart from continual reflection we are at best sensitive only to the value of special and limited ends.

The larger and remoter values of an act form what is ordinarily termed an ideal. About nothing, perhaps, is misconception more current than as to the nature of ideals. They are thought of sometimes as fixed, remote goals, too far away to be ever realized in conduct and sometimes as vague emotional inspirations which take the place of thought in directing conduct. Thus the "idealist" is thought of as either an impractical person, concerned with the unattainable, or else as a person who is moved by aspirations for something intangible of a vague spiritual sort having no concrete reference to actual situations. The trouble with ideals of remote "perfection" is that they tend to make us negligent of the significance of the special situations in which we have to act; they are thought of as trivial in comparison with the ideal of perfection. The genuine ideal, on the contrary, is the sense that each of these special situations brings with it its own inexhaustible meaning, that its value reaches far beyond its direct local existence. Its nature is perhaps best expressed in the verses of George Herbert:

Who sweeps a room as for Thy Laws
Makes that and th' action fine.

As we have said, reflection when directed to practical matters, to determination of what to do, is called deliberation. A general deliberates upon the conduct of a campaign, weighing possible moves of the enemy and of his own troops, considering pros and cons; a business man deliberates in comparing various modes of investment; a lawyer deliberates upon the conduct of his case, and so on. In all cases of deliberation, judgment of *value* enters; the one who engages in it is concerned to weigh values with a view to discovering the better and rejecting the worse. In some cases, the value of ends is thought of and in other cases the value of means. Moral deliberation differs from other forms not as a process of forming a judgment and arriving at knowledge but in the kind of value which is thought about. The value is technical, professional, economic, etc., as long as one thinks of it as something which one can aim at and attain by way of having, *possessing*; as something to be got or to be missed. Precisely the same object will have a moral value when it is thought of as making a difference in the *self*, as determining what one will *be*, instead of merely what one will *have*. Deliberation involves doubt, hesitation, the need of making up one's mind, of arriving at a decisive choice. The choice at stake in a moral deliberation or valuation is the worth of this and that kind of character and disposition. Deliberation is not then to be identified with calculation, or a quasimathematical reckoning of profit and loss. Such calculation assumes that the nature of the self does not enter into question, but only how much the self is going to *get* of this and that. Moral deliberation deals not with quantity of value but with quality.

We estimate the import or significance of any present desire or impulse by forecasting what it will come or amount to if carried out; literally its consequences define its *consequence*, its meaning or import. But if these consequences are conceived *merely as remote*, if their picturing does not arouse a present sense of peace, of fulfillment, or of dissatisfaction, of incompletion and irritation, the process of thinking out consequences remains purely intellectual. It is as barren of influence upon behavior as the mathematical speculations of a disembodied angel. Any actual experience of reflection upon conduct will show that every foreseen result at once stirs our present affections, our likes and dislikes, our desires and aversions. There is developed a running commentary which stamps objects at once as good or evil. It is this direct sense of value, not the consciousness of general rules or ultimate goals, which finally determines the worth of the act to the agent. Here is an inexpugnable element of truth in the intuitional theory. Its error lies in conceiving this immediate response of appreciation as if it excluded reflection instead of following directly upon its heels. Deliberation is actually an imaginative rehearsal of various courses of conduct. We give way, *in our mind*, to some impulse; we try, *in our mind*, some plan. Following its career through various steps, we find ourselves in imagination in the presence of the consequences that would follow: and as we then like and approve, or dislike and disapprove, these consequences, we find the original impulse or plan good or bad. Deliberation is dramatic and active, not mathematical and impersonal; and hence it has the intuitive, the direct factor in it. The advantage of a mental trial, prior to the overt trial (for the act after all is itself also a trial, a proving of the idea that lies back of it), is that it is retrievable, whereas overt consequences remain. They cannot be recalled. Moreover, many trials may mentally be made in a short time. The imagining of various plans carried out furnishes an opportunity for many impulses which at first are not in evidence at all, to get under way. Many and varied direct sensings, appreciations, take place. When many tendencies are brought into play, there is clearly much greater probability that the capacity of self which is really needed and appropriate will be brought into action, and thus a truly reasonable happiness result. The tendency of deliberation to "polarize" the various lines of activity into opposed alternatives, into incompatible "either this or that," is a way of forcing into clear recognition the importance of the issue.

§ 5. The Nature and Office of Principles

It is clear that the various situations in which a person is called to deliberate and judge have common elements, and that values found in them resemble one another. It is also obvious that general ideas are a great aid in judging particular cases. If different situations were wholly unlike one another, nothing could be learned from one which would be of any avail in any other. But having like points, experience carries over from one to another, and experience is intellectually cumulative. Out of resembling experiences general ideas develop; through language, instruction, and tradition this gathering together of experiences of value into generalized points of view is extended to take in a whole people and a race. Through intercommunication the experience of the entire human race is to some extent pooled and crystallized in general ideas. These ideas constitute *principles*. We bring them with us to deliberation on particular situations.

These generalized points of view are of great use in surveying particular cases. But as they are transmitted from one generation to another, they tend to become fixed and rigid. Their origin in experience is forgotten and so is their proper use in further experience. They are thought of as if they existed in and of themselves and as if it were simply a question of bringing action under them in order to determine what is right and good. Instead of being treated as aids and instruments in judging values as the latter actually arise, they are made superior to them. They become prescriptions, rules. Now a genuine principle differs from a rule in two ways: (a) A principle evolves in connection with the course of experience, being a generalized statement of what sort of consequences and values tend to be realized in certain kinds of situations; a rule is taken as something ready-made and fixed. (b) A principle is primarily intellectual, a method and scheme for judging, and is practical secondarily because of what it discloses; a rule is primarily practical.

Suppose that one is convinced that the rule of honesty is made known just in and of itself by a special faculty, and has absolutely nothing to do with recollection of past cases or forecast of possible future circumstances. How would such a rule apply itself to any particular case which needed to be judged? What bell would ring, what signal would be given, to indicate that just *this* case is the appropriate case for the application of the rule of honest dealing? And if by some miracle this question were answered, if we could know that here is a case for the rule of honesty, how should we know just what course in detail the rule calls for? For the rule, to be applicable to all cases, must omit the conditions which differentiate one case from another; it must contain only the very few similar elements which are to be found in all honest deeds. Reduced to this skeleton, not much would be left save the bare injunction to be honest whatever happens, leaving it to chance, the ordinary judgment of the individual, or to external authority to find out just *what* honesty specifically means in the given case.

This difficulty is so serious that all systems which have committed themselves to belief in a number of hard and fast rules having their origin in conscience, or in the word of God impressed upon the human soul or externally revealed, always have had to resort to a more and more complicated procedure to cover, if possible, all the cases. The moral life is finally reduced by them to an elaborate formalism and legalism.

Suppose, for example, we take the Ten Commandments as a starting-point. They are only ten, and naturally confine themselves to general ideas, and ideas stated mainly in negative form. Moreover, the same act may be brought under more than one rule. In order to resolve the practical perplexities and uncertainties which inevitably arise under such circumstances, *Casuistry* is built up (from the Latin *casus*, case). The attempt is made to foresee all the different cases of action which may conceivably occur, and provide in advance the exact rule for each case. For example, with reference to the rule "do not kill," a list will be made of all the different situations in which killing might occur:—accident, war, fulfillment of command of political superior (as by a hangman), self-defense (defense of one's own life, of others, of property), deliberate or premeditated killing with its different motives (jealousy, avarice, revenge, etc.), killing with slight premeditation, from sudden impulse, from different sorts and degrees of provocation. To each one of these possible cases is assigned its exact moral quality, its exact degree of turpitude and innocency. Nor can this process end with overt acts; all the inner springs of action which affect regard for life must be similarly classified: envy, animosity, sudden rage, sullenness, cherishing of sense of injury, love of tyrannical power, hardness or hostility, callousness—all these must be specified into their different kinds and the exact moral worth of each determined. What is done for this one kind of case must be done for every part and phase of the entire moral life until it is all inventoried, catalogued, and distributed into pigeon-holes definitely labeled.

Dangers and evils attend this way of conceiving the moral life. (a) *It tends to magnify the letter of morality at the expense of its spirit.* It fixes attention not upon the positive good in an act, not upon the underlying agent's disposition which forms its spirit, nor upon the unique occasion and context which form its atmosphere, but upon its literal conformity with Rule A, Class I., Species 1, subhead (1), etc. The effect of this is inevitably to narrow the scope and lessen the depth of conduct. (i.) It tempts some to hunt for that classification of their act which will make it the most convenient or profitable for themselves. In popular speech, "casuistical" has come to mean a way of judging acts which splits hairs in the effort to find a way of acting that conduces to personal interest and profit, and which yet may be justified by some moral principle. (ii.) With others, this regard for the letter makes conduct formal and pedantic. It gives rise to a rigid and hard type of character conventionally attributed to the Pharisees of olden and the Puritans of modern time—the moral schemes of both classes being strongly impregnated with the notion of fixed moral rules.

(b) *This ethical system also tends in practice to a legal view of conduct.* Historically it always has sprung from carrying over legal ideas into morality. In the legal view liability to blame and to punishment inflicted from without by some superior authority, is necessarily prominent. Conduct is regulated through specific injunctions and prohibitions: Do this, Do not do that. Exactly the sort of analysis of which we have spoken above (p. 277) in the case of killing is necessary, so that there may be definite and regular methods of measuring guilt and assigning blame. Now liability, punishment, and reward are important factors in the conduct of life, but any scheme of morals is defective which puts the question of avoiding punishment in the foreground of attention, or which tends to create a pharisaical complacency in the mere fact of having conformed to command or rule.

(c) *Probably the worst evil of this moral system is that it tends to deprive moral life of freedom and spontaneity* and to reduce it (especially for the conscientious who take it seriously) to a more or less anxious and servile conformity to externally imposed rules. Obedience as loyalty to principle is a good, but this scheme practically makes it the only good and conceives it not as loyalty to ideals, but as conformity to commands. Moral rules exist just as independent deliverances on their own account, and the right thing is merely to follow them. This puts the centre of moral gravity outside the concrete processes of living. All systems which emphasize the letter more than the spirit, legal consequences more than vital motives, put the individual under the weight of external authority. They lead to the kind of conduct described by St. Paul as under the law, not in the spirit, with its constant attendant weight of anxiety, uncertain struggle, and impending doom. Many who strenuously object to all of these schemes of conduct, to everything which hardens it into forms by emphasizing external commands, authority, and punishments and rewards, fail to see that such evils are logically connected with any acceptance of the finality of fixed rules. They hold certain bodies of people, religious officers, political or legal authorities, responsible for what they object to in the scheme; while they still cling to the idea that morality is an effort to apply to particular deeds and projects a certain number of absolute unchanging moral rules. They fail to see that, if this were its nature, those who attempt to provide the machinery which would render it practically workable deserve praise rather than blame. In fact, the notion of absolute rules or precepts cannot be made workable except through certain superior authorities who declare and enforce them. Said Locke: "It is no small power it gives one man over another to be the dictator of principles and teacher of unquestionable truths."

There is another practically harmful consequence which follows from the identification of principles with rules. Take the case of, say, justice. There may be all but universal agreement in the notion that justice is the proper rule of conduct—so universal as to be admitted by all but criminals. But just what does justice demand in the concrete? The present state of such things as penology, prison reform, the tariff, sumptuary laws, trusts, the relation of capital and labor, collective bargaining, democratic government, private or public ownership of public utilities, communal versus private property, shows that persons of equally well-meaning dispositions find that justice means opposite things in practice, although all proclaim themselves devoted to justice as the rule of action. Taken as a principle, not as a rule, justice signifies the will to *examine* specific institutions and measures so as to find out how they operate with the view of introducing greater impartiality and equity into the consequences they produce.

This consideration brings us to the important fact regarding the nature of true moral principles. *Rules are practical; they are habitual ways of doing things. But principles are intellectual; they are the final methods used in judging suggested courses of action.* The fundamental error of the intuitionalist is that he is on the outlook for rules which will of themselves tell agents just what course of action to pursue; *whereas the object of moral principles is to supply standpoints and methods which will enable the individual to make for himself an analysis of the elements of good and evil in the particular situation in which he finds himself.* No genuine moral principle prescribes a specific course of action; rules,[1] like cooking recipes, may tell just what to do and how to do it. A moral principle, such as that of chastity, of justice, of the Golden Rule, gives the agent a basis for looking at and examining a particular question that comes up. It holds before him certain possible aspects of the act; it warns him against taking a short or partial view of the act. It economizes his thinking by supplying him with the main heads by reference to which to consider the bearings of his desires and purposes; it guides him in his thinking by suggesting to him the important considerations for which he should be on the lookout.

A moral principle, then, is not a command to act or forbear acting in a given way: *it is a tool for analyzing a special situation,* the right or wrong being determined by the situation in its entirety, and not by the rule as such. We sometimes hear it stated, for example, that the universal adoption of the Golden Rule would at once settle all industrial disputes and difficulties. But suppose that the principle were accepted in good faith by everybody; it would not at once tell everybody just what to do in all the complexities of his relations to others. When individuals are still uncertain of what their real good may be, it does not finally decide matters to tell them to regard the good of others as they would their own. Nor does it mean that whatever in detail we want for ourselves we should strive to give to others. Because I am fond of classical music it does not follow that I should thrust as much of it as possible upon my neighbors. But the "Golden Rule" does furnish us a *point of view from which to consider acts;* it suggests the necessity of considering how our acts affect

---

1. Of course, the word "rule" is often used to designate a principle—as in the case of the phrase "Golden Rule." We are speaking not of the words, but of their underlying ideas.

the interests of others as well as our own; it tends to prevent partiality of regard; it warns against setting an undue estimate upon a particular consequence of pain or pleasure, simply because it happens to affect us. In short, the Golden Rule does not issue special orders or commands; but it does clarify and illuminate the situations requiring intelligent deliberation.

The same distinction is implied in what was brought out in the last chapter between happiness (in the sense of general welfare) as an end and as a standard. If it were regarded as the direct end of acts, it might be taken to be something fixed and inflexible. As a standard it is rather a cautionary direction, saying that when we judge an act, accomplished or proposed, with reference to approval and disapproval, we should first consider its consequences in general, and then its special consequences with respect to whatever affects the well-being of others. As a standard it provides a consistent point of view to be taken in all deliberation, but it does not pretend to determine in advance precisely what constitutes the general welfare or common good. It leaves room open for discovery of new constituents of well-being, and for varying combinations of these constituents in different situations. If the standard were taken as a rule, in the sense of a recipe, it would signify that one comes to each case with a prior hard and fast, Procrustean, and complete conception of just and only what elements form happiness, so that this conception can be applied like a mathematical formula. "Standards" interpreted after this fashion breed self-righteousness, moral conceit, and fanaticism. The standard as a standpoint for survey of situations allows free play to the imagination in reaching new insights. It requires, rather than merely permits, continual advance in the conception of what constitutes happiness in the concrete.

It follows accordingly that the important thing about knowledge in its moral aspect is not its actual extent so much as it is the *will* to know—the active desire to examine conduct in its bearing upon the general good. Actual information and insight are limited by conditions of birth, education, social environment. The notion of the intuitional theory that all persons possess a uniform and equal stock of moral judgments is contrary to fact. Yet there are common human affections and impulses which express themselves within every social environment;—there is no people the members of which do not have a belief in the value of human life, of care of offspring, of loyalty to tribal and community customs, etc., however restricted and one-sided they may be in the application of these beliefs. Beyond this point, there is always, on whatever level of culture, the possibility of being on the alert for opportunities to widen and deepen the meaning of existing moral ideas. The attitude of *seeking* for what is good may be cultivated under any conditions of race, class, and state of civilization. Persons who are ignorant in the conventional sense of education may display an interest in discovering and considering what is good which is absent in the highly literate and polished. From the standpoint of this interest, class divisions vanish. The moral quality of knowledge lies not in possession but in concern with increase. The essential evil of fixed standards and rules is that it tends to render men satisfied with the existing state of affairs and to take the ideas and judgments they already possess as adequate and final.

The need for constant revision and expansion of moral knowledge is one great reason why there is no gulf dividing non-moral knowledge from that which is truly moral. At any moment conceptions which once seemed to belong exclusively to the biological or physical realm may assume moral import. This will happen whenever they are discovered to have a bearing on the common good. When knowledge of bacteria and germs and their relation to the spread of disease was achieved, sanitation, public and private, took on a moral significance it did not have before. For they were seen to affect the health and well-being of the community. Psychiatrists and psychologists working within their own technical regions have brought to light facts and principles which profoundly affect old conceptions of, say, punishment and responsibility, especially in their place in the formation of disposition. It has been discovered, for example, that "problem children" are created by conditions which exist in families and in the reaction of parents to the young. In a rough way, it may be asserted that most of the morbid conditions of mind and character which develop later have their origin in emotional arrests and maladjustments of early life. These facts have not as yet made their way very far into popular understanding and action, but their ultimate moral import is incalculable. Knowledge once technically confined to physics and chemistry is applied in industry and has an effect on the lives and happiness of individuals beyond all estimate. The list of examples might be extended indefinitely. The important point is that any restriction of moral knowledge and judgments to a definite realm necessarily limits our perception of moral significance. A large part of the difference between those who are stagnant and reactionary and those who are genuinely progressive in social matters comes from the fact that the former think of morals as confined, boxed, within a round of duties and sphere of values which are fixed and final. Most of the serious moral problems of the present time are dependent for their solution upon a general realization that the contrary is the case. Probably the great need of the present time is that the traditional barriers between scientific and moral knowledge be broken down, so that there will be organized and consecutive endeavor to use all available scientific knowledge for humane and social ends.

There is, therefore, little need of calling attention to the point with which we have concluded the previous chapters: namely, the influence of the social environment upon the chief ethical concepts. Only if some rigid form of intuitionalism were true, would the state of culture and the growth of knowledge in forms usually called non-moral, be without significance for distinctively moral knowledge and judgment. Because the two things are connected, each generation, especially one living in a time like the present, is under the responsibility of overhauling its inherited stock of moral principles and reconsidering them in relation to contemporary conditions and needs. It is stupid to suppose that this signifies that all moral principles are so relative to a particular state of society that they have no binding force in any social condition. The obligation is to discover *what* principles *are* relevant to our own social estate. Since this social condition is a fact, the principles which are related to it are real and significant, even though they be not adapted to some other set and style of social institutions, culture, and scientific knowledge. It is the insistence on a uniform and unchanging code of morals, the same at all times and places, which brings about the extreme revolt which says that they are all conventional and of no validity. Recognition of their close and vital relationship to social forces will create and reenforce search for the principles which are truly relevant in our own day.

Literature

Original material for the earlier history of intuitionalism is found in Selby-Bigge, *British Moralists*, I. and II., from Butler and Price respectively. Selections from Butler, Price, and Reid are found in Rand's *Classical Moralists*. For the "moral sense" theory, see Shaftesbury, *Characteristics*; Hutcheson, *System of Moral Philosophy*. Consult also Sidgwick, *History of Ethics, passim*; and Rogers, *Morals in Review*, 1927. Bonar, *Moral Sense*, 1930, contains an excellent account of the development of the moral sense theory in British thought.

For the relation between sympathy and moral judgment, see Smith, *Theory of Moral Sentiments*, especially Part III., chs. i. and iv., and Part IV., chs. i.–iii., and Stephen, *Science of Ethics*, 1882, pp. 228–238.

For the controversy between the emotional and rational theories of moral judgment see Rashdall, *Is Conscience an Emotion?* 1914, defending the rational theory against McDougall, *Social Psychology*, 1909, and Westermarck, *The Origin and Development of Moral Ideas*, 1906. Fite's *Moral Philosophy*, 1925, is noteworthy for the importance attached to insight in the moral life. See also Aristotle, *Ethics*, Book III., chs. ii.–iii., and Book VI. The nature of deliberation is discussed at greater length in Dewey, *Human Nature and Conduct*, 1922, pp. 189–209. Dewey, *The Quest for Certainty*, 1930, ch. viii., discusses the difference between the immediate sense of value and the judgment of value.

For intuitionalism, see Calderwood, *Handbook of Moral Philosophy*; Maurice, *Conscience*; Whewell, *The Elements of Morality*; Martineau, *Types of Ethical Theory*, Vol. II., 1901, pp. 96–115; Mezes, *Ethics*, 1901, ch. iii.; Sidgwick, *Methods of Ethics*, Book I., chs. viii.–ix., and Book III. entire, but especially ch. i., *History of Ethics*, pp. 170–204, and 224–236, and *Lectures on Ethics of Green, Spencer, and Martineau*, 1902, pp. 361–374.

15. The Moral Self

§ 1. The Self and Choice

The self has occupied a central place in the previous discussions, in which important aspects of the good self have been brought out. The self should be *wise* or prudent, looking to an inclusive satisfaction and hence subordinating the satisfaction of an immediately urgent single appetite; it should be *faithful* in acknowledgment of the claims involved in its relations with others; it should be solicitous, *thoughtful*, in the award of praise and blame, use of approbation and disapprobation, and, finally, should be *conscientious* and have the active will to discover new values and to revise former notions. We have not, however, examined just what is the significance of the self. The important position of the self in morals, and also various controversies of moral theory which have gathered about it, make such an examination advisable. A brief reference to the opposed theories will help to indicate the points which need special attention.

A most profound line of cleavage has appeared in topics already discussed. Some theories hold that the self, apart from what it does, is the supreme and exclusive moral end. This view is contained in Kant's assertion that the Good Will, aside from consequences of acts performed, is the only Moral Good. A similar idea is implicit whenever moral goodness is identified in an exclusive way with virtue, so that the final aim of a good person is, when summed up briefly, to maintain his own virtue. When the self is assumed to be the *end* in an exclusive way, then conduct, acts, consequences, are all treated as *mere* means, as external instruments for maintaining the good self. The opposed point of view is found in the hedonism of the earlier utilitarians when they assert that a certain kind of consequences, pleasure, is the only good end and that the self and its qualities are mere means for producing these consequences.

Our own theory gives both self and consequences indispensable roles. We have held, by implication, that neither one can be made to be merely a means to the other. There is a circular arrangement. The self is not a *mere* means to producing consequences because the consequences, when of a moral kind, enter into the formation of the self and the self enters into them. To use a somewhat mechanical analogy, bricks are means to building a house, but they are not *mere* means because they finally *compose* a part of the house itself; if being a part of the house then reacted to modify the nature of the bricks themselves the analogy would be quite adequate. Similarly, conduct and consequences are important, but instead of being separate from the self they form, reveal, and test the self. That which has just been stated in a formal way will be given concrete meaning if we consider the nature of choice, since choice is the most characteristic activity of a self.

Prior to anything which may be called choice in the sense of deliberate decision come spontaneous selections or *preferences*. Every appetite and impulse, however blind, is a mode of preferring one thing to another; it selects one thing and rejects others. It goes out with attraction to certain objects, putting them ahead of others in value. The latter are neglected although from a purely external standpoint they are equally accessible and available. We are so constructed that both by original temperament and by acquired habit we move toward some objects rather than others. Such preference antecedes judgment of comparative values; it is organic rather than conscious. Afterwards there arise situations in which wants compete; we are drawn spontaneously in opposite directions. Incompatible preferences hold each other in check. We hesitate, and then hesitation becomes deliberation: that weighing of values in comparison with each other of which we have already spoken. At last, a preference emerges which is intentional and which is based on consciousness of the values which deliberation has brought into view. We have to make up our minds, when we want two conflicting things, which of them we *really* want. That is choice. We prefer spontaneously, we choose deliberately, knowingly.

Now every such choice sustains a double relation to the self. It reveals the existing self and it forms the future self. That which is chosen is that which is found congenial to the desires and habits of the self as it already exists. Deliberation has an important function in this process, because each different possibility as it is presented to the imagination appeals to a different element in the constitution of the self, thus giving all sides of character a chance to play their part in the final choice. The resulting choice also shapes the self, making it, in some degree, a new self. This fact is especially marked at critical junctures (p. 171), but it marks every choice to some extent however slight. Not all are as momentous as the choice of a calling in life, or of a life-partner. But every choice is at the forking of the roads, and the path chosen shuts off certain opportunities and opens others. In committing oneself to a particular course, a person gives a lasting set to his own being. Consequently, it is proper to say that in choosing this object rather than that, one is in reality choosing what kind of person or self one is going to be. Superficially, the deliberation which terminates in choice is concerned with weighing the values of particular ends. Below the surface, it is a process of discovering what sort of being a person most wants to become.

Selfhood or character is thus not a *mere* means, an external instrument, of attaining certain ends. It *is* an agency of accomplishing consequences, as is shown in the pains which the athlete, the lawyer, the merchant, takes to build up certain habits in himself, because he knows they are the causal conditions for reaching the ends in which he is interested. But the self is more than an external causal agent. The attainment of consequences reacts to form the self. Moreover, as Aristotle said, the goodness of a good man shines through his deeds. We say of one another's conduct, "How characteristic that was!" In using such an expression we imply that the self is more than a cause of an act in the sense in which a match is a cause of a fire; we imply that the self has entered so intimately into the act performed as to qualify it. The self reveals its nature in what it chooses. In consequence a moral judgment upon an act is also a judgment upon the character or selfhood of the one doing the act. Every time we hold a person responsible for what he has done, we acknowledge in effect that a deed which can be judged morally has an intimate and internal connection with the character of the one from whom the deed issued. Metaphorically, we speak of the virtues of a medicinal plant, meaning that it is efficient for producing certain effects which are wanted, but the virtuous dispositions of the self enter into what the self does and remain there, giving the act its special quality.

If the earlier utilitarians erred in thinking that the self with its virtuous and vicious dispositions was of importance only as a means to certain consequences in which all genuine good and evil are found, the school which holds that consequences have no moral significance at all, and that only the self is morally good and bad, also falls into the error of separating the self and its acts. For goodness and badness could, on this theory, be attributed to the self apart from the results of its dispositions when the latter are put into operation. In truth, only that self is good which wants and strives energetically for good consequences; that is, those consequences which promote the well-being of those affected by the act. It is not too much to say that the key to a correct theory of morality is recognition of the *essential unity of the self and its acts*, if the latter have any moral significance; while errors in theory arise as soon as the self and acts (and their consequences) are separated from each other, and moral worth is attributed to one more than to the other.

The unity of self and action underlies all judgment that is distinctively moral in character. We may judge a happening to be useful or harmful in its consequences, as when we speak of a kindly rain or a destructive torrent. We do not, however, imply moral valuation, because we do not impute connection with character or with a self to rain or flood. On similar grounds, we do not attribute moral quality to acts of an infant, an imbecile or a madman. Yet there comes a time in the life of a normal child when his acts are morally judged. Nevertheless, this fact does not imply, necessarily, that he deliberately intended to produce just the consequences which occurred. It is enough if the judgment is a factor in *forming* a self from which future acts deliberately, intentionally, proceed. A child snatches at food because he is hungry. He is told that he is rude or greedy—a moral judgment. Yet the only thing in the child's mind may have been that the food taken would satisfy hunger. To him the act had no moral import. In calling him rude and greedy, the parent has made a connection between something in himself and a certain quality in his act. The act was performed in a way which discloses something undesirable in the self. If the act be passed without notice, that tendency will be strengthened; the self will be shaped in that direction. On the other hand, if the child can be brought to see the connection, the intimate unity, of his own being and the obnoxious quality of the act, his self will take on another form.

§ 2. The Self and Motivation: Interests

The identity of self and an act, morally speaking, is the key to understanding the nature of *motives* and *motivation*. Unless this unity is perceived and acknowledged in theory, a motive will be regarded as something external acting upon an individual and inducing him to do something. When this point of view is generalized, it leads to the conclusion that the self is naturally, intrinsically, inert and passive, and so has to be stirred or moved to action by something outside itself. The fact, however, is that the self, like its vital basis the organism, is always active; that it acts by its very constitution, and hence needs no external promise of reward or threat of evil to induce it to act. This fact is a confirmation of the moral unity of self and action.

Observation of a child, even a young baby, will convince the observer that a normal human being when awake is engaged in activity; he is a reservoir of energy that is continually overflowing. The organism moves, reaches, handles, pulls, pounds, tears, molds, crumples, looks, listens, etc. It is continually, while awake, exploring its surroundings and establishing new contacts and relations. Periods of quiescence and rest are of course needed for recuperation. But nothing is more intolerable to a healthy human being than enforced passivity over a long period. It is not action that needs to be accounted for, but rather the cessation of activity.

As was intimated earlier in another context, this fact is fatal to a hedonistic psychology (p. 194). Since we act before we have experience of pleasures and pains, since the latter follow as results of action, it cannot possibly be true that desire for pleasure is the source of conduct. The implications of the fact extend, moreover, to the entire concept of motivation. The theory that a motive is an inducement which operates from without upon the self confuses motive and *stimulus*. Stimuli from the environment are highly important factors in conduct. But they are not important as causes, as generators of action. For the organism is already active, and stimuli themselves arise and are experienced only in the course of action. The painful heat of an object stimulates the hand to withdraw but the heat was experienced in the course of reaching and exploring. The function of a stimulus is—as the case just cited illustrates—to *change the direction of an action* already going on. Similarly, a response to a stimulus is not the beginning of activity; it is a *change*, a shift, of activity in response to the change in conditions indicated by a stimulus. A navigator of a ship perceives a headland; this may operate to make him alter the course which his ship takes. But it is not the cause or "moving spring" of his sailing. Motives, like stimuli, induce us to alter the trend and course of our conduct, but they do not evoke or originate action as such.

The term "motive" is thus ambiguous. It means (1) those *interests* which form the core of the self and supply the principles by which conduct is to be understood. It also (2) signifies the *objects*, whether perceived or thought of, which effect an alteration in the direction of activity. Unless we bear in mind the connection between these two meanings along with the fundamental character of the first signification, we shall have a wrong conception of the relation of the self to conduct, and this original error will generate error in all parts of ethical theory.

Any concrete case of the union of the self in action with an object and end is called an interest. Children form the interest of a parent; painting or music is the interest of an artist; the concern of a judge is the equable settling of legal disputes; healing of the sick is the interest of a physician. An interest is, in short, the dominant direction of activity, and in this activity desire is united with an object to be furthered in a decisive choice. Unless impulse and desire are enlisted, one has no heart for a course of conduct; one is indifferent, averse, not-interested. On the other hand, an interest is objective; the heart is set on something. There is no interest at large or in a vacuum; each interest imperatively demands an object to which it is attached and for the well-being or development of which it is actively solicitous. If a man says he is interested in pictures, he asserts that he *cares* for them; if he does not go near them, if he takes no pains to create opportunities for viewing and studying them, his actions so belie his words that we know his interest is merely nominal. Interest *is* regard, concern, solicitude, for an object; if it is not manifested in action it is unreal.

A motive is not then a drive *to* action, or something which moves *to* doing something. It *is* the movement of the self as a whole, a movement in which desire is integrated with an object so completely as to be chosen as a compelling end. The hungry person seeks food. We may say, if we please, that he is moved by hunger. But in fact hunger is only a name for the tendency to move toward the appropriation of food. To create an entity out of this active relation of the self to objects, and then to treat this abstraction as if it were the cause of seeking food is sheer confusion. The case is no different when we say that a man is moved by kindness, or mercy, or cruelty, or malice. These things are not independent powers which stir to action. They are designations of the kind of active union or integration which exists between the self and a class of objects. It is the man himself in his very self who is malicious or kindly, and these adjectives signify that the self is so constituted as to act in certain ways towards certain objects. Benevolence or cruelty is not something which a man *has*, as he may have dollars in his pocket-book; it is something which he *is*; and since his being is active, these qualities are *modes of activity*, not forces which produce action.

Because an interest or motive is the union in action of a need, desire of a self, with a chosen object, the object itself may, in a secondary and derived sense, be said to be the motive of action. Thus a bribe may be called the motive which induces a legislator to vote for a particular measure, or profit-making may be called the motive a grocer has for giving just weights. It is clear, however, that it is the person's own make up which gives the bribe, or the hoped for gain, its hold over him. The avaricious man is stirred to action by objects which mean nothing to a generous person; a frank and open character is moved by objects which would only repel a person of a sly and crafty disposition. A legislator is tempted by a bribe to vote against conviction only because his selfhood is already such that money gain has more value to him than convictions and principles. It is true enough when we take the whole situation into account that an object moves a person; for that object as a moving force *includes the self within it*. Error arises when we think of the object as if it were something wholly external to the make-up of the self, which then operates to move the foreign self.

The secondary and derived sense that identifies "motive" with the object which brings about an *alteration* in the course of conduct has a definite and important practical meaning. In a world like ours where people are associated together, and where what one person does has important consequences for other persons, attempt to influence the action of other persons so that they will do certain things and not do other things is a constant function of life. On all sorts of grounds, we are constantly engaged in trying to influence the conduct of others. Such influencing is the most conspicuous phase of education in the home; it actuates buyers and sellers in business, and lawyers in relation to clients, judge and jury. Lawmakers, clergymen, journalists, politicians are engaged in striving to affect the conduct of others in definite ways: to bring about *changes*, redirections, in conduct. There is a common *modus operandi* in all these cases. Certain objects are presented which it is thought will appeal to elements in the make-up of those addressed, so as to induce them to shape their action in a certain way, a way which in all probability they would not have taken if the object in question had not been held up to them as an end. These objects form what in the secondary and directly practical sense of the word are called motives. They are fundamentally important in attempts to influence the conduct of others. But moral theory has often committed a radical mistake in thinking of these objects which call out a change in the direction of action as if they were "motives" in the sense of originating movement or action. That theory logically terminates in making the self passive—as if stirred to action only from without.

§ 3. Egoism and Altruism

Aside from the bearing of the right conception of motivation upon the unity of self and action, it is particularly important in connection with another problem. In British ethical theorizing this had been so much to the fore that Herbert Spencer called it the "crux of moral speculation." The problem is that of the relation of egoism and altruism, of self-regarding and other-regarding action, of self-love and benevolence. The issue concerns the motivation of *moral* action; discussion has been confused because of failure to examine the underlying problem of the nature of all motivation. This failure is perhaps most evident in those who have held that men are naturally moved only by self-love or regard for their own profit. But it has affected those who hold that men are actuated also by benevolent springs to action, and those who hold that benevolence is the sole motive which is morally justifiable.

A correct theory of motivation shows that both self-love and altruism are acquired dispositions, not original ingredients in our psychological make-up, and that each of them may be either morally good or morally reprehensible. Psychologically speaking, our native impulses and acts are neither egoistic nor altruistic; that is, they are not actuated by *conscious* regard for either one's own good or that of others. They are rather direct responses to situations. As far as self-love is concerned, the case is well stated by James. He says: "When I am moved by self-love to keep my seat whilst ladies stand, or grab something first and cut out my neighbor, what I really love is the seat; it is the thing itself which I grab. I love *them* primarily, as the mother loves her babe, or a generous man a heroic deed. Whenever, as here, self-seeking is the outcome of simple instinctive propensity, it is but a name for certain reflex acts. Something rivets my attention and fatally provokes the 'selfish' response. . . . In fact the more thoroughly selfish I am in this primitive way, the more blindly absorbed my thought will be in the *objects* and impulses of my lust and the more devoid of any inward looking glance."[1] There is, in other words, no reflective quality, no deliberation, no conscious end, in such cases. An observer may look at the act and call it selfish, as in the case of the reaction of a parent to the child's grabbing of food. But in the beginning, this response signifies that the act is one which is *socially* objected to, so that reproof and instruction are brought to bear to induce the child in question to become conscious of the consequences of his act and to aim, *in the future*, at another kind of consequences.

The analysis of James applies equally well to so-called unselfish and benevolent acts—as is, indeed, suggested in the pas-

1. *Principles of Psychology*, I., p. 320. The entire passage, pp. 317–329 should be consulted.

sage quoted in the statement about the mother's response to the needs of her babe. An animal that cares for its young certainly does so without thinking of their good and aiming consciously at their welfare. And the *human* mother in many instances "just loves," as we say, to care for her offspring; she may get as much satisfaction out of it as the "selfish" person does from grabbing a seat when he has a chance. In other words, there is a natural response to a particular situation, and one lacking in moral quality as far as it is wholly unreflective, not involving the idea of *any* end, good or bad.

An adult, however, observing acts of a child which, independently of their aim and "motive," show disregard or regard for others in their *results*, will reprove and approve. These acts tend to dissuade the child from one course of action and encourage him in the other. In that way the child gradually becomes conscious of himself and of others as beings who are affected for good and evil, benefit and detriment, by his acts. Conscious reference to one's own advantage and the good of others may then become definitely a part of the *aim* of an act. Moreover, the ideas of the two possibilities develop together. One is aware of his own good as a definite end only as he becomes aware of the contrasted good of others, and *vice versa*. He thinks consciously of himself only in distinction from others, as set over against them.

Selfishness and unselfishness in a genuinely moral sense thus finally emerge, instead of being native "motives." This fact, however, is far from implying that conscious regard for self is morally bad and conscious regard for others is necessarily good. Acts are not selfish because they evince consideration for the future well-being of the self. No one would say that deliberate care for one's own health, efficiency, progress in learning is bad just because it is one's own. It is moral duty upon occasion to look out for oneself in these respects. Such acts acquire the quality of moral selfishness only when they are indulged in so as to manifest obtuseness to the claims of others. An act is not wrong because it advances the well-being of the self, but because it is unfair, inconsiderate, in respect to the rights, just claims, of others. Self-sustaining and self-protective acts are, mooreover, conditions of all acts which are of service to others. Any moral theory which fails to recognize the necessity of acting sometimes with especial and conscious regard for oneself is suicidal; to fail to care for one's health or even one's material well-being may result in incapacitating one for doing anything for others. Nor can it be argued that every one naturally looks out for himself so that it is unnecessary to give thought to it. It is as difficult to determine what is really good for oneself as it is to discover just where the good of others lies and just what measures will further it. It may even be asserted that *natural* self-interest tends to blind us to what constitutes our own good, because it leads us to take a short-sighted view of it, and that it is easier to see what is good for others, at least when it does not conflict with our own interests.

The real moral question is what *kind of* a self is being furthered and formed. And this question arises with respect to both one's own self and the selves of others. An intense emotional regard for the welfare of others, unbalanced by careful thought, may actually result in harm to others. Children are spoiled by having things done for them because of an uncontrolled "kindness"; adults are sometimes petted into chronic invalidism; persons are encouraged to make unreasonable demands upon others, and are grieved and hurt when these demands are not met; charity may render its recipients parasites upon society, etc. The goodness or badness of *consequences* is the main thing to consider, and these consequences are of the same nature whether they concern *my*self or *your*self. The kind of objects the self wants and chooses is the important thing; the *locus* of residence of these ends, whether in you or in me, cannot of itself make a difference in their moral quality.

The idea is sometimes advanced that action is selfish just because it manifests an interest, since every interest in turn involves the self. Examination of this position confirms the statement that everything depends upon the *kind* of self which is involved. It is a truism that all action springs from and affects a self, for *interest* defines the self. Whatever one is interested in is in so far a constituent of the self, whether it be collecting postage stamps, or pictures, making money, or friends, attending first nights at the theater, studying electrical phenomena, or whatever. Whether one obtains satisfaction by assisting friends or by beating competitors at whatever cost, the interest of the self is involved. The notion that therefore all acts are equally "selfish" is absurd. For "self" does not have the same significance in the different cases; there is always a self involved but the different selves have different values. A self changes its structure and its value according to the kind of object which it desires and seeks; according, that is, to the different kinds of objects in which active interest is taken.

The identity of self and act, the central point in moral theory, operates in two directions. It applies to the interpretation of the quality and value of the act and to that of the self. It is absurd to suppose that the difference between the good person and the bad person is that the former has no interest or deep and intimate concern (leading to personal intimate satisfaction) in what he does, while the bad person is one who does have a personal stake in his actions. What makes the difference between the two is the *quality* of the interest that characterizes them. For the quality of the interest is dependent upon the nature of the object which arouses it and to which it is attached, being trivial, momentous; narrow, wide; transient, enduring; exclusive, inclusive in exact accord with the object. When it is assumed that because a person acts from an interest, in and because its fulfillment brings satisfaction and happiness, he therefore always acts selfishly, the fallacy lies in supposing that there is a separation between the self and the end pursued. If there were, the so-called end would in fact be *only* a means to bringing some profit or advantage to the self. Now this sort of thing does happen. A man may use his friends, for example, simply as aids to his own personal advancement in his profession. But in this case, he is *not* interested in them as friends or even as human beings on their own account. He is interested in what he can get out of them; calling them "friends" is a fraudulent pretense. In short, the essence of the whole distinction between selfishness and unselfishness lies in what sort of object the self is interested. "Disinterested" action does not signify *un*interested; when it has this meaning, action is apathetic, dull, routine, easily discouraged. The only intelligible meaning that can be given to "disinterested" is that interest is intellectually fair, impartial, counting the same thing as of the same value whether it affects my welfare or that of some one else.

So far we have been dealing with cases wherein action manifests and forms the self. In some of these cases the *thought* of the self definitely influences the passage of desire into choice and action. Thus we may say of an act that it manifests self-respect, or that it shows the agent to have no longer any sense of shame. The use of such terms as self-respect, sense of dignity, shame, in approbation is enough to show that conduct is not of necessity worse because the thought of self is a weighty factor in deciding what to do. When, however, we attribute an act to conceit or to false pride we disapprove. The conclusion, obviously, is that the issue is not whether the thought of self is a factor or not, but *what kind of self* is thought of, and in what way, to what purpose. Even "self-respect" is a somewhat ambiguous term. It may denote a sense of the dignity inhering in personality as such, a sense which restrains from doing acts which would besmirch it. It may mean respect for one's personal standing or repute in a community. Again, it may mean attachment to the family name which one bears, or a pride in some personal past achievement which one feels one must live up to. In the latter forms, it may be a definite support and safeguard to wise choice, or it may become a pretentious and hollow sham. It all depends, not on the general name employed, but on the constituents of the particular case. About the only general proposition which can be laid down is that the principle of equity and fairness should rule. The dividing line between, say, genuine and "false" pride is fixed by the equality or inequality of weight attached to the thought of one's own self in comparison with other selves. It is a matter of the intellectual attitude of objectivity and impartiality. The trouble with conceit, vanity, etc., is their warping influence on *judgment*. But humility, modesty, may be just as bad, since they too may destroy balance and equity of judgment.

Regard for others like regard for self has a double meaning. It may signify that action as a matter of fact contributes to the good of others, or it may mean that the *thought* of others' good enters as a determining factor into the conscious aim. In general, conduct, even on the conscious plane, is judged in terms of the elements of situations without explicit reference either to others or to oneself. The scholar, artist, physician, engineer, carries on the great part of his work without consciously asking himself whether his work is going to benefit himself or some one else. He is interested in the *work* itself; such objective interest is a condition of mental and moral health. It would be hard to imagine a situation of a more sickly sort than that in which a person thought that every act performed had to be actuated consciously by regard for the welfare of others; we should suspect the merchant of hypocrisy who claimed his motive in every sale was the good of his customer.

Nevertheless, there are occasions when *conscious* reference to the welfare of others is imperative. Somewhat curiously, at first appearance, this conscious reference is particularly needed when the immediate impulse is a sympathetic one. There is a strong natural impulse of resentment against an individual who is guilty of anti-social acts, and a feeling that retributive punishment of such a person is necessarily in the social interest. But the criterion of the interest actually served lies in its consequences, and there can be no doubt that much punishment, although felt to be in the interest of social justice, fosters a callous indifference to the common good, or even instills a desire in the one punished to get even in return by assailing social institutions. Compassion ranks ordinarily as a social motive-force. But one who consciously cultivates the emotion may find, if he will but consider results, that he is weakening the character of others, and, while helping them superficially, is harming them fundamentally.

Such statements do not signify, of course, that a passion for justice or the emotion of pity should be suppressed. But just as the moral change in the person who thoughtlessly grabs something he wants is an expansion of interest to the thought of a wider circle of objects, so with the impulses which lie at the other pole. It is not easy to convert an immediate emotion into an interest, for the operation requires that we seek out indirect and subtle relations and consequences. But unless an emotion, whether labeled selfish or altruistic, is thus broadened, there is no reflective morality. To give way without thought to a kindly feeling is easy; to suppress it is easy for many persons; the difficult but needed thing is to retain it in all its pristine intensity while directing it, as a precondition of action, into channels of thought. A union of benevolent impulse and intelligent reflection is the interest most likely to result in conduct that is good. But in this union the role of thoughtful inquiry is quite as important as that of sympathetic affection.

§ 4. The Inclusive Nature of Social Interest

The discussion points to the conclusion that neither egoism nor altruism nor any combination of the two is a satisfactory principle. Selfhood is not something which exists apart from association and intercourse. The relationships which are pro-

duced by the fact that interests are formed in this social environment are far more important than are the adjustments of isolated
selves. To a large extent, the emphasis of theory upon the problem of adjustment of egoism and altruism took place in a time
when thought was decidedly individualistic in character. Theory
was formed in terms of individuals supposed to be naturally isolated; social arrangements were considered to be secondary and
artificial. Under such intellectual conditions, it was almost inevitable that moral theory should become preoccupied with the
question of egoistic *versus* altruistic motivation. Since the prevailing individualism was expressed in an economic theory and
practice which taught that each man was actuated by an exclusive regard for his own profit, moralists were led to insist
upon the need of some check upon this ruthless individualism,
and to accentuate the supremacy in *morals* (as distinct from
business) of sympathy and benevolent regard for others. The ultimate significance of this appeal is, however, to make us realize
the fact that regard for self and regard for others are both of
them secondary phases of a more normal and complete interest:
regard for the welfare and integrity of the social groups of which
we form a part.

The family, for example, is something other than one person,
plus another, plus another. It is an enduring form of association
in which the members of the group stand from the beginning in
relations to one another, and in which each member gets direction for his conduct by thinking of the whole group and his place
in it, rather than by an adjustment of egoism and altruism. Similar illustrations are found in business, professional, and political
associations. From the moral standpoint, the test of an industry
is whether it serves the community as a whole, satisfying its
needs effectively and fairly, while also providing the means of
livelihood and personal development to the individuals who
carry it on. This goal could hardly be reached, however, if the
business man (a) thought exclusively of furthering his own interests; (b) of acting in a benevolent way toward others; or
(c) sought some compromise between the two. In a justly organized social order, the very relations which persons bear to one
another demand of the one carrying on a line of business the
kind of conduct which meets the needs of others, while they also
enable him to express and fulfill the capacities of his own being.

Services, in other words, would be reciprocal and cooperative in their effect. We trust a physician who recognizes the social import of his calling and who is equipped in knowledge and skill, rather than one who is animated exclusively by personal affection no matter how great his altruistic zeal. The political action of citizens of an organized community will not be morally satisfactory unless they have, individually, sympathetic dispositions. But the value of this sympathy is not as a direct dictator of conduct. Think of any complex political problem and you will realize how short a way unenlightened benevolence will carry you. It has a value, but this value consists in power to make us attend in a broad way to all the social ties which are involved in the formation and execution of policies. Regard for self and regard for others should not, in other words, be *direct* motives to overt action. They should be forces which lead us to *think* of objects and consequences that would otherwise escape notice. These objects and consequences then constitute the *interest* which is the proper motive of action. Their stuff and material are composed of the relations which men actually sustain to one another in concrete affairs.

Interest in the social whole of which one is a member necessarily carries with it interest in one's own self. Every member of the group has his own place and work; it is absurd to suppose that this fact is significant in other persons but of little account in one's own case. To suppose that social interest is incompatible with concern for one's own health, learning, advancement, power of judgment, etc., is, literally, nonsensical. Since each one of us is a member of social groups and since the latter have no existence apart from the selves who compose them, there can be no effective social interest unless there is at the same time an intelligent regard for our own well-being and development. Indeed, there is a certain *primary* responsibility placed upon each individual in respect to his own power and growth. No community more backward and ineffective *as* a community can be imagined than one in which every member neglected his own concerns in order to attend to the affairs of his neighbors. When selfhood is taken for what it is, something existing in relationships to others and not in unreal isolation, independence of judgment, personal insight, integrity and initiative, become indispensable excellencies from the social point of view.

There is too often current a conception of charity which illustrates the harm which may accrue when objective social relations are shoved into the background. The giving of a kindly hand to a human being in distress, to numbers caught in a common catastrophe, is such a natural thing that it should almost be too much a matter of course to need laudation as a virtue. But the theory which erects charity in and of itself into a supreme excellence is a survival of a feudally stratified society, that is, of conditions wherein a superior class achieved merit by doing things gratuitously for an inferior class. The objection to this conception of charity is that it too readily becomes an excuse for maintaining laws and social arrangements which ought themselves to be changed in the interest of fair play and justice. "Charity" may even be used as a means for administering a sop to one's social conscience while at the same time it buys off the resentment which might otherwise grow up in those who suffer from social injustice. Magnificent philanthropy may be employed to cover up brutal economic exploitation. Gifts to libraries, hospitals, missions, schools may be employed as a means of rendering existing institutions more tolerable, and of inducing immunity against social change.

Again, deliberate benevolence is used as a means of keeping others dependent and managing their affairs for them. Parents, for example, who fail to pay due heed to the growing maturity of their children, justify an unjustifiable interference in their affairs, on the ground of kindly parental feelings. They carry the habits of action formed when children were practically helpless into conditions in which children both want and need to help themselves. They pride themselves on conduct which creates either servile dependence or bitter resentment and revolt in their off spring. Perhaps no better test case of the contrast between regard for personality bound up with regard for the realities of a social situation and abstract "altruism" can be found than is afforded in such an instance as this. The moral is not that parents should become indifferent to the well-being of their children. It is that *intelligent* regard for this welfare realizes the need for growing freedom with growing maturity. It displays itself in a change of the habits formed when regard for welfare called for a different sort of conduct. If we generalize the lesson of this instance, it leads to the conclusion that overt acts of charity and benevolence are incidental phases of morals, demanded under certain emergencies, rather than its essential principle. This is found in a constantly expanding and changing sense of what the concrete realities of human relations call for.

One type of moral theory holds up self-realization as the ethical ideal. There is an ambiguity in the conception which will serve to illustrate what has been said about the self. Self-realization may be the end in the sense of being an outcome and limit of right action, without being the end-in-*view*. The *kind* of self which is formed through action which is faithful to relations with others will be a fuller and broader self than one which is cultivated in isolation from or in opposition to the purposes and needs of others. In contrast, the kind of self which results from generous breadth of interest may be said alone to constitute a development and fulfillment of self, while the other way of life stunts and starves selfhood by cutting it off from the connections necessary to its growth. But to make self-realization a conscious aim might and probably would prevent full attention to those very relationships which bring about the wider development of self.

The case is the same with the interests of the self as with its realization. The final happiness of an individual resides in the supremacy of certain interests in the make-up of character; namely, alert, sincere, enduring interests in the objects in which all can share. It is found in such interests rather than in the accomplishment of definite external results because this kind of happiness alone is not at the mercy of circumstances. No amount of outer obstacles can destroy the happiness that comes from lively and ever-renewed interest in others and in the conditions and objects which promote their development. To those in whom these interests are alive (and they flourish to some extent in all persons who have not already been warped) their exercise brings happiness because it fulfills the self. They are not, however, preferred and aimed at *because* they give greater happiness, but as expressing the kind of self which a person fundamentally desires to be they constitute a happiness unique in kind.

The final word about the place of the self in the moral life is, then, that the very problem of morals is to form an original body of impulsive tendencies into a voluntary self in which desires and affections centre in the values which are common; in which interest focusses in objects that contribute to the enrichment of the lives of all. If we identify the interests of such a self with the virtues, then we shall say, with Spinoza, that happiness is not the reward of virtue, but is virtue itself.

§ 5. Responsibility and Freedom

The ethical problems connected with the fact of selfhood culminate in the ideas of responsibility and freedom. Both ideas are bound up with far-reaching issues which have produced great controversy in metaphysics and religion as well as in morals. We shall consider them only with respect to the points in which these concepts are definitely connected with the analysis which precedes. So considered, an important side of responsibility has been already touched upon in connection with the transformation of native and psychological tendencies into traits of a self having moral significance and value.

Social demands and social approvals and condemnations are important factors in bringing about this change, as we had occasion to notice (p. 288). The point which is important is that they be used to produce a change in the attitude of those who are subject to them, especially the intellectual change of recognizing relations and meanings not hitherto associated with what they do. Now the commonest mistake in connection with the idea of responsibility consists in supposing that approval and reprobation have a retrospective instead of prospective bearing. The possibility of a desirable *modification* of character and the selection of the course of action which will make that possibility a reality is the central fact in responsibility. The child, for example, is at first held liable for what he has done, not because he deliberately and knowingly intended such action, but in order that *in the future* he may take into account bearings and consequences which he has failed to consider in what he *has* done. Here is where the human agent differs from a stone and inanimate thing, and indeed from animals lower in the scale.

It would be absurd to hold a stone responsible when it falls from a cliff and injures a person, or to blame the falling tree which crushes a passer-by. The reason for the absurdity is that such treatment would have and could have no conceivable influence on the future behavior of stone or tree. They do not interact with conditions about them so as to learn, so as to modify their attitudes and dispositions. A human being is held accountable in order that he may learn; in order that he may learn not theoretically and academically but in such a way as to modify and—to some extent—remake his prior self. The question of whether he might when he acted have acted differently from the way in which he did act is irrelevant. The question is whether he is capable of acting differently *next* time; the practical importance of effecting changes in human character is what makes responsibility important. Babes, imbeciles, the insane are not held accountable, because there is incapacity to learn and to change. With every increase of capacity to learn, there develops a larger degree of accountability. The fact that one did not deliberate before the performance of an act which brought injury to others, that he did not mean or intend the act, is of no significance, save as it may throw light upon the kind of response by others which will render him likely to deliberate next time he acts under similar circumstances. The fact that each act tends to *form*, through habit, a self which will perform a certain kind of acts, is the foundation, theoretically and practically of responsibility. We cannot undo the past; we can affect the future.

Hence responsibility in relation to control of our reactions to the conduct of others is twofold. The persons who employ praise and blame, reward and punishment, are responsible for the selection of those methods which will, with the greatest probability, modify in a desirable way the future attitude and conduct of others. There is no inherent principle of retributive justice that commands and justifies the use of reward and punishment independently of their consequences in each specific case. To appeal to such a principle when punishment breeds callousness, rebellion, ingenuity in evasion, etc., is but a method of refusing to acknowledge responsibility. Now the consequence which is most important is that which occurs in personal attitude: confirmation of a good habit, change in a bad tendency.

The point at which theories about responsibility go wrong is the attempt to base it upon a state of things which *precedes* holding a person liable, instead of upon what ensues in consequence of it. One is held responsible in order that he may *become* responsible, that is, responsive to the needs and claims of others, to the obligations implicit in his position. Those who hold others accountable for their conduct are themselves accountable for doing it in such a manner that this responsiveness develops. Otherwise they are themselves irresponsible in their own conduct. The ideal goal or limit would be that each person should be completely responsive in all his actions. But as long as one meets new conditions this goal cannot be reached; for where conditions are decidedly unlike those which one has previously experienced, one cannot be sure of the rightness of knowledge and attitude. Being held accountable by others is, in every such instance, an important safeguard and directive force in growth.

The idea of freedom has been seriously affected in theoretical discussions by misconceptions of the nature of responsibility. Those who have sought for an antecedent basis of and warrant for responsibility have usually located it in "freedom of the will," and have construed this freedom to signify an unmotivated power of choice, that is an arbitrary power to choose for no reason whatever except that the will does choose in this fashion. It is argued that there is no justice in holding a person liable for his act unless he might equally have done otherwise—completely overlooking the function of being held to account in improving his future conduct. A man might have "acted otherwise than he did act" *if* he had been a different kind of person, and the point in holding him liable for what he did do (and for being the kind of person he was in doing it) is that he may *become* a different kind of self and henceforth choose different sorts of ends.

In other words, freedom in its practical and moral sense (whatever is to be said about it in some metaphysical sense) is connected with possibility of growth, learning and modification of character, just as is responsibility. The chief reason we do not think of a stone as free is because it is not capable of changing its mode of conduct, of purposely readapting itself to new conditions. An animal such as a dog shows plasticity; it acquires new habits under the tutelage of others. But the dog plays a passive role in this change; he does not initiate and direct it; he does not become interested in it on its own account. A human being, on the other hand, even a young child, not only learns but is capable of being interested in learning, interested in acquiring new attitudes and dispositions. As we mature we usually acquire habits that are settled to the point of routine. But unless and until we get completely fossilized, we can break old habits and form new ones. No argument about causation can affect the fact, verified constantly in experience, that we can and do learn, and that the learning is not limited to acquisition of additional information but extends to remaking old tendencies. As far as a person becomes a different self or character he develops different desires and choices. Freedom in the practical sense develops when one is aware of this possibility and takes an interest in converting it into a reality. Potentiality of freedom is a native gift or part of our constitution in that we have *capacity* for growth and for being actively concerned in the process and the direction it takes. Actual or positive freedom is not a native gift or endowment but is acquired. In the degree in which we become aware of possibilities of development and actively concerned to keep the avenues of growth open, in the degree in which we fight against induration and fixity, and thereby realize the possibilities of recreation of our selves, we are actually free.

Except as the outcome of arrested development, there is no such thing as a fixed, ready-made, finished self. Every living self causes acts and is itself caused in return by what it does. All voluntary action is a remaking of self, since it creates new desires, instigates to new modes of endeavor, brings to light new conditions which institute new ends. Our personal identity is found in the thread of continuous development which binds together these changes. In the strictest sense, it is impossible for the self to stand still; it is becoming, and becoming for the better or the worse. It is in the *quality* of becoming that virtue resides. We set up this and that end to be reached, but *the* end is growth itself. To make an end a final goal is but to arrest growth. Many a person gets morally discouraged because he has not attained the object upon which he set his resolution, but in fact his moral status is determined by his movement in that direction, not by his possession. If such a person would set his thought and desire upon the *process* of evolution instead of upon some ulterior goal, he would find a new freedom and happiness. It is the next step which lies within our power.

It follows that at each point there is a distinction between an old, an accomplished self, and a new and moving self, between the static and the dynamic self. The former aspect is constituted by habits already formed. Habit gives facility, and there is always a tendency to rest on our oars, to fall back on what we have already achieved. For that is the easy course; we are at home and feel comfortable in lines of action that run in the tracks of habits already established and mastered. Hence, the old, the habitual self, is likely to be treated as if it were *the* self; as if new conditions and new demands were something foreign and hostile. We become uneasy at the idea of initiating new courses; we are repelled by the difficulties that attend entering upon them; we dodge assuming a new responsibility. We tend to favor the old self and to make its perpetuation the standard of our valuations and the end of our conduct. In this way, we withdraw from actual conditions and their requirements and opportunities; we contract and harden the self.

The growing, enlarging, liberated self, on the other hand, goes forth to meet new demands and occasions, and readapts and remakes itself in the process. It welcomes untried situations. The necessity for choice between the interests of the old and of the forming, moving, self is recurrent. It is found at every stage of civilization and every period of life. The civilized man meets it as well as the savage; the dweller in the slums as well as the person in cultivated surroundings; the "good" person as well as the "bad." For everywhere there is an opportunity and a need to go beyond what one has been, beyond "himself," if the self is identified with the body of desires, affections, and habits which has been potent in the past. Indeed, we may say that the good person is precisely the one who is most conscious of the alternative, and is the most concerned to find openings for the newly forming or growing self; since no matter how "good" he has been, he becomes "bad" (even though acting upon a relatively high plane of attainment) as soon as he fails to respond to the demand for growth. Any other basis for judging the moral status of the self is conventional. In reality, direction of movement, not the plane of attainment and rest, determines moral quality.

Practically all moralists have made much of a distinction between a lower and a higher self, speaking of the carnal and spiritual, the animal and the truly human, the sensuous and the rational, selves which exist side by side in man and which war with one another. Moralists have often supposed that the line between the two selves could be drawn once for all and upon the basis of definite qualities and traits belonging respectively to one and the other. The only distinction, however, that can be drawn without reducing morals to conventionality, self-righteous complacency, or a hopeless and harsh struggle for the unattainable, is that between the attained static, and the moving, dynamic self. When there is talk of the lower animal self, and so on, it is always by *contrast*, not on the basis of fixed material. A self that was truly moral under a set of former conditions may become a sensuous, appetitive self when it is confronted with a painful need for developing new attitudes and devoting itself to new and difficult objectives. And, contrariwise, the higher self is that formed by the step in advance of one who *has* been living on a low plane. As he takes the step he enters into an experience of freedom. If we state the moral law as the injunction to each self on every possible occasion to identify the self with a new growth that is possible, then obedience to law is one with moral freedom.

In concluding the theoretical discussion of Part Two, we sum up by stating the point of view from which all the different problems and ideas have been looked at. For this point of view it is, which supplies the unifying thread: *Moral conceptions and processes grow naturally out of the very conditions of human life.* (1) Desire belongs to the intrinsic nature of man; we cannot conceive a human being who does not have wants, needs, nor one to whom fulfillment of desire does not afford satisfaction. As soon as the power of thought develops, needs cease to be blind; thought looks ahead and foresees results. It forms purposes, plans, aims, ends-in-view. Out of these universal and inevitable facts of human nature there necessarily grow the moral conceptions of the Good, and of the value of the intellectual phase of character, which amid all the conflict of desires and aims strives for insight into the inclusive and enduring satisfaction: wisdom, prudence.

(2) Men live together naturally and inevitably in society; in companionship and competition; in relations of cooperation and subordination. These relations are expressed in demands, claims, expectations. One person has the conviction that fulfillment of his demands by others is his *right*; to these others it comes as an *obligation*, something owed, due, to those who assert the claim. Out of the interplay of these claims and obligations there arises the general concept of Law, Duty, Moral Authority, or Right.

(3) Human beings approve and disapprove, sympathize and

resent, as naturally and inevitably as they seek for the objects they want, and as they impose claims and respond to them. Thus the moral Good presents itself neither merely as that which satisfies desire, nor as that which fulfills obligation, but as that which is *approvable*. From out of the mass of phenomena of this sort there emerge the generalized ideas of Virtue or Moral Excellence and of a Standard which regulates the manifestation of approval and disapproval, praise and blame.

Special phenomena of morals change from time to time with change of social conditions and the level of culture. The facts of desiring, purpose, social demand and law, sympathetic approval and hostile disapproval are constant. We cannot imagine them disappearing as long as human nature remains human nature, and lives in association with others. The fundamental conceptions of morals are, therefore, neither arbitrary nor artificial. They are not imposed upon human nature from without but develop out of its own operations and needs. Particular aspects of morals are transient; they are often, in their actual manifestation, defective and perverted. But the framework of moral conceptions is as permanent as human life itself.

Literature

For self in general, see Bosanquet, *Psychology of the Moral Self*, 1897; Otto, *Things and Ideals*, 1924, ch. vi.; Cooley, *Human Nature and the Social Order*, 1922, chs. v.–ix.; Dewey, *Human Nature and Conduct*, 1922, pp. 134–139 and see Index. The conception of altruism under that name was introduced by Comte. See his *System of Positive Politics*, Introduction, ch. iii., and Part II., trans. 1854, ch. ii.; a good summary is contained in Lévy-Bruhl's *Philosophy of Comte*, trans. 1903, Book IV.; see Spencer, *Principles of Ethics*, Vol. I., Part I., chs. xi.–xiv.; Stephen, *Science of Ethics*, 1882, ch. vi.; Sorley, *Recent Tendencies in Ethics*, 1904; Sidgwick, *Methods of Ethics*, 1901, pp. 494–507; Adler, *An Ethical Philosophy of Life*, 1918; Hastings' *Encyclopaedia of Religion and Ethics*, 1922, article on "Altruism"; Sharp, *Ethics*, 1928, ch. v., on self-sacrifice, chs. xxii. and xxiii.; H. E. Davis, *Tolstoy and Nietzsche*, 1929; Calkins, *The Good Man and the Good*, 1918.

On freedom and responsibility, Sharp, *Ethics*, 1928, ch. xiii.; James, *Will to Believe*, 1915, essay on "Dilemma of Determinism"; G. E. Moore, *Ethics*, 1912, ch. vi.; *Freedom in the Modern World*, 1928, edited by

H. M. Kallen, especially Essays i., iii., x., xi., xii.; Dewey, *Human Nature and Conduct*, 1922, pp. 303–317; Everett, *Moral Values*, 1918, ch. xxi.; Stapledon, *A Modern Theory of Ethics*, 1929, ch. xi. On self-interest, see Mandeville, *Fable of Bees*.

Sidgwick, *Methods of Ethics*, 1901, Book I., ch. vii. and Book II., ch. v. Self-realization: Wright, *Self-Realization*, 1913; Aristotle, *Ethics*; Green, *Prolegomena to Ethics*, 1890 (for criticism of Green, see Dewey, *Philosophical Review*, Vol. II., pp. 652–664); Palmer, *The Nature of Goodness*, 1903.

Part III

The World of Action

General Literature for Part III

Addams, *Democracy and Social Ethics*, 1902, *Newer Ideals of Peace*, 1907; Santayana, *The Life of Reason*, Vol. II., 1905; Bergemann, *Ethik als Kulturphilosophie*, 1904, especially pp. 154–304; Wundt, *Ethics*, Vol. III., *The Principles of Morality and the Departments of the Moral Life* (trans. 1901); Spencer, *Principles of Ethics*, 1893, Vol. II., *Principles of Sociology*, 1882, Vol. I., Part II.; Ritchie, *Studies in Political and Social Ethics*, 1902; Bosanquet, *Philosophical Theory of the State*, 1899; Willoughby, *Social Justice*, 1900; Cooley, *Human Nature and the Social Order*, 1902; Paulsen, *System der Ethik*, 5th ed., 1900, Book IV.; Runze, *Praktische Ethik*, 1891; Janet, *Histoire de la Science Politique dans ses Rapports avec la Morale*, 3d ed., 1887; Plato, *The Republic*; Aristotle, *Ethics*, Book V., and *Politics* (trans. by Welldon, 1883); Hegel, *Philosophy of Right* (pub. 1820, trans. by Dyde, 1896); Mackenzie, *An Introduction to Social Philosophy*, 1890; Dunning, *History of Political Theories*, Vol. I., 1902, Vol. II., 1905; Stein, *Die Sociale Frage im Lichte der Philosophie*, 1897.

Morals and Social Problems

§ 1. The Moral Significance of Social Questions

Part II undertook an analysis of the most important concepts of morals. The analysis was carried on in the interest of reflective morality. Now reflection goes on within the minds of individuals. Consequently the emphasis fell upon the attitudes and responses of individual persons. We repeatedly noted, however, that the social environment has great influence in calling out and repressing the thought of individuals, and in sharpening or dulling their moral sensitiveness. From the social human environments proceed ultimately the problems which reflection has to deal with (pp. 212, 233).

In Part III we propose to consider these problems from the social side, especially those problems which demand solution in the existing conditions of social life. The analysis of the previous Part may be called *formal*, since it deals with basic conceptions of morals, such as Good, Right, Duty, Approbation, Standard, Virtue, etc. Now we shall consider the content or *material* of these ideas which is provided by contemporary organization of life.

When social life is stable, when custom rules, the problems of morals have to do with the adjustments which individuals make to the institutions in which they live, rather than with the moral quality of the institutions themselves. Men take their social relations for granted; they are what they are and, in being that, are what they *should* be. If anything is wrong it is due to the failure of individuals to do what social customs tell them to do. Only a few daring persons criticize ancestral habits, and then only guardedly. When social life is in a state of flux, moral issues cease to gather exclusively about personal conformity and deviation. They centre in the value of social arrangements, of laws, of inherited traditions that have crystallized into institutions, in changes that are desirable. Institutions lose their quasi-sacredness and are the objects of moral questioning. We now live in such a period. Concerning our condition, Jane Addams has said:

> Certain forms of personal righteousness have become to a majority of the community almost automatic. It is as easy for most of us to keep from stealing our dinners as it is to digest them, and there is quite as much voluntary morality involved in one case as in the other. . . . To attain personal morality in an age demanding social morality, to pride one's self upon the results of personal effort when the time demands social adjustment is utterly to fail to apprehend the situation. . . . All about us are men and women who have become unhappy in regard to their attitude toward the social order itself. The test which they would apply to their conduct is a social test. . . . They desire both a clearer definition of the code of morality applied to present day demands and a part in its fulfilment, both a creed and a practice of social morality.[1]

Some of these problems of "social order and social test", will now engage our attention. We noticed, in an earlier discussion, that the problem of egoism and altruism arose in a time when morality was thought of chiefly in personal terms. At that time, social relations were thought of in terms of relations to other individuals as individuals, and then egoism and altruism exhaust the alternatives (p. 298). Utilitarianism with its social criterion tended, however, to bring to the fore issues which question the moral worth of existing social arrangements themselves. The opposed theory of Kant was also actuated by ideals which ran counter to the then existing organization of political society. In fact, ever since the latter half of the eighteenth century the interesting and stirring human problems for intellectual inquiry as well as for practical application have arisen out of criticism of existing social arrangements and traditions, in State, government, law, church, family, industry, business, international relations. So far as moral theories have kept aloof from perplexities about social policies in these fields, so far as they have merely

1. *Democracy and Social Ethics*, pp. 1–4, *passim*. The book as a whole is a consideration of the application of this point of view to such questions as family life, domestic adjustments, charity, industry, city politics, education, etc.

repeated commonplaces about personal conduct in isolation from social issues, they have become anemic and sterile.

Indeed, one of the chief values, from the standpoint of theory, of considering the moral bearing of social problems is that we are then confronted with live issues in which vital choices still have to be made, and with situations where principles are still in process of forming. We are thus saved from the "moralistic" narrowing down of morals to which reference has been made from time to time; we appreciate that morals are as wide as the area of everything which affects the values of human living. These values are involved on the widest scale in social issues. Hence critical questioning of existing institutions and critical discussion of changes, proposed on the theory that they will produce social betterment, are the best means of enforcing the fact that moral theory is more than a remote exercise in conceptual analysis or than a mere mode of preaching and exhortation. When we take the social point of view we are compelled to realize the extent to which our moral beliefs are a product of the social environment and also the extent to which *thinking*, new ideas, can change this environment.

Study from this point of view also enforces, as nothing else can, a conclusion reached in our theoretical analysis. It discloses in a concrete fashion the limitation of moral theory and the positive office which it can perform. It shows that it is *not* the business of moral theory to provide a ready-made solution to large moral perplexities. But it also makes it clear that while the solution has to be reached by *action* based on personal choice, theory can enlighten and guide choice and action by revealing alternatives, and by bringing to light what is entailed when we choose one alternative rather than another. It shows, in short, that the function of theory is not to furnish a substitute for personal reflective choice but to be an instrument for rendering deliberation more effective and hence choice more intelligent (p. 165).

Again, conventionalized morals conceal from view the uncertainty which attends decision as to what is good in a concrete case, and covers up the problematic nature of what is right and obligatory. But consideration of social questions and conflicting proposals brings just these things home to us. It puts before us situations where the moral struggle is not just to be kept from departing from what we know already to be good and right, but where we need to *discover* what *is* good and right, and where reflection and experimentation are the sole means of discovery. There are still those who think they are in possession of codes and principles which settle finally and automatically the right and wrong of, say, divorce, the respective rights of capital and labor, the exact limits of private property, the extent to which legislation should go in deciding what individuals shall eat, drink, wear, etc. But there are also many other persons, an increasing number, who see that such questions as these cannot be settled by deduction from fixed premises, and that the attempt to decide them in that fashion is the road to the intolerant fanaticism, dogmatism, class strife, of the closed mind. Wars waged in the alleged interest of religion, or in defense of particular economic conceptions, prove the practical danger of carrying theoretical dogmatism into action. Since the right course is to bring the best intelligence we can command to bear upon such social problems, theory has a definite function in establishing the value of such intelligence and in promoting it by clarifying issues, proposing solutions, guiding the action which tests the worth of these proposals.

The foregoing remarks should make clear what is meant by that change from personal to social morality which has been referred to. It does *not* signify that morality becomes impersonal and collective; it remains and must remain personal in that social problems have to be faced by individuals, and decisions reached in the forum of individual minds have to be carried into effect by individual agents, who are in turn personally responsible for the consequences of their acts. Morals are personal because they spring from personal insight, judgment, and choice. Such facts as these, however, are wholly consistent with the fact that *what* men think and believe is affected by common factors, and that the thought and choice of one individual spreads to others. They do not militate against the fact that men have to act together, and that their conjoint action is embodied in institutions and laws; that unified action creates government and legislative policies, forms the family, establishes schools and churches, manifests itself in business corporations of vast extent and power, in clubs and fraternities for enjoyment and recreation, and in armies which set nation against nation. In other words, it is a *fact* that a vast network of relations surrounds the individual: indeed, "surrounds" is too external a term, since every individual lives *in* the network as a part of it. The material of personal reflection and of choice comes to each of us from the customs, traditions, institutions, policies, and plans of these large collective wholes. They are the influences which form his character, evoke and confirm his attitudes, and affect at every turn the quality of his happiness and his aspirations. This statement is true not only of the associations of which he is a direct member but also of those which seem external to him; since through commerce, war, and intercommunication the action of one territorial nation affects the members of another, while the standards set by one social group, say that of wealth and prestige, affect the desires and the capabilities of individuals in other groups.

At the present time, almost all important ethical problems arise out of the conditions of associated life. As we have previously noted, in a stationary society, in one dominated by custom, the existing social order seems to be like the order of nature itself; as inevitable, and as necessary or as capricious as the case may be. Any suggestion for change is regarded as "unnatural." Even in present social life, any deep-seated change is opposed as contrary to nature; such was the case, for example, in the case of "votes for women" a short time ago. Such is the case still with proposals for, say, doing away with war, or the elimination of the pecuniary profit motive from industry. Nevertheless, when inventions modify social conditions, when new wants and new satisfactions abound, when dislocations of elements of population through migration take place on a large scale, when cultures once separated mix and influence one another, when new modes of industry invade domestic life, when the emergence of increased leisure time coincides with new opportunities for amusement, when great combinations of capital arise which determine the opportunities of individuals for finding work, attention is forced to note the influence exerted upon individuals by collective conditions. Personal selves are forced, unless they are merely to drift, to consider their own action with respect to social changes. They are forced, if they engage in reflection at all, to determine what social tendencies they shall favor and which ones they shall oppose; which institutions they will strive to conserve and which they will endeavor to modify or abolish. That the present is a time of social changes such as have been mentioned is a commonplace; the mere existence alone of democratic government, for example, raises social issues for moral decision which did not exist for most men and women so long as government was autocratic and confined to a "few."

The change from "personal" to "social" morality concerns then the kind of moral questions which are uppermost. For many individuals it is not now a question of whether they individually will appropriate property belonging to another, but whether existing large-scale economic arrangements operate to effect an equitable distribution of property; and if not, what they as individuals shall do about it. In one sense the change to social morality makes morals more acutely personal than they were when custom ruled. It forces the need of more personal reflection, more personal knowledge and insight, more deliberate and steadfast personal convictions, more resolute personal attitudes in action—more personal in the sense of being more *conscious* in choice and more voluntary in execution. It would then be absurd to suppose that "social morals" meant a swallowing up of individuality in an anonymous mass, or an abdication of personal responsibility in decision and action. It signifies that the social conditions and social consequences of personal action (which always exist in any case), are now brought to explicit consciousness so that they require searching thought and careful judgment in a way practically unprecedented formerly. It indicates that reflection is morally indispensable. It points out the material of reflection: the sort of things to which moral inquiry and judgment must go out.

There are countless illustrations of the way in which a problem of personal conduct is so complicated by social conditions that a person has to decide about the latter in order to reach a conclusion in the former. His problem thus takes the form: What attitude shall I adopt towards an issue which concerns many persons whom I do not know personally, but whose action along with mine will determine the conditions under which we all live? A person may have reached a conclusion satisfactory to himself about his own use or non-use of alcoholic liquors, but he finds that this matter runs out into the question of legislative and constitutional action by the nation as a whole. He may find the comparatively simple problem of his relations to members of his own family running out into problems of marriage and divorce which require collective and conjoint action. An individual who takes regard for human life as an unquestioned matter of course suddenly finds that the matter assumes an entirely new face when his nation is at war. A person engaged in making a livelihood for himself and his family finds himself out of work for causes over which he has no personal control, and he may be then called upon to reach a judgment regarding large matters of economic and political policy which can be settled only by collective action. These are but samples of the broadening out of issues of personal conduct till they include the formation of intelligent judgments upon great social institutions, family, property, political states. Unless men are to surrender to chance, to caprice, to prejudice, they must have some general moral principles by which to guide themselves in meeting such questions.

§ 2. The Underlying Issue: Individual and Social

While the problems themselves are concrete and particular, experience shows that, in dealing with them, most persons, from temperament, education, or environment, lean in one direction or another. Some incline to favor private as against combined action. They think that the presumption is always in favor of leaving individuals to themselves, and that collectively organized action is to be looked upon with suspicion, since to them it involves invasion of the realm of personal liberty; every such intervention is, according to them, an interference which has to be especially justified. There are others who incline to reverse the presumption; they place the burden of evidence *against* the isolated individual. They think of him as egoistic in the main, seeking his own private gain, lacking in consideration of the rights of others, and needing to be guided by the laws of a group if he is not to become a social menace. Or, they think of an individual as in and of himself an ignorant barbarian, living on a level deprived of art and science, and requiring the beneficent activity of society to develop him into any worthy culture of mind and spirit.

It is easy to verify the existence of these opposite tendencies in the issues which we cited as samples. There are those who hail the conscientious objector in war as a moral hero and who regard any degree of conscription of an individual by the state for war as moral tyranny of the worst kind. There are others, doubtless many more in number, who regard such a person as a moral shirker, ungrateful to the society which has educated and protected him, as one who prefers from cowardice his own personal safety to the values, perhaps the life, of the community. There are those who think the maximum amount of liberty should be accorded to individuals in their sex relations; that marriage should not be a fixed institution but rather a voluntary contract, to be broken at will provided the interests of the offspring are duly protected. There are others who regard such opinions as a form of moral anarchy, entertained only because of desire for satisfaction of lawless appetites, and destructive of the basic stability of social life. With respect to property and the economic situation, the strife between the upholders of private property as sacred and those in favor of communal ownership is too well known to need more than a reference.

The tendency to split into opposed camps concerning the respective moral claims of unrestrained individuality and of social control affects all phases of life, education, politics, economics, art, religion. It also determines the attitude taken toward more imponderable things. On one side, it is asserted that collective action tends toward regimentation into mechanical uniformity; towards a mass production of people turned out in a common mold, with individual differences wiped out, that social influence is leveling, that it obliterates distinction and tends toward an average which spells mediocrity. Democracy, as compared with aristocracy, is condemned for its alleged tendencies in this direction. Organized society, it is contended, favors censorship; it tends to meddle constantly with private affairs; to interfere with what the individual thinks, eats, and drinks; by its nature it is hostile, so it is said, to freedom of inquiry, discussion, criticism, since such freedom almost certainly produces variation of judgment and action. Thinking is sure to bring some phase of the established social order under adverse criticism and hence is suppressed by those who have more concern for society than for individuals.

Thus there develops a definite school of thought which holds that the action of society in its collective and organized capacity should be limited to a minimum; that its action should be mainly negative, restricting privately initiated action only when it operates to harm others. All, except the most extreme, of this school, admit the necessity of occasional interference of this negative sort, but urge that it should be confined to what men do externally and should never be extended to the essentials of individuality, to desire, emotion, thought, belief. And they support themselves by pointing to a long and disastrous historical persecution of variation in belief; to the fanaticism and intolerance which have been bred in desire for social conformity.

On the other side stands the collectivist school. Some of its members assume that individuals left to themselves are actuated only by "self-love," which is so powerful as to produce, when it is left to itself, a "war of all against all." Others point to the influence of social connection in the culture of individuals who left to themselves are at best raw and crude. They point to the fact that, from the standpoint of original nature, individuals hardly rise above the animal level; that what they possess in the way of civilization comes to them through nurture and not from nature; that culture is transmitted not by means of biological heredity, but by tradition, transmission of education, books, art products, and the influence of enduring institutions. Maintenance and strengthening of these collective social forces is, therefore, the primary duty of all those who are interested in the moralization of individuals. At the present time, the point more emphasized is a practical one. It is claimed that only organized social action can remake the old social institutions which persist because of mere inertia and the self-interest of a privileged few. Hence they are unfitted to serve the needs of the present day, a reconstruction especially of economic and industrial conditions being imperatively demanded. Such a change is obviously upon a large scale and of vast extent. It can be effected, therefore, only by collective organized action.

§ 3. Three Aspects of the Conflict

While persons incline in one direction or another, only confusion results from lumping together all issues as so many species of a more general issue of individual *versus* social. In fact, there are a number of questions which are distinct, each of which must be met and dealt with on its own merits, and in which the individual and the social are not opposed terms. Indeed, in the strict sense of the terms, *no* question can be reduced to the individual on one side and the social on the other. As is frequently pointed out, society consists of individuals, and the term "social" designates only the fact that individuals are in fact linked together, related to one another in intimate ways. "Society" cannot conflict, it is pointed out, with its own constituents; one might as well put number in general in opposition to integers taken severally. On the other hand, individuals cannot be opposed to the relations which they themselves maintain. Only an unreal and impossible being, one completely isolated, disconnected, can be put in opposition to society.

It is surely a fact that there is nothing called society over and above John Smith, Susan Jones, and other individual persons. Society as something apart from individuals is a pure fiction. On the other hand, nothing in the universe, not even physical things, exists apart from some form of association; there is nothing from the atom to man which is not involved in conjoint action. Planets exist and act in solar systems, and these systems in galaxies. Plants and animals exist and act in conditions of much more intimate and complete interaction and interdependence. Human beings are generated only by union of individuals; the human infant is so feeble in his powers as to be dependent upon the care and protection of others; he cannot grow up without the help given by others; his mind is nourished by contact with others and by intercommunication; as soon as the individual graduates from family life he finds himself taken into other associations, neighborhood, school, village, professional, or business associates. Apart from the ties which bind him to others, he is nothing. Even the hermit and Robinson Crusoe, as far as they live on a plane higher than that of the brutes, continue even in physical isolation to be what they are, to think the thoughts which go through their minds, to entertain their characteristic aspirations, because of social connections which existed in the past and which still persist in their imagination and emotions.

The facts urged are all of them true. They bear *upon false statements of the nature of the problems at issue; they do not in any way resolve the actual and important conflicts which exist.* It is important to bear them in mind because they protect us from misconceiving the nature of the problem. For reasons just stated, there can be no conflict between *the* individual and *the* social. For both of these terms refer to pure abstractions. What do exist are conflicts between *some* individuals and *some* arrangements in social life; between groups and classes of individuals; between nations and races; between old traditions imbedded in institutions and new ways of thinking and acting which spring from those few individuals who depart from and who attack what is socially accepted. There is also a genuine difference of convictions as to the way in which, at any given time, these conflicts should be met and managed. There are reasons for holding that they are best settled by private and voluntary action and also for holding that they are best settled by means of combined organized action. No general theory about the individual and the social can settle conflicts or even point out the way in which they should be resolved.

But conflicts nevertheless do exist; they are not got rid of by asserting, what is perfectly true, that there can be no wholesale opposition between society and individuals. How are they to be explained, and to what general kinds can they be reduced? In the first place, there is no single thing denominated "society"; there are many societies, many forms of association. These different groups and classes struggle in many ways against one another and have very diverse values. Men associate in friendship and in antagonism; for recreation and for crime; they unite in clubs and fraternities, in cliques and sects, in churches and armies; to promote science and art and to prey upon others; they unite in business partnerships and corporations. Then these social units compete vigorously against one another. They unite in nations and the nations war with one another; workers combine in trade unions and employers in trade associations and association intensifies struggle between opposite interests. Political life is carried on by parties which oppose each other, and within each party there are contending factions or "wings." Struggle within an organization is indeed a common phenomenon; in trade unions the central organization and the local units often pull different ways, just as in politics there is usually a struggle between forces making for centralization and for local autonomy. Economically, individuals form into groups, and the union accentuates struggle between producer, distributor, and consumer. Church has vied with State for supremacy; the scientific group has at times had to contend with both. Different groups try to get hold of the machinery of government. Officials tend to combine to protect their special interests and these interests are contrary to those of private individuals; it is a recurrent phenomenon for rulers to use power to oppress and harass their subjects. Indeed, so common is it that the whole struggle for political liberty has been represented as a struggle of subjects to emancipate themselves from the tyranny of rulers.

There are then a multitude of conflicts not between individuals and society but between groups and other groups, between some individuals and other individuals. Analysis shows that they tend to fall into classes marked by similar traits, and these traits help explain why there arose the idea that the conflict is between individual and society.

1. There is the struggle between the *dominant* group and the group or groups, occupying, at the time, an *inferior* position of power and economic wealth. The superior group under such circumstances always thinks of itself as representing the social interest, and represents other groups which challenge its power as rebels against constituted authority, as seeking for the satisfaction of their personal appetites against the demands of law and order. A somewhat striking example of this phase of the matter is seen at the present time in the split between those who hold up the political state as the supreme social form, the culminating manifestation of the supreme common moral will, the ultimate source and sole guarantor of all social values, and those who regard the state as simply one of many forms of association, and as one which by undue extension of its claims into virtual monopoly has brought evils in its train. The conflict is not, as was believed earlier, between the state and individual but between the state as the dominant group and other groups seeking greater liberty of action. It is similar in principle, though often opposite in point of material constituents, to the earlier struggle of political groups to get free from the dominant authority of the church.

2. At a certain stage of such conflicts, the inferior but growing group is not organized; it is loosely knit; its members often do not speak for a group which has achieved recognition, much less for social organization as a whole. The dominant group on the

other hand is not only well established, but it is *accepted*, acknowledged; it is supported by the bulk of opinion and sentiment of that time. A government which at a later period is regarded as thoroughly despotic cannot always have been so regarded. In that case it would have been easily overthrown.

To remain in power a dominant class must at least seem to the mass to represent and to sustain interests which they themselves prize. There is thus added to the conflict of the old and established class with the inferior but developing group, the conflict of values that are generally accepted with those which are coming into being. This for a time takes the form of a struggle between a majority *conserving* the old, and a minority interested in the generation of something new, in *progress*. Since it takes time for an idea to gain recognition and for a value to become appreciated and shared, the new and relatively unorganized, although it may represent a genuinely important social value, is felt to be that of dissenting individuals. The values of a past society which are to be conserved are recognized as social, while those of a future society which has yet to be brought into being are taken to be those of individuals only.

In these two instances, the conflict is commonly thought to be between those interested in order and those concerned in progress, where maintenance of order is interpreted as "social" and the initiation of progress as the function of individuals. Even those whose activity in the end establishes a new social order often feel at the time that the enemy is social organization itself. Moreover, every social order has many defects, and these defects are taken to be signs of evils inhering in every kind of social organization. The latter is felt to be nothing but a system of chains holding individuals in bondage. This feeling grows up particularly when old institutions are decaying and corrupt. As in France in the latter eighteenth century and Russia in the later nineteenth, they then call out an intense moral individualism like that of Rousseau and that of Tolstoi respectively. When organization needs to be changed all organization is likely to be felt oppressive. The temporary phenomenon is taken as an illustration of an eternal truth, and the needs of a particular situation frozen into a universal principle.

3. There are also cases in which the troubles of the present are associated with the breakdown of a past order, while existing

evils are capable of being remedied only by organized social action. Then the alignment of so-called individual and social is altered, indeed, is virtually reversed. Those who profit by the existing régime and who wish to have it retained are now the "individualists," and those who wish to see great changes brought about by combined action are the "collectivists." These latter feel that institutions as they exist are a repressive shell preventing social growth. They find disintegration, instability, inner competition to be so great that existing society is such only in outward appearance, being in reality what Carlyle called the "society" of his day, namely, "anarchy plus the constable." On the other hand stand those who are at a special advantage in the situation. They extol it as the product of individual energy, initiative, industry, and freedom; these precious qualities will be imperiled by adoption of a plan of conjoint collective activity. They represent the social order desired by others to be one of servility which crushes out the incentives to individual effort, and which creates dependence upon an impersonal whole, putting a vicious paternalism in place of self-reliance. "Collectivism" in their mouths is a term of reproach. In short, those who are on the side of keeping the *status quo* intact are now the "individualists," those who want great social changes are the "collectivists," since the changes desired are on so large a scale that they can be effected only through collective action.

We shall accordingly substitute the consideration of definite conflicts, at particular times and places, for a general opposition between social and individual. Neither "social" nor "individual," in general, has any fixed meaning. All morality (including immorality) is both individual and social:—individual in its immediate inception and execution, in the desires, choices, dispositions from which conduct proceeds; social in its occasions, material, and consequences. That which is regarded as anti-social and immoral at one time is hailed later on as the beginning of great and beneficent social reform—as is seen in the fate of those moral prophets who were condemned as criminals only to be honored later as benefactors of the race. Organizations that were punished as conspiracies by despotic governments have been regarded as the authors of a glorious liberty after their work has succeeded. These facts do not signify that there is no enduring criterion for judgment but that this criterion is to be found in consequences, and not in some general conception of individual and social.

The points just made suggest three angles from which a social problem may be analyzed in detail in order to decide upon the moral values involved. First, the struggle between a dominant class and a rising class or group; secondly, between old and new forms and modes of association and organization; thirdly, between accomplishing results by voluntary private effort, and by organized action involving the use of public agencies. In historic terms, there is the struggle between class and mass; between conservative and liberal (or radical); and between the use of private and public agencies, extension or limitation of public action.

An illustration of the first issue is seen in the origin of states organized on a popular instead of upon an autocratic dynastic basis. This origin involved the overthrow of the established institutions which for a long time had regulated social affairs; it emancipated many individuals. But at the same time, it generated new types of social institutions and organizations. It was not in other words a movement toward mere individualism. The second mentioned struggle, that between conservative (or, as his opponents term him, reactionary) and liberal, between those who want to preserve intact what has been already attained and who fear and oppose all social change, and those who aim at social modifications more or less profound, is seen in all phases of life; in religious organizations, with the cleavage into fundamentalist and modernist; in education, with the traditionalist and the "progressive"; in politics, with its divisions into right and left; in industrial society, between capitalism and communism as extreme illustrations. The controversy between believers in private and in public action is manifested in every issue which concerns the extent and area of governmental action. At one extreme, are anarchists shading off into those who believe in *laissez faire* and hold that government is best which governs least, through those who believe in enlargement of governmental functions to serve the general interest, over to state socialists who would have government assume control of all means of production and distribution that are of any great size.

§ 4. The Problem of Method

The attempt to settle these issues in our discussion of ethics would obviously involve an exhibition of partisanship. But, what is more important, it would involve the adoption of a method which has been expressly criticized and repudiated. It would assume the existence of final and unquestionable knowledge upon which we can fall back in order to settle automatically every moral problem. It would involve the commitment to a dogmatic theory of morals. The alternative method may be called experimental. It implies that reflective morality demands observation of particular situations, rather than fixed adherence to *a priori* principles; that free inquiry and freedom of publication and discussion must be encouraged and not merely grudgingly tolerated; that opportunity at different times and places must be given for trying different measures so that their effects may be capable of observation and of comparison with one another. It is, in short, the method of democracy, of a positive toleration which amounts to sympathetic regard for the intelligence and personality of others, even if they hold views opposed to ours, and of scientific inquiry into facts and testing of ideas.

The opposed method, even when we free it from the extreme traits of forcible suppression, censorship, and intolerant persecution which have often historically accompanied it, is the method of appeal to authority and to precedent. The will of divine beings, supernaturally revealed; of divinely ordained rulers; of so-called natural law, philosophically interpreted; of private conscience; of the commands of the state, or the constitution; of common consent; of a majority; of received conventions; of traditions coming from a hoary past; of the wisdom of ancestors; of precedents set up in the past, have at different times been the authority appealed to. The common feature of the appeal is that there is some voice so authoritative as to preclude the need of inquiry. The logic of the various positions is that while an open mind may be desirable in respect to physical truths, a completely settled and closed mind is needed in moral matters.

Adoption of the experimental method does not signify that there is no place for authority and precedent. On the contrary, precedent is, as we noted in another connection, a valuable *instrumentality* (p. 275). But precedents are to be *used* rather than to be implicitly followed; they are to be used as tools of analysis of present situations, suggesting points to be looked into and hypotheses to be tried. They are of much the same worth as are personal memories in individual crises; a storehouse to be drawn upon for suggestion. There is also a place for the use of authorities. Even in free scientific inquiry, present investigators rely upon the findings of investigators of the past. They employ theories and principles which are identified with scientific inquirers of the past. They do so, however, only as long *as no evidence is presented calling for a reexamination of their findings and theories*. They never assume that these findings are so final that under no circumstances can they be questioned and modified. Because of partisanship, love of certainty, and devotion to routine, accepted points of view gain a momentum which for long periods even in science may restrict observation and reflection. But this limitation is recognized to be a weakness of human nature and not a desirable use of the principle of authority.

In moral matters there is also a presumption in favor of principles that have had a long career in the past and that have been endorsed by men of insight; the presumption is especially strong when all that opposes them is the will of some individual for exemption because of an impulse or passion which is temporarily urgent. Such principles are no more to be lightly discarded than are scientific principles worked out in the past. But in one as in the other, newly discovered facts or newly instituted conditions may give rise to doubts and indicate the inapplicability of accepted doctrines. In questions of social morality more fundamental than any particular principle held or decision reached is the attitude of *willingness to reexamine and if necessary to revise current convictions, even if that course entails the effort to change by concerted effort existing institutions, and to direct existing tendencies to new ends.*

It is a caricature to suppose that emphasis upon the social character of morality leads to glorification of contemporary conditions just as they are. The position does insist that morals, to have vitality, must be related to these conditions or be up in the air. But there is nothing in the bare position which indicates whether the relation is to be one of favor or of opposition. A man walking in a bog must pay even more heed to his surroundings than a man walking on smooth pavement, but this fact does not mean that he is to surrender to these surroundings. The alternative is not between abdication and acquiescence on one side, and neglect and ignoring on the other; it is between a morals which is effective because related to what is, and a morality which is futile and empty because framed in disregard of actual conditions. Against the social consequences generated by existing conditions there always stands the idea of other and better social consequences which a change would bring into being.

§ 5. Historic Individualism

Examination of the special moral problems presented by existing social conditions is reserved for subsequent chapters. We shall here attempt to illustrate what has been said by a reference to the movement termed "individualism" in a particular sense determined by historical causes.

1. In economics, it is the notion that individuals left free to pursue their own advantage in industry and trade will not only best further their own private interests but will also best promote social progress and contribute most effectively to the satisfaction of the needs of others and hence to the general happiness.

2. Since the "left free" in this statement signifies in point of practice freedom from regulation by legislation and governmental administration, the doctrine has its political side. It signifies that the activities of government shall be restricted as closely as possible to policing society; that is, to keeping order, to preventing encroachments by one person upon the lawful rights of others, and to securing redress when such interference with the rights of others has occurred. In current phrases, it signifies "keep government out of business"; at least keep it out as much as possible.

3. Since the doctrine has an "ideological" support, it also signifies a certain general philosophy, which may be called that of the "natural" *versus* "artificial." Economic activities on this view are natural and governed by natural laws. Men naturally seek to satisfy their wants; labor or the expenditure of energy is naturally economized so that there will be the utmost return for the minimum outgo; to make the future secure men naturally abstain from consuming all they produce, thus laying by capital to

increase their future productivity. Since the output of work is greatest when there is the skill which comes with restriction of effort to one field, division of labor is inherent in the development and this division brings about exchange and trade. There results a general interdependence in which each is forced to find the line of work in which he is most productive and to do the things which, in order to bring the most return to himself, will best serve the needs of others. In contrast with the "natural laws" of this economic process, political laws are artificial; the first are implanted by nature (often conceived of as vice-regent of God) in the human frame. The second are man-made. The presumption is always in favor of natural laws and their workings and against human "interference."

4. To this idea of natural laws, identical with economic laws, was joined an idea of natural *rights*. According to this view, certain rightful claims belong inherently to individuals apart from civil society and the State. The right to life, to property which one has personally produced, to contract or make agreements with others, are such rights; they contrast with civil and political rights which are dependent upon the civil and political organization of society. Being innate and inalienable, they set fixed limits to the activity of government. Government exists in order to protect them; if it infringes on them, it violates its own function so that citizens are released from an obligation to obedience. At the least, courts must pronounce such action invalid because in violation of natural rights.

5. There was often, although not always, associated with the above mentioned four points, the doctrine of self-interest, taken as a scientific support based on psychology. According to this view, human nature is so constituted as to be averse to all activity involving the sacrifice of abstinence and toil except when an incentive of the prospect of a greater advantage or profit is offered. All individuals are supposed to be on the alert for their own interest and to be skilled in calculating where it lies—provided at least that they are not paralyzed or confused by oppressive laws and artificial social institutions.

These various considerations taken as a whole constitute the doctrine of "individualism" in its narrower historic sense. It was formulated during the eighteenth century. It had immense influence—far from extinct as yet—in shaping legal and political institutions throughout the nineteenth century. There were definite causes for its appearance and its growth. Newly invented machines, run by steam power instead of by hand, were creating a new industrial development, while existing laws and customs expressed an agrarian culture and contained many feudal survivals. They were filled with regulations which obstructed commerce, foreign and domestic, which hampered the development of the new type of industry, and which favored landlords at the expense of the manufacturing and mercantile class. European governments regulated (in fact obstructed) international trade in the interest of accumulation of specie in the governmental treasury, at the expense of industry and commerce. The doctrine of economic *laissez faire* then presented itself as an unshackling of human initiative, energy, and inventive skill, as opening a definite road of progress. Established organization on the other hand represented inertia, sloth, and repression. This temporary historic conflict was generalized into an inherent and absolute opposition between the "individual" and the "social," the "natural" and the "artificial."

The period coincided with the beginnings of what we now term popular and democratic government. Governments in general were either corrupt or oppressive or both. They were felt—and at the time with good reason—to mark arbitrary limitations on the legitimate freedom of individuals. In the United States, this feeling was reenforced by the struggle between the colonists and the home government in Great Britain. It was an easy step from the restrictions imposed on the colonies by Great Britain to the idea that all government by its very nature tends to be repressive, and that the great aim in political life is to limit the encroachments of governments in order to make secure the liberty of citizens. The United States was born in the atmosphere of jealousy and fear of State action; the tradition has persisted; it forms a large part of the present power of individualistic philosophy. This feeling, combined with the personal initiative, independence, and self-help that were so indispensable under pioneer conditions in a country of small population and having seemingly unbounded natural resources, operated to create a moral background for the doctrine of individualism. Although the idea of democracy was that of self-rule, the traditions and emotions generated under conditions of alien rule persisted to such an ex-

tent that any conception that the people could use their own instrument, government, as a constructive agency for furthering
their own well-being, was confined at most to the administration
of local communities. The doctrine of the superiority of "natural
laws" to man-made law led to an abdication of effort at intelligent control; economic processes were supposed to work of
themselves and to a beneficent end. The idea of natural rights
was interpreted by courts to forbid legislation which in any way
disturbed the *status quo* in the distribution of property, or which,
in the interest of workers, limited the power of free contract—
the legal fiction being that all parties to an industrial arrangement were equally free to enter or not into the arrangement.

Meantime the original circumstances, economic and political,
under which the philosophy of so-called individualism grew up
and had had, upon the whole, a useful effect, changed completely. Industrialism supplanted agrarianism as the ruling force.
The machine became the regular instead of the novel and exceptional means of production. Impersonal corporations, instead of
individual employers in personal contact with workmen, became
the rule. Accumulations of capital grew large, and then merged
into larger units. The doctrine of liberty and contract and of
non-interference with the customary rules of industry inured to
the benefit of the employer and investor, and to the detriment
of the workers—that of the mass of people. Protective legislation
began to make its way and was followed by the development of a
"collectivist" point of view in opposition to the older "individualism." The roles were reversed. The accepted, the established,
social order came to include the things which earlier had had to
be striven for by a minority. The social order was now itself "individualistic" in the sense defined above, and the doctrines and
slogans which had been used earlier by dissidents and reformers
were now used to defend the *status quo*. "Liberty" meant *in
effect* the legally unrestrained action of those advantageously
placed in the existing distribution of power, through possession
of capital and ownership of the means of production.

The ethical formula of the individualistic philosophy was and
still remains: The greatest possible freedom of individuals as
long as that freedom is not used to the detriment of equal or
similar liberty on the part of other individuals. The formula has
had great vogue; as already intimated, it once did a useful service

in getting rid of laws and institutions that had outlived their value. But there is, as an intellectual statement, a flaw in it, a "catch." What is meant by *like* or *equal* freedom? If it signified materially alike, equal in actual power, it would be difficult to take objection to it. The formula would be compatible with the efforts of organized society to *equalize conditions*. It would, for example, justify public action to secure to all an education which would effect a complete development of their capacities, so that they might meet one another on a plane of knowledge and trained intelligence as nearly even as possible. It would justify legislation to equalize the standing of those now at a disadvantage because of inequality in physical power, in wealth, in command of the machinery of employment. It would justify, in other words, a vast amount of so-called social legislation which the individualistic theory as usually held condemns.

But the interpretation given to the ideal of equality was formal, not material; it was legalistic not realistic. Individuals were said to be equal provided they were equal *before the law*. In legal theory, the individual who has a starving family to support is equal in making a bargain about hours and conditions of labor and wages, with an employer who has large accumulated wealth to fall back on, and who finds that many other workers near the subsistence line are clamoring for an opportunity to earn something with which to support their families.

Morally speaking, individuals cannot be split up into a number of isolated and independent powers, all of which can be compared, one by one, with like powers of others so as to determine their equality. The individual person is a whole; what he labors at and the reward he gets are things which affect all his capacities, desires, and satisfactions—and not only his own but those of the members of his family. Just as we cannot tell what is "due" a man until we have taken his whole self into account, so we cannot tell whether a man's freedom is furthered or is interfered with until we have taken into account not just some single point, formally and legally defined, but the bearing of the factor in question (for example, "freedom" of contract) upon his whole plane of living, his opportunities for development, and his relations to others.

The purpose of this historical survey is not to indicate that some anti-"individualistic" principle is correct, so that we should supplant it by a collectivistic formula and program in order to meet the moral requirements of society. It is, first, to suggest the *relativism* of social formulae in their ethical aspect. No single formula signifies the same thing, in its consequences, or in practical meaning under different social conditions. That which was on the side of moral progress in the eighteenth and early nineteenth centuries may be a morally reactionary, doctrine in the twentieth century; that which is serviceable now may prove injurious at a later time. This fact is but a statement in more definite form of the impossibility of deriving concrete directions for moral action from the general concepts of individual and social.

From this fact follows the second point. We have to consider the probable consequences of any proposed measure with reference to the situation, as it exists at some defined time and place in which it is to apply. There cannot be any universal rule laid down, for example, regarding the respective scopes of private and public action. All but the most extreme "individualists" stop short of the logical conclusion that there should be no public schools supported by taxation. They are aware of how many children might, under a purely voluntary system, fail to get any education, and they know what inequalities in society would thereby be fostered. Yet, it does not follow that public education is always and only good. A ruling class and the government may use the schools to inculcate particular doctrines in plastic minds; to suppress freedom of inquiry; to turn out minds in a common mold, and a mold favorable to their own special interest. Under such conditions, there is justification for upholding, on moral grounds, the claims of other schools than those supported by the state.

Every question for the extension or restriction of public action should, then, be considered on its merits. There was a time when religion and religious worship were public functions. Almost all peoples are now convinced that it is better that they should be a private, a voluntary, affair. There was a time in English history when the courts of law were not indeed exactly private, but were attached to the domain of feudal lords; few there are today who would question the value of the transfer of the judicial function to the State. But even this transfer is not inconsistent with the growth, under the jurisdiction of government, of private arbitration as a method of settling commercial disputes. If we go further back in history we find the administration of justice in savage tribes a matter of "self-help." There may have been those who opposed its transfer to the public on the ground that it would weaken individual initiative and responsibility and create a servile dependence on state paternalism. In general, we can say that many interests have shifted from public to private and *vice versa* in connection with changes in science, industry, and public sentiment. Every proposed measure of public policy should, therefore, be considered on the ground of its own effects on the welfare of the members of a community, and not be disposed of on the basis of some abstract theory of either the individual or the social.

Finally, while we have taken our examples for the most part from the controversy concerning public *versus* private action, the principle that conclusions should be reached by analysis of consequences in definite situations holds good of the whole range of problems that have been mentioned. Take, for example, the respective moral claims of conservatism and radicalism. It is impossible to imagine a situation in which there are no values worked out in the past which need to be conserved. But their conservation may demand a change in the *means* by which they are maintained, a change in laws and habits. It is evident that not all customs and ways of doing things can be changed simultaneously. The inertia of habit renders it impossible in the first place, and any attempt in that direction would simply throw everything into chaos. Some habits must remain intact in order to get a positive leverage by which to effect changes desired in other institutions. The problem is always one of discrimination and emphasis: What social arrangements at any given time and place should be kept relatively stable and what arrangements should be modified, in order that values may be rendered more secure, more equitably distributed, richer and more diversified? As long as the issue is conceived in a wholesale manner, conservatism will tend to be blind and reactionary, and radicalism will tend to be abrupt and violent. In a normal society, there would be no class of professional reformers. Some social institutions, some phase of every institution, would be continually re-forming, in the literal sense of remaking, in order to be better adapted to its contemporary conditions of social life.

To some persons it may seem an academic matter whether

their attitude and the method they follow in judging the ethical values of social institutions, customs, and traditions, be experimental or dogmatic and closed; whether they proceed by study of consequences, of the working of condition, or by an attempt to dispose of all questions by reference to preformed absolute standards. There is, however, no opening for application of scientific method in social morals unless the former procedure is adopted. There is at least a presumption that the development of methods of objective and impartial inquiry in social affairs would be as significant there as it has proved in physical matters. The alternative to organic inquiry is reliance upon prejudice, partisanship, upon tradition accepted without questioning, upon the varying pressures of immediate circumstance. Adoption of an experimental course of judgment would work virtually a moral revolution in social judgments and practice. It would eliminate the chief causes of intolerance, persecution, fanaticism, and the use of differences of opinion to create class wars. It is for such reasons as these that it is claimed that, at the present time, the question of method to be used in judging existing customs and policies proposed is of greater moral significance than the particular conclusion reached in connection with any one controversy.

Literature

Addams, *Democracy and Social Ethics*, 1902; Dewey, *The Public and Its Problems*, 1927, *Individualism, Old and New*, 1930; Hobhouse, *Morals in Evolution*, 1907, Vol. II., ch. vii.; Sidgwick, *Elements of Politics*, 1897; Rickaby, *Political and Moral Essays*, 1902; Fite, *Individualism*, 1911; Bonar, *Philosophy and Political Economy*, 1893; Cooley, *Social Organization*, 1912, ch. i. and Part III.; Gide and Rist, *History of Economic Doctrines from the Time of the Physiocrats to the Present Day*, 1915; Wallas, *The Great Society*, 1914, *Human Nature in Politics*, 1909; Wells, *The Work, Wealth and Happiness of Mankind*, 1931, especially Vol. II., chs. xv. and xvi.; Lippmann, *Drift and Mastery*, 1914, *Preface to Politics*, 1913, *The Phantom Public*, 1925; Dicey, *Law and Opinion in England*, 1914; Ogburn, *Social Change*, 1922; Ogburn and Goldenweiser, *The Social Sciences and Their Interrelations*, 1927, with extensive bibliographies; Follett, *The New State*, 1918; Laski, *Authority in the Modern State*, 1919; Catlin, *A Study of the Principles of Politics*,

1930, especially ch. viii.; Godwin, *Political Justice*; Spencer, *Man versus the State*, 1884; Hobson, *Free-Thought in the Social Sciences*, 1926; Green, *Principles of Political Obligation*, 1879; Cooley, *Social Process*, 1918; MacIver, *The Modern State*, 1926; Wilde, *The Ethical Basis of the State*, 1924; Tufts, *Our Democracy, Its Origins and Its Tasks*, 1917.

§ 1. Does the Social Environment Have Moral Import?

Previous discussion has virtually taken for granted a principle which is not admitted by all moralists and which must be made explicit, especially since it is fundamental to the whole range of questions we are to consider. The hypothesis in question is that the social environment has intrinsic moral significance; that it enters intimately into the formation and the substance of the desires, motives, and choices which make up character. There are those who hold the contrary. They assert that the environment is morally indifferent and neutral. This view is a perfectly logical conclusion from the tenet that moral goodness is wholly a matter of motives and that motives (and will) have nothing to do with consequences; it follows logically from the divorce of "inner" and "outer" and the identification of morals with the "inner." To one who adopts this view, such things as the legal system, the political régime, the dominant economic order with whatever distribution of wealth and income, opportunity for work, control of the machinery of production and distribution, happens to exist, may have much to do with material prosperity but nothing to do with morality. For an individual in any system can have a righteous will. Social conditions, upon this theory, affect such things as comfort and happiness, but not moral selfhood; they influence the external execution of the motive but not the motive itself.

We shall not repeat the criticism already passed (p. 173) upon the dualism set up between the inner motive or will and the outer act and consequences, beyond a reminder that this view deliberately and avowedly narrows the scope and contents of the "moral." The theory of such a separation eliminates all concrete elements from character, reducing it to mere arbitrary power of choice, the same in all, a purely formal matter. The notion that there is such a power of choosing, having no ground or reason outside the arbitrary choice itself, isolates the moral agent from all social relations. "Will" on this view is what it is, and acts as it does act, wholly independently of all environing conditions—domestic, economic, penal, political, legal, educational, those of friendship, etc. Although this conclusion follows logically from the premise, few who hold the premise carry the idea to its final conclusion. If social institutions and arrangements are without moral significance then the individual has no moral responsibility with respect to them; one system of, say, punishment, government, distribution of wealth, is just as good morally as any other. No one has any moral ground for trying to bring one system into existence in preference to another: social reform has no *moral* signification.

If we surrender preconceived theories as to the nature of "will," if we extend the meaning of character to include the whole body of desires, purposes, convictions, manifested in deliberation and choice, then surrounding conditions which arouse desires; which direct wants toward one object rather than another for satisfaction; which confirm certain purposes and weaken others; which lead to prizing some objects and disparaging others, have intrinsic moral meaning. It is empirically evident that the social world into which each of us is born exercises a constant stimulative and inhibitory effect upon desire and intent. The environment also acts in a *non-moral* fashion, like a physical force, in as far as we are unaware of its working. But its operation in shaping character comes into moral account as soon as we become aware of it and judge its quality, its direction, its value. Probably at the present time some social habits are so engrained that we, or at least most of us, are not even aware that they influence us. But as soon as they are perceived, they cease to operate in isolation or merely externally. As we become aware of them, we like or dislike their effects; we actively approve and support them; we tolerate them, we are willing to have them exist rather than take the trouble to change them; or we are moved to active opposition. In any case, there is human complicity, an assumption of responsibility. To many persons at present the economic system, in all probability, seems to exist in the same way that the order of nature exists. It is something to which we must accommodate ourselves as to sunshine and storms, taking advantage of it when possible, protecting ourselves against its inclemencies when necessary, and so on. But in the degree in which there develops in the mind of any one a consciousness of its operation and effects, it is no longer the bare institution which acts, but that institution as it is reflected in the imagination; in desire, hope, fear, intention to support or to change. In short, the contention is not in the least that our will, the body of our desires and purposes, is subservient to social conditions, but that the latter are incorporated into our attitudes, and our attitudes into social conditions, to such an extent that to maintain one is to maintain the other, to change one is to change the other.

It is possible to indicate some of the typical ways in which the social environment enters into the stuff of character. (a) It determines opportunities. We never think of expecting the same desires and aims from the savage as from the civilized man. Ends open to one are non-existent for the other. An individual under any circumstances may have a desire to extend his knowledge, to enlarge his sensitiveness to whatever is lovely in his surroundings. The savage, barbarian, and cultivated man may have the same *quality* of responsiveness on their different levels, and so have the same kind of goodness of character (p. 281). But the actual material of character is different because opportunities for thought and choice vary so much. (b) Different types of institutions, customs, traditions stimulate and evoke different powers. The virtues of a militant society are not those of an industrialized community, nor are these the excellencies which would be especially prized in a society where science and art flourish. The pattern of social organization tends to be reflected in the pattern of character that obtains. (c) Since institutions relate persons to one another in definite ways, as for instance in some type of family organization, in such economic forms as contract and limited liability corporation, private property, business for pecuniary profit, etc., they define the prevailing scheme of recognized obligations (pp. 227–229). (d) As their strong points, their valuable contributions to life, reenforce character, so their weaknesses and defects evoke those adverse reactions out of which grow plans of betterment. Effective plans of improvement are not born of empty aspiration, miscalled idealism, but out of experience of the concrete evils wrought by institutions as they are. We often overlook the fact that the moral prophet who stands out against the dominant conditions of his age is as much influenced by social conditions as is the conformist, more deeply so in fact. The positive and negative values of existing institutions are more truly reflected in his desire and imagination than in those of the conformist: otherwise his protest is sentimental and futile. While the negative values call out desire for something different and better, the positive values supply the content and material attributed to the better. There is no source save past experience out of which the concrete stuff of new aspirations can be formed.

We are not concerned here to do more than to point out that the hypothesis adopted in the text is that social conditions enter integrally and intrinsically into the formation of character, that is, the make-up of desires, purposes, judgments of approval and disapproval. If this positive contention concerning the intimate connection of social conditions is admitted, the immediate problem of theory is the question of what criterion is to be used in judging social conditions as they exist at any time. The last chapter indicated the method by which the criterion should be reached and the spirit in which it should be employed, namely, the *experimental*. That statement concerns the form of the criterion rather than its content or substance. It indicates what has just been intimated, that it should be a generalization from the experiences of the past; a generalization which does not, however, merely repeat or restate in a literal fashion the experience of the past, but is stated in such a way that it will apply to changed conditions of the present and future; that it will serve as an intellectual instrument of survey and criticisms and will point out the direction in which efforts at change and betterment should move. It indicates that the generalization should be a hypothesis, not a dogma; something to be tried and tested, confirmed and revised in future practice; having a constant point of growth instead of being closed.

It would be hard to say whether the world has suffered more from the attempt to regulate social affairs by a rule of thumb empiricism, by sticking to precedent and such rules as have evolved in the past, by refusing to admit constructive imagination and rational insight, or from doctrinaire creeds framed without reference to actual conditions, from dogmas supposed to proceed from some source beyond all experience and immutable. The experimental method looks to past experience not for authoritative rules, but as the indispensable source of suggestions to be worked over in thought. It has respect to intelligence, not as supplying final truths and rigid rules, but as the organ of putting past experience into the form in which it can be useful in the future, and projecting the plans which are to be experimentally tried out.

It is also doubtful whether the world has suffered more from a sheer acquiescence in existing social conditions and from conformity to the rules and conventions they set before us, or from an abstract idealism which sets up vast and vague aims in separation from a basis and leverage in existing conditions. Ideals that are framed without reference to existing social conditions set up ends without means for their realization; since effective means must be found in what already exists. The habit of setting up ideals of this sort eventuates either in blind, passionate revolt which trusts to destruction of what exists to bring forth by some miracle a better estate of things, or, more commonly, in an esthetic disgust with the present which seeks refuge in what is aloof and which through refusal to face existing conditions actually operates to perpetuate them. An experimental method in social morality acknowledges existing conditions to the full; it insists upon facing them intellectually, that is by way of observation and record; it also recognizes that criticisms and plans of betterment are mere indulgences unless they are based upon taking existing conditions into account. But as experimental, it recognizes that these conditions are not fixed and final; that they are both means of change and something to be changed by intelligently directed action. Our position is that past experience enables us to state a criterion of judgment which is sufficiently definite to be usable and sufficiently flexible to lead to its own reinterpretation as experience progresses.

§ 2. The Nature of the Criterion of Social Conditions

In the earlier discussion we arrived at the conclusion that the effect of acts upon the common welfare, the general well-being, is the criterion for judging the moral worth of personal acts and dispositions (pp. 238–248). The presumption is that the same criterion holds with respect to social institutions and in projecting plans of social change. The idea of common good, general welfare, needs, however, careful interpretation. We may say of welfare what was said of the kindred idea of happiness, that we must beware of giving it a fixed meaning. Since it includes the harmonious fulfillment of all capacities, it grows as new potentialities are disclosed; it develops as social changes present new opportunities for personal development.

Such terms as "general" and "common" need, perhaps, even more careful interpretation. The words come easily to the tongue and too readily give a wrong impression. They do *not* mean a sacrifice of individuality; it would be a poor kind of society whose members were personally undeveloped. It does not mean the submergence of what is distinctive, unique, in different human beings; such submergence would produce an impoverishment of the social whole. The positive import of "common good" is suggested by the idea of sharing, participating—an idea involved in the very idea of *community*. Sharing a good or value in a way which makes it social in quality is not identical with dividing up a material thing into physical parts. To partake is to *take* part, to *play* a role. It is something active, something which engages the desires and aims of each contributing member. Its proper analogue is not physical division but taking part in a game, in conversation, in a drama, in family life. It involves diversification, not sameness and repetition. There could be no communication of feeling and idea in a conversation if each one parrot-like said the same sentence over and over, and there could be no game played if all made the same motions at the same time. Each contributes something distinctive from his own store of knowledge, ability, taste, while receiving at the same time elements of value contributed by others. What is contributed to each is, first, a support, a reenforcement, of his own action; thereby each receives from others the factors which give his own position greater *security*—a fact illustrated by the mutual aid given to one another by the partners, the partakers on the same side of a game. In the second place what is contributed is enjoyment of new meanings, new values. In a debate each debater on the same "side" tries to strengthen or reenforce the position of every other one on that side. But in a genuine conversation the ideas of one are corrected and changed by what others say; what is confirmed is not his previous notions, which may have been narrow and ill-informed, but his capacity to judge wisely. What he gains is an expansion of experience; he learns; even if previous ideas are in the main confirmed, yet in the degree in which there is genuine mutual give and take they are seen in a new light, deepened and extended in meaning, and there is the enjoyment of enlargement of experience, of growth of capacity.

What has been said helps to an understanding of the idea of equality as part of the social ideal. It does not mean sameness; it is not to be understood quantitatively, an interpretation which always ends in ideas of external and mechanical equality. Children gain enrichment of experience from parents precisely because of *disparity*. There is quantitative inequality—inequality in *possession* of skill, knowledge, but qualitative equality, for when children are *active*, when they give as well as receive, the lives of parents are fuller and richer because of what they receive from their children as well as because of what they put forth. There is a great deal of discussion of equality which is meaningless and futile because the conception is taken in a static instead of in a functional way. One person is morally equal to others when he has the same opportunity for developing his capacities and playing his part that others have, although his capacities are quite unlike theirs. When there is an equation in his *own* life and experience between what he contributes to the group activity and experience and what he receives in return in the way of stimulus and of enrichment of experience, he is *morally* equal. The equality is one of *values*, not of materials and quantities, and equality of value has on this account to be measured in terms of the intrinsic life and growth of each individual, not by mechanical comparisons. Each individual is incommensurable as an individual with every other, so that it is impossible to find an external measure of equality. Concretely, one person is superior in one particular respect and inferior in some other to many others. He is morally equal when his values with respect to his own possibilities of growth, whatever they are, are reckoned with in the social organization as scrupulously as those of every other. To employ a somewhat mechanical analogy, a violet and an oak tree are equal when one has the same opportunity to develop to the full as a violet which the other has as an oak.

The conception of community of good may be clarified by reference to attempts of those in fixed positions of superiority to confer good upon others. History shows that there have been benevolent despots who wished to bestow blessings on others. They have not succeeded except when their actions have taken the indirect form of changing the conditions under which those lived who were disadvantageously placed. The same principle holds of reformers and philanthropists when they try to do good to others in ways which leave passive those to be benefited. There is a moral tragedy inherent in efforts to further the common good which prevent the result from being either good or common—not good, because it is at the expense of the active growth of those to be helped, and not common because these have no share in bringing the result about. The social welfare can be advanced only by means which enlist the positive interest and active energy of those to be benefited or "improved." The traditional notion of the great man, of the hero, works harm. It encourages the idea that some "leader" is to show the way; others are to follow in imitation. It takes time to arouse minds from apathy and lethargy, to get them to thinking for themselves, to share in making plans, to take part in their execution. But without active cooperation both in forming aims and in carrying them out there is no possibility of a common good.

The other side of this picture is the fact that all special privilege narrows the outlook of those who possess it, as well as limits the possibilities of development of those not having it. A very considerable portion of what is regarded as the inherent selfishness of mankind is the product of an inequitable distribution of power—inequitable because it shuts out some from the conditions which evoke and direct their capacities, while it produces a one-sided growth in those who have privilege. Much of the alleged unchangeableness of human nature signifies only that as long as social conditions are static and distribute opportunity unevenly, it is absurd to expect change in men's desires and aspirations. Special privilege always induces a standpat and reactionary attitude on the part of those who have it; in the end it usually provokes a blind rage of destruction on the part of those who suffer from it. The intellectual blindness caused by privileged and monopolistic possession is made evident in "rationalization" of the misery and cultural degradation of others which attend its existence. These are asserted to be the fault of those who suffer; to be the consequence of their own improvidence, lack of industry, wilful ignorance, etc. There is no favored class in history which has not suffered from distorted ideas and ideals, just as the deprived class has suffered from inertia and undevelopment.

The tenor of this discussion is that the conception of common good, of general well-being, is a criterion which demands the full development of individuals in their distinctive individuality, not a sacrifice of them to some alleged vague larger good under the plea that it is "social." Only when individuals have initiative, independence of judgment, flexibility, fullness of experience, can they act so as to enrich the lives of others and only in this way can a truly common welfare be built up. The other side of this statement, and of the moral criterion, is that individuals are free to develop, to contribute and to share, only as social conditions break down walls of privilege and of monopolistic possession.

The fallacies which most often lead to putting individual development in opposition to attainment of a common good are (a) restricting the number of individuals to be considered, and (b) taking these individuals statically instead of dynamically, that is, with reference to what they are at a given time instead of in connection with their possibilities of growth. The historic "Individualism" criticized in the last chapter went astray at both these points. It confined its outlook to a particular class of individual, the industrialists, leaving out of account the much greater number of men, women, and children who were employees attached to machinery. And it treated the latter as if their efficiency, skill, intelligence, and character could be determined by their existing status, without regard to the developments which would take place if institutions were changed. The moral criterion attaches more weight to what men and women are capable of becoming than to their actual attainments, to possibilities than to possessions, even though the possessions be intellectual or even moral. Generosity in judgment of others as distinct from narrowness is largely a matter of estimating what they can grow into instead of judging them on the basis of what conditions have so far made of them.

The criterion is identical in its political aspect with the *democratic ideal.* For democracy signifies, on one side, that every individual is to share in the duties and rights belonging to control of social affairs, and, on the other side, that social arrangements are to eliminate those external arrangements of status, birth, wealth, sex, etc., which restrict the opportunity of each individual for full development of himself. On the individual side, it takes as the criterion of social organization and of law and government release of the potentialities of individuals. On the social side, it demands cooperation in place of coercion, voluntary sharing in a process of mutual give and take, instead of authority imposed from above. As an ideal of social life in its political phase it is much wider than any form of government, although it includes government in its scope. As an ideal, it expresses the need for progress beyond anything yet attained; for nowhere in the world are there institutions which in fact operate equally to secure the full development of each individual, and assure to all individuals a share in both the values they contribute and those they receive. Yet it is not "ideal" in the sense of being visionary and utopian; for it simply projects to their logical and practical limit forces inherent in human nature and already embodied to some extent in human nature. It serves accordingly as basis for criticism of institutions as they exist and of plans of betterment. As we shall see, most criticisms of it are in fact criticisms of the imperfect realization it has so far achieved.

Democracy as a moral ideal is thus an endeavor to unite two ideas which have historically often worked antagonistically: liberation of individuals on one hand and promotion of a common good on the other. In the famous motto of the French Revolution "Liberty and Equality" represent the values which belong to individuals in their severalty, their distinction from one another; "Fraternity" represents the value that belongs to them in their relations with one another. All history proves, however, that there is no automatic equation of liberty and fraternity with each other. How can fraternal relations be secured without putting individual freedom under restraint? History proves also that liberty and equality do not automatically tend to generate and support one another. Granting liberty to all has a tendency to produce inequalities, since those who have superior capacities or superior opportunities, rise, while those of inferior capacity remain stationary or sink. It has been frequently remarked that the

American nation is more interested in equality than in liberty, and willingly places great restrictions on freedom of action if it thinks thereby to secure a greater amount of social uniformity.

From the ethical point of view, therefore, it is not too much to say that the democratic ideal poses, rather than solves, the great problem: How to harmonize the development of each individual with the maintenance of a social state in which the activities of one will contribute to the good of all the others. It expresses a postulate in the sense of a demand to be realized: That each individual shall have the opportunity for release, expression, fulfillment, of his distinctive capacities, and that the outcome shall further the establishment of a fund of shared values. Like every true ideal, it signifies something to be done rather than something already given, something ready-made. Because it is something to be accomplished by human planning and arrangement, it involves constant meeting and solving of problems—that is to say, the desired harmony never is brought about in a way which meets and forestalls all future developments. There is no short-cut to it, no single predestined road which can be found once for all and which, if human beings continue to walk in it without deviation, will surely conduct them to the goal.

The conditions and the concrete significance of liberty, of equality, of mutual respect, and reciprocal service, change from generation to generation, in some degree from year to year. The change in their significance for thought, purpose, and choice, since this country was founded, is simply enormous. The change from a small population to a large one, from rural to urban, from agricultural to industrial, from hand to machine production, from comparative economic equality to great disparity of fortunes, from free land and unused natural resources to their appropriation—merely to point to some of the larger alterations—has given the terms of the problem a radically new significance, and demands, therefore, new thoughts and new measures if ideals remaining formally and nominally the same, are to be maintained. Because of these facts, the approach must be experimental. The alternative to the adoption of an experimental method is not the attainment of greater security by adoption of fixed method (as dogmatists allege), but is merely to permit things to drift: to abdicate every attempt at direction and mastery.

§ 3. Some Special Political Problems

The particular questions which are involved in the concrete application of the democratic criterion to social issues are numerous and, as just indicated, shifting. All that can be done here is to select a few, and those few as samples rather than as questions which all would agree to be of the highest importance. The first one to be discussed concerns the *status of the idea of democratic government.* In the later eighteenth and early nineteenth century it was virtually an axiom among enlightened thinkers that self-government is the only morally justifiable form of government; they believed that its establishment would usher in a new historic epoch of virtue and happiness. We are living in a time of disillusionment concerning claims once sincerely put forth; in a time of reaction so extreme that many declare the whole idea to be a superstition. It is worth while, accordingly, to consider some of the aspects and causes of the change.

One of its manifestations is the spread of political apathy and indifference. When only about one-half of the potential electorate exercises the right of franchise, there is not only a contradiction of the early assumption that democratic government would of necessity call out political interest in all citizens, but proof that in its present form it lacks vitality. When disinterested exhortation to rise to political responsibility, plus partisanship, plus vast expenses of well-organized party machines, fail to stir more than fifty per cent of the voting population to the attempt to influence governmental action, there is some serious flaw either in democratic policy or in the way in which it is expressed at the present time.

A more overt illustration of the reaction is found in the rise of dictatorships. In some countries they supplant previous autocratic governments, but in others they take the place of supposedly popular and representative governments. In countries which have not adopted dictatorships, there is general decline of faith in Parliamentary institutions, growing disrespect for political leaders of the traditional type, and desire for more direct and effective methods of meeting social questions than are provided by existing democratic machinery. Attacks upon popular government are now claiming scientific support, particularly that of biology and psychology. It is alleged that the democratic theory implies a much wider distribution of a high degree of intelligence than actually exists; that scientific inquiry reveals the prevalence of constitutional and hence unalterable inferiority in capacity for education and for understanding in masses of the population; the doctrine of heredity is appealed to in support of belief in inherent inequalities so great as to substantiate an oligarchical theory of government.

Without raising ulterior questions, it may be pointed out that political questions have increased enormously in scope and in internal complexity since the democratic movement originated. This is especially true in the United States where the experiment began with a small rural population, located on a comparatively limited territory having large and still unappropriated natural resources, at a time when the problems set by the industrial revolution had not yet emerged, and when the town-meeting was competent to take care of the local questions which arose in face-to-face communities. The questions which now come up for political action are vast in extent. Those of the tariff and of finance, for example, are world-wide in their scope, beside involving a tremendous amount of intricate detail. The increase of physical mobility and transportation has produced an interknitting of forces which complicates every issue while it has not effected any corresponding unity of aim and harmony of sentiment. It has merely created a situation too vast for the imagination to grasp and too involved to judge.

With respect to internal problems, a very long road has been traveled since the formation of the American State. Our Constitution was framed and the system of government formulated in the later decades of the eighteenth century. Since then inventions have occurred which have produced more social changes in a hundred and fifty years than the world had experienced in a thousand preceding years, but our governmental mechanisms have, relatively speaking, stood still. As is often said, we deal with the problems of the age of the airplane with the political machinery of the stage-coach period. Actual problems, actual in the sense of being contemporary, were not dreamed of when our political forms took shape. Those of tariff, money and credit, public utilities, power, management of municipalities with respect to housing, traction, water, light, schools, sanitation, are technical requiring the special knowledge and trained ability of the expert rather than the general judgment of the average voter. Along with the growing complexity of all political questions there has come into being a number of powerful rivals to political interest. Individuals absorbed in business and professional affairs leave politics to those who can work political machinery for their own private profit. The automobile, radio, movie, have become rivals of politics; men have hundreds of outlets unthought of when the conduct of the State was entrusted to popular guidance.

With increased complexity and intricacy of public affairs, the demand for efficiency becomes greater, at the very time when doubts as to the possible efficiency of representative government also increase. The mental model of efficiency is set largely by the impersonal processes of the machines which dominate our industrial society, since men's mental habits are largely formed by what they are accustomed to in their everyday surroundings. Present society is used to, almost built upon, mechanical standards and methods. Control of industry is from the top downwards, not from the bottom upwards. The greater number of persons engaged in shops and factories are "subordinates." They are used to receiving orders from their superiors and acting as passive organs of transmission and execution. They have no active part in making plans or forming policies—the function comparable to the legislative in government—nor in adjudicating disputes which arise. In short their mental habits are formed under conditions which render their minds unfit for accepting the intellectual responsibilities involved in political self-government. In pioneer days, the greater number of persons worked "on their own," directed their own activities, and lived in frontier conditions which exercised personal initiative and independence.

Since the idea of efficiency in an industrialized society tends to assume a mechanical and external form, discussion, consultation, deliberation which involves much talking, seem inefficient. A demand grows up for concentration of power in making and executing plans similar to that which we have become accustomed to in industry. The demand is reenforced by the fact that because of the apathy of large numbers, the actual management of politics falls into the hands of professionals who are interested not in principles or issues, but in keeping or getting power by winning elections, and who use the spoils of office to strengthen their own machines and not for public ends. Dissatisfaction with the class of office-holders who are in power or who want to be is one of the chief causes, the world over, of disgust with politics and support of dictatorships. In addition, there are those who believe that it is to their own pecuniary advantage to disparage political action, to belittle governmental agencies as incompetent meddlers, and who therefore discredit lawmakers on every occasion.

We shall make no attempt to settle the particular questions which are involved in the contemporary predicaments of democracy, but shall speak rather of certain underlying general factors which determine the spirit in which they should be met. The first point concerns the need of a change in the earlier *theory* of democracy if it is to be adapted to present conditions. The second point has to do with the extent to which our political problems have become predominantly economic in nature. The two points are, as the discussion will disclose, intimately bound up together.

The democratic theory took articulate shape in a pre-industrial and a prescientific age. And it bears the marks of the time of its origin. Although both the democratic theory and practice are recent, although they have endured but a short portion of the recorded time of history, there has been more human history, measured in terms of change and its rapidity, since they came into existence than in all previous ages. The validity of the ideal and criterion is questionable if the theory cannot be readapted and restated in terms of present-day life. (a) Intellectually, conditions during the late eighteenth century tended to give all social theory a fixed and absolutistic form. The consequence was that adherents and opponents of democracy alike often assume the identity of the theory with particular governmental methods and instruments that came into being at an early date. In the United States, the tendency to rigidity of interpretation and corresponding fixity of governmental institutions was favored by a written constitution and its provisions. (b) Moreover, as has already been noted, the theory of government was formulated during a period of struggle against governments which then existed, a revolt which was especially strong in the American colonies when the system took shape. The fear of government resulted in keeping the organs of government rudimentary; developments have for the most part taken place either covertly or only under the stress of a great crisis. The clumsiness of governmental procedure in contrast with the constant invention and use of new mechanisms and methods in industrial production has led upon the whole to distrust of governmental action rather than to an attempt to create new political organs.

(c) The scheme of government was conceived in individualistic terms. The best immediate service that could be rendered society in the pioneer days of the republic was to give individuals a free chance to employ their personal abilities and energies in coping with the abundant resources of an undeveloped country. The "sovereignty of the individual" was supposed to be amply secured in politics by the grant of the suffrage in which every individual could exercise his independent judgment. The theory worked well enough as long as the country was agrarian and the population mainly rural. Problems were then comparatively simple, within the range of the personal experience of citizens, while the persons voted for were generally known personally or by repute. It is not necessary to point out how completely conditions have altered.

(d) The conception of majority rule, determined by counting of individual ballots has, to take only one example, tended to work out in the opposite direction to that which was anticipated. It rested upon a kind of quantitative individualism, but it often operates to set up a new kind of despotism, in that ideas uncongenial to the majority are discouraged and their expression not only frowned upon but often prevented by violence. The individualistic conception, summed up into the rule of a majority, has put a false value upon mere uniformity, and created to some extent jealousy of distinction, fear of the dissenter and nonconformist in social matters, a fear increased as population has become heterogeneous through immigration. The result is obviously adverse to progress except in technical and material lines, since cultural progress must always start from a minority. Many instances can be found where dependence upon the false individualistic theory has operated to repress and hamper individuality of thought and expression.

(e) As long as social life was relatively simple, it could be served by correspondingly simple machinery. As new conditions emerged, they were met, if at all, by a process of mechanical addition, not by one of internal readaptation. The consequence was the production of a clogged and cumbrous political machinery, creaking and often breaking down from its own weight. Moreover, as long as economic conditions were simple, as long as comparative, though of course not absolute, equality of industrial opportunity existed, there was no great motive for special interests to get hold of governmental agencies in order to use them for their own ends. Yet, even in the days of the adoption of the Constitution there was enough of a propertied class over against an unpropertied one to add fear of the populace to general fear of government, and to force a compromise with the freer democratic ideals of the Declaration of Independence, concessions to the manufacturing class of the North being balanced with concessions to the slave-owners of the South. The further development of this point takes us over into the second main point. But the conclusion to be drawn from the combined force of the items just mentioned is clear. The translation of the democratic ideal into governmental terms cannot safely be left to statements made on the basis of eighteenth century conditions. Political organs must be modified to meet new conditions. Until they are so modified, there is no way of telling how much of the current criticism and protest against democracy has to do with inherent values and how much with external defects of application.

The second point concerns the modification in political theory and practice demanded by the developments which have come about because of the industrial revolution, the larger part of which has taken place since democratic ideas took political form. Economic questions as such are considered in later chapters. Here we have to note that, putting the matter in the most moderate terms, industrial development during the past century, occurring largely since the Civil War, has put a tremendous strain upon the governmental machinery which was created before it took place. Most political issues of the present arise out of economic conditions; they have to do with the distribution of wealth and income, the ownership and control of property. Taxation, tariff, money and credit, security of employment, unemployment insurance, regulation of rates of railways and public utilities, control of super-power, child labor, pensions of mothers and for old age, are economic in nature, while they are also questions on which citizens divide politically. The chief significance of the Fourteenth Amendment, under the decisions of the courts, has been the protection given to property because of the "due process of law" clause. Radicals insist that the fundamental political issue is now whether the rights of human beings or of property shall be supreme. In any case, there is a problem of value of a moral nature beneath all these politico-economic questions. The question of how far and by what means political agencies shall be used to promote social welfare is itself ultimately a moral question.

While honest differences of judgment arise among persons equally well-intentioned on the subject of both social end and political means, we may be sure upon one point: Political thought and action will be confused and insincere as long as the importance of economic issues in political life is kept from view. Recognition by the general public of their central position in political theory and action would clear the air and make honest differences of conviction more to the point and more fruitful. As long as those who wish to preserve intact certain privileges, of which they have become possessed, successfully prevent the recognition of the presence of economic issues, and of the human import of the decision of economic questions, the workings of professedly democratic governments will be so crude and one-sided as to give ground for attack on the whole democratic idea in politics. Meantime a special complication has been introduced into the machinery of governmental action.

Because political questions are now economic in nature, because governmental action affects seriously the conduct of manufacturing, trade, banking, railways, those who have large pecuniary stakes in the success of these industrial undertakings, have a business motive for getting control of the agencies of government. Municipalities, for example, have valuable franchises to grant for public utilities in lighting, power, traction; they can enter into competition with private corporations through public ownership; the Federal government regulates the tariff, banking, interstate commerce, and the income tax. Hence some business interests have a direct stake in influencing the election of officers, legislative and administrative, and in controlling their action, whether the end is attained by corrupting officials, by large campaign contributions, by pushing into public places those favorable to the business interests involved. A complication and a skew-factor are introduced into democratic government not contemplated by the authors of our system. Where corrupt means, bribery, graft, are resorted to, the business interests concerned have also an interest in keeping a venal machine in power, a fact which explains in part the alliance between municipal officials and the criminal and gangster class found in some of our larger cities. The effective power of these interests in states and in the nation is increased because they are organized in corporate form, and, extending over the whole country, are ready to mobilize their forces quickly at any spot, while those who suffer from their predatory action remain unorganized and scattered, and are appealed to by the slogan of "individualism," even when they are faced by vast consolidated associations.

§ 4. Liberty of Thought and Expression

Liberty to think, inquire, discuss, is central in the whole group of rights which are secured in theory to individuals in a democratic social organization. It is central because the essence of the democratic principle is appeal to voluntary disposition instead of to force, to persuasion instead of coercion. Ultimate authority is to reside in the needs and aims of individuals as these are enlightened by a circulation of knowledge, which in turn is to be achieved by free communication, conference, discussion. Exchange of ideas, distribution of knowledge, imply a previous possession of ideas and information which is dependent upon freedom of investigation. Free circulation of intelligence is not enough barely of itself to effect the success of democratic institutions. But apart from it there is no opportunity either for the formation of a common judgment and purpose or for the voluntary participation of individuals in the affairs of government. For the only alternative to control by thought and conviction is control by externally applied force, or at best by unquestioned custom. Even the ballot, as the alternative to the bullet, has its ultimate value as a form of articulate expression of need and intention. The opportunity to communicate desire in this way is of value ultimately because it is a stimulus to the formation of informed judgment. As Justice Holmes has said, it is the theory of our Constitution "that the ultimate good desired is better reached by free trade in ideas—that the best test of truth is the power of the thought to get itself accepted in the market"; that is, the market where ideas are exchanged.

The idea is implicit in our Constitution because whatever interferes with the free circulation of knowledge and opinions is adverse to the efficient working of democratic institutions. Adulteration of intellectual material is as harmful socially as adulteration of foods is physiologically. Secrecy and falsification are the chief enemies which democratic ideals have to contend with. Intellectual apathy leads to toleration of ignorance and to willingness to be misled and to see others misled. It is an ally of the deliberate concealment and misrepresentation which are undertaken in order to subserve private at the expense of public interest. The unexpected difficulties which democracy has had to meet are largely connected with the fact that it is much more of a task to maintain intellectual courage and energy than the founders of the system contemplated. Dispositions like love of ease, of sensational excitement, and desire to be relieved from responsibility for obtaining information and for careful reflection, are the internal forces which reenforce the suppression of truth and the distortion of fact which come from without. Mental passivity probably accounts for more failures in democratic government than does actual corruption, since it plays such a large part in making the latter tolerable. Honesty of purpose is universally recognized to be a condition of successful government, but it may be doubted whether intellectual activity has been sufficiently emphasized as a condition of the success of democracy.

At the present time, liberty of thought and of expression is threatened, curiously enough, from two opposite sources. The dictatorships referred to in the previous section hold that any amount of suppression of individual belief and of its oral and written manifestation is justified when it is a matter of bringing a new social order into being and getting it thoroughly established. They agree with those persons who assume that since they are in possession of final truth, whether from revelation or from some other source, dissent is a dangerous heresy which must be suppressed. Like other absolute orthodoxies, they hold that the suppression of all but official doctrines is ultimately in the interest of the welfare of all, even of those whose liberties are for the time crushed out. They hold that in the time of creation of a new social order, until it is thoroughly established, freedom of expression is a form of anti-social egoism, as harmful as is any other kind of rebellion against the state, and to be put down by the same drastic measures. Rousseau himself, the prophet of many of the democratic ideas, had said that it was necessary sometimes to *force* individuals to be free.

The opposite attack on freedom comes from those who are already entrenched in power, economic and political, and who fear that general exercise of civil rights, such as freedom of speech, writing, press, assembling, although guaranteed by the Constitution, will disturb the existing order. Accordingly, they claim that every such expression, when it takes the form of criticisms of the *status quo* and of proposal of significant change, is a dangerous radicalism, seditious, subversive of law and order. They believe in freedom of thought and communication as long as it repeats their own convictions, but only under this condition. While the upholders of the first type of restraint wish to suppress everything that would retard revolutionary change, those of this second school oppose as revolutionary all ideas which go contrary to the existing distribution of privilege and power. Their use of power to maintain their own interests is met, from the other side, by widespread fear of any disturbance, lest it be for the worse. This fear of any change is greatly enhanced by the complexity of the existing social scheme, where a change at one point may spread in unforeseen ways and perhaps put all established values in peril. Thus an active and powerful self-interest in maintaining the *status quo* conspires with dread and apathy to identify loyal citizenship with mental acquiescence in and blind laudation of things as they are. Those who strive to sustain even the rights nominally guaranteed by the Bill of Rights of the Constitution find themselves attacked as dangerous enemies of the nation and its Constitution.

Direct and violent encroachments on liberty of thought and speech are perpetrated by police and by organized bands of persons when suggestions for important social change in economic lines are put forth. A still greater invasion of freedom of thought comes about by subtler and more insidious means. Just because public opinion and sentiment are so powerful in a democratic country, even when its democracy is largely nominal, it is immensely worth while for any group which wishes to control public action to regulate their formation. This is best done at their source—while, that is, they are still in process of forming. Propaganda is the method used. Hence we have today a multitude of agencies which skilfully manipulate and color the news and information, which circulate, and which artfully instill, under the guise of disinterested publicity, ideas favorable to hidden interests. The public press, which reaches almost every individual and which circulates cheaply and rapidly, affords an organ of unprecedented power for accomplishing a perversion of public opinion. Favorable and unfavorable presentation of individuals, laudation and ridicule, subtle suggestion of points of view, deliberate falsification of facts and deliberate invention of half-truth or whole falsities, inculcate by methods, of which those subject to them are not even aware, the particular tenets which are needed to support private and covert policies.

On its lowest level, freedom of speech is literally what it is so often said to be, a safety-valve. Until the social order is much more perfected than it is as yet, there will always be those who are discontented. The resulting emotional disturbance must find some outlet. "Blowing off steam" is one way of forestalling a more disastrous explosion. This motive of expediency, however, does not touch the positive values involved. Except for those who are most completely hardened in their own opinion and conceit, public expression gives opportunity for growth; it calls out the ideas and experiences of others and enables one to learn. In general it is the best method humanity has discovered for combining conservation of attained values with progress toward new goods. It is the chief means of uniting order with change, by bringing about a process of orderly development.

The ultimate reason for permitting and actively encouraging freedom of expression is the organic relation which exists between thought and its manifestation. There are those who say that mind is free in any case; that there is no way in which force exercised from without can reach down into mind and stop its operations. They divorce freedom of thought from freedom of communication. There can be no greater fallacy. This particular separation is but another instance of the division erected between inner and outer, between self and action, will and consequences, to which reference has frequently been made (see pp. 286–292). The mind cannot develop in a vacuum; the evil of repressing freedom of expression in speech and print is twofold. On the one hand, an individual is deprived of the material which would otherwise reach him from others, material which is the nutriment and sustenance of thought. He has no opportunity to hear and attend to a variety of points of view. His ideas are almost of necessity kept in a single channel, and the restriction is highly favorable to prejudice and mental apathy. Divergence, movement, is the great stimulus of curiosity, and where curiosity is not aroused, mind remains dormant. On the other hand, without expression, such ideas as one has are likely to die from inanition; or to take an emotional turn at the expense of calm inquiry and understanding; or else to find some indirect channel which is remote and technical and hence, safe. One of the main reasons for the ultra-technical character of scientific knowledge at the present time, for example, is precisely the deflection of inquiry into things apparently so remote from conduct that it does not occur to any one that what is found out will injure any vested interest. No general culture has anywhere developed without freedom of discussion; a small aristocratic class has achieved intellectual distinction even in despotisms, but it has always been by assuming an introvert form. There can be no surer method of preventing the growth of a high level of mind in this country, no more certain way of keeping intellectual life on the plane of mediocrity, than repression of freedom of communication. It is not merely the liberty of the individual that suffers, but the health of society and the development of its culture.

There are two criticisms made of democratic society with respect to its intellectual status which should be directed elsewhere. One of these adverse comments rests on the notion that since in a democracy the majority rules, the majority is always hostile to permitting a minority to develop ideas which are opposed to its own. Since new ideas and points of view necessarily begin with a minority, at first a very small minority, this antagonism, it is said (and truly so if the premises are correct) prevents intellectual and artistic progress. But as a matter of fact, a genuine democracy will always secure to every individual a maximum of liberty of expression and will establish the conditions which will enable the minority by use of communication and persuasion to become a majority. The real culprit is always some powerful minority which prefers to use methods of suppressive force or of perversion and degradation of opinion by means of propaganda. One minority, entrenched economically, does suppress and misrepresent another minority which is at an economic disadvantage, if it is permitted to do so. The responsibility of the actual majority is not for originating the suppression but for standing passively by and permitting it to occur. Any fair-minded survey of suppressive acts in this country will demonstrate that their ultimate source is always a privileged minority. Attacks upon the democratic principle as being their cause merely reacts to strengthen the power of this minority.

The other criticism starts from the premise that the number capable of independent and original thinking and of significant artistic production is always a small minority; that the great mass is inherently on a plane of permanent, because organic, intellectual inferiority. From this it is concluded that democracy is intrinsically unfavorable to intellectual and artistic distinction. In the first place, if we take the matter purely comparatively as between democracies and oligarchies or tyrannies, there is of course no assurance that in the latter the wise and competent minority is going to be in power or have an opportunity to develop and to influence progress. The presumption against this result is indeed somewhat stronger than it is in a democracy. The contrast always drawn by critics is with some ideal aristocracy, too ideal to have ever had a chance to exist. But apart from comparison, the argument suffers from a fallacy. Admitting the most extreme statement that can be rendered plausible concerning the innate intellectual inferiority of the mass, the alleged inferiority concerns their ability to originate and create, not to take in and to follow. They may be, as Plato said, predestined to live on the level of opinion rather than of understanding, but also, as he pointed out, they may absorb and be guided by right opinion. It is a commonplace that many an ordinary man today is in possession of knowledge and ideas which the wisest men of antiquity were unacquainted with. Cultural material is now incarnate in the environment and even a low intelligence can appropriate it. The real issue, in short, comes back to the forces which prevent the free circulation of the discoveries and ideas of the supposedly small superior class, and which prevent the masses from coming in contact with them and taking them over. Examination will show that the obstacles always proceed from a privileged group who are afraid of losing something of their power and prestige.

The moral function of law and institutions, as well as of freedom of inquiry and expression, is in last analysis educative.

Their final test is what they do to awaken curiosity and inquiry in worthy directions; what they do to render men and women more sensitive to beauty and truth; more disposed to act in creative ways; more skilled in voluntary cooperation. In the sense in which culture signifies nurture of powers of growth and increased fullness of the life of mind, the ulterior function of all definite modes of organization, political and otherwise, is cultural. Freedom itself is an end only because it is such an organic and internal means of cultural development. Historic democracies have perhaps erred in overlooking the educative effect of legal and economic institutions and in exaggerating the educative office of a special instrument, the schools. But the latter error, if it exists, at least testifies to a sound, instinctive recognition that the cause of democracy is bound up with development of the intellectual capacities of each member of society. For this reason, we are committed to a system of public schools supported at public expense, open and free to all, and with, in theory, an uninterrupted ladder from infancy up to the mature training of the university and professional school.

It would be possible to illustrate and expand both the criticisms and the problems already suggested by taking educational institutions as the text. We can only note a few points. (a) The "individualistic" tradition was rife when our educational system took shape and its influence has endured. Schooling was counted a means to "getting on" in the world, an aid to individuals in making their own way, getting ahead, carving out their personal fortunes. After pioneer conditions had given away, the idea persisted in the interpretation given to the practical aim of education. It was narrowed down to the "utilitarian" meaning of practical, where utilitarian signifies assisting individuals in making a material living. The wider meaning of practical, viz., related to action as a freely cooperating participant in a community, has been obscured from view. (b) The schools like other agencies have been laid hold of by strong minorities and used to subserve their own ends. The studies which have been made of the factors which influence school administration and instruction in large centres bear out what was said about the suppressive influence of powerful minorities.

(c) The schools, like definitely political agencies of society, have grown by piece-meal extension rather than by internal reorganization. Studies, methods, and ideals appropriate to and inherited from non-democratic societies have been retained with slight modification, to which other studies and methods more directly related to contemporary social conditions have been externally added. The result is often a conglomeration in which older ideals of culture and discipline have lost their vitality while the newer possibilities have been forced into narrow and superficial channels, reenforcing the kind of harsh "practicality" mentioned above. Schools have been accommodated in a passive way to existing industrial conditions instead of being employed to wrest humane culture from them. The result is the current dualism of a refined and remote culture on one side and a harsh and inhumane vocationalism on the other. (d) The struggle said to exist in democracy between quantity and quality is illustrated in a current controversy regarding the scope of higher education. The recent tendency has been for a much larger number of pupils to go to high schools and colleges. It is objected that many go who are not fit by native constitution, and the outcome is said to be lowering and dilution of standards—all professedly in the name of loyalty to democratic ideals. Aside from the point that this movement is still too new to enable us to assess its value, the question arises whether the difficulties which exist could not be met by greater systematic differentiation in the agencies of higher education, together with greater attention in them all to development of the capacity for thought and for creative work. It may be admitted that many go to higher educational institutions where they are misfits. The unsettled question is whether this fact signifies that their schooling should be cut short, or whether it is a reflection upon the curriculum and methods of the institutions which they attend.

The one fact which is most certain is that throughout social life as a whole the older idea and practice which made knowledge a monopolistic possession still persist in a way which prevents the realization and even the fair trial of the democratic ideal. Formerly, cultivation was, especially in its higher forms, the special property of a "spiritual" class or churchly authority. Now, those who are advantageously placed in industry can use superior knowledge and intellectual ability rather to take advantage of others than to contribute to their development. The problem of bringing about an effective socialization of intelli-

ETHICS

gence is probably the greatest problem of democracy today. The case of physical science is typical. As merely theoretical knowledge it is confined to specialists. In its practical applications it affects all persons. But it does so under conditions where its generic social usefulness is limited by consideration of private profit. Applied science works powerfully upon society but not so much as application of *science* as of the mechanism of pecuniary profit, to which science itself is subordinated.

On the other hand, economic limitations prevent many persons, probably the greater number, from effective access to the means of real cultivation of their capacities. They are taken up with the bare processes of making a living, and even when they have leisure they have not been educated to make a significant use of it. Preoccupation with mechanical operations—employees in factories being just "operators" of machines—deadens susceptibilities, and produces by reaction a demand for outside abnormal stimulations. Insecurity of employment and income deprives them of effective use of the freedom of thought and expression they nominally possess. The maldistribution of material goods is reflected in an even greater maldistribution of cultural goods. There is great suffering due to inequality in distribution of material things. But the greater moral loss comes from the effect of this inequality upon participation in the higher values of friendship, science, art, taking an active part in public life, in all the variety of forms which these things are capable of assuming. What the democratic ideal emphasizes in the idea that there is an ethical criterion for social institutions—a conception as old as Plato—is that every human being must count in applying the test, and that the enormous diversification of capacities and interests among individuals must be taken into account so as to realize the distinctive, the unique potentialities of each one.

§ 5. Nationalism, International Relations, Peace and War

History discloses a fairly uninterrupted movement toward widening the area of units of political organization. The ancient world knew empires but they were loose aggregates of local units whose internal customs were not disturbed, save for levying of taxes and drafting of soldiers, by the conquering military dynasty. Otherwise, until the formation of the Roman Empire, the units were hardly wider than the tribe, a confederation of tribes, or a city-state. The most characteristic political phenomenon of recent centuries is the development of national states. These states often, practically always if strong enough, display imperialistic tendencies toward nations that are economically backward. Internally they presuppose or aim at a certain unity of culture, and a system of common laws supported, usually, by some sort of representative government. The gradual substitution of the word "nation" for other terms which designate supreme political units implies, if not actual popular participation in government, at least a personal attachment and loyalty which had previously been found only among the members of small city-states.

The emergence into being of national states has been accompanied by the development of a certain state of mind described as follows by a contemporary writer: "a state of mind in which loyalty to the ideal or to the fact of one's national state is superior to all other loyalties and of which pride in one's nationality and belief in its intrinsic excellence and its 'mission' are integral parts."[1] Historically, national states are results of the break-up of the feudally organized Holy Roman Empire, and the rise of dynastic monarchies; of the substitution of literatures written in the vernacular for Latin as the literary language; of control of the constantly increasing commerce by the government in the interest of accumulation of specie in its own treasury; of the gradual substitution of loyalty to the country for loyalty to the sovereign; of the disruption of the common religion of medieval Europe. Such diverse causes as these somehow blended to effect a large transfer of what we now call "social consciousness" from family, town, and church over to the state. The new attachment and emotional loyalty intensified when dependent and oppressed groups struggled for emancipation from the rule of some empire which held them in subjection; the most acute nationalistic feeling today is found in states which have recently become independent or are still struggling to throw off what they regard as a foreign yoke.

There can be no doubt that one effect of this change has been

1. Carlton J. H. Hayes, *Essays on Nationalism*, p. 6.

to widen the sense of social unity, to deepen the civic sense and to generate public spirit, which may be defined as interest in the affairs of the community as if they were one's own concern; to break down clannishness and provincialism. But on the side in which public spirit is popularly known as patriotism this widening of the area of interest has been accompanied by increased exclusiveness, by suspicion, fear, jealousy, often hatred, of other nations. The stranger, alien, foreigner, has always, for psychological reasons, tended to be an object of dread to all but the most enlightened. The growth of national states carried this feeling over from individuals and small groups and concentrated it upon other states. The self-interest of the dynastic and military class persistently keeps the spark of fear and animosity alive in order that it may, upon occasion, be fanned into the flames of war. A definite technique has grown by which the mass of citizens are led to identify love of one's own country with readiness to regard other nations as enemies. Economic rivalries in trade, desire for markets, for control of raw materials, in some cases for man power to be conscripted for war, for coaling stations, are seized upon as means of exacerbating nationalistic feeling. Public spirit is often converted into a belief in the inherent superiority of all significant virtues of one's nation; the native egoism of individuals is swollen to identify itself with an entity designated *the* "State."

No emotion has ever governed large numbers of mankind for any great length of time unless it had its ideal side. Love of country is intrinsically extension of love for one's friends and neighbors. Men and women who are not animated by public spirit limit their activities to causes and ends which obviously bring profit to themselves and their immediate clique and sect. There are, for example, large parts of the world where transportation is extremely difficult just because individual families hang on to their land and refuse to part with it for any public use. Even in nominal democracies, it is still extremely difficult to induce persons, occupied with what they regard as being in a transcendent sense their "own affairs," to attend to the business of the organized community. Corrupt politicians and those who use public agencies for private profit trade systematically upon this fact. In such directions as these, the development of national sentiment has been in the direction of moral advance.

But, on the other hand, public spirit under the guise of patriotism has been turned increasingly into negative channels; it is used to stir up hostility against other countries and is a potent factor in causing wars, and in making private citizens willing to bear the immense sacrifices they have to make in war and in carrying in peace-time the burden of taxation due to wars. And in many cases, it is becoming clear that particular economic interests hide behind patriotism in order to serve themselves. So far has this feeling gone that on one side there is a definite attempt to attach the stigma of "unpatriotic" to everything designated "international"; to cultivate that kind of "hundred-per-cent Americanism" which signifies practically suspicion and jealousy of everything foreign; to identify national self-respect and independence of character with an isolationism which is based on contempt of other peoples. Along with these sentiments there has grown up a belief that war is inevitable as long as nations retain their present system of industry for private profit, and as long as the manufacture of munitions and war equipment is a source of gain. Economic rivalry and war both react into domestic policies to complicate and confuse the problems of internal political life. Every war, for example, brings about suppression of civil rights; the feeling which is then engendered persists to bring about later encroachments which would not otherwise be endured. Witness the intolerance and lawless violence that developed in this country after the World War. The oft-cited but little heeded fact that some eighty per cent of national taxes is levied because of wars past and prospective carries its benumbing effect into almost every phase of social life. Competition between nations is a strong force in maintaining high tariffs on imported goods, and these tariffs again are used to stir up animosity. We might, in fact, go through every aspect of domestic political organization and activity, and show how the difficulties in finding morally satisfactory solutions of internal problems are increased by hostility between nations.

The increased destructiveness of war due to the ability to employ scientific discoveries is now a subject become almost trite through reiteration. It is used as an argument against further wars. The command not to kill, the sentiment in favor of the sanctity of human life, have also long been used to cultivate pacific feelings. In the past neither self-interest, nor belief that war is wholesale murder, nor the fear of returning civilization to the level of barbarism, have, however, been efficacious in preserving peace. Desire to preserve life, fear of loss of property, dread of the destruction of civilization itself, have been impotent when put in the scales against a scheme of national independent egoism, which is, from the international point of view, a state of anarchy. The fact is that most persons are pacific in times of peace and are easily stirred at those times by personal appeals to kindly feeling and opposition to war, but that these personal sentiments melt away for lack of objective organized support at the very time when they are needed to influence action.

Because of the growing feeling that as long as organized institutional forces of politics and of industry tend toward war, personal sentiments of peace and good will are impotent in a crisis, movements for peace have of late tended to take on new forms, raising new moral questions. In order to preserve, when war impends, the human sympathies and pacific feelings which are normal when peace exists, many persons are pledging themselves as "war resisters" to refuse every form of war service, at no matter what cost to themselves. They hold the conviction that if even a comparatively small proportion of the male population were to pledge themselves to such a course and were to congest the prisons in time of war, wars would soon become impossible. Another approach by means of institutional action is the removal of the sanction of law. According to the international law of the past, war is a legitimized means of settling disputes between nations; indeed, it has been the high court of last resort not metaphorically but in a definite jural sense. The Paris Pact pledged the nations of the world to settle their disputes by peaceful means and formally abrogated their right under international law to resort to arms, thus outlawing war as an institution. Whether, as its critics claim, this is a mere gesture or will be efficacious depends, as in the case of all laws, upon whether there is sufficient conviction behind it. If there is, the declaration of the illegality of recourse to war to settle disputes does what a law always does, namely, provides an orderly channel through which moral conviction will express itself. Movements for disarmament, for arbitration and conciliation, the institution of a World Court, of a permanent council for deliberation through the medium of a League of Nations are other efforts to attack the problem of war by means of the mechanisms of organized society instead of by appealing to pacific sentiment. All such attempts have to reckon, however, not only with the ambition, land hunger, and greed of nations, but with injustices which are fixed by the *status quo*. In the past, war has been a means of rectifying settled injustices. Whether peaceful means will do so in the future when they involve change in boundaries, in the allegiance of populations, in possession of economic resources, is the final moral issue which is involved. Those who are devoted to peace must recognize the scope of the issue and be willing to bear the cost, largely moral and intangible, of sacrificing their nationalistic sentiments to broader conceptions of human welfare. The criterion of the greater good of all must be extended beyond the nation, as in the past it has been expanded beyond confines of family and clan.

Literature

On freedom from the social point of view: Mill, *Liberty*, 1859; *Freedom in the Modern World*, 1928, essays edited by Kallen; Laski, *Liberty in the Modern State*, 1930; Martin, *Liberty*, 1930; Hays, *Let Freedom Ring*, 1928; Chafee, *Freedom of Speech*, 1920, contains complete information as to attitude of American administrative officers and courts, together with an extensive bibliography; Lippmann, *Liberty and the News*, 1920, and *Public Opinion*, 1922, for allied topics; Drake, *The New Morality*, 1920, chs. xiv.–xvii. There is no adequate treatment of the whole subject of propaganda, but the series of volumes edited by Professor Merriam on civic training in various countries and summed up in his own volume on *The Making of Citizens*, 1931, indicates the chief ways in which conformity to national types is effected; Bent, *Ballyhoo: The Voice of the Press*, 1927, discusses it from the standpoint of the newspaper.

Beard, *The Economic Basis of Politics*, 1922; Beard, editor, *Whither Mankind*, 1928, a collection of essays; Bent, *Machine Made Man*, 1930; Hocking, *Man and the State*, 1926; Smith, "Contemporary Perplexities in Democratic Theory," *International Journal of Ethics*, 1928, pp. 1–14.

On international relations, war and peace, Addams, *Newer Ideals of Peace*, 1907; James, "Moral Equivalent of War," in *Memories and Studies*, 1912; Stratton, *Social Psychology of International Conduct*, 1929; Jordan, *War and Waste*; Page, *National Defense*, 1931; Morrison, *The*

Outlawry of War, 1927; Crosby, *International War*, 1919; Wells, *The Work, Wealth and Happiness of Mankind*, 1931, ch. xii.; Russell, *Why Men Fight*, 1917; Hayes, *Essays on Nationalism*, 1926; Angell, *The Unseen Assassins*, 1932.

18. Ethical Problems of the Economic Life

The economic problems of life may not be more important now than heretofore, since it has always been necessary for man to get a living; but they certainly stand out in more striking fashion. The difference is illustrated by the character of the conspicuous buildings in the cities. The visitor to Athens would have been struck by the temples on the Acropolis; the observer in ancient Rome by the temples and the forums with their story of government. The medieval city had its cathedral rising above the market place and the dwellings of merchants and craftsmen. But the modern city is above all the place of manufacture, commerce, and finance. Factories filled with steam-driven machines, and surrounded by rather dismal dwellings, occupy the outer regions; shops, offices, banks, tower commandingly above the central portion. Government is less prominent; the churches follow the residences into the suburbs; business reigns.

If one looks more closely he sees other signs of the economic influence. The shops provide necessaries and luxuries in profusion unknown at earlier times; transport is swift, night is made day, enormous sums of money are transferred; loans of millions and tens of millions are arranged. About half our citizens neglect to vote; at least as many abstain from the services of the churches; but business and industry admit no absence.

Men of eminent ability are found increasingly in the world of industry, commerce, and finance, whereas in earlier periods they were likely to be found in State or church. The power wielded by those highest in economic fields is actually greater, at least in times of peace, than the power exercised by religious or political leaders. The rise to power seems to be more within the individual's own control, and its security less precarious, than in those fields where it depends to a greater degree upon popular favor.

Furthermore the influence of business and wealth appears in subtler forms. Men used to buy what they needed. Now the great production of goods not only invites the satisfaction of needs; it creates needs hitherto undreamed of. It determines the location of residences, the family circle of acquaintance, the selection of schools.

The primacy of economic power in our time is due chiefly to the discoveries and inventions which have given man such control over natural resources and forces, such new techniques through machines, and such advantages from association and cooperation, as the world has not previously known. These have changed the conditions of our work, have made a greater plenty, have brought people to live in cities instead of in rural conditions, and have occasioned tensions and conflicts between economic and political interests.

These changes and conflicts create moral problems of fundamental character. A large part of the life of nearly all except the very young and the very aged is occupied with some form of work. We all have wants to be satisfied, and the more basic of these—for food and shelter, for comforts and enjoyments—depend upon economic conditions. These bring us into relations with our fellow men in the exchange of goods and services, in contracts, in the status of employer or employed, of buyer and seller, of competition or cooperation. If we own property or have to do with the policies of business, or if as individual workers we seek to improve our conditions by concerted action, we are inevitably brought into contact with the laws of the land and the policies of government. Let us consider some of the chief ethical problems which these various phases of economic life have forced upon our attention.

§ 1. Production, Capitalism, Competition

1. Man has been defined as a tool-using or as a tool-inventing animal. It has been suggested that his very defects in natural means of offense and defense have stimulated him to invent the bow and arrow and other weapons, and that the lack of certain capacities for assimilating raw foods has stimulated inventions for increasing and preparing his food-supply. Unable

like the birds to migrate, he builds more elaborate shelters and discovers fire. The fundamental crafts of building, weaving, metal-working, agriculture, have not only supplied needs but have given scope for the early artist. Skill of hand and development of brain have gone side by side. The sequence of sowing and harvest, of work and achievement, of skill and success, has helped to shape character as well as to provide the means of living. The social influences of work are no less striking. It makes a difference whether a workman works for himself as an independent farmer and craftsman, or whether he works for another in a factory or a shop. It makes a difference whether he is forced to spend his strength upon hard and heavy tasks, or whether by using ox, horse, or machine to do the heavier tasks, he can substitute work of guiding or controlling. It makes a difference whether his work is relatively regular and his reward dependent upon his own exertions, or whether it is uncertain and dependent largely upon market conditions over which the individual worker has no control. And finally it makes a difference whether his relations with his fellow workers or employers are of a family or neighborly or friendly character, or whether the relation is purely impersonal and the motive for work is the acquisition of money in some form as wage or salary or profits.

2. The single word which includes in large measure the outstanding features of the present methods of production and economic organization is *capitalism*. This may be contrasted with the system of primitive society in which each group for the most part supplied its own needs; or with that of feudalism, in which agriculture was the main industry, and the land was worked and household tasks performed by tenants who were not paid in money for their services but were required to give part of their time to the services of the lord as a condition of occupying a portion of the land, and utilizing this for their own support. As crafts and trade increased in importance the merchant and the banker accumulated wealth and could venture upon enterprises which required considerable sums of money, but the craftsmen continued for the most part to own their own tools and therefore to retain a certain measure of independence. They associated in gilds for mutual aid.

It was the great inventions of the eighteenth and nineteenth centuries which replaced the independent crafts of textile workers, smiths, and a multitude of other trades, by factories with machines driven by water or steam power. These displaced hand work, and compelled the advance of large sums of money for building factories, equipping them with machines, supplying them with raw materials, marketing goods, and paying wages of workmen. The system in which the capitalist—that is, the man who can provide the necessary sums for factories, railroads, ships, and all other instruments of modern industry and commerce—is so important, is then very properly called capitalism. It may be contrasted, not only with the simpler systems of earlier times, but with a system such as that of socialism in which production is carried on more or less completely by society as organized in the State or otherwise. Russia is an example of a society which is very largely carrying on its manufactures through public ownership and direction as contrasted with private ownership and management.

Two corner stones of capitalism are private property and freedom of enterprise. It is assumed that, barring violence and certain kinds of fraud, a man is free to enter upon any kind of enterprise which he chooses, and to hold as his own whatever he may acquire. Both these "rights" are indeed subject to certain limitations. He may not engage in an enterprise which perils his neighbors, such as the manufacture of explosives, without due precaution, or require his employees to operate dangerous machinery in unsanitary mines or factories, or engage in the sale of certain drugs, and in some countries, of alcoholic liquors, without government supervision, and as regards property he must pay taxes. Limitations of private enterprise and of property rights will be considered under a later head, but the general theory of capitalism is stated above.

3. To insure that the system of private ownership with freedom of enterprise works for the general good, the reliance has been chiefly upon *competition*. This has been regarded as a sort of balance wheel which keeps wages, profits, and prices in a fair adjustment. It is supposed to secure just treatment of workmen, of owners, and of consumers. It is also supposed to stimulate the inventor and the manufacturer or trader to take the risks necessary for progress. If wages tend to be too low, competition between employers, it is held, will raise them. If profits under a monopoly or in any business are too great, other firms will be tempted to enter and thus reduce prices. If a manufacturer is too

conservative in his policies, or is reluctant to abandon outworn machinery or processes, he will be forced by the competition of more progressive firms to adopt new inventions and new methods, all of which will be for the public advantage in the long run. Capitalism therefore has seemed to many to provide a self-regulating principle which secures the best interests of all concerned, and needs no attention from the point of view of ethics except admiration and approval, and no interference by the government.

In addition to the above, competition has seemed to be especially adapted to bring out and strengthen qualities of independence of character and self-reliance. It seems to offer a "fair field and no favors" to every one. Instead of relying upon personal favor of some one in power, or upon family prestige or inherited property, it seems to make the individual's own ability and efforts the test for success. It has been especially in favor in the United States, because it has seemed to be in accord with conditions in a relatively new country where family and inherited wealth count for less than in older societies. The ethical problems which have arisen in relation to competition are due largely to changes in conditions of industry or business which have either interfered with competition or have caused its failure to work as anticipated.

The system has, as it were, grown of itself, fed by the progress of invention, and the enormous increase in production attending this progress, rather than as a result of any definite plan. Nevertheless as the various phases and results of the system have come to be clearly seen, its merits and demerits have been vigorously stated. It secures certain kinds of liberty; does it, or can it, also secure justice? Is it in harmony with the political system of democracy? These questions may be conveniently considered in their ethical aspects under two divisions: on the one hand the industrial process; on the other the business enterprise which owns and manages the industry, markets its products, and receives the profits or incurs the losses.

§ 2. Some Ethical Problems of Industry

1. In the earlier years of the nineteenth century the textile industries were the first to take advantage of machines and the new power of steam. The great ethical problems were those

of protecting the lives and health of workmen. In the language of the economist, Henry Clay,

> Competition, coupled with the defenseless condition of the workers, tended to make the worst conditions of employment into the standard conditions. The abandonment of sanitary conditions, hours of work, speed of work, exposure to risk of accident from machinery, and the age of the workers to the regulation of competition, made hells of mines and factories.

Child labor was used to a degree which now seems incredibly cruel. Factory legislation, first in England where factories began, much later in the United States, checked the worst of these processes. But there is little protection for children in certain of the United States; and it is only in very recent years that any provision has been made for adequate care of sufferers from industrial accidents through workmen's compensation acts. The courts prevailingly took the position that if a workman was of sound mind he assumed the risks of employment, and especially the risks due to the fault of his fellow workmen. The employer could not be held responsible unless he were in some way shown to be at fault, and the State itself assumed no responsibility except that of poor relief to individuals or families in extreme destitution.

For the evils of industrial accidents and of child labor, and of excessively long hours for women, competition gave no remedy. As is stated by Henry Clay in the quotation above, it tended to increase rather than diminish these evils; for it tended to make the worst conditions of employment into the standard conditions. An employer who wished to maintain high standards of health and safety, and to pay good wages, was likely to find that a less scrupulous competitor could manufacture at a lower cost. It was therefore only by the intervention of the State that just conditions in industry could be secured. The State could require standards of health and safety, insurance against accidents, and an age limit for the employment of children.

This first ethical problem of responsibility for working conditions dangerous to health or to childhood may be said to be decided in principle, however backward certain communities and courts may be in its recognition. That the enormous profits of industry as a whole should disclaim any responsibility for the life and health of those whose labor makes them possible is too out-rageous a proposition to be publicly maintained. The labor office connected with the League of Nations is an important recognition of the wide acceptance among all peoples of the principle of social responsibility for conditions which competition tends to make worse instead of to improve.

The problems which are most prominent at the present day are rather those of a subtler influence of the machine upon civilization, of security, and of the relations of workers and their organizations to owners and management, including the relations of wages to profits.

2. The beginnings of machines in the most general sense are as old as civilization. But it is since the industrial revolution, in which the new power of steam began to be applied through machines of rapidly increasing efficiency and complexity, that men have begun to speak of a "machine age." Samuel Butler in his *Erewhon* imagined the machines as ultimately becoming all-powerful and ruling the men who had made them. Thorstein Veblen saw the machine as bringing about a division of society into two classes—those who work with machines, and those who do not. Machine-workers, he thought, tend to become mechanized in their habits of thought and thus to resemble the machines which they operate. Machines know nothing of good or bad, right or wrong, joy or pity. They are an embodiment of cause and effect, of force and its channels or modes of working. Men whose whole life is spent with machines tend to adopt similar conceptions, as contrasted with those who deal with legal doctrines, or with money and buying and selling. The machine-workers are thus constantly molded by rigid and grim realities. The other classes deal with symbols and ideas that are more or less artificial and conventional.

The influence of machines in industry is reenforced by a trend in industrial management which has tended to substitute for older, closer, and more personal relationships between workmen and employers, a more distant and impersonal relationship between workmen and a corporation. The huge railroads, mines, factories of today are too vast to be owned and controlled, like the old-time stagecoach or loom, by a single individual. The United States Steel Corporation was the first to be capitalized at a billion dollars; but it is no longer alone in this class. General

Motors, which manufactures various patterns of automobiles, the American Telephone and Telegraph Company, several railroads and banks have capital in excess of a billion.

The owners of such enormous properties are the stockholders, but they seldom have any direct knowledge of the industry or share in its management. Management is in the hands of a board of directors who determine its general policies, and trust the carrying out of these policies to an operating staff. And when the property includes various mines, factories, and railway systems, scattered over the country, the central management entrusts local management to subordinate officials. The effect is therefore to remove the workmen farther and farther from the owners, and to make the relationships so impersonal as to resemble the machines. A working class and a white-collar class have come to be recognized as divisions of modern society which have taken the place of the old-time divisions into landlord and tenant, or gentry and common-folk. When we add to the influence of the machine and the corporation the very obvious difference in wealth between the working class and the high executives or principal owners of modern industry, we have the basis for various ethical problems, some of which are on the way to a solution whereas others are far from that point.

As regards the immediate effects of the machine upon those who tend it, another charge is that the monotony in certain processes, and the nervous tension occasioned by the high speed or extreme heat or other strains, produce fatigue or exhaustion which deadens the mind or demands some form of exciting diversion, in place of the simpler forms of healthful recreation which really give rest and refreshment to body and mind. The restless and noisy forms of entertainment, the stimulation of vicious indulgence of passions in gambling and sex, the demand for alcoholic stimulants or narcotic drugs, have been attributed to the subtle influence of a machine civilization.

Over against such evils, real or alleged, are set unquestioned advantages. The machines are doing the heavy drudgery. They have replaced the slave power of older civilizations. They have broken down the isolation between villages and nations, between regions and continents. They have increased enormously the total of available wealth, and have raised the general standard of comfort. Sir Josiah Stamp, the eminent English statistician, has computed that the level of goods and comfort available for the ordinary man has been increased four times by the industrial revolution. The actual number of people who are deadened in mind and body by machine operation is small in comparison with the proportion of society who were formerly deadened by long hours and laborious, heavy work. The working day for a great number has been cut in half. Leisure for various purposes has been made available. An automobile is owned by nearly every family in the United States. And one thing is certain, we cannot drop machinery to go back to the age of handicraft.

What then is the ethical problem, and how can it be met? The problem is that of minimizing the bad effects, and of supplying positive values to replace those which have been lost. Under the first head fall such measures as those of restricting the hours of employment to prevent exhaustion or excessive fatigue. The further progress of invention in making it possible for machines to do some of the most monotonous tasks is also not to be overlooked. But the most promising remedy for the mechanizing influence of the machine, and for its displacement of the old-time skill of the craftsman and pride in the workmanlike or artistic value of the product, is to be found in education. Education works at the problem from both ends—that of the producer and that of the consumer. Education, including training in art, enables the manager and his staff to design better garments, better furnishings, better automobiles, better houses. Education of the consumer fits him—or her, for it is in most cases the woman who buys—to appreciate and demand better products in all fields.

3. One of the unsolved problems of capitalism is that of insuring measurable *stability and security*. Under feudal economy there might be a shortage of crops and consequent scarcity, but there was little chance for unemployment. Under machine industry and business management there are fairly regular cycles of prosperity, crisis, depression. In the periods of depression there are surpluses of food and manufactured goods, but little money in the hands of buyers and small confidence in the future. Some depressions may be due to wars. Civilization, however secure, could scarcely sacrifice 13,000,000 men and throw billions of dollars—three hundred or more according to some estimates—

into war without suffering, especially when it continues to keep millions under arms and to expend billions for armament yearly. But many panics and depressions occur which are not traceable to wars. They seem rather to result from production with no plan except that of making a profit, and to a reckless speculation based on inflated expectation of future profits and their capitalization. The single-minded pursuit of profit, combined with lack of any far-reaching plans for stabilizing industry, is all that business has thus far been able to offer, and this affords little hope for anything better in the future.

The situation is aggravated by the resistance of business and the Federal government to any attempt to deal with unemployment as a national rather than as a local problem. No doubt economy of administration and greater local responsibility are secured. But the effects upon character of making every community look out for its own burdens with no central coordinating agency are deplorable. Each city endeavors to keep its expenditures as low as possible. It fears to get a reputation for generosity lest it be flooded with applicants for aid. It naturally tends to limit relief to residents, and to a single meal or night's lodging for others. "The next freight train out leaves in an hour. Don't let me see you after it has gone," is quoted as a typical warning of the police. So the stream drifts or is driven from city to city, old, middle-aged, and boys. It is not a good training school for the young.

Those who do not drift about are little better off. To be idle day after day, month after month, is calculated to discourage the young who need the educative and stabilizing influence of regular employment. For the older worker who has a family dependent on his earnings it presents, at least for the more self-respecting, a desperate alternative. He must suffer himself and see his family suffer, or seek relief from public agencies or private charity. Charity seems a gracious help when flood, fire, earthquake, or pestilence comes as a calamity that could not have been anticipated, but to resort to charity to remedy a situation which ought to be prevented by the economic system is a confession of weakness. For charity places the burden not on those who are able, nor on those who have profited most from previous prosperity, but on those who are willing. Such a method of dealing with a situation is not efficient, to say nothing as to justice. To a greater degree than in previous depressions leaders in government and business are now [1] recognizing the responsibility of the community. But it is doubtful whether there will be any escape from the cycle so long as business and industry are left to the unlimited control of the profit motive.

It is not so much a question of who is to blame, as it is of what we propose to do about it. Business wishes to be let alone by government, but at the same time it virtually admits that it has no plan, except to make as large profits as possible in times of prosperity, and when depression comes to throw the burdens of unemployment upon charity.

The public has thus far been content to deal with the situation as a local matter. But a situation in which six millions out of fifty are unemployed is not a local matter. To treat it as such is to prevent national consideration of the problem and adequate plans for dealing with the whole conduct of industry.

The dilemmas would be ironic if they were not tragic. The Public says to Business, "You are managing industry, why don't you plan intelligently instead of by rule of thumb?" Business answers, "We have to compete. The Government will not permit planning on a national scale; it calls this an agreement in restraint of trade and threatens prosecution." The Public then asks, "If Business cannot be trusted to consider the public welfare unless it is forced to compete, and if competition prevents Business from intelligent planning on a national scale, why does not the Government plan?" But both Business and Government are aghast at such an idea. It would contradict the fundamental policy of American Individualism which we have inherited from the eighteenth century. Then the Public asks once more, "At least if we can do nothing to prevent unemployment can we not look at the problem of relief nationally?" But the answer is: "Relief is under our system of government a local problem. It would be calamitous if we should deal with it as we deal with war, or floods, on a national scale." We must stick to the eighteenth century at all costs!

1. This paragraph was written in the period of depression which followed the crash of 1929, and which still continues in 1932.

Literature

The classic treatises of Adam Smith, J. S. Mill, and Karl Marx are still important as furnishing the background of present discussion. The following give prominence to the ethical problems involved: Carver, *The Present Economic Revolution in the United States*, 1925, *Essays in Social Justice*, 1922; Chase, *Men and Machines*, 1929; Clay, *Economics for the General Reader*, 1923; Donham, *Business Adrift*, 1931; Faulkner, *The Quest for Social Justice, 1898–1914*, 1931; Hadley, *Economic Problems of Democracy*, 1923, *Standards of Public Morality*, 1912; Hamilton, *Current Economic Problems*, 1925; Hobson, *Evolution of Modern Capitalism*, 1894, *Work and Wealth*, 1914; Marshall, *Industrial Society*, 1929; Slichter, *Modern Economic Society*, 1931; Tawney, *The Acquisitive Society*, 1920; Tugwell, ed., *The Trend of Economics*, 1924; Veblen, *The Theory of Business Enterprise*, 1904; Williams, *Principles of Social Psychology*, 1922; Wormser, *Frankenstein, Incorporated*, 1931; Beveridge, *Unemployment, 1909 and 1930*; Douglas and Director, *The Problem of Unemployment*, 1931.

19. Collective Bargaining and the Labor Union

§ 1. Conflicting Interests of Employer and Employed

1. The industrial revolution has brought a division between classes of employers and employed, and a number of conflicts between their respective interests. Doubtless both classes have a common interest in the prosperity of industry, yet there are several fundamental causes of conflicting interests which give rise to moral problems.

Class division is very old. In earlier times it arose largely from conquest of one group by another. The defeated group might become serfs or villeins; the ruling class was free. In England after the Norman conquest the survey recorded in Domesday Book showed that the unfree were greatly in excess of the free. In the following centuries the villein class disappeared. Farmers and farm laborers who worked for wages carried on agriculture; independent traders and craftsmen carried on trade and industry. But the industrial revolution brought back in a new form a distinction between those who owned factories and tools, and directed work, on the one side, and those who performed assigned tasks for wages, on the other. As the revolution has developed through successive stages, there have been shifts in the particular conflicts; in certain respects employers have gained in strength, in others the employed have improved their conditions. But certain conflicts of interest are due, not to any desire on the part of either employer or employed to take an unfair advantage, but rather to the complexity of the question, what is fair? and to the system of bargaining. What are the conflicting interests which divide the community sharply at times of special stress? We select five:

(1) The division of the income from the industry; how much to wages, how much to profits?

(2) When work is paid by the hour or day, what is a fair (or honest) pace or rate of speed? What justification, if any, for restriction of output?

(3) Which party shall control working conditions? Shall shop-rules, and other necessary regulation be determined absolutely by employer, or should there be citizenship in industry as well as in government?

(4) Which shall bear the risks of industry? the risks of accident? of unemployment? of premature old age? of disease?

(5) Since all four of the above conflicts are bound to be decided, under the system of competition, in favor of the party that holds superior bargaining power, each party will seek to strengthen itself by (1) Organization, massing of forces; (2) Political alliance, either through legislation, or the courts, or by electing friends to office, or by forming a political party. A further factor in bargaining power is the degree to which invention and the machine lessen the requirement of trained skill on the workman's part. If a worker can be taught in a day, the old-time worker's asset of skill acquired by years of experience is lost.

Moral considerations appear when we ask, Is it possible to introduce reason and justice into the settlement of these conflicts, or must they be decided solely by force, and the preponderance of power?

2. The *impersonal character* of the relation between employer and employed, while it clarifies certain issues by freeing them from personal ties, sharpens the conflicts. Many problems have their roots in stresses between older policies for carrying on industry, and new methods of machine production and corporation ownership and management. The older policies were based on personal as well as upon employment relations. They were suited to a stage of industry when an employer was himself a worker in the industry, had journeymen and apprentices in his employ, knew them intimately, shared the work with them, needed their labor as they needed his wages, and would not be shocked if his son should marry a daughter of one of the workmen, or conversely if his daughter should marry one of the young workmen who might then aspire to a share in the business. Under those conditions the workman was very nearly upon the same financial and social level as the employer. On the one hand he was fairly able to look out for himself; on the other the

personal relations made it natural for the employer to deal with the workman as a co-worker rather than as either an inferior or merely as a "hand"—No. 12,376 on the pay roll.

Contrast the present situation. From the very necessities of machine industry, mass production, and huge factories or other plants, the most effective methods and agencies of production are enormous corporations controlling millions or even billions of capital and employing thousands of laborers. The gap between employer and workman is financial, educational, and social. They live in distinct districts, have different schools, are frequently from different races, and seldom intermarry. The bargaining power of an individual workman when set over against that of a million dollar corporation is practically zero. The personal claim for consideration in case of illness, accident, debt, or other contingency, is also nearly zero. The limit of the impersonal and detached character of modern industrial relations is perhaps the doctrine that labor is a commodity. No doubt it is—like raw materials, rent, and interest—one of the factors to be reckoned with in determining the cost of production. No doubt wages like other factors are subject to market conditions. But to the mind of the worker the implication goes further. It signifies that labor may be bought in the cheapest market irrespective of long and faithful service, that it may be scrapped when the worker is past his period of maximum speed, that in any business depression workmen may be laid off or discharged without regard to the possibility of finding other employment. Even if individual employers may regret such extreme measures, competition of other firms less scrupulous, and the demands of absentee owners for dividends, leave no alternative. It may appear to be an empty gesture to enact, as in Section Six of the Clayton Act of 1914, "that the labor of a human being is not a commodity or article of commerce," yet the sentiment of protest behind it has its roots in hard facts.

§ 2. Bargaining Power Determines

1. Under older conditions it seemed easier to estimate what might be regarded as a *fair wage*. Older industry was on a comparatively individual basis of production. When the wheel-

wright made a wagon or the cobbler a shoe, or a tailor a suit it was comparatively easy to figure his cost of materials and the time spent in making the product. It was not impossible to reach some estimate of a fair price based on these factors. "It took me two days and I ought to have four dollars," was a common enough formula even within the memory of some now living. But modern enterprise has become cooperative instead of individual. It brings together hundreds or thousands to make the different parts of the tool, the shoe, or the clothing. It takes advantage of a long series of inventions and discoveries. It maintains an extensive selling department. Its prices are necessarily fixed, not by a calculation of the proper return for the worker's time, but upon the market or, in the case of transportation, upon "what the traffic will bear." The cooperative process, combined with the enormous efficiency of power-driven machinery, provides in ordinarily prosperous times a highly profitable enterprise.

Who is entitled to the surplus? Evidently three main claims may be put forward—that of the owner-employer, that of the workman, and that of the general public: profits, wages, lower prices to consumers. The older theory considered that competition would be the fairest way to adjust these claims, but it is obvious that in the actual adjustment much will depend upon which of the three is in the stronger strategic position. And thus far the owner-employer has usually been in this stronger position. Nor has he been slow to strengthen it at vulnerable points. To avoid too severe competition he has sought to gain control of natural resources, to prevent by protective tariff foreign competition, to combine forces with competitors, to gain legal protection for a minimum return upon invested capital, and especially, as will be brought out later, to have his capital investment measured for this purpose not by what actually has been put into it but by its income producing capacity. The enormous fortunes built up in America and Western Europe have been acquired largely by the employer-owner class. The consumer may benefit to some extent; and wages have slowly risen in the period since the War, although there was a period from 1900 to 1914 during which no gain in wages was made. But on the whole the immense gains made by modern industrial processes, including those due to science, to invention, and to education, have gone to the owner-employer group.

2. What is a *fair pace* or day's work? Two systems are in use for reckoning the adjustment of wages to work: piece-work, and work by the hour or day, or by some longer period. On the piece-work plan the conflict of interest enters in fixing the price to be paid per piece. On the day-wage plan, since the wage is fixed, the conflict appears in the question, How much work shall be given in return? Even in piece-work the question of pace or speed enters, for the workman may calculate that if he works too fast and thereby earns what may seem a high wage, the price per piece will be reduced. Under older conditions, when the employer worked side by side with the other workmen it was easier to set a "fair" pace. But under present conditions this question, like that of wages, depends for its answer largely upon the market, i.e., upon supply and demand. At least the workman is likely to look at it from this point of view, whereas the employer is likely to hold to the older conception of an honest day's work.

Limitation of output is of course a well-recognized and fundamental principle of business management. To make more goods than can be sold at a profit is to invite loss, if not disaster. The universally recognized and legitimate method of maintaining prices is to limit the output to what can be sold at a price which will yield a profit. The labor union has adopted a similar policy from motives which illustrate the difference between the psychology of business and that of labor. The laborer feels that in his case, as in that of the employer, the value of his labor depends on supply and demand. If he supplies too much he diminishes to some extent the demand. With a vague fear, especially in seasonal occupations, that there may not be work enough to last he hesitates to "work himself out of his job." This attitude is reenforced by a motive based on the welfare of his fellow workmen, namely, reluctance to set too swift a pace which may result in lowering the rate of wages for piece-work, or in making excessive demands upon the pace of others, or still further in diminishing the amount of work available for others. The constant tendency of invention and scientific management is to displace laborers. The workman sees this process continually going on, as inventions increase. It is liable at any time to deprive him or his fellows of the job which means perhaps the investment of his total training and experience. He has no contract which insures him against dismissal at any moment when the contingencies of

business and industry make it prudent for the employer to reduce expenses. Why then should he not adopt the policy of
sound business management and limit output? But such a policy
is not accepted as reasonable either by the employer or by the
"general public." The employer argues, "I pay a fair wage and
have right to a full day's work." The welfare of industry demands a constant effort to produce goods at low prices, and
thereby to extend the market by placing goods within the means
of larger and larger numbers of consumers. One way of doing
this is by improvements in machinery and management. The
other way is by increasing the efficiency of labor. It is only as
these two factors are combined that industry can prosper, and
employment be stabilized. The general public is naturally interested in low prices for the goods which it must buy. It is therefore
inclined to agree with the employer's point of view rather than
with that of the union.

It is frequently supposed that restriction of output is exclusively a union device and policy. It is true that certain unions,
notably in the building trades, have insisted upon fixing a maximum output as a standard, and have thus made a definite claim
for a standard of production to match a standard of wages. But a
recent investigation has shown that the practice of restriction is
by no means confined to organized labor. The same motives assert themselves with unorganized workmen. The practice appears to be general. The answer is to be sought, as in the wage
question, in measures to render the bargaining clear in its provisions and standards, and fair in its terms, and this, as will be seen
later, means a more nearly equal bargaining power.

3. *Who shall make working rules and regulate shop conditions, management, or workmen?* Perhaps this question has been
more bitterly debated than the two preceding questions. This,
too, results from the changes introduced by the industrial revolution. For under older conditions the craft-gild determined many
matters and the master who determined others was himself also
a workman. Under present large-scale production in which ten
thousand or a hundred thousand workmen may be employed by
a single firm, the separation of management from workmen is inevitable. The plan by which the management makes rules and directs all details of shop conditions has seemed equally inevitable
to many employers. On railroads the safety of the traveling pub-

lic is an additional ground for concentrating authority in the body which is sure to be held responsible for accidents. In some cases the employer has built up the industry largely by his own efforts. He regards it quite naturally as "his business." And there is the general human trait of reluctance to yield power once exercised. Many firms have been willing to grant increases of wages to a point as high as competition with other firms would admit, but have preferred to do this under the pressure of supply and demand, or from their own free will, rather than to admit the union to a voice in shop management. Similarly many firms have found it good policy to reduce excessive hours of labor, to introduce protective devices against dangerous machinery, and to inculcate the maxim, "Safety First," but have been reluctant to accept these same policies when proposed by a labor union. On the other side, the laborer is also human. He likes to have some say about the rules under which he spends the larger part of his day. Moreover, he lives in a democratic age and in a more or less democratic country. If citizenship is a good principle in political life, is there no application for it in industry? To be hired and fired at the will of a superior official, is not made more agreeable by the statement that market conditions require a reduction of the force. To be subject to the whims of a foreman or to impersonal authority seems to lessen not only his security but his self-respect. He probably has never read Aristotle's classification of mankind into the two classes of those fitted by nature to direct, and those fit only to obey the directions of others, but he rebels at Aristotle's conclusion that some men are "natural slaves."

4. *Which shall bear the risks of industry?* We have already mentioned the risks of accident and unemployment, especially unemployment of the seasonal or cyclical type. There is also the unemployment which confronts the workman in all kinds of industry but particularly in machine industry, namely, that due to advancing age. Maximum speed is reached early in life in manual operations; the man of forty who finds himself out of work has a serious problem before him. Under older conditions personal feeling might prevent the discharge of one who had passed his age of greatest efficiency. Many employers have recognized the situation by a system of retiring allowances, but a corporation established for profit is under pressure to keep expenses down and labor efficient. And yet, what can be more dishearten-

ing than the fear of dismissal in middle life with the attendant difficulty—or impossibility—of securing another job?

§ 3. How Can Bargaining Power Be Kept Equal?

Under the system of private property, contract, prices governed by the market, and free competition, the outcome of each of the four conflicts is usually decided largely by the respective bargaining powers of the parties, that is, of owner-employer and of workmen. All the influences of humaneness and instinct of workmanship which enter into the dealings of the parties are liable under pressure to yield to considerations of a seemingly more urgent character. Profits and the maintenance of business standing, on one side, a standard of living and of security, on the other, may drive both parties into positions where self-defense seems to be the first law of nature. The firmest protection against injustice under a capitalistic system is to be sought first of all in keeping the conditions of bargaining such that the two parties shall be as nearly equal as possible in bargaining power. As in military operations, three sources of strength are (1) organization, (2) equipment and (3) allies.

1. In organization the employing side has taken and held a strong advantage. The business corporation not only combines the wealth and resources of thousands and even hundreds of thousands of individuals, but it is given immortality by law. As a corporate person it enjoys the protection of the government in the rights of property, and yet it cannot be imprisoned if it defies the law. It is so advantageous a plan for the conduct of great enterprise that it is displacing individual ownership. More than twenty corporations in America have assets of over one billion each. Some of these are banks and insurance companies which employ chiefly salaried and clerical personnel; others such as the United States Steel Corporation and the railroads employ all grades. The United States Steel Corporation has employed at times 250,000 men. A recent study states that two hundred large corporations controlled in 1927 almost half the corporate wealth of the country and more than half of the industry. The figures are significant for several purposes, but just now they force the ques-

tion, How can the laborer possibly stand upon a platform of equality in dealing with a billion dollar corporation? As if such enormous power were not enough, there are also associations of manufacturers engaged in the same line of production, and if necessary they can usually be relied upon to give moral support and perhaps material support to a fellow member.

Confronted with such huge combinations of capital, workmen have believed that their only hope of equal bargaining power is in meeting organization with organization. If all workmen in a plant, and still more if all workmen in the same kind of production, unite they will be less at a disadvantage, although, even so, the corporation usually has a strategic advantage in that it can afford to wait, whereas the workman ordinarily cannot. The corporation may lose profits by waiting to conclude a bargain, but the workman out of a job is soon at the end of his resources. Some labor unions seek to include all the workers in a given plant or industry, others limit their membership to the skilled workmen. The American Federation is a federation of organizations of skilled trades. The Amalgamated Clothing Workers includes all operatives in the making of men's clothing. The Railway Brotherhoods include in four groups engineers, firemen, trainmen, and conductors. In the earlier history of unionism strikes were the frequent resort. When a strike seemed to be losing there was not infrequently violence. Some employers have not scrupled to introduce spies into the union ranks, whose mission is to provoke violence in order to alienate public favor from the union. Such methods of industrial war are not, however, likely to continue as unions succeed in securing strong organizations and employers become more reasonable. The Railway Brotherhoods seldom strike, and the managements negotiate with them on a basis of mutual respect. The Amalgamated Clothing Workers have agreements with clothing manufacturers in the larger cities which provide for permanent arbitration boards, to the end that "reason may take the place of force." In England the principle of collective bargaining is general; in the United States only a minority of workmen are organized. The rest may or may not receive approximately the same wage as that of union labor; their working conditions may or may not be good; this will depend largely upon the attitude of the management and the prosperity of the industry. But it may easily be a question of "Take it or leave it. If you don't like my terms, go." Some large firms which are unwilling to bargain with a union have sought to organize "company unions" which afford opportunity for discussion of wages and grievances with representatives of the management.

2. A second factor in bargaining power is what may be called the equipment of the parties. The employer's great weapon—to use the military parallel—is the machine. The workman's greatest asset was his skill. An all-round workman—carpenter, smith, mason, tailor, weaver—could not be trained in a day. Experience increased his competence. He could not be easily replaced by a casual and ignorant applicant for a job. Machinery brings about the splitting-up of such a task as making a coat or shoe or tool into a number of distinct steps, each performed by a machine. To learn to tend these machines requires various periods of time, but seldom if ever does it require anywhere nearly as much time as to learn the whole craft; and many machines require in the operator neither intelligence nor skill. Under these conditions the strongest asset and source of security which the old-time workman possessed tends to become less and less. How can he bargain on equal terms when he not only must deal with a vast corporation, but has less protection through the very mechanism of modern industry? So far as equality in bargaining power is dependent on equipment, the balance is hopelessly weighted against the workman.

3. Neither side is content to rely solely on its own strength. Each seeks aid from the government in securing its ends. The employer seeks protection for his property; the workman seeks protection for his life, health, and safety, and for prevention from competition by child labor and unlimited immigration. The workman has sought help from legislatures, and these have responded with child-labor laws, and employers' liability laws. Workmen have joined forces with other groups to secure from Congress restriction of immigration. Limitation of the hours of employment for women, and in certain occupations, such as work in mines and smelters, for men has been enacted into law and upheld by the courts as a proper exercise of the so-called "police power." Limitation of hours for men where the danger to health is not so evident has been declared unconstitutional by the United States Supreme Court.

The employer has relied for help chiefly upon the courts. For what he seeks is defense of property, and since the courts have held that the rights secured by the Fourteenth Amendment to the Constitution include the right to maintain a business as a going concern without molestation he is protected by the law from any action by a union which interferes with his business.

Law is usually more backward than public opinion. Especially is this true of the decisions of the courts, because these are based in part upon custom which in turn reflects past opinion and past habits of thought. In both English and American law, the tradition has been that of individual rights with assumed equality of bargaining power. Monopolies, i.e., special privileges given by grants of king or Parliament, were indeed jealously watched. But no differences arising from wealth or poverty were taken into account. It was, however, also in the tradition that what might be lawful for one person might be unlawful if done by a group; for in the latter case it might fall under the conception of a conspiracy. The individual laborer in dealing with the corporation may be, in actual bargaining power, in the ratio of one to a million. The court refuses to recognize the facts, and finds it more in accordance with the principles of American life to regard every person as equal to every other person. Further, when the individuals in a union try to bring combined strength, the corporation is treated as a single person although it consists of many owners. It is therefore entitled to all the economic standing of a single person, and according to the Fourteenth Amendment to the Federal Constitution cannot be deprived of its property by any state without "due process of law." For their resistance to trade unions certain employers have adopted the policy of the "open shop," meaning by this that no one belonging to a union will be employed. Believing that it is lawful for workmen to unite, and that this affords a means to give them a measure of equality in bargaining power with the great corporations, both Congress and the state of Kansas passed laws forbidding the discharge of workmen, or refusal to hire workmen, because of membership in a union. But the United States Supreme Court in each case declared such a law to be unconstitutional.[1]

In the Adair case the decision of the court, as formulated by

1. Adair v. U.S., 208 U.S. 161 (1908); Coppage v. Kansas, 236 U.S. 1 (1915).

Justice Harlan states clearly the legal theory that employer and employee have equal rights:

> The right of a person to sell his labor upon such terms as he deems proper, is in its essence, the same as the right of the purchaser of labor to prescribe the conditions upon which he will accept such labor from the person offering to sell it. So the right of the employee to quit the service of the employer, for whatever reason, is the same as the right of the employer, for whatever reason, to dispense with the services of such employee. . . . In all such particulars the employer and the employee have equality of right, and any legislation that disturbs that equality is an arbitrary interference with the liberty of contract, which no government can legally justify in a free land.

This statement excludes from consideration all questions of actual equality as regards bargaining power between the great railway and the individual laborer. In the decision upon the Kansas law, Justice Pitney, speaking for the majority of the court, noted the actual inequality, but held frankly that we cannot have freedom of contract and private property without having also inequality. And apparently he regards it not only difficult but legally unjustified for the courts to recognize any attempt to compensate such inequality by protecting the right of workingmen to combine. The Kansas state court had previously upheld the law which made it unlawful "to coerce, require, demand or influence any person not to join or become or remain a member of any labor organization or association, as a condition of, securing employment." The Kansas court said, "the employees as a rule are not financially able to be as independent in making contracts for the sale of their labor as are employers in making contracts of purchase thereof." But Justice Pitney said in reply:

> No doubt, wherever the right of private property exists, there must and will be inequalities of fortune; and thus it naturally happens that parties negotiating about a contract are not equally unhampered by circumstances. . . . Since it is self-evident that, unless all things are held in common, some persons must have more property than others, it is from the nature of things impossible to uphold freedom of contract

and the right of private property without at the same time recognizing as legitimate those inequalities of fortune that are the necessary result of the exercise of those rights.[2]

There are two principles at stake in both the Adair case and the Coppage case: in the first place, whether the courts can recognize economic inequality as something which justifies public interference with contracts, as they have for a long time recognized physical force, or threats, or undue influence of some superior, as constituting a proper ground for such interference; and, in the second place, whether some public purpose is clearly discernible in such a measure as the Kansas law, in as much as laws forbidding employment in dangerous occupations, e.g., mines and smelters, have been upheld in a previous leading case.[3]

On both points it was possible, so far as legal precedents were concerned, to decide either for or against the law in question, as is evidenced by the fact that the dissenting opinion in Coppage v. Kansas was signed by three justices of the Court whose learning in the law cannot be questioned (Day, Holmes, and Hughes). The issue was not one of law but of public policy and justice in the broad sense. On the side of the majority it may fairly be said that, if economic inequality were recognized as having coercive power, many contracts would be rendered uncertain; for it is frequently possible for debtor or creditor, merchant or manufacturer, as well as for the laborer, to find himself under such financial stress as leads to contracts which he would not make if he could wait for a more favorable time, and the courts are therefore reluctant to make a decision which might involve such possibilities of indefinite voiding of contracts. On the other hand the court in Holden v. Hardy had very definitely recognized that new conditions might arise in the development of industry which would call for the protection of the weaker party by the State. Shall such protection be extended to the laborer's wage contract as well as to his health? Those who adhere to one type of public policy—and to a conception of justice which implies the maxim, "Hands Off! Let the strongest win!" (barring violence and fraud) —decide against the laws in question; those who have a concep-

2. These cases are discussed in Commons, *Legal Foundations of Capitalism*, 288–297; see also Cook, 27 *Yale Law Journal*, 779 (1918) and Powell, 33 *Political Science Quarterly*, 396 (1918).
3. Holden v. Hardy, 169 U.S. 366 (1898).

tion of public policy of a different type, such as is implied in the term, *commonwealth*, and regard justice as involving not only formal freedom but protection against such inequality as involves real coercion, decide to uphold the law.

And as regards the second point, the majority of the court recognize no public purpose in a trade union which would justify the government in protecting it, whereas in the case of protection for health and morals the right of the State had a clear precedent in its favor. On the other hand it may be urged that if it is regarded as lawful for workmen to associate in order to improve their conditions, it is only logical to prevent action by corporations designed to destroy such associations. Undoubtedly earlier conditions of business and industry made policies of individualism, of "let-alone," seem not only wise but just. The spirit of the frontier, and the approximate economic equality of the people of the United States in the earlier years, fixed such policies firmly in legal attitude and precedent. The ethical question turns thus on how far the changed conditions require a different conception.

The question of economic inequality receives further treatment in the so-called Hitchman case.[4] In this case the matter at issue was not a statute passed by a legislature but an injunction forbidding a union and its agents from persuading employees of a coal company to join a union, as a step toward unionizing the mines. It appeared that all employees of the company were required as a condition of employment to agree not to belong to a union while working for the company. The injunction forbade the labor union to interfere with such contracts. Injunctions are issued by the court to prevent some damage to property for which there would be no adequate legal remedy in an ordinary suit. For example, to use Justice Taft's illustration, if a man attempts to cut down a tree to which I claim ownership it will give me little or no satisfaction to collect damages after the tree has been cut down. I want the tree, and no damages will replace it. Hence it is the part of equity to prevent the cutting of the tree until it is determined whose tree it is. In this case the court held that the company was entitled to the good will of its employees, and the minority (Brandeis, Holmes, and Clarke) held that the

4. Hitchman Coal and Coke Co. *v.* Mitchell, 245 U.S. 229 (1917).

effort of the union to persuade employees of the company was "a reasonable effort to improve the condition of workingmen engaged in the industry by strengthening their bargaining power through unions, and extending the field of union power." The majority opinion reenforced the argument for the right of good will by the old law of master and servant: "The plaintiff was and is entitled to the good will of its employees, precisely as the merchant is entitled to the good will of his customers. . . . The right of action for persuading an employee to leave his employer is universally recognized." This appears to be in many respects the severest ruling since the days when all unions were treated as conspiracies. If any company can prevent any union of its employees by the simple method of requiring a contract, and then can summon to its support all the forces of government under a legal process which makes the judge who issues the injunction the authority to decide upon its alleged violations, and to punish all violators for contempt of court, what remains of the alleged lawfulness of associations for mutual benefit? This is apparently reduced to an ironical mockery. It amounts to saying, "Organize if you dare!" The contract which the injunction supports has been called by union sympathizers a "yellow dog contract." It is certainly one-sided. The company is supposed to offer a job; the employee to agree not to belong to a union. But the company is under no obligation to continue to employ the laborer for as long as he stays out of the union. It is under no obligation to employ him for more than a single day. The consideration offered, namely, that of a job, may be canceled at any time at the whim of a foreman, or by conditions in the market over which the workman has no control, or by the illness of the employee. If there was ever a case of "Heads I win; tails you lose," this may fairly claim to be the outstanding example. With the forces of the law so heavily against them, it is small wonder that labor unions have not been more successful in the United States. It is not surprising that laboring men have great distrust of the courts, and believe that their point of view has little chance of receiving fair treatment.

One reason for the unfavorable situation of the laborer before the law is that whereas the employer can stand upon the well-recognized rights of property, the workman's interest is in securing and maintaining a standard of living.

The law does not recognize that the workman has any legal claim to a standard of living. It holds that if there is no physical coercion every one has an equal chance; and that justice consists in just this. The workman feels the pressure of supporting a family, and perhaps compares his lot with that of others more favored; he feels justified in bringing all pressure possible upon the employer. Those who would take his place he calls "scabs," and regards them as traitors to their fellows. The public sides sometimes with one party, sometimes with the other. It is likely to sympathize with workmen as against a great corporation, unless the strike causes serious inconvenience not only to the employer but to the public itself, as, for example, when a railroad is forced to cease from running trains.

When the alternative for the workman is between a job on his employer's conditions, on the one hand; and no job, which spells starvation, on the other, his "freedom" does not seem to be of great value. Of course the theory of competition is that different employers will be competing for the services of the workman, and this will insure good wages. In highly prosperous times this has a measure of truth. But when in accordance with modern tendencies various competing firms in a given type of industry combine, competition is reduced to a minimum; and when times are not prosperous the competition is all for jobs and not for the services of workmen.

Attempts to prevent wages from sinking below what is necessary for support have been made in the form of minimum wage laws. These have usually applied to women's wages only, although Congress in the so-called Adamson law indirectly legislated regarding wages for railroad employees, in that it declared the regular day to be of eight hours—thereby implying that overtime might be subject to a higher rate. Massachusetts has a law providing that wage boards may be appointed to consider whether wages paid to women in a given industry are sufficient. A law was passed by Congress fixing a minimum wage for women in the District of Columbia, but this was held by the Supreme Court to be unconstitutional.[5]

It is generally recognized that when two nations are at war it is very difficult to obtain an impartial view of their respective mer-

5. Adkins *v.* Children's Hospital, 261 U.S. 525.

its in the case. The same is true when employer and workman become engaged in bitter strife. Each is likely to resort to measures which are unwise if nothing worse. Instead of attempting the difficult task of estimating which is more in the right or wrong, it is more hopeful to consider what may be done to prevent conflicts—and thus to substitute reason for force, cooperation for conflict. That this is not impossible is evident from the record of many great industries, such as that of the Railway Brotherhoods and the men's clothing industry. The principle of collective bargaining is recognized. Readjustments are made from time to time in hours and wages. The men enjoy a relative security. In the men's clothing industry differences are referred to a permanent board of arbitration which makes a record of its decisions. It thus gradually establishes principles of justice which recognize the interests of both parties to an extent to which the courts have not yet gone. Many other firms which have not accepted the principle of collective bargaining have organized systems of employee representation or "works councils." Such systems have had the advantage from the employer's point of view of not involving negotiations with outsiders not in the employ of the firm concerned. At the same time they afford a method by which grievances may be redressed and conditions improved. The moral questions involved in the relations hinge largely upon whether under the theory of "free bargaining" justice is possible. If the theory is to be retained, is it possible to make the bargaining really free unless there is approximate equality in bargaining power? Is there any way to secure such equality except by organization of workmen to conduct collective bargaining? If we admit that justice cannot be secured under the system of free bargaining, we must consider what the alternatives would be. But this involves the whole economic and political system. It is a serious indictment of a system if it does not secure justice, as well as liberty, or if it cannot be so modified as to permit justice.

Literature

Burns, *The Philosophy of Labour*, 1925; Cole, *Labour in the Commonwealth*, 1919; Commons, and Associates, *History of Labour in the United States*, 1918; Douglas, Hitchcock, and Atkins, *The Worker in*

Modern Economic Society, 1923; Perlman, *A Theory of the Labor Movement*, 1928; S. and B. Webb, *The History of Trade Unionism*, rev. ed., 1920, *Industrial Democracy*, 1902; Frankfurter, *The Labor Injunction*, 1930; Commons, *Legal Foundations of Capitalism*, 1924.

20. Moral Problems of Business

In this chapter we consider certain moral problems connected with the other half of our productive process, namely, with the business side.

§ 1. The Profit Motive

Industry is the making and distributing and in general the providing of goods. Business has to do with the management and financing of industry. Its primary purpose is profits. The theory of capitalism is that this motive will secure the greatest efficiency in business and therefore the greatest production, that it will secure the production of the kind of goods which society most needs and wants, and thus will secure the greatest welfare of all in the long run. The theory as formulated by Adam Smith presupposed that if each seeks his own advantage he will necessarily prefer that employment which is most advantageous to society.

> The individual neither intends to promote the public interest nor knows how much he is promoting it by directing industry in such a manner as its produce may be of the greatest value, but intends only his own gain, and he is in this, as in many other cases, led by an invisible hand to promote an end which was no part of his intention.[1]

There are many industries in which this seems to be the case. To furnish an article which many want is one way to large profits. Makers of automobiles, of telephones, of radios, have profited by supplying necessary and eagerly desired goods and services.

1. Adam Smith, *Wealth of Nations*.

On the other hand it is by no means so easy at the present time to suppose that the profit motive is the infallible key to a just distribution of benefits, or to fine types of products, or to social welfare. Let us examine certain of the facts which give rise to the above queries.

1. The great advantage which is claimed for the profit motive is that it gets things done. It is efficient. It stimulates invention and production, and results in greater wealth than can be produced in any other way. The rapid increase in the total wealth of England during the earlier part of the nineteenth century, of the United States since the Civil War, and of Germany in the early years of this century, are cited in support of this claim.

The per capita wealth and income of the United States certainly show an enormous and fairly steady increase. The estimate of the national income in the United States by the National Bureau of Economic Research in 1921 was that the national income had increased in the period, 1909 to 1918, from 28.8 billions to 61 billions; or, making allowance for the rise of prices during the war, from 30 to 38.8 billions, giving a per capita income in 1918 of $372.00. Since 1918 the increase has continued until the total income is estimated at 84 billions, and the per capita income at $692.00. It is of course true that much of this increase is due to invention under the guidance of science; and that the motive of great scientists is seldom predominantly that of profits. Nevertheless the figures are certainly impressive. And it may further be said, as Professor Mitchell has stated, that if a business man cannot secure profits he will soon be compelled to go out of business. No one has unlimited resources, and to conduct a business at a loss for an indefinite period is merely a form of economic suicide.

Some work is fascinating. On the other hand, many kinds of work are not. The most successful way to get such kinds of work done appears to be that of offering a reward adequate to call out the effort of those who will take great risks, or do difficult and irksome tasks for the sake of large returns. Under the regulation of competition it is held that rewards cannot long continue to be excessive, and that the simplest way to find out what the community wants and needs is to make it profitable to supply wants and needs.

2. The first defect alleged is that the profit motive by no means

always leads to service of the public by supplying public wants. Sometimes greater profits can be made by restricting the supply, and thus raising the price of goods and services. With the organization of the principal lines of business and industry in great corporations, which frequently control the supply of natural resources, it is increasingly difficult to suppose that competition automatically turns the seeker for profits to methods which supply public needs. A considerable portion of profits is sought, not by the supply of necessities as such, but by *control* over the supply, or by speculation in which there is no thought of rendering any equivalent to the public for the profits received. Such a craze for unearned profits as marks various periods of wildcat speculation—such as, for example, culminated in 1929 in the United States, in what was characterized by a financial authority as the most gigantic gamble of history—result in transfer of profits from the less shrewd to the more shrewd, but divert the interests and activities of many from serving the public to a method of getting something for nothing.

Nor does the profit motive necessarily give to consumers what they need or want. It is now a commonplace that the balance has shifted. Instead of making what consumers want, the theory now is to produce large supplies, and then to sell them to consumers. If the consumers do not want the things offered, then their "sales resistance" must be overcome. Salesmanship and advertising are relied upon to awaken new wants where none exist, and the total effect is often discontent rather than content.

A third charge is that the profit motive fails to secure production of fine quality. Frequently there is more profit in cheap and shoddy goods than in durable and substantial articles. It has even been found profitable to appeal to the salacious and unwholesome in commercial amusements. Those who are concerned for the higher and finer types of work in education, in drama, in music, and in many other fields, fear the profit motive. "Commercialized" art or literature or journalism seems as contrary to the best types as "commercialized" medicine or religion.

3. Highly important is the question of *waste of natural resources*. Under the administration of President Roosevelt attention was called to the exhaustion of the great natural resources of forests, mines, oil, which was threatened by the methods of treatment then practiced. Under the influence of the profit mo-

tive, forests were cut off with no provision for replanting. It would not pay a private owner to make such provision for the needs of future generations, and so nothing was done to replace forests, even on land unsuitable for any other purpose. The methods of mining coal were wasteful in that they extracted only a part of the coal in a given tract, and left the remainder in such condition as would not permit any further extraction. Attempts have been made to guard against waste in oil, but the desire for immediate profits has been so strong as to encourage a large amount of wasteful exploitation. Even more disastrous in its ultimate possibilities is the exhaustion of the soil in certain parts of the country by the washing away of exposed bare soils into the rivers, and so into the ocean or the Gulf of Mexico.

The difficulty is not that corporations or individual farmers are more shortsighted and wasteful than the average of mankind but rather that the profit motive itself works directly against the future welfare of the country, instead of toward a far-sighted policy which takes account of the welfare of coming generations. The whole tendency of American conditions, due to the seemingly inexhaustible supplies of coal, oil, metals, timber, and virgin soil, has been to encourage the wasteful tendency. The profit motive, which in the case of many a small business encourages thrift and saving, has not only been powerless in the case of these large resources but has reenforced the natural carelessness and free spending attitude. "Easy come, easy go" has in large measure been true of our capitalistic system in respect to natural resources.

§ 2. The Difficult Problem of Justice

We have seen that capitalism has proved to be an effective method of increasing the total wealth and income of the countries in which it has had its fullest trial. The question which has been raised with increasing insistence is, how are the wealth and income distributed among the different members of the various peoples under this system? This is to raise the question of justice.

So far as the average man, and particularly the laboring man or farmer or the man in petty trade or in clerical work is concerned, it may be that the question of productive efficiency is more important than the question of distribution. If there is so meager a total production as to permit no comfort for the mass of people it would not better their condition greatly if there were an equal distribution. In times past this has largely been the case. When the per capita income was only $300.00, few could have more than the bare necessities. Now that the per capita income has increased greatly, comforts and even luxuries such as automobiles, radios, modern plumbing, well-heated dwellings, are within the possibility of a large number of the population. Arguing from this it is sometimes thought foolish to raise the question of distribution. So long as the general level is rising, what does it matter if some are rising faster than others? The general spirit of American life has undoubtedly been to think of success as a game which is open to all, with prizes for those who win. The disposition has been to applaud the winner rather than to complain because he was more successful than his fellows. And a further fact of importance was that nothing was definitely known as to the distribution of wealth in the United States, although European countries were better informed. At present the distribution of wealth is less accurately known than the distribution of incomes, but there are sufficient data to afford basis for discussion of the principle involved. So far as opportunities to enjoy comforts and goods of life including education, as well as material necessities, are concerned, income is the more important. Many persons who receive good salaries spend them as they go along. They provide for death or old age by insurance. On the other hand when we think of influence and power in society, wealth is the more important. The individuals or corporations that have great available wealth can undertake great enterprises. They control for better or worse the wages and living conditions of great numbers. They exercise influence in church and state. If then we are thinking of social welfare in all its aspects we cannot pass by the question of justice.

But what is a "just" distribution? Several answers have been given of which we mention four which are typical.

§ 3. Four Theories of Just Distribution

1. Give to each what he earns. This sounds fair. In simpler conditions of society, when each man made an entire product

such as a bow or a piece of cloth, it might be possible so to arrange prices as roughly to give to each man what he earned. But in the present age of industry, when the labor of hundreds or thousands enters in a complex process of manufacture, transportation, and sale, this is obviously impossible.

2. Give every man what he can get through his ability, his shrewdness, his advantageous economic position due to inherited wealth, and every other factor which adds to his bargaining power, as regulated by free competition. This is the existing method under capitalism.

Here once more present conditions have profoundly changed the rules of the contest. On the one hand, corporations with enormous aggregations of wealth have taken the place of individual bargaining; on the other, labor unions have endeavored to even up conditions, to strengthen their bargaining power, by collective strength. The interest of the consumer who does not belong to either class is to some extent protected in Europe by cooperative societies; in the United States, however, these have not been successful. This method is no doubt a practicable method of division, but there is a serious question whether it can be called just. So far as the working of the system is concerned it appears that the outcome is similar in Prussia, France, Great Britain, and the United States. The concentration of wealth in the richest group is highest in Great Britain where capitalism has been in effect longest. But the trend is similar.

According to the estimates of W. I. King, if we divide the population in the four countries into four classes—(1) the poorest, comprising sixty-five per cent; (2) the lower middle, comprising fifteen per cent; (3) the upper middle, comprising eighteen per cent; and (4) the richest, comprising two per cent—the first class owns approximately five per cent, the second class five per cent, the third class thirty per cent, the fourth class sixty per cent of the wealth. If one had a hundred dollars to divide among one hundred people it is doubtful whether one would divide it in this proportion, although of course the question as to whether this would be just would depend upon principles which we have not yet fully examined. Many defenders of capitalism have been shocked by the extraordinary inequality shown in this estimated division by which two out of every hundred have more wealth than the other ninety-eight, and have challenged the accuracy of the figures. The Federal Trade Commission, however, in its report for 1926 studied and estimated the disproportion to be even greater.

If we turn to the distribution of income we have more adequate data. The National Bureau of Economic Research in 1921 estimated that, in 1918,

> the most prosperous one per cent of the income receivers had nearly 14 per cent of the total income, the most prosperous 5 per cent of the income receivers had nearly 26 per cent of the total, the most prosperous 10 per cent of the income receivers had nearly 35 per cent of the total, and the most prosperous 20 per cent of the income receivers had about 47 per cent of the total income.[2]

More recent estimates in the report of the Hoover Commission show a slight gain in the proportion of income going to the less well-to-do.

What gives us pause in accepting the distribution of wealth as just, is the fact that the modern world and especially the people of the United States entertain two social theories with which it is difficult to reconcile the existing distribution. The first is the theory that, in certain respects at least, men are equal. In political affairs we give each man and each woman one vote. We have never on any general scale attempted to apply this to wealth, and yet it is hard for us to suppose that an inequality of a million to one (if we take extremes) is quite representative of justice in a democratic society.

The second doctrine is that to some extent at least reward ought to be proportionate to the service or contribution which the individual makes to the common wealth. Some of the great fortunes are unquestionably the result of great services, but others are acquired through shrewdness in diverting the flow of wealth into the individual's pocket rather than by any actual contribution to this flow. In other words, "something for nothing" is not infrequently a maxim which yields a great fortune to the shrewd manipulator of securities or gambler in futures.

3. A third possible theory of just distribution would be to give an equal share to every one. Mr. Bernard Shaw, a member of the

2. *Income in the United States*, 1921, p. 147.

group of so-called Fabian socialists, advocates this as the right principle.[3] The difficulty with this from the point of view of justice is that it too fails to give sufficient weight to the differences among men, not only in ability but in willingness to do their share of work. In other words it applies one type of equality, but fails to make the further application of distributing equal returns to equal contributors, and proportionate returns to the unequally valuable contributions.

4. A fourth principle would abandon, in part at least, the attempt to distribute justly on the basis of giving to each man a precise equivalent for his contribution, or of giving him an equal share on the basis of the assumed equality of all human beings, or on the basis of what he can get in the market. It substitutes as the primary consideration, a regard for the public good or what the common law and the older writers had in mind by the common wealth. It asks what is a good condition of society, and what standard of living is necessary or conducive to a good society. The best example of the working of this principle is seen in our system of public education. The leading concern in our public school system has been, not primarily to produce a few exceptional scholars, nor to give superior advantages to members of certain social or economic classes; but to give all a minimum of education, and to those who can profit by it such opportunities for further education as are believed to be essential and desirable for the welfare of people as a whole. If we should apply this same principle to economic distribution it would insist upon a minimum that would not merely prevent actual starvation, but would in any country of abundant wealth make possible the necessaries and some of the comforts of present civilization.

Yet while it may be impossible to give to each a precise equivalent for his contribution, the principle that every man who receives should make his contribution is fundamental to this fourth theory of just distribution. One of the greatest sources of the feeling of injustice is that too often those who work hardest—such as the laborers in many kinds of agriculture and industry, and those whose contributions are of the highest value to civilization, such as the inventor or scientist—are poorly paid; whereas many who have never done a stroke of useful work enjoy by in-

3. *The Intelligent Woman's Guide to Socialism and Capitalism.*

heritance, or by luck, or by shrewd manipulations of securities and monopolistic privileges, enormous wealth.

The fourth principle as stated above is the principle of what has been called by Mr. Tawney a *functional*, as contrasted with an acquisitive society. The term goes back to Plato's study of justice in his dialogue, *The Republic*. His thought is that a just society is that in which each performs his own part or function, and in which the good of the individual members is inseparable from that of the whole social body. As contrasted with modern theories it undoubtedly emphasizes the good of the whole society, whereas since Adam Smith modern individualism has assumed that if every one looks out for "Number One" the result will be the greatest prosperity for all, or at least the sum total of wealth will be greatest even if it is not widely distributed. The question is whether—now that the individual has almost ceased to exist as a power, and when his place has been taken by a corporation or a trade union or other organization—we can continue to hold to a theory of individualism and free acquisition, which worked fairly well when there were individuals, and when there was (apart from conquests and war and grabbing of land) much truth in Adam Smith's theory.

Literature

In addition to the references in the two preceding chapters: Chase, *The Tragedy of Waste*, 1926; Hobhouse, *The Elements of Social Justice*, 1922; Various Writers (Hobhouse et al.), *Property, Its Duties and Rights*, 1913; King, *The Wealth and Income of the People of the United States*, 1915; Mitchell and Associates, *Income in the United States*, 1921; Veblen, *The Vested Interests*, 1919.

21. Social Control of Business and Industry

If there are such defects and injustices in the present capitalistic order, the question may naturally arise—why does not society do something about it? The answer is that there have been several policies adopted in capitalistic countries which aim toward mitigating the evils which have been pointed out. At the present time also, in two countries—Italy and Russia— experiments with a radically different system have been undertaken. Let us consider first, modifications in countries which are still on the whole capitalistic.

§ 1. Factory Legislation

This began in Great Britain where the industrial revolution first made its appearance. The shocking abuses in the employment of women and children, with long hours and under conditions dangerous to health, led Parliament to enact a child-labor law in 1802, which was followed by a series of factory laws for the protection of those classes. The United States and Germany followed later. In the United States the situation was complicated by the fact that whereas one state might adopt protective legislation, another state with industries which competed with those of the first state might neglect or refuse to adopt such measures. This continues to a considerable degree to be the case.

Congress attempted to control child labor by a law taxing such goods produced by child labor as should enter into interstate commerce. The United States Supreme Court decided that such a use of taxing power would be unlawful, since the purpose of the bill was not to raise money but to prevent child labor. The court had previously held that it was lawful for the Federal government to tax out of existence the issues of currency by state banks. The implication would seem to be that the familiar principle of protecting business against loss was regarded as so important as to justify a stretching of the taxing power of the Federal government. To avoid the objections of the court to the child-labor bill, a constitutional amendment was passed by Congress and submitted to the state legislatures. Unfortunately this proposal came at a time of conservative reaction following the World War; and there is at present little prospect of its adoption by the necessary number of states. It is not without an ironical feature that Massachusetts, which was one of the first to reject the proposed amendment, is now suffering from competition of states which have little or no protective legislation, as is shown by the decrease of population in the Massachusetts textile cities, according to the census of 1930.

Germany and England have not only adopted factory legislation but unemployment insurance to provide for the seemingly inevitable periods of unemployment, and for the inevitable reaching of an age when employment can no longer be expected in a business governed by competitive principles. Until recently the United States had done nothing in these directions in the way of action by the government. A strong sentiment in favor of government aid for those incapacitated by old age has led in many states, however, to proposals for legislation, and in December, 1931, measures for such aid had been adopted by seventeen states and one territory. Provisions for retirement with a pension or other allowance have been made in many business firms, and provisions against unemployment have been adopted in a few cases, notably in the men's clothing industry.

In the Middle Ages the church felt a responsibility for the poor. Its possessions of land were partly no doubt used to maintain the communities of monks and nuns, but were also in part devoted to charity. When the church property in England was largely confiscated by the State a certain measure of responsibility for care of the poor was recognized by secular authorities. But there was always a stigma connected with poor relief. The theory was that a man who was willing to work could support himself and his family. In earlier times in the United States there was a feeling that it was a disgrace to "come on the town." The man who did this was suspected of being "shiftless," and shiftlessness was as deeply abhorred as vice.

Here again, however, the complete change in economic conditions is slowly compelling recognition of the fact that men are likely to be thrown out of work by a general business depression without the least fault or possibility of escape on their part. It is also apparent that, in so far as labor is regarded as a commodity to be bought in the cheapest market and scrapped like a machine when it is no longer at its maximum efficiency, the older protection against poverty and old age—which existed when the employer had a personal interest in his workman—no longer exists. A society which claims to be just, to say nothing of being humane, must take account of these changed conditions and make provision, either through the industries themselves, or through government administration, against those contingencies which the present development of industry has brought about. The old legal maxim was, "Where the tree falls, there let it lie." The modern conscience believes that a society which makes any pretense to understand what it is about should prevent trees from falling—or when this is not possible should at least prevent the fall from crushing the helpless members of the commonwealth.

The exercise of the power of government to control conditions of employment in the interest of health, safety, and morals, is justified in the so-called "police power" of the State. The leading decision in the United States for the exercise of this power in the regulation of dangerous occupations is that of Holden v. Hardy, rendered in 1897. The opinion of Justice Brown in this case may well be called the Magna Carta of the laboring people. And a still broader statement of the police power was given in the opinion of Justice Holmes:

> It may be said in a general way that the police power extends to all the great public needs (167 U.S. 518). It may be put forth in aid of what is sanctioned by usage or held by the prevailing morality or strong and preponderant opinion to be greatly and immediately necessary to the public welfare.[1]

Thus far the courts have been reluctant to justify under the police power, legislation which does not fall directly under health, safety, or morals.[2]

1. Noble State Bank v. Haskell, 219 U.S. 111 (Oct., 1911).
2. E. Freund, *The Police Power.*

In the case of Lochner *v.* New York,[3] a law limiting the hours of work in bakeshops was declared unconstitutional by the Federal Supreme Court. In 1911, the New York Court of Appeals annulled the Workmen's Compensation Act, designed to afford compensation to workmen injured by accidents even when the employer was not necessarily at fault. The Federal Supreme Court declared unconstitutional a minimum wage law for the District of Columbia, enacted by Congress. On the other hand, it sustained in 1908 an Oregon law limiting women's hours of labor.[4] In the case of legislation affecting wages the issue is between the older individualistic principle of freedom in the wage contract, on the one hand; and on the other the more recently affirmed principle that in the interest of social welfare it may be wise for a state to protect its members against exploitation.

§ 2. Property Affected with a Public Interest

A second attempt to protect the common welfare against the power of wealth was the doctrine affirmed by the courts of "property affected with a public interest." In this case it was the protection of farmers against exorbitant prices by railroads and warehouses which prompted the legislation. The increasing dependence of business and private life upon such public utilities as telephones, electric-lighting plants, gas companies, street railways, or public bus lines, has favored the extension of the principle that states and cities and the United States may prescribe "reasonable" rates. The leading case of Munn *v.* Illinois justifies such control as follows:

> Property does become clothed with a public interest when used in a manner to make it of public consequence and affect the community at large. When, therefore, one devotes his property to a use in which the public has an interest, he, in effect, grants to the public an interest in that use, and must submit to be controlled by the public for the common good to the extent of the interest he has thus created.[5]

3. 198 U.S. 45 (1905).
4. Muller *v.* Oregon, 208 U.S. 412.
5. 94 U.S. 113 (1877).

The United States Interstate Commerce Commission, and various commissions in the several states supervise, and to a certain extent regulate, rates of railroads and public utilities. Evidently the crucial question in these cases is, what is a reasonable rate? Two methods have been proposed for fixing the basis of such a rate: (a) Rates should be such as to pay a fair interest upon the money actually invested in the railroad or other utility. (b) Rates should be such as to yield a fair return upon what it would at present cost to reproduce the plant.

The great difference between the two is likely to be, first, that a plant built when materials and wages were low would cost very much more to build at a subsequent period when materials and wages are higher. And in the second place, plants or terminals which are located in cities gain in value by growth of those cities, so that if it were necessary at present to purchase a new location the cost would be very much greater than the cost at an earlier date. In presenting a case on the part of the public utility the aim is naturally to make the capital as high as possible, on which a return to the stockholders is to be based. The interest of the consumer, on the other hand, is in keeping the authorized capital at as low a figure as possible. Opinions differ as to the extent to which this regulation has been proved successful. Some declare that, if the second principle is adopted for estimating rates, the consumer might as well have no protection at all. On the other hand, the investor does not see why he should not share in the general advance of urban values, or in the general advance in prices. The remedy which some cities have adopted is to provide their own lighting, as they have provided their own water supplies and sewage systems. In Europe municipal ownership of street railways is common, and Germany has operated its railroads profitably. The United States took control of the railroads during the War when private management had completely broken down. In Chicago, as one incidental feature of public convenience, it brought together under one roof something like a dozen ticket offices which had been scattered about the city and had on principle made it a policy to decline any information except for their own individual road. But at the close of the War the outcry of those opposed to any extension of government administration was so great that the railroads were returned to private ownership. Whether because of the wholesome shock to the management given by the period of government administration, or for some other reason, the railroads have greatly improved their freight service. But the charges have been regarded by farmers and certain other classes of shippers as excessive. In earlier times a favorite method of making high rates seem "reasonable" was by issuing so-called watered stock; i.e., stock which did not represent any investment, but which was rather a title to share in possible profits. The right to issue such stock has been restrained in the case of railroads and public utilities; but there is a continuous duel between the resourceful advisors of railroads and utilities, on the one hand, and the guardians of the public interest, on the other.

§ 3. The Sherman Act of 1890

In the '80's and still more in the '90's, a movement was in progress toward a consolidation of smaller industrial and business firms into larger corporations; and these were at first called "trusts," from the legal device under which the combinations were at first effected. There was fear that these would become monopolies and would then be free from the self-regulation by competition which had been supposed to regulate prices.

The Sherman Act prohibited the formation of monopoly, and of combinations in restraint of trade. Evidently this act proceeded under the theory that if competition could be preserved the public would be protected. As a matter of fact the efforts of the government to dissolve certain great combinations seemed to be effective only in changing the paper certificates of ownership without affecting actual ownership. As one owner of stock in two railroads which had merged under the control of a single holding corporation is said to have remarked, "The principal difference seems to be whether I shall have one white certificate in one pocket or two certificates, one blue and one pink, in two separate pockets." In other words he and his fellow stockholders owned both roads, and did not care particularly whether they had to keep their stock certificates separate or could combine them in one legal corporation. The main point was that they owned the railroads.

§ 4. Fair Competition

Competition was relied upon by the supporters of capitalism to regulate business and industry. But here again changed conditions interfered with the working of the principle. Not only were various fraudulent practices attempted—such as imitating trade-marks, or palming off goods under some device which deceived the purchaser—but it was found that great combinations or associations were able to exert such pressure upon smaller firms as to drive them out of business. Older forms of unfair competition, based on fraud or slander, had from time to time been condemned by the courts. But the more explicit formulation of public opinion was reached in the Federal Trade Commission Act of 1914 and the Clayton Anti-Trust Act passed by Congress very nearly at the same time.

The former enacted "that unfair methods of competition in commerce are hereby declared unlawful." The latter forbade certain definite practices supposed to lessen competition. Certain corporations had charged a very low price in one town in order to drive out all competition there, while at the same time they charged a higher price in some other town where there was no competition, and thus made up the loss. A similar practice was to cut prices on some one article called a "fighting brand." A very effective use of power, when the same group of owners controls both the railroads and coal or iron mines, is to charge competitors high freight rates. In other cases it may secure such special rates or rebates from a railroad as to place competitors at a disadvantage. To a certain extent the courts recognized that the power of association might be used unfairly. The Supreme Court of the United States declared that

An act harmless when done by one may become a public wrong when done by many acting in concert, for it then takes on the form of a conspiracy; and may be prohibited or punished, if the result be hurtful to the public, or to the individual against whom the concerted action is directed.

But since the great corporation is in many respects treated as a person it is still able to exert extraordinary power without violating law.

In the field of industry the term, *unfair*, as used by labor unions, has a somewhat special meaning. It is applied to a shop in which the union is not recognized for purposes of collective bargaining, and in which non-union men are employed. The union claims that one of two things is true: either the non-union man cuts under the regular union scale of wages; or he gets the union wage and the other advantages of shorter hours, better workrooms, and more healthful conditions which the union has aided in securing. If he cuts under he is unfair, because he tends to pull down others; if he gets all the advantages gained by union efforts he is unfair, because he does not take his part in helping those who make these advantages possible. The law has recognized the right of union men to refuse to work with non-union men, and thus to bring pressure on the employer to discharge such non-union men. But it has not usually upheld unions when they have tried to bring further pressure upon "unfair" employers by boycotting them. In this respect it has treated associations of laborers on the same principle as associations of business men who have combined to boycott or blacklist.

In general it may be said that in so far as competition is directed toward discovering new secrets of nature, and more efficient practices of production or marketing, it is in the interest of the public. But in so far as in business it aims to foul a competitor and thus put him out of the game, or in industry to depress standards of living by taking advantage of superior bargaining power, or defeating attempts of workmen to better their conditions, competition is morally unfair whether legally so or not.

§ 5. Restriction of Immigration

This may be regarded as in a sense another effort to restrict unfair competition; but it is sufficiently distinctive to deserve separate mention. Earlier efforts to protect American industry and business by tariffs levied on goods imported from other countries had been directed primarily to aid business, although it was also claimed that, since wages in other countries were usually lower than in the United States, such tariffs were also a protection to American standards of wages. Nevertheless since there was no protective tariff upon the importation of la-

borers from other countries it is evident that the laborer was subjected to severe competition in his efforts to maintain wages.

In a period of enormous development of industry, such as took
place in railway building, or in the manufacture of iron and steel,
great numbers of sturdy workmen who were eager to work for
almost any wage were brought to the United States. Multitudes
were employed at an average wage of about ten dollars a week,
which was in the case of city-dwellers supplemented by taking
boarders and various other methods. In slack times or financial
crises, multitudes were thrown out of work, and added to the
burdens of charity and public support. It was believed by many
that the addition of such great numbers of unskilled laborers
—coming as they did from countries which differed from the
United States, not only in language, but in social and political
institutions, and in general levels of education—was a danger
not only to economic standards but to cultural and political standards as well. In many localities the foreign vote was organized
by skilful politicians and wielded as a unit, particularly in great
cities. Here then was a case where an economic policy was affecting injuriously other departments of society, and threatening
to destroy some of the things which had been fundamental in
American life.

The combined influence of labor unions, and of those who
feared unrestricted immigration on civic grounds, resulted in the
adoption by Congress of measures to restrict immigration. The
tendency has been to tighten rather than relax these restrictions.

§ 6. The Income Tax

The most radical measure in the field of social control
which the United States has thus far adopted is the Sixteenth
Amendment to the Federal Constitution. This authorizes Congress to lay a tax upon incomes. The amendment was adopted
in 1913.

There was, to be sure, nothing novel in its principle. European
countries had for a long time relied upon an income tax for a
substantial part of their revenue, and had employed a graded
scale by which those who received larger incomes should pay a
higher rate of tax. In the original Federal Constitution of the

United States was a provision that Congress should have no power to levy a direct tax except on the basis of population. This meant that a tax levied upon the rich could be no larger than the tax upon the poor. Since a tax levied on this basis would be obviously impossible unless it were extremely small, the result was that Congress resorted to other forms of taxation in order to raise money needed for carrying on the Federal government. The chief reliance was upon customs, i.e., taxes upon articles imported from other countries; and upon "internal revenue," taxes levied chiefly upon manufacture and sale of alcoholic liquors and tobacco. Both these forms of taxation were upon articles of consumption. A poor man with a large family might need to purchase more sugar than a rich man with a small family. In so far as the tax on such necessaries as sugar was concerned, the tax fell far more heavily in proportion upon the poor than upon the rich. With regard to alcoholic liquors and tobaccos the theory was that these were luxuries rather than necessities. But after all the taxes were burdens which pressed heavily upon the poor. No attempt was made to distribute burdens in proportion to ability to pay. The same feeling of discontent with existing inequalities which had already led to factory legislation, to control of public utilities, and to restraint of monopolies and trusts—culminating in the so-called Progressive movement in President Roosevelt's administration—led to agitation on existing inequality in burdens of taxation.

An income tax had been in force during the Civil War but had gone into disuse. The Supreme Court in 1895 had declared such a tax unconstitutional, to the bitter disappointment of many. The only legal way to overcome this obstacle was by an amendment to the Constitution; but amendments to the Constitution had usually up to this time been adopted only under circumstances of great stress. Since the adoption of the Thirteenth, Fourteenth, and Fifteenth Amendments, at the close of the Civil War, no serious proposal for such a step had been entertained. Such, however, was the rising tide of feeling in the then prevalent temper of the people that political parties favored an amendment, and President Taft recommended to Congress that it should propose such an amendment to the state legislatures for ratification. Announcement of its adoption was made in 1913.

During the World War the tax levied upon the largest incomes was for a time eighty per cent. In the prosperous '20's taxes on all classes of income were reduced. But in order to balance the national budget they were raised in 1932.

Professor Burgess, the political scientist, who had admired the previous balance between legislative power and constitutional limitations in our government, was quick to point out the revolutionary nature of this amendment.[6] Of course the actual application of taxation is subject to the discretion of Congress from time to time; but there is no doubt that in principle it makes possible a far more just distribution of burdens than existed prior to its adoption.

Literature

Clark, *Social Control of Business*, 1926; Commons, *Legal Foundations of Capitalism*, 1924; Freund, *Standards of American Legislation*, 1917; Goodnow, *Social Reform and the Constitution*, 1911; Slichter, *Modern Economic Society*, 1931; Stimson, *Popular Law-Making*, 1910; Taeusch, *Policy and Ethics in Business*, 1931; Gruening, *The Public Pays: A Study of Power Propaganda*, 1931; Levin, *Power Ethics*, 1931; Laidler, *Socialism in Thought and Action*, 1920; Stevens, *Unfair Competition*, 1917; Davies, *Trust Laws and Unfair Competition* (Government Printing Office), 1915; Radin, *The Lawful Pursuit of Gain*, 1931; Wormser, *Frankenstein, Incorporated*, 1931.

6. *The Reconciliation of Government with Liberty*, 1915.

22. Toward the Future

§ 1. Tendencies within the Capitalistic System

In addition to efforts of organized society to right some of the wrongs of the capitalistic system there are also certain tendencies at work which are believed by many to have great promise. Perhaps the most conspicuous is that given prominence by Mr. Henry Ford. This speaks with greater authority because it has actually worked to a considerable degree in Mr. Ford's own industry. Mr. Ford holds that the method of *mass production* enables the efficient manager to do four things:

(1) To reduce prices and thereby benefit consumers and extend the use of products; (2) to raise wages and thereby, not only to improve morale, but still further to extend the market for products by enabling workmen to become customers; (3) to shorten hours; and (4) to increase profits.

It may be alleged that the automobile industry offered an exceptionally favourable field for mass production; and that other factors, for example, national prohibition of the manufacture and sale of intoxicants, have operated to increase the purchasing power of the people. Nevertheless, the policy of high wages and low prices, as contrasted with the earlier theory that low prices could be achieved only by low wages, is a genuine contribution to business principles.

Another tendency, to which Professor Carver has directed attention, is called by him "the present economic revolution in the United States."[1] "It is a revolution," he claims,

> that is to wipe out the distinction between laborers and capitalists by making laborers their own capitalists and by com-

1. T. N. Carver, *The Present Economic Revolution in the United States*, Boston, 1926.

pelling most capitalists to become laborers of one kind or
another, because not many of them will be able to live on the
returns from capital alone. This is something new in the history of the world.

Instead of continuing to fight capital they [laborers] are
beginning to recognize its power and to use it as an imple-
ment for their own improvement. There are at least three
kinds of evidence that indicate roughly the extent to which
laborers are becoming capitalists: first, the rapid growth of
savings deposits; second, the investment of laborers in the
shares of corporations; third, the growth of labor banks.

It may well be doubted whether the extent to which laborers
own stocks and bonds is likely to give them any large measure of
participation in the control of industry. It is usually the preferred
stock, which has no voice in the control of industry, that is offered to employees. And yet of course the common stock with its
risks is frequently purchasable in the market, and in time laborers may come in this way to have a voice in control.

A third tendency, emphasized by Mr. Owen D. Young of the
General Electric Company, is that of separating management
from ownership. This separation has been carried far in certain
great corporations. When ownership and management were
combined in the same individual, ownership, actuated by the
profit motive, was likely to dictate policies without sufficient regard to any other consideration than that of profits. But when
ownership comes to be vested in a great number of stockholders,
and when an industry such as the electric industry, involves technical skill, scientific research, and the ability to secure harmonious working relations with great numbers of employees, the
situation requires an expert and broad-minded staff for its successful management. Such a staff cannot so easily be compelled
to think only of profits. It is itself largely on a salaried basis. It
is frequently more interested in making an excellent grade of
goods, and in gaining public favor, than it is in immediate profits. Such a management, Mr. Young claims, considers not only
the advantage of the owner but also the welfare of workmen and
responsibility to the public.

A fourth tendency has been the formation of associations
which have adopted codes of business ethics, or have emphasized

the standard of "service." Certain practices calculated to lower the public esteem for business morals have been condemned by such ethical codes. It is true that they have not usually attacked fundamental issues; and such associations as the Rotary, Kiwanis, Lions, Optimists, have been more or less derided as aiming rather at good luncheons than at drastic reforms. And yet they are symptomatic of a tendency to be dissatisfied with present conditions; and the maxim of "service" is certainly better than the all too general maxim—none the less acted upon, even if not so openly expressed—of "something for nothing," which so largely governs speculation.

A drastic change in the attitude and conduct of corporations is believed by many to be imperative. It is claimed that since corporations are given valuable privileges by the public they should make the public interest primary. This is already the theory as regards the so-called public service corporations; other corporations should adopt the same view of their responsibility; if they will not do so of their own accord, they should be placed under government supervision and control. This would give what Professor Wormser calls "a socialized corporate capitalism."[2] The corporation is organized "for profit," and hence is a conspicuous example of what the naked profit motive may induce. The profit often seems to be regarded as profit for the promoters at the expense of credulous investors, as when stock of no actual value is issued and sold. Again it is interpreted as profit for the high officials, as when a corporation pays millions in bonuses to its already well-paid officers, and yet pays no dividends. Again it is interpreted as profit for an inside ring at the expense of investors, as when stock is manipulated in such a way as to deceive the public as to its security and value. Again it is interpreted as profit for stockholders in periods of prosperity without any provision for its employees in subsequent periods of depressions. Business must clean house if the capitalistic system is to endure. "Corporate capitalists," says Professor Wormser, "if they would meet the serious situation which now confronts them, must regard themselves as 'trustees.'"

Such an extension of the principle of property affected with a public interest would be in accord with the spirit of the earlier

2. *Frankenstein, Incorporated.*

movement of public opinion and constitutional law that resulted in the Supreme Court's enunciation of the doctrine in Munn *v.* Illinois. There may be doubt as to whether the Supreme Court would regard such an extension as constitutional, but, as James Bryce remarked, the American people have bent their Constitution to prevent it from breaking, and may do it again. And we have learned that it is not impossible to amend the Constitution.[3]

§ 2. Radical Alternatives to Capitalism

Russia and Italy at the present time are conducting great experiments in economic systems. It is still too early to attempt a judgment as to the outcome, but we may use these as illustrations of other methods than capitalism.

1. Russia is putting into effect on a large scale the ideas of Karl Marx. In the *Communist Manifesto*, written jointly by Marx and Engels in 1848, and in the massive work called *Capital* by Marx, the foundations of so-called scientific socialism, as distinguished from former idealistic projects for a better society called Utopias, were laid. These foundations were: (1) The materialistic—or better, the economic—interpretation of history which regards economic forces as basic in determining religious, political, and cultural ideas and institutions. (2) Class struggle, seen as a factor ever present hitherto in society, whether between patrician and plebeian, or between lords and villeins, or between bourgeoisie and proletariat. Conflict between bourgeoisie and proletariat is bound to reach a crisis in the social revolution out of which will emerge the dictatorship of the proletariat and finally the withering away of the State and abolition of classes. (3) Surplus value, a doctrine that present conditions of manufacture and commerce yield a large surplus value beyond the maintenance wages allotted to labor. This surplus value is appropriated by the capitalist who owns the factories and tools. Labor is therefore exploited. The remedy for this exploitation, as for class conflict, lies in the dictatorship of the proletariat and the socialization of wealth.

3. On this topic of reform of business, see, Ripley, *Main Street and Wall Street*, 1927; Donham, *Business Adrift*, 1931; Taeusch, *Policy and Ethics in Business*, 1931; Wormser, *Frankenstein, Incorporated*, 1931.

Various parties in European countries and in the United States have advocated socialist principles, in a more or less modified form. But Russia is the first country to try the experiment of a complete "dictatorship of the proletariat," with an equalization of income and a large degree of State control of industry and land. It was pointed out by many that Marx himself did not contemplate the social revolution as occurring in an agricultural country such as Russia. He had in mind an industrialized society as the intermediate stage between agriculture and the revolution. The Russian peasants have thus far been reluctant to raise crops for the State. But the Soviet government is pushing toward a collective organization of agriculture; and toward driving out, or forcing into submission, the Kulaks or wealthy landowners. Moreover, concessions to carry on some of the large industries have been made to private capital. Conflicting reports as to the success of the movement render it impossible as yet to make an impartial estimate of its successes and defects. The ruthlessness with which opponents were treated is probably to be attributed in part to the long period of repression, and the extreme inequalities and cruelties, which existed under the government of the Czar. Yet it is not surprising that peoples in other countries have not been attracted by the prospect of a similar dictatorship of the proletariat.

2. Italy is attempting an experiment of a different sort. Whereas in Russia political power is subordinated to the control of an economic class, in Italy economic interests are subordinated to national power. After a short trend toward socialism the Fascist Revolution under Mussolini reversed the balance of power and proceeded to supervise or administer the economic life in a way to subserve national power and prestige. On the one hand employers, on the other workmen, were admonished that nothing in business policy or workingmen's efforts must interfere with efficiency of economic operations and national strength.

The traditions of the Empire when Rome ruled the world were appealed to in order to inspire devotion to the supreme cause of national welfare. In the interest of this purpose, criticism of the government by the press or by individuals was severely restrained. As one sympathetic defender of the system stated to an American audience, "In America you may be able to combine liberty with efficiency; in Italy apparently we are not yet able to do this and must choose between the two." At present Fascism seems to be as firmly the policy of Italy as communism is of Russia. Meanwhile the peoples of other countries may well be interested in studying the outcomes.

§ 3. If Capitalism Is to Continue

The extreme individualism of *laissez faire*, with competition as the only regulator of the economic process, has been shown to be no longer tolerable in present conditions. Just as the congested traffic of a modern city demands a traffic officer to regulate the streams of rushing automobiles and to protect pedestrians—so the necessities of public welfare, and of the large numbers who are economically in the status of pedestrians, require the supremacy of an authority which aims at justice and not at profits; and which interprets justice, not merely as keeping order while the contestants fight it out, but as revising the rules of the contest in the interest of the common good when this is made necessary by the changed conditions of industrial life.

The issue is then between a modified capitalism—in which the democratic principle, embodied in our political and educational systems, shall have increasing recognition, and in which liberty, efficiency, and justice shall be combined so far as possible—as over against policies of a more radical character, such as are on trial in Russia and Italy.

In another aspect the issue is one between the democratic principle of equality, which has more and more gained recognition in the modern world in political, religious, and educational life; and the principle of inequality which formerly obtained in the three areas just mentioned, and which now seems to be essential to efficiency in economic life.

Perhaps the deepest reason for distrust in Western Europe, and particularly in the United States, of either the Russian or the Fascist system is unwillingness to be subject to *absolute control of a single master*. In Russia this master is an economic class; in Italy it is a nationalist group. Both profess to be acting for the general welfare, but the fact remains that a single master is in absolute control. In a system such as obtains in Western Europe and the United States, the masters of the economic system and those of the political system form two distinct groups selected on different principles. Economic leaders are chosen principally by competition in the market. This selects men of certain types of ability, and gives them wide scope for the exercise of that ability to organize which is so largely responsible for the efficiency of modern business and industry. Leaders in the political sphere are selected by votes on the basis of their ability to win public approval. They represent a distinctly different phase of society, and a distinctly different interest from that represented by economic leaders. Perhaps the interests of the public are safer when control is thus divided than when it is concentrated in one hand.

It is probably safe to assume that in the immediate future a modified capitalism is likely to continue. The present owners of the vast proportion of the national wealth in Western Europe and America, even though a small minority of the total population, wield a power and influence proportionate to their wealth rather than to their numbers. The agricultural group, although in the United States the least prosperous as measured by income (the per capita income of those engaged in agriculture for 1926 was estimated by Professor Copeland to be $265.00, as contrasted with the average income of the whole population for that same year estimated at $750.00), nevertheless have a relatively large investment in land and are therefore favorable to private property, which is one of the fundamentals of the existing system. The industrial workers are the class which might be supposed to be most inclined toward change. In European countries this class has been largely favorable to a socialistic trend, although for the most part committed to constitutional and legal methods of change toward State control, rather than to a violent social revolution. In the United States, however, the American Federation of Labor has been strongly opposed to socialism. There has been a widespread feeling among industrial workers that it is a more prudent and wiser policy to give a free hand to owners and employers in developing improved methods of production, distribution, and selling of goods; and to concentrate efforts rather upon obtaining as large a share as possible of the increasingly profitable returns from such efficient industry. In other words, it may be better to let the capitalist make money and to depend upon coming in on an increasing share of the income, than to take the risks of making a mess of things if either workmen themselves or the State should displace the capitalist in ownership and control of the productive, distributing, and financial machinery.

A further and perhaps the main reason why economic socialism has as yet made little headway in the United States is the great and liberal scale on which public education has been conceived and measurably carried out in the United States. The aim, as stated by the late President Angell of the University of Michigan, that every child might see a path from the door of his home to the state university, has been generously furthered, particularly in the newer states. And despite the expressed fears of some, that too many are seeking higher education, it is not likely that the public system will close its doors to its young people.

If then the present economic system is likely to continue, it is all the more important to consider how some of its worst abuses, wastes, injustices, may be remedied at least partially. We have already noted six points at which organized society has interfered with the extreme individualistic program based on private property, free enterprise, free contract, and free competition. Some of these measures—notably factory laws, stabilization of finance and to some extent of public utility charges, the income tax— have marked progress. Others such as the Sherman Act have been of doubtful value. It is moreover evident that though for certain ends we may properly rely upon law and public administration, there are other ends which can be gained only through education and a change of attitude both in producers and in consumers. We may roughly divide the field into (1) problems of increasing production and decreasing waste; (2) problems of security; (3) problems of protecting workmen and especially women and children against dangerous processes and machinery, against excessive hours, fatigue, and unsanitary conditions; (4) problems of improving the wisdom and good taste of consumers of goods, and of raising standards for recreation, as contrasted with commercialized standards; (5) problems of juster distribution of the enormous gains in economic processes—juster both as measured by service to the community, and as measured by the requirements of a functional society.

§ 4. Improvements Needed

1. Increasing production and decreasing waste. Increasing production is largely an engineering problem. Great strides have been made in this direction. A constantly increasing ratio of power—hydraulic, steam, electric—available through tapping new sources of supply and through its more efficient utilization, constantly improved organization, and in many cases better cooperation between management and workmen, have resulted in a rising rate of efficiency. The profit motive is of course enlisted toward this end. It is not wholly an engineering problem in the ordinary sense of the term, because the willingness of workmen to cooperate in increased production, is dependent in part upon their expectation of sharing in the returns created by this cooperation. Yet if we take engineering in the most inclusive sense this may well comprise such a consideration of the human factor as will lead to juster distribution.

Prevention of waste might also be thought to be an engineering problem. As regards methods, it is such. Extraordinary savings have been made in electric lighting, in the generation of power from steam, in the means of transportation.[4] And these economies have resulted in lowering of costs, in preventing waste of coal, and in many cases in the lowering of prices to consumers, and thus to a wider market. But the engineer under capitalism does not always have a free hand. Whether he is permitted to save or not depends on whether it is more profitable to save or to waste. In the case of the management of forests and the reforestation of cut-over areas, it has thus far seemed more profitable to waste than to save or reforest. European countries have been successful in keeping forests and their management under public ownership and control. The Federal government still has a considerable area under the charge of a national forestry system, and a few experiments have been made in state or municipal forestry. Even in Massachusetts, where the courts have been extremely conservative in protecting private business from public

4. An example of this on a small scale which nevertheless is typical came under the writer's observation. A coal distributing business is now carried on with two trucks and their drivers, which formerly required forty men and one hundred twenty horses.

competition, towns are allowed to own forests. In the extraction of oil a recent movement of owners to cooperate in reducing waste has promise. But natural gas has for the most part been recklessly wasted.

2. A further field in which up to the present time the engineer has been unable to prevent waste is that of unemployment. In this case his inability is not due directly to the profit motive, because the recurring periods of depression in industry and business are as yet imperfectly understood. Government supervision of banking has indeed reduced the "money panics" which private management was utterly incapable to prevent. But the business cycle is still not under control. Certain shrewd and powerful individuals may very likely profit by the opportunity to buy back at a low price the securities which at the crest of a prosperity wave they sold to the trustful public. Yet they cannot be charged with total responsibility for depressions. The heaviest burden rests upon the shoulders of those who are thrown out of employment, and who never had sufficient margin of income over expense to lay by for the rainy day. The American plan has been to let them look out for themselves, and to let their families suffer except as relieved by charity. Europe has provided for the risks of unemployment, as well as for those of accident, illness, and old age. Mr. Rubinow says:

> Every period of unemployment in this country [the United States] results in increased mendicancy, increased applications to charitable organizations, both private and public, increased crime, disease, and general demoralization, a sum total of social results which surely is much graver than the presumed demoralizing effect of the English so-called dole system.[5]

And a measure for old age has been adopted by seventeen state legislatures. But the very fact that American workmen have been able to be more provident than those of Europe has delayed measures to remove the manifest injustice of allowing the calamity of unemployment to rest upon those least able to bear it. Until scientists and engineers have discovered the way to prevent unemployment and its wastes, social insurance or some form of large

5. *A New Economic Order*, edited by Kirby Page, p. 168.

public works undertaken by the state is the only practicable remedy. It is absurd to object to a national plan for mitigating suffering and injustice on the ground that it was first tried in Europe. The argument that social insurance is "paternalistic" or "socialistic" or "German" is convenient hokum.

3. The principle that life and health should not be sacrificed to profits is seldom denied openly. Much has been done both by private initiative and by public control to safeguard workmen, and especially women and children. Much, however, still remains to be done. Since the Great War some of the states have undertaken to rehabilitate and reeducate those crippled in industry, following the example of the nation in rehabilitating those crippled in war. The general reaction against liberal and humanitarian activities on the part of government, which was manifest in many directions, has apparently postponed any successful attempt to establish a national protection of children against premature employment. Nevertheless it may be doubted whether state action will be adequate. In the meantime, however, those who live in states which have no protection against child labor, or inadequate protection, may work to improve local standards. The whole movement for labor legislation is scarcely more than a generation old in the United States, and it is premature to despair of further progress. Some form of public health insurance is probably also necessary to provide adequate medical and hospital service for those with small incomes.

4. Improvement of taste on the part of consumers, and of better standards of goods. If problems under (1) were primarily for the engineer, and problems under (2) primarily for government, problems of improving the taste of consumers and the standards of goods are primarily problems of education. The profit motive is not adequate as we have already seen. This has worked well in the case of automobiles, for these have improved in both beauty and utility.

On the other hand, this motive has failed almost utterly in providing dwellings of better quality. No doubt modern dwellings are better equipped as to plumbing, lighting, and heating, than those available a generation ago. But the congestion of cities, the hideous surroundings of the ordinary workingman's home which is near a factory or a railroad, the almost universal practice under the profit motive of covering the ground in cities with multiple dwellings, leaving no space for the play of children or for the recreation of adults, except in so far as the city itself has stepped in to provide parks and playgrounds—these show the profit motive nearly at its worst. As engineers are limited by profits, so architects who would like to plan generously are restricted by rents and profits. Courts do not allow the government to supply more healthful dwellings, and hence the ultimate remedy appears to be in the general education of the consumer to demand a different type of dwelling. The sphere of government is limited to preventing, under housing and zoning laws, the more outrageous violations of sanitation and good taste, and to the positive provision of free spaces for public parks and playgrounds. The newer parts of the country have been able to secure far more adequate space for children's play, than the older portions in which it was assumed that no provision need be made by the public. Adulteration of foods is another instance in which the profit motive cannot be trusted. Law in this case has stopped some of the worst practices in the case of foods. It is, however, impossible to prevent by law all kinds of trickery and deception.

Education, with the increased application of scientific standards for quality, is indispensable. Above all, it is education to which we must look for improvement in standards of art, literature, and recreation. Legislation may prevent some of those practices of commercial recreation, and commercial art and literature, which are most shocking to morality. But it cannot insure a more healthful taste. In this field, as distinguished from that of the automobile, the greater profit seems to lie in the worse products. The moving pictures, the jazz music, the comic strips, and various other forms of popular entertainment, are not an object of pride to those who have learned to know good art, good music, and good literature. A civilization, in which the average man spends his day in a factory and his evening at a movie, has still a long way to go.

5. Just distribution. As already noted, the conception of just distribution may be approached in several ways. We found it extremely difficult and indeed impossible to say how much each contributes, and hence that it is impracticable to determine how much each deserves to receive from the great pool into which go the accumulated knowledge and skill of past generations, the genius of the discoverer and inventor, the patient labors of the sci-

entist, the order and tranquillity and social standards so necessary for peaceful production, and the taste and sensitiveness to color, form, and sound which are our inheritance from the past. The only promising approach is rather by the path which Plato suggested when he asked what was necessary for a good society. On behalf of inequality in wealth it may be argued that more capital will be available for business enterprise if wealth is distributed as at present, and it may be granted that in the past this has in many if not in all cases been true. If we take the illustration of dividing a thousand dollars among one hundred men it is probable that if each received $10.00 he would expend it on some present need; whereas if ninety men received $1.00 each, and if nine more received $40.00 each, and the one hundredth man received the balance of $550.00, it is probable that the last named man would be inclined to use at least a part of the $550.00 for some new venture. But at present we recognize that this may be overdone. If the great mass have only sufficient income to maintain a meager standard of living, the market for goods will be correspondingly limited. The rich man cannot consume indefinitely. The mass of men provide the great market. It is by the constant education of greater and greater numbers to use more and better goods that the market is widened and sustained. The movement, which some far-sighted employers have initiated, of paying better wages in order to increase the number of consumers is commended by economists as tending in a wise direction.

Unfortunately the case of the farmer is more difficult. There are many advantages from the point of view of the general welfare in the continuance of small holdings and independent farms. On the other hand, it may be that it will prove impossible to resist the trend toward larger units, which has gone so far in the industrial world. In the meantime the farmer receives low prices for his goods, and pays high prices for what he must buy; while if he needs help he must compete with the wages paid by industry.

Efforts toward a juster distribution of gains need not be limited to better wages. Society through public agencies is constantly doing more for its members. The outstanding example is of course the system of public education. Most communities provide books as well as buildings and teachers. Public libraries, public parks and playgrounds, have done much to counteract the evils of city congestion. Such inventions as the automobile and the radio have made available to the multitude the advances of science. Generous gifts to hospitals and education, and endowments for research in all lines, are continually making better standards of life possible.

It is sometimes objected that such activities by the public tend to limit private enterprise, with the self-help and independence which has been so important a factor in modern society. On the other hand, it is more probable that the opening of wider doors, to all sorts and conditions of men, by education and acquaintance with the finer things of life, will more than even the balance.

Looking at our economic life in the light of what we have learned from Hebrew and Greek, and from modern conceptions of scientific method and fuller life—we may say that a good society should aim to secure justice, should keep a right perspective as to the various goods which are desirable, should take account of all the human relations, and should move toward raising all men toward that measure of equality and democracy which has been the ideal and aspiration not only of the finer spirits but of increasing multitudes in the modern world.

§ 5. A Distorted Perspective

We have considered some of the merits and defects of our present order with respect to justice, liberty, and equality. In conclusion, we note what is perhaps the most serious question of all, namely, that of the proper perspective. If the economic dominates life—and if the economic order relies chiefly upon the profit motive as distinguished from the motive of professional excellence, i.e., craftsmanship, and from the functional motive of giving a fair return for what is received—there is danger that a part of life, which should be subordinate or at most coordinate with other interests and values, may become supreme. It is as true now as when the words were uttered that life is more than meat. And when wealth is made a chief if not the sole interest, some of the precious and finer things of life—love, justice, knowledge, beauty—are liable to be displaced. Referring to the unlimited exercise of powers in the acquisition of wealth, and the conception that to this pursuit there is no limit other than that which individuals think advisable, Mr. Tawney says:

Under the impulse of such ideas men do not become religious or wise or artistic; for religion and wisdom and art imply the acceptance of limitations. But they become powerful and rich.[6]

It is by no means intended that all men who engage in business and industry become absorbed wholly in the pursuit of wealth. Every one knows conspicuous instances which would refute such a judgment. The point which it is intended to urge is that exclusive reliance upon the profit motive and upon the supreme importance of wealth tends to distort the proper perspective for life as a whole.

Literature

Beard (Editor), *Whither Mankind*, 1928; Donham, *Business Adrift*, 1931; Hamilton, "Freedom and Economic Necessity," in *Freedom in the Modern World*, edited by Kallen, 1928; Page (Editor), *A New Economic Order*, 1930; Slichter, *Modern Economic Society*, Part IV., 1931; Tawney, *Equality*, 1931; Tufts, *The Ethics of Coöperation*, 1918.

6. *The Acquisitive Society*, p. 31.

The family ideally considered has one end, the common good of all its members, but this has three aspects. (1) Marriage converts an attachment between man and woman, either of passion or of friendship, into a deliberate, intimate, permanent, responsible union for a common end of mutual good. It is this common end, a good of a higher, broader, fuller sort than either could attain in isolation, which lifts passion from the impulsive or selfish to the moral plane; it is the peculiar intimacy and the peculiar demands for common sympathy and cooperation, which give it greater depth and reach than ordinary friendship. (2) The family is the great social agency for the care and training of the race. (3) This function reacts upon the character of the parents. Tenderness, sympathy, self-sacrifice, steadiness of purpose, responsibility, and activity, are all demanded and usually evoked by the children. A brief sketch of the development of the family will prepare the way for a consideration of its present problems.

§ 1. Historical Antecedents of the Modern Family

The division of the sexes appeals to the biologist as an agency for securing greater variability, and so greater possibility of adaptation and progress. It has also to the sociologist the value of giving greater variety in function, and so a much richer society than could exist without it. Morally, the realization of these values, and the further effects upon character noted above, depend largely upon the terms under which the marriage union is formed and maintained. The number of parties to the union, the mode of forming it, its stability, and the relations of husband and wife, parents and children, while in the family relation, have shown in western civilization a tendency toward certain lines of progress, although the movement has been irregular and has been interrupted by certain halts or even reversions.

The early family, certainly in many parts of the world, was formed when a man left his father and mother to "cleave unto his wife," that is, when the woman remained in her own group and the man came from his group to live with her. This tended to give the woman continued protection—and also continued control—by her own relatives, and made the children belong to the mother's clan. As recent ethnologists seem inclined to agree, this does not mean a matriarchal family. The woman's uncle and brothers, rather than the woman, are in the last analysis the authority. At the same time, at a stage when physical force is so large a factor, this type of family undoubtedly favors the woman's condition as compared with the next to be mentioned.

When the woman leaves her own group to live in the house of her husband, it means a possible loss of backing and position for her. But it means a great gain for the influence which insures the wife's fidelity, the father's authority over the children and interest in them, and finally the permanence of the family. The power of the husband and father reached its extreme among western peoples in the patriarchate at Rome, which allowed him the right of life and death. At its best the patriarchal type of family fostered the dignity and power of a ruler and owner, the sense of honor which watched jealously over self and wife and children to keep the name unsullied; finally the respective attitudes of protector and protected enhanced the charm of each for the other. At its worst it meant domineering brutality, and either the weakness of abject submission or the misery of hopeless injustice.

Along with this building up of "father right" came variations in the mode of gaining a wife. When the man takes a wife instead of going to his wife, he may either capture her, or purchase her, or serve for her. In any of these cases she may become to a certain extent his property as well as his wife. This does not necessarily imply a feeling of humiliation. The Kafir women profess great contempt for a system in which a woman is not worth buying. But it evidently favors a commercial theory of the whole relation. The bride's consent may sometimes be a necessary part of the transaction, but it is not always.

This family of "father right" is also likely to encourage a theory that the man should have greater freedom in marriage than the woman. In the lowest types of civilization we often find marital relations very loose from our point of view, although, as was noted in Chapter 2, these peoples usually make up for this in the rigidity of the rules as to who may marry or have marriage relations. With some advance in civilization and with the father right, we are likely to find polygamy permitted to chiefs or those who can afford it, even though the average man may have but one wife. In certain cases the wives may be an economic advantage rather than a burden. It goes along with a family in which father and children are of first importance that a wife may even be glad to have her servant bear the children if they may only be reckoned as hers. The husband has thus greater freedom—for polyandry seems to have been rare among civilized peoples except under stress of poverty. The greater freedom of the husband is likely to appear also in the matter of divorce. Among many savage peoples divorce is easy for both parties if there is mutual consent, but with the families in which father right prevails it is almost always easier for the man. The ancient Hebrew might divorce his wife for any cause he pleased, but there is no mention of a similar right on her part, and it doubtless did not occur to the lawgiver. The code of Hammurabi allows the man to put away the mother of his children by giving her and her children suitable maintenance, or a childless wife by returning the bride price, but a wife who has acted foolishly or extravagantly may be divorced without compensation or kept as a slave. The woman may also claim a divorce "if she has been economical and has no vice and her husband has gone out and greatly belittled her." But if she fails to prove her claim and appears to be a gadder-about, "they shall throw that woman into the water." India and China have the patriarchal family, and the Brahmans added the obligation of the widow never to remarry. Greater freedom of divorce on the part of the husband is also attended by a very different standard for marital faithfulness. For the unfaithful husband there is frequently no penalty or a slight one; for the wife it is frequently death.

The modern family in western civilization is the product of three main forces: the Roman law, the Teutonic custom, and the Christian church. Early Roman law had recognized the extreme power of the husband and father. Wife and children were in his "hand." All women must be in the *tutela* of some man. The woman, according to the three early forms of marriage, passed completely from the power and hand of her father into that of her husband. At the same time she was the only wife, and divorce was rare. But by the closing years of the Republic a new method of marriage, permitting the woman to remain in the *manus* of her father, had come into vogue, and with it an easy theory of divorce. Satirists have charged great degeneracy in morals as a result, but Hobhouse thinks that upon the whole the Roman matron would seem to have retained the position of her husband's companion, counselor, and friend, which she had held in those more austere times when marriage brought her legally under his dominion.[1]

The Germanic peoples recognized an almost unlimited power of the husband. The passion for liberty, which Caesar remarked as prevalent among them, did not seem to require any large measure of freedom for their women. In fact, they, like other peoples, might be said to have satisfied the two principles of freedom and control by allotting all the freedom to the men and all, or nearly all, the control to the women. Hobhouse thus summarizes the conditions:

The power of the husband was strongly developed; he might expose the infant children, chastise his wife, dispose of her person. He could not put her to death, but if she was unfaithful, he was, with the consent of the relations, judge and executioner. The wife was acquired by purchase from her own relatives without reference to her own desires, and by purchase passed out of her family. She did not inherit in early times at all, though at a later period she acquired that right in the absence of male heirs. She was in perpetual ward, subject, in short, to the Chinese rule of the three obediences, to which must be added, as feudal powers developed, the rule of the king or other feudal superior. And the guardianship or *mundium* was frankly regarded in early law rather as a source of profit to the guardian than as a means of defense to the ward, and for this reason it fetched a price in the market, and was, in fact, salable far down in the Middle Ages. Lastly, the German wife, though respected, had not the certainty en-

1. *Morals in Evolution*, Part I., p. 216.

joyed by the early Roman Matron of reigning alone in the household. It is true that polygamy was rare in the early German tribes, but this, we have seen, is universally the case where the numbers of the sexes are equal. Polygamy was allowed, and was practiced by the chiefs.

The influence of the church on marriage and family life was in two conflicting lines. On the one hand, the homage and adoration given to Mary and to the saints, tended to exalt and refine the conception of woman. Marriage was, moreover, treated as a "sacrament," a holy mystery, symbolic of the relation of Christ and the church. The priestly benediction gave religious sacredness from the beginning; gradually a marriage liturgy sprang up which added to the solemnity of the event, and finally the whole ceremony was made an ecclesiastical instead of a secular function.[2] The whole institution was undoubtedly raised to a more serious and significant position. But, on the other hand, an ascetic stream of influence had pursued a similar course, deepening and widening as it flowed. Although from the beginning those "forbidding to marry" had been denounced, it had nearly always been held that the celibate life was a higher privilege. If marriage was a sacrament, it was nevertheless held that marriage made a man unfit to perform the sacraments. Woman was regarded as the cause of the original sin. Marriage was from this standpoint a concession to human weakness. "The generality of men and women must marry or they will do worse; therefore, marriage must be made easy; but the very pure hold aloof from it as from a defilement. The law that springs from this source is not pleasant to read."[3] It must, however, be noted that, although celibacy by a selective process tended to remove continually the finer, more aspiring men and women, and prevent them from leaving any descendants, it had one important value for woman. The convent was at once a refuge, and a door to activity. "The career open to the inmates of convents was greater than any other ever thrown open to women in the course of modern European history."[4]

Two important contributions to the justice of the marriage relation, and therefore to the better theory of the family, are in any

2. Howard, *History of Matrimonial Institutions*, I., ch. vii.
3. Pollock and Maitland, *Hist. Eng. Law*, II., 383, quoted in I., Howard, 325–326.
4. Eckenstein, *Woman under Monasticism*, p. 478.

case to be set down to the credit of the church. The first was that the consent of the parties was the only thing necessary to constitute a valid marriage. "Here the church had not only to combat old tradition and the authority of the parents, but also the seignorial power of the feudal lord, and it must be accounted to it for righteousness that it emancipated the woman of the servile as well as of the free classes in relation to the most important event of her life."[5] The other was that in maintaining as it did the indissolubility of the sacramental marriage, it held that its violation was as bad for the husband as for the wife. The older theories had looked at infidelity either as an injury to the husband's property, or as introducing uncertainty as to the parenthood of children, and this survived in Dr. Johnson's dictum of a "boundless" difference. The feelings of the wife, or even of the husband, aside from his concern for his property and children, do not seem to have been considered.

The church thus modified the Germanic and Roman traditions, but never entirely abolished them, because she was divided within herself as to the real place of family life. Protestantism, in its revolt from Rome, opposed both its theories of marriage. On the one hand, the Reformers held that marriage is not a sacrament, but a civil contract, admitting of divorce. On the other hand, they regarded marriage as the most desirable state, and abolished the celibacy of the clergy. The "subjection of women," especially of married women, has, however, remained as the legal theory until very recently. In England it was the theory in Blackstone's time that "The very being or legal existence of the woman is suspended during the marriage, or at least is incorporated and consolidated into that of the husband, under whose wing, protection, and cover, she performs everything." According to the old law, he might give her "moderate correction." "But with us in the politer reign of Charles II., this power of correction began to be doubted." It was not until 1882, however, that a married woman in England gained control of her property. In the United States the old injustice of the common law has been gradually remedied by statutes until substantial equality in relation to property and children has been secured.

5. Hobhouse, op. cit., I., 218.

§ 2. Recent Changes in Society and Ideas
Which Affect the Family

As the family is probably the oldest among human institutions—older than government as a separate factor, and probably older than separately organized religion—it is also eminently the institution which concerns men and women in daily living. Rooted biologically in sex it has drawn strength from economic, religious, political, and artistic sources. Shifts from the maternal to the paternal type, or from polygamy to monogamy, have been so gradual as to tend toward greater strength rather than toward a lessening of permanence and community of relationship. The gradual lengthening of the period of education has been an influence toward a continuance of the bond of common interest in children, which has made for greater unity between parents. At the present time, however, a conjunction of forces seems to be working in the opposite direction. Economic, political, religious conditions form a background for revolutionary ideas.

Economic changes, and the urban life which is largely the result of them, are the first and perhaps the most serious underlying factor in the situation. The family and home of former times, while rooted in sex and parental relations assumed a pattern largely shaped by the need of division of labor between husband, wife, and children, and by community of property, particularly of a stable dwelling, the home. This dwelling was often a centre of industry, recreation, and religion. The division of labor between man and woman, after culture had reached the higher hunting or agricultural stage, was that man should bring home the game or work in the field while woman prepared food and cared for the house. They were thus interdependent. A man found himself largely helpless in preparing food and especially in caring for children. The woman was correspondingly at a disadvantage in hunting game or working in the fields, although in many cases she might take part in this. All the work as well as the enjoyments of life tended to centre in the home.

The industrial revolution sent both men and women into factories. It took even children in large numbers. The first effect of industrial change was therefore upon the working class—the economically poorer strata of society—in which the work of both man and wife was necessary to maintain existence and support children. While this did little to break legal ties which bound husband and wife, it did impoverish the life of the home. Even from well-to-do families it removed nearly all the domestic arts and crafts, except that of preparing food, and thus left the business of the housewife far less important and interesting. The Civil War in the United States was the occasion for the entrance of larger numbers of women into the teaching profession. Inventions such as the telephone called for women operators; business development made room for stenographers, clerks, secretaries, department heads, and executives. Many women from middle and well-to-do classes have come to enjoy the outside contacts and economic independence which such employments make possible. Public education fits them for efficient service.

The drift of population to the cities affects marriage and family life in several ways. The marriage rate in cities is lower than in the country, due in part to the higher cost of renting and furnishing dwellings in the city. Expense tends to discourage many young married people from raising a family. Children seem particularly out of place in a modern city apartment; but any city dwelling, with little or no opportunity for convenient play space, seems a poor place for a child to thrive in. No one, says Russell, would undertake to grow young trees in separate cellars in the city.

Modern inventions have displaced the home as a centre of enjoyment also. The automobile to some extent opposed family disintegration, because the tendency was for the family to move about together, but it brought also new perils. The moving-picture which has become a leading type of recreation also invites the whole family, but like the automobile it takes the family away from home. The city dwelling tends to become smaller and smaller. It has no best room, in which the young people can entertain their friends. The old neighborhood relationships which were based on the mutual acquaintance of families have practically ceased to exist. The younger generation finds its own recreation and enjoyment not only apart from the parents but without the supervision of parents and neighbors, which although usually friendly was nevertheless real under older conditions.

The automobile, the night club or dance hall, and other present forms of diversion, are not favorable to common participation by parents and children.

Changes in the external conditions of family and home have been accompanied by radical changes in ideas.

First came a modification of view as to *divorce*. In England until 1857 absolute divorce with the right to remarry had been possible only by an act of Parliament. Between 1800 and 1850 only ninety such acts were passed. The Act of 1857 established a court to hear and adjudicate procedures. Divorce was granted to the husband on the ground of adultery and to the wife if she could prove not only adultery on the part of the husband but also some aggravation of that act or addition to it, as by desertion. But even after this Act of 1857 divorce continued to be infrequent in England, ranging for the remainder of the century from about 300 to about 1,000 divorces (including judicial separations) annually. In the United States (except in South Carolina which grants no divorce) legal divorce has been easier than in England. It has, however, increased rapidly since 1870. In that year 10,962 divorces were granted; in 1930 there were 191,591. The population had increased from 38.5 millions to about three times that number; the divorces had increased to about seventeen times as many as the number in 1870. Or looking at the matter from another angle, the divorces now average about one to every six marriages—fewer in the East, more in the West and Southwest; fewer in agricultural life, more among actors, musicians, telegraph and telephone operators, and commercial travelers; fewer among rural, more among urban residents.

Change in social attitude has been correspondingly striking. In 1870, divorce in the Eastern states, at least, was not good form. The view, which is still registered by the British royal court in the regulation that divorced persons are not presented at court, was virtually the prevailing view in American society. At present, however, when religious restraints are no longer so widely felt, and when the ratio of divorce to marriages is about one to six or seven, there is little mental and social opposition to be overcome if husband or wife becomes dissatisfied. The increase of divorce, which has been steady since 1870 and as yet shows no sign of lessening, has given rise to anxiety, for it seems to indicate a radical change in the attitude toward marriage.

Yet this increase in divorce, unfortunate as it often is for the children, is not the most serious phase of the situation. With the common tendency in America to enter upon marriage chiefly upon the basis of emotion, it is not surprising that difficulties of adjustment—intellectual, economic, social, and sexual—often prove too great. Companionship may then fail to supervene when the first flush of emotion has passed. Statistics show that where there are no children, discontent is especially likely to follow. Divorce, however, does not necessarily imply that the institution of marriage is a failure, for divorced persons not infrequently marry again in the hope of a more successful union. The more radical threats to the family are found, not in divorce, but in certain attitudes toward the desirability of any family life.

The first of these attitudes is that sex relations are a purely individual matter, in which no one except the parties concerned has any rightful interest. It is held by some representatives of this view that the coming of children does create a situation which society may properly recognize in requiring provision for their care. The second attitude goes still further. It would not place responsibility for the care and upbringing of children upon the parents. It maintains that this responsibility can better be assumed by society itself through proper experts. The tendency of either of the above theories would be to remove much if not all social, legal, and moral support from the institution of the family, and to encourage casual attachments instead of permanent unions. We may consider the bearings of these theories first from the point of view of the man and woman, and secondly as they affect children.

These more radical questionings of the institutions of marriage and family spring from (1) an increased emphasis upon sex, and (2) an expansion of individualism, already powerful economically and politically, to a new significance in personal relations, particularly those of sex.

The significance of sex has been emphasized recently along two lines—the one esthetic, the other psychological.

In the esthetic field the modern novel has focussed attention upon the emotional life, and especially upon its stresses and conflicts. Romances have magnified the charm of idealized sex interest. Realistic schools have magnified physiological aspects. The problem novel has portrayed the waywardness of sex passion, as over against the restraints of law or convention, in the often used "triangle." The total effect has tended to make men, and especially women—since these are perhaps greater readers of fiction —probably more sex conscious than any previous generation. The high degree of this interest is indicated by the enormous circulation of the magazines which publish "true stories" or "confessions" of what profess to be actual life experiences.

The psychological influence is found in the school of Freud. This school has magnified the place of sex and has emphasized dangers of repression of this primitive urge. It has professed to find evidences of sex, not merely in the adolescent and later years, but from infancy on. Taking various forms the libido becomes, like Schopenhauer's Will to Live or Nietzsche's Will to Power, the fundamental drive in all human life, waking or dreaming. The Unconscious is constantly carrying on and watching an opportunity to slip by the "censor." It is perilous to repress so fundamental a drive, since this is likely to force a disastrous introversion, or to lead to an exaggeration of the very interest temporarily repressed. Asceticism may thus, according to this theory, plunge its victim into disorganized passions. It is no doubt true that in their concern to control this passion of sex, religion and society have too often relied upon asceticism, or repression, or upon ignoring facts, rather than upon frank and intelligent consideration of its meaning and implications. The recent tendency, however, to emphasize sex in fiction and in psychological theory has brought the subject into the open. Whether the effect has been to exaggerate by isolation, or to prepare the way for a truer estimate of the significance of sex in its relations to other life interests, is not yet apparent.

The extension of individualism to the sphere of marriage is not surprising. The age recognizes both the right of the individual to be himself, and the importance for society that each individual should respect himself and set a high worth upon his own life, his own ends, and his own method of finding and making his peculiar contribution to the whole of human living. Not merely writers who express the drive of selfish enjoyments or egoism, but still more strongly those who have thought in high terms of broadly human ends, have insisted on the worth of the individual. The worth of the soul was the dominant conception of Christian thought which found expression in the challenge—

what shall it profit a man if he shall gain the whole world and lose his own soul? Kant, the great representative of the place of duty in the moral life, laid down as one of his universal principles: "man and generally any rational being exists as an end in himself, not merely as a means to be arbitrarily used by this or that will," and adds, "man necessarily conceives his own existence as being so" [i.e., as an end in itself].

New applications of this principle of the worth of the individual appeared in the last century in movements for emancipation of slaves, for extension of suffrage—first to wider number of males and then to women—in the philosophy of the social settlement as contrasted with earlier philanthropies, in the general extension of the opportunities of education. In the economic world, freedom of initiative has been prized, even if not secured. In the political sphere, individual rights have been zealously guarded by constitutional law. The whole trend of the age is away from the ascetic ideal, which would repress certain aspects of human nature, particularly those renounced in the threefold vow of poverty, chastity, and obedience. The age is no less against institutions or modes of securing or maintaining social ends which require sacrifice of individual life and happiness. Such methods as war, which formerly seemed necessary, are coming more and more to seem futile. If marriage and the family are in opposition to the fundamental worth and development of the individual, they have a difficult case to plead before the bar of present opinion.

And as a preliminary to a consideration of the values of marriage and the family, it should be repeated that the question is one to be settled, not by a general rule, but by taking into account the special and peculiar factors in each case. While this is true of all moral action it is eminently true of a relationship so personal and intimate as that of marriage and the family. It should further be said that conditions of health and temperament may very properly preclude marriage for some. A decided bent toward certain careers, such as in older days would have been regarded as a "call," is also a factor to be considered. In former times such a "call" was not uncommon in the field of religious service. Today a similar sense of social responsibility may be felt with reference to other lines of work. Yet with due recognition of the individual nature of all choice, and of the exceptional factors in certain cases, we may consider important reasons to be weighed by the average person and especially by the college student.

§ 3. Marriage from the Individual Point of View

To begin with the more immediate factors we have first of all to recognize that in normal individuals the sex impulse, on the one hand, needs expression or satisfaction, and, on the other, needs to be so refined and related to the individual's total interests and emotional life as to remain in due perspective. Sex impulse thwarted or repressed may give rise to abnormality, to coldness and narrowness, or even to psychoses and neuroses. Sex impulse uncontrolled—or without the refining and intimate association with intellectual, esthetic, and social interests and influences—may coarsen and distort personality. If women have suffered more from the first of these alternatives, men in resorting to a sex satisfaction separated from all other steadying and elevating contacts have suffered more from the second.

Consider next other needs which are to be met in some way—for companionship, stability, mutual encouragement. It is not necessary to praise friendship. "No one," says Aristotle, "would care to live without friends though he had all other good things." Moreover, he continues, "friendship is not only an indispensable but also a beautiful or noble thing." And still further, the truest and best love and friendship "requires long and familiar intercourse." For, as the proverb says, "it is impossible for people to know one another till they have consumed the requisite quantity of salt together." And while friendship between men or between women is entitled to all the encomia which have been given it, there are certain respects in which the friendship between man and woman which marriage affords when at its best is more intimate, more beautiful, and more mutually helpful than any other. The fact of sharing ambitions, hopes, experiences of joy and sorrow, especially of united planning and concern for the welfare and futures of children, builds up a certain community of life which is found in no other type of experience.

Recognizing then the facts of sex and friendship, the question from the individual point of view is (1) whether it is better to keep these interests relatively fluid so that they may be changed at will, or to plan for a permanent structure with the hope that they will gain by stability; and (2) whether it is better to keep one or both of these interests separate from others, or to combine them with each other and with cooperation for further ends.

In favor of keeping sex and friendship ties fluid is the consideration that one is doubtless freer in certain respects if one can make and break relations as tastes and moods change. In the case of friendships it is not infrequent to find ourselves outgrowing youthful attachments—although probably few intimate friendships are formed after middle life, or even after thirty. Emotion and passion are susceptible to ebb as well as flood; why commit oneself? In favor of keeping sex a separate, as well as an easily changed interest, it may be argued that sex attraction is notoriously not based on rational grounds, and is with difficulty subject to rational control. Conceivably one might prefer to keep this separate from friendship based on mutuality of interests and community of tastes.

In favor of permanence of commitment and of combining sex with friendship and other interest is the consideration that a great factor in human advance from the relatively planless and casual existence of the animal world to a significant and worth while life has been the ability and disposition of civilized man to plan and work continuously for distant ends, and to build institutions to give strength and support to his plans and efforts. The wise individual, instead of abdicating control over passion, so organizes his life as to make passion and emotion contribute to its fullness. To this end he has to commit himself and undertake responsibilities. Fullness of life and the more lasting joys are not attained by a casual dependence upon whatever allures. And the gratification of sex makes its finest contribution when it is associated with the refining influences of art, the dignity of intelligent guidance, a "partnership in the whole of life" as the Roman jurist defined marriage, the grace of affection, and for many, the sacredness of a religious institution. It suffers by isolation.

Much depends upon what standard for decision is, perhaps unconsciously, used. Some frankly ask primarily, Will marriage and family give me pleasure? "Now," writes Professor Groves, "it is demanded of both matrimony and the family that they accept the testing of the pleasure standards which in our time are commonly used as a means of measurement for all sorts of social activities."[6] The question of pleasure is doubtless one of the factors that must be considered. Feeling is an important part of life, and an anticipation of happiness is an almost indispensable condition of a successful marriage.

But granting the relevance of the question whether marriage and family give pleasure, two other points demand a hearing. In the first place, am I to expect that I as an already completely finished individual, am to be made happy without effort, and without adjustment to the other member of the partnership? or are mutual adjustment, give and take, and cooperation for a common end, to be presupposed as the necessary conditions of a fair test? In the second place, is it possible that the venture of creating something not yet experienced, of building a structure in which new values will find a dwelling place, ought to count in our final weighing and testing?

Ambitious young men find an opportunity for self-development and for usefulness in the community by creating or building something—a business, an industry, a church, a school, a "practice," a professional reputation. They expect difficulties, anxieties, disappointment, but hold to their purpose in the belief that such creative work will yield increasing and substantial satisfaction.

Plato finely expressed one aspect of this, when he said that the fundamental principle in love is not merely the love of beauty but the love of creation. Whether creative in bodies or in souls, men seek immortality through offspring, through a fair name, through the ordering of States and families. Viewed as an opportunity to create a new sphere of enhanced living the community of marriage and family may make a strong appeal.

§ 4. Marriage from the Social Point of View

The growth of the consciousness of individuality fosters a disposition to decide problems on an individualistic basis. And yet few of us wish to decide a highly important question without

6. Groves and Ogburn, *American Marriage and Family Relationships*, p. 26.

looking at it in all its bearings. Least of all the college student who inherits from all the ages and is in a fuller sense than most persons profiting from the community of which he is a member. The seriousness and devotion, with which the young people of all the countries engaged in the World War showed their willingness to give themselves to what they believed to be a worthy cause, is a sufficient proof if any were needed that our younger generations are made of the same stuff as that which has been shown through the ages in the service of social ends.

"If," writes America's great legal and social philosopher, Mr. Justice Holmes,

> we think of our existence not as that of a little God outside [the universe] but as that of a ganglion within, we have the infinite behind us. It gives us our only but our adequate significance. . . . If our imagination is strong enough to accept the vision of ourselves as parts inseparable from the rest, and to extend our final interest beyond the boundary of our skins, it justifies the sacrifice even of our lives for ends outside of ourselves.[7]

"The motive, to be sure," adds Justice Holmes to the thought of the quotation above, "is the common wants and ideals that we find in man." But the adjustment of the claims, on the one hand, of individual ambitions, development, and joys; on the other, of social claims, is a problem which each must work out anew. In an ideal stage of human development, the issue might be less that of "either-or" and more that of "both" than it is at present, but in the language of the chapter on the self, this adjustment will always be a moral question. Each must make his own decision, but we may present some of the considerations to be taken into account.

When we think of ourselves as parts of the human family, and when we think of our life as an opportunity not merely for enjoyment or even for liberty but for creative work, we have to recognize that for most of us this means cooperation with others to accomplish what no individual can accomplish by himself. We find ourselves here entering upon opportunities made possible by ages of struggle, by patient researches of scientists, by brilliant

7. *Collected Legal Papers*, New York, 1920, p. 316.

discoveries of inventors, by the labor of countless "unknown soldiers" of the common good. We feel it a privilege as well as an obligation to "carry on." If we have healthy bodies—and with the growing progress of hygiene and medicine, health is becoming more and more part of our morality as well as of our pleasure—one of the ways in which we may make our contribution is through bringing new life into being, and giving to our children the best in our power.

It has been suggested by a recent writer[8] that today we are not so sure, as men once were, that the world needs to increase its population. Rapid growth of population with a large birth rate has been characteristic of cruder civilizations which sought to gain superior advantage in man-power or to compensate for the high death rate incidental to ignorance and lack of sanitation. Further the overpopulation of certain countries has been alleged as a justification for invasion of other lands, or for planting colonies where they are not wanted. Why then add to the evil of overpopulation? In answer it may be freely granted that there is no good reason for increasing the total population of the world, and that some countries are already overpopulated. The question is one of quality rather than of quantity. Admitting that as yet our knowledge of eugenics is very imperfect it is still reasonable to hold that on the whole children of healthy parents inherit a better physical organism than children of diseased or feeble-minded parents, and that children of educated parents are likely to be better cared for and better prepared to play their part in life than children of ignorant parents.

In fact at the present time many thoughtful students believe that the problem of maintaining the best stocks is one of the most serious which confronts us. For it is evident that the birth rate among the better educated as well as the more prosperous financially is decreasing both absolutely and relatively to the birth rate among other elements of the population. Dr. Cattell, editor of the volume, *American Men of Science*, has found that the completed family of contemporary scientific men is about two, and the number of surviving children for each scientific man about 1.6. The tendency of those in professional occupa-

8. Ruth Reed, *The Modern Family*, 1929.

tions is to postpone marriage until about thirty. Reasons of health or expense tend to limit the number of children after marriage. Among the well-to-do, reasons of expense can scarcely be recognized, and it must be assumed that luxury and convenience play a large role. In an agricultural population children were an economic asset and a provision for old age. The modern man is more likely to think of them as an expense, and to seek provision for old age through insurance. But the very fact that many fail in their contribution to the membership of a better society makes it all the more important that those who are well and able should do their share. In so doing they may find that enlargement of life, that joy in expectation and fulfillment of promise, that oneness with the great stream of living and working which is one of the deeper sources of satisfaction.

To look at marriage and family from the social point of view requires us to consider also the part they play in social structure. Society through language, tradition, mutual aid, varied stimulation, largely makes human life what it is. And of all its units kin and family have been the most firmly knit and influential. The researches of anthropology show flexibility of form, with emphasis now on the father, now on the mother; they show, however, the persistent, steady power of the institution into which every one is born and by which he receives his earliest impressions. The biological drives lead on to sentiments. If trade calls out shrewdness, and government teaches justice, it is kin and family which develop sympathy and kindness. Because a human being is by nothing so eminently human and richly individual as by the fact that he is a person, so he gets his personality through a personal group—not in an impersonal relation. For the personal is evoked by personal relations. Cultural influences, art, poetry, on the one hand find emotional sources in love, and on the other reach to refine and enrich passional and parental influences. Religion has found in father and mother symbols of tenderness and unforgetting care, and in turn has lent to human ties additional sacredness. The anthropologist Malinowski, in concluding an investigation of parenthood from a functional point of view, says, "the institutions of marriage and the family are indispensable."

Do children need parents? For even if parents do need children to make life full, and to provide objects on which affection may find its appropriate expression, it may seem that the family is after all less competent than society at large to bring up children. There is very general assent to the wisdom of taking children from home for at least part of their education after they have reached a certain age. The environment of home is too narrow, too strongly personal and emotional. The child in school is likely to behave better and to be better taught by the experts that society at large can provide. Hence the query, may not the same principle be applied to the care of infancy and early childhood? Would not a corps of physicians, nurses, and nursery teachers, get better results than the present more or less haphazard practices of feeding and forming habits, under ignorant parental care or lack of care? In reply to these questions it must be agreed that there is a great deal of ignorance on the part of parents as to the care of children's bodies, and still greater ignorance as to the proper care of their minds and especially their morals. And yet it does not logically follow that impersonal care by experts will be a better way on the whole. The past few years have seen a wide spread among parents of knowledge as to the proper feeding of children. This is an encouragement to look for similar improvement in knowledge along the more difficult lines of behavior and moral education. The best scientific opinion thus far is that the infant under the impersonal care of an institution misses something vital, namely, that some one loves him.

Granted that an exclusive home environment is too strongly personal and emotional, we yet know too little about the conditions of normal balance between the intimately personal, on the one hand, and the general, social, and impersonal, on the other, to warrant the entire abandonment of the former. If the child who lives too exclusively in the family environment may become an "introvert," it is quite possible that the child who has no specific and personal relationships of sympathy and affection may be so exclusively "extrovert" as to lack valuable elements of talent and character. As the attending nurse in an institution that cares exceptionally well for the bodily and mental welfare of children put it, in speaking of those under her care, "They haven't any insides."

§ 5. Special Sources of Friction and Needs for Adjustment

To believe profoundly in marriage and family for the normal human being does not imply that we ignore the many defects and sources of friction in these institutions. Some of these have lessened in importance with the general progress of education and culture; others have become more acute. Among the sources of unhappiness with respect to which conditions have improved in recent years may be included economic and "political" attitudes. Among those which have come more acutely to consciousness are those of sex.

Under economic conditions a distinction must first be made between industry and business. Industry has thus far affected chiefly the less well-to-do and the less highly educated. In this field there has been little recent change in the situation so far as it affects women and children. The numbers of women in industry tend somewhat slowly to increase, but among women in industry the radical change for marriage and the home took place at an earlier period. Business and professional careers, on the contrary, have recently been opening progressively to the entrance of women of the well-to-do and educated members of the community. It has thus made these women less ready to accept marriage and domestic life, except on the basis of affection. Economic stress is no longer so important as in the days when the alternative was marriage or dependence upon some male relative. At first the alternatives of marriage *or* a career seemed mutually exclusive. No doubt it is still frequently difficult to do justice to both, but that it is not impossible is being proved by an increasing number.

In two respects the situation seems easier. When women at first began to consider gainful occupations after marriage there was a distinct prejudice against this on the part of husbands. It appeared to them to be a reflection upon their ability to support a wife. Support was a duty recognized by law. It was perhaps not surprising that they failed to recognize that a woman might have as strong a bent toward some profession or career other than housework as her husband, and that it would be unjust to deprive her of an opportunity for constructive work and a creative life. The general ability and vigor shown by women in various occupations to which they were new has done much to change this attitude on the part of intelligent men. The point is not at all that a man cannot "give her what she wants" in the way of money. The point is rather that she wishes the opportunity to do her own work in the world. For some the work she may prize most and find best suited to her capacities will lie in the making of a home and in the care and education of her children. But something like twenty per cent of college women have no children, and for many of these a life entirely limited to a city apartment would be empty. The woman of today does not care to live in "The Doll's House." In another respect, economic conditions have improved with the general advance of woman to suffrage and citizenship, namely, in provision for a proper distribution of family income between husband and wife without the necessity for the wife's "asking the husband for money." No one of mature years likes to be put in the position of asking another for money. Husband and wife are supposed to engage in a partnership according to the old Roman formula, "a partnership in the whole of life." Income may be earned by one or by both. In any case, expense ought to be shared, and the necessary income distributed according to the items for which each partner is individually responsible. Twenty-five years ago, the irritation caused by the status which was then common was frequently severe, and was rather general. Today, among educated people it is apparently much less. Joint checking accounts or individual checking accounts are convenient methods of adjustment. Among the working classes, family income is frequently handed over almost entire to the wife.

The question of authority within the home is likewise progressing with the general advance in educational and political emancipation. The word "obey" has been largely dropped from wedding ceremonies. In certain matters the husband may be better fitted to take final responsibility, in other matters the wife. In any case there should be consultation and give and take rather than assertion.

In sex relations between husband and wife the situation has undoubtedly become more conscious. The older policy of refraining from all discussions of this highly critical factor is undergoing a change. Along with educational and political emancipation has come the possibility of freer recognition of woman's sex life. Studies by Dr. Davis with the aid of an advisory committee of professional women, studies by several physicians, and by experts in social observation, have at least made a beginning in this direction. The study by Dr. Davis[9] of 1,000 married women and of 1,200 unmarried women has confirmed opinions from other sources that there is far less difference between men and women in both physical and emotional aspects of sex life than was formerly assumed to be the case. One of the facts brought out most clearly has been the value of preparation for marriage by instruction as to sex life, its meaning, its responsibilities, and its management, so as to insure a minimum of marital unhappiness and a maximum of harmony and mutual satisfaction. Dr. Davis found that among the 1,000 married women, 846 classed themselves as happy; but a considerable proportion of these underwent a period of unhappiness at the beginning of married life, which in their judgment would have been helped by proper previous instruction. Studies of the 1,200 unmarried women in Dr. Davis's survey show that among a considerable proportion those who have not married have nevertheless felt the need or desire for some form of sex satisfaction.

Another aspect of married life which has come especially under discussion is that of birth control or, as many prefer to call it, the proper spacing of children. Mankind from early times has controlled the birth—or at least the life of the newly born—in some fashion. Infanticide and abortion have been widely practiced. The more humane and intelligent have found less violent ways to limit births, by prevention of conception. In general, vigorous stocks under conditions of plentiful food-supply or agricultural life have had large families—and likewise the very poor and ignorant. In the early colonial period of the United States, families of the English and French emigrants were large. In recent years the birth rate among the native born of native parents in New England has sunk to 2.61, and the surviving family to 1.92. Similarly, Professor Cattell's study[10] has shown that whereas the families from which scientific men have come averaged 4.65, the families of these scientific men themselves average 2.28 children. Information given by 461 leading scientific men showed that the families of 176 had not been limited; that the

9. *Factors in the Sex Life of Twenty-two Hundred Women*, 1929.
10. *American Men of Science*, 3rd ed., 1921.

families of 285 had been voluntarily limited. Of these 285, the reasons assigned were: on account of health, 133; of expense, 98; of other causes, 54. Vigorous discussion has been called out on the one hand by these and other figures which reflect conditions among the educated and well-to-do classes; and on the other hand by the problems of social workers who find the poor and ignorant bringing large numbers of children into the world, whom they can neither feed nor educate properly, and doing this frequently at the serious cost of the mother's health. The two types of cases are evidently not of the same order. In the one case, there are too few children, in the other too many.

Birth control clinics to the number of seventy at this writing have been set up in various cities of the United States and Europe, primarily for the instruction of the poor and ignorant. The aim is to substitute medically approved methods of control for violent and criminal methods. The need for such control to meet conditions of health and expense has recently received recognition from the Lambeth Conference, which by a considerable majority recognizes the propriety of such control when not dictated by "selfishness, luxury, or convenience." It may be remarked parenthetically that these three motives are very poor motives for the guidance of any of the more serious affairs of life. For the well educated and well-to-do the apparent need is all in the direction of maintaining at least such a number of children as will serve to continue the family stock wherever conditions of health permit.

It is amusing and perhaps instructive to note that nature has made an experiment in the direction of separating sex satisfaction from parental care and of entrusting the nurture and rearing of the community's offspring entirely to workers that are not parents. Many of the hymenopterous insects have successfully followed this plan. The queen bee and the males have no further social responsibilities beyond production of progeny. The neutral workers care very efficiently for the young. In view of this the eminent biologist H. S. Jennings comments on the suggestion for public care of children, and isolation of sex life from parental functions.

As we find it in popular proposals, this aspiration appears largely dominated by the desire to set free and give full satisfaction to the mating impulse; to facilitate change in mates, making it unnecessary for them to remain tied to one another longer than fancy dictates. If we examine this aspect of the matter in the animals that have fully carried out this system of public care for the progeny, we find a surprising result. The system has resulted, not in the freeing of the mating impulses, but in their suppression; their almost complete extinction; in the essential desexualization of society. Only a few isolated individuals continue to be occupied with mating and propagation; the rank and file are sexless. If man must look to this result, possibly the enthusiasm for this system will abate.[11]

The facts are that whereas insects have successfully followed the proposed plan, mammals and in particular human beings have followed a line of development which has involved, for instance, long and intimate physical union between mother and offspring, helpless infancy, care of both mother and child by the male, education of the child by the parents, with an almost equally prominent reflex influence of the child upon the parents. To make a thorough success of the proposal, says Professor Jennings, man should have begun aeons ago, before he became a mammal. In that case, by the present time he might perhaps hope to rival the ants in social organization.

One of the broadest-minded of the writers upon women's sex life and the family is Ellen Key. She holds that the way out of some at least of our present difficulties lies in the direction of emphasizing rather than minimizing the importance of sex and motherhood in woman's life. She is distrustful of the effect upon woman's life of organized business and industry. She goes further than many in her concern that freedom and personality of the woman be not sacrificed to the supposed necessities of an institution. But she insists that it is not necessary to destroy the family in order to secure the right relationships for the personality of the wife and the development of the children.

It is not the family that ought to be abolished, but the rights of the family that must be reformed; not education by parents that ought to be avoided, but education of parents

11. Jennings, *The Biological Basis of Human Nature*, New York, 1930, p. 266.

that must be introduced; not the home that ought to be done away with, but homelessness that must cease.[12]

Fear has been expressed from time to time, and especially since the World War with its succeeding disillusionments, that the moral ideals and standards, the bonds of sympathy and duty, which have played so significant a role in individual character and social order are in danger of disappearing. The authors do not share this fear. They believe that the moral life is too deeply rooted in human nature and human needs to be either lost or discarded. For the moral life is a *life*, and life means power to adjust to changing conditions. It is precisely the new and serious situations that call out new vigor and lift to new levels. Ethical science, tracing and interpreting this process of growth and adjustment, has as its task, not to create moral life—for that life is already present—but to discover its laws and principles, and thereby aid in making its further advance stronger, freer, and more assured because more intelligent.

Literature

On the early forms of the Family, see the literature cited at the close of Chapters 2 and 4; also Goodsell, *A History of the Family as a Social and Educational Institution*, 1923; Howard, *A History of Matrimonial Institutions*, 3 vols., 1904; Westermarck, *The History of Human Marriage*, 1901; Sumner and Keller, *The Science of Society*, vol. 3, 1927; Briffault, *The Mothers*, 1927; on present problems: Bosanquet, *The Family*, 1906; A. W. Calhoun, *A Social History of the American Family*, 3 vols., 1917; Briffault, *op. cit.*, last chapter; Goodsell, *op. cit.*; Groves and Ogburn, *American Marriage and Family Relationships*, 1928; Jennings, *The Biological Basis of Human Nature*, 1930; McDougall, *Character and the Conduct of Life*, 1927; Malinowski, "Parenthood—The Basis of Social Structure," in Calverton and Schmalhausen, *The New Generation*, 1930; Popenoe, *The Conservation of the Family*, 1926; Reed, *The Modern Family*, 1929.

12. Ellen Key, *Love and Marriage*, p. 240.

Checklist of References

This section gives full publication information for each work cited. Books in Dewey's personal library (John Dewey Papers, Special Collections, Morris Library, Southern Illinois University at Carbondale) have been listed whenever possible. When Dewey or Tufts gave page numbers for a reference, the edition has been identified by locating the citation; for other references, the edition listed here is the most likely source by reason of place or date of publication, general accessibility during the period, or evidence from correspondence and other materials.

Adams, George Burton. *Civilization during the Middle Ages, Especially in Relation to Modern Civilization*. New York: Charles Scribner's Sons, 1894.

Addams, Jane. *Democracy and Social Ethics*. New York: Macmillan Co., 1902.

———. *Newer Ideals of Peace*. New York: Macmillan Co., 1907.

Adler, Felix. *An Ethical Philosophy of Life*. New York: D. Appleton and Co., 1918.

Albee, Ernest. *A History of English Utilitarianism*. New York: Macmillan Co., 1902.

Alexander, Samuel. *Moral Order and Progress: An Analysis of Ethical Conceptions*. London: Trübner and Co., 1889. [2d ed. London: Kegan Paul, Trench, Trübner, and Co., 1891.]

———. "The Meaning of 'Motive.'" *International Journal of Ethics* 4 (1894): 233–36.

Angell, Norman. *The Unseen Assassins*. New York: Harper and Bros., 1932.

Aristotle. *The Nicomachean Ethics of Aristotle*. 2d ed. Translated by F. H. Peters. London: Kegan Paul, Trench and Co., 1884.

———. *The Politics of Aristotle*. Translated by J. E. C. Welldon. London: Macmillan and Co., 1883.

Ashley, William James. *An Introduction to English Economic History and Theory*. 2 vols. London: Longmans, Green, and Co., 1888. [2d ed., 1892–93.]

Atkins, Willard E.; Douglas, Paul H.; and Hitchcock, Curtice N. *The*

Worker in Modern Economic Society. Chicago: University of Chicago Press, 1923.

Augustine, Saint. *The City of God*. Translated by John Healey. London: J. M. Dent and Sons, 1931.

Austin, John. *Lectures on Jurisprudence; or, The Philosophy of Positive Law*. Edited by Robert Campbell. 2 vols. London: John Murray, 1869. [4th ed., rev., 1873.]

Bacon, Francis. *New Atlantis*. Edited by G. C. Moore Smith. Cambridge: Cambridge University Press, 1919.

Bagehot, Walter. *Physics and Politics*. International Scientific Series, vol. 2. New York: D. Appleton and Co., 1890.

Bain, Alexander. *The Emotions and the Will*. London: John W. Parker and Son, 1859.

———. *Moral Science: A Compendium of Ethics*. New York: D. Appleton and Co., 1882.

Baldwin, James Mark. *Social and Ethical Interpretations in Mental Development: A Study in Social Psychology*. 3d ed., rev. and enl. New York: Macmillan Co., 1902.

———, ed. *Dictionary of Philosophy and Psychology*. 3 vols. in 4. New York: Macmillan Co., 1901–5.

Barker, Ernest. *Greek Political Theory: Plato and His Predecessors*. London: Methuen and Co., 1918.

Barton, George Aaron. *A Sketch of Semitic Origins, Social and Religious*. New York: Macmillan Co., 1902.

Beard, Charles Austin. *The Economic Basis of Politics*. New York: Alfred A. Knopf, 1922.

———, ed. *Whither Mankind: A Panorama of Modern Civilization*. New York: Longmans, Green and Co., 1928.

Benn, Alfred William. *The Philosophy of Greece Considered in Relation to the Character and History of Its People*. London: G. Richards, 1898.

Bent, Silas. *Ballyhoo: The Voice of the Press*. New York: Boni and Liveright, 1927.

———. *Machine Made Man*. New York: Farrar and Rinehart, 1930.

Bentham, Jeremy. *An Introduction to the Principles of Morals and Legislation*. New ed. 2 vols. London: Printed for W. Pickering, 1823.

Bergemann, Paul. *Ethik als Kulturphilosophie*. Leipzig: J. Hoffman, 1904.

Beveridge, William Henry. *Unemployment: A Problem of Industry (1909 and 1930)*. New imp. New York: Longmans, Green and Co., 1931.

Beyschlag, Willibald. *New Testament Theology*. Translated by Rev. Neil Buchanan. 2 vols. Edinburgh: T. and T. Clark, 1895.

Boas, Franz. *The Mind of Primitive Man*. New York: Macmillan Co., 1911.

————. "Anthropology." In *Encyclopaedia of the Social Sciences*, edited by Edwin R. A. Seligman, 2:73–110. New York: Macmillan Co., 1930.

Bonar, James. *The Intellectual Virtues*. New York: Macmillan Co., 1894.

————. *Moral Sense*. London: George Allen and Unwin, 1930.

————. *Philosophy and Political Economy in Some of Their Historical Relations*. London: Swan Sonnenschein and Co., 1893.

Bonner, Robert J., and Smith, Gertrude. *The Administration of Justice from Homer to Aristotle*. Vol. 1. Chicago: University of Chicago Press, 1930.

Bosanquet, Bernard. *The Philosophical Theory of the State*. New York: Macmillan Co., 1899.

————. *Psychology of the Moral Self*. New York: Macmillan Co., 1897.

Bosanquet, Helen. *The Family*. New York: Macmillan Co., 1906.

Bowne, Borden P. *The Principles of Ethics*. New York: Harper and Bros., 1892.

Bradley, Andrew Cecil. "Aristotle's Conception of the State." In *Hellenica: A Collection of Essays on Greek Poetry, Philosophy, History and Religion*, edited by Evelyn Abbott, pp. 181–243. New York: Longmans, Green, and Co., 1880.

Bradley, Francis Herbert. *Ethical Studies*. New York: G. E. Stechert and Co., 1904. [2d reprint, 1927.]

Brandes, George. *Main Currents in Nineteenth Century Literature*. Translated by Diana White and Mary Morison. 6 vols. London: William Heinemann, 1901–5.

Briffault, Robert. *The Mothers: A Study of the Origins of Sentiments and Institutions*. 3 vols. London: George Allen and Unwin, 1927.

Brimhall, Dean R., and Cattell, J. McKeen, eds. *American Men of Science: A Biographical Directory*. 3d ed. Garrison, N.Y.: Science Press, 1921.

Broad, Charlie Dunbar. *Five Types of Ethical Theory*. London: Kegan Paul, Trench, Trubner and Co., 1930.

Bruce, William Straton. *The Ethics of the Old Testament*. Edinburgh: T. and T. Clark, 1895.

Bryce, James. *The Holy Roman Empire*. New ed., rev. and enl. New York: Macmillan Co., 1904.

————. *Modern Democracies*. 2 vols. New York: Macmillan Co., 1921.

————. *Studies in History and Jurisprudence*. 2 vols. Oxford: At the Clarendon Press, 1901.

Bücher, Karl. *Arbeit und Rythmus*. 3d ed., enl. Tübingen: H. Laupp, 1901.

————. *Industrial Evolution*. 3d ed. Translated by S. Morley Wickett. New York: Henry Holt and Co., 1901.

Budde, Karl Ferdinand Reinhart. *Religion of Israel to the Exile*. American Lectures on the History of Religions, 4th series, 1898–99. New York: G. P. Putnam's Sons, 1899.

Burckhardt, Jakob Christoph. *The Civilisation of the Renaissance in Italy*. Half Guinea International Library. Translated by S. G. C. Middlemore. London: Swan Sonnenschein and Co., 1892.

Burgess, John William. *The Reconciliation of Government with Liberty*. New York: Charles Scribner's Sons, 1915.

Burnet, John. "Law and Nature in Greek Ethics." *International Journal of Ethics* 7 (1897): 328–33.

Burns, Cecil Delisle. *The Philosophy of Labour*. London: George Allen and Unwin, 1925.

Bury, John Bagnell. *A History of Freedom of Thought*. New York: Henry Holt and Co., 1913.

Butler, Joseph. *Fifteen Sermons*. London: Longman, Brown, Green, and Longmans, 1856.

Butler, Samuel. *Erewhon; or, Over the Range*. New York: E. P. Dutton and Co., 1917.

Caesar. *Caesar's Gallic War*. Reëdited from Allen and Greenough's ed. by James B. Greenough, Benjamin L. D'Ooge, and M. Grant Daniell. Boston: Ginn and Co., 1898.

Caird, Edward. *The Evolution of Theology in the Greek Philosophers*. 2 vols. Glasgow: James Maclehose and Sons, 1904.

Calderwood, Henry. *Handbook of Moral Philosophy*. 14th ed. London: Macmillan and Co., 1888.

Calhoun, Arthur Wallace. *A Social History of the American Family from Colonial Times to the Present*. 3 vols. Cleveland: Arthur H. Clark Co., 1917.

Calkins, Mary Whiton. *The Good Man and the Good: An Introduction to Ethics*. New York: Macmillan Co., 1918.

Carlyle, Alexander James. *A History of Mediaeval Political Theory in the West*. Vol. 1, *The Second Century to the Ninth*. Edinburgh: William Blackwood and Sons, 1903.

Carlyle, Thomas. *The Works of Thomas Carlyle*. Centenary ed. 31 vols. London: Chapman and Hall, 1898–1907. [*Past and Present*, vol. 10, 1899; *Latter-Day Pamphlets*, vol. 20, 1907.]

Carriere, Moriz. *Die Kunst im Zusammenhang der Culturentwickelung und die Ideale der Menschheit*. 3d ed., rev. 5 vols. Leipzig: F. A. Brockhaus, 1877–86.

Carver, Thomas Nixon. *Essays in Social Justice*. Cambridge: Harvard University Press, 1922.

————. *The Present Economic Revolution in the United States.*
Boston: Little, Brown, and Co., 1925.

Catlin, George Edward Gordon. *A Study of the Principles of Politics.*
New York: Macmillan Co., 1930.

Cattell, J. McKeen, and Brimhall, Dean R., eds. *American Men of Science: A Biographical Directory.* 3d ed. Garrison, N.Y.: Science
Press, 1921.

Chafee, Zechariah, Jr. *Freedom of Speech.* New York: Harcourt, Brace
and Howe, 1920.

Chase, Stuart. *Men and Machines.* New York: Macmillan Co., 1929.

————. *The Tragedy of Waste.* New York: Macmillan Co., 1926.

Cicero, Marcus Tullius. *De finibus bonorum et malorum libri V,* 3d ed.,
rev. Edited by Johan Nicolai Madvig. Copenhagen: Glydendal, 1876.

————. *De legibus libri tres.* Edited by W. D. Pearman. Cambridge:
J. Hall and Son, 1881.

————. *De natura deorum libri tres.* Edited by J. H. Swanson. 3 vols.
Cambridge: Cambridge University Press, 1883–91.

————. *De officiis libri tres.* 7th ed. Edited by Hubert Ashton Holden.
Cambridge: Cambridge University Press, 1891.

————. *De re publica.* In *Scripta Quae Manserunt Omnia,* edited by
Reinholdus Klotz, vol. 2. Leipzig: B. G. Teubneri, 1874.

Clark, John Maurice. *Social Control of Business.* Chicago: University
of Chicago Press, 1926.

Clay, Henry. *Economics: An Introduction for the General Reader.*
New York: Macmillan Co., 1923.

Clifford, William Kingdon. *Lectures and Essays.* 2d ed. Edited by Leslie Stephen and Frederick Pollock. New York: Macmillan Co., 1886.

Clutton-Brock, Arthur. *The Ultimate Belief.* New York: E. P. Dutton
and Co., 1916.

Cole, George Douglas Howard. *Labour in the Commonwealth.* New
York: B. W. Huebsch, 1919.

Commons, John Rogers. *Legal Foundations of Capitalism.* New York:
Macmillan Co., 1924.

————, et al. *History of Labour in the United States.* New York: Macmillan Co., 1918.

Comte, Auguste. *The Positive Philosophy of Auguste Comte.* Translated by Harriet Martineau. 2 vols. London: Trübner and Co., 1875.

————. *System of Positive Polity.* Translated by John Henry Bridges et
al. 4 vols. London: Longmans, Green, and Co., 1875–77.

Cone, Orello. *Paul: The Man, the Missionary, and the Teacher.* New
York: Macmillan Co., 1898.

Cook, Walter Wheeler. "Privileges of Labor Unions in the Struggle for
Life." *Yale Law Quarterly* 27 (1918): 779–801.

Cooley, Charles Horton. *Human Nature and the Social Order.* New York: Charles Scribner's Sons, 1902. [Rev. ed., 1922.]

——. *Social Organization: A Study of the Larger Mind.* New York: Charles Scribner's Sons, 1912.

——. *Social Process.* New York: Charles Scribner's Sons, 1918.

Coulanges. *See* Fustel de Coulanges.

Crawley, Alfred Ernest. *The Mystic Rose: A Study of Primitive Marriage and of Primitive Thought in Its Bearings on Marriage.* New York: Macmillan Co., 1902.

Crosby, Oscar T. *International War: Its Causes and Its Cure.* London: Macmillan and Co., 1919.

Cunningham, William. *An Essay on Western Civilization in Its Economic Aspects.* Cambridge Historical Series, edited by G. W. Prothero, 2 vols. Cambridge: Cambridge University Press, 1898–1900.

——. *The Growth of English Industry and Commerce.* 3d ed. 2 vols. Cambridge: Cambridge University Press, 1896–1903.

Darwin, Charles Robert. *The Descent of Man.* 2 vols. New York: D. Appleton and Co., 1871.

Davies, Joseph Edward. *Trust Laws and Unfair Competition.* March 15, 1915. Washington, D.C.: Government Printing Office, 1916.

Davis, Helen Edna. *Tolstoy and Nietzsche: A Problem in Biographical Ethics.* New York: New Republic, 1929.

Davis, Katharine Bement. *Factors in the Sex Life of Twenty-two Hundred Women.* New York: Harper and Bros., 1929.

Denis, Jacques François. *Histoire des théories et des idées morales dans l'antiquité.* 2d ed. 2 vols. Paris: E. Thorin, 1879.

Dewey, John. *Human Nature and Conduct.* New York: Henry Holt and Co., 1922. [*The Middle Works of John Dewey, 1899–1924*, edited by Jo Ann Boydston, vol. 14. Carbondale and Edwardsville: Southern Illinois University Press, 1983.]

——. *Individualism, Old and New.* New York: Minton, Balch and Co., 1930. [*The Later Works of John Dewey, 1925–1953*, edited by Jo Ann Boydston, 5:41–123. Carbondale and Edwardsville: Southern Illinois University Press, 1984.]

——. *Logical Conditions of a Scientific Treatment of Morality.* Chicago: University of Chicago Press, 1903. [*Middle Works 3*: 3–39.]

——. *Outlines of a Critical Theory of Ethics.* Ann Arbor: Register Publishing Co., 1891. [*The Early Works of John Dewey, 1882–1898*, edited by Jo Ann Boydston, 3:237–388. Carbondale and Edwardsville: Southern Illinois University Press, 1969.]

——. *The Public and Its Problems.* New York: Henry Holt and Co., 1927. [*Later Works 2*:235–372.]

———. *The Quest for Certainty*. New York: Minton, Balch and Co., 1929; London: George Allen and Unwin, 1930. [*Later Works* 4.]

———. *Reconstruction in Philosophy*. New York: Henry Holt and Co., 1920; London: University of London Press, 1921. [*Middle Works* 12:77–201.]

———. *The Study of Ethics: A Syllabus*. Ann Arbor: Register Publishing Co., 1894. [*Early Works* 4:219–362.]

———. "The Evolutionary Method as Applied to Morality. I. Its Scientific Necessity." *Philosophical Review* 11 (1902): 107–24; "II. Its Significance for Conduct." Ibid., pp. 353–71. [*Middle Works* 2:3–38.]

———. "Interpretation of Savage Mind." *Psychological Review* 9 (1902): 217–30. [*Middle Works* 2:39–52.]

———. "Moral Theory and Practice." *International Journal of Ethics* 1 (1891): 186–203. [*Early Works* 3:103–9.]

———. "Self-Realization as the Moral Ideal." *Philosophical Review* 2 (1893): 652–64. [*Early Works* 4:42–53.]

Dicey, Albert Venn. *Lectures on the Relation between Law and Public Opinion in England during the Nineteenth Century*. London: Macmillan and Co., 1905. [2d ed., 1914.]

Dinsmore, Charles Allen. *Atonement in Literature and Life*. Boston: Houghton, Mifflin and Co., 1906.

Director, Aaron, and Douglas, Paul H. *The Problem of Unemployment*. New York: Macmillan Co., 1931.

Donham, Wallace Brett. *Business Adrift*. New York: McGraw-Hill Book Co., Whittlesey House, 1931.

Döring, August. *Die Lehre des Sokrates als sociales Reformsystem: Neuer Versuch zur Lösung des Problems der Sokratischen Philosophie*. Munich: C. H. Beck, 1895.

Dorsey, James Owen. "Omaha Sociology." In *Third Annual Report of the Bureau of Ethnology to the Secretary of the Smithsonian Institution 1881–'82*, pp. 205–370. Washington, D.C.: Government Printing Office, 1884.

———. "A Study of Siouan Cults." In *Eleventh Annual Report of the Bureau of Ethnology to the Secretary of the Smithsonian Institution 1889–'90*, pp. 361–544. Washington, D.C.: Government Printing Office, 1894.

Douglas, Paul H., and Director, Aaron. *The Problem of Unemployment*. New York: Macmillan Co., 1931.

Douglas, Paul H.; Hitchcock, Curtice N.; and Atkins, Willard E. *The Worker in Modern Economic Society*. Chicago: University of Chicago Press, 1923.

Drake, Durant. *The New Morality*. New York: Macmillan Co., 1928.

Draper, John William. *History of the Intellectual Development of Europe.* Rev. ed. 2 vols. New York: Harper and Bros., 1876.

Driesch, Hans. *Ethical Principles in Theory and Practice: An Essay in Moral Philosophy.* Translated by W. H. Johnston. London: George Allen and Unwin, 1930.

Dunning, William Archibald. *A History of Political Theories Ancient and Medieval.* New York: Macmillan Co., 1902.

———. *A History of Political Theories from Luther to Montesquieu.* New York: Macmillan Co., 1905.

Durkheim, Émile. *De la division du travail social: Étude sur l'organisation des sociétés supérieures.* Paris: F. Alcan, 1893.

Eastman, Charles Alexander. *Indian Boyhood.* New York: McClure, Phillips and Co., 1902.

Eaton, Howard Ormsby. *The Austrian Philosophy of Values.* Norman: University of Oklahoma Press, 1930.

Eckenstein, Lina. *Woman under Monasticism: Chapters on Saint-Hood and Convent Life between A.D. 500 and A.D. 1500.* Cambridge: Cambridge University Press, 1896.

Eicken, Heinrich von. *Geschichte und System der mittelalterlichen Weltanschauung.* Stuttgart: J. G. Cotta, 1887.

Eliot, George. *Romola.* London: J. M. Dent and Co., 1907.

Encyclopedia Biblica. Edited by Thomas Kelly Cheyne and John Sutherland Black. 4 vols. New York: Macmillan Co., 1899–1903.

Epictetus. *The Discourses of Epictetus.* Translated by George Long. 2 vols. London: George Bell and Sons, 1903.

Erdmann, Johann Eduard. *A History of Philosophy.* 2d ed. Translated by Williston S. Hough. 3 vols. London: Swan Sonnenschein and Co., 1892–97.

Everett, Walter Goodnow. *Moral Values: A Study of the Principles of Conduct.* New York: Henry Holt and Co., 1918.

Falckenberg, Richard Friedrich Otto. *History of Modern Philosophy from Nicolas of Cusa to the Present Time.* Translated by Andrew Campbell Armstrong, Jr. New York: Henry Holt and Co., 1893.

Farnell, Lewis Richard. *The Cults of the Greek States.* 3 vols. Oxford: At the Clarendon Press, 1896.

Faulkner, Harold Underwood. *The Quest for Social Justice, 1898–1914.* A History of American Life, vol. 11. New York: Macmillan Co., 1931.

Fewkes, Jesse Walter. "Hopi Katcinas." In *Twenty-First Annual Report of the Bureau of Ethnology to the Secretary of the Smithsonian Institution 1899–1900,* pp. 13–126. Washington, D.C.: Government Printing Office, 1903.

———. "Tusayan Katcinas." In *Fifteenth Annual Report of the Bureau of Ethnology to the Secretary of the Smithsonian Institution*

1893–'94, pp. 245–313. Washington, D.C.: Government Printing Office, 1897.

Fichte, Johann Gottlieb. *The Characteristics of the Present Age.* In *The Popular Works of Johann Gottlieb Fichte*, 4th ed., translated by William Smith, vol. 2, pp. 1–288. London: Trübner and Co., 1889.

Fischer, Kuno. *History of Modern Philosophy.* Translated by J. P. Gordy. Edited by Noah Porter. New York: Charles Scribner's Sons, 1887.

Fiske, John. *Outlines of Cosmic Philosophy.* 4 vols. Boston: Houghton Mifflin Co., 1903.

———. *Through Nature to God.* Boston: Houghton Mifflin Co., 1899.

Fison, Lorimer, and Howitt, Alfred William. *Kamilaroi and Kurnai.* Melbourne: G. Robertson, 1880.

Fite, Warner. *Individualism: Four Lectures on the Significance of Consciousness for Social Relations.* New York: Longmans, Green, and Co., 1911.

———. *An Introductory Study of Ethics.* New York: Longmans, Green, and Co., 1903.

———. *Moral Philosophy: The Critical View of Life.* New York: Dial Press, 1925.

Fletcher, Alice C. "The Hako: A Pawnee Ceremony." In *Twenty-Second Annual Report of the Bureau of Ethnology to the Secretary of the Smithsonian Institution 1900–1901*, part 2, pp. 1–368. Washington, D.C.: Government Printing Office, 1904.

Follett, Mary Parker. *The New State: Group Organization the Solution of Popular Government.* New York: Longmans, Green and Co., 1918.

Fowler, Thomas, and Wilson, John Matthias. *The Principles of Morals.* 2 vols. Oxford: At the Clarendon Press, 1886–87.

Francke, Kuno. *Social Forces in German Literature: A Study in the History of Civilization.* New York: Henry Holt and Co., 1896.

Frankfurter, Felix, and Greene, Nathan. *The Labor Injunction.* New York: Macmillan Co., 1930.

Frazer, James George. *The Golden Bough: A Study in Magic and Religion.* 2d ed., rev. and enl. 3 vols. New York: Macmillan Co., 1900.

———. *Totemism and Exogamy: A Treatise on Certain Early Forms of Superstition and Society.* London: Macmillan and Co., 1910.

Freund, Ernst. *The Police Power: Public Policy and Constitutional Rights.* Chicago: Callaghan and Co., 1904.

———. *Standards of American Legislation: An Estimate of Restrictive and Constructive Factors.* Chicago: University of Chicago Press, 1917.

Fustel de Coulanges, Numa Denis. *The Ancient City: A Study on the Religion, Laws, and Institutions of Greece and Rome.* Translated by Willard Small. Boston: Lee and Shepard, 1874.

Genung, John Franklin. *The Epic of the Inner Life: Being the Book of Job.* Boston: Houghton Mifflin Co., 1900.

Giddings, Franklin Henry. *Inductive Sociology: A Syllabus of Methods, Analyses and Classifications, and Provisionally Formulated Laws.* New York: Macmillan Co., 1901.

————. *The Principles of Sociology: An Analysis of the Phenomena of Association and of Social Organization.* 3d ed. New York: Macmillan Co., 1896.

Gide, Charles, and Rist, Charles. *A History of Economic Doctrines from the Time of the Physiocrats to the Present Day.* Boston: D. C. Heath and Co., 1915.

Gillen, Francis James, and Spencer, Baldwin. *The Native Tribes of Central Australia.* London: Macmillan and Co., 1899.

————. *The Northern Tribes of Central Australia.* London: Macmillan and Co., 1904.

Godwin, William. *An Enquiry concerning Political Justice and Its Influence on General Virtue and Happiness.* New York: Alfred A. Knopf, 1926.

Goldenweiser, Alexander A. *Early Civilization.* New York: Alfred A. Knopf, 1922.

Goldenweiser, Alexander A., and Ogburn, William Fielding, eds. *The Social Sciences and Their Interrelations.* Boston: Houghton Mifflin Co., 1927.

Goldsmith, Oliver. *The Vicar of Wakefield.* Edited by Mary A. Jordan. New York: Longmans, Green, and Co., 1898.

Gomperz, Theodor. *Greek Thinkers: A History of Ancient Philosophy.* 3 vols. [Vol. 1 translated by Laurie Magnus; vols. 2 and 3 translated by George Godfrey Berry.] London: John Murray, 1901–5.

Goodnow, Frank Johnson. *Social Reform and the Constitution.* New York: Macmillan Co., 1911.

Goodsell, Willystine. *A History of the Family as a Social and Educational Institution.* New York: Macmillan Co., 1923.

Grandgent, Charles Hall. *Dante.* New York: Duffield and Co., 1916.

Gray, John Henry. *China: A History of the Laws, Manners, and Customs of the People.* Edited by William Gow Gregor. 2 vols. London: Macmillan and Co., 1878.

Green, Thomas Hill. *Lectures on the Principles of Political Obligation.* In *Works of Thomas Hill Green,* edited by R. L. Nettleship, vol. 2. London: Longmans, Green, and Co., 1886.

————. *Prolegomena to Ethics.* Edited by A. C. Bradley. Oxford: At the Clarendon Press, 1883. [3d ed., 1890.]

Greene, Nathan, and Frankfurter, Felix. *The Labor Injunction*. New York: Macmillan Co., 1930.

Grosse, Ernst. *Die Formen der Familie und die Formen der Wirthschaft*. Freiburg and Leipzig: J. C. B. Mohr, 1896.

Grote, George. *A History of Greece*. 4th ed. Vol. 3. London: John Murray, 1872.

———. *Plato, and the Other Companions of Sokrates*. London: John Murray, 1888.

Grote, John. *An Examination of the Utilitarian Philosophy*. Cambridge: Deighton, Bell, and Co., 1870.

Groves, Ernest Rutherford, and Ogburn, William Fielding. *American Marriage and Family Relationships*. New York: Henry Holt and Co., 1928.

Gruening, Ernest Henry. *The Public Pays: A Study of Power Propaganda*. New York: Vanguard Press, [1931].

Gummere, Francis Barton. *The Beginnings of Poetry*. New York: Macmillan Co., 1901.

Guyau, Jean Marie. *A Sketch of Morality Independent of Obligation or Sanction*. 2d ed. Translated by G. Kapteyn. London: Watts and Co., 1898.

Hadley, Arthur Twining. *Economic Problems of Democracy*. New York: Macmillan Co., 1923.

———. *The Relations between Freedom and Responsibility in the Evolution of Democratic Government*. New York: Charles Scribner's Sons, 1903.

———. *Standards of Public Morality*. New York: Macmillan Co., 1912.

Halévy, Élie. *La Formation du radicalisme philosophique*. 3 vols. Paris: F. Alcan, 1901–4.

Hall, Thomas Cuming. *The Religious Background of American Culture*. Boston: Little, Brown, and Co., 1930.

Hamilton, Walton Hale. *Current Economic Problems*. 3d ed. Chicago: University of Chicago Press, [1925].

———. "Freedom and Economic Necessity." In *Freedom in the Modern World*, edited by Horace M. Kallen, pp. 25–49. New York: Coward-McCann, 1928.

Hammurabi, King of Babylonia. *The Oldest Code of Laws in the World*. Translated by C. H. W. Johns. Edinburgh: T. and T. Clark, 1911.

Hardy, Edmund. *Der Begriff der Physis in der griechischen Philosophie*. Vol. 1. Berlin: Weidmann, 1884. [No more published.]

Harnack, Adolf von. *What Is Christianity?* 2d ed., rev. Translated by Thomas Bailey Saunders. New York: G. P. Putnam's Sons, 1901.

Harris, George. *Moral Evolution*. Boston: Houghton, Mifflin and Co., 1896.

Harrison, Jane Ellen. *Prolegomena to the Study of the Greek Religion*. Cambridge: Cambridge University Press, 1903.

Hartmann, Nicolai. *Ethics*. Translated by Stanton Coit. Vol. 1. London: George Allen and Unwin, 1932.

Hastings, James, ed. *Encyclopaedia of Religion and Ethics*. 13 vols. New York: Charles Scribner's Sons, 1922. ["Altruism" by James Iverach, 1:354–58; "Summum Bonum" by Paul Shorey, 12:44–48.]

————, et al., eds. *A Dictionary of the Bible*. 5 vols. New York: Charles Scribner's Sons, 1898–1904.

Hayes, Carlton J. H. *Essays on Nationalism*. New York: Macmillan Co., 1926.

Hays, Arthur Garfield. *Let Freedom Ring*. New York: Boni and Liveright, 1928.

Hazlitt, William. "Jeremy Bentham." In *The Spirit of the Age; or, Contemporary Portraits*. The World's Classics, vol. 57. *The Works of William Hazlitt*, 4:1–16. London: Henry Frowde, 1904.

Hearn, Lafcadio. *Japan: An Attempt at Interpretation*. New York: Macmillan Co., 1904.

Hearn, William Edward. *The Aryan Household, Its Structure and Development: An Introduction to Comparative Jurisprudence*. London: Longmans, Green, and Co., 1879.

Hegel, Georg Wilhelm Friedrich. *Lectures on the Philosophy of History*. Translated from the 3d German ed. by John Sibree. London: George Bell and Sons, 1881.

————. *Philosophy of Right*. Translated by S. W. Dyde. London: George Bell and Sons, 1896.

Held, Adolf. *Zwei Bücher zur socialen Geschichte Englands*. Leipzig: Duncker and Humblot, 1881.

Herbert, George. *The Temple: Sacred Poems and Private Ejaculations*. New York: Baker and Taylor, n.d.

Hirn, Yrjö. *The Origins of Art: A Psychological and Sociological Inquiry*. New York: Macmillan Co., 1900.

Hitchcock, Curtice N.; Douglas, Paul H.; and Atkins, Willard E. *The Worker in Modern Economic Society*. Chicago: University of Chicago Press, 1923.

Hobbes, Thomas. *Leviathan; or, The Matter, Form and Power of a Commonwealth, Ecclesiastical and Civil*. 3d ed. London: George Routledge and Sons, 1887.

Hobhouse, Leonard Trelawney. *The Elements of Social Justice*. New York: Henry Holt and Co., 1922.

————. *Morals in Evolution: A Study in Comparative Ethics*. 2 vols.
New York: Henry Holt and Co., 1906.

————. *The Rational Good*. New York: Henry Holt and Co., 1921.

————, et al. *Property, Its Duties and Rights*. London: Macmillan and
Co., 1913.

Hobson, John Atkinson. *The Evolution of Modern Capitalism: A
Study of Machine Production*. London: George Allen and Unwin,
1894.

————. *Free-Thought in the Social Sciences*. New York: Macmillan
Co., 1926.

————. *Work and Wealth: A Human Valuation*. New York: Macmillan
Co., 1916.

Hocking, William Ernest. *Man and the State*. New Haven: Yale University Press, 1926.

Höffding, Harald. *Ethik*. Translated by F. Bendixen. Leipzig: Reisland,
1888.

————. *A History of Modern Philosophy: A Sketch of the History of
Philosophy from the Close of the Renaissance to Our Own Day*.
Translated by B. Ethel Meyer. 2 vols. London: Macmillan and Co.,
1900.

Holmes, Oliver Wendell. *Collected Legal Papers*. New York: Harcourt,
Brace and Howe, 1920.

————. *U.S. Supreme Court Reports*, 63 Law. Ed., pp. 1173–80.

Howard, George Elliott. *A History of Matrimonial Institutions*. 3 vols.
Chicago: University of Chicago Press, 1904.

Howitt, Alfred William. *The Native Tribes of South-East Australia*.
London: Macmillan and Co., 1904.

Howitt, Alfred William, and Fison, Lorimer. *Kamilaroi and Kurnai*.
Melbourne: G. Robertson, 1880.

Hume, David. *A Treatise of Human Nature*. Edited by T. H. Green
and T. H. Grose. 2 vols. London: Longmans, Green, and Co., 1898.

————. "An Enquiry concerning the Principles of Morals." In *Essays:
Moral, Political, and Literary*, edited by T. H. Green and T. H.
Grose, 2:169–287. London: Longmans, Green, and Co., 1875.

Hutcheson, Francis. *A System of Moral Philosophy*. 2 vols. London:
A. Millar, 1755.

Ihering, Rudolph von. *Der Kampf um's Recht*. Vienna: G. J. Manz, 1872.

————. *Der Zweck im Recht*. 3d rev. ed. Leipzig: Breitkopf and
Härtel, 1893.

Jackson, Abraham Valentine Williams. *History of India*. 9 vols. London: Grolier Society, [1906–7].

James, William. *The Principles of Psychology*. 2 vols. New York:
Henry Holt and Co., 1890.

————. *The Will to Believe and Other Essays in Popular Philosophy.* New York: Longmans, Green and Co., 1915. ["The Dilemma of Determinism," pp. 145–83; "The Moral Philosopher and the Moral Life," pp. 184–215.]

————. "The Moral Equivalent of War." In *Memories and Studies,* edited by Henry James, Jr., pp. 265–96. London: Longmans, Green, and Co., 1912.

————. "The Moral Philosopher and the Moral Life." *International Journal of Ethics* 1 (1891): 330–54.

Janet, Paul Alexandre René. *Histoire de la science politique dans ses rapports avec la morale.* 3d ed. 2 vols. Paris: F. Alcan, 1887.

————. *The Theory of Morals.* Translated by Mary Chapman. Edinburgh: T. and T. Clark, 1884.

Jennings, Herbert Spencer. *The Biological Basis of Human Nature.* New York: W. W. Norton and Co., 1930.

Jewish Encyclopedia. Edited by Isidore Singer et al. 12 vols. New York: Funk and Wagnalls Co., 1901–6.

Jodl, Friedrich. *Geschichte der Ethik in der neueren Philosophie.* 2 vols. Stuttgart: Cotta, 1882–89.

Jones, William Henry Samuel. *Greek Morality in Relation to Institutions.* London: Blackie and Son, 1906.

Jordan, David Starr. *War and Waste.* Garden City, N.Y.: Doubleday, Page and Co., 1913.

Kallen, Horace Meyer, ed. *Freedom in the Modern World.* New York: Coward-McCann, 1928.

Kant, Immanuel. *Critique of Practical Reason and Other Works on the Theory of Ethics.* 4th rev. ed. Translated by Thomas Kingsmill Abbott. London: Longmans, Green, and Co., 1889.

————. *Fundamental Principles of the Metaphysics of Ethics.* 3d ed. Translated by Thomas Kingsmill Abbott. London: Longmans, Green, and Co., 1907.

————. "The Idea of a Universal Cosmopolitical History." In *Kant's Principles of Politics, Including His Essay on Perpetual Peace,* edited and translated by William Hastie, pp. 1–29. Edinburgh: T. and T. Clark, 1891.

Karsten, Rafael. *Blood Revenge, War, and Victory Feasts among the Jibaro Indians of Eastern Ecuador.* Smithsonian Institution, Bureau of American Ethnology, Bulletin 79. Washington, D.C.: Government Printing Office, 1923.

Keller, Albert Galloway, and Sumner, William Graham. *The Science of Society.* Vol. 3. New Haven: Yale University Press, 1927.

Key, Ellen Karolina Sofia. *Love and Marriage.* New York: G. P. Putnam's Sons, 1911.

Kidd, Dudley. *The Essential Kafir.* London: A. and C. Black, 1904.

————. *Savage Childhood: A Study of Kafir Children*. London: A. and C. Black, 1906.

King, Willford Isbell. *The Wealth and Income of the People of the United States*. New York: Macmillan Co., 1915.

Köstlin, Karl Reinhold von. *Geschichte der Ethik*. Vol. 1. Tübingen: H. Laupp, 1887. [No more published.]

Kovalevsky, Maxime. *Tableau des origines et de l'evolution de la famille et de la propriété*. Stockholm: Samson and Wallin, 1890.

Krauss, Friedrich Salomon. *Sitte und Brauch der Südslaven*. Vienna: A. Holder, 1885.

Kroeber, Alfred Louis. *Zuñi Kin and Clan*. Anthropological Papers of the American Museum of Natural History, vol. 18, pt. 2. New York: Museum Trustees, 1917.

Kropotkin, Petr Aleksievich. *Mutual Aid: A Factor of Evolution*. New York: McClure, Phillips and Co., 1902.

Ladd, George Trumbull. *Philosophy of Conduct: A Treatise of the Facts, Principles, and Ideals of Ethics*. New York: Charles Scribner's Sons, 1902.

Laidler, Harry Wellington. *Socialism in Thought and Action*. New York: Macmillan Co., 1920.

Laski, Harold Joseph. *Authority in the Modern State*. New Haven: Yale University Press, 1919.

————. *Liberty in the Modern State*. New York: Harper and Bros., 1930.

Lecky, William Edward Hartpole. *History of European Morals: From Augustus to Charlemagne*. 3d ed., rev. 2 vols. New York: D. Appleton and Co., 1877.

Levin, Jack. *Power Ethics*. New York: Alfred A. Knopf, 1931.

Lévy-Bruhl, Lucien. *Ethics and Moral Science*. Translated by Elizabeth Lee. London: Archibald Constable and Co., 1905.

————. *The Philosophy of Auguste Comte*. New York: G. P. Putnam's Sons, 1903.

Lippmann, Walter. *Drift and Mastery; An Attempt to Diagnose the Current Unrest*. New York: Mitchell Kennerley, 1914.

————. *Liberty and the News*. New York: Harcourt, Brace and Howe, 1920.

————. *The Phantom Public*. New York: Harcourt, Brace and Co., 1925.

————. *A Preface to Morals*. New York: Macmillan Co., 1929.

————. *A Preface to Politics*. New York: Mitchell Kennerley, 1913.

————. *Public Opinion*. New York: Harcourt, Brace and Co., 1922.

Locke, John. *An Essay concerning Human Understanding*. In *The Works of John Locke*, 1:1–282. London: Bye and Law, 1801.

————. *A Letter concerning Toleration*. 2d ed., corrected. London: A. Churchill, 1690.

————. *Some Thoughts concerning Education.* In *The Works of John Locke,* 9:1–205. London: T. Davison, 1801.

Lowie, Robert Harry. *Primitive Society.* New York: Boni and Liveright, [1920].

Lucretius Carus, Titus. *T. Lucreti Cari de rerum natura libri sex.* 4th ed., rev. Translated by Hugh A. J. Munro. 3 vols. London: George Bell and Sons, 1898–1900.

Lyall, Alfred Comyn. *Asiatic Studies, Religious and Social.* 2d ed. London: John Murray, 1882.

McDougall, William. *Character and the Conduct of Life.* New York: G. P. Putnam's Sons, 1927.

————. *An Introduction to Social Psychology.* Boston: J. W. Luce and Co., 1909.

McGilvary, Evander Bradley. "The Consciousness of Obligation." *Philosophical Review* 11 (1902): 333–52.

MacIver, Robert Morrison. *The Modern State.* London: Oxford University Press, 1926.

Mackenzie, John Stuart. *An Introduction to Social Philosophy.* Glasgow: James Maclehose and Sons, 1890.

————. *A Manual of Ethics.* 4th ed. London: University Correspondence College Press, 1900.

————. "The Meaning of 'Motive.'" *International Journal of Ethics* 4 (1894): 231–33.

————. "Moral Science and the Moral Life." *International Journal of Ethics* 4 (1894): 160–73.

McLennan, John Ferguson. *Studies in Ancient History: Comprising a Reprint of Primitive Marriage.* New ed. London: Macmillan and Co., 1886.

Maine, Henry Sumner. *Ancient Law: Its Connection with the Early History of Society, and Its Relation to Modern Ideas.* 10th ed. London: John Murray, 1885.

————. *Dissertations on Early Law and Custom.* New York: Henry Holt and Co., 1886.

————. *Lectures on the Early History of Institutions.* New York: Henry Holt and Co., 1888.

Maitland, Frederic William, and Pollock, Frederick. *The History of English Law before the Time of Edward I.* 2 vols. Cambridge: Cambridge University Press, 1895. [2d ed., 1899.]

Malinowski, Bronislaw. *Crime and Custom in Savage Society.* New York: Harcourt, Brace and Co., 1926.

————. *The Family among the Australian Aborigines: A Sociological Study.* London: University of London Press, 1913.

————. "Parenthood—The Basis of Social Structure." In *The New*

Generation: The Intimate Problems of Modern Parents and Children, edited by Victor Francis Calverton and Samuel D. Schmalhausen, pp. 113–68. New York: Macaulay Co., 1930.

Mandeville, Bernard. *The Fable of the Bees*. Edinburgh: Mundell and Sons, 1806.

Marcus Aurelius. *Meditations of Marcus Aurelius*. Translated by John Jackson. Oxford: At the Clarendon Press, 1906.

———. *The Thoughts of the Emperor Marcus Antoninus 'Aurelius*. Translated by George Long. Boston: Little, Brown and Co., 1899.

Marett, Robert Ranulph. "Is Taboo a Negative Magic?" In *Anthropological Essays Presented to Edward Burnett Tylor*, edited by W. H. R. Rivers, R. R. Marett, and Northcote W. Thomas, pp. 219–34. Oxford: At the Clarendon Press, 1907.

Marshall, Leon Carroll, ed. *Industrial Society*. 3 vols. Chicago: University of Chicago Press, 1929–30.

Marti, Karl. *The Religion of the Old Testament: Its Place among the Religions of the Nearer East*. Translated by Rev. Gustav Adolph Bienemann. Edited by Rev. William Douglas Morrison. New York: G. P. Putnam's Sons, 1907.

Martin, Everett Dean. *Liberty*. New York: W. W. Norton and Co., 1930.

Martineau, James. *Types of Ethical Theory*. 2 vols. Oxford: At the Clarendon Press, 1885. [3d ed., rev., 1891; 3d ed., rev., 1901.]

Marvin, F. S., and Stawell, Florence Melian. *The Making of the Western Mind*. London: Methuen and Co., 1923.

Matthews, Shailer. *The Social Teaching of Jesus: An Essay in Christian Sociology*. New York: Macmillan Co., 1897.

Maurice, John Frederick Denison. *The Conscience*. London: Macmillan and Co., 1868.

Merriam, Charles Edward. *The Making of Citizens: A Comparative Study of Methods of Civic Training*. Chicago: University of Chicago Press, 1931.

Merz, John Theodore. *A History of European Thought in the Nineteenth Century*. 2 vols. Edinburgh: William Blackwood and Sons, 1903–4.

Mezes, Sidney Edward. *Ethics: Descriptive and Explanatory*. New York: Macmillan Co., 1901.

Mill, James. *Analysis of the Phenomena of the Human Mind*. 2 vols. New ed. Edited by John Stuart Mill. London: Longmans, Green, Reader, and Dyer, 1873.

Mill, John Stuart. *Autobiography*. London: Longmans, Green, Reader, and Dyer, 1874.

————. *Dissertations and Discussions: Political, Philosophical, and Historical.* 4 vols. Boston: William V. Spencer, 1868.

————. *Early Essays by John Stuart Mill.* London: George Bell and Sons, 1897.

————. *On Liberty.* New York: Henry Holt and Co., 1859.

————. *Utilitarianism.* 2d ed. London: Longman, Green, Longman, Roberts, and Green, 1864.

Millay, Edna St. Vincent. *A Few Figs from Thistles.* New York: Harper and Bros., 1922.

Milton, John. *Areopagitica.* New York: Grolier Club, 1890.

————. *The Tenure of Kings and Magistrates.* In *The Prose Works of John Milton,* edited by J. A. St. John, 2:1–47. London: George Bell and Sons, 1888.

Mindeleff, Cosmos. "The Repair of Casa Grande Ruin, Arizona, in 1891." In *Fifteenth Annual Report of the Bureau of Ethnology to the Secretary of the Smithsonian Institution 1893–'94,* pp. 315–49. Washington, D.C.: Government Printing Office, 1897.

Mitchell, Wesley Clair, et al. *Income in the United States, Its Amount and Distribution, 1909–1919.* 2 vols. New York: Harcourt, Brace and Co., 1921–22.

Moore, George Edward. *Ethics.* New York: Henry Holt and Co., 1912.

————. *Principia Ethica.* Cambridge: Cambridge University Press, 1903.

————. "The Nature of Moral Philosophy." In his *Philosophical Studies,* pp. 310–39. New York: Harcourt, Brace and Co., 1922.

Morgan, Lewis Henry. *Ancient Society; or, Researches in the Lines of Human Progress from Savagery through Barbarism to Civilization.* New York: Henry Holt and Co., 1877.

————. *Houses and House-Life of the American Aborigines.* Contributions to North American Ethnology, vol. 4. Washington, D.C.: Government Printing Office, 1881.

————. *League of the Ho-de-no-sau-nee, or Iroquois.* Rochester, N.Y.: Sage and Bros., 1851.

————. *Systems of Consanguinity and Affinity of the Human Family.* Smithsonian Contributions to Knowledge, vol. 17. Washington, D.C.: Smithsonian Institution, 1870.

Morrison, Charles Clayton. *The Outlawry of War: A Constructive Policy for World Peace.* Chicago: Willett, Clark and Colby, 1927.

Muirhead, J. H. "The Meaning of 'Motive.'" *International Journal of Ethics* 4 (1894): 229–31.

Murray, Gilbert. "The Value of Greece to the Future of the World." In *The Legacy of Greece,* edited by Richard Winn Livingstone, pp. 1–23. Oxford: At the Clarendon Press, 1924.

Newman, William Lambert. Introduction to *The Politics of Aristotle*, vol. 1, edited by W. L. Newman. Oxford: At the Clarendon Press, 1887.

Nietzsche, Friedrich. *The Will to Power: An Attempted Transvaluation of All Values*. Translated by Anthony M. Ludovici. 2 vols. New York: Macmillan Co., 1924.

Nitobé, Inazo Ota. *Bushido, The Soul of Japan: An Exposition of Japanese Thought*. 10th rev. and enl. ed. New York: G. P. Putnam's Sons, 1905.

Ogburn, William Fielding. *Social Change with Respect to Culture and Original Nature*. New York: B. W. Heubsch, 1922.

Ogburn, William Fielding, and Groves, Ernest Rutherford. *American Marriage and Family Relationships*. New York: Henry Holt and Co., 1928.

Ogburn, William Fielding, and Goldenweiser, Alexander, eds. *The Social Sciences and Their Interrelations*. Boston: Houghton Mifflin Co., 1927.

Otto, Max C. *Things and Ideals: Essays in Functional Philosophy*. New York: Henry Holt and Co., 1924.

Page, Kirby. *National Defense: A Study of the Origins, Results and Prevention of War*. New York: Farrar and Rinehart, 1931.

————, ed. *A New Economic Order*. New York: Harcourt, Brace and Co., 1930.

Palmer, George Herbert. *The Field of Ethics*. Boston: Houghton, Mifflin and Co., 1902.

————. *The Nature of Goodness*. Boston: Houghton Mifflin Co., 1903.

Parrington, Vernon Louis. *Main Currents in American Thought*. 3 vols. New York: Harcourt, Brace and Co., 1927–30.

Pater, Walter Horatio. *Marius the Epicurean: His Sensations and Ideas*. 2d ed. London: Macmillan and Co., 1885.

Paulsen, Friedrich. *A System of Ethics*. Edited and translated by Frank Thilly. New York: Charles Scribner's Sons, 1899.

————. *System der Ethik*. 2 vols. in 1. Berlin: Besser, 1889. [5th rev. ed. 2 vols. Berlin: W. Hertz, 1900.]

Peake, Arthur Samuel. *The Problem of Suffering in the Old Testament*. London: Robert Bryant, 1904.

Perlman, Selig. *A History of Trade Unionism in the United States*. New York: Macmillan Co., 1922.

————. *A Theory of the Labor Movement*. New York: Macmillan Co., 1928.

Perry, Ralph Barton. *General Theory of Value: Its Meaning and Basic Principles Construed in Terms of Interest*. New York: Longmans, Green and Co., 1926.

————. *The Moral Economy*. New York: Charles Scribner's Sons, 1909.

Pfleiderer, Otto. *Paulinism: A Contribution to the History of Primitive Christian Theology*. 2d ed. Translated by Edward Peters. 2 vols. London: Williams and Norgate, 1891.

Plato. *The Dialogues of Plato*. Translated by Benjamin Jowett. 4 vols. Boston: Jefferson Press, 1871. [*Protagoras*, 1:97–162; *Apology*, 1:303–39; *Crito*, 1:341–59; *Republic*, 2:1–452; *Gorgias*, 3:1–119; *Theaetetus*, 3:301–419; *Laws*, 4:1–480.]

Pöhlmann, Robert von. *Geschichte des antiken Kommunismus und Sozialismus*. 2 vols. Munich: C. H. Beck, 1893–1901.

Pollock, Frederick. *The Expansion of the Common Law*. London: Stevens and Sons, 1904.

Pollock, Frederick, and Maitland, Frederic William. *The History of English Law before the Time of Edward I*. 2 vols. Cambridge: Cambridge University Press, 1895. [2d ed., 1899.]

Popenoe, Paul. *The Conservation of the Family*. Baltimore: Williams and Wilkins Co., 1926.

Post, Albert Hermann. *Die Grundlagen des Rechts und die Grundzüge seiner Entwicklungsgeschichte*. Oldenburg: Schulze (A. Schwartz), 1884.

————. *Grundriss der ethnologischen Jurisprudenz*. 2 vols. Oldenburg: Schulze, 1894–95.

Powell, John Wesley. "On the Evolution of Language"; "Sketch of the Mythology of the North American Indians"; "Wyandot Government: A Short Study of Tribal Society." In *First Annual Report of the Bureau of Ethnology to the Secretary of the Smithsonian Institution 1879–'80*, pp. 1–16; 17–56; 57–86. Washington, D.C.: Government Printing Office, 1881.

Powell, Thomas Reed. "Collective Bargaining before the Supreme Court." *Political Science Quarterly* 33 (1918): 396–429.

Pratt, James Bissett. *The Psychology of Religious Belief*. New York: Macmillan Co., 1907.

Radin, Max. *The Lawful Pursuit of Gain*. Boston: Houghton Mifflin Co., 1931.

Rambaud, Alfred Nicolas. *Histoire de la civilisation française*. 2 vols. Paris: Armand Colin, 1897–98.

Rand, Benjamin. *The Classical Moralists: Selections Illustrating Ethics from Socrates to Martineau*. Boston: Houghton Mifflin Co., 1909.

Randall, John Herman, Jr. *The Making of the Modern Mind*. Boston: Houghton Mifflin Co., 1926.

Rapson, E. J., ed. *The Cambridge History of India*. Vol. 1. New York: Macmillan Co., 1922.

Rashdall, Hastings. *Is Conscience an Emotion? Three Lectures on Re-*

cent Ethical Theories. Boston: Houghton Mifflin Co., 1914.
————. *The Theory of Good and Evil: A Treatise on Moral Philosophy*. Oxford: At the Clarendon Press, 1907.
————. *The Universities of Europe in the Middle Ages*. 2 vols. in 3. Oxford: At the Clarendon Press, 1895.
Ratzel, Friedrich. *The History of Mankind*. Translated from the 2d German ed. by Arthur John Burler. 2 vols. London: Macmillan and Co., 1896–98.
Reed, Ruth. *The Modern Family*. New York: Alfred A. Knopf, 1929.
Reinach, Salomon. *Cultes, mythes et religions*. 3 vols. Paris: E. Leroux, 1905–8.
Rickaby, Joseph John. *Moral Philosophy; or, Ethics and Natural Law*. New York: Benziger Brothers, 1888.
————. *Political and Moral Essays*. New York: Benziger Brothers, 1902.
————, trans. *Aquinas Ethicus; or, The Moral Teaching of St. Thomas*. 2 vols. London: Burns and Oates, 1896.
Ripley, William Zebina. *Main Street and Wall Street*. Boston: Little, Brown, and Co., 1927.
Rist, Charles, and Gide, Charles. *A History of Economic Doctrines from the Time of the Physiocrats to the Present Day*. Boston: D. C. Heath and Co., 1915.
Ritchie, David George. *Natural Rights: A Criticism of Some Political and Ethical Conceptions*. London: Swan Sonnenschein and Co., 1895.
————. *Philosophical Studies*. Edited by Robert Latta. London: Macmillan and Co., 1905.
————. *Studies in Political and Social Ethics*. London: Swan Sonnenschein and Co., 1902.
————. "The Meaning of 'Motive.'" *International Journal of Ethics* 4 (1894): 236–38.
————. "On the Meaning of the Term 'Motive,' and on the Ethical Significance of Motives." *International Journal of Ethics* 4 (1893): 89–94.
Rivers, William Halse Rivers. *The History of Melanesian Society*. 2 vols. Cambridge: Cambridge University Press, 1914.
————. *The Todas*. London: Macmillan and Co., 1906.
————. "On the Origin of the Classificatory System of Relationships." In *Anthropological Essays Presented to Edward Burnett Tylor*, edited by W. H. R. Rivers, R. R. Marett, and Northcote W. Thomas, pp. 309–23. Oxford: At the Clarendon Press, 1907.
Robertson, John Mackinnon. *A Short History of Freethought: Ancient and Modern*. London: Swan Sonnenschein and Co., 1899.

Rogers, Arthur Kenyon. *Morals in Review*. New York: Macmillan Co., 1927.

Rohde, Erwin. *Psyche: Seelencult und unsterblichkeitsglaube der Griechen*. 2 pts. Freiburg and Leipzig: J. C. B. Mohr, 1894.

Ross, Edward Alsworth. *Foundations of Sociology*. New York: Macmillan Co., 1905.

Ross, William David. *Aristotle*. London: Methuen and Co., 1923.

Royce, Josiah. "The Problem of Job." In *Studies of Good and Evil: A Series of Essays upon Problems of Philosophy and of Life*, pp. 1–28. New York: D. Appleton and Co., 1898.

Runze, Georg. *Praktische Ethik*. Ethik: Encyklopadische Skizzen u. Literaturangaben, vol. 1. Berlin: Carl Duncker, 1891.

Russell, Bertrand. *Why Men Fight: A Method of Abolishing the International Duel*. New York: Century Co., 1917.

Russell, Dora Winifred. *The Right to Be Happy*. New York: Harper and Bros., 1927.

Santayana, George. *Reason in Science*. Vol. 5 of *The Life of Reason; or, The Phases of Human Progress*. New York: Charles Scribner's Sons, 1906.

————. *Reason in Society*. Vol. 2 of *The Life of Reason; or, The Phases of Human Progress*. New York: Charles Scribner's Sons, 1905.

Schmidt, Leopold Valentine. *Die Ethik der alten Griechen*. 2 vols. Berlin: W. Hertz, 1882.

Schneider, Herbert Wallace. *The Puritan Mind*. New York: Henry Holt and Co., 1930.

Schoolcraft, Henry Rowe. *Historical and Statistical Information Respecting the History, Condition and Prospects of the Indian Tribes of the United States*. 6 vols. Philadelphia: Lippincott, Grambo and Co., 1851–57.

Schultz, Hermann. *Old Testament Theology: The Religion of Revelation in Its Pre-Christian Stage of Development*. Translated from the 4th German ed. by Rev. James Alexander Paterson. 2 vols. Edinburgh: T. and T. Clark, 1892.

Schurman, Jacob Gould. *The Ethical Import of Darwinism*. New York: Charles Scribner's Sons, 1888.

Schurtz, Heinrich. *Altersklassen und Männerbünde*. Berlin: G. Reimer, 1902.

————. *Urgeschichte der Kultur*. Leipzig and Vienna: Bibliographisches Institut, 1900.

Seebohm, Frederic. *Tribal Custom in Anglo-Saxon Law*. London: Longmans, Green, and Co., 1902.

————. *The Tribal System in Wales: Being Part of an Inquiry into the Structure and Methods of Tribal Society*. London: Longmans, Green, and Co., 1895.

Selby-Bigge, Lewis Amherst, ed. *British Moralists: Being Selections from Writers Principally of the Eighteenth Century.* 2 vols. Oxford: At the Clarendon Press, 1897.

Seligman, Charles Gabriel. *The Melanesians of British New Guinea.* Cambridge: Cambridge University Press, 1910.

———. *The Veddas.* Cambridge: Cambridge University Press, 1911.

Seneca. *Moral Essays.* Vol. 2. Translated by John W. Basore. London: William Heinemann, 1928.

Seth, James. *A Study of Ethical Principles.* 3d ed. New York: Charles Scribner's Sons, 1898.

———. "The Evolution of Morality." *Mind* 14 (1889): 27–49.

Shaftesbury, Anthony Ashley Cooper, 3d earl of. *Characteristics of Men, Manners, Opinions, Times, etc.* Edited by John M. Robertson. 2 vols. London: Grant Richards, 1900. ["An Inquiry concerning Virtue or Merit," 1:235–338.]

Sharp, Frank Chapman. *Ethics.* New York: D. Appleton-Century Co., 1928.

———. "An Analysis of the Idea of Obligation." *International Journal of Ethics* 2 (1892): 500–513.

Shaw, George Bernard. *The Intelligent Woman's Guide to Socialism and Capitalism.* New York: Brentano's, 1928.

Sidgwick, Henry. *The Elements of Politics.* New York: Macmillan Co., 1897.

———. *Lectures on the Ethics of T. H. Green, Mr. Herbert Spencer, and J. Martineau.* London: Macmillan and Co., 1902.

———. *The Methods of Ethics.* London: Macmillan and Co., 1874. [2d ed., 1877; 6th ed., 1901.]

———. *Outlines of the History of Ethics, for English Readers.* 3d ed. London: Macmillan and Co., 1892.

Simcox, Edith J. *Natural Law: An Essay in Ethics.* English and Foreign Philosophical Library, vol. 4. London: Trübner and Co., 1877.

Simmel, Georg. "The Sociology of Secrecy and of Secret Societies." *American Journal of Sociology* 11 (1906): 441–98.

Simmons, Duane B. "Notes on Land Tenure and Local Institutions in Old Japan." Edited by John H. Wigmore. *Transactions of the Asiatic Society of Japan* 19 (1891): 37–270.

Skeat, Walter William. *Malay Magic: Being an Introduction to the Folklore and Popular Religion of the Malay Peninsula.* London: Macmillan and Co., 1900.

Slichter, Sumner H. *Modern Economic Society.* New York: Henry Holt and Co., 1931.

Small, Albion Woodbury. *General Sociology: An Exposition of the Main Development in Sociological Theory from Spencer to Ratzenhofer.* Chicago: University of Chicago Press, 1905.

————. *The Significance of Sociology for Ethics.* Chicago: University of Chicago Press, 1902.

Smith, Adam. *The Theory of Moral Sentiments.* London: A. Millar, 1759. [New ed. London: George Bell and Sons, 1892.]

————. *The Wealth of Nations.* 3 vols. New York: American Home Library Co., 1902.

Smith, Arthur Henderson. *Chinese Characteristics.* 2d ed., rev. New York: Fleming H. Revell Co., 1894.

————. *Village Life in China: A Study in Sociology.* New York: Fleming H. Revell Co., 1899.

Smith, Gertrude, and Bonner, Robert J. *The Administration of Justice from Homer to Aristotle.* Vol. 1. Chicago: University of Chicago Press, 1930.

Smith, Henry Preserved. *Old Testament History.* New York: Charles Scribner's Sons, 1903.

————. *The Religion of Israel.* Edinburgh: T. and T. Clark, 1914.

Smith, John Merlin Powis. *The Moral Life of the Hebrews.* Chicago: University of Chicago Press, 1923.

————. *The Prophets and Their Times.* Chicago: University of Chicago Press, 1925.

Smith, Thomas Vernor. "Contemporary Perplexities in Democratic Theory." *International Journal of Ethics* 39 (1928): 1–14.

Smith, William Robertson. *Kinship and Marriage in Early Arabia.* Cambridge: Cambridge University Press, 1885.

————. *Lectures on the Religion of the Semites.* New ed., rev. London: A. and C. Black, 1894.

————. *The Prophets of Israel and Their Place in History to the Close of the Eighth Century B.C.* New ed. London: A. and C. Black, 1895.

Sneath, Elias Hershey, ed. *The Evolution of Ethics as Revealed in the Great Religions.* New Haven: Yale University Press, 1927.

Sophocles. *The Tragedies of Sophocles.* Translated by E. H. Plumptre. New York: George Routledge and Sons, 1881. [*Oedipus at Colonos,* pp. 57–125; *Antigone,* pp. 127–77; *Philoctetes,* pp. 341–97.]

Sorley, William Ritchie. *On the Ethics of Naturalism.* London: William Blackwood and Sons, 1885.

————. *Recent Tendencies in Ethics: Three Lectures to Clergy, Given at Cambridge.* London: William Blackwood and Sons, 1904.

Spencer, Baldwin, and Gillen, Francis James. *The Native Tribes of Central Australia.* London: Macmillan and Co., 1899.

————. *The Northern Tribes of Central Australia.* London: Macmillan and Co., 1904.

Spencer, Herbert. *The Data of Ethics.* New York: D. Appleton and Co., 1879.

————. *The Man versus the State.* New York: D. Appleton and Co., 1884.

————. *The Principles of Ethics.* 2 vols. New York: D. Appleton and Co., 1892–93.

————. *The Principles of Psychology.* 2 vols. New York: D. Appleton and Co., 1872–73.

————. *The Principles of Sociology.* 3 vols. London: Williams and Norgate, 1876–96. [3 vols. in 4. New York: D. Appleton and Co., 1880–97.]

Spinoza, Benedict de. *The Ethics of Benedict de Spinoza.* Translated by Daniel Drake Smith. New York: D. Van Nostrand, 1876.

Stapledon, William Olaf. *A Modern Theory of Ethics: A Study of the Relations of Ethics and Psychology.* London: Methuen and Co., 1929.

Starcke, Carl Nicolai. *The Primitive Family in Its Origin and Development.* New York: D. Appleton and Co., 1889.

Stawell, Florence Melian, and Marvin, F. S. *The Making of the Western Mind.* London: Methuen and Co., 1923.

Stein, Ludwig. *Die sociale Frage im Lichte der Philosophie.* Stuttgart: F. Enke, 1897.

Steinmetz, Sebald Rudolf. *Ethnologische Studien zur ersten Entwicklung der Strafe.* 2 vols. Leipzig: O. Harrassowitz, 1894.

Steinthal, Heymann. *Allgemeine Ethik.* Berlin: G. Reimer, 1885.

Stephen, Leslie. *The English Utilitarians.* 3 vols. New York: G. P. Putnam's Sons, 1900.

————. *History of English Thought in the Eighteenth Century.* 3d ed. 2 vols. New York: G. P. Putnam's Sons, 1902.

————. *The Science of Ethics.* London: Smith, Elder, and Co., 1882.

Stevens, William Harrison Spring. *Unfair Competition.* Chicago: University of Chicago Press, 1917.

Stevenson, James. "Ceremonial of Hasjelti Dailjis and Mythical Sand Painting of the Navajo Indians." In *Eighth Annual Report of the Bureau of Ethnology to the Secretary of the Smithsonian Institution 1886–'87,* pp. 229–85. Washington, D.C.: Government Printing Office, 1891.

Stevenson, Matilda Coxe. "The Zuñi Indians: Their Mythology, Esoteric Fraternities, and Ceremonies." In *Twenty-Third Annual Report of the Bureau of Ethnology to the Secretary of the Smithsonian Institution 1901–'02,* pp. 3–608. Washington, D.C.: Government Printing Office, 1904.

Stimson, Frederic Jesup. *Popular Law-Making: A Study of the Origin, History, and Present Tendencies of Law-Making by Statute.* New York: Charles Scribner's Sons, 1910.

488 CHECKLIST OF REFERENCES

Stratton, George Malcolm. *Social Psychology of International Conduct*. New York: D. Appleton and Co., 1929.

Stuart, Henry Waldgrave. *The Logic of Self-Realization*. University of California Publications in Philosophy, vol. 1, no. 9. Berkeley: University of California Press, 1904.

Sturt, Henry. *Human Value: An Ethical Essay*. Cambridge: Cambridge University Press, 1923.

Sumner, William Graham. *Folkways: A Study of the Sociological Importance of Usages, Manners, Customs, Mores, and Morals*. Boston: Ginn and Co., 1906.

Sumner, William Graham, and Keller, Albert Galloway. *The Science of Society*. Vol. 3. New Haven: Yale University Press, 1927.

Sutherland, Alexander. *The Origin and Growth of the Moral Instinct*. 2 vols. London: Longmans, Green, and Co., 1898.

Taeusch, Carl F. *Policy and Ethics in Business*. New York: McGraw-Hill Book Co., 1931.

Tarde, Gabriel de. *Les Lois de l'imitation: Étude sociologique*. 2d ed., rev. and enl. Paris: F. Alcan, 1895.

Tawney, Richard Henry. *The Acquisitive Society*. New York: Harcourt, Brace and Co., 1920.

———. *Equality*. New York: Harcourt, Brace and Co., 1931.

———. *Religion and the Rise of Capitalism*. New York: Harcourt, Brace and Co., 1926.

Taylor, Alfred Edward. *Plato: The Man and His Work*. London: Methuen and Co., 1926.

———. *The Problem of Conduct: A Study in the Phenomenology of Ethics*. London: Macmillan and Co., 1901.

Taylor, Henry Osborn. *Ancient Ideals: A Study of Intellectual and Spiritual Growth from Early Times to the Establishment of Christianity*. 2 vols. New York: Macmillan Co., 1900.

———. *The Mediaeval Mind: A History of the Development of Thought and Emotion in the Middle Ages*. 2d ed. 2 vols. London: Macmillan and Co., 1914.

Thomas, Northcote Whitridge. *Kinship Organisations and Group Marriage in Australia*. Cambridge: Cambridge University Press, 1906.

———, ed. *The Native Races of the British Empire*. 4 vols. London: A. Constable and Co., 1906–7.

Thomas, William Isaac. *Sex and Society: Studies in the Social Psychology of Sex*. Chicago: University of Chicago Press, 1907.

Thomas Aquinas, Saint. *Aquinas Ethicus; or, The Moral Teaching of St. Thomas*. Translated by Joseph John Rickaby. 2 vols. London: Burns and Oates, 1896.

Traill, Henry Duff, ed. *Social England.* 6 vols. London: Cassell and Co., 1894–98.

Troeltsch, Ernst. *The Social Teaching of the Christian Churches.* 2 vols. Translated by Olive Wyon. Glencoe, Ill.: Free Press, 1931.

———. *Die Soziallehren der christlichen Kirchen und Gruppen.* 2 vols. Tübingen: J. C. B. Mohr, 1912.

Tufts, James Hayden. *The Ethics of Coöperation.* New York: Houghton Mifflin Co., 1918.

———. *Our Democracy, Its Origins and Its Tasks.* New York: Henry Holt and Co., 1917.

———. "On Moral Evolution." In *Studies in Philosophy and Psychology,* edited by J. H. Tufts et al., pp. 3–39. Boston: Houghton Mifflin Co., 1906.

———. "Some Contributions of Psychology to the Conception of Justice." *Philosophical Review* 15 (1906): 361–79.

Tugwell, Rexford Guy, ed. *The Trend of Economics.* New York: Alfred A. Knopf, 1924.

Tylor, Edward B. *Primitive Culture: Researches into the Development of Mythology, Philosophy, Religion, Language, Art, and Culture.* 4th ed., rev. 2 vols. London: John Murray, 1903.

Ueberweg, Friedrich. *History of Philosophy, from Thales to the Present Time.* Translated by George Sylvester Morris. 2 vols. New York: Charles Scribner's Sons, 1892.

Urban, Wilbur Marshall. *Fundamentals of Ethics: An Introduction to Moral Philosophy.* New York: Henry Holt and Co., 1930.

Veblen, Thorstein. *The Theory of Business Enterprise.* New York: Charles Scribner's Sons, 1904.

———. *The Vested Interests and the State of the Industrial Arts.* New York: B. W. Huebsch, 1919.

Vinogradoff, Paul. *Outlines of Historical Jurisprudence.* 2 vols. London: Oxford University Press, 1920–22.

Voigt, Moritz. *Das jus naturale, aequum et bonum und jus gentium der Römer.* 4 vols. Leipzig: Voigt and Günther, 1856–75. [Vol. 1. *Die Lehre vom jus naturale, aequum et bonum und jus gentium der Römer,* 1856.]

Waitz, Theodor. *Anthropologie der Naturvölker.* 6 vols. Leipzig: F. Fleischer, 1859–72.

Wallace, William. *Epicureanism.* New York: Pott, Young, and Co., 1880.

———. *Lectures and Essays on Natural Theology and Ethics.* Edited by Edward Caird. Oxford: At the Clarendon Press, 1898.

Wallas, Graham. *The Great Society: A Psychological Analysis.* New York: Macmillan Co., 1914.

————. *Human Nature in Politics*. Boston: Houghton Mifflin Co., 1909.

Watson, John. *Hedonistic Theories from Aristippus to Spencer*. New York: Macmillan Co., 1895.

Webb, Beatrice, and Webb, Sidney. *The History of Trade Unionism*. Rev. ed. London: Longmans, Green and Co., 1920.

————. *Industrial Democracy*. 2 vols. in 1. London: Longmans, Green and Co., 1902.

Weber, Max. *The Protestant Ethic and the Spirit of Capitalism*. Translated by Talcott Parsons. London: George Allen and Unwin, 1930.

Webster, Hutton. *Primitive Secret Societies: A Study in Early Politics and Religion*. New York: Macmillan Co., 1908.

Wells, H. G. *The Work, Wealth and Happiness of Mankind*. 2 vols. Garden City, N.Y.: Doubleday, Doran and Co., 1931.

Wendt, Hans Hinrich. *The Teaching of Jesus*. Translated by Rev. John Wilson. 2 vols. Edinburgh: T. and T. Clark, 1892–99.

Westermarck, Edward. *The History of Human Marriage*. 3d ed. London: Macmillan and Co., 1901.

————. *The Origin and Development of the Moral Ideas*. 2 vols. London: Macmillan and Co., 1906–8.

————. "The Influence of Magic on Social Relationships." *Sociological Papers* 2 (1906): 141–74.

Whewell, William. *The Elements of Morality, Including Polity*. New York: Harper and Bros., 1856.

————. *Lectures on the History of Moral Philosophy in England*. London: John W. Parker and Son, 1852. [New ed. Cambridge: Deighton, Bell, and Co., 1862.]

Wilamowitz-Moellendorff, Ulrich von. *Aristoteles und Athen*. 2 vols. Berlin: Weidmann, 1893.

Wilde, Norman. *The Ethical Basis of the State*. Princeton: Princeton University Press, 1924.

Williams, Cora May. *A Review of the Systems of Ethics Founded on the Theory of Evolution*. New York: Macmillan Co., 1893.

Williams, James Micke. *Principles of Social Psychology*. New York: Alfred A. Knopf, 1922.

Willoughby, Westel Woodbury. *Social Justice: A Critical Essay*. New York: Macmillan Co., 1900.

Wilson, John Matthias, and Fowler, Thomas. *The Principles of Morals*. 2 vols. Oxford: At the Clarendon Press, 1886–87.

Windelband, Wilhelm. *History of Ancient Philosophy*. Translated by Herbert Ernest Cushman. New York: Charles Scribner's Sons, 1899.

————. *A History of Philosophy with Especial Reference to the Formation and Development of Its Problems and Conceptions*. 2d ed., rev. and enl. Translated by James Hayden Tufts. London: Macmillan and Co., 1901.

Wormser, I. Maurice. *Frankenstein, Incorporated.* New York: McGraw-Hill Book Co., Whittlesey House, 1931.

Wright, Henry W. *Self-Realization: An Outline of Ethics.* New York: Henry Holt and Co., 1913.

Wright, William Kelley. *General Introduction to Ethics.* New York: Macmillan Co., 1929.

Wundt, Wilhelm Max. *Ethics: An Investigation of the Facts and Laws of the Moral Life.* 2d ed. 3 vols. London: Swan Sonnenschein and Co., 1897–1901.

———. *Ethik: Eine Untersuchung der Thatsachen und Gesetze des sittlichen Lebens.* Stuttgart: F. Enke, 1886. [3d rev. ed. 2 vols. 1903.]

———. *Geschichte der griechischen Ethik.* Vol. 1. Leipzig: W. Engelmann, 1908.

Xenophon. *The Anabasis; or, Expedition of Cyrus.* Translated by Rev. John Selby Watson. Boston: W. Small, 1893.

Zeller, Eduard. *Aristotle and the Earlier Peripatetics.* Translated by B. F. C. Costelloe and J. H. Muirhead. London: Longmans, Green, and Co., 1897.

———. *Plato and the Older Academy.* New ed. Translated by Sarah Frances Alleyne and Alfred Goodwin. London: Longmans, Green, and Co., 1888.

———. *Socrates and the Socratic Schools.* 3d ed., rev. Translated by Oswald J. Reichel. London: Longmans, Green, and Co., 1885.

———. *The Stoics, Epicureans and Sceptics.* New ed., rev. Translated by Oswald J. Reichel. London: Longmans, Green, and Co., 1880.

Ziegler, Theobald. *Die geistigen und socialen Strömungen des neunzehnten Jahrhunderts.* Berlin: G. Bondi, 1901.

Index

Family (*continued*)
440–41; from social stand-
point, 452–56
Father Anchises, 34
Federal Trade Commission Act,
408–9, 418
Feudalism: contrasted with indi-
vidualism, xxix
"Feudal Principle in Modern Law,
A" (Pound), xxix
Folkways. *See* Customs; Mores
Ford, Henry: on mass produc-
tion, 423
Fourteenth Amendment, 356,
395
Freedom, xxv; attacks on, 359–
60; economic, 141–44; of en-
terprise, 376; and individuality,
334–35; nature of, 305–6;
Pauline conception of, 95. *See
also* Liberty
Freud, Sigmund, 448
Friendship: Aristotle on, 450;
Epicureans on, 114; and mar-
riage, 450–52; pleasure in,
200–201; "political," 113
Fries, Horace S., xxx
Fulfillment: as quality of desire,
247
Fustel de Coulanges, 24

Galileo, Galilei, 144, 145
Genetic method: coupled with
experimental, xxxii; growth in,
xxxii
Gentleman: as class ideal, 143;
Greek conception of, 98, 101,
118*n*
Genung, John Franklin, 90
Germans: family among, 441;
landholding among, 23; responsibility of, 33
Germany: factory legislation in,
412–13

Gillen, Francis James, 26*n*–27*n*,
56
Goethe, Johann Wolfgang von,
190
Golden Rule, 178, 242, 280 and
n, 281
Goldsmith, Oliver, 171
Good: as central, xi; common,
xii, 347–48; Cynics on, 203–
4; as definition of morality, xiv;
and desire, 73, 190–91; double
meaning of, 265; Epicurean
theory of, 199–202; Greek
conception of, 98–99, 104,
115–17, 119–20; in group
morals, 64; Hebrew ideal of,
94; natural vs. moral, 207; as
objective interests, 208–12;
and pleasure, 195–96; pluralistic, xxxi; qualifications of,
271–72; relation to right,
215–17, 224–25, 229; role of,
xxxi; as ultimate, 181–82; in
utilitarianism, 242–43; and
wisdom, 191
Government: functions of, 332;
and labor, 394–95
Gratian, 137
Gray, J. H., 22–23
Great Britain: divorce in, 446;
factory legislation in, 412–13;
utilitarianism in, 251; women
in, 443
Greeks: on art, 97–98; on beauty,
102; on character, 121–23; on
commerce, 103–4; customs of,
23–24; on emotions, 92–93;
on evil, 89; on good, xxvii;
group authority of, 97; individuality among, 97; political authority among, 103–4; on
propriety, 101; on wisdom,
203–5
Grote, George, 24

Pagination Key to the 1932 Edition

Scholarly studies in the past have usually referred to the 1932 Henry Holt and Company edition. The list below relates that pagination to the pagination of the present edition. Before the colon appear the 1932 edition page numbers; after the colon are the corresponding page numbers from the present edition.

109:104–5	153:144–45	197:184	241:221–22
110:105–6	154:145	198:184–85	242:222–23
111:106–7	155:145–46	199:185–86	243:223–24
112:107–8	156:146–47	200:186–87	244:224–25
113:108–9	157:147–48	201:187–88	245:225
114:109–10	158:148–49	202:188–89	246:225–26
115:110–11	159:149–50	203:189–90	247:226–27
116:111–12	160:150	204:190–91	248:227–28
117:112–13	161:150–51	205:191	249:228–29
118:113–14	162:151–52	206:191–92	250:229
119:114	163:152–53	207:192–93	251:229–30
120:114–15	164:153–54	208:193–94	252:230–31
121:115–16	165:154–55	209:194–95	253:231–32
122:116–17	166:155–56	210:195–96	254:232–33
123:117–18	167:156	211:196	255:233–34
124:118–19	168:156–57	212:197	256:234
125:119–20	169:159	213:197–98	257:235
126:120–21	170:161	214:198–99	258:235–36
127:121–22	171:162	215:199–200	259:236–37
128:122–23	172:162–63	216:200–201	260:237–38
129:123–24	173:163–64	217:201–2	261:238–39
130:124	174:164–65	218:202–3	262:239–40
131:125	175:165–66	219:203	263:240–41
132:125–26	176:166–67	220:203–4	264:241–42
133:126–27	177:167	221:204–5	265:242
134:127–28	178:167–68	222:205–6	266:242–43
135:128–29	179:168–69	223:206–7	267:243–44
136:129–30	180:169–70	224:207–8	268:244–45
137:130	181:170–71	225:208	269:245–46
138:130–31	182:171–72	226:208–9	270:246–47
139:131–32	183:172–73	227:209–10	271:247–48
140:132–33	184:173	228:210–11	272:248–49
141:133–34	185:173–74	229:211–12	273:249
142:135	186:174–75	230:212–13	274:249–50
143:135–36	187:175–76	231:213	275:250–51
144:136–37	188:176–77	232:214	276:251–52
145:137–38	189:177–78	233:214–15	277:252–53
146:138–39	190:178–79	234:215–16	278:253–54
147:139–40	191:179	235:216–17	279:254
148:140	192:179–80	236:217–18	280:254–55
149:140–41	193:180–81	237:218–19	281:255–56
150:141–42	194:181–82	238:219–20	282:256–57
151:142–43	195:182–83	239:220	283:257–58
152:143–44	196:183	240:220–21	284:258–59